REA ACCOUNTING SYSTEMS AND ANALYTICS

Cheryl L. Dunn
Gregory J. Gerard

REA ACCOUNTING SYSTEMS AND ANALYTICS

© 2020, Cheryl L. Dunn and Gregory J. Gerard.

ISBN 978-1-5342-9985-6

JWD   *JSG*

We dedicate this book to our families. We could not have done this without their love, sacrifice, patience, and understanding. Thank you Jim, Jimmy, Sarah, Theresa, Jayne, Joey, and Kaitlyn, and our wonderful parents, Bob & Issie Scott, and Jim & Mary Ann Gerard.

We also dedicate this book to Bill McCarthy, the REA guru, for his guidance, instruction, mentorship, and friendship.

BRIEF CONTENTS

DETAILED CONTENTS

PREFACE

REA is an acronym that stands for the words *resources*, *events*, and *agents*. More importantly, REA is a model of economic exchange, and by extension, a model of accounting and accountability. In this textbook, we focus on REA-driven data representation, data storage, data reporting, and data analytics. REA is an innovative approach to teaching and developing accounting and enterprise information systems, developed by Bill McCarthy of Michigan State University. Students will benefit from this theoretical foundation for enterprise systems because it provides a glimpse of what is possible in enterprise systems, yet also permits comparison to existing systems. While existing software can demonstrate the constructs in this approach, REA is software-independent and therefore stands the test of time.

One objective of this book is to give students a pattern-based framework for thinking about enterprise systems. People use patterns every day in learning. We apply patterns we have seen before to help us understand new situations. This book encourages students to apply the object patterns (things and relationships between them) and script patterns (logical sequences of events) that make up the REA enterprise ontology to help them understand enterprises and business processes. We focus on the core business processes – acquisition, payroll, conversion, and revenue – from an REA value chain perspective and from an REA data modeling (representation) perspective. While these perspectives are independent of specific technologies, we ultimately choose to implement our models using relational databases due to their role in current implementations of enterprise systems. We use Microsoft Access because of its wide availability and ease of use in the classroom. Even students who have never used Access should find it easy to use as they follow the examples explained in narrative form and illustrated with screen captures. The actual implementation of the conceptual models as illustrated by the screen captures helps students to make abstract concepts more concrete.

The second objective of this book is to give students a framework for thinking about accounting and business analytics. Our use of REA data models and structured data (relational databases) naturally extends to using structured query language (SQL) as the basis of our analytics. Our approach to analytics covers accounting analytics, such as the materialization of financial statement information, as well as business analytics, such as understanding the most profitable product sold to customers living in the state of California during the month of June this year. These analytics are best realized when using a well-designed database; a database designed based on REA. While unstructured data and statistical data analysis can complement REA data, those topics are beyond the scope of this text. We believe students should master structured data management and analytics before moving on to unstructured data management and analytics.

Instructors may use this text in an undergraduate or graduate accounting information systems course; we have used it at both levels. This text could be used in an MIS enterprise systems course or a database course, although students using the book should have some prerequisite knowledge of accounting. Because it is unrealistic for instructors to use all 15 chapters in a one semester course, we offer some thoughts on chapter coverage.

In an undergraduate course, one might choose to limit the business process coverage to acquisition and revenue, and to avoid the advanced REA topics, thereby skipping chapters 5 (payroll), 7, (conversion) 10 (advanced topics) and 14 (payroll and conversion querying and analytics). Such an approach would provide good coverage of REA along with the system documentation, and risks and controls topics that are important for the CPA exam.

In a graduate course, materials in chapters 3 (relational databases and Microsoft Access), 8 (workflow and system documentation) and 9 (enterprise risks and controls) may have already been covered in other courses, such as undergraduate AIS, MIS, audit or IT audit courses Having chapter 3 available, even if unassigned, will help students who have forgotten the relational database and Access concepts from previous coursework. This is important, as later chapters will require knowledge of chapter 3 concepts. Later chapters do not require knowledge of chapter 8 and 9 concepts, thus eliminating coverage of those chapters will not detract from the others. These are just some possible considerations; we understand there will be instructor-specific preferences.

In addition to our student audience, professionals who use or develop enterprise systems will find interesting ideas in this text because it allows for some understanding of things happening "behind the software interface." When people use an enterprise system, the interface usually hides the data structure – in other words, the user looks at a web page, not the relational database itself. Our approach connects the business process to the database directly. Once the database structure is understood, the next step is developing the analytics skills, such as the skills presented in this text. Enterprise software developers will likely also be intrigued by the notion that debits, credits, accounts, and financial statements need not lay the foundation for accounting and enterprise software, but rather can be derived as views from the underlying transactional data as demonstrated in chapters 12-14.

Instructors' supplements, including PowerPoint presentations, Microsoft Access databases, additional assessment questions and solutions, and a test bank, will be available to verified instructors who adopt this book. To obtain the supplements, please contact dunnc@gvsu.edu.

ACKNOWLEDGMENTS

We were both extremely fortunate to have Bill McCarthy as a teacher, advisor, mentor, role model, and friend. Simply put, this book would not exist without Bill and our relationships with him. Bill is the founder of the REA enterprise ontology that forms the focal point of this textbook. We have done our best to faithfully present his ideas so as to make them more accessible to instructors, students, and practitioners across the globe. We appreciate Bill's many insights and his permission to use or adapt many of the examples he himself uses in teaching REA to his students. Our heartfelt thanks to you, Bill!

We also acknowledge insights gained over the past two decades from participants at various REA-related research and teaching workshops, including SMAP (Semantic Modeling of Accounting Phenomena) workshops, the American Accounting Association's Intensive Workshops on Teaching AIS (also known as the REA Boot Camps) organized by Julie Smith David of the American Accounting Association (and formerly at Arizona State University) and Bill McCarthy of Michigan State University, and the AIS Educators' REA Mini-Bootcamps organized by Sarah Bee of Seattle University and Cheryl Dunn of Grand Valley State University and held in conjunction with the AIS Educators Conference. We have learned from all of you, as you have helped contribute to what REA is today.

We thank Julie Smith David of the American Accounting Association for the wonderful idea of using cookie-baking as an example to which students can easily relate in understanding the conversion process.

We thank the many students and alumni at Florida State University, Grand Valley State University, Michigan State University, University of Notre Dame, and Rice University who have used materials that are now part of this book. Nothing helps one learn something better than to teach it to someone else. Thank you for helping us to learn REA better than we otherwise could have.

We thank those who read drafts of our book and provided us with valuable feedback:

Geoffrey Adams, *Florida State University*

Elizabeth Connors, *Michigan State University*

Kevin Kobelsky, *University of Michigan-Dearborn*

ABOUT THE AUTHORS

Cheryl L. Dunn, **Grand Valley State University**

Cheryl (PhD, Michigan State University) is a Professor and Interim Associate Director of the School of Accounting in the Seidman College of Business at Grand Valley State University. She was formerly an Associate Professor at Florida State University and has held visiting positions at Rice University, University of Notre Dame, and Michigan State University. She has also served as an instructor at the American Accounting Association's Workshop on Teaching Accounting Information Systems and has led the REA Accounting & Analytics Workshop for the Accounting Information Systems Educator's Conference. Cheryl has written many articles for scholarly journals, including *Journal of the Association for Information Systems, Decision Sciences, Communications of the Association for Information Systems, Journal of Information Systems, International Journal of Accounting Information Systems, Issues in Accounting Education, Strategic Finance*, and *Journal of Emerging Technologies in Accounting*. Cheryl has taught graduate and undergraduate accounting information systems courses as well as graduate accounting theory and undergraduate principles of financial and managerial accounting. Cheryl's primary research interests are in business ontologies, conceptual modeling, enterprise system design, and corporate financial reporting.

Gregory J. Gerard, **Florida State University**

Greg (PhD, Michigan State University) is an Associate Professor in the Department of Accounting at Florida State University. He teaches accounting information systems courses at both the undergraduate and graduate levels. He has published articles in scholarly journals such as *Journal of the Association for Information Systems, Communications of the Association for Information Systems, Journal of Information Systems, International Journal of Accounting Information Systems, Auditing: A Journal of Practice & Theory, Review of Accounting and Finance*, and *Issues in Accounting Education*. He was the president of both the Accounting Information Systems Section and the Strategic and Emerging Technologies Section of the American Accounting Association. He was the editor of a special issue of Issues in Accounting Education that focused on information technology. He is currently an editor for *Journal of Information Systems*, an associate editor for *International Journal of Accounting Information Systems* and *Journal of Emerging Technologies in Accounting*. His primary research interests are conceptual modeling, and the design, use, and audit of enterprise information systems.

CHAPTER 1

Why REA? Economic Storytelling – Accountants as Enterprise Historians, Visionaries, and Data Scientists

LEARNING OBJECTIVES

Throughout history, accountants assumed the role of economic historians. That is, accountants are responsible for recording, storing, and reporting details of activities that affect enterprises' financial positions. This chapter examines how accountants have accomplished this goal and evaluates opportunities for improvement. Reporting the past is not enough to satisfy the information needs of investors, creditors, and corporate managers. In the constantly-changing information age, accountants must also be visionaries, adapting to accelerating changes in technology, globalization, and the environment. The fundamental skill underlying the information age is accountants' ability to manage and analyze vast amounts of data. After highlighting accounting history, we will consider the effect new technologies may have on accounting practice.

After studying this chapter, you should be able to

1. Identify the core components of the Resources-Events-Agents (REA) model
2. Describe the role of accountants as economic historians throughout time
3. Describe the need for accountants to be visionaries
4. Describe the need for accountants to be data scientists
5. Explain what it means for accountants to have an analytics mindset

ECONOMIC STORYTELLING: ACCOUNTANTS AS ENTERPRISE HISTORIANS

Enterprises and accountants existed long before computers, calculators, formal corporations, and the double-entry bookkeeping system. Historians have described many attempts by ancient agrarian enterprises to account for their activities. As far back as 5000 B.C. in Babylonia, Egypt, China, and Greece, concepts of economic value and profit existed, as did attempts to record information regarding enterprise activities or business transactions.[1] Among the earliest enterprises were families who labored together in fields tending to crops, trees, or animals; and families who fished, hunted, or trapped in order to have enough food to eat. These families traded goods with other families who grew different crops, herded, or successfully hunted different types of animals; or who created other products (such as furniture) from their land's resources (such as trees).

Accounting consisted of methods such as making notches in sticks to indicate quantities of goods for which one was responsible, or having scribes write business transactions onto moist lumps of clay using wooden rods with blunt triangular ends. Such records noted the names of the parties involved in the transactions, the items paid or received, promises made, and any other pertinent

---

[1] Chatfield, M. 1977. *A History of Accounting Thought*. Huntington, New York: Robert E. Krieger Publishing.

details. The clay tablets were then dried and kept as accounting records. Ancient records also include periodically prepared inventory lists of assets on hand and evidence of audit examinations. Furthermore, taxation is traced back to Egyptian pharaohs; tax collection efforts required accounting (record keeping, counting, measuring, and calculating).

The Sumerians in 3250 B.C. used sealed clay receptacles containing tokens that represented the portion of one person's wealth on loan to another.[2] Imprints on the seals indicated the contents. See Exhibit 1-1 for examples of artifacts used for ancient accounting. The ball in the upper left is an accountancy envelope. To its right is a similar receptacle that has been broken to reveal the counters inside of it. On the top right are various types of tokens, each representing a different type of physical item (e.g., pigs, chickens, tea, and bolts of cloth). The clay tablets in the bottom row demonstrate the increasing amount of transaction detail recorded and stored over time.

**Exhibit 1-1: Artifact display at the Oriental Institute Museum at the
University of Chicago[3]**

The ancient agrarian systems were not just "accounting" systems recording transactions; they were "enterprise" systems allowing for a broad description, and history, of what had occurred – including non-accounting information. The same "systems" supported managers and other decision-makers. Accountants reported the economic story of the enterprise – that is, they described economic activity details such as who, what, when, where, why, and how. Granted, such enterprises were much smaller than modern enterprises and just a few descriptive records for each business transaction or audit activity were sufficient to augment the enterprise owner's memory, where much of the information was stored, and thus to meet their information needs. Enterprise

---

[2] Mattesich, R. 1989. Accounting and the input-output principle in the prehistoric and ancient world. *ABACUS*. September. 74-84.

[3] Downloaded from
https://commons.wikimedia.org/wiki/File:Clay_accounting_ball_with_calculi,_counters,_and_evolution_of_cuneifo
rm_-_Oriental_Institute_Museum,_University_of_Chicago_-_DSC07070.JPG, with attribution to By Daderot (Own work) [CC0], via Wikimedia Commons.

owners and accountants measured the success of such enterprises in terms of asset increases; income was not isolated. *Accountability* was the focus – keeping track of the assets and measuring the give and the take of economic transactions. Making notches in sticks, putting tokens in clay pots, or creating laborious carvings on clay tablets limited the quantity of data captured and stored. Proprietors remembered details that could not be stored, and then verbally conveyed those details to other interested parties.

As society progressed to the mercantile and industrial ages, new technologies and new forms of business organizations emerged. Merchant voyagers, also called adventurers, journeyed to distant places to trade their goods. Some traveled by land, others by sea. See Exhibit 1-2 for a merchant caravan traveling over land.

Exhibit 1-2: Merchant's Caravan[4]

Because a merchant trading voyage was expensive and labor-intensive, the joint venture form of business emerged. The adventurer (owner of the ship or caravan) typically did not own the merchandise to be traded during the journey. The merchant (owner of the goods) entrusted his goods to the adventurer who, if all went well, returned many months later with return cargo – new merchandise obtained in exchange for the original goods. The merchant and adventurer divided the return cargo according to their joint venture agreement and the venture ended. Because the merchants were entrusting their goods to the adventurers, this joint venture and the return cargo needed to be divided up, and the quality and quantity of information needed to increase – certainly beyond the primitive methods of lists, clay tablets, and notched sticks of earlier times. Archaeologists have recovered records indicating two primary information records: the value of the initial cargo entrusted to the adventurer, and the value of the adventurer's return cargo. Merchants measured the success of each venture by the increase in (cargo) assets. The more valuable the return cargo relative to the initial cargo, the more profitable the venture. The *double-entry bookkeeping* system formally described by Pacioli in 1494 met most of the enterprise information needs, at least in terms of written records kept. However, no financial statements were prepared, probably because each joint venture was its own enterprise. There was no concept of a

---

[4] Downloaded from https://commons.wikimedia.org/wiki/File:Pieter_van_der_Borcht_(I)_-_Merchants%27_Caravan.jpeg, with attribution to Pieter van der Borcht [Public domain], via Wikimedia Commons.

business as an ongoing entity.[5,6] Once a voyage was over, and the profits were split among the merchant and adventurer, the corresponding joint venture ended. Although there were no financial statements, the focus on assets sets the stage for what would become the balance sheet. The income statement would come much later (1700s) after the development of corporate forms of ownership where shares could be traded. These shareholders would not have much direct information about the companies that they owned – therefore, they needed additional information and modern financial reporting was born.

As the Industrial Revolution spread throughout the world, manufacturing enterprises emerged that required substantial purchases of fixed assets beyond the financial means of most sole proprietors and joint ventures. See Exhibit 1-3 for an early assembly line at Ford Motor Company.

Exhibit 1-3: Assembly line at Ford Motor Company in 1913[7]

The corporation as a business entity thus evolved, allowing many investors (shareholders) to contribute relatively small amounts of capital in exchange for partial ownership.[8] Merchants began to form corporations for their trading voyages, re-investing the profits from one voyage in the next voyage. Salaried managers took over the administration of enterprises in many sectors. Because many shareholders were not involved in managing the corporations in which they had invested,

---

[5] Irish, R.A. 1968. The evolution of corporate accounting. *Contemporary Studies in the Evolution of Accounting Thought*. Dickenson Publishing. 57-85.

[6] Littleton, A.C. 1968. Ancient and modern bookkeeping compared. (ed. Chatfield) *Contemporary Studies in the Evolution of Accounting Thought*. Dickenson Publishing. 48-56.

[7] Downloaded from https://commons.wikimedia.org/wiki/File:Ford_assembly_line_-_1913.jpg. Picture is in the public domain.

[8] ten Have, O. 1976. *The History of Accountancy*. Bay Books. Palo Alto, California.

they did not have ready access to the bookkeeping records. Companies created periodic financial statements to summarize the corporations' profit and loss activities; and to list the corporations' assets and equities, enabling shareholders to track the performance of their investments. Double-entry bookkeeping worked well for many years and was appropriate, given available technologies and forms of business. As additional types of business emerged, double-entry was generic enough to be adapted for all of them. Because bookkeepers performed calculations manually or with the assistance of adding machines, errors were certain to occur. Double-entry provided an important check to identify many types of bookkeeping errors so that accountants could locate the errors and fix them before preparing financial statements.

As the Industrial Age progressed, manufacturers needed data beyond that typically stored in traditional accounting systems. As corporations grew larger and encompassed multiple geographical locations (sometimes in multiple countries), managers could not observe corporate operations first-hand. Instead, managers needed to make decisions based on operational data. Cost and managerial accounting thus emerged to support internal decision-makers, while financial accounting continued to support external decision-makers. Unfortunately, bookkeepers summarized the original data from the underlying transactions before entering them into journals and posting the entries to ledger accounts, thus destroying the level of detail needed to support cost and managerial decisions. Accountants also journalized and posted accrual accounting entries thus making the accruals part of the account balances, further obscuring the original data. To obtain the detail needed for cost accounting would require reverting to the original source documents and re-summarizing according to the cost and managerial accounting decision needs. To circumvent the need to re-process the original source documents, cost and managerial accountants developed estimation techniques based on the financial accounting journal entries and other readily available data to meet their information needs.

As enterprises became more complex, with numerous employees working in various departments, and multiple layers of management, the demand grew for all types of information needed to run the enterprises. People designed machines such as typewriters, telephones, cash registers, and tabulating equipment to assist with information gathering, processing, and communicating. Sales of such machines grew rapidly as enterprise information needs increased. Some enterprises became global conglomerates, some achieved their growth through numerous mergers and acquisitions, and some developed alliances and cooperatives with other enterprises. Still, as long as financial accountants used the same measures and reports to assess and communicate financial performance – i.e., balance sheets, income statements, statements of stockholders' equity, and statements of cash flow – the double-entry mechanics worked reasonably well to support those information needs.

As computers became readily available to companies, accountants used general ledger software that forced journal entries to balance before accepting their entry, automatically posted the journal entries to the appropriate ledger accounts, and automatically prepared financial statements based on the general ledger account balances. As Professor Bill McCarthy of Michigan State University said in a speech given to the American Accounting Association's *Accounting is Big Data* workshop in September 2016, the automation of double-entry accounting was like "putting rocket propulsion behind a stagecoach." See Exhibit 1-4.

Exhibit 1-4: A stagecoach and a rocket – different designs for different uses[9],[10]

General ledger software certainly makes double-entry bookkeeping faster and more accurate. However, much as a stagecoach isn't built for flight into orbit, double-entry bookkeeping is not built for the dizzying volume, velocity, variety, and veracity of data available in today's enterprises. Double-entry bookkeeping made sense as the foundation for accounting information systems when the most important data to be captured, stored, and reported was that describing *accounting transactions* – defined as those events that directly affected a company's assets, liabilities, or owners' equity accounts.

Today's business people demand much more information than can be provided by double-entry bookkeeping systems. They want financial reports that have predictive value, not just those that report historical results. Cost and managerial accountants should not need to make estimates for allocating shared costs and other tasks after data are summarized, mixed in with accruals, and stored in general ledger accounts. Technology today can store transactions such that the original data is preserved and people can retrieve and manipulate it in various ways to support different decisions. Accountants can apply accruals after retrieval of the original data when producing financial views, rather than forever altering that data for all views. Some complain that accountants have not kept pace with the vast changes in business and technology that occurred throughout the Information Age and that continue to occur in the current age, whether you believe we are still in the Information Age or whether you believe we have moved into a new age called the Connected Age[11], the Experience Age[12], the Age of Accelerations[13], or something else. Exhibit 1-5 illustrates a claim by responsive.org that we have progressed to a new age.

---

[9] George Arents Collection, The New York Public Library. *The Burton coach.* Retrieved from http://digitalcollections.nypl.org/items/510d47de-3387-a3d9-e040-e00a18064a99.

[10] George Arents Collection, The New York Public Library. *Rocket booster parts from rocket.* Retrieved from http://digitalcollections.nypl.org/items/5e66b3e9-05fc-d471-e040-e00a180654d7.

[11] Pisoni, A. "The Responsive Organisation: A Framework for Changing How Your Organisation Works." Presentation published to slideshare.net in April 2014, downloaded in July 2017 from https://www.slideshare.net/responsiveorg/the-responsive-organisation-a-framework-for-changing-how-your-organisation-works

[12] Wadhera, M. "The Information Age is Over: Welcome to the Experience Age." *Tech Crunch*, posted May 9, 2016, downloaded July 2017 from https://techcrunch.com/2016/05/09/the-information-age-is-over-welcome-to-the-experience-age/.

[13] Friedman, T.L. 2016. *Thank You For Being Late: An Optimist's Guide to Thriving in the Age of Accelerations.* Farrar, Straus and Giroux: New York.

Exhibit 1-5: Major Eras; image credit responsive.org[14]

Whether or not we are living in a new age, many corporate phenomena today do not meet the traditional asset or liability definitions that were conceptualized centuries ago. For example, many contracts do not qualify as liabilities despite the fact that they obligate companies to future payments. A company that signed a two-year agreement with a cellular service provider for cell phone service for its CEO, will simply record telephone expense as the service is used and the monthly invoices are received. The overall obligation for two years of payments does not appear on the company's balance sheet. Many companies have so much difficulty keeping track of such commitments, that software developers created contract management software to assist in that endeavor.

Human capital and other intangibles that have significant value to companies do not qualify as assets and thus do not appear on corporate balance sheets. The market capitalization of some of today's largest companies (e.g., Alphabet, Amazon, or Facebook) differs vastly from those companies' balance sheets, primarily because their value lies in their knowledge, expertise, and digital assets that their balance sheets do not reflect. Traditional accounting methods and definitions were not created with these new business models in mind. Note that most such companies are less than 25 years old.

ECONOMIC STORYTELLING: ACCOUNTANTS AS VISIONARIES

How can accountants tell a more complete economic story, such that the story not only reports historical accounting transactions, but also facilitates predictions about future economic results? Ironically, the answer may lie in reporting a greater percentage of the economic history. Current accounting information systems begin telling the story of each transaction when the story is over or nearly over. Accountants do not journalize transactions until the transactions have directly affected an asset, liability, and/or an owners' equity account. Yet transactions do not magically

---

[14] Pisoni, A. "The Responsive Organisation: A Framework for Changing How Your Organisation Works." Slide 33 from presentation published to slideshare.net in April 2014, downloaded in July 2017 from https://www.slideshare.net/responsiveorg/the-responsive-organisation-a-framework-for-changing-how-your-organisation-works

materialize! Other preceding events lead to those transactions. A salesperson calling on a customer triggers a sale order, which leads to a sale and *cash receipt*, i.e., an event that has the effect of increasing cash. People identify an internal need for a good or service, then they initiate a purchase requisition. A purchase requisition leads to a purchase order, which leads to a purchase and *cash disbursement*, i.e., an event that has the effect of decreasing cash, also called a payment.

Double-entry bookkeeping systems do not capture sales calls, sale orders, purchase requisitions, or purchase orders. Why? Because those transactions do not affect any asset, liability, or owners' equity accounts. Would decision-makers benefit from knowing the dollar value of open sale orders a company has at the end of a given period? Presumably, such data would help predict the dollar value of sales likely to occur in the next period. Similarly, data about a company's sales call volume, its marketing and advertising promotions, and its customer inquiries in one period may help predict the dollar value of sale orders likely to occur in the next period. The dollar value of open purchase orders would likely help predict the dollar value of purchases likely to occur in the next period, and data about a company's purchase requisitions and the volume of receiving vendor sales calls may help predict the dollar value of purchase orders likely to occur in the next period.

Some would argue that accountants should not report such activities because of too much uncertainty as to whether they will progress to completion. Would such predictions be perfectly accurate? No, of course not. Does that mean they would not be useful? Does that mean they are not an important part of the company's economic story? No, of course not. Even events that currently qualify as accounting transactions have less than 100% certainty. Accountants record credit sales without knowing for sure that the sales will result in cash receipts. How do accountants handle the uncertainty? They create allowances for bad debts based on the companies' accounts receivable collection histories. Could accountants establish similar allowances for unfilled or cancelled sale orders and for unfilled or cancelled purchase orders? Yes. The difficulty is that such commitments nor their related allowances do not meet the definitions of assets, liabilities, or equities, and thus do not fit within the traditional double-entry bookkeeping model. If we want to expand the possibilities for financial reporting and business management, we must change the method by which we capture and store transaction data.

Transformative Technologies in Accounting
Which technologies may facilitate accountants telling economic stories of their companies that are more complete than the stories they tell today? One obvious technology for accountants to know is database software. Whether relational, graph, array, object-oriented, flat-file, or another, company data must be stored in some type of database. Most large companies today have ERP (Enterprise Resource Planning) systems built on relational databases. An *ERP system* is a group of software applications integrated to form an enterprise-wide system solution. Therefore, accountants should understand the mechanics of relational databases – how to best structure that data for storage, and how to retrieve such data to facilitate decision-makers. Accountants should also understand the risks and controls associated with both the ERP systems and the underlying databases – which will partly depend on whether the systems and database(s) are cloud-based or onsite. Cybersecurity should be of concern to nearly all enterprises, large and small, as even owners' and employees' smartphones are potential points of access for hackers.

Accountants as visionaries, should be actively engaged in researching new technologies and new business models to determine the potential impacts on their companies and/or on the field of accounting in general. In this textbook we will discuss technologies such as ERP and relational databases that are not new, but until recently have been largely ignored by most accountants. Some relatively new technologies for which we will examine potential impacts include artificial intelligence/cognitive technologies, blockchain, cloud computing/software as a service, crowdsourcing and social media, and robotic process automation/machine learning.

In a 1982 article[15], Professor William McCarthy at Michigan State University proposed an alternative method for capturing and storing multi-dimensional data at its most disaggregated levels such that it supports multiple views and could facilitate expanded financial reporting. He called his method the REA (resources-events-agents) accounting model. In the four decades since his initial REA article's publication, McCarthy and other researchers have more fully developed this model. REA is more than just a method for capturing, storing, and reporting data. Rather, REA is an *enterprise ontology* – a vocabulary useful for understanding business processes that can guide system implementation using many different technologies. *REA accounting* supports all of the traditional accounting needs, but it goes beyond that – it can plan and set policies for future accounting transactions and additionally support the decision-making needs of all people in the organization because it considers non-accounting events and activities in addition to accounting events and activities.

The core of REA is made up of specific economic resources, economic events, and economic agents. *Economic resources* have a broader definition than traditional accounting assets. Tangible and intangible assets, skills, knowledge, and digital assets are all economic resources. While REA does not solve the measurement difficulty for such resources, REA allows storage of multiple measurements for them so that people can use the measurements that most appeal to them. *Economic events* are activities that change the quantity or value of economic resources. There are two types: *economic increment events*, which increase related resources; and *economic decrement events* which decrease related resources. More generally, the term events includes economic events, commitment events, instigation events, and other business events (these will be discussed later; for now, know that the different types of events relate to whether or not they have implications for accounting). *Economic agents* are people, departments, divisions, and organizations who participate in, authorize, record, or play other roles in the various events in enterprise business processes. We will discuss REA in more detail in later chapters.

ECONOMIC STORYTELLING: ACCOUNTANTS AS DATA SCIENTISTS

Data scientist is a title used to describe jobs that sometimes have very different responsibilities and require different knowledge and skill sets, so let us clarify what we mean by accountants needing to be data scientists. Most enterprises' economic stories are buried amidst vast quantities of data. Some of the data are structured; some of the data are unstructured. Some of the data are captured

---

[15] McCarthy, W.E. "The REA Accounting Model: A Generalized Framework for Accounting Systems in a Shared Data Environment." *The Accounting Review*, July 1982, pp. 554-578.

and stored within enterprises' own systems; some of the data are available from outside sources, such as social media, news outlets, and blog posts. The quantity of data captured and stored within companies' own systems has skyrocketed in recent years. Gone are the days when the captured data that could be relevant to a company's economic story were all housed in the company's accounting journals and ledgers. Now accountants also need to consider data that is captured by the non-accounting modules of the company's ERP system, data that is captured by Internet of Things (IoT) enabled machines and equipment, and data that is captured by the company's website. Some such data can provide verification of data that resides within the accounting records. Auditors are particularly interested in that type of data, as it helps provide assurance that the company's financial statements have been prepared in accordance with generally accepted accounting principles (GAAP). Other such data may alert company management and/or its auditors to potential product issues. Some alerts may be negative – such as a large number of complaints and/or threats of lawsuits regarding a new product. Other alerts may be positive – such as a large number of rave reviews that could indicate greater than anticipated demand. Either way, monitoring and analysis of such data can help ensure prompt response that could maximize the economic benefit or minimize the economic harm to the company.

To be effective data scientists, accountants must become proficient with database tools, advanced spreadsheet functions, visualization software, and even some basic programming and statistics. Pattern-based thinking is important. Perhaps the most important *data science skills* for accountants to have are being able to (1) ask the right questions, (2) manipulate data to answer those questions, and (3) create data visualizations to effectively communicate those answers (a form of storytelling). These skills are fundamental for developing an analytics mindset.

CONCLUDING COMMENTS

Most businesses today have surpassed the ability of the 500+ year old double-entry bookkeeping system to adequately capture, store, and report the data needed to satisfy internal and external decision-makers. A new method of accounting should take advantage of the capabilities provided by new technologies, including artificial intelligence, cognitive computing, database and big data analytics tools, machine learning, semantic technologies, and others. A team of accounting professors, led by Dr. William McCarthy at Michigan State University, has been continually developing a model that can preserve the accountability needed for accounting, while expanding the flexibility to incorporate other types of data to flesh out enterprise's economic stories. Throughout the rest of this textbook, we will study this model, known as REA, and see its potential to contribute to accounting in the future.

KEY TERMS AND CONCEPTS
Accountability (in early accounting)
Accountants as visionaries
Accounting transaction
Cash disbursement
Cash receipt
Data science skills
Double-entry bookkeeping
Economic agent
Economic decrement event
Economic event
Economic increment event
Enterprise ontology
ERP system
Joint venture
REA accounting

REVIEW QUESTIONS
R1-1. What does it mean for accountants to have played the role of economic historian?
R1-2. Why should accountants become visionaries?
R1-3. What do the letters in the acronym REA stand for?
R1-4. Who invented the REA ontology, and for what purpose?
R1-5. Why should accountants become data scientists?

MULTIPLE CHOICE QUESTIONS
MC1-1. The R in REA stands for
      A) Reality
      B) Resources
      C) Revenues
      D) Relationships

MC1-2. The earliest accounting-like activities identified by historians trace back to
      A) 5000 BC
      B) 3250 BC
      C) 1494
      D) The 1700s

MC1-3. Why do double-entry bookkeeping systems not capture sales calls, sale orders, purchase requisitions, or purchase orders?
      A) Double-entry bookkeeping systems do capture those activities
      B) Because they are not an important part of a company's economic story
      C) Because such activities have no predictive value
      D) Because those activities do not affect any asset, liability, or owners' equity accounts

MC1-4. How does REA solve the measurement difficulty for assets such as skills, knowledge, and digital assets?
  A) By tracking the agents responsible for those assets
  B) By storing data about the events in which those assets are acquired and used
  C) While not solving the measurement difficulty, REA allows storage of multiple measurements for them so that people can use the measurements that most appeal to them
  D) REA doesn't solve the measurement difficulty for such assets, and therefore prescribes that such assets be ignored in accounting systems

MC1-5. Skills that are fundamental for developing an analytics mindset include
  A) Asking the right questions
  B) Manipulating data to answer questions
  C) Creating data visualizations to effectively communicate answers
  D) All of the above

CHAPTER 2

Representation and Patterns: Give & Take in Enterprise Business Processes and the REA Ontology

LEARNING OBJECTIVES

The objective of this chapter is to help you understand how to analyze and create enterprise representations that serve as the core foundation for their information systems. After studying this chapter, you should be able to

1. Explain the importance of representation and modeling in enterprise system design and use
2. Identify various types of patterns and recognize patterns in the world around you
3. Describe the purpose and the components of the four levels of the Resources-Events-Agents (REA) ontology
4. Identify an enterprise's external business partners
5. Identify the resources that are exchanged between an enterprise and its business partners
6. Develop an REA value system model for an enterprise
7. Identify the scenes in the entrepreneur script as the foundation for enterprise value chains
8. Identify an enterprise's business processes
9. Identify the resource flows between an enterprise's business processes and the economic events that cause those resource flows
10. Develop an REA value chain model for an enterprise

REPRESENTATION AND MODELING[16]

You may wonder why representation and modeling are important for understanding accounting and enterprise systems. The general answer to this question is that we cannot understand accounting and enterprise systems without models that serve as representations of the systems and their underlying reality. The systems are too large and complex for most people to comprehend in their entirety. People create and use models to help manage the complexity inherent in the real world. Engineers who build automobiles create models before they create the real cars. Automotive repairmen use models to help them understand the cars on which they work. Architects create drawings, models, and blueprints as representations of the buildings they design; once the building is built, other users often refer to those representations to understand some aspect of the building (such as where the support beams are located). See Exhibit 2-1.

---

[16] Much of the material on representation and patterns is adapted from work of Professor William E. McCarthy at Michigan State University and is used with his permission.

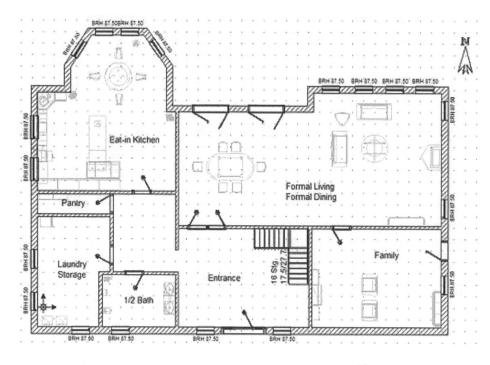

Exhibit 2-1: Architectural drawing[17]

We develop and analyze representations of an enterprise's context and activities (i.e., the enterprise's reality) in order to design and understand the enterprise's accounting and enterprise system. Representations are surrogates for the real constructs; in other words, they are symbols of those constructs. The more faithfully and completely a system represents the underlying enterprise's reality, the more useful the system will be for analyzing and managing the enterprise. To design an information system that closely resembles the underlying reality of the enterprise about which the information is stored, we must build a set of symbols that represents that reality. Some models are more completely and faithfully representative than other models. Consider model cars as an example. First, envision a molded plastic toy car (Exhibit 2-2) created for use by toddlers.

Exhibit 2-2: Plastic toy car[18]

---

[17] Drawing courtesy of Boereck https://commons.wikimedia.org/wiki/File:Sample_Floorplan.jpg, public domain
[18] Picture courtesy of Alf van Beem (Own work) [CC0], via Wikimedia Commons

For safety reasons, such a toy may be created with no removable parts that could choke a baby – the wheels don't turn, and the doors don't open. Contrast that image with that of a model car (Exhibit 2-3) created for use by adults or teenagers – for example one that they might build from a kit. Such a model car may have doors and a trunk that open, headlights that light up, perhaps a battery operated convertible top or even a power source that propels the car across the floor.

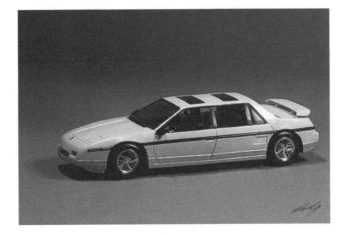

Exhibit 2-3: Model car from kit[19]

Which model car is more completely and faithfully representative of a real car? Obviously the adult version portrays more features of a real car than does the toddler's toy, and is thus a more complete and faithful representation.

A symbolic model of an enterprise that is to be implemented as an information system should map as directly as possible to the underlying reality, and the model should also be convertible into a computerized format. Most database designers start by drawing a model of the enterprise reality and then they convert the model into a format that is compatible with a database software package. Database designers use software modeling tools, but as you are learning you will begin by drawing symbols on paper.

Representations may include symbols of objects at different levels of abstraction. *Token level representation* uses symbols that each have a one-for-one correspondence to the physical object it represents. Such symbols are token symbols. *Type level representation* uses symbols that each represents multiple physical objects. Such symbols are type symbols. For example, see Exhibit 2-4.

---

[19] Picture courtesy of F84Thunderjet (Own work) [CC BY-SA 3.0 (http://creativecommons.org/licenses/by-sa/3.0)], via Wikimedia Commons

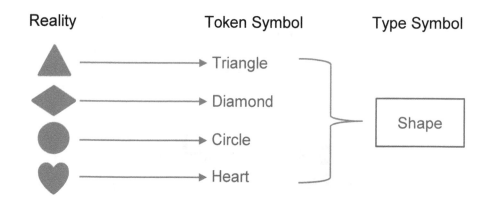

Exhibit 2-4: Token and Type Symbols

Exhibit 2-4 demonstrates that the reality of shapes can be represented in different formats and at various levels of abstraction. Each shape is represented at the token level by a word that once upon a time was created as a representation for that shape. The string of characters h-e-a-r-t is a representation of the drawn heart shape. A token is an individual instance of something. For example, *Fred's little red corvette,* that has vehicle identification number C21350313651-QET, is a single instance of an automobile and is thus a token. Please understand that the middle column's use of words to represent the shapes is not what makes the middle column a token representation; rather, it is the use of a separate symbol in the second column for each physical instance in the first column. The one-for-one correspondence of symbols to actual instances in reality is a token level representation.

The box with the word shape inside it in the third column of Exhibit 2-4 is a type-level representation of the individual shape instances. A type is a category of instances that have something in common with each other. Each separate shape fits into the shape category. Representation at the type level yields a one-to-many correspondence of symbols to actual instances in reality. This reality-to-category mapping is a very important concept in building enterprise system models, because often the models represent categories of objects as well as the individual objects. Imagine an enterprise that has 4,000 different types of inventory items, 895 employees, 25 different cash accounts, 12 branch locations, and this enterprise engages in thousands of transactions each day. The enterprise system must store data about all of the individual instances, but the conceptual model of the system must represent those instances as types to manage the complexity.

Types can even exist at various levels of abstraction – super-types are categories of sub-types. For example, consider separating the shapes in the first column of Exhibit 2-4 into two categories: straight-edged shapes and rounded-edge shapes. Those two categories are sub-types of the shape super-type.

PATTERNS

A *pattern* is an arrangement of repeated or recognizably consistent objects or actions. People use patterns every day to understand their environment. Patterns allow us to make predictions about future events and to make sense of present and past events. We learn with patterns from the time that we are very young children throughout the rest of our lives. Preschoolers and early elementary school students may be given a row of symbols such as that below, and asked to fill in the blank with the appropriate next symbol.

What is the most appropriate next symbol in the pattern? It probably didn't take you very long to identify the most appropriate symbol as the diamond. As the students progress, they might be asked to identify the most appropriate next symbol in a slightly more difficult pattern, such as the following.

Of course the correct answer is the club symbol. Try to complete this pattern, which is a little more complex.

Complete the pattern: Which symbol should be next in the above pattern?

As you can see, the answer requires recognition of one pattern (the + X - pattern) inside of another pattern (the circle square pattern).

Object Patterns

An *object pattern* is a commonly observed constellation of things and relationships between those things. For example, an early learning pattern made popular by the children's television show "Sesame Street" presented groups of four objects on the screen and sang a song that said something like "One of these things is not like the others; one of these things just doesn't belong." They made it a game for children to select the object that did not belong because it was different from the other three objects. Simple patterns of this type might include three things that are identical (e.g., three copies of the same picture of a cow) and one unique thing (e.g., a picture of an airplane). A slightly more difficult pattern of this type could include three things that fit into a category contrasted with another thing that does not fit the category. For example, a group could include a cow, a dog, a monkey, and an airplane; of course, the airplane is not like the others.

More advanced patterns of this type might include three things that are related to each other by some kind of domain (e.g., a cow, a barn, and a tractor are related to each other as part of the farm domain) and one thing that is unrelated to that domain (e.g., a monkey). It is especially complicated if a subset of objects is part of a different domain; in this example, cow and monkey are part of the animal domain, but barn and tractor are not.

In conceptual modeling, object patterns consist of expected groupings of things and the relationships between them. Consider the farm example. What things would you expect to find on a farm? A partial list would include

- Farm Animals
- Crops
- Barn
- Silo
- Farmer
- Tractor
- Harvesting Equipment
- Field
- Harvesting of Crops
- Feeding of Farm Animals
- Caring for Farm Animals

What relationships between these objects would you expect to find on the farm? A partial list would include

- Farm animals take shelter in the barn
- Crops (unharvested) grow in the field
- Crops (harvested) are stored in the silo
- Farmer participates in the harvesting of crops
- Crops participate in the harvesting of crops
- Farmer responsible for caring for farm animals
- Animals benefit from caring for farm animals
- Farmer drives the tractor
- Harvesting equipment is used in harvesting of crops

These are incomplete lists that make up only a part of the overall farm object pattern. Undoubtedly, you can think of additional objects and relationships between them that should also be part of the overall farm object pattern. How do you know what things are likely to be part of the farm's reality? You probably know what to expect to find on a farm from one or more experiences in your past. That experience could have been personal (from visiting or growing up on a farm) or second-hand (e.g., from seeing a farm on television or hearing stories about a farm on which your grandfather was raised).

You may not have realized you have at least parts of the farm object pattern stored in your memory! In fact, you have many object patterns stored in your long-term memory. Whether the information is actually stored as patterns or whether you simply have an indexing scheme that triggers recall of those objects from various parts of your memory is a matter of debate among academic researchers, but that distinction is unimportant for purposes of this book. Our goal is to teach you to use pattern matching to solve data-related problems. When you are faced with what looks like a new problem, we want you to treat it as one you have solved before by leveraging the power of patterns. This approach requires you to find some similarity to old problems for which you have already developed a solution. You may then apply the old solution to the new problem, adapting the solution for anything that is different in the new problem situation. You may be thinking, "I haven't solved any data-related problems like this before." That is OK; others have solved these problems using a pattern – so all you need to do is learn this pattern. For enterprise system modeling, you will need to consider the objects you expect to find in an enterprise, match the reality to your expectations, and adapt as necessary. Such an approach enables you to avoid the need to reinvent the wheel every time you design or evaluate a new enterprise system.

Script Patterns

Whereas object patterns focus on objects and the relationships between them, a *script pattern* is a sequence of events that typically occur in combination. Although an object pattern can include activities (recall the harvesting of crops activity in the farm object pattern), a script pattern establishes a sequence of those activities. For example, a script pattern for the farm would likely include plowing fields, then planting seeds, then weeding and watering periodically while waiting for the crops to grow, then harvesting the crops.

Imagine you are in a friend's house and your friend came in from his car and said he had just come from the grocery store. If you are a polite person, you will likely ask if he would like you to help him carry in the groceries. How do you know he has groceries to carry? Based on experience, you have stored in your memory a script pattern for a sequence of events that frequently occur when someone goes to the grocery store. That script leads you to infer he drove to the grocery store, took groceries off the store shelves, transported the groceries to the checkout lane, placed the groceries on the checkout counter so the prices could be summed and the groceries could be bagged, paid for the groceries, and drove home. The script evoked in your mind is not necessarily accurate for the particular situation. Perhaps your friend went to the grocery store because it contained a postal station and he needed to mail a letter. Despite exceptions that often occur, the script patterns you develop based on experiences you have will help you more often than not in understanding your present and future experiences.

Context is important in determining which script your brain will invoke. Part of what determines someone's knowledge is that person's ability to invoke the most appropriate script for a situation. For example, imagine that someone starts to tell you a story that begins with the following sentences. "Once upon a time a boy named Jimmy met a girl named Theresa. They fell in love." You likely have at least two scripts to invoke based on those sentences, but you need more information about the context in order to guess the ending. If informed that the story is a traditional romance, you are likely to guess the ending "They lived happily ever after." If informed that the story is a romantic tragedy, you are likely to guess the ending reads more like "One of them died and the other was very sad."

You may be surprised to learn that many of the critical steps of building an information system have little to do with programming a computer. The process begins with identifying the need for a business solution and acquiring a better understanding of the environment you plan to represent with the information system. You must examine that environment from different perspectives and at different levels of detail. Using object patterns to communicate enterprise objects and relationships between them, and using script patterns to communicate typical sequences of events, we may gain sufficient understanding of the enterprise domain to represent the relevant enterprise activities in its information system. A domain ontology is a combination of such patterns for a particular domain.

THE REA ENTERPRISE ONTOLOGY

William McCarthy proposed a generalized model for accounting systems after analyzing many accounting transactions and identifying the common features of the transactions. McCarthy named this model REA because three of the principle constructs: Resources, Events, and Agents. McCarthy and Guido Geerts further developed and extended the constructs of the original model to form an enterprise domain ontology[20]. You can think of the REA ontology as the formal representation of the sets of objects and relationships that may exist within an enterprise. We use the REA ontology to help us create REA models.

Resources are things of economic value (with or without physical substance) that enterprise activities provide, use, consume, and manage. Resources include cash, raw materials, finished goods inventory, equipment, employee labor, land, and various kinds of rights. (Note: this is not a comprehensive list!)

Events are activities that enterprises plan, control, execute, and evaluate. You should also think about events as occurrences in time. Economic events are those events that increase or decrease

---

[20] The REA Ontology material included in this chapter is based on the McCarthy 1982 paper (see footnote 15) and on the following papers:

Geerts, G. and McCarthy, W.E. "Modeling Business Enterprises as Value-Added Process Hierarchies with Resource-Event-Agent Object Templates" in J. Sutherland and D. Patel, eds., *Business Object Design and Implementation*, London: Springer-Verlag, 1997, pp. 94-113.

Geerts, G. and McCarthy, W.E. "Using Object Templates from the REA Accounting Model to Engineer Business Processes and tasks." *The Review of Business Information Systems*, Fall 2001, vol. 5, no. 4, pp.89-108.

Geerts, G. and McCarthy, W.E. "An Accounting Object Infrastructure for Knowledge-Based Enterprise Models." *IEEE Intelligent Systems and Their Application*. Vol. 14, Issue 4, 1999, pp. 89-94.

Geerts, G. and McCarthy, W.E. "The Ontological Foundation of REA Enterprise Information Systems." Presented to the American Accounting Association annual meeting, Philadelphia, Pennsylvania, 2000.

Geerts, G. and McCarthy, W.E. "An Ontological Analysis of the Economic Primitives of the Extended-REA Enterprise Information Architecture." *International Journal of Accounting Information Systems* 3, no. 1 (2002), pp. 1-16.

either the quantity or the value of one or more resources. Other types of events (non-economic events) include commitment events, instigation events, and reversal events. A carefully designed REA model will include only those events that are necessary and in a sense natural, as opposed to those that could be eliminated without changing the substance of the enterprise and thus are in a sense artificial. We return to this distinction later.

Agents are individuals, departments, divisions, or organizations that participate in the planning, control, execution, and evaluation of events. Agents may be internal (working on behalf of the enterprise being modeled) or external (working at an arm's length with the enterprise being modeled). Agents may also have custody of resources and do resource-related planning.

The REA ontology views enterprises at four levels of detail (see Exhibit 2-5):

1) An *REA value system model* focuses on the resources exchanged between the enterprise and its various business partners. Business partners are people or organizations with which the enterprise trades resources. Examples include suppliers, customers, creditors, investors, and employees. A supply chain is made of value system models of interconnected business partners.

2) An *REA value chain model* focuses on the internal resources that flow between interconnected business processes, and on the economic events that affect the resource flows. Economic events cause increases (economic increments) or decreases (economic decrements) in the economic value of resources. In a value chain, the resource flows indicate either the transfer of availability of, or responsibility for, the resource as it moves from one business process to another. Once a resource is made available to a different business process, that process needs to do something with it and will therefore include an economic decrement event to use up the resource. The economic decrement event is connected to an economic increment event that acquires or produces a different resource, typically explaining why the enterprise participates in the decrement event. The enterprise must then make the acquired or produced resource available to another business process.

The term *business process* is widely used in practice to mean anything ranging from the act of producing a report to the entire set of activities in a transaction cycle. In this textbook, business process is the term used to describe an entire transaction cycle. The commonly interconnected business processes included in a typical REA value chain are financing, acquisition, payroll, conversion, and revenue.

3) An *REA business process model* is a representation of an enterprise's resources, events, agents, and appropriate associations between them within one or more business processes in an enterprise value chain. We will discuss a common pattern for each business process.

4) An *REA task level model* focuses on workflow – the individual steps involved in accomplishing events in an enterprise. Researchers have not yet discovered and published a pattern for the task level; however, consultants recommend best practices for some tasks. Tasks may include activities that can be changed or eliminated, and therefore should not serve as foundational elements in a well-designed enterprise system.

Types of Patterns in REA

The value system REA model is an object pattern that depicts a macro-level view of the enterprise, with the objects being the enterprise itself, its external business partners, and the resources exchanged between them. An exchange is a trade or swap of one (or more) resource for a different resource between business partners.

The value chain REA model is a script pattern. McCarthy proposes that there is a ***business entrepreneur script*** (with several possible variations) that serves as a starting point for modeling enterprises. The script says (from the enterprise's perspective)

1) The enterprise gets some cash

2) The enterprise engages in value-added exchanges, such as (but not limited to)
   • Purchase equipment and raw materials in exchange for cash
   • Purchase labor in exchange for cash
   • Manufacture finished goods in exchange for labor and raw materials
   • Sell finished goods in exchange for cash

3) The enterprise pays back the cash and lives off the profit

Variations on this script include value-added exchanges that involve performing services rather than manufacturing and selling finished goods, renting of equipment instead of purchasing equipment, renting of goods rather than selling goods, and many other possible revenue-generating and resource-expending activities. REA value chain models should be created with this overall script in mind, but adjusted and embellished as appropriate for the specific enterprise being modeled.

Scripts consist of scenes and involve actors, roles, and props. You have probably experienced a dramatic production (e.g., a play, musical, or opera) either as an actor or as an audience member. Printed programs that outline the scenes to take place in the production help people in the audience follow the action on stage. Each scene involves actors playing roles according to a written script. Sometimes props (physical items used to help communicate the message of the scene) are used. An REA value chain model is somewhat analogous to the program given to the audience – it provides an outline of the scenes (business processes) that will take place in the enterprise.

The REA business process model is an object pattern portraying more detail of each scene in the value chain. The REA business process object pattern relates events within a business process to each other and connects each event to participating roles (agents) and props (resources).

The REA task level model has had no pattern identified. Although many industries recommend best practices in workflow, much variation exists among companies. Still, it is important to consider and document workflow when designing, using, and auditing enterprise systems. Even though there is no general pattern to tasks, tasks still have a sequential component like scripts do. They also have an accountability component in which we need to know who is responsible for each task.

Exhibit 2-5 illustrates the relationships between the four levels of the REA ontology; we briefly discuss exhibit 2-5 before elaborating on the four levels. The value system model identifies the enterprise and its four trading partners in this example. It also shows the resources being exchanged between the enterprise and its trading partners. The emphasis at this level is on the Resources and Agents. Resources are denoted with arrows; Agents are in boxes.

As we move from the value system model to the value chain model, we show how the acquired resources are coordinated in time to add value. This model is meant to be read counter-clockwise beginning at the top (financing process). The emphasis at this level is on the Resources and Events. Resources are denoted with arrows; Events are in boxes. An arrow going to a circle represents giving a resource; an arrow coming from a circle represents taking a resource. Inside the circle are the related give (decrement) and take (increment) events.

As we move from the value chain model to the business process model, we show on the left how one particular business process – payroll – is expanded to a complete object model that specifies Resources, Events, and Agents. While payroll is shown in this example, all business processes from the value chain above would have related REA business process models. On the right of the figure we show how this business process model might look as a relational database. It is at the business process level that we consider the data necessary to manage the enterprise.

Finally, as we move from the business process level to the task level, we show an example of how the tasks would be configured for the payroll process. The emphasis at this level is on Agents and Events/Tasks. Again, each business process would have a set of tasks associated with it.

REA Value System Models

The most general level of REA ontology is the value system. You may have heard the saying "they couldn't see the forest for the trees" to describe people so mired in detail that they forget the big picture of what they are trying to accomplish. We want to avoid that problem by examining the "forest level" (value system) of an enterprise first. This will provide structure for the more detailed model-levels and will help you keep your perspective and avoid getting mired in the detail.

Analyzing a firm's value system includes thinking about the enterprise's mission and strategy; that is, an enterprise's planned course of action for achieving its objectives. Understanding this level is crucial because later you must ensure that activities within the enterprise's business processes are consistent with its overall mission and strategy. The REA ontology is about much more than developing information systems; it is about understanding enterprises.

To really understand and analyze an enterprise, you must understand more than internal operations and functions. You must look outside the enterprise at the industry, the enterprise's suppliers (people or organizations from which the enterprise purchases goods or services), its customers (people or organizations to whom the enterprise sells goods or services) and all the other parties that affect enterprise performance. In other words, you must examine the enterprise at its value system level, and consider how the enterprise value system interacts with the value systems of the other enterprises in its supply chain. An enterprise supply chain encompasses all of the enterprises involved in providing a product or service to an end customer. For example, a manufacturer may purchase materials and equipment from suppliers, then the manufacturer may sell its finished products to wholesalers, which then sell the products to retail stores, which then sell the products to the end customers.

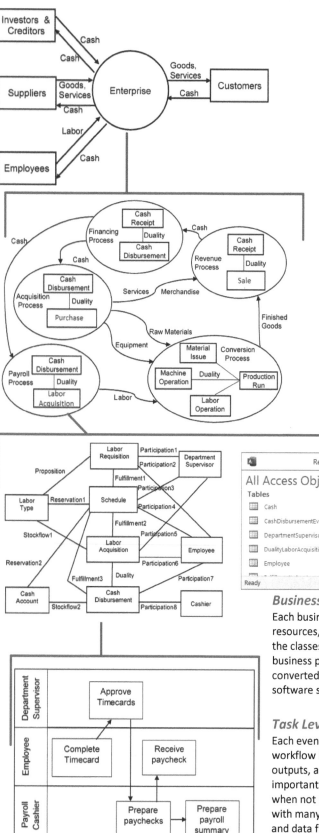

Value System Level

Resource exchanges (bi-directional resource flows) connect the enterprise to its various business partners.

Value Chain Level

Unidirectional resource flows connect enterprise business processes. The value chain level describes what occurs inside the bubble labeled Enterprise at the value system level.

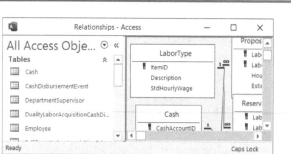

Business Process Level

Each business process from the value chain is decomposed into the resources, events, agents, and other classes, with associations between the classes including duality, stockflow, participation, and more. These business process class diagrams are integrated into one conceptual model, converted into database table structures, and implemented in database software such as Microsoft Access or Oracle.

Task Level

Each event from the business process level is decomposed into the detailed workflow by which the event is accomplished, including inputs, processes, outputs, and areas of responsibility. Some activities identified as especially important at the task level may be added to business process models even when not normally prescribed by REA. Task level models may be portrayed with many different notations, including BPMN, flowcharts, process maps, and data flow diagrams. The swimlane diagram shown at left is a small piece of a larger diagram to represent payroll activities for an enterprise.

Exhibit 2-5: Four levels of the REA Ontology

REA Value Chain Models

Everything an enterprise does should create value for its customers, according to Michael Porter in Competitive Advantage[21]. However, creating value has a cost. For example, an enterprise that assembles automobiles creates something of value, but also must pay for various inputs (e.g., materials, supplies, and time of employees). Porter computes an organization's margin as the difference between value and cost. This calculation includes all value and all cost, much of which is difficult to measure, but which the REA value chain model can capture in theory, even if current measurements are unavailable. Geerts and McCarthy define a value chain as "a purposeful set of economic exchanges where an initial outlay of cash is successively converted into some types of more valuable intermediate resource and then finally converted back to cash." McCarthy has also defined value chain as "a purposeful network of business processes aimed at assembling the individual components of a final product (i.e., its portfolio of attributes) of value to the customer."

Relating value chains back to the script, there are five standard scenes in the value chain: financing, acquisition, payroll, conversion, and revenue. Each of these five standard scenes involves the exchange of resources via give and take events (normally a one-to-one relationship between a give or take event and its related resource). While there are various financing sources, the *financing process* involves the enterprise getting the cash resource from these sources and giving cash to these sources (give event: cash disbursement; take event cash receipt). The *acquisition process* involves giving the resource cash in exchange for various resources like raw materials and equipment (give event: cash disbursement; take event: acquisition). The *payroll process* is a special type of acquisition where the resource cash is exchanged for the resource labor (give event: cash disbursement; take event labor acquisition). The *conversion process* takes resources like raw materials, equipment, and labor, and gives them in exchange for the production of a finished good resource (give events: material issue, machine operation, and labor operation; take event: production run). The *revenue process* involves giving goods or services resources in exchange for the cash resource (give event: sale; take event: cash receipt). After the revenue process is complete, cash can be returned to financing sources.

The concept of creating value applies to both for-profit and not-for-profit organizations. For-profit organizations try to maximize their margins. Not-for-profit organizations, such as charitable or governmental entities, seek to maximize the goods and services they provide with the resources (funds) they receive. Over the long run, charitable and governmental organizations seek to optimize their services (and minimize costs) while matching outflows to inflows. Whether for-profit or not-for-profit, viable organizations provide goods and services that customers value in a cost-effective way. The main difference between for-profit and not-for-profit enterprises is that at the value system level, the input resources and output resources are paired with different external business partners. That is, some of the partners who give resources to the not-for-profit enterprises do not receive resources directly from the not-for-profit enterprises and some of the partners who receive resources from the not-for-profit enterprises do not give resources to the not-for-profit enterprises. The overall notion of input resources being transformed into output resources is still valid, however, because one would expect that if the not-for-profit organization failed to provide the expected goods and services, its contributing external business partners would discontinue their contributions.

---

[21] M. Porter, *Competitive Advantage: Creating and Sustaining Superior Performance* (New York: The Free Press, 1985), p. 12.

Every organization seeks to create value by providing goods and services that customers want. We want to think of this good or service as bundling a portfolio of attributes of value to the customer. For example:

- A grocery store creates value by providing fresh organic food in a clean and convenient location for customers to purchase.
- An airline company creates value by safely transporting passengers and cargo in a timely manner.
- An automobile manufacturer creates value by manufacturing safe, reliable, stylish vehicles with various technologies to transport people and cargo.
- A municipality creates value by providing essential community services (e.g., police protection, fire protection, emergency services, and utilities) to its citizens.

Enterprises that provide goods and services of value to their customers will survive and grow while those that do not will shrink and die. Due to competition for scarce resources, each enterprise must provide value in a cost-effective manner. Although some organizations manage to defer their demise through deceit, disguise, or political influence, ultimately every organization must answer to the final arbiter of value – the customer.

REA Business Process Models

The act of developing REA value system and value chain models provides a great deal of insight about the enterprise's mission, strategy, and overall operations. Facilitating high-level strategic analysis is certainly a goal of the REA enterprise ontology. The ultimate goal, though, is to provide a structure for the creation of an enterprise database in which to store disaggregated data. The physical implementation of the shared data storage may vary; the relational database is the most widely used format as of this book's publication and is the format demonstrated herein.

To develop the REA business process model, each exchange (scene/bubble) in the REA value chain model is expanded to include specifications of resources, events, agents, and various types of associations among them. At this level, the external business partners are once again included – you may think of the REA business process model as a combination of value system and value chain components but at a more detailed level. Later we discuss in more detail the specific components of the REA business process model; for now, an illustration of the basic REA business process model for the acquisition of labor is included within Exhibit 2-5, together with some example corresponding relational tables. Exhibit 2-5 is over-simplified in order to provide a manageable example; additional complexities that provide more realism are introduced and discussed in later chapters.

In a later chapter, we describe how to derive business process models like the one in Exhibit 2-5 and we further explain the symbols and the names of the constructs. For now, you need to understand that each rectangle represents a resource, an event, or an agent. You also need to understand that each of these rectangular constructs corresponds to a table in the enterprise-wide database and that the notations on the relationships between the rectangles determine how the database tables connect to each other. The procedures for converting the REA business process model (the diagram with the boxes and lines between them) to relational database tables will be detailed later, so don't be concerned that you don't know how that works yet. For now, the purpose of Exhibit 2-5 is to show you a small piece of a deliverable obtained from the REA ontology: an operational enterprise database.

One goal of this book is to teach you the basics involved in designing such a deliverable as the partial relational database illustrated in Exhibit 2-5. Complexities involved in scaling up such a design, optimizing its performance, and designing effective user interfaces are beyond the scope of this book. Once you master the material covered in this book you will have only a partial tool set to use in designing a working database for a real-world enterprise. However, the tool set you acquire by mastering the material in this book can help you to use and evaluate relational database tables in actual enterprises.

REA Task Models

The final level of detail in the REA ontology is the task level. Recall that any activities that are not essential to an enterprise's operation – in other words, those activities that can be re-engineered away – should not serve as foundational building blocks of an enterprise system and thus should not become base objects in the enterprise database. However, enterprises need to document all activities and to include information about them in their enterprise systems. A variety of workflow activities are possible and no pattern has emerged to represent the task level. Further, a variety of representation techniques for documenting workflow activities are used in practice, including narrative descriptions, system flowcharts, data flow diagrams, process models, fishbone diagrams, and others. Although no one has discovered a specific pattern for tasks, in a later chapter of this book we introduce some commonly used workflow representation techniques. The ability to document tasks and to interpret task documentation is important for designing, using, and evaluating enterprise systems. The task level of Exhibit 2-5 shows a tiny portion of a diagram representing part of a company's payroll system workflow. The portion of the diagram included in this exhibit does not represent the entire workflow needed by a typical company; the complete flowchart would take multiple pages.

AN EXAMPLE ENTERPRISE: RSWS AND ITS REA MODELS

This chapter introduced several abstract concepts that we make concrete using Robert Scott Woodwind Shop (RSWS), a fictitious enterprise based on a real former enterprise. To help separate fact from fiction, until he passed away in 2018 at age 93, Robert Scott was a real person and a truly accomplished woodwind instrument repairman, player, and teacher. Customer demand kept him working until just a few months before his death, when he simply could no longer do what he loved. See Exhibit 2-6 for a photo of Robert Scott.

Exhibit 2-6: Robert Scott

RSWS's primary line of business was woodwind instrument repair. Many concert musicians claim Mr. Scott was the best in the world because he had nearly perfect pitch and could detect subtle tone and pitch changes that other repairmen are unable to distinguish. Mr. Scott provided repair services and he manufactured clarinet mouthpieces, clarinet barrels, oboe reeds, and bassoon reeds. He sold a few instruments and taught some lessons to a few lucky students. He never took on more work than he could perform by himself, with occasional help from whichever one of his children showed an interest in learning how to perform some of the simpler repair or manufacturing activities. To keep his workload manageable, he never advertised; word of mouth proved sufficient to generate enough business to support his family while doing something he loved with a minimal amount of administrative work. Mr. Scott needed only a simple information system to maintain complete control of his tiny sole proprietorship.

We have therefore embellished the real Robert Scott Woodwinds (with Mr. Scott's permission) to describe an enterprise with a need for a fully integrated enterprise information system capable of a high volume of transactions, multiple locations, multiple employees with division of labor, and other complicating factors. In this fictitious enterprise, Mr. Scott is still very much alive and working hard.

RSWS has two types of financing: debt and equity. The debt financing reflects occasional loans RSWS obtains from banks to help with short-term cash flow needs. As RSWS expanded in volume and needed additional cash infusions to purchase new equipment, rent new store buildings, and pay employees, Robert Scott decided to change from a sole proprietorship to a corporation, completed all the necessary legal paperwork, and sold shares of stock representing ownership interest to a dozen of his concert musician friends.

RSWS generates revenues in four ways. First, RSWS purchases woodwind instruments from suppliers at wholesale prices and sells them to customers at retail prices. Second, RSWS purchases woodwind instruments from suppliers at wholesale prices and rents them to customers. Most often, these rentals are made to the parents of schoolchildren who are just beginning to play an instrument; the parents want some evidence that their child's interest in the instrument is more than just a passing fancy. Third, RSWS manufactures various instrument parts and accessories and sells them to customers. For example, RSWS manufactures clarinet barrels, clarinet mouthpieces, oboe reeds, and bassoon reeds. This involves purchasing the equipment and raw materials and then performing the labor and machine operations needed to transform the raw materials into finished goods. Fourth, RSWS performs repair services for customers. This involves evaluating customers' instruments to diagnose any problems, purchasing any needed repair parts, and performing the labor and machine operations needed to repair the instruments.

REA Value System Modeling

One question to answer when developing an REA value system model is "Who are the enterprise's external business partners?" To answer this question, it is helpful to focus on resource flows and ask the question this way, "To whom does the enterprise give resources and from whom does the enterprise receive resources?" Recall that resources have economic value to the enterprise. Recall also our pattern-based approach to developing enterprise information systems. This means that we should consider what is true for most enterprises and then make adjustments as necessary for our specific enterprise. Most enterprise resources fit into one of the following categories:

- Cash
- Inventory (raw materials, finished goods, merchandise, parts, and supplies)
- Labor
- Property, plant and equipment
- Insurance
- Rights (such as copyrights, patents, or trademarks)
- Services (such as accounting, advertising, cleaning, or government services)
- Utilities (water and energy)

To determine an enterprise's external business partners, a helpful step is to examine cash -- the universal resource for which most other resources are exchanged in today's economy. Very seldom do companies engage in *barter transactions* (exchanges of a non-cash resource for a different non-cash resource); our modeling approach can still handle such transactions, they just will not be our focus. Therefore, if you identify the various external partners to whom the enterprise pays cash and from whom the enterprise receives cash, you will very likely have identified all the appropriate external business partners. Typically, the external business partners fit into the following categories:

- Vendors or suppliers (of inventory, equipment, utilities, insurance, and services)
- Employees

- Investors and creditors
- Customers

Sometimes examining the cash outflows of an enterprise does not reveal a resource received in exchange. For example, when an enterprise pays cash to government agencies (such as the Internal Revenue Service) what resource does the enterprise receive in exchange? Some resources the government provides are easy to identify, such as a license to do business, or police and fire protection services. However, the amounts paid in taxes and fees to the government often exceed identifiable resources received in exchange, and we must simply label the resource as government services.

Payments to charitable organizations pose a similar dilemma. If an enterprise donates money to a university, what resource does it receive in exchange? We assume that enterprises make economically rational decisions; therefore, the enterprise presumably expects at least one resource in exchange. The enterprise may expect goodwill, an increased reputation in the community (in effect, advertising), or an advantage in recruiting the university's students. Based on the assumption that the enterprise does in fact receive resources in exchange for these payments, hopefully, you have figured out that government agencies and charitable organizations would be included in the external business partner category of vendors or suppliers.

Once we determine the resources an enterprise uses and we identify the external business partners with whom these resources are exchanged, we portray the information in a diagram called a value system model. We draw a circle or oval in the center of the diagram to represent the enterprise. We draw a separate square or rectangle outside the circle to represent each type of external business partner. We draw arrows between the enterprise circle and each square as appropriate to indicate the resource exchanges between the enterprise and its external business partners. Arrows from the enterprise to the external business partners represent resources given by the enterprise to the external partners; arrows from the external partners to the enterprise represent resources received by the enterprise from the external partners.

REA Value System Model for RSWS
The narrative summary of RSWS's operations provided earlier in this chapter identified RSWS's external business partners and the resources exchanged among them. Exhibit 2-7 illustrates RSWS's REA Value System model.

The external business partners for RSWS include investors, creditors, suppliers, customers, and employees. At first glance, you may wonder why employees are external business partners. After all, they perform services on behalf of RSWS. Although employees are internal agents as they perform services on behalf of RSWS, employees are external business partners in that they are exchanging their labor resource for RSWS's cash resource.

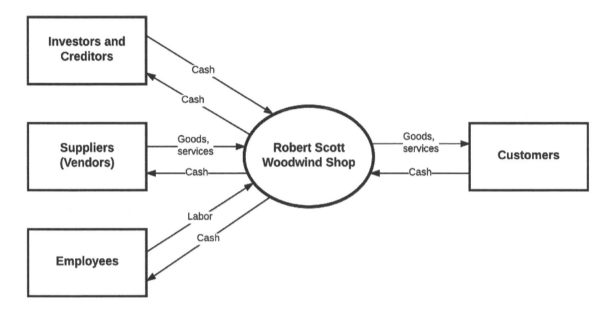

Exhibit 2-7: Robert Scott Woodwind Shop Value System

The first step in constructing this model is to draw a circle or oval in the middle of the diagram and label it Robert Scott Woodwind Shop. The second step in constructing this model is to identify the various resources RSWS uses in its operations. RSWS certainly uses cash. Consider the sources from which RSWS receives cash, the parties to whom RSWS pays cash, and how the cash is used. We note that cash is received from investors (for equity financing), from creditors (for debt financing), and from customers (for sales and rentals of goods and services). Because equity financing and debt financing both represent cash for cash exchanges, we can combine the investors and creditors into a single rectangle. Because sales and rentals of goods and services represent exchanges of cash for non-cash resources, we draw a separate rectangle to represent the set of customers.

Investors and creditors are willing to give cash to RSWS because they expect to receive an amount of cash that is worth more to them than the cash they initially gave up (with the excess being interest, dividends, and/or capital appreciation). Therefore, we draw one arrow from investors and creditors to RSWS labeled cash to represent cash inflows from investors and creditors, and we draw another arrow labeled cash from RSWS to investors and creditors to represent cash outflows to investors and creditors (e.g., for interest payments, dividends, principal repayments, and treasury stock purchases).

Customers are willing to give RSWS cash because they expect RSWS to provide goods (e.g., instruments, accessories), repair services, or the use of goods (i.e. rental of instruments). Therefore, we draw an arrow labeled cash from customers to RSWS to represent the cash inflows from customers and we draw an arrow labeled goods and services from RSWS to customers to indicate that RSWS provides those resources to its customers.

We then inspect the narrative to determine what types of cash payments RSWS makes and to whom. We identify cash payments made to employees and realize that those payments are made in exchange for labor provided by the employees (we assume labor encompasses skills, knowledge, and time). Therefore, we draw a rectangle to represent the set of employees. We draw an arrow labeled cash from RSWS to employees to represent the cash outflows to employees, and we draw an arrow labeled labor from employees to RSWS to represent the labor inflow from employees. You might notice that there is no arrow to represent benefits such as health insurance paid to employees. Is it because RSWS does not offer any such benefits or is it because they have forgotten to represent them? The answer is neither. Payments made for health insurance for employees are cash outflows to suppliers made by RSWS on behalf of the employees. The actual insurance benefit is an outflow from the health insurance supplier to the employees and is outside the scope of RSWS's value system model, which only examines the direct resource flows between RSWS and its external business partners.

This leads us to the other external business partner for RSWS – the suppliers (some enterprises may call these vendors). Suppliers are all non-employee individuals or organizations from which an enterprise acquires goods and services. We draw a rectangle to represent the set of suppliers, an arrow labeled cash from RSWS to suppliers to indicate the cash outflow, and an arrow labeled goods and services from suppliers to RSWS to indicate the inflow of goods and services.

The REA value system model represents expectations rather than actuality (as do all levels of the REA ontology). Some customers may not fulfill their end of the exchange bargain and RSWS will have given up goods or services without receiving the expected cash. Likewise, RSWS may not succeed in its endeavors, in which case its investors will not receive cash returns. Regardless of what actually occurs, the model must allow for the expected exchanges. Furthermore, the exchange of resources does not have to be simultaneous. For example, RSWS may purchase materials and pay for them at a later date. When the "give side" and "take side" of the exchange are separated across time it leads to certain accounting concepts such as receivables and payables. However, when you think of the exchange, you should focus on the resources related to the ultimate settlement of the exchange.

You may have some questions about how to create the REA value system model from the narrative. For example, how do you choose how many different external partner categories to represent? As alluded to earlier, we could have made separate boxes for investors and creditors. We chose to combine them because both were trading cash for cash with RSWS. Similarly, we could have made separate boxes for suppliers of goods and suppliers of services. In fact, we did make a separate box for employees, who are essentially suppliers of one type of service.

As guidance for your decision about what to combine and what to separate, consider the types of resources expected to be exchanged and the types of information you want to capture about the external partners. If the same types of resources are to be exchanged with two different types of external parties, and the same types of information need to be captured about those external parties, then it makes sense to combine them to simplify the picture. If different types of resources are to be exchanged and/or different types of information need to be captured about the external parties, then it makes sense to separate them.

For example, the exchange between RSWS and its employees is cash for services. That is similar to the exchange between RSWS and some types of suppliers (advertising agencies, accountants, and lawyers). However, RSWS needs to capture much more information about its employees than about its other suppliers. To process payroll and comply with government reporting requirements, RSWS must store employees' social security numbers, number of dependents, tax filing status, bank account numbers for direct deposit, and so forth. RSWS would not capture, much less store such details about its non-employee suppliers.

REA Value Chain Modeling

Completion of the value system analysis leads to the initial value chain analysis. The value chain analysis focuses on the resource flows between the enterprise's internal business processes. Because you have already identified the resources flowing into and out of the enterprise when analyzing the value system, what remains at the value chain level is to examine what the company does with its input resources and how it generates its output resources. As business processes consume resources, they should also produce or acquire resources that are worth more to the enterprise than those consumed. As noted earlier, enterprises create value by developing and providing the goods and services customers desire. Enterprises have at least three business processes.

1. Acquisition: The objective of the acquisition process is to acquire, maintain, and pay for the resources needed by the enterprise. The acquisition process has many synonyms: expenditure cycle, purchasing cycle, procurement process, procure-to-pay, and purchase-to-pay. Enterprises need many resources: financial, human, raw materials, supplies, property, plant, and equipment. Resources are acquired from external suppliers or vendors. These are the inputs required by the organization to provide goods and services to its customers. Because the acquisition of financial resources and the acquisition of human resources have complexities not found in the acquisition of other goods and services, many enterprises separate these activities into additional business processes, called the financing process and the payroll (or human resource) process.

2. Conversion: Sometimes called the manufacturing process, the objective of the conversion process is to convert the acquired resources into goods and services for customers. Raw inputs, such as materials and labor, are transformed into finished goods and services, while using other inputs such as equipment, within this process.

3. Revenue: Sometimes called the revenue process, the objective of the revenue process is to sell and deliver goods, services, or the temporary use of goods to customers and to collect payment from customers. The finished goods and services sold to customers may have come from the conversion process or from the acquisition process. The cash received from customers will then be used for other purposes in the company. Other synonyms include: sale-to-cash, order-to-cash, quote-to-cash, and contact-to-contract-to-cash.

Creating a value chain model that illustrates the linkages between these processes requires understanding of two very important concepts in the REA ontology: duality and stockflow. These concepts characterize a core economic phenomena – that of an exchange. As noted earlier, we presume that enterprises make rational economic decisions. Rational economic theory precludes decision-makers from giving something up with no expectation of getting anything in exchange. For every event in which an enterprise gives something up we expect a related event in which the enterprise receives something. The causal relationship between a give event and a take event is a *duality* association.

Stockflow is defined generally as a relationship between an economic event and a related resource. "Stock" means increase (increment, take) and "flow" means decrease (decrement, give); therefore, we could separate Stockflow into Stock and Flow to represent the two types of relationships. Stockflow relationships between give events and resources show specific resources given in an exchange. Stockflow relationships between take events and resources show specific resources taken in an exchange. These flows may be economic value increases and decreases rather than physical quantity increases and decreases. For example, adding a logo to a shirt increases the economic value of the shirt rather than increasing the quantity of shirts. Duality and stockflow are foundational concepts in the REA ontology's value chain level. Geerts and McCarthy say "Duality relationships are the glue that binds a firm's separate economic events together into rational economic processes, while stock-flow relationships weave these processes together into an enterprise value chain[22]. (p. 98)"

The first step in REA value chain modeling is writing the enterprise script – identifying the business processes. We use the REA value system model along with whatever other information we have, such as a narrative description of the enterprise activities. The second step in REA value chain modeling is to draw the resource flows to link the business processes together. The third step is to determine the economic exchange events and the duality relationships that make up the core of each business process in the value chain. We next revisit our RSWS example to clarify these steps.

REA Value Chain Model for RSWS
Once we have identified the external business partners and the resource exchanges with them, we can develop the REA value chain model for RSWS. See Exhibit 2-8. To understand how we created this value chain, consider the following steps.

---

[22] Geerts, G. and McCarthy, W.E. "Modeling Business Enterprises as Value-Added Process Hierarchies with Resource-Event-Agent Object Templates" in J. Sutherland and D. Patel, eds., *Business Object Design and Implementation*, London: Springer-Verlag, 1997, pp. 94-113.

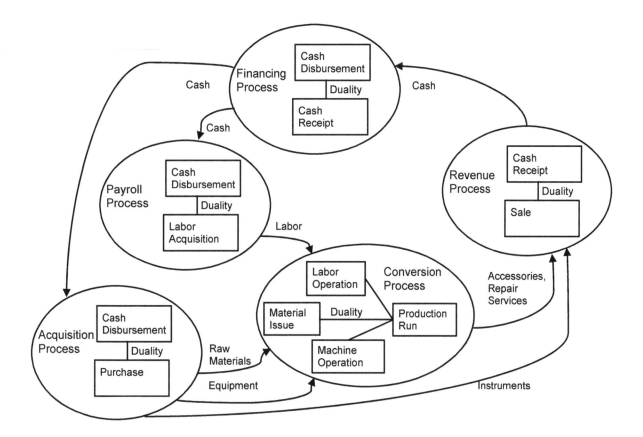

Exhibit 2-8: Robert Scott Woodwind Shop (RSWS) Value Chain Model

Step 1: Write the business entrepreneur script

To complete this step, we examine the typical scenes of the business entrepreneur script to see which of the scenes apply for RSWS. Based on our value system level analysis, the typical script pattern, and the narrative description of RSWS we write the script as follows:

Scene 1. RSWS gets cash from investors and creditors

Scene 2. RSWS uses cash to acquire labor from employees

Scene 3. RSWS uses cash to buy instruments, raw materials, and overhead from vendors

Scene 4. RSWS uses materials, equipment, and overhead to manufacture accessories, and to provide repair services

Scene 5. RSWS sells instruments, accessories, and repair services to customers for cash

Scene 6. RSWS pays cash to investors and creditors

Scenes 1 and 6 in the script comprise the financing business process. Scenes 2, 3, 4, and 5 represents the payroll, acquisition, conversion, and revenue business processes, respectively. All of these scenes come directly from our value system analysis except for scene 4. Because the conversion process does not include resource exchanges with external business partners, it does not appear on the value system model. Effective value chain modeling requires that you include not only the scenes that you derive from the value system level, but you also include any business processes that add value via internal resource transformations.

To begin re-creating the model in Exhibit 2-8, draw one bubble for each business process identified in step 1. Label each bubble with the business process name.

Step 2: Connect the business processes with resource flows

Once you identify all the business processes, combine them to form a value chain. The resource flows provide the links from one business process to the next.

Look first at the financing process bubble for RSWS. Once the cash resource is received, it must be made available to at least one other business process. In this case, cash is made available as a resource for the acquisition and payroll processes. Therefore, draw arrows labeled cash from financing to acquisition and from financing to payroll.

Value chain models do not depict agents. The goal is to show how business processes within the enterprise add value to the resources. The arrows depicted on the models do not necessarily represent physical flows, but represent resource availability passing from one process to another. RSWS's acquisition process uses up the cash resource and obtains raw material, equipment, overhead, and instrument resources. RSWS's payroll process uses up the cash resource and obtains labor resources. RSWS's conversion process transforms the labor, raw material, equipment, and overhead resources into the accessories and repair service resources. To depict the latter, draw an arrow labeled labor from payroll to conversion and draw arrows labeled raw materials, equipment, and overhead from acquisition to conversion.

RSWS's revenue process consumes the resources: instruments, accessories, and repair services, and obtains the resource cash. To depict these concepts, draw an arrow labeled Instruments from acquisition to revenue, and draw arrows labeled accessories and repair services from conversion to revenue. The cash obtained within the revenue process is made available to the financing process. Therefore, draw an arrow labeled cash from revenue to financing. The assumption is that in each business process the taken resources are worth more than the given resources, thus value is added in each link of the chain.

Step 3: Specify the economic exchange events within each scene

The third step in creating the value chain model adds economic events that are associated with the resources identified in step 2; the events are drawn inside each scene's bubble. Each scene must contain at least one economic decrement (give) event and at least one economic increment (take) event. Resource flows help to determine what events to include; ask yourself what event caused this resource to decrease or increase in value? This analysis will also help you to determine whether any scene in your value chain should be decomposed into multiple scenes.

The general rule to follow for this step is that each business process should include an economic decrement event that corresponds to each resource outflow and an economic increment event that corresponds to each resource inflow. In other words, if a resource is given, the business process must include an event that consumes it (either by transferring it to an external partner or by transforming it into a different resource). Similarly, if a resource is taken, the business process must include an event that obtains or produces the resource (either by transferring it in from an external business partner or by creating it as a transformation of some other resources).

Consider RSWS's financing process. When a company needs financing it needs the resource cash. The increment (take event) associated with receiving the cash is called a cash receipt. From step 2, you saw the revenue process leads to a receipt of cash; that received cash is returned to the financing process where a cash disbursement event occurs (and the financing agents receive a return on their investment). Draw two event boxes inside the financing process bubble, and label them as cash receipt and cash disbursement. Connect them by drawing a line between them and labeling the relationship line duality. This relationship indicates the disbursement is being made because of a previous cash receipt (e.g. repaying a loan).

Next, consider RSWS's payroll process. If RSWS wants to obtain a labor resource, what does it have to give in exchange? Cash. The payment of cash for payroll purposes is identified by a cash disbursement event The enterprise will likely only have one cash disbursement event set that will encompass all cash disbursements made for all purposes, but we must depict that cash disbursement event set in each business process that consumes cash. The labor resource increases in the payroll process, so we include a take event that obtains the labor (e.g., labor acquisition). Therefore, draw two event boxes inside the payroll process bubble and connect them via a relationship line labeled duality. Label the events cash disbursement and labor acquisition.

Next, consider RSWS's acquisition process. The acquisition process must include a give event that consumes cash (i.e., a cash disbursement event). In exchange for the cash, RSWS gets instruments, materials, services, and equipment, so the process must include at least one take event that obtains those items from external sources (i.e., an acquisition event). To decide whether to include multiple take events, we determine whether the enterprise requires the same data attributes for acquisitions of each item type. We recommend making separate acquisition process bubbles with separate take events for those that require different data attributes. Assuming that RSWS records all acquisitions of goods, services, and equipment using a common set of forms and captures the same data attributes for them, we need only one acquisition event set and only one acquisition process bubble. Draw two event boxes inside the acquisition process bubble and connect them via a relationship line labeled duality. Label the events cash disbursement and purchase.

Next, consider RSWS's conversion process. The conversion process is typically the most complicated. RSWS's value chain model shows input resources as materials, equipment, labor, and overhead, indicating the conversion process must include events that consume each of those inputs. Materials are consumed as they are issued into manufacturing or repair jobs so draw a box and label it material issue. Employee labor is consumed when employees perform labor operations, so draw a box and label it labor operation. Equipment and overhead are consumed in machine operations, so draw a box and label it machine operation. RSWS's value chain model shows output resources as finished accessories and repaired instruments. Mr. Scott tells us that RSWS calls every repair service and each job to produce a batch of parts or accessories a production run, so we draw a box and label it production run. We realize that the material issues, labor operations, and machine operations are economic decrement events (they use up resources) that are matched with the production run, which is an economic increment event (it produces resources). Therefore, we draw relationship lines to connect material issues, labor operations, and machine operations to the production run and label each line as duality. The conversion process illustrates that exchanges are not limited to one give event and one take event.

Finally, consider RSWS's revenue process. Input resources include new instruments from the acquisition process, and manufactured accessories and repaired instruments from the conversion process. RSWS exchanges the new instruments for cash by either selling them or renting them to customers. RSWS exchanges repaired instruments and manufactured accessories for cash by delivering them to customers. As with the acquisition process, we need to make a choice as to whether there is a common sale event set for which the same set of data attributes will be maintained, or whether the activities are dissimilar enough to warrant being maintained as separate event sets. Mr. Scott tells us that RSWS uses the same set of forms and captures the same data attributes for each of these revenue-generating activities, so we will combine them into one economic decrement event called sale. The output resource is cash, indicating that the process must include an event that produces or obtains the cash, in other words an economic increment event called cash receipt. We draw two boxes with a duality relationship line connecting them; we label one box sale and the other box cash receipt. Now the value chain is complete and we can use it to facilitate creation of the REA business process models for RSWS.

REA Business Process Modeling – the Core Pattern

ISO (the International Organization for Standardization), and IEC (the International Electro-technical Commission) form the specialized system for worldwide standardization. A 2007 ISO/IEC standard for business transactions formalized most of the terminology and REA constructs introduced in this chapter[23]. The three object categories that comprise the core REA business process pattern are Resources, Events, and Agents.

As you read above, resources are things such as goods, services, or rights that have value and are under the control of a person or enterprise. Enterprises may track resources at the individual instance (token) level if the enterprise can differentiate each specific physical object, even though their nature and appearance may be identical. Such tracking is typically accomplished through some type of tags, each of which has a unique identifier such as a serial number. Alternatively, enterprises often track resources only by categories, and we thus refer to them as **resource types**. The enterprise assigns one identifier such as a part number or stock keeping unit (SKU) to represent each resource type; individual instances of a resource type are interchangeable and indistinguishable. Resource types are sometimes called bulk resources.

An automobile is an example of a resource. Each specific physical automobile has a unique vehicle identification number (VIN) that differentiates that automobile from all others (specific-identification). At first, thinking about these concepts can be confusing, because cars can also be

---

[23] ISO/IEC 2007, ISO 15944-4 Information technology -- Business Operational View -- Part 4: Business transaction scenarios -- Accounting and economic ontology. http://standards.iso.org/ittf/PubliclyAvailableStandards/index.html

represented as types like a "Ford Mustang" – that is a type of car or type or resource. A stapler is another example of a resource type. Each specific physical stapler has a label that identifies the type of product – brand, size, and color, but all staplers that share that brand, size, and color have the same label. Staplers with the same label are interchangeable and indistinguishable from each other (type-identification). Most mass produced items are type-identified.

The REA business process model has its economic events at its core. As discussed earlier, economic increment events increase resources, either in quantity or in value; and economic decrement events decrease resources, either in quantity or in value. All events are occurrences in time and therefore have either dates to timestamps as essential data. A purchase (receipt of goods) is an example of an economic increment event in the acquisition process. Cash receipt is an example of an economic increment event in the revenue process. Cash disbursement is an example of an economic decrement event commonly found in the acquisition process. Sale is an example of an economic decrement event commonly found in the revenue process.

Agents are individuals, enterprises, or agencies who participate in events or who control resources. Agents acting on behalf of the enterprise are internal agents. Agents operating on behalf of themselves or on behalf of other enterprises are external agents. Because employees primarily operate on behalf of their enterprises, we consider them to be internal agents. However, be aware that when representing themselves within the payroll process (operating at an arms' length with the enterprise, exchanging their labor for cash), their connection to events would be outside participation rather than inside participation.

Core REA Associations

When Bill McCarthy examined hundreds of accounting transactions in search of an underlying pattern, he noted that every accounting transaction represented part or all of an economic exchange made up of at least one economic increment event and at least one economic decrement event. In other words, each economic exchange involved the company giving up one resource or combination of resources to get another resource or combination of resources. In this textbook, we define and use associations as relationships between two sets of objects (although there are other types of associations beyond the scope of this textbook); rectangle symbols represent sets of objects in the REA business process model, and lines connecting the rectangles represent associations between those objects. Duality is the causal association between the economic increment and decrement events that make up an economic exchange.

McCarthy also noticed that the exchange was not always immediate and that there was no rule as to whether the increment or the decrement event happened first. Sometimes there was a significant time lag between the events, for which double-entry bookkeeping entries created an account to allow its entries to balance – i.e., to keep both sides of the Assets = Liabilities + Equity equation equal with each other. McCarthy labeled these timing differences between related economic decrement and increment events *claims* and emphasized the fact that the exchanges were incomplete until corresponding economic events occurred to satisfy the claims. Claims in financial accounting include accounts receivable (sale happens before the related cash receipt), deferred revenue (cash receipt happens before the related sale), prepaid expenses (cash disbursement happens before the related acquisition event), accounts payable (acquisition event happens before the related cash disbursement event), and wages payable (acquisition of labor happens before the related cash disbursement event). You may already know the related terminology of accruals and deferrals from your financial accounting classes.

McCarthy also noticed that although what was received or given up varied for different transactions, that thing always had economic value and could be thought of as a resource. He emphasized that the claims are not resources and should not be used as foundational elements in an information system. McCarthy used the term stockflow to describe the association between an economic event and the resource that event increases or decreases. Associations between economic increment events and the resources they increase are inflow relationships. Associations between economic decrement events and the resources they decrease are outflow relationships.

Finally, McCarthy noticed that each event that made up an economic exchange involved more than just a "what" (the resource) but also a "who." In fact, each event typically involved at least one person operating as an agent of the enterprise and at least one other person or company serving as an external business partner. *Participation* associations relate events to the internal and external agents who participate in those events. Whenever an event occurs, it is essential to know the agents participating in the event. This allows for management control and accountability.

Exhibit 2-9 illustrates McCarthy's 1982 core REA pattern, modified to the present UML class diagram format.

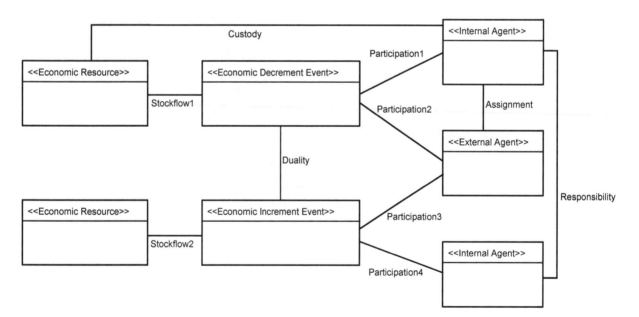

Exhibit 2-9: Core REA Pattern[24]

---

[24] Adapted from McCarthy, W.E. "The REA Accounting Model: A Generalized Framework for Accounting Systems in a Shared Data Environment." *The Accounting Review*, July 1982, pp. 554-578.

McCarthy realized that enterprises do not record accounting transactions until part of the economic story is already over. He also understood that enterprises were not capturing their full economic stories because the accounting view driven by the content of traditional financial statements did not require all the details of the economic stories. Because in 1982 McCarthy intended REA as an accounting model, he included only the economic events needed to generate financial accounting figures. In addition to the core REA associations called duality, stockflow, and participation, McCarthy discussed three additional types of associations that he believed enterprises should track: custody, assignment, and responsibility. In later years, he and other colleagues further developed the REA ontology to include events that happen before and after the actual economic exchange. These concepts are further illustrated in chapters 4 through 7 and in chapter 10.

Custody associates an agent and a resource such that the agent has physical control over the resource or the agent controls access to the resource. Such a relationship is separate from any event involving the resource. If an event involves a resource and an agent, the participation of both the resource and the agent in that event does not constitute a custody association. The agent who has custody of a resource may be an internal agent or an external agent. For example, banks have custody of an enterprise's cash held in accounts at their locations. Consignees have custody of goods that they have been contracted to sell on the enterprise's behalf.

Assignment is an association between an internal agent and an external agent that is separate from any event in which they might both participate. For example, say salesperson S42's assigned territory includes customer number 43BYZ. That relationship exists even if S48 makes a sale to customer 43BYZ while S42 is on vacation.

Responsibility is an association between two types of internal agents that is separate from any event in which they might both participate. For example, a partner in a public accounting firm may have responsibility for ten of the staff accountants in that firm. Specific responsibilities may include the partner mentoring the staff accountants, reading supervisors' reviews of the staff accountants' performance, reviewing the staff accountants' training programs and career plans, and conducting their annual evaluations. Such a relationship exists even if those staff accountants never work on a client engagement with that partner.

If enterprises stopped modeling their business processes after they have finished the core REA pattern, their models would be woefully incomplete. In later chapters, we will expand the core pattern to flesh out the business process models so that they capture a more complete picture of the enterprise's economic story. We will add even more details to the business process models, demonstrate how to convert those models into relational databases, and develop queries to extract information from the databases to support financial reporting and decision-making.

REA Business Process Model for Acquisition Process
The REA business process modeling constructs may seem abstract to you. Let us make those constructs more concrete by first discussing them in the general context of the acquisition process, and then in the following section, applying the constructs to RSWS's REA acquisition business process model.

The acquisition process includes the activities associated with buying, maintaining, and paying for goods and services needed by enterprises. Exhibit 2-10 illustrates three typical REA business process models for acquisition: a) for inventory acquisitions, b) for operating asset acquisitions or rentals, and c) for service acquisitions. The REA pattern aids in analyzing business processes and events by highlighting "what" (the resources involved in the event) and "who" (the internal and external agents) that are associated with each event. The where and the when of the events are also relevant; however, they are most often stored as attributes of each event - a topic illustrated in a later chapter. The events, agents, and resources involved in the acquisition process may vary from enterprise to enterprise – but the general pattern discussed in this chapter can easily be adapted and applied to meet the exact requirements of any enterprise.

Economic Increment Event
The economic increment event in the acquisition process may take on one of several labels: acquisition, purchase, rental, or receipt of goods are typical. This event is normally associated with resources such as supplies, inventory, or operating assets.

Purchase is the label used for the economic increment event when the acquired resource is a tangible asset such as inventory or equipment. Rental is the label used for the economic increment event when the acquired resource is a temporary right to use some type of tangible asset. A rental acquisition begins when the right to temporary possession of the asset transfers from the supplier to the enterprise, and ends when possession of the asset transfers back from the enterprise to the supplier. Service acquisition or general and administrative service acquisition are among the labels used for the economic increment event when the acquired resources are services.

Whatever the labels, the important consideration is that an increment event must represent the point at which the enterprise received benefit. It is at this point that a liability is incurred (unless the corresponding payment has already been made).

Enterprises usually purchase several types of resources (e.g., inventory, operating assets, and general and administrative services) and therefore must decide whether to combine the different acquisitions into one acquisition event object (associated with multiple resource objects) or to create separate acquisition event objects based on the type of resource being acquired.

The decision to combine or separate acquisitions of different resources usually depends on whether the data differ based on type of acquisition. Types of acquisitions with different data should be separate objects, whereas acquisitions with identical data should be combined, especially if they are captured with the same set of sequentially numbered documents or software interfaces.

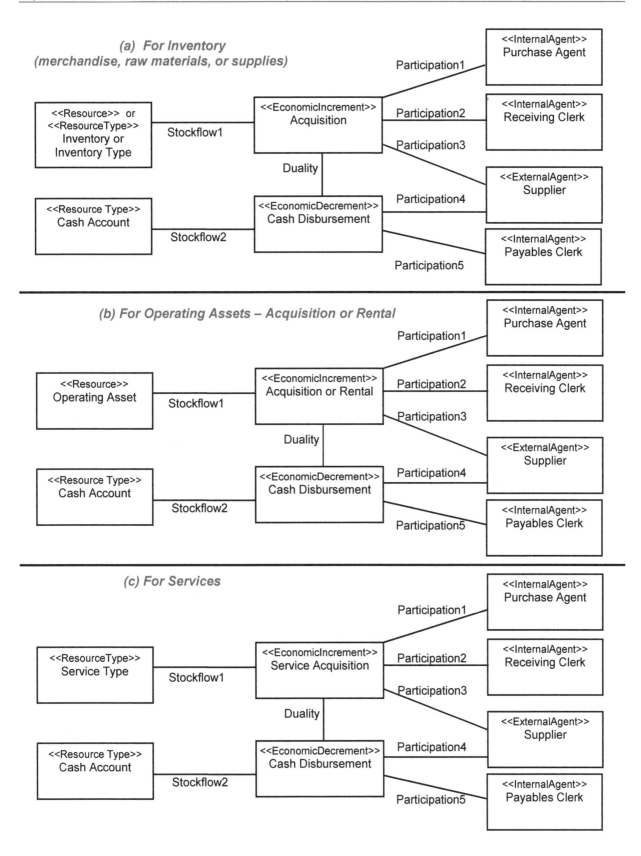

Exhibit 2-10: REA Acquisition Process Model

Internal agents are typically associated with economic increment events via participation associations; these agents include purchase agents and receiving clerks. External agents are typically associated with economic increment events via participation associations; these agents include suppliers, common carriers (such as UPS or Federal Express), and credit card companies.

The resources typically associated with the economic increment event via stockflow associations in the acquisition process are inventory, inventory type, service type, supply type, or operating asset. The resource typically associated with the economic decrement event via stockflow associations in the acquisition process is cash.

Most manufacturers and merchandisers do not specifically identify inventory, so the resource that participates in the stockflow1 association for inventory acquisition is usually inventory type. For those enterprises that do specifically identify individual inventory items, the resource in the stockflow1 association is inventory. For general and administrative service acquisitions, the resource involved in the stockflow1 association is usually service type. For supply acquisitions the associated resource is usually supply type, and for operating asset acquisitions the associated resource is usually operating asset (note that typically operating assets are individually identified, either with serial numbers or enterprise-generated asset tags).

Economic Decrement Event

Cash disbursements are economic decrement events that decrease the enterprise's cash resource balance. The company may disburse cash via paper check, debit card, electronic funds transfer, or with currency and coins. Realize that if the enterprise uses a credit card to pay a supplier, the enterprise has not yet disbursed cash; the cash disbursement does not occur until the enterprise pays the credit card company.

In the last section, we discussed the various types of acquisitions and potential resources acquired. Regardless of the type of resource acquired or the type of acquisition, if there is an acquisition, there must be an associated economic decrement event because of duality. Cash disbursement is the decrement event typically associated with an acquisition (increment) event.

REA Business Process Model for RSWS's Acquisition Process

Recall that RSWS generates revenue through several different activities:
- selling instruments
- renting instruments
- providing repair services
- selling manufactured accessories such as clarinet barrels and mouthpieces

To engage in its revenue-generating activities, RSWS must first purchase instruments, raw materials, fixed assets, and various services from suppliers.

The first step in creating RSWS's REA acquisition process model is to draw boxes for its economic increment and decrement events and to connect them via a duality association. We know from

RSWS's value chain model that the economic exchange events in RSWS's acquisition process are purchase (increment event) and cash disbursement (decrement event). We represent those with boxes and connect the boxes as shown in Exhibit 2-11.

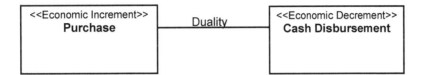

Exhibit 2-11: RSWS Acquisition Process Step 1

The second step is to connect the economic events to the resources they affect. The value chain assists in identifying the resources. Cash is the resource being given (decremented) in the acquisition process, so the decrement event is cash disbursement. Thus, we attach the cash resource type to the cash disbursement decrement event via a stockflow association, as shown below.

Instruments, raw materials, and overhead are the resources being taken (incremented) in the acquisition process, so the increment event is purchase. We next need to decide whether we should combine the resources into a single object, or to portray them as separate objects. We make this decision based on the data attributes to be stored for the various resource types. In this example, let us say we will track the same attributes for instrument inventory and raw materials so we combine them into one object (inventory type). However, we determine the data for the overhead items/services we acquire are different from the inventory data so we create a separate object to represent overhead. We create two resource objects; one called inventory and the other called overhead, and we link them to the acquisition increment event via two stockflow associations, as shown in Exhibit 2-12.

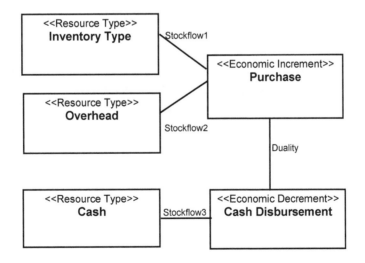

Exhibit 2-12: RSWS Acquisition Process Step 2

The third step is to add objects representing the external and internal agents and create appropriate associations between the agents and related events. The value system model helps with this step, as we identified external agents with which RSWS exchanges resources. For RSWS, we identified suppliers as the external agent with whom RSWS exchanges cash for goods and services. Thus, we add suppliers as an external agent and we create two participation associations; one between supplier and purchase and the other between supplier and cash disbursement.

Neither the value system, nor the value chain models identify internal agents for specific events. The narrative description for RSWS does not include enough detail to determine the applicable internal agents for specific events. Thus, we ask Robert Scott, "who processes acquisitions and cash disbursements on behalf of RSWS," and we receive the following reply: "Johnny Arthur and Cheri Lynn make the acquisitions; Lorie Lisbet, Linda Kay, and Timothy Rob process the cash disbursements – those for acquisitions and all other payments we make. Oh, and Ray Edwards approves all checks that are written."

Notice that the response we received was at the token level of detail. We need to raise the level of abstraction for our conceptual model, using employee type descriptions rather than individual employee names. Some companies may choose simply to create one employee object rather than creating separate objects for different employee types. Whether that is a good idea depends on whether we want to store the same attributes for all categories of employee. If we need to store different attributes about different sets of employees (e.g., if we need different attributes for purchasing agents than we do for accounts payable clerks or managers) then we may choose to represent each category of employee as a separate object and show associations between the events and the appropriate employee category agents. If we represent all employees as a single class, we must take care to identify separate associations to represent different roles involving different individuals with respect to each event. For example, processing cash disbursements is a different role from authorizing them. If RSWS chooses to maintain one overall class for employee, it should create two associations between the cash disbursement event and the employee agent. RSWS wants to keep its employees in separate objects depending on their positions.

When we interview Mr. Scott further, he tells us that Johnny and Cheri are purchasing agents; Lorie, Linda, and Timothy are cashiers, and Ray is a manager. We add purchasing agent as an object and connect it to purchase via a participation association. We add cashier as an object and connect it to cash disbursement via a participation association. We add manager as an object and connect it to cash disbursement via an authorization association (thus distinguishing the role of the manager with respect to the cash disbursement from that of the cashiers). See Exhibit 2-13 for the result of this step – the core business process model for RSWS's acquisition process.

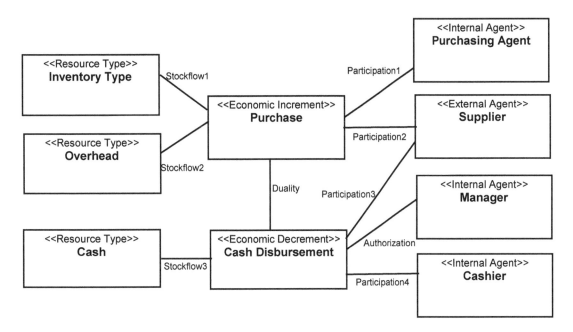

Exhibit 2-13: RSWS Acquisition Process Step 3

REA Task Modeling

As noted earlier in the chapter, an REA task model contains the detailed procedures by which information is obtained, stored, maintained, and reported with regard to each event in an REA business process model. Researchers have yet to identify patterns at the task level. Enterprises may employ any number of different procedures to accomplish the events about which data are captured in REA business process models. If covering the entire REA business process model for each process is too much for one chapter, covering the entire task level would be even more voluminous. For that reason, Chapter 3 provides additional detail about the events to be included in REA business process models and the documents often used to capture data describing those events. Chapter 8 discusses and provides examples of methods for documenting task models.

CONCLUDING COMMENTS

In this chapter we discussed techniques for representing elements of an enterprise's reality in a conceptual model. Such representations serve both as a basis for designing an enterprise wide database, and for understanding and analyzing the enterprise's strategies and operations. We discussed the four levels of the REA enterprise ontology, and illustrated how to view the enterprise from multiple perspectives to ensure the database can capture information consistent with the enterprise's value-adding activities and overall strategy.

Value system and value chain analyses are valuable because they compel you to understand both the internal operations of a firm as well as the environmental forces and parties outside the firm that affect its ability to create value. The direct actions of an organization are only part of its overall value chain process. External linkages, such as the activities of customers and suppliers are also important to understand the ability of an organization to create value. For example, some organizations may succeed in creating value because they elicit quality response from their customers and use the feedback to quickly change or upgrade their products. Other organizations may achieve success because they have worked effectively with their suppliers to reduce costs and to improve their ability to respond to customer desires. A thorough analysis of the value system and value chain helps your thought process by enabling you to understand all the activities that are strategically relevant to an organization, not just the activities in which an organization directly participates or controls.

KEY TERMS AND CONCEPTS
Acquisition process
Assignment
Barter transaction
Business entrepreneur script
Business process
Claim
Conversion process
Custody
Duality
Event
Object pattern
Participation
Pattern
Payroll process
REA business process model
REA task level model
REA value chain model
REA value system model
Resource
Responsibility
Script pattern
Stockflow
Token level representation
Type level representation

REVIEW QUESTIONS
R2-1. What is the difference between token level and type level representation?
R2-2. What is the difference between an object pattern and a script pattern?
R2-3. To begin creating a value system level REA model, this chapter recommends that you first try to identify what?
R2-4. What are the five major business processes found in most enterprises?
R2-5. When a REA value chain level model includes a business process that has three economic decrement events and one economic increment event, what should you know about that business process' resources?

MULTIPLE CHOICE QUESTIONS

MC2-1. Which of the following is true about script patterns?
- A) Script patterns are sequence of events that occur in combination with each other.
- B) Script patterns focus on objects and relationships between them.
- C) Script patterns are always accurate.
- D) Past script patterns rarely help you for the future

MC2-2. Which of the following models focuses primarily on the resource exchanges between the enterprise and its various external business partners such as suppliers, customers, creditors/investors, and employees?
- A) REA value system level model
- B) REA value chain level model
- C) REA business process level model
- D) REA task level model

MC2-3. In database design, individual objects are sometimes referred to as _____, and categories of objects are known as _____.
- A) Symbols, Types
- B) Types, Token
- C) Tokens, Types
- D) Symbols, Tokens

MC2-4. Employees of Brymer Bridge Design (BBD) can elect to have $50 per month deducted from their paychecks to pay for dental insurance. BBD transmits the insurance premiums to DentaRight Dental Insurance (DRDI). When an insured BBD employee visits a participating dentist, the employee pays only half the bill. The remaining half is paid by DRDI. Which of the following statements best describes why the dental benefits paid by DRDI to the dentists should not be included on BBD's REA Value System Model?
- A) Payment of employee benefits such as dental insurance falls within the scope of BBD's conversion cycle, and conversion cycles are typically not depicted on value system models.
- B) Payment of the dental benefits relates to the resource exchanges between DRDI and its suppliers, therefore it is outside the scope of BBD's value system model.
- C) Payment of the dental benefits by DRDI to the dentists should be included on BBD's value system model.
- D) Payment of dental benefits is an event, not a resource exchange; therefore it should not appear on a value system level model.

MC2-5. The relationship between a give event and a take event is a _____, and _____ is defined as the relationship between an event and a resource.
- A) Difference association; Process
- B) Duality association; Stockflow
- C) Conversion association; Timing
- D) Value Chain association; Resource flow

MC2-6. Resource flow connections between the internal business processes of an enterprise are most commonly illustrated in:
A) REA Value System models
B) REA Value Chain models
C) REA Business Process models
D) REA Task models

MC2-7. What is likely the most appropriate label to put on the arrow going into the financing process for this partial value chain level model for a privately held pharmacy?

A) Loan
B) Common stock
C) Cash
D) Pharmaceuticals

MC2-8. In a REA value chain level model, what event should be added inside the financing process bubble corresponds to the arrow coming into the financing process bubble?

A) Cash disbursement
B) Cash receipt
C) Labor acquisition
D) Purchase

MC2-9. In an enterprise value chain, to which other internal business process are manufactured goods typically made available by the conversion business process?
A) Financing
B) Revenue
C) Payroll (Human Resources)
D) Acquisition

MC2-10. In top-down order, the hierarchy levels in the REA enterprise ontology are
A) Task, business process, value system, value chain
B) Business process, task, value system, value chain
C) Value chain, value system, business process, task
D) Value system, value chain, business process, task

CHAPTER 3

UML Class Diagrams and Relational Databases

LEARNING OBJECTIVES

The primary focus of this chapter is on developing Unified Modeling Language (UML) Class Diagrams and creating relational databases. UML and relational database technology are not specific to REA; computer scientists created these tools. REA models are created and implemented using other tools too; we have chosen to demonstrate REA with UML and relational database technology due to their widespread use and availability to universities. In the previous chapter, while learning how to create REA business process models, you actually learned some basic concepts of UML. The primary objectives of this chapter are (1) to provide additional details of conceptual modeling with UML class diagrams, (2) to explain how to convert conceptual models into logical relational database models, and (3) to demonstrate how to create physical implementations of such models using Microsoft Access. After studying this chapter, you should be able to:

1. Explain the difference between conceptual, logical, and physical database models
2. Describe constructs of UML class diagrams and relational databases
3. Prepare and interpret UML class diagrams
4. Convert conceptual models into logical models in relational database format
5. Interpret logical relational models to determine what the underlying conceptual models must have been
6. Create data consistent with multiplicities
7. Convert a logical relational model into a Microsoft Access physical implementation
8. Enter transaction data into a relational database in Microsoft Access
9. Interpret a physical database implemented in Microsoft Access to determine what the underlying conceptual model must have been
10. Recognize and implement application level controls to facilitate the integrity of data entered into a relational database

INTRODUCTION

We organize this chapter around three levels of database models: conceptual, logical, and physical. *Conceptual database models* are representations of objects and their relationships. As such, they are not tied to a specific software package; conceptual models are hardware and software-independent. Because current enterprise systems use relational database technology, we will convert conceptual models to a specific type of logical model – the relational model. At the physical level, we are going to work with Microsoft Access as an example of one type of relational database (others you may know of are Microsoft's SQL Server and Oracle's Oracle Database).

This chapter is about the effective modeling and use of data. When we create a conceptual model, a UML class diagram, we are structuring data in a way that allows for effective and efficient data management. The purpose of the conceptual models created in this chapter is very different from the workflow models that we discuss in Chapter 8. Workflow models represent the sequential flow of documents and other information through a system, showing the areas of responsibility for the information and documents, as well as data's sources, destinations, and formats. Conceptual models design a structure for the data an enterprise needs to store to meet its information needs. Conceptual models are converted into logical models once the type of software to be used is known; therefore, you may think of them as blueprints with the specifications for the resulting database table structures. In sum, conceptual models are about effective and efficient data representation; workflow models are about the sequences of steps that workers do to complete their tasks.

Several different conceptual modeling languages exist. The REA ontology is independent of any specific modeling language and can be implemented using many different types of models and software. REA can be communicated using (1) narrative descriptions, (2) diagrams of various types with different notations (3) structured grammar, (4) predicate logic notation, (5) tags such as are used in XML and XBRL, and (6) programming language notation. It is very difficult for some people to separate the REA pattern from the notation that is used to communicate the REA pattern.

Unified Modeling Language (UML) is a widely accepted notation for system analysis and design that includes several types of diagrams for different levels of analysis; its *class diagrams* are appropriate for conceptual modeling of data, as well as modeling specific REA concepts.

In database design, a conceptual model is converted into a logical model once the type of database to be used has been determined. *Logical database models* are independent of any specific software package, but may only be implemented using a software package based on the logical model choice. Logical models may be relational, object-oriented, graph databases, and so forth. Logical models are converted into physical database implementations using the chosen vendor-specific software (e.g., Microsoft sells both the Access relational database software as well as the SQL Server relational database software).

Exhibit 3-1 illustrates the difference between conceptual, logical, and physical models.

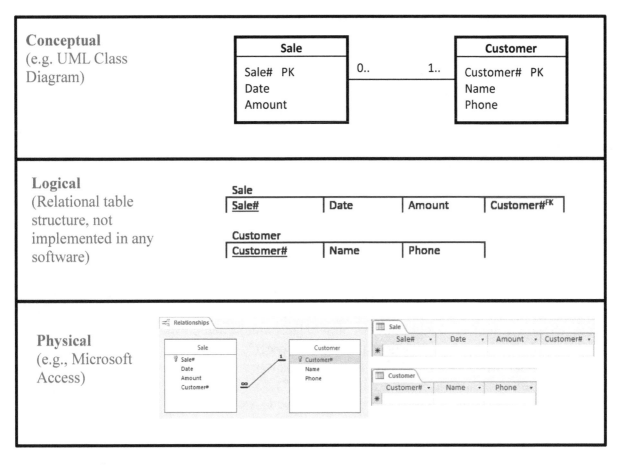

Exhibit 3-1: Conceptual, Logical, and Physical Model Comparison

Once a conceptual model is converted to a relational logical format, it can no longer be implemented in object-oriented, graph or other database software (unless you go back to the original conceptual model and re-convert it to the corresponding format). Instead, the relational logical model must be implemented using one of many relational database software packages. Similarly, if a conceptual model is converted into an object-oriented format, it can no longer be implemented in non-object-oriented software, but may be implemented in a variety of object-oriented software packages.

The third type of model used in database design is the *physical database model*, which is an implementation of the logical model. Such an implementation is created using a specific database software package, thus clearly depends on the software choice.

Because most enterprises use relational database software of some kind (it is used in most ERP software), and because most universities make relational database software available to students, we have chosen in this book to focus only on the relational database logical model. For the physical database implementation, we illustrate the concepts discussed in this chapter with Microsoft Access because of its wide availability in both academia and in practice, and because of its ease of use. Please understand that the logical constructs also apply to other relational database software; the skills you learn are generalizable.

CONCEPTUAL MODELING WITH UML CLASS DIAGRAMS

From conception, conceptual models have represented REA business processes. Before we re-examine the details of the REA business process pattern, we need to introduce the constructs of conceptual modeling using UML class diagrams. The five UML class diagram constructs we discuss are classes, associations, attributes, association classes, and multiplicities. Keep in mind that the class diagram constructs are independent from the REA constructs; class diagrams can model any data, and REA constructs can be represented with various alternative notations.

An *entity* is a real world object that has a separate existence (either physical or conceptual). Entities that share the same types of characteristics (but may each have different values for those characteristics) form an entity set, which may also be called a *class*. The individual members of that set are called instances. For example, each individual customer of an enterprise is an instance of the customer class. The customers share a set of characteristics (e.g., CustomerID, name, address, telephone number, credit limit, account balance due) Each customer in the set may have different values for these characteristics, but they are expected to possess these characteristics. The specific customer whose ID is C1234, named Brenda Brenton, who lives at 236 Bonair St., Lansing, MI 48917, whose telephone number is (517) 555-2236, whose credit limit is $4,000, whose account balance due is $100 is an instance of the Customer class.

An *association* is a relationship between classes. Associations are represented in UML class diagrams as lines drawn between the related classes; the lines are labeled with the association names. Notice that because classes are set level constructs, associations represent sets of relationships between entities. Consider a Student class and a Course class. The association between them may be called Enrollment, and that association represents the set of all associations between individual students and the individual courses in which they are or have been enrolled. Exhibit 3-2 illustrates an association between the student class and the course class.

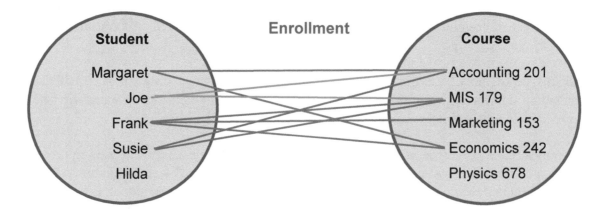

Exhibit 3-2: Students, Courses, and the Enrollment Association

To describe instances of the association, we need to use characteristics of both of the related classes. Instances of the enrollment set in Exhibit 3-2 are

- ❑ Margaret enrolled in Accounting 201
- ❑ Margaret enrolled in Economics 242
- ❑ Joe enrolled in Accounting 201
- ❑ Joe enrolled in MIS 179
- ❑ Frank enrolled in MIS 179
- ❑ Frank enrolled in Marketing 153
- ❑ Frank enrolled in Economics 242
- ❑ Susie enrolled in Accounting 201
- ❑ Susie enrolled in MIS 179

An *attribute* is a characteristic possessed by a class or an association. There are several attribute types. A *primary key attribute* must uniquely and universally describe each instance of a class or association. For a primary key to be unique, each instance must have a different data value for that attribute. For a primary key to be universal, each instance must possess a data value for that attribute; the absence of a data value is called a *null value* (and null values are not allowed for a primary key). Consider the Student class – what would be a good primary key for it? Could we use Last Name? No; it is likely that more than one student will share the same last name so it would not be unique. Could we use Driver's License Number? No; it is likely that some students will not possess a driver's license so it would not be universal. If the school in question is in the United States, it may be reasonable to use social security number, substituting an equivalent government-assigned identification number for non-US citizens. In cases where there is not a naturally occurring attribute that uniquely and universally describes each instance a primary key may be arbitrarily assigned (usually with a system-generated number that increments by one for each new instance). For example, while social security numbers are possible primary keys, most organizations avoid using them as primary keys because of privacy issues. Most universities choose to assign student ID numbers to use as the primary key for students.

In some cases, it may be necessary to combine two (or more) attributes to uniquely and universally identify an instance of a class or association. This is a special type of primary key known as a composite primary key or a *concatenated primary key*. A class representing employee education might use the combination of employee ID plus degree earned as a composite primary key; because employees can have multiple degrees earned, the employee ID is not unique – imagine employee 101 with a BS degree and an MBA – that would result in 101 & BS and 101 & MBA as two unique instances.

Related to the idea of using composite primary keys, is the association class. An *association class* is a relationship between classes wherein the association has characteristics of its own and for which there can be only one link between the related classes. The purpose of an association class is to store association, as opposed to class, attributes. An association must have at least one attribute to be an association class. Consider an association between purchase and inventory types, wherein a purchase may include multiple types of inventory (e.g., eggs, soup, and ramen noodles) and the same type of inventory may be purchased multiple times. Quantity purchased (the number of a specific inventory type purchased on a specific purchase transaction) is an association attribute. One may purchase 1 carton of eggs, 4 cans of soup, and 10 packets of ramen noodles on one purchase, and one may purchase 2 cartons of eggs and 7 ramen noodle packets on another purchase. Actual unit cost is another association attribute. On the first purchase described above, one might have paid $1.69 for the carton of eggs, $2.09 for each can of soup, and $.29 for each packet of ramen noodles. On the second purchase, one may have paid $1.48 for each carton of eggs and $.32 for each ramen noodle packet. Quantity purchased and actual unit cost are attributes of the association between purchase and inventory type. They are not attributes of purchase by itself (on a single purchase there are multiple quantities and multiple unit costs), nor are they attributes of inventory type (each inventory type has multiple values of purchase quantity and unit cost). It takes the combination of purchase id and product id to uniquely and universally identify each instance of purchase quantity and each instance of unit cost. The association is therefore an association class with a concatenated primary key.

A *simple attribute* is an attribute that cannot be further decomposed (e.g., city name); whereas a *composite attribute* may be decomposed into other attributes. A commonly used composite attribute is address, which may be decomposed into street address, city, state or province, country, and postal code. In general, it is best to store only simple attributes to facilitate querying and maintenance of the data once it is entered. For example, to query all customers who live in a particular city, it will be most efficient if city is stored as a separate attribute rather than as part of address.

A *derivable attribute* is an attribute that can be derived (computed) from the values of other attributes in the database. For example, the total number of items purchased on a purchase transaction may be computed as the sum of the quantity purchased for each inventory type on the transaction. Similarly, the dollar value of a purchase transaction may be computed by first multiplying the quantities purchased by the actual unit costs of each inventory type and then summing the products. There are two types of derivable attributes: *static derivable attributes* are those for which the derived value will not change if new data records (also called rows) are entered into the database, and *volatile (dynamic) derivable attributes* are those for which the derived value will change if new data are entered into the database and the new data are related to the derivable attribute. Student's overall grade point average is an example of a volatile derivable attribute. Each time a student completes another course, the value for overall grade point average must be re-calculated. "Total sale dollar amount" as an attribute of a Sale class is an example of a static derivable attribute. The total dollar amount of any sale may be calculated as the sum of the quantity sold multiplied by the unit selling price of each item sold. The total dollar amount of one sale will not change when new sales or other data are entered into the database. For example, we may compute the total sale dollar amount for Sale #1 as $100. As we enter data for Sales #2 through #50 into the database, Sale #1's $100 amount is unaffected.

Relational theory says that derivable attributes should not be stored in a relational database, because they add unnecessary storage space, which creates bulk and adds cost. However, relational theory was proposed when storage space was very expensive relative to processing power costs. Today, storage is inexpensive, therefore in some cases one may decide to store derivable attributes. We recommend storing static derivable attributes if they are likely to be base elements in queries, because those queries will be much less complex and more efficient. For example, "total sale amount" is often a base element in other queries such as "accounts receivable as of the balance sheet date" or "total sales for region Y during the marketing campaign." We do not recommend storing <u>volatile</u> derivable attributes unless the database software is capable of storing them as triggers (in essence storing the formula that computes the data value instead of storing an actual data value).

However, keep in mind that the conceptual model is independent of any specific logical model or physical implementation. Therefore, the conceptual model (UML class diagram) <u>should</u> include derivable attributes if and when they are identified in the modeling process. In fact, one should not decide to exclude derivable attributes from the company database tables until the physical implementation level, at which point the specific software and its capability of storing triggers is known, and cost/benefit decisions can be made.

Multiplicities (also called cardinalities) represent business rules describing how instances of a class participate in an association with instances of another class. In this book, we will always use binary associations – that is, the associations will always be between two classes. Therefore, our associations will always have four multiplicities; both a minimum and a maximum multiplicity for each class connected to the association.

Minimum multiplicities represent the minimum number of times each instance of a class must participate in an association with another class. Sometimes instances of a class "may or may not" associate with instances of another class; this is known as *optional participation* and corresponds to a minimum multiplicity of "0". However, sometimes instances of a class "must" associate with instances of another class; this is known as *mandatory participation* and corresponds to a minimum multiplicity of "1".

Maximum multiplicities represent the maximum number of times instances of a class may participate in an association with another class. The most common possible values for a maximum multiplicity are one ("1") and many ("*"). The term many for multiplicities is somewhat misleading because it actually means more than one. So if the maximum participation of a class is two or three, it could be depicted as many. Maximum multiplicities may be set to a specific number when appropriate. For example, if a store says each customer may redeem a special offer coupon a maximum of 2 times; the maximum multiplicity could be specified as 2 – rather than *.

Exhibit 3-3 displays a UML class diagram depicting Purchase and Employee classes and a Participation association between them. Also shown are the multiplicities; note that the minimum and maximum multiplicities are always shown in pairs of minimum..maximum (with two pairs per association). The pair of multiplicities 1..1 represent how purchases (instances) relate to employees (instances). The minimum 1 indicates that each purchase must have an employee. The maximum of 1 indicated that each purchase has (a maximum of) one employee. Likewise, the pair of multiplicities 0..* represent how employees (instances) relate to purchases (instances). The minimum 0 indicates that an employee does not have to be associated with a purchase. The maximum * indicates that an employee can relate to (make) many purchases.

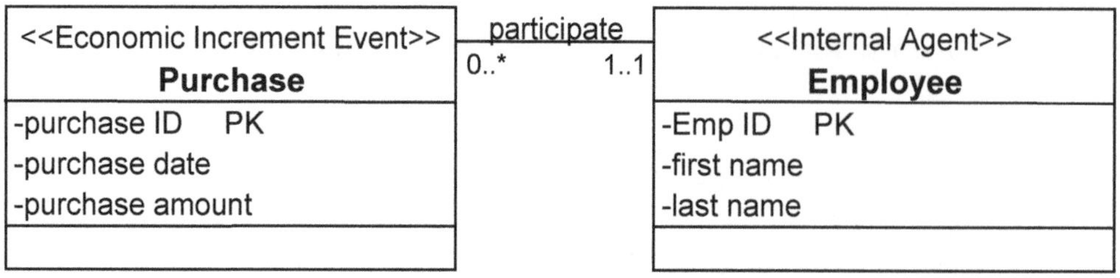

<<Economic Increment Event>> **Purchase**	participate	<<Internal Agent>> **Employee**
-purchase ID PK	0..* 1..1	-Emp ID PK
-purchase date		-first name
-purchase amount		-last name

Exhibit 3-3: UML Class Diagram

UML Class diagrams represent classes as rectangles with three compartments. The top section of the box is the class name compartment; that section shows the name of the class and, optionally, a stereotype for the class (in this book we use stereotypes to map classes to REA constructs). In Exhibit 3-3, <<Economic Increment Event>> and <<Internal Agent>> are stereotypes.

The middle section of the box is the attribute compartment. We list only the attribute names in this compartment plus PK next to the primary key attribute(s); more complicated UML class diagrams may also list data types, attribute multiplicities, visibility (whether an attribute is public or private), and other aspects of the attributes.

The bottom section of the box is the operation compartment. An operation is a method or function that can be performed by instances of the class in object-oriented programming. These concepts are beyond the scope of this textbook. Therefore, we use a simplified class with two compartments, or we will leave the third compartment blank.

Let us return to Exhibit 3-2 and demonstrate how to represent the sets with a UML class diagram. The sets of students and courses will be represented as classes; see Exhibit 3-4. The set of lines drawn between the instances of the Student and Course in Exhibit 3-2 are represented by an association called enrollment in Exhibit 3-4. These lines between student instances and course instances in Exhibit 3-2 provide multiplicity information. See if you can fill in the multiplicities labeled A, B, C, and D on the association between Student and Course (in Exhibit 3-4).

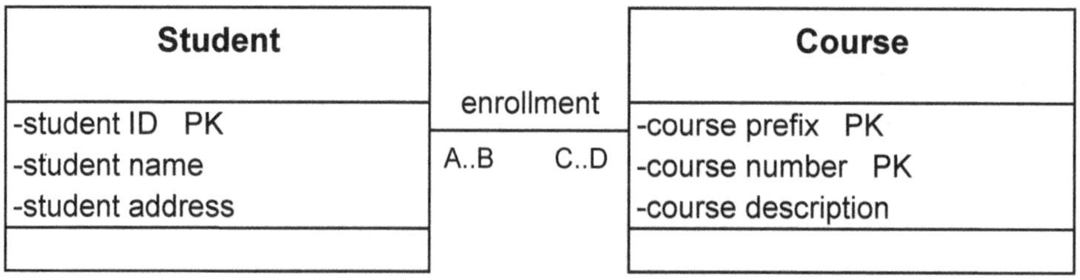

Student	enrollment	**Course**
-student ID PK	A..B C..D	-course prefix PK
-student name		-course number PK
-student address		-course description

Exhibit 3-4: Student Enrollment in Course in UML Class Diagram format

The A represents the minimum participation of Course in its association with related Students. Physics 678 is an example of a course for which no students have yet enrolled, therefore the participation of course in that association is optional and the appropriate value for A is 0.

The B represents the maximum participation of Course in its association with related Students and Accounting 201 has multiple students enrolled; therefore, the appropriate value for B is *. Notice that MIS 179 and Economics 242 also have multiple students; however, once you identify any one instance of course that has multiple related students you don't have to look any further.

The C represents the minimum participation of Student in its association with related Courses. Hilda is an example of a (perhaps new) student who has not (yet) enrolled in any courses; therefore, the participation of student in that association is optional and the appropriate value for C is 0.

The D represents the maximum participation of Student in its association with related Courses. Margaret has enrolled in multiple courses; therefore, the appropriate value for D is *. Although Joe, Frank, and Susie have also enrolled in multiple courses, once you notice that Margaret has, you need look no further.

CONVERTING CONCEPTUAL MODELS INTO RELATIONAL LOGICAL MODELS

To understand the rules for converting a conceptual data model (UML class diagram) into a relational logical model, you must first understand the structure of the *relational model*. Codd developed the relational model based on set theory and predicate logic. [25,26] The primary construct in the relational model is the *relation*, which is a two-dimensional storage structure (i.e., a storage structure with rows and columns) more commonly referred to as a table. Each table in the relational model represents either a class or an association between classes. The columns in a relational database table are formally called the table *intension*, *schema*, or *fields*, and they represent the attributes of the class or association. The rows in a relational database table are formally called the table *extension*, *tuples*, or *records*, and they represent the specific instances that are members of the classes or associations.

The order of columns in a table does not matter, nor does the order in which rows appear. This is because the tables are created in such a way that the rows and columns may be sorted as desired through the use of queries. For this to be possible, one requirement is that all data values in a column must conform to the same data format (e.g., date, text, currency). Another requirement is that each cell (row-column intersection) in a relational table can contain only one value. Multiple values stored in the same cell form a *repeating group*; a table containing a repeating group is not a relational table.

The tables in a relational database are linked to each other through primary keys and foreign keys. Recall that a primary key consists of one or more characteristics of a class that uniquely and universally identifies each instance of the class. Every table must have a primary key (and some tables have composite primary keys). A *foreign key* is a column of data that relates to the primary

[25] Codd, E.F. "Derivability, Redundancy, and Consistency of Relations Stored in Large Data Banks." *IBM Research Report* RJ599, August 19, 1969.
[26] Codd, E.F. "A Relational Model of Data for Large Shared Data Banks." CACM 13, No. 6, June 1970. Republished in *Milestones of Research: Selected Papers 1958-1982.* CACM 25th Anniversary Issue, CACM 26, No. 1, January 1983.

key column of a related table. The purpose of the foreign key is to implement an association (this allows rows of one table to be associated with rows of a related table). We also say that primary keys get "posted" (added as another column) into related tables as foreign keys. Relationships between primary keys and foreign keys will allow tables to be joined together in a query (a topic of a later chapter).. Note that we are focusing on the logical model; foreign keys are <u>not</u> shown in the conceptual model (UML class diagram).

Exhibit 3-5 illustrates an example of a foreign key attribute. Salesperson ID is the primary key of the Salesperson table, and is posted into the Sale table to establish a relationship, or link, between the Sale and Salesperson tables. Notice that the name of the foreign key attribute is not required to match the name of the primary key attribute. What must match across primary keys and foreign keys is the chosen data type (e.g., number, text) and any data values common to both.

(a) meets referential integrity principle

Sale

SaleID	Date	Amount	Salesperson
061401A	6/14	$4,218	*123456*
061401B	6/14	$6,437	*654321*
061501A	6/15	$1,112	*654321*
061501B	6/15	$3,300		★
061501C	6/15	$1,776		★

★ Null values do not violate referential integrity.

Salesperson

SalespersonID	Name	Telephone
123456	Fred	555-0063
654321	Francis	555-0007

(b) violates referential integrity principle

Sale

SaleID	Date	Amount	Salesperson
061401A	6/14	$4,218	*123456*
061401B	6/14	$6,437	*654321*
061501A	6/15	$1,112	*654321*
061501B	6/15	$3,300	
061501C	6/15	$1,776	*234567*

Violation, as 234567 doesn't exist in the Salesperson table.

Salesperson

SalespersonID	Name	Telephone
123456	Fred	555-0063
654321	Francis	555-0007

Exhibit 3-5: Referential Integrity Illustrated

Almost all types of relational database software support referential integrity, an important control on the data found in foreign keys. *Referential integrity* ensures that new data values entered into a foreign key (column) must already exist in the related primary key (column). When we discussed multiplicities, we noted that sometimes the minimum participation is optional. Whenever a foreign key is optional, it is possible to have null values in the foreign key without violating referential integrity.

In Exhibit 3-5, example (a) on the left side meets referential integrity because each value for salesperson in the Sale table is either null or it matches a data value from the Salesperson table. This example is contrived; it would be unusual for a sale to not have a salesperson (or another specific internal agent) because some employee needs to be responsible for the sale. Example (b) on the right side of Exhibit 3-5 violates referential integrity because it includes a data value for a salesperson in the Sale table for salesperson 234567, but there is no salesperson 234567 in the Salesperson table.

It is important to understand that referential integrity does not guarantee the accuracy of the data. Returning to Exhibit 3-5 (a), assume that the very first sale was really made by salesperson 654321, but the salesperson was entered as shown. This is not a referential integrity violation, so that row of data can be saved in the database. However, the data would be inaccurate.

Another important point is that certain tables that contain composite primary keys will have referential integrity enforced, so even though our example above was about foreign keys, referential integrity isn't limited to foreign keys. One more point about Microsoft Access – referential integrity has to be configured after the tables are designed. When a new row of data is being entered into a table, that data is stored in temporary memory until you hit the enter key to move to the next row of the table. When you hit the enter key, you commit the data – permanently save it – to the database. Before this commitment occurs any foreign keys in the table will receive a one-by-one referential integrity check; any identified referential integrity violations will prevent saving the row of data (until the violation is resolved). We will return to these points when we look at Microsoft Access and the implementation of relationships.

Referential integrity is only one principle to which relational databases must adhere. A second principle is that of entity integrity. *Entity integrity* means that the values of a relational table's primary key are (1) unique and (2) non-null (i.e., every row of data must have a primary key value that is different for each row). Entity integrity guarantees the uniqueness of entities and enables proper referencing of primary key values by foreign key values. As an example, consider the common practice of using telephone numbers as identifiers for customers. Among the issues associated with this practice is the problem that some customers may not have telephone numbers. If a customer, Joe Smith, does not have a telephone number and telephone number is used as the primary key for the Customer table, the entity integrity principle would prohibit entering a row for Joe Smith in the Customer table (at least until Joe obtains a telephone number).

One Fact-One Place

A third principle to which relational databases must adhere is the *"one-fact, one-place" rule*.[27] To understand this rule, you must understand the definition of a fact in the context of database design. A *fact* in database design is the pairing of a candidate key attribute value with another attribute value. A *candidate key* is an attribute value that could be used as a primary key for a class table. Because the facts consist of pairs of actual data values (found in the table rows), one must consider the likely data entry possibilities to ensure that each fact will appear only one time. In database design, *redundancy* is duplicate storage of the same information. One fact stored in multiple places is redundancy and should be avoided, as redundancy nearly always causes data inconsistencies.

The typical use of the term candidate key is to suggest that there are two, and in some cases more, choices for uniquely representing the same set of objects. For example, student number and social

---

[27] The "one-fact, one-place" rule was developed by William McCarthy in class notes as a simplified approach to normalization of relational database tables to approximately 3rd normal form.

security number are both candidate keys for a student table; either one could be the primary key of a student table. Facts are found in the extension (rows) of the database tables.

The important issue with the fact rule is that sometimes errors are made, and instead of having two or more candidate keys representing the same set of objects, there are actually two (or more) candidate keys that are meant to represent two (or more) different set of objects. Furthermore, the second candidate key has one (or more) related attribute(s) stored in a table that already has its own primary key (and the candidate key stored in the table is not a candidate key for that table – it is a candidate key for a different table). The following example will help to clarify this issue.

Example of One Fact Multiple Places

Consider the Sale table in Exhibit 3-6, and examine each of its attributes. What attributes are candidate keys? Are any other attributes paired with a candidate key for which duplicate data is expected?

Sale

SaleID	Date	Amount	CustomerID	CustomerName	CustomerAddress
8532	Oct. 2	$13	C422	Andy	456 Pine St.
9352	Oct. 14	$14	C821	Jennifer	987 Forest St.
10215	Oct. 27	$20	C363	Arlie	321 Beech St.
14332	Nov. 5	$18	C422	Andy	456 Pine St.
17421	Nov. 16	$22	C363	Arlie	321 Beech St.

Exhibit 3-6: Sale table (poorly designed)

Two attributes in Exhibit 3-6 are candidate keys: SaleID (which actually is the primary key for this table) and CustomerID, which would be a logical primary key for a class of customers – an entirely different set of objects. Next, examine the data in the table to see if there are any duplicate combinations of candidate keys and other attribute values. Each SaleID is unique, so there is no duplication of facts containing that attribute. However, values for CustomerID are not unique in the Sale table. To determine whether there is any one fact in multiple places we must examine whether the repeated customer IDs are associated with the same data values for another attribute (remember the definition of a fact is a pairing of a candidate key data value with another attribute data value). Inspection of the data reveals that every time C422 is listed as the customer ID, Andy is listed as the customer name and 456 Pine St. is the customer address. Similarly, each time C363 is listed as the customer id, Arlie is listed as the customer name and 321 Beech St. is the customer address. This pairing is not coincidental – it is systematic. We would expect the next time a sale is made to C422, the customer name would be Andy and the address 456 Pine St. because Andy is customer C422. Therefore, the "one-fact, one-place" rule is violated in this table.

The type of rule violation we just presented sometimes occurs because of attribute overload in the UML class diagram. For example, the UML class that would have been converted into the Sale table in Exhibit 3-6 is shown in Exhibit 3-7. This class is overloaded, in that it contains attributes that in fact describe multiple classes.

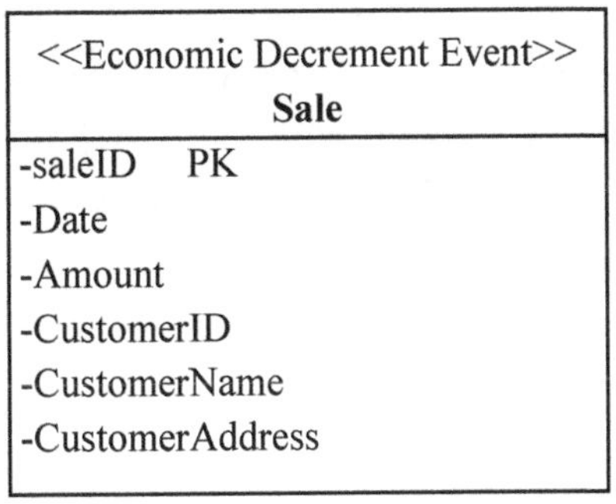

```
        <<Economic Decrement Event>>
                  Sale
    -saleID    PK
    -Date
    -Amount
    -CustomerID
    -CustomerName
    -CustomerAddress
```

Exhibit 3-7: Sale UML Class (poorly designed)

Note how the UML class diagram improves with the addition of a Customer class, as illustrated in Exhibit 3-8. The attributes that will store the facts are logically grouped together.

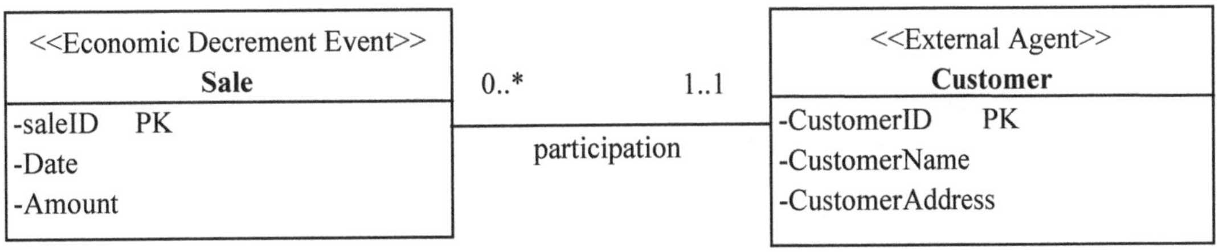

```
  <<Economic Decrement Event>>                          <<External Agent>>
            Sale                  0..*        1..1           Customer
  -saleID    PK                                        -CustomerID    PK
  -Date                             participation       -CustomerName
  -Amount                                               -CustomerAddress
```

Exhibit 3-8: Sale-Customer participation UML Class diagram

Example of Multiple Facts in One Place

Another violation of the one-fact, one-place rule occurs when multiple facts are stored in one place. This phenomenon is commonly known as a repeating group. Consider the table in Exhibit 3-9.

Employee

EmployeeID	Name	Office	Degree Earned
1	Tony	Cleveland	BS,MBA
2	Emily	New York	BA,MBA,PhD
3	Leigh	Birmingham	BA

Exhibit 3-9: Employee table (poorly designed)

Because employees may have earned multiple degrees, the placement of the "degree earned" attribute in the Employee table creates multiple facts in the same row. That is, there are multiple pairings of a candidate key (EmployeeID) and another attribute (Degree Earned) in at least one row. Similarly, if we tried to store any other attribute (telephone number, vehicle owned, etc.) for which an employee may have multiple values, we would end up with a repeating group. To be able to retrieve and manipulate data in accordance with set theory and predicate logic, the relational model does not allow repeating groups. Therefore, the Employee table above is not a well-designed relational table.

Remember that we always build conceptual models prior to building tables. Therefore, it is useful to think about the related UML class diagram shown in Exhibit 3-10:

<<Internal Agent>> **Employee**
-EmployeeID   PK
-Name
-Office
-Degree Earned   1..*

Exhibit 3-10: Employee UML Class with Multi-valued Attribute

Close inspection of this Employee class reveals that the attribute "Degree Earned" possesses multiplicities. The 1 indicates that each employee must have a data value for Degree Earned; the * indicates that each employee could have more than one data value for Degree Earned. The * represents a "multivalued attribute." So referring to the Employee table in Exhibit 3-9, there are two reasons such a table would be incorrectly created. First, the database designer may have failed to recognize that Degree Earned was a multivalued attribute. Second, the database designer may have recognized the need for a multivalued attribute, but made an error in implementing the multivalued attribute – multivalued attributes need to be stored in a separate table; the primary key of that table is a composite primary key made up of the primary key of the original table (in this example, "EmployeeID") and the multivalued attribute itself (in this example, "Degree Earned").

As you see in the discussion above, there is a correspondence between the relational tables and the UML class diagram. Any errors occurring in the UML class diagram will be "carried forward" into the relational tables unless those errors are detected. Therefore, quality control procedures should be implemented to review the UML class diagram prior to converting it to relational tables. When conceptual modeling is done well, and the appropriate steps are followed for mapping the UML class diagram to the relational tables, the tables tend to comply with the fact rule. However, as an additional quality control procedure, each relational table should be evaluated for compliance with the fact rule; this evaluation should happen prior to implementing the tables in database software.

Next we present the steps for converting conceptual model UML class diagrams to logical model relational tables and demonstrate the application of these steps.

Step 1: Create a separate table to represent each class. Make each class attribute a column in the relational table. Use the class' primary key as the table's primary key.

Step 2: Create a separate table to represent each association class (remember that association classes store association attributes) and create a separate table to represent each many-to-many association. Create a concatenated primary key for the association table made up of the individual primary keys of the two associated classes. Add columns to the association table for any association attributes.

Step 3: Post a foreign key from the table of any class that has a 1..1 multiplicity next to it into the associate class table. Note: for any association that has 1..1 next to both classes, (i.e. 1..1 to 1..1), first consider whether the two classes should be collapsed into one. If the representation as two separate classes is accurate, post a foreign key from one class' table into the other, but do not post both (i.e., do not double-implement the association).

Step 4: Once you complete steps 1 through 3, the only remaining associations should have 0..1 participation by at least one of the classes, and something other than 1..1 by the other class. Create a separate table to represent each of these associations, using a composite primary key made up of the individual primary keys of the two associated classes.

These steps are derived from two overall goals. One is to avoid repeating groups (attributes that have multiple values that correspond to the same primary key value) and the second is to avoid the storage of null values. Repeating group avoidance is crucial in relational database design – a table that contains repeating groups is not relational. The most critical rule to apply to avoid causing repeating groups is to never post a foreign key from a class that has a * (many) next to it. By definition of that multiplicity, that class would potentially have multiple values to post into the foreign key field. Consider the conceptual model shown in Exhibit 3-11.

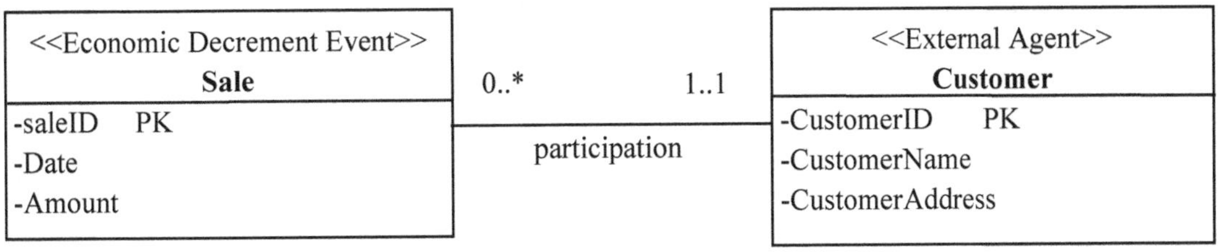

<<Economic Decrement Event>> **Sale**	0..* 1..1	<<External Agent>> **Customer**
-saleID PK	participation	-CustomerID PK
-Date		-CustomerName
-Amount		-CustomerAddress

Exhibit 3-11: Sale-Customer Association Conceptual Model

Our Step 1 rule requires that we create tables to represent the Customer and Sale classes, as shown in Exhibit 3-12.

Customer

CustomerID	Name	Address

Sale

SaleID	Date	Dollar Value

Exhibit 3-12: Step 1 Result - Customer and Sale class tables

Before following the remaining steps to complete this example, consider the 0..* describing customer participation with sales; that indicates a customer may exist without participating in a sale (the 0 minimum) and that a customer may participate in many sales (the * maximum). If SaleID were posted as a foreign key in the Customer table, both null values and repeating groups may result. A customer who has not yet participated in a sale would have a null value in the SaleID field. A customer who has participated in multiple sales would have a repeating group. See Exhibit 3-13 for an illustration with data that represents the multiplicities.

Customer

CustomerID	Name	Address	SaleID
C1	Henri	12 Elm	S1, S3
C2	Faith	27 Oak	
C3	Deonte	33 Fir	S2

Sale

SaleID	Date	Dollar Value
S1	1/3	$400
S2	1/3	$600
S3	1/5	$700

Exhibit 3-13: Tables with Null and Repeating Group Foreign Keys (poor design)

The customer table shown in Exhibit 3-13 is a non-relational table. To avoid causing a repeating group, do not post a foreign key from a class that has a * maximum next to it into a related class's table. To avoid causing a null value, do not post a foreign key from a class that has a 0 minimum next to it into a related class's table.

Examine the possibility of posting the primary key from the Customer class' table into the Sale class' table as a foreign key. The 1..1 next to customer reveals that a sale cannot exist without a customer, and that a sale involves no more than 1 customer. Therefore, if CustomerID is posted into the Sale table, it will not contain any null values (because of the 1 minimum) and, more importantly, it will not contain multiple values (because of the 1 maximum). See Exhibit 3-14 for an illustration of this result.

Customer

CustomerID	Name	Address
C1	Henri	12 Elm
C2	Faith	27 Oak
C3	Deonte	33 Fir

Sale

SaleID	Date	Dollar Value	CustomerID
S1	1/3	$400	C1
S2	1/3	$600	C3
S3	1/5	$700	C1

Exhibit 3-14: Tables without Null or Repeating Group Foreign Keys (good design)

The general rule to follow, then, is to post foreign keys from classes that have maximum participation of 1 and mandatory minimum participation in the associations. Steps 2 through 4 are derived from this general rule.

Along with following the rules for multiplicities, steps 2 through 4 also provide guidance for what columns to include in any association and association class tables you create. Consider the stockflow association class between Sale and Inventory in Exhibit 3-15.

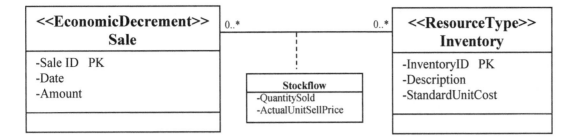

Exhibit 3-15: Sale-Inventory Stockflow Association

Step 1 requires that we make a separate table for the Sale class and a separate table for the Inventory class, with each table having a column for each class attribute. Step 2 requires that we create a separate table to represent the stockflow association class, using the primary keys of Sale and Inventory as a concatenated primary key and making additional columns in the stockflow table for the quantity sold and unit selling price attributes. Exhibit 3-16 illustrates these table structures with some representative data.

Sale

SaleID	Date	Amount
S1	1/3	$400
S2	1/3	$600
S3	1/5	$700

Inventory

InventoryID	Description	StandardUnitCost
A1	Large agleclap	$25
B1	Large widget	$45
B2	Medium widget	$32

Stockflow

SaleID	InventoryID	QuantitySold	ActualUnitSellingPrice
S1	A1	10	$40
S2	A1	5	$40
S2	B1	5	$80
S3	B2	10	$70

Exhibit 3-16: Association Class Table Implementation Example

Why do the stockflow association class attributes need to be placed in the stockflow table rather than in either the sale or the inventory table? If we placed quantity sold and actual unit selling price in the inventory table, we would have a problem entering the data for A1, as we would have two values for each of those attributes. If we placed quantity sold and actual unit selling price in the sale table, we could enter sale S1's values without causing a problem. However, when we got to sale S2, we would have two values for each of those attributes. To avoid such problems, we must place quantity sold and actual unit selling price in the stockflow association table.

Next, examine Step 3 more closely. Step 3 applies to associations with the multiplicity pattern 1..1--1..1. The first part of the step says to consider whether the two classes are conceptually separate or whether they should be combined. Consider an enterprise that earns its revenue by setting up hot dog stands between the hours of 11:00 a.m. and 2:00 p.m. each day that classes are in session on college campuses. The enterprise places its stands in areas where many students are likely to be walking, and likely to be hungry because no alternative food vendors are nearby. The enterprise sells hot dogs, lemonade, chips, fruit, and cookies. All sales are made on a cash basis. The food and the cash change hands simultaneously. Therefore a sale doesn't exist without a related cash receipt, and the sale only involves one cash receipt since it must be paid in full. So the multiplicity next to cash receipt is 1..1.

Next we make a rather bold assumption that sales are the only source of cash for this enterprise (that is, they haven't borrowed money or obtained contributed cash from its owners). That is probably not realistic, but is within the realm of possibility as the owners could have contributed the equipment as capital instead of cash, and the enterprise could have purchased its initial inventory on credit, and then generated enough cash flow from sales to pay for the purchases and make new purchases. If we accept these assumptions, the minimum multiplicity next to sale in the association with cash receipt is 1 (mandatory). It also seems reasonable to assume maximum multiplicity next to sale in the association with cash receipt is also 1; that says that a cash receipt applies to only one sale. In this scenario, if we receive cash from a customer for a hot dog and lemonade, the cash receipt applies only to that sale.

You may wonder whether the maximum of 1 next to Cash Receipt is valid if two friends approach the stand and one friend pays for both their lunches. The hot dog vendor would view that as one sale and one cash receipt, with the paying friend as the customer. Thus we have a reasonable Sale 1..1 − 1..1 Cash Receipt association. Now you must determine whether these two classes are conceptually separate (in the context of this enterprise) or whether they should be combined into one class. To make this determination, you must consider the future of this enterprise, allowing for reasonably possible growth, as well as the present circumstances. If you determine this enterprise will never sell lunches on credit and will never obtain cash from a source other than sales, you may reasonably combine them into a single class.

If you determine that someday the enterprise might obtain cash from other sources, then you should maintain Sale and Cash Receipt as separate classes and create separate tables for them. If you decide to keep the classes separate, and to keep the multiplicity pattern as 1..1—1..1 then you can either post the primary key from Sale into Cash Receipt or post the primary key from Cash Receipt into Sale to establish the association in the tables. Consider the tables and information about their association in Exhibit 3-17.

Sale

SaleID	Date	Amount
S1	6/5	$4.25
S2	6/5	$3.75

CashReceipt

ReceiptID	Date	Amount
CR1	6/5	$4.25
CR2	6/5	$3.75

Association Information:
Cash Receipt CR1 paid for Sale S1
Cash Receipt CR2 paid for Sale S2

Exhibit 3-17: Sale and Cash Receipt Class Tables and association information

Given the association information (notice that the association information is consistent with the multiplicities) you can see that posting ReceiptID from the Cash Receipt table as a foreign key in the Sale table creates no problems. No repeating groups result, and no facts end up stored in multiple places. Similarly, you could post SaleID from the Sale table as a foreign key in the Cash Receipt table without any problem. However, you must choose one or the other. Don't post both.

If you post both foreign keys, you will have created one fact (a pairing of a candidate key attribute SaleID with another attribute ReceiptID) in multiple places (in this case, in two different tables). Our recommendation for this particular situation is to post the ReceiptID into the Sale table because that allows the most flexibility in case of future changes in the enterprise (as it seems more likely the company would add cash receipts unrelated to sales than for the company to add sales that don't yield cash receipts). Thus, our recommended solution is as shown in Exhibit 3-18.

Sale

SaleID	Date	Amount	ReceiptID
S1	6/5	$4.25	CR1
S2	6/5	$3.75	CR2

CashReceipt

ReceiptID	Date	Amount
CR1	6/5	$4.25
CR2	6/5	$3.75

Exhibit 3-18: Recommended implementation for 1..1-1..1 association between Sale and Cash Receipt

PHYSICAL IMPLEMENTATION OF RELATIONAL MODELS IN MICROSOFT ACCESS

Once the relational tables are derived, forming a logical model, the model may be implemented in physical form using a vendor-specific database software. We use Microsoft Access in this chapter to demonstrate the conversion of a logical model to a physical model. Keep in mind that the procedures will be similar but not identical with other vendor-specific relational database software.

This chapter is not intended to provide you with comprehensive assistance on every aspect of Access. Instead, it will provide you with an introduction to creating tables and relationships in Access. If you need additional Access instructions, you may use the electronic help facility provided in Access or consult an Access reference manual (perhaps search your library for an e-book).

If you have Access installed on your computer, you can identify it with the icon below or you can find it with the search bar. Note that Access only operates on the Windows operating system.

To use the help facility, once Access is open, click on the white question mark inside the blue circle near the top right corner of your Access window. If you are connected to the Internet, the help function will default to Office.com and the Access Help window will appear as illustrated in Exhibit 3-19. The help available offline is not nearly as extensive as that available when you are connected.

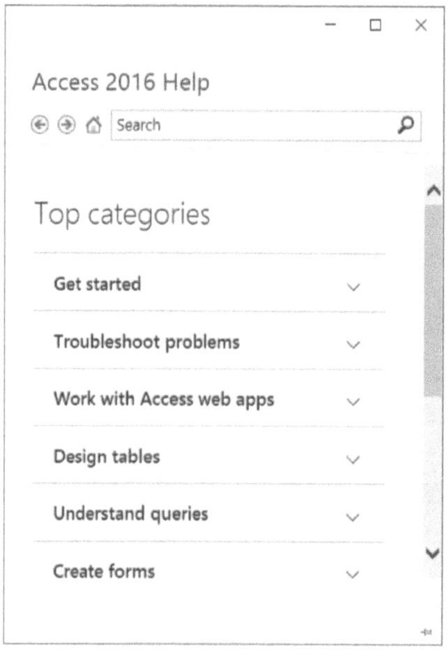

Exhibit 3-19: Microsoft Access Help Window if Connected to Office.com

For material related to this chapter, you are most likely to use the Design tables category.

Creating and Working with Databases

When you start Microsoft Access, you may select Open to resume working on an existing database file, or you may select New to begin a new database. Selecting New produces numerous template options. When you use Microsoft Access in conjunction with materials in this textbook, do NOT use any wizards or templates. These wizards and templates use defaults that you must understand and know when and how to override when appropriate. We do not cover that knowledge in this book, so we caution you not to use wizards or templates at all, or to use them at your own risk.

To begin without a template, select Blank Desktop Database. You will then see a popup window asking you to name your new database file. See Exhibit 3-20. This is somewhat different from other Microsoft software products, most of which allow you to begin creating content in a blank document or spreadsheet and later save that content to a file. Microsoft Access requires you to name your file before you add any content, and Access then automatically saves additions and changes as they are accepted. As you see in Exhibit 3-20, Access suggests a default name such as Database1, or in this case, Database10 and lists the folder in which it will store your database file (unless you choose to change this location). To provide a more meaningful name for the file, simply type a different name in the box that says Database10. If you want the file to be stored in a different folder, click on the folder icon to the right of the file name box and browse to the location in which you want to store your database.

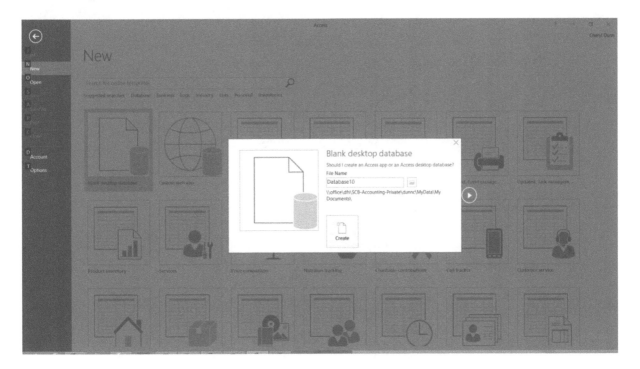

Exhibit 3-20: Create a Database as a Blank Desktop Database

When you create, Microsoft Access by default displays its database window with the Table Tools section open, and a Table1 open in datasheet view. The *database window* is a container for all objects stored in the database, including tables, queries, forms, and reports. In this chapter, we will focus only on tables.

As shown in Exhibit 3-21, when you create a new database, Access automatically opens a new table for you in *datasheet view*, a mode that presents a relational table or query result in row/column format. Datasheet view assumes you want to create a table simply by entering data. This is not the option we recommend using. Instead, change the view to design view by clicking on the *View* icon near the top left corner of the Table Tools window and then click on *Design view*. Design view gives you control over all choices that need to be made during table creation, such as specifying data types and field (attribute) properties for each field in the table. *Field properties* are additional field characteristics (e.g., is the field required or not), sometimes called metadata (people usually define metadata as "data about data" – in this context the "data" is the rows of table data, and the "data about data" is the field properties). The most important field property is the *data type,* which determines what kind of data values may be entered into a database table's column. Commonly used data types include text, numbers, currency, and date/time.

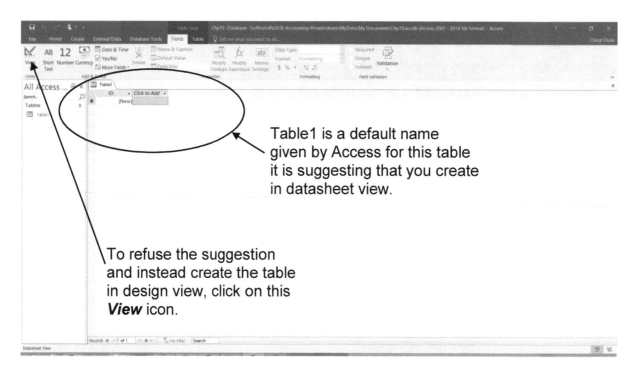

Exhibit 3-21: Microsoft Access Database Window – Table Tools

In response to clicking on the *View* icon, Access prompts you with a popup window to save the table and offers you a chance to give it a different name instead of the default. See Exhibit 3-22. For example purposes, we will change the table's name to Sale.

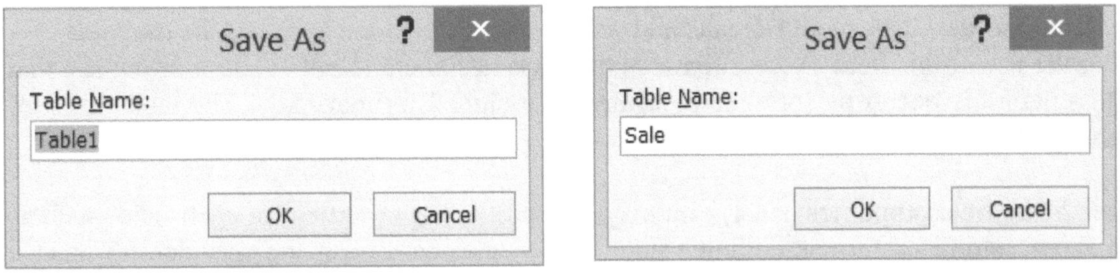

Exhibit 3-22: Popup Window to Save and Rename Table When Switching to Design View

Once the table is saved as Sale in design view, the resulting window appears as illustrated in Exhibit 3-23.

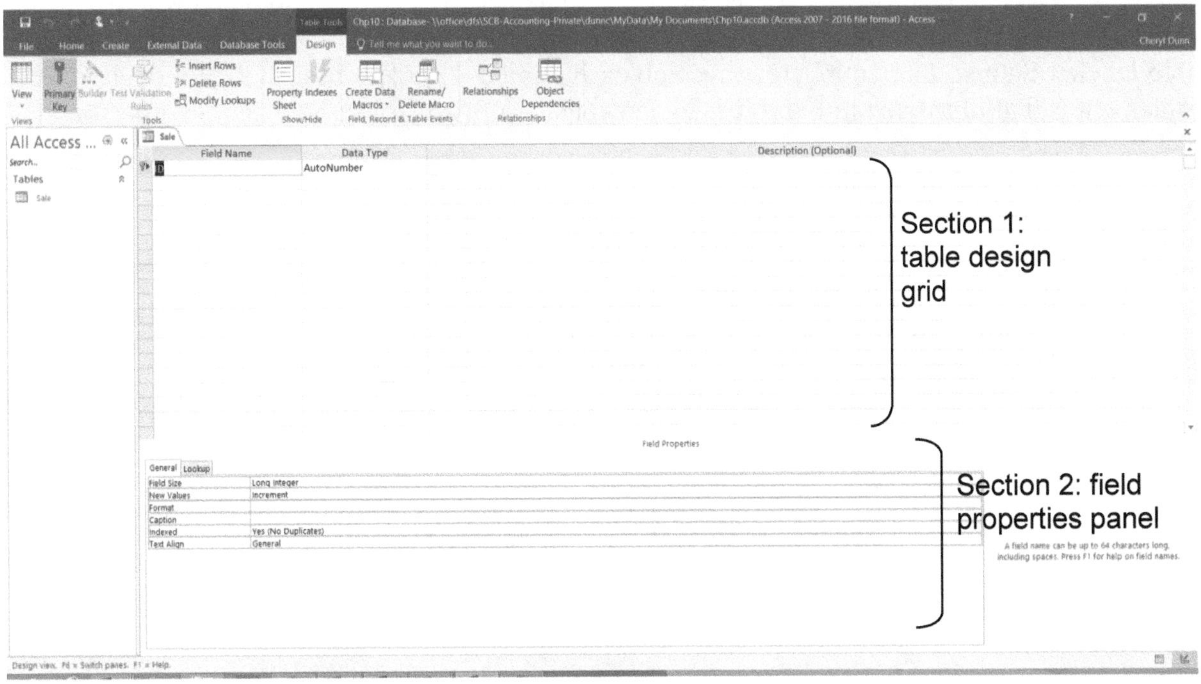

Exhibit 3-23: Microsoft Access Table Design View

Section 1 of Exhibit 3-23 shows the overall layout of the table design. The fields (attributes) of the table are listed on the left; in the middle column you can choose the appropriate data type for each field (e.g., text, currency, date, number). The right-hand column provides space for the table designer to write a description of what that field represents. The description may be left blank; however, a description should be added when deemed useful.

A quick note about the default attribute that Access displays: ID with AutoNumber as its Data Type (note that this attribute resulted from starting in datasheet view and switching to design view, and would not automatically appear if you started in design view). Access knows that every table should have a primary key attribute and that if a naturally occurring primary key does not exist, then the database designer should create and assign numbers to each record in the table. By suggesting the use of this field, Access reminds database designers to either use it or replace that field with a naturally occurring (or already arbitrarily assigned) primary key. The table designer should change the data type to whatever is appropriate.

In Section 2 (the field properties panel) you may set additional properties for each field, such as the field size, customized format, default value (the value to be used if the user doesn't enter a value), validation rules, or a specification as to whether the field is required to contain data (or can be null). The panel and properties in section 2 change based on the field that is active in Section 1. That is because the field property options for one field can be different from the options for a different field.

We next work through two examples to give you some experience creating physical implementations of relational logical models in Access. You may want to work through these examples on a computer as you read the rest of this chapter. (If you have not been working along up to this point, you will want to catch up by creating a new blank database, then creating a new table labeled Sale so that your screen resembles Exhibit 3-23). The first logical model we will implement is that illustrated in Exhibit 3-24 and consists of two tables: Sale and Salesperson.

Sale

SaleID	Date	Amount	Salesperson
061401A	6/14	$4,218	*123456*
061401B	6/14	$6,437	*654321*
061501A	6/15	$1,112	*654321*
061501B	6/15	$3,300	*123456*
061501C	6/15	$1,776	*654321*

Salesperson

SalespersonID	Name	TelephoneNumber
123456	Fred	555-0063
654321	Francis	555-0007

Exhibit 3-24: Sale – Salesperson Logical Model

Example 1: Creating and Connecting Class Tables

To finish creating the Sale table, enter the four fields (SaleID, Date, Amount, and Salesperson) in the leftmost column and change each data type to its appropriate value. You may have noticed that Access set a default data type as "Short Text." Move to the middle column of Section 1 of Exhibit 3-23. Click on the arrowhead next to "Short Text" and a popup list of data type choices will appear. Here are some general rules to follow:

- If a field will contain dates or times, use the *date/time* data type.
- If a field will contain data that will be used in mathematical calculations, use the *number* data type; if you want numbers to be formatted to appear as currency, then use the *currency* data type.
- Otherwise, use the *short text* data type.

These rules are simplistic, but work well for most situations. For our example, we will specify SaleID as *Short Text*, Date as *Date*, Amount as *Currency*, and Salesperson as *Short Text*. (Date is a reserved Word in Access so you will likely receive a message; simply click **Yes** and keep going). Notice the field properties panel change as you click from one field to the next in the top section – but don't change anything in the field properties section yet. You may wonder why we used "Short Text" for Salesperson, when all the data values we have are numeric. Go back to the rule of thumb. Are we likely to need to calculate anything based on the salesperson ID? No. And it is possible that someday we may start adding letters into our salesperson IDs, so we are better off specifying the type as short text. Why short text instead of the long text data type? Short text allows up to 255 characters, which should be long enough for most identifiers. Long text should be used only when a field's value may exceed 255 characters.

Now let us think about the field properties section, but without going into detail on most of these settings. One thing you need to be aware of with respect to field properties (and data type, which is also a field property) is that if the properties of two fields are different, then Access considers the values in those fields to be different even if the content is the same. Why is that important? Think about posted foreign keys. In our example, the identification number for salesperson is a field in both of our tables. In the Salesperson table (which we haven't yet created) it will be the primary key. In the Sale table (which we are currently creating) it is a foreign key. Now, recall from earlier in this chapter the referential integrity principle — in this case, the principle implies that for a data value entered in the Salesperson field in the Sale table, that particular data value must already exist in the in the SalespersonID (primary key) column of the Salesperson table The data type for a foreign key must be identical to the data type of the related primary key. (A related concept that is not in this example, is when primary keys from two individual tables are concatenated to become a primary key of a third table; this concatenated primary key must have data types that match the primary key data types in the two related tables.)

Getting back to our example from Exhibit 3-24, because the SalespersonID field is a foreign key that we do not want to allow users to leave blank, we should change the *required data entry field property* "Required" to Yes. Once you do that, your table design should look like Exhibit 3-25 below.

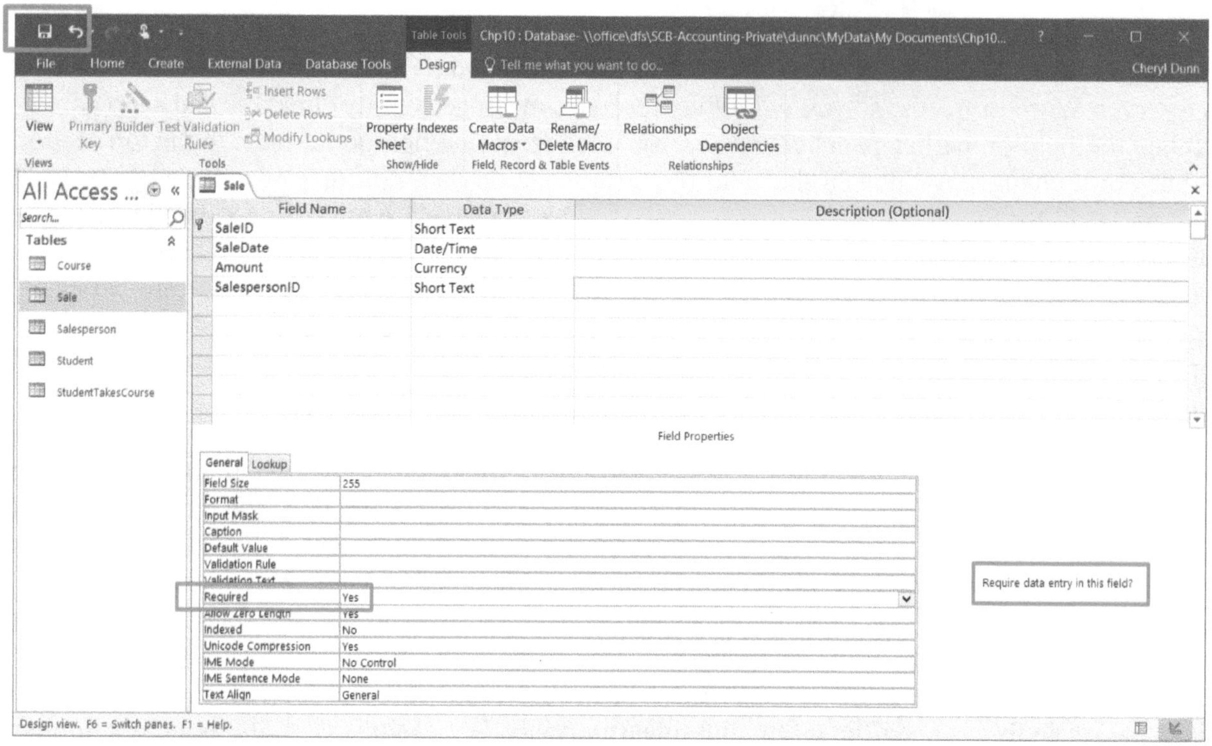

Exhibit 3-25: Example Sale table design

Look on your screen in the grey box immediately to the left of SaleID. If it has a small key symbol in it as is shown in Exhibit 3-25, that resulted from replacing the autonumbered id field suggested by Access with the text SaleID field. If instead of replacing that initial field you had deleted it and then added SaleID as a new field, you may not have a key icon next to the SaleID. If that is the case, you need to add it to define the primary key of the Sale table: click on the small gray box to the immediate left of the field, and then click on the Primary Key icon near the top left corner of the TableTools window. (If you do not see the Primary Key icon, you may have to click the Design tab.) Once you do that, your window should look like Exhibit 3-25. For the moment, we are finished with the Sale table's design, so we need to save the table. You may either choose File, Save from the top menu bar, or simply click on the disk icon (highlighted in Exhibit 3-25) Close the table by right-clicking on the table's tab (named Sale).

Next, create the Salesperson table, following similar steps. From the database window, click on Create and then Table Design. Enter the three fields: SalespersonID, SalespersonName, and SalespersonTelephoneNumber. None of these fields are dates, and none are fields that would likely be part of a calculation, so don't change the default short text data type or any field properties. Set SalespersonID as the primary key. Save the table, giving it the name Salesperson, and close the table. Your database window should now resemble Exhibit 3-26.

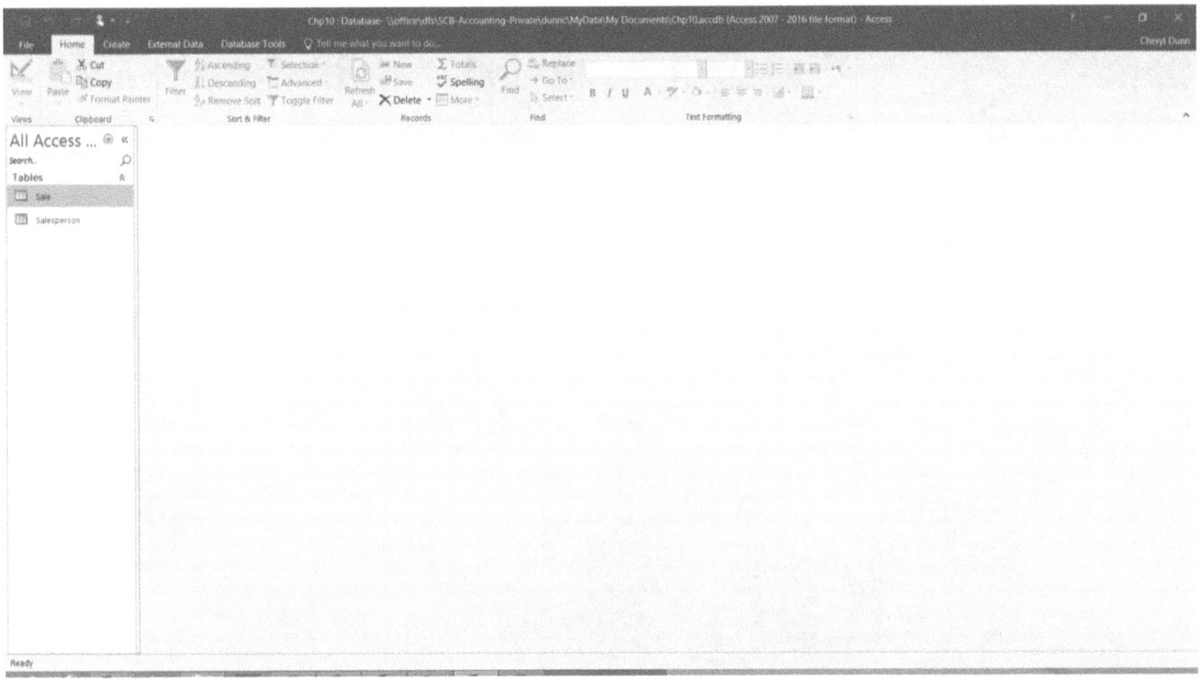

Exhibit 3-26: Database Window after Designing Sale and Salesperson Tables

Did you notice that we left out one very important piece of information we designed these tables?

No, we are not talking about the entry of data values into the tables, although that certainly also needs to be done (after the database definition is complete). Instead, we are talking about showing how the tables should connect to each other. At this point, Access "understands" that we have two tables representing the Sale and Salesperson classes, respectively, but Access does not "understand" there is an association between sale and salesperson. These associations are called relationships in Access.

Recall that we established that association in our logical model by posting salesperson as a foreign key into the Sale table. To Access, salesperson looks like just another attribute, because we have done nothing to differentiate it from any other attribute in the Sale table. We could, of course, type "foreign key from Salesperson table" in the description area for that field (and for system documentation purposes that is a very good thing to do). However, Access doesn't understand natural language and Access doesn't process anything based on information in description cells. The way to communicate foreign keys (as well as concatenated primary keys that are formed from posting two different class' primary keys into an association table) to Access is by establishing a relationship between the two tables. To do this, go to the *relationship layout*, which is a window that visually depicts relationships between tables. To go to the relationship layout, click on the menu choice for Database Tools and then click on the icon labeled Relationships (see circled items on Exhibit 3-27). When you enter the relationship layout, it is typically a good idea to make sure all of the tables are closed (or at least saved); open tables can sometimes interfere with the process of creating relationships.

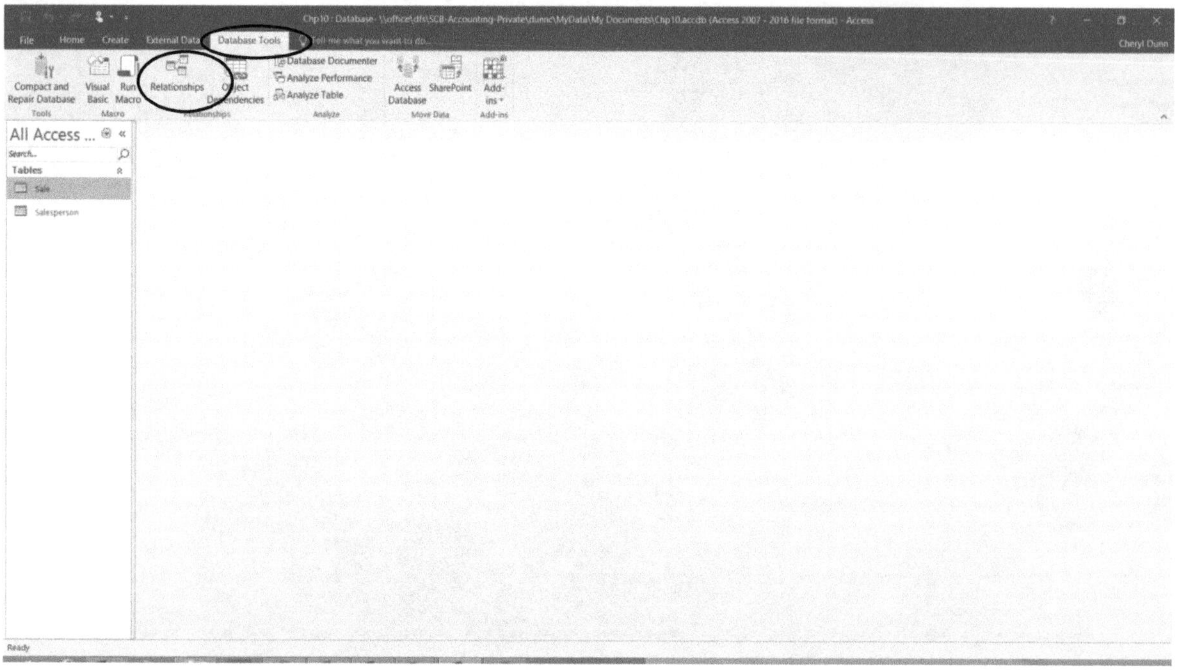

Exhibit 3-27: Database Tools, Relationships

The screen that initially appears when you open the relationship layout is the ***show table window*** – that is a screen from which the user may choose the tables to include in the relationship layout. See Exhibit 3-28. This screen automatically appears if there are no tables already in the relationship layout; if you want to add more or different tables later you must go to the relationship tools menu and click on the icon labeled Show Table.

Exhibit 3-28: "Show Table" Window

Highlight both tables and add them to the layout by clicking Add after they are both highlighted. Then close the "show table" window (but leave the relationship layout window open). Hover your cursor near the right edge of the Salesperson object until it becomes a double-ended arrow. This allows you to increase the width so that you can see the entire name of each field. Your relationship layout should look like Exhibit 3-29 (without the arrows and labels that we added to instruct you as to what to do next).

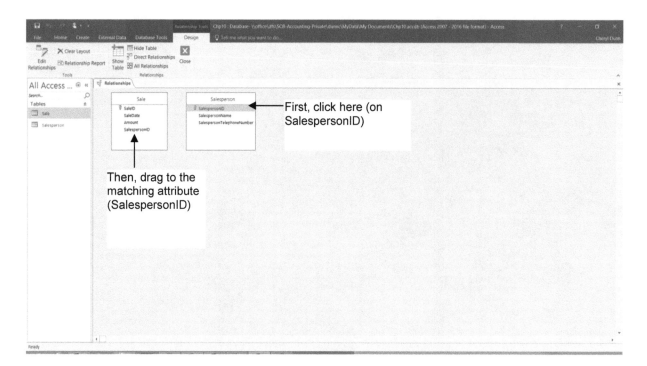

Exhibit 3-29: Relationship Layout with tables added

You may move a table around on the layout by clicking on its title bar and dragging it to the desired location. You may also resize the table windows as necessary.

Next, define a relationship between the two tables (i.e., "explain" to Access that you posted a foreign key). To do this, start with your cursor on SalespersonID in the Salesperson table. Click and drag the cursor to SalespersonID in the Sale table. Make sure you drag the primary key to the posted foreign key because those are the fields that you expect to have matching data values. Note that the field names do not have to match (but the data types do as we said above; we repeat the point here, because sometimes people make mistakes and this mistake will prevent relationships from being created). We could have labeled the primary key of Salesperson as EmployeeID, but named the foreign key in Sale as SalespersonID without causing any problem; however, if we had set EmployeeID as Number and SalespersonID as Short Text, we would not be able to *enforce referential integrity* (a choice selected in the relationship layout to determine whether data entry will be disallowed if it does not match between the two key fields as the user enters data into the database), as the different data types would cause Access to consider any entered values as different.

When you "drop" the primary key onto the matching foreign key to which you dragged it, Access will display an "Edit Relationships" window, as shown in Exhibit 3-30.

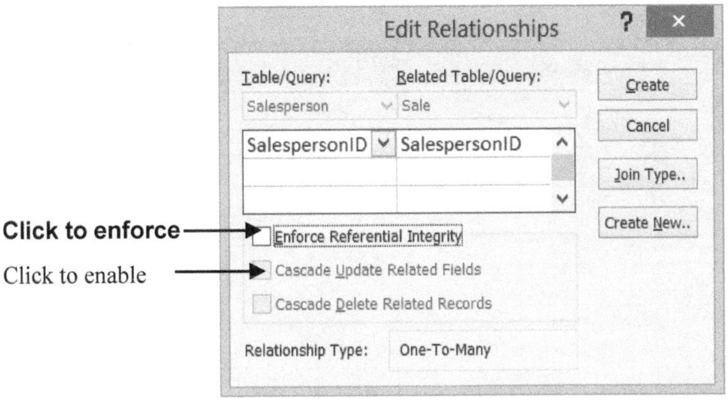

Exhibit 3-30: Edit Relationships Window

This window allows you to verify that you are establishing the relationship between the correct two attributes (in this example, the attribute that is the primary key in one table and the attribute that is the posted foreign key value in the other table). This window also allows you to enforce referential integrity – to do so, simply click on the check box.

You also have the option of setting updates in the primary key field to "cascade" such that it will also update the related field if a specific primary key value changes for some reason. The option of setting cascade deletions of related records means that if a primary key value is deleted (which also means the entire row of data would be deleted; rows cannot have null primary key values) the related rows in the other table will also be deleted.

Cascade update is usually a good option, because if you change the value of a primary key such as SalespersonID in the Sale table, then you want the corresponding posted foreign key values (such as Salesperson values in the Sale table) to also be changed. Cascade delete is somewhat risky, because you could unintentionally lose data that you may later need.

One important note regarding cascade updates: Many people get the false impression that enabling this option causes data entry of new primary key values to automatically become entered into the related foreign key fields. That cannot happen, because based solely on entering a value for a primary key, Access does not have any way of "knowing" which specific records in the related table (in which the foreign key is posted) are related until the data itself is actually entered. In our sales-salesperson example, when we enter a record (e.g., a new salesperson) into the Saleperson table, Access cannot possibly know which sale(s) will be made by that salesperson until the individual sales actually occur. However, after you have created a relationship between the fields, enabled cascade updates, and entered common data (123456) into the primary and foreign key fields, if you were to later decide to re-number salesperson 123456 to be 1234560, when you change that primary key data value in the Salesperson table, the change will flow through and will change to 1234560 all the foreign key values in the Sale table that were 123456.

After enforcing referential integrity and enabling cascade updates, click on "Create" to establish the relationship. The relationship layout will appear, and will now display the relationship you just created, as shown in Exhibit 3-31.

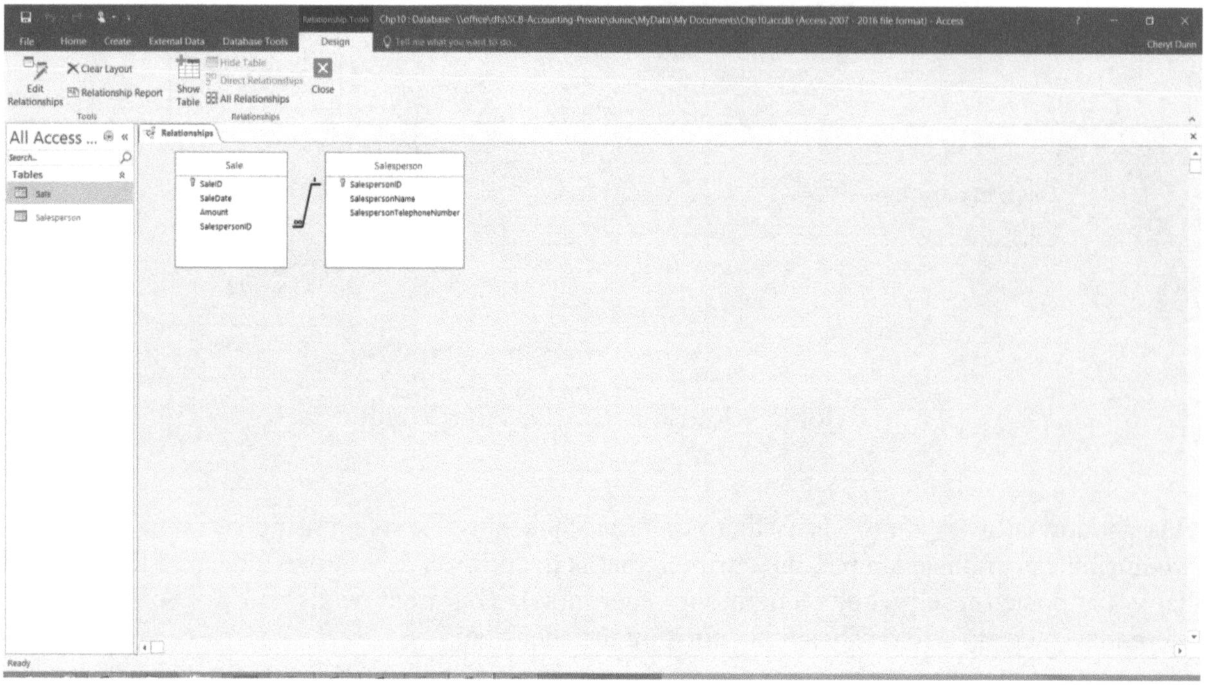

Exhibit 3-31: Relationship Layout

Although the relationship layout resembles a UML class diagram, they are not the same thing. Remember, the only purpose of the relationship layout is to communicate to Access information about posted key relationships – including the posting of foreign keys and the posting of concatenated primary keys.

The 1 and ∞ symbols in the Relationship Layout resemble multiplicities, however, they are not exactly the same concept. The 1 and ∞ reveal how many times the same data value can be stored in that field of the table to which the symbol is connected; for 1, think "duplicate values NOT allowed" and for ∞ think "duplicate value allowed." For example, the 1 next to Salesperson says that a particular data value for SalespersonID can exist in the Salesperson table only one time. That is, there can be no duplicate values, which makes sense because SalespersonID is the primary key and must be unique. The ∞ next to SalespersonID in the Sale table indicates that the same data value for that attribute may exist multiple times in the Sale table (duplicate values allowed). That also makes sense given that there is no restriction on foreign key fields to be unique (unless dictated by the related maximum multiplicity). In this example, had the multiplicity unrealistically indicated that "a salesperson can have at most one sale," then no duplicates would be allowed in the foreign key – this restriction would have to be implemented in the field properties in the design view of the table that has the foreign key; the foreign key's index would be specified as " no duplicates." That restriction would be unrealistic in this case – the company hires salespersons to make sales on a regular basis, not to terminate them once they have made one sale. Thus, for example, salesperson 654321 can only be entered in one row of the Salesperson table (in which it is the primary key), but can be entered in as many rows as appropriate in the Sale table (in which it is a foreign key) – that is, as many rows as that salesperson made sales.

Example 2: Creating and Connecting Association Class Tables to Class Tables
The second example demonstrates the physical implementation of the tables from Exhibit 3-32.

Student	0..*			0..*	Course
-Student ID PK					-CourseID PK
-Name		Takes			-Description
-Address		-grade earned			-Credits

Student

StudentID	Name	Address
999888	Mildred	123 Almanac St.
888777	Kent	456 Market Dr.
777666	Candace	789 Harriet Ave.

Course

CourseID	Description	Credits
ACG611	Advanced AIS	3
FIN642	Financial Markets	3
MIS650	IT Management	3

Takes

StudentID	**CourseID**	Grade earned
999888	ACG311	B
999888	MIS350	A-
888777	MIS350	B+

Exhibit 3-32: Student-Course Association: Conceptual Model with Association Class and Corresponding Relational Database Tables with Example Data

To begin, create a new blank database following the steps in Exhibit 3-12. Following the same basic procedure that was illustrated in Exhibits 3-13 through 3-15, add two new tables in design view. One should be named Student, and should include the following fields: StudentID (short text, primary key), Name (short text), Address (short text). (Name is a "reserved word" in Access, so you will probably get an error message when you enter it; just click OK and keep going because it won't matter for what we are doing here.) The other should be named Course, and should include the following fields: CourseID (short text, primary key), Description (short text), and Credits (number).

Next, create a third new table in design view and include the following fields: Student ID (short text), CourseID (short text) and Grade earned (short text). For this third table, we need to specify a concatenated primary key made up of both StudentID and CourseID. To represent this in Access, click on the grey box immediately to the left of Student ID. Hold the shift key and click on the grey box immediately to the left of Course ID. If you did this correctly, the rows of those two fields are highlighted. With those rows highlighted, click on the icon that looks like a key. Keys should appear in the grey boxes next to the field names as illustrated in Exhibit 3-33.

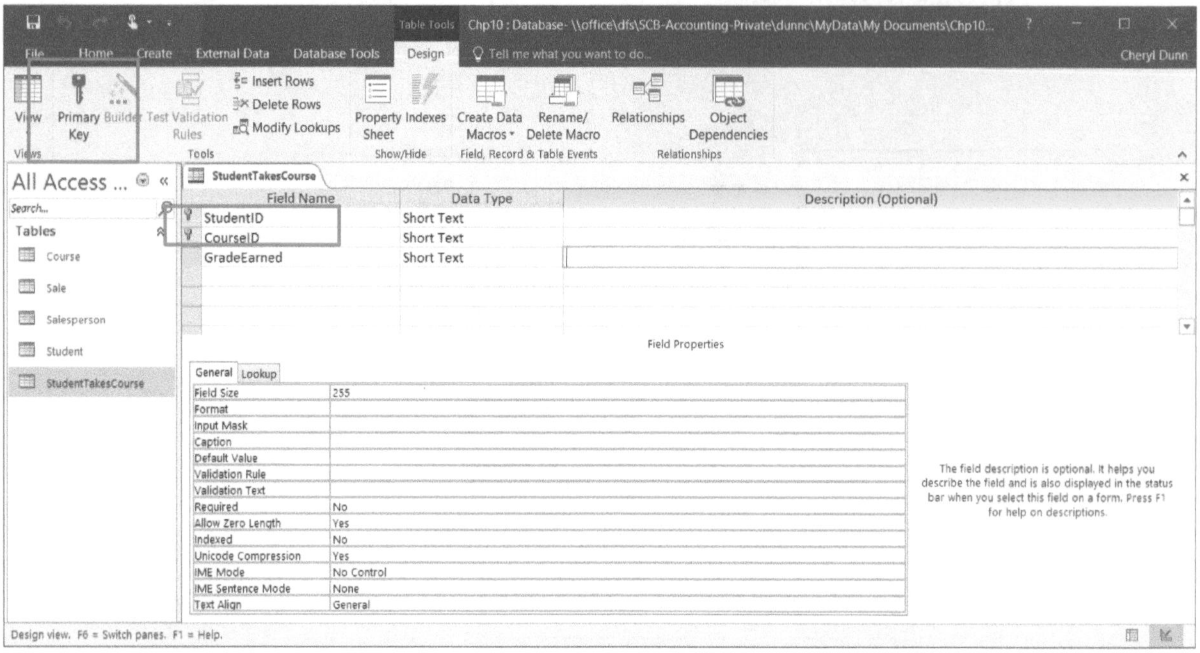

Exhibit 3-33: Specifying a concatenated primary key in Microsoft Access

Name/Save the table "StudentTakesCourse." Next, add the Student, Course, and StudentTakesCourse tables to the relationship layout following the same basic procedure used in Exhibits 3-27 and 3-28. Recall that the relationship layout informs Access as to the existence of primary keys posted into other tables either as foreign keys **or**, in this example, as parts of concatenated primary keys. Therefore, you need to inform Access that you posted the primary keys from Student and Course into the StudentTakesCourse table to form its concatenated primary key. To do this you simply click on StudentID in the Student table and drag the cursor to StudentID in the StudentTakesCourse table, similar to what was done in Exhibit 3-29. When you release the mouse, the "Edit Relationships" window will appear, as it did in Exhibit 3-30. Check the appropriate boxes to enforce referential integrity and enable cascade updates, similar to what you did for Exhibit 3-31. Click on OK. A relationship should appear connecting StudentID in the Student table to StudentID in the StudentTakesCourse table. Next, click on CourseID in the Course table and drag the cursor to CourseID in the StudentTakesCourse table and check the boxes in the "Edit Relationships" window to enforce referential integrity and enable cascade updates. Your relationship layout should resemble Exhibit 3-34.

Notice that any given value for StudentID can exist in the Student table only once because it is the primary key of that table and must be unique; however, that same value for StudentID can exist multiple times in the StudentTakesCourse table because it is only a part of the concatenated primary key and it is the <u>combination</u> of StudentID and CourseID that must be unique. Likewise, the primary key of Course is CourseID, so any given value for CourseID can exist only once in the Course table, but can exist multiple times in the StudentTakesCourse table – as long as each time it appears in that table it is paired with a different StudentID (again, it is the <u>combination</u> of individual students and individual courses that must be unique).

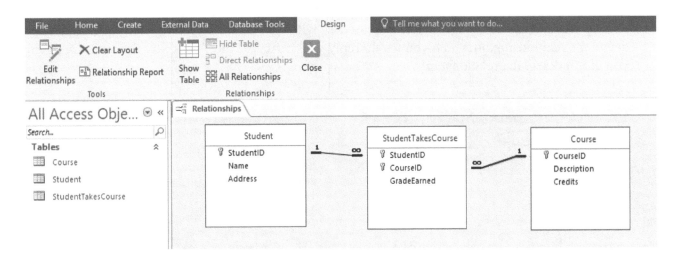

Exhibit 3-34: Association Class Table Linked to Two Class Tables

In our example from Exhibit 3-32, Mildred's student ID of 999888 can appear in the Student table only once, because there can't be another student with that same ID. However, Mildred's student ID 999888 can appear multiple times in the StudentTakesCourse table as long as that value is paired with different values of CourseID, such as ACG311 and MIS350. The course number MIS350 can appear only once in the Course table because there can't be another course with the same ID. However, Course MIS350 may be taken by multiple students and therefore can appear in the StudentTakesCourse table multiple times – as long as it is paired with different values of Student ID such as 999888 and 888777.

Deleting Existing Relationships in the Relationship Layout

What if you make a mistake and create a relationship you didn't really want? Open the relationship layout. Single-click the line for the relationship you want to delete (**make sure it's highlighted**), and then press the Delete key (you will receive a message asking you to confirm the deletion because deletions are important actions). Notice that you must delete the relationship itself, not just delete one table that was part of the relationship. If you delete a table from the relationship layout (by selecting the table and pressing the Delete key) the relationship will appear to be gone (when the table disappears, the relationship disappears; note we are deliberately saying "disappear" as opposed to "deleted"). However, if you click on "Design" on the top menu bar and then click "Show All" as circled on Exhibit 3-35 (this will show all existing relationships), you will see that the relationship was retained in Access's memory.

Similarly, if you are frustrated with your relationship layout and decide you want to start over, you may notice the "Clear Layout" icon that is also circled on Exhibit 3-35. Beware! The layout will be cleared, but all the relationships are still in Access's memory so you have not actually deleted them. As soon as you click on "Relationships, Show All" they will be back. The reason for this (at-first-glance) counterintuitive feature is that complex databases can contain a significant number of tables and relationships. There can be so many that you cannot see everything at once on the screen. So if you want to see just a portion of the relationships, you have that option. Just remember -- if you want to delete relationships from your relationship layout, you MUST highlight each relationship line and press the Delete key. Access will ask you if you really want to permanently delete the relationship, to which you would reply yes. If Access didn't ask you that question, then you didn't delete the relationship!

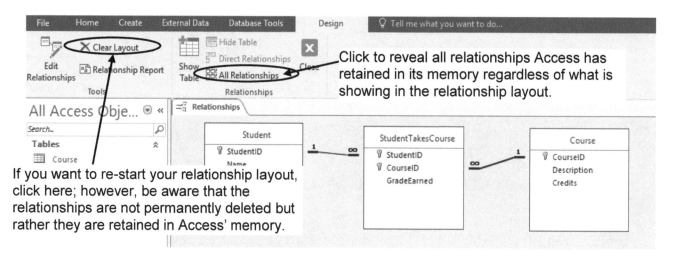

Exhibit 3-35: Relationship Layout Design Tools

Relationship Layout Summary
As the sale/salesperson example illustrated, relationships must be created between foreign keys and their related primary keys. And as the student/course example illustrated, relationships must also be created between composite primary keys and the individual primary keys in related tables. You should typically enforce referential integrity on all relationships. You will visually know referential integrity is enforced for a relationship because you will see the 1 and ∞ symbols on the relationship – unless it is a one-to-one relationship – and you should choose to cascade update fields.

Entering Data into Microsoft Access Tables
Once all of your tables are created and you have defined the relationships, you are ready to begin entering data into the tables in datasheet view. (Note: Access has the ability to create "forms" to facilitate data entry into tables; however, forms are beyond the scope of this chapter).

Enter the appropriate data records, using the TAB key to move between fields. You can also use the mouse to move the cursor to a desired field or record. As you tab out of one record to another record, the software automatically saves the record, displaying an error message if it was unable to save the record because of a data entry problem (such as violations of referential integrity). Often, you may see a pencil icon in the left hand, gray column. The pencil indicates the current record (the one being "pointed to" in temporary memory). You must completely enter through a row of data to save (commit) the entire row (at which point the pencil will disappear from that particular row and you will know it is saved).

After you finish adding records, choose File, Close from the main menu. Experiment with the arrow keys at the bottom of the table window. They allow you to view different fields and records.

Do not worry about entering data in alpha or numeric order. The computer will sort the data via the primary key attribute field.

Keep in mind that if you have enforced referential integrity (as you should have) and established mandatory data entry for appropriate fields (e.g., foreign keys posted from a 1..1 class table), you must be careful about the order in which you enter the data (you cannot add data to foreign keys or composite primary keys until that data "exists" in the related primary key(s). Consider the multiplicities in your underlying conceptual model and picture the company's reality in your mind. Think about the order in which data would be entered in real life. Generally, information about resources and agents (sometimes called master data) is input to corporate databases before any transactions involving them occur. Most of the time, you should enter your resource and agent data before you enter your event data. If you encounter error messages while you are entering data, try to figure out whether you are entering the data incorrectly, or whether you have a flaw in your table design, or relationship layout.

CONCLUDING COMMENTS

In this chapter, we introduced the UML class diagram notation used for conceptual modeling, including the creation of classes and associations and the definition of minimum and maximum multiplicities for each association. We then introduced a set of 6 steps that can be applied in an algorithmic manner to convert any UML class diagram into a set of relational database tables. If you apply steps 1 through 6 to a UML class diagram and then are careful when assigning attributes to ensure you don't cause one fact to be multiple places or multiple facts in one place, you will end up with a set of well-organized relational database tables.

Keep in mind, though, that we have not discussed (and will not discuss) technical issues such as optimization and database performance that would be necessary for scaling databases to be able to handle the enormous volume required by large corporations. Such a discussion is beyond the scope of this book, but would need to be considered in large scale implementations.

KEY TERMS AND CONCEPTS
Association (in UML)
Association class
Attribute
Candidate key
Class
Composite attribute
Concatenated primary key
Conceptual (database) model
Database window (in Access)
Datasheet view (in Access)
Data type
Design view (in Access)
Enforce referential integrity (in Access)
Entity

KEY TERMS AND CONCEPTS (continued)
Entity integrity
Extension
Fact (in database design)
Field
Field property
Foreign key
Intension
Logical (database) model
Mandatory participation
Maximum multiplicity
Minimum multiplicity
Multiplicities
Null value
One fact, one place rule
Optional participation
Physical database model
Primary key attribute
Record
Redundancy
Referential integrity
Relation
Relational model
Relationship layout (in Access)
Repeating group
Required data entry field property
Schema
Show table window (in Access)
Simple attribute
Static derivable attribute
Tuple
Unified Modeling Language (UML)
Volatile derivable attribute

REVIEW QUESTIONS
R3-1. What is the purpose of a foreign key?
R3-2. Does every table in a relational database contain a foreign key? Explain.
R3-3. Explain the difference between conceptual, logical, and physical database models.
R3-4. What is referential integrity, and how can one tell whether or not a relational database has referential integrity?
R3-5. How do you establish a concatenated primary key in Microsoft Access?

MULTIPLE CHOICE QUESTIONS

MC3-1. Which statement accurately interprets one or more of the multiplicities that are depicted below in the Alpha to Omega relationship?

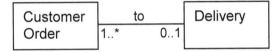

      A) An Alpha is related to at most one Omega
      B) An Omega can be related to many Alphas
      C) An Omega can happen before an Alpha
      D) Omegas can be related only to Alphas

MC3-2. Which statement accurately explains one or more of the following multiplicities between the "Customer Order" and the "Delivery" events?

Customer Order	to	Delivery
1..*	0..1	

      A) Each delivery can be associated with only one order
      B) A delivery must be associated with an order
      C) An order must be associated with a prior delivery to the customer
      D) Any order can be associated with several delivery events

MC3-3. Customers that come in to Furniture Galore, Inc. may be helped by any available salesperson. If more than one salesperson helps the same customer with the same merchandise, any resulting sale to that customer will be credited to all involved salespeople, who will split the sale commission. Salespeople are added to the database as soon as they are hired. A sale cannot be made without a salesperson. The multiplicities for the association between Sale and Salesperson for Furniture Galore, Inc. are:
      A) Sale 0..* to 1..1 Salesperson
      B) Sale 1..1 to 0..* Salesperson
      C) Sale 1..* to 0..* Salesperson
      D) Sale 0..* to 1..* Salesperson

MC3-4. Any attribute that may be decomposed into other attributes is called a
      A) Simple attribute
      B) Complex attribute
      C) Static derivable attribute
      D) Candidate key attribute

MC3-5. Which of these are <u>invalid</u> multiplicities for a class' participation in an association?
   A) 0..1
   B) *..1
   C) 1..1
   D) 1..*

MC3-6. Which of the following minimum and maximum multiplicities represent a class that has optional participation in an association and can participate in the association multiple times?
   A) 1..0
   B) 1..*
   C) 0..1
   D) 0..*

MC3-7. In relational database design, a primary key of one table that is also included in another table
   A) Usually indicates that someone made a mistake in deriving the tables and has added undesirable data redundancy into the database.
   B) Usually results in null values being introduced into the database.
   C) Usually ensures that we can get all the information we need to make a decision by querying only one table or the other (i.e., we would not need both tables in the same query).
   D) Usually establishes a connection between the tables so they can be linked to generate useful information.

MC3-8. Which of the following is NOT another name for the column names in a relational database?
   A) Intension
   B) Schema
   C) Fields
   D) Records

MC3-9. Which of the following describes referential integrity?
   A) A primary key of a relational table must not contain a null value
   B) One fact must not be in multiple places
   C) The value for a foreign key attribute must match one of the data values of that attribute in the table in which the attribute is a primary key
   D) A principle that prevents the use of redundancy, avoids null values, and creates a minimal database

MC3-10. Which example relational tables below contain data that best represents the multiplicities for the Location association Warehouse 1..* - 0..* Inventory.

A)

Warehouse	
WarehouseID	Address
WH138	11 Oak
WH479	321 East
WH702	929 Paris

Location	
WarehouseID	InventoryID
WH138	BVL489
WH138	ANK18
WH702	BVL489

Inventory	
InventoryID	Description
ANK18	Rough
BVL489	Smooth

B)

Warehouse	
WarehouseID	Address
WH138	11 Oak
WH479	321 East

Location	
WarehouseID	InventoryID
WH138	BVL489
WH138	ANK18

Inventory	
InventoryID	Description
ANK18	Rough
BVL489	Smooth

C)

Warehouse	
WarehouseID	Address
WH138	11 Oak
WH479	321 East
WH702	929 Paris

Location	
WarehouseID	InventoryID
WH138	BVL489
WH479	ANK18
WH702	BVL489

Inventory	
InventoryID	Description
ANK18	Rough
BVL489	Smooth

D)

Warehouse	
WarehouseID	Address
WH138	11 Oak
WH479	321 East
WH702	929 Paris

Location	
WarehouseID	InventoryID
WH138	BVL489
WH138	ANK18
WH702	BVL489

Inventory	
InventoryID	Description
ANK18	Rough
BVL489	Smooth
CRW177	Bumpy

APPENDIX 3A: ALTERNATIVE CONCEPTUAL MODELING NOTATIONS

UML class diagrams are a popular conceptual modeling notation, but there are alternatives – both diagrammatic and not. Chen introduced one of the first conceptual modeling notations: the entity-relationship model. [28] In Chen's notation, rectangles represent entities and diamonds represent relationships between entities. Chen's notation uses cardinalities instead of multiplicities; the concepts are very similar but the notation placement is slightly different. Other information systems and computer science courses use other notations such as crow's feet diagrams.

You may feel disconcerted that there is not just one notation that everyone uses for conceptual modeling. The differences in notation are especially pronounced for multiplicities/cardinalities. You must not let these differences frustrate you any more than you can let the fact that there are many different languages spoken globally frustrate you. Be aware of the different notations and be sure you understand which "language" an enterprise has used when you try to interpret its system documentation. At least when different spoken languages are written, they look different on paper so that when you are presented with גדול, for example, you immediately recognize that you are not reading English. While you may not be able to tell exactly what language the non-familiar notation is, you will at least recognize that you don't know the language. With conceptual modeling notation (especially for multiplicities) you must be very careful because at first glance the notation may look similar but upon closer examination you may find it is backward from your familiar approach. You must become multi-lingual with regard to conceptual modeling notations!

UML Class diagrams are similar to Chen's entity-relationship models. Classes are similar to entities and Associations are similar to relationships. Multiplicities are similar to participation cardinalities. Nearly every diagrammatic notation in practice represents entities with rectangles (or rounded rectangles). Notations vary as to whether they represent relationships using diamonds, some other symbol, or just connection lines. It is usually reasonably easy to tell at a glance what the entities and relationships are in any notation. Cardinalities or multiplicities are sometimes more difficult to interpret across notations. To clarify cardinalities and to illustrate the difference between the Chen notation and two other notations, examine Exhibit 3A-1.

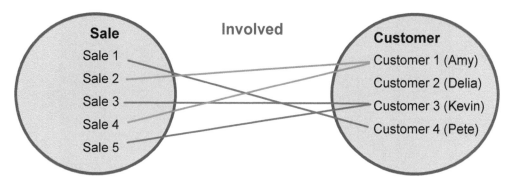

Exhibit 3A-1: Example Comparing Multiplicity (Cardinality) Notations

---

[28] Chen P.P. 1976. The entity relationship model—toward a unified view of data. *ACM Transactions on Database Systems* (March) pp. 9-36.

We ask (and answer) 4 questions about the sets above:

- ❑ Q1: Must every sale relate to a customer?
  - o Yes, each instance of sale involves a customer = mandatory participation
    minimum multiplicity = 1
- ❑ Q2: Can any sale relate to multiple customers?
  - o No, each instance of sale involves only one customer
    maximum multiplicity = 1
- ❑ Q3: Must every customer relate to a sale?
  - o No, Customer 2 (Delia) is unrelated to any sale = optional participation
    minimum multiplicity = 0
- ❑ Q4: Can any customer relate to multiple sales?
  - o Yes, Customer 1 (Amy) is related to Sale 2 and to Sale 4
    maximum multiplicity = *

These same four questions are asked and answered no matter what multiplicity or cardinality notation is used; the difference is simply where the answers to the questions are placed in the conceptual model and what notation is used to communicate the answers. (As an aside, you may wonder how a customer, Customer 2 – Delia, can be a customer without relating to a sale. One reason is that Delia might be defined as a customer because she placed her first order, but that order has not yet been filled or converted into an actual sale.)

UML class diagrams put the answers next to the opposite class, with the minimum participation followed by two periods and then the maximum participation. The Chen notation puts the answers next to the first entity in the question inside parentheses, with the minimum participation followed by a comma and then the maximum participation. Another cardinality notation widely used in practice, Crow's Foot, places the answers to the minimum and maximum cardinality questions next to the second entity in the questions, with the minimums closest to the center of the relationship and the maximums closest to the entities.

Exhibit 3A-2 shows a side-by-side comparison of the notation used to describe the reality depicted in Exhibit 3A-1 for the association/relationship and its multiplicities/cardinalities based on the answers to the four questions above.

	UML Class Diagrams	Chen	Crow's foot
Notation for each multiplicity/ cardinality	Min Zero = 0. Min One = 1. Max One = .1 Max Many = .*	Min Zero = (0, Min One = (1, Max One = ,1) Max Many = ,N)	Min Zero = ──o── Min One = ──┼── Max One = ──┼ Max Many 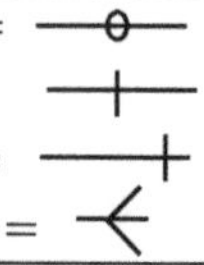 = ──<

Answer Placement	Sale (Q3..Q4)
	   (Q1..Q2) Customer
		Sale (Q1, Q2)
		   (Q3, Q4) Customer
			Min symbol closest to relationship center on opposite entity's side; Max symbol closest to opposite entity; Sale (Q4, Q2) ------ (Q1, Q3) Customer

Solution to Exhibit 3-A1	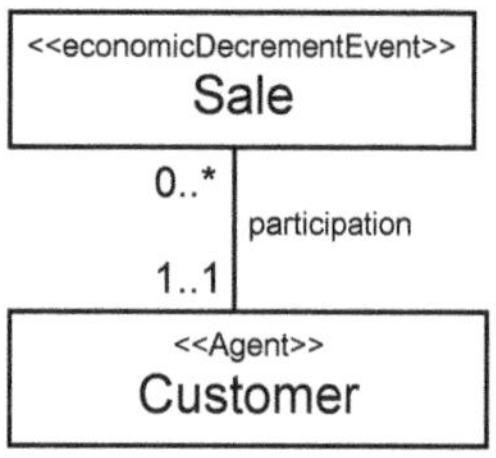	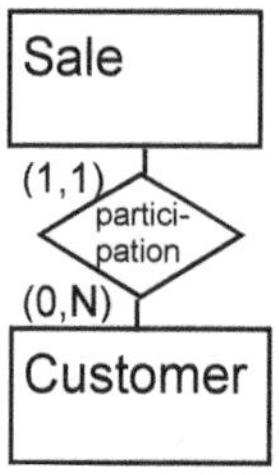	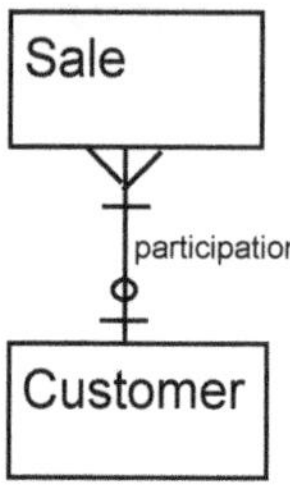

Exhibit 3A-2: Conceptual Modeling Notation Comparison

Expanded REA Business Process Models and Modeling Acquisition Business Processes with REA

LEARNING OBJECTIVES

The first objective of this chapter is to introduce some of the expanded concepts added to the core REA pattern in the decades since 1982, and to provide additional insight for assigning attributes and multiplicities to any REA business process model. You will want to keep the first part of this chapter in mind as you move on to chapters 5 through 7, as the insights we share also apply to the payroll, revenue, and conversion processes. The second primary objective of this chapter is to create detailed REA (Resource-Event-Agent) business process models for acquisition business processes. We expand the REA models originally seen in chapter 2 for acquisition business processes, and we also illustrate various types of business documents companies use to capture data about tasks and events in their acquisition business processes. After studying this chapter, you should be able to

1. Describe the typical tasks, instigation events, commitment events, economic events, economic reversal events found in most enterprises' business processes
2. Identify attributes commonly assigned to Resources, Events, Agents, and various associations in the REA ontology across business processes
3. Explain multiplicity heuristics that commonly apply to stockflow, participation, and duality associations across business processes
4. Identify the documents commonly used to capture data about the various types of tasks and events in acquisition business processes
5. Create a REA business process model for a company's acquisition business process
6. Apply multiplicity heuristics for selected relationships in REA acquisition models

EXPANSIONS TO THE CORE REA BUSINESS PROCESS MODEL

In chapter 2, we introduced the REA business process model with only its core pattern. Exhibit 4-1 illustrates an expanded model that includes several additional constructs. We discussed three of these in chapter 2: the custody, assignment, and responsibility associations. To refresh your memory, custody associates an agent and a resource such that the agent has physical control over the resource or the agent controls access to the resource. Such a relationship is separate from any event involving the resource. If an event involves a resource and an agent, the participation of both the resource and the agent in that event does not constitute a custody association. The agent who has custody of a resource may be an internal agent or an external agent. For example, banks have custody of an enterprise's cash held in accounts at their locations. Consignees have custody of goods that they have been contracted to sell on the enterprise's behalf.

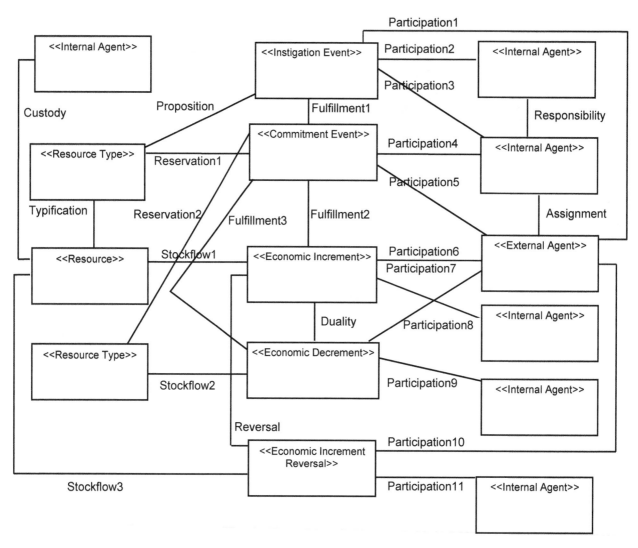

Note: Internal agents are depicted on this diagram as separate classes to indicate that different employees are responsible for different events, and to allow for the illustration of the Custody, Assignment, and Responsibility associations. These associations are just examples, custody may occur between any agent and any resource or resource type; assignment may occur between any internal agent and any external agent; and responsibility may occur between any two internal agents. Additionally, often the same internal agent connects to multiple events (e.g., a purchase agent might relate both to a purchase requisition and to a purchase order).

Exhibit 4-1: Expanded REA Business Process Pattern

Assignment is an association between an internal agent and an external agent that is separate from any event in which they might both participate. For example, say salesperson S42's assigned territory includes customer number 43BYZ. That relationship exists even if S48 makes a sale to customer 43BYZ while S42 is on vacation.

Responsibility is an association between two types of internal agents that is separate from any event in which they might both participate. For example, a partner in a public accounting firm may have responsibility for ten of the staff accountants in that firm. Specific responsibilities may include the partner mentoring the staff accountants, reading supervisors' reviews of the staff accountants' performance, reviewing the staff accountants' training programs and career plans, and conducting their annual evaluations. Such a relationship exists even if those staff accountants never work on a client engagement with that partner.

We illustrate these associations and expand our illustration with additional constructs that help to complete the economic story that the REA ontology supports. With only the core pattern, the economic story is incomplete – the storytelling does not begin until an economic event increases or decreases a resource. Yet other events had to occur before that, and additional events could happen afterward. Starting to tell a story only after it is nearly complete does not seem as informative as starting to tell a story from the time it begins. The Exhibit 4-1 model helps us to tell an informative story. Therefore, we need to understand the purpose of the various classes and associations. Your first attempt to understand this model will probably be challenging. As you proceed through the chapter, we will make this model more concrete with specific examples and your understanding will improve. It may be necessary to read this chapter more than once.

A typical business process begins with *instigation events* - events that identify the need for future commitment and economic events, thus triggering other activities and events in the business process. *Commitment events* are events in which the enterprise enters into agreements expected to result in future economic events. In theory, the agreements may consist of separate commitments to future economic increment events and to future economic decrement events. Commitments that happen simultaneously may be bundled into a *mutual commitment* event.

Is the economic story complete once we add instigation and commitment events on the front end? Not necessarily. The core REA pattern tells the "happy path" in which expectations are met as intended for all involved parties. For example, goods or services are exchanged for cash and both buyer and seller are satisfied. Unfortunately, sometimes buyers or sellers (or both) are dissatisfied and the story ends unhappily rather than happily. For example, a purchase (economic increment event) may result in a purchase return (economic increment reversal event) instead of resulting in a payment (economic decrement event). A sale (economic decrement event) may result in a sale return (economic decrement reversal) instead of resulting in a cash receipt (economic increment event). Such events that reverse or negate previous economic events are *economic reversal* events.

Once we flesh out the economic story with instigation, commitment, and economic reversal events, we must connect those events to the core pattern constructs. Some *fulfillment associations* connect instigation events to the resulting commitment events (see fulfillment1 in Exhibit 4-1), and other fulfillment associations connect commitment events to the resulting economic events (see fulfillment2 and fulfillment3 in Exhibit 4-1). For example, purchase orders (commitment event) fulfill purchase requisitions (instigation event) and both purchases (economic event) and payments (economic event) fulfill purchase orders (commitment event).

All events represent occurrences in time. Therefore, they must contain a date or time attribute. We define two event types: economic events and business events. Each of these event types is associated with resources; the key difference is that an economic event causes a change to the value of a resource (increase or decrease – meaning there can be economic events that increase resource values, and economic events that decrease resource values), whereas a business event does not. Business events can be divided into instigation events and commitment events. Before discussing the stereotypical events and associations, we want to point out that any time an event occurs, regardless of event type, we must show any agents who are, or may be, participating in the event or authorizing the event. Those associations between events and agents are called participation associations. We next focus on specific events and how they relate to resources and other events.

The stereotypical event series is shown in Exhibit 4-2; the exhibit also shows how that event series would look in the acquisition process.

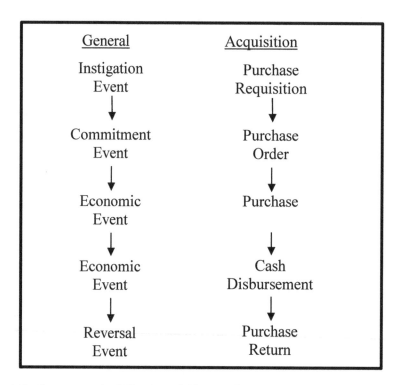

Exhibit 4-2: Stereotypical Series of General and Acquisition Process Events

Instigation Events

Instigation events identify a need that will begin a series of events in a business process. The need is associated with a resource. Instigation events may, or may not, lead to commitment events. Because of the tentative nature of instigation events, we say that we are proposing resources associated with instigation events; a *proposition association* connects an instigation event to a resource or resource type. A proposition association is essentially a proposed (potential) future stockflow association.

Exhibit 4-1 illustrates a proposition association between the instigation event and the resource type, but could have instead connected the instigation event to the resource. To refresh your memory from chapter 2, each instance of a resource type class is a category that may represent many separate physical objects, whereas each instance of a resource class is a uniquely identified separate physical object. For example, the car type Chevrolet Trax LT is a category for many different physical cars, and each of those physical cars has its own unique VIN (vehicle identification number) that differentiates that vehicle from all others.

Most proposition associations connect to the resource type rather than to the resource, because at the time of proposition, physical objects within the same category are viewed as interchangeable. For example, someone who requisitions a new computer is likely to specify the brand and model that has the desired features – processor speed, amount of RAM, hard drive size, and so forth – but would be unlikely to specify the serial number of a specific physical computer. This is not always the case – in some business processes the proposition is for a specific physical object (think about many E-bay listings that solicit bids on uniquely identified items) – so one must be careful to determine which scenario best fits the business process one is modeling.

Commitment Events

Commitment events are contracts, or contract components, that delineate future economic exchanges. An order is an example of a commitment event: an order will result in both a transfer in ownership of inventory, and a transfer in ownership of cash (inventory and cash will be exchanged). *Reservation associations* connect commitment events to the resources or resource types. In Exhibit 4-1, the commitment event has a reservation association with a resource type. But note that this resource type has a *typification association* (i.e., an association between a category and individual instances of that category) with a specifically-identified resource. This is because the commitment event is for a type of resource, yet to be specifically-identified; the specifically-identified resource is known when the economic event takes place. A reservation association is essentially an agreed upon future stockflow association (theoretically, it is an agreed upon two future stockflow associations, one representing the resource to be transferred to the external agent, and one representing the resource to be transferred from the external agent).

There can be a specific commitment event associated with an economic increment event, and there can be a separate specific commitment event associated with an economic decrement event (the increments and decrements would represents transfers from and to an external agent in an exchange). When separate, but related commitment events are modeled, reciprocal associations occur between those commitment events; one commitment is for a future economic increment, and a related commitment is for a future economic decrement. *Reciprocal associations* are the commitment equivalent of duality associations. Bundling separate commitments into a single mutual commitment event eliminates the reciprocal association. Because the commitment event illustrated in Exhibit 4-1 is a mutual commitment (one commitment is associated with two different economic events), that commitment is also associated with two different resources or resource types. It is possible to have a contracting event that bundles together separate commitments, so a bundling associating could connect the contract to its defined commitments (this is not illustrated in Exhibit 4-1).

Economic Events

In Chapter 2, we discussed economic events and stockflow associations that connect economic events to resources or resource types. Recall that in an exchange, the enterprise gives up one or more resources (or resource types) in exchange for one or more resources (or resource types). An exchange is therefore a give-take relationship; something (a resource) is given, and something (a resource) is taken. The "give event" is an economic decrement event; the "take event" is an economic increment event. Economic decrement events decrease the value of resources: think "flow." Economic increment events increase the value of resources: think "stock." So while the general term "stockflow" can be used to name an association between an economic event and a resource, whether the association is a "stock" or a "flow" depends on whether the related economic event is an increment or a decrement. You will note three stockflow associations in Exhibit 4-1. Two of those associations are related to the original economic exchange, "the happy path," and one association is related to "the unhappy path."

Reversal Events

Reversal events are "unhappy path" events. Perhaps you received some unsatisfactory raw material inventory that you would like to return to the vendor (increment reversal event), or you sold a product to an unhappy customer who wants to return the product (decrement reversal event). Such reversal events essentially reverse, or annul, a prior economic event. *Reversal associations* connect economic reversal events to the economic events being reversed or annulled. Exhibit 4-1 includes a reversal association between the economic increment event and the economic increment reversal event classes. If the modeled company also tracked reversals of economic decrement events, the model would include a second class for the economic decrement reversal events and another reversal association to connect that event class to the economic decrement event class. Reversal events are also connected by stockflow associations to related resources that are incremented or decremented by the reversals.

REA AND ATTRIBUTES

REA does not prescribe specific attributes as part of its enterprise ontology. Enterprises may use whatever attributes are appropriate to describe its classes and associations. With that said, events are expected to have at least one temporal attribute. Attribute determination and assignment is a very important step attributes will store the economic story (data) of the enterprise. In order to correctly assign attributes to classes and associations, you must understand what information the attribute is supposed to communicate. You must understand exactly what "thing" in reality each class and each association represents, and at what level of detail the data will exist. This may seem like an easy task, and for some classes it is quite simple. For other classes, and for many associations, it takes considerable thought. Sometimes a designer will realize he or she misunderstood what reality a class was intended to represent and attribute assignment errors occur. Such misunderstandings are best corrected before the conceptual model is converted into a physical implementation. The longer it takes to identify an error, the costlier the error is to fix.

In the remainder of this chapter, the documents discussed for each business process include many fields that we should include in REA business process models. Header data (fields that apply to the document as a whole) are often appropriate attributes of the event the document represents, or for the associations between the event and any other classes with which the event has maximum multiplicities of 1 (meaning the table for the event will have foreign keys – most often associated with specific agents). Line item data (fields that have multiple values within a document) are often appropriate attributes of associations between the event and other classes with which the event has maximum multiplicities of * (many). It is important to recognize that the documents may be computerized or have computerized equivalents (many times with a web page).

Attributes can be class attributes or association attributes. Class attributes are shown inside UML classes; association attributes are shown inside UML association classes. However, recall that we are using UML class diagrams in conjunction with the REA ontology. In the REA ontology, resources, events, and agents, are represented as classes. Therefore, we can think about certain attributes for resources, events, and agents. Many times, but not always, certain REA associations (like stockflow or duality) will have attributes. We elaborate on this paragraph below.

Class or Association Attribute?

As implied in the previous section, specific types of documents usually signal specific types of events. The document header fields typically contain event class attributes, whereas document line item fields are often association attributes (and therefore, modeled with an association class). To determine whether an attribute describes an instance of a class or an instance of an association, you need to be able to isolate whether the attribute describes just one thing or whether it describes a combination of things. For example, consider the attribute quantity sold of an inventory item in a sale event. Assume each sale event can involve multiple inventory items and that an inventory item represents a type of inventory (i.e., a model number and description) that can be sold multiple times. Should this attribute be assigned to the inventory class, to the sale class, or to the stockflow association? To answer this question, think about what the attribute quantity sold describes. Does it describe inventory separately from sale? Could you find a data value for that attribute if you knew which inventory item it was but you didn't know which sale it was related to? That is, if you knew it was Model KXPJ432, but you didn't know whether you wanted the quantity sold on Sale #2, 46, or 79? No, you could not find the data value, because different quantities may have been sold on each of those sales! So quantity sold is not an attribute of inventory.

Does quantity sold describe sale separately from inventory? Could you find a data value for that attribute if you knew which sale it was but you didn't know which inventory item was involved? That is, if you knew it was Sale #17 but you didn't know whether the quantity sold was of Model AFLQ127 or Model CLDJ1110? No! That tells you that quantity sold is not an attribute of sale. To fill in a data value for the attribute "quantity sold" you must know both the inventory item (e.g., KXPJ432) and the sale (e.g., #2) because it is really describing the relationship between them. Thus, quantity sold is an association attribute, not a class attribute (remember that association attributes get modeled in an association class).

If, on the other hand, the attribute of interest was not the quantity of a specific item sold in a specific sale event, but rather the total quantity sold of an inventory item throughout the company's history (a volatile derivable attribute considering all sale events that have involved that inventory model) then the attribute is a class attribute assigned to inventory. Similarly, if the attribute of interest was the total count of all individual inventory items included in a sale event, then it is a class attribute assigned to the sale class. You must verify that you understand what data the enterprise wants for each of the attributes on your list and model the attribute accordingly.

Resource Attributes

Although REA does not prescribe a set of required attributes, we have repeatedly seen some attributes based on experience. Resources can be difficult classes to grasp in terms of the underlying reality and what attributes we should use to identify and describe them. Cash is a class that many people who are new to REA modeling have difficulty conceptualizing. When you pictured cash as a resource in thinking about the value system and value chain levels in a previous chapter, you probably thought about physical cash – the actual coins and banknotes of currency. Most of the time we do not need information about each specific coin and each specific banknote that enters and exits an enterprise; therefore we do not usually represent cash at the specific instance level. Instead, we typically represent cash at an aggregated level, representing characteristics of the accounts in which cash is stored. The instances of a cash class are usually cash accounts that have attributes such as cash account number, cash account location (e.g., "Fourth Street Bank," "Cash register #42," or "secretary's file cabinet drawer in room 144"), cash account type (e.g., checking, savings, money market, petty cash, or cash on-hand), and account balance.

Inventory is another resource class in which the related attributes take some thought: sometimes instances of the inventory class are specifically identified physical items, and other times, instances of the inventory class are categories (types) into which the physical items are grouped – these instances typically are model or SKU numbers. What determines whether the instances are separate physical items or whether they are categories (types)? As discussed earlier, if the enterprise does not separately identify each physical unit of inventory, then the instances must be categories. For example, consider bags of potato chips at the grocery store. When a bag of potato chips is sold, the cashier scans the UPC code that tells the system what brand and what size package was just scanned. Scanning another bag of chips (of the same brand and size) communicates exactly the same information to the system. There is no way for the system to distinguish between the first physical bag of chips and the second physical bag of chips.

Contrast bags of chips with personal computers that have serial numbers separately identifying each physical computer. When the serial number is entered into the system for a sale, the system "knows" exactly which physical unit is being sold. Technically, the class that represents category level inventory should be called Inventory Type, and the class that represents each physical unit of inventory should be called Inventory; those two classes should have a typification association between them if an enterprise chooses to collect data about each class. If an enterprise has no need to separately identify each physical unit of inventory, then often a compromise is made and Inventory Type is substituted for Inventory and used as if it were a resource instead of a resource type.

Because of the inventory distinction just described, it is important to understand your primary key attributes for inventory and inventory type. Specifically identified inventory has a unique data value for every physical instance of inventory; e.g., Vehicle Identification Numbers (VINs). With inventory types, a unique value for a specific inventory type represents multiple physical instances of inventory; e.g., International Standard Book Numbers (ISBNs), catalog part numbers, or SKUs. Non-primary key attributes that are commonly stored for resources include descriptions, dimensions, valuations, and locations.

Event Attributes

Assignment of attributes to events is usually straightforward. Consider the information that is typically needed regarding events. The five "journalism 101" questions – who, what, why, when, and where – are a good representation of what people (and enterprises) want to know about events. The "who and why" questions are answered by the participation and duality associations in which the event class participates. The "what" question actually contains two parts. One part is "what happened" and the other part is "what things were affected by the event." The "what happened" is answered by the name of the event and its identifier attribute. The "what things were affected by the event" is answered by the stockflow associations between the event and the related resources and sometimes by the inclusion of a dollar value attribute. The remaining attributes needed to fill out the whole picture, then, are those that will answer the "when" and the "where" questions. For "when," the date attribute is needed. Time is also sometimes included as an attribute of an event. For "where," the location may be stored. If there is no question as to the where for an event set, then the enterprise may exclude the location attribute. For example, if an enterprise only has one location at which it makes sales, or if the location of a sale doesn't matter for decision-making purposes, then there is no need to record location as an attribute of sale.

Agent Attributes

To consider what attributes are likely to be assigned to agents, think about what you typically want to know about people or companies with which you do business. An identifier is needed, of course, to be able to tell one agent from another, especially if two agent instances may have the same name. EmployeeID (or something similar) is very common as a primary key. Social Security Number used to be a common primary key for employees, but has fallen into disuse because of privacy and identity theft concerns. What else do you need to know about agents? You probably want to know their name and some means of contacting them, such as addresses and telephone numbers. You may also need to keep attributes that tell you something about their qualifications and their performance. For example, one might store the CPA license number as an attribute of accountant, and one might store year-to-date sales as an attribute of salesperson if the database is capable of storing formulas for volatile derivable attributes.

REA AND MULTIPLICITIES: SOME HEURISTICS

As with attributes, REA does not specifically prescribe any multiplicities as part of its enterprise ontology. However, years of practice have produced heuristics, i.e., rules of thumb, that usually apply. Therefore, your assignment of multiplicities is not completely ad hoc; however, you must carefully consider whether the situation you are modeling is an exception to the heuristics. We have listed some common exceptions along with the heuristics, but other exceptions certainly exist!

Resource Type-Economic Event (Stockflow) Multiplicity Heuristics

If a resource type substitutes for a resource in a stockflow association with an economic event (increment or decrement), then the general multiplicity heuristics are:

Resource Type 1..* – 0..* Economic Event

The minimum of zero (0) for the participation of resource types in the association with economic events reflects the common business practice of entering data about resource types before recording any economic events involving those resource types. Also, often resource type data is entered in conjunction with instigation or commitment events that precede the economic event that causes the resource inflow or outflow.

The maximum of many (*) for the participation of resource type in the association with economic events reflects the fact that resource type is a category level class; a resource type can be associated with many events (e.g., a particular ISBN could be associated with many sales).

The minimum of one (1) for the participation of economic event in the association with resource type reflects the fact that an economic event must involve a resource flow – by definition an economic event either gives or takes something of economic value.

The maximum of many (*) for the participation of economic event in the association with resource type reflects the fact that seldom does an enterprise design its business processes such that each event may involve only one instance of a resource. When an enterprise makes a sale, it would hope at least some of its sales consist of multiple items. When an enterprise purchases merchandise, it would be inefficient to create a separate purchase for each separate item it purchases, especially if multiple resources are purchased on the same day from the same vendor.

Common exception that changes the 1 minimum participation of Economic Event
If the event could involve alternative kinds of resource types that are stored in different classes, then the minimum participation for Event in its association with Resource Type would change from one (1) to zero (0) or mandatory to optional. For example, if a purchase could involve a fixed asset or an inventory item (assuming those are maintained as separate classes) then the participation of purchase with fixed assets would be optional, because the purchase could instead involve an inventory item.

Resource-Economic Event (Stockflow) Multiplicity Heuristics
If a resource class represents specifically identified resources, the expected multiplicities are:

Resource 1..* – 0..1 Economic Event

The reasoning for the minimum of zero (0) participation of Resource in its association with the related Economic Event, the minimum of one (1) participation of Economic Event in its association with the related Resource and the maximum of many (*) for Economic Event in its association with the related Resource is the same as in the expected multiplicity for Resource-Type – Economic Event, so we do not repeat that logic here. The only difference between the pattern for stockflow associations involving resources as opposed to resource types is the expected maximum participation of the Resource in its association with the Economic Event. Because resources are specifically identified physical units (as opposed to categories) each can typically only be involved in one (1) economic event. Usually the same physical unit of something can only be produced or purchased or sold one time.

Common Exceptions that change the 1 maximum participation of Resource

One exception that changes the one (1) maximum participation of Resource to many (*) in its association with Economic Event occurs when the economic event involves the <u>rental</u> of the resource rather than the permanent transfer of the resource. In this case, what is being exchanged for cash is actually the right to use a resource for a contracted period of time, rather than the resource itself. For example, a video store can rent the same specific copy of a video many times.

Another exception that changes the one (1) maximum participation of Resource in its association with Economic Event to a maximum of many (*) occurs when the same resource may be sold and reacquired multiple times. For example, a car dealership that handles both new and used vehicles may sell a car, then acquire the same car when the owner decides to trade it in for another new vehicle, then sell the car to another customer, eventually re-acquire it again, etc. In some such cases an enterprise may decide to assign a different identifier to the resource each time it is re-acquired (an argument in favor of this approach is that the condition of the resource is likely different each time) and then the maximum of one would still be appropriate. However, in some cases the history of the specific physical item may be important and the enterprise may choose to keep using the same identifier and the maximum participation needs to be many.

Economic Event-Agent (Participation Association) Multiplicity Heuristics

The general participation heuristic for internal agent-event associations is:

> Economic Event 0..* - 1..1 Internal Agent

The one (1) minimum participation of the Economic Event in its association with an internal agent signifies that enterprises want to record an Internal Agent responsible for each economic event. If we don't know who represented each enterprise involved in the exchange, it will be difficult to resolve any future discrepancies about the exchange events.

The one (1) maximum participation of the Economic Event in its association with an Internal Agent indicates that most enterprises hold one internal agent accountable for (or give them credit for) each economic event.

The zero (0) minimum participation of Internal Agent in its association with an economic event indicates that Internal Agents exist and entered into the database before they begin participating with economic events.

The many (*) maximum participation of Internal Agent in its association with an economic event indicates that an Internal Agent can participate with many economic events (e.g., a salesperson can make many sales).

The general participation heuristic for external agent-event associations is:

> Non-cash-related Economic Event 0..* - 1..1 External Agent
> Cash-related Economic Event 0..* - 0..1 External Agent

The non-cash-related economic event multiplicities are the same for External Agents as the general heuristic for economic events to Internal Agents (the same logic applies). And the only difference between cash-related and non-cash-related economic events and external agents is because of the following. With either cash receipt or cash disbursement economic events, there are usually multiple associations with multiple types of external agents – therefore, any particular cash receipt (cash disbursement) will be from (to) one type of external agent and not the other types of external agents. For example, a cash disbursement could be made to an employee or to a vendor or to a creditor (and if those are maintained as separate classes), then the participation of cash disbursement with employee would be optional (because it could involve a vendor or creditor instead) and for the same reason, participation with vendor would be optional and participation with creditor would be optional. Participation with an employee as processor rather than payee of the cash disbursement may still be mandatory.

Typical exceptions to the Economic Event-Agent multiplicity heuristics are as follows:

Common exceptions that change the 1 minimum participation of Economic Event
If alternative types of internal agents can process an event, then the minimum participation of the Event in the association with Internal Agent would change from 1 to 0. For example, if a sale could be made by either a salesperson or by a manager (and if those are maintained as two separate classes), then the participation of sale with salesperson would be optional (because it could involve a manager instead) and the participation of sale with manager would be optional (because it could involve a salesperson instead).

Common exception that changes the 1 Maximum participation of Economic Event
If multiple internal agents share responsibility (or credit) for an economic event, then the maximum participation for the Economic Event in its association with Internal Agent would change to *. For example, if two different salespeople assist a customer in selecting the product he or she wants to buy, and they split the commission resulting from the sale, the sale event is associated with multiple salespeople.

Economic Event – Economic Event (Duality Association) Multiplicity Heuristics
Duality associations typically allow any number of different multiplicities, thus are limited as to heuristics. One reliable heuristic is the optional participation of cash-related economic events in the duality association. For example, cash disbursement's participation in a duality association with inventory acquisition should usually be optional, because most enterprises pay for other types of acquisitions such as labor acquisitions in the payroll process.

Exhibit 4-1 and its related discussion may have seemed abstract to you because it is the generic pattern for the expanded REA business process models. We next apply that pattern to the specific context of the main four enterprise business processes to help concretize those abstract concepts. We begin with the acquisition process.

ACQUISITION BUSINESS PROCESSES IN ENTERPRISE VALUE SYSTEMS

At the value system level, the acquisition process is the point of contact between the enterprise and its vendors, as shown in Exhibit 4-3.

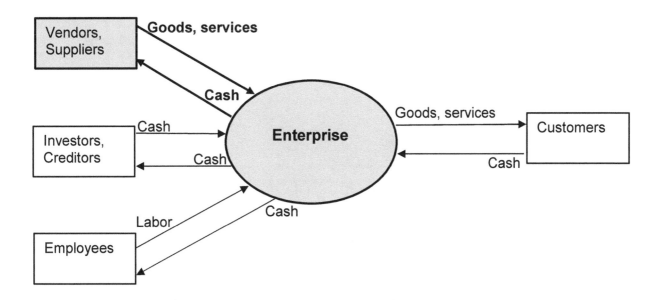

Exhibit 4-3: Acquisition Process in the Enterprise Value System

The enterprise gives cash to the vendors in exchange for goods, services, or the right to use goods for a specified time period. Services are intangible – we cannot directly see or touch most services, therefore when modeling service acquisition processes, we often substitute service types for actual services.

ACQUISITION BUSINESS PROCESSES IN ENTERPRISE VALUE CHAINS

The value chain reveals interfaces between the acquisition process and other business processes. Exhibit 4-4 illustrates a partial value chain with typical value chain interfaces.

Partial Value Chain

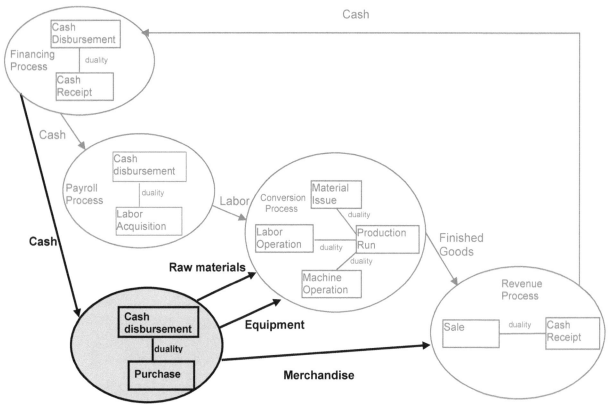

Exhibit 4-4: Acquisition Process in the Value Chain

The financing process makes cash available to the acquisition process. The acquisition process then uses that cash in cash disbursement (economic decrement) events, in which the company pays for various purchase events (economic increments). The resources obtained in the various purchase events include raw materials, equipment, and merchandise. Additional purchase events not pictured in Exhibit 4-4 include service acquisitions and supply purchases. The raw materials, equipment, and merchandise acquired within the acquisition process are made available to various other business processes that track their usage. Raw materials and equipment are made available to the conversion process, in which the materials usage is tracked via material issuances and the equipment usage is tracked via machine operations. Merchandise is made available to the revenue process, in which its usage is tracked via sales. Note that a company could also track equipment usage in a revenue process, in which case an arrow would be added from acquisition to revenue, with a corresponding economic decrement event inside the revenue process connecting to cash receipt via another duality association. For example, if a company wanted to track the use of a delivery truck in making sales without adding a logistics process to its value chain, it would add a delivery truck arrow from acquisition to revenue. Then in the sale event or in another event connected to sale and to cash receipt, the company would track the truck usage, with attributes such as miles driven for this sale or time used for this sale.

Note that although Exhibit 4-4 illustrates just one acquisition process with three resource arrows going to other processes, some companies may instead make three separate acquisition processes. To decide whether to separate the processes, determine whether the purchase events for the various resources require or facilitate capture of different attributes. If, for example, the attributes a company captures for purchases of operating assets are the same as those the company captures for purchases of inventory, then it is likely more convenient to combine those types of acquisitions into one process.

EXPANDED REA ACQUISITION PROCESS MODEL

Exhibit 4-5 illustrates the acquisition process for an enterprise that purchases inventory that is identified at the type level for purposes of need identification and ordering, but for which the inventory is specifically identified and tracked by serial numbers upon receipt.

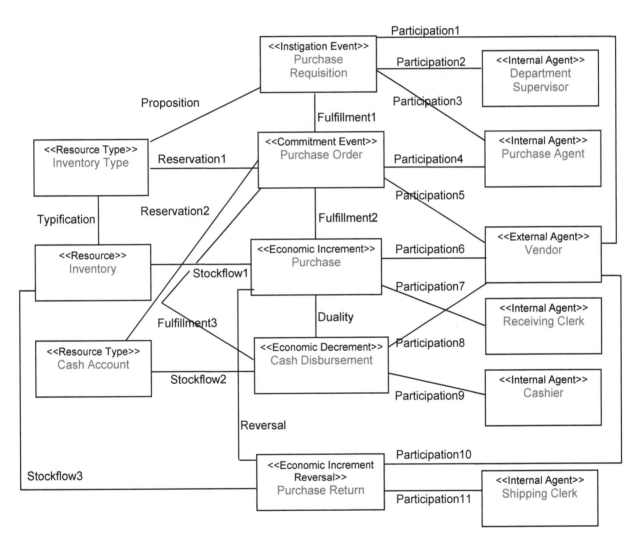

Exhibit 4-5: Expanded Acquisition REA Business Process Model

We next discuss the events that comprise the expanded acquisition model within the context of the common documents used by many companies. We also show relational tables related to the documents.

Need Identification – Purchase Requisitions (Instigation Events)

The acquisition process begins with someone in an enterprise identifying and communicating a need to acquire a good or service, an event sometimes called a *purchase requisition*. The need may exist to satisfy a new requirement or to replenish an existing supply that is low in quantity (e.g., a supply item, inventory item, or an advertising services contract) or that is low in useful life (e.g., property, plant, and equipment items). The identification of the need for additional goods and services may be triggered externally, such as by a vendor's presentation of a new product and its capabilities. Alternatively, the need identification trigger may be internal: various supervisors identify the need for goods and services by monitoring enterprise activities such as production levels, sales levels, capital improvement plans, capital budgets, sales forecasts, trends and projections. Once supervisors or other authorized individuals (or even automated bots, programmed to reorder when an item's quantity on hand falls below its reorder point) identify a need for goods, they communicate that need to an authorized buyer (internal purchase agent) via a purchase requisition form such as that shown in Exhibit 4-6. This form may be either a paper document or it may be a software interface or web page. In either case, similar data are captured and transmitted from user departments to authorized purchase agents. Data from Exhibit 4-6's purchase requisition have been entered into the database tables that follow Exhibit 4-6; however, some of these data (e.g. inventory, vendor, and employee information) would have existed already in the database tables before the requisition data was added to the tables such that only the association information that links them to the event is recorded for those objects. New data recording the purchase requisition event is shown in bold italic red font.

YOUR SOURCE COMPANY PURCHASE REQUISITION			No. ___R17___
Date Prepared: 4/20/2020	Prepared by: E5		Suggested Vendor: V7
Deliver To: Product Warehouse Attention: Patrick Wellesley			Date Needed: 5/2/2020
Item ID	Quantity	Description	Price/Unit
BIS1	100	Big Stuff	$20.00
LIS1	200	Little Stuff	$36.00
HUS1	100	Huge Stuff	$30.00
TIS1	300	Tiny Stuff	$48.00
Reason Needed: To meet customer demand.			

Approved by:
        E12
	Department:
	        Sales
		Date Approved:
		4/22/2020	

Exhibit 4-6: Purchase Requisition

PurchaseRequisition (Instigation Event)

Purch ReqID	Date	Maximum Budget for this purchase	Date Needed	Deliver to Location	Deliver to Whose Attention	Reason Needed	SuperID[FK]	Purch AgentID[FK]	Suggested VendorID[FK]
R17	04/20/2020	$30,000	05/02/2020	Product Warehouse	Patrick Wellesley	To meet customer demand.	E5	E12	V7

Proposition2PurchaseRequisitionInventoryType

PurchReqID	Item ID	QuantityNeeded	EstimatedUnitCost
R17	BIS1	100	$20.00
R17	LIS1	200	$36.00
R17	HUS1	150	$30.00
R17	TIS1	300	$48.00

InventoryType (Resource Type)

Item ID	Description	UnitOfMeasure	Standard Cost	List Price
BIS1	Big Stuff	Each	$20.00	$50.00
HUS1	Huge Stuff	Each	$30.00	$70.00
LIS1	Little Stuff	Box of 6	$36.00	$72.00
MIN1	Miniature Stuff	Box of 24	$56.00	$110.00
TIS1	Tiny Stuff	Box of 12	$48.00	$96.00
TTP12	Tiara	Each	$10.00	$25.00

PurchaseAgent (Internal Agent)

PurchaseAgentID	Name	Address	Telephone	DateOfBirth
E12	Joy Berwick	437 Oak Dr.	555-9617	04/20/1982

DepartmentSupervisor (Internal Agent)

DeptSupervisorID	Name	Address	Telephone	DateOfBirth
E5	Patrick Wellesley	53125 Fenton Dr.	555-1112	03/04/1958

Vendor (External Agent)

VendorID	Name	Address	Telephone	PerformanceRating
V7	Joe's Favorite Vendor	89056 Ransom Hwy.	555-7655	Excellent

Agreements/Contracts (Mutual Commitment Events)

Once the enterprise identifies a need for goods or services, a purchase agent places an order with a vendor on behalf of the enterprise. The *purchase order* is a mutual commitment event in which a vendor agrees to transfer title of goods to an enterprise at an agreed upon future time and price, and the enterprise agrees to pay for those goods. If the agreement involves the temporary use of an asset to which title is not transferred, the mutual commitment is typically called a rental agreement. If the commitment involves the vendor performing a service rather than providing goods, the event is typically called a *service agreement* or *service order*. In most states, purchase, rental, and service agreements are enforceable as contracts.

Commitments to purchase products or services have important data such as date, time, a list of products or services, the quantities needed and unit prices of each, the total dollar amount of the order or agreement, the date by which the enterprise needs the goods or services delivered, the delivery method to be used (e.g., Federal Express, UPS, or customer pick-up), the desired location of the delivery, and the payment terms. Such data are often captured on a purchase order form such as that shown in Exhibit 4-7. This form may be either a paper document or a software interface (web page) used to update the enterprise database. Similar types of data would be captured on similar types of documents regarding service and rental agreements. Until the vendor delivers the products or services specified, the purchase order is considered unfilled or open. The phrase *open purchase order* simply means a purchase order for which the ordered products or services have not yet been received. Database tables that include data to record purchase orders follow Exhibit 4-7, with the new data needed to record purchase order 16 appearing in red, bold, italic font.

Your Source Company
Your Source for Everything You Need
123 Main St.
Anytown, USA 12345

Purchase Order
NO. ____16____

This number must appear on all related correspondence, shipping papers, and invoices

To: Joe's Favorite Vendor
89056 Ransom Hwy.
Metro Village, USA 54321

Ship To: Your Source Company
123 Main St.
Anytown, USA 12345

P.O. DATE	DATE NEEDED	REQUISITION#	REQUISITIONER	SHIP VIA	F.O.B. POINT	TERMS
4/24/2020	5/2/2020	R17	E5	UPS	Shipping	N/30

QTY	UNIT	ITEM NO.	DESCRIPTION	UNIT PRICE	TOTAL
100	Each	BIS1	Big Stuff	$20.00	$2,000.00
150	Each	HUS1	Huge Stuff	$29.00	$4,350.00
200	Box/ 6	LIS1	Little Stuff	$35.50	$7,100.00
300	Box/12	TIS1	Tiny Stuff	$50.00	$15,000.00

SUBTOTAL	$28,450.00
SALES TAX	$0.00
SHIPPING & HANDLING	$0.00
OTHER	$0.00
TOTAL	$28,450.00

1. Please send two copies of your invoice.

2. Enter this order in accordance with the prices, terms, delivery method, and specifications listed above.

3. Please notify us immediately if you are unable to ship as specified.

4. Send all correspondence to:
Purchasing Manager
Your Source Company
123 Main St., Anytown, USA

Joy Berwick   E12   4/24/2020
Authorized by   Date

Exhibit 4-7: Purchase Order

PurchaseOrder (Mutual Commitment)

Purchase OrderID	OrderDate	DateNeeded	DollarTotal	DateAuthorized	Purchase ReqID[FK]	Purchase AgentID[FK]	Vendor ID[FK]
PO16	04/24/2020	05/2/2020	$28,450.00	04/24/2020	R17	E12	V7

Reservation3PurchaseOrderInventoryType

PurchOrderID	ItemID	QuantityOrdered	QuotedUnitPrice
PO16	BIS1	100	$20.00
PO16	LIS1	200	$35.50
PO16	HUS1	150	$29.00
PO16	TIS1	300	$50.00

InventoryType (Resource Type)

Item ID	Description	UnitOfMeasure	Standard Cost	List Price
BIS1	Big Stuff	Each	$20.00	$50.00
HUS1	Huge Stuff	Each	$30.00	$70.00
LIS1	Little Stuff	Box of 6	$36.00	$72.00
MIN1	Miniature Stuff	Box of 24	$56.00	$110.00
TIS1	Tiny Stuff	Box of 12	$48.00	$96.00
TTP12	Tiara	Each	$10.00	$25.00

DepartmentSupervisor (Internal Agent)

DeptSupervisorID	Name	Address	Telephone	DateOfBirth
E5	Patrick Wellesley	53125 Fenton Dr.	555-1112	03/04/1958

Vendor (External Agent)

VendorID	Name	Address	Telephone	PerformanceRating
V7	Joe's Favorite Vendor	89056 Ransom Hwy.	555-7655	Excellent

PurchaseAgent (Internal Agent)

PurchaseAgentID	Name	Address	Telephone	DateOfBirth
E12	Joy Berwick	437 Oak Dr.	555-9617	04/20/1982

Performance by Vendor – Delivery of Goods or Services (Economic Increment Event)

In contract law, *performance* is the fulfillment of an obligation in a manner that releases the performer from all liabilities. The vendor's performance is typically the delivery of the products or services specified in a commitment. If the vendor delivered products to the enterprise, this activity is called a *purchase*, an acquisition, or a receipt of goods (from the perspective of the enterprise, a perspective maintained through this paragraph). If the vendor provided a temporary right to use goods, the event is called a *rental*; the rental begins when the right to temporary possession of the goods transfers from the vendor to the enterprise; the rental ends when possession of the goods transfers back from the enterprise to the vendor. If the vendor provided services or utilities, the event is usually called a *service acquisition* or a general and administrative service acquisition. Whatever label is used, the important consideration is that performance represents the enterprise receiving a resource or a benefit that it didn't previously possess. Therefore, an economic increase has occurred and this is called an economic increment event. At this point, unless the enterprise pre-paid for the product or service, a liability is incurred. While many companies do not record the liability until the vendor sends an invoice to document its performance, in theory, the performance is what causes the liability. Therefore, systems in which the liability is not recorded until the vendor invoice is received are technically inaccurate.

Receiving reports (Exhibit 4-8) are documents indicating the quantities and condition of goods received by an enterprise from an external business partner. These reports are typically completed by inventory or receiving clerks when goods or services are received from vendors (or from customers in the case of sale returns). Similar to Exhibit 4-8, such reports list the items, quantities, and condition of each item received. In general, we consider it unwise for an enterprise to use an externally prepared document as a base object in its system when an internally prepared alternative is available. Because receiving reports are typically prepared as the vendor's performance occurs and the liability is thereby incurred, most enterprises should consider using the receiving report together with the underlying commitment documents to record the liability rather than waiting for the *vendor invoice* – a document sent by a vendor to the enterprise to communicate the fact that the vendor has fulfilled its commitment to transfer title of the goods to the enterprise. While data captured on vendor invoices may provide additional details of the acquisition; such data could be used to update the data captured via the receiving report and underlying agreement. Meanwhile the system would be more accurate than it is when nothing is recorded until the invoice arrives. Exhibit 4-9 illustrates a vendor invoice.

Following Exhibit 4-9, database tables show the purchase data, with the new data to be added for receiving report 18 indicated in red, bold, italic font.

RECEIVING REPORT		NO.	18	

Your Source Company
Your Source for Everything You Need
123 Main St.
Anytown, USA 12345

DATE	4/30/2020	PURCH ORD NO./ SALE RETURN AUTH NO.	PO16	
RECEIVED FROM	Joe's Favorite Vendor			PREPAID XX
ADDRESS	89056 Ransom Hwy. Metro Village, USA 54321			COLLECT
FREIGHT CARRIER UPS		FREIGHT BILL NO. XYAT31253		

	QUANTITY	ITEM NO	DESCRIPTION
1.	100	BIS1	Big Stuff
2.	200	LIS1	Little Stuff
3.	150	HIS1	Huge Stuff
4.	300	TIS1	Tiny Stuff
5.			
6.			
7.			
8.			
9.			

REMARKS: CONDITIONS, ETC.
Perfect condition

RECEIVED BY E247	DELIVERED TO Product Warehouse

BE SURE TO
MAKE THIS RECORD
ACCURATE AND COMPLETE

Exhibit 4-8: Receiving Report

```
┌─────────────────────────────────────────────────────────────────────────────────┐
│  Invoice                                     Joe's Favorite Vendor                │
│                    NO:  __4167__             Let us be your favorite too!          │
│                    DATE: 5/3/2020            89056 Ransom Hwy.                      │
│                                              Metro Village, USA 54321              │
│                                                                                    │
│  Sold To:                             Ship To:                                     │
│     Your Source Company                  Same                                      │
│     123 Main St.                                                                   │
│     Anytown, USA 12345                                                             │
└─────────────────────────────────────────────────────────────────────────────────┘
```

P.O. NUMBER	SALESPERSON	PACKING LIST#	DATE SHIPPED	SHIPPED VIA	TERMS
16	Veronica	4199	4/27/2020	UPS	N/30

QUANTITY	STOCK #	DESCRIPTION	UNIT PRICE	AMOUNT
100	BIS1	Big Stuff	$20.00	$2,000.00
200	LIS1	Little Stuff	$35.50	$7,100.00
150	HUS1	Huge Stuff	$29.00	$4,350.00
300	TIS1	Tiny Stuff	$50.00	$15,000.00

SUBTOTAL	$28,450.00
SALES TAX	0
SHIPPING & HANDLING	0
TOTAL DUE	$28,450.00

Make all checks payable to: Joe's Favorite Vendor
Please make sure your account number is on all correspondence and checks.

THANK YOU!

Exhibit 4-9: Vendor Invoice

Purchase (Economic Increment Event)

Receiving ReportID	Date	Dollar Amount	Remarks	Receiving ClerkID[FK]	VendorID[FK]	Vendor Invoice#	InvoicedAmount ForPurchase
RR18	04/30/2020	$28,450.00	Perfect condition	E111	V7	VI4167	$28,450.00

Note: At the time when goods are received, there may not be a vendor invoice (which may arrive at a later date) so the VendorInvoice# and InvoicedAmountForPurchase would be null. Because these fields are not foreign keys and we don't expect them to stay null, we do not need to create a separate table in which to store them.

Stockflow4PurchaseInventoryType

ReceivingReportID	ItemID	PurchaseQuantity	ActualUnitCost
RR18	BIS1	100	$20.00
RR18	LIS1	200	$35.50
RR18	HUS1	150	$29.00
RR18	TIS1	300	$50.00

InventoryType (Resource Type)

Item ID	Description	UnitOfMeasure	Standard Cost	List Price
BIS1	Big Stuff	Each	$20.00	$50.00
HUS1	Huge Stuff	Each	$30.00	$70.00
LIS1	Little Stuff	Box of 6	$36.00	$72.00
MIN1	Miniature Stuff	Box of 24	$56.00	$110.00
TIS1	Tiny Stuff	Box of 12	$48.00	$96.00
TTP12	Tiara	Each	$10.00	$25.00

Fulfillment4PurchaseOrderPurchase

PurchaseOrderID	PurchaseID
PO16	RR18

ReceivingClerk (Internal Agent)

ClerkID	Name	Address	Telephone	DateOfBirth
E247	Kenneth Barki	4312 Monticello Dr.	556-4891	04/14/1955
E251	Rita Barki	4312 Monticello Dr.	556-4891	05/22/1958

Vendor (External Agent)

VendorID	Name	Address	Telephone	PerformanceRating
V7	Joe's Favorite Vendor	89056 Ransom Hwy.	555-7655	Excellent

Performance by Enterprise - Payments (Economic Decrement Events)

The commitment made by the enterprise was to pay for the goods or services detailed in the purchase order, rental agreement, or service agreement. Contracts may require the enterprise to pay for the goods or services in advance, at the time of vendor performance, or within a specified time after the vendor performance. The payment made by the enterprise is also sometimes called a *cash disbursement*. Payments may be made via *check* (a document used to authorize the transfer of cash from one entity to another, as illustrated in Exhibit 4-10), debit card, electronic funds transfer, or with currency and coins. If the enterprise uses a credit card to pay a vendor, the enterprise has not yet disbursed cash. Such a payment does decrease the accounts payable balance with the vendor to whom the payment was rendered; however, it creates a new payable balance with the credit card company. Therefore, the cash disbursement does not occur until the enterprise pays the credit card company.

Several documents may be involved in task activities that comprise the cash disbursement event: checks, vendor invoices, purchase orders, and receiving reports. Most enterprises require that an employee verify that various fields on the vendor invoices, purchase orders, and receiving reports match before authorizing payment. This common internal control procedure, which will we discuss further in chapter 8, is called a three-way match. Two main concerns in the acquisition process are for enterprises to ensure they do not receive goods or services they did not order, and more importantly, to ensure they do not disburse cash for goods or services that they did not receive.

Some enterprises have reengineered the workflow in the acquisition process to eliminate vendor invoices and disbursement vouchers. Rather than an individual employee performing the three-way match after the events had occurred, the information system may instead match the purchase to the purchase order as the receipt of goods occurs, and then automatically trigger payment based on the quantities received and the contractual costs per the purchase order. Tables following Exhibit 4-10 illustrate data related to cash disbursements, with new data to be added when check 41235 is written indicated in red, bold, italic font.

Your Source Company
Your Source for Everything You Need
123 Main St.
Anytown, USA 12345   41235

                                                                    DATE   *5/25/2020*

PAY TO THE
ORDER OF   *Joe's Favorite Vendor* $ *28,500.00*

Twenty-eight thousand, five hundred, and no/100 ------------------------------ DOLLARS

MEMO *Invoice 4167*   *Diane Bowersox*

    000000000   000000000   41235

Exhibit 4-10: Check

CashDisbursement (Economic Decrement Event)

CashAcctID	CheckNbr	CheckDate	DollarAmount	CashierID^FK	PayeeID^FK
Ca123501	41234	05/15/2020	$746.57	E36	E23
Ca123501	*41235*	*05/25/2020*	*$28,450.00*	*E36*	*V7*

DualityPurchaseCashDisbursement

RecReportID	CashAcctID	CheckNbr
RR18	*Ca123501*	*41235*

Cash (Resource Type)

CashAccountID	AccountType	Location	DateAccountEstablished
Ca123501	Checking	1st Local Bank	04/01/2020
Ca789125	Savings	1st Local Bank	04/01/2020
Ca351235	Petty	Onsite - Cashier Desk drawer	04/15/2020
Ca351327	Petty	Onsite - CEO Assistant's File Cabinet	04/22/2020

Cashier (Internal Agent)

CashierID	Name	Address	Telephone	DateOfBirth
E36	Diane Bowersox	9115 Wolfgang Ct.	555-7244	09/15/1963

Vendor (External Agent)

VendorID	Name	Address	Telephone	PerformanceRating
V7	Joe's Favorite Vendor	89056 Ransom Hwy.	555-7655	Excellent

Post-Purchase Activities: Returns & Allowances (Economic Increment Reversal Events)
If goods and services received do not meet the identified needs (i.e., the enterprise has a divergence from the "happy path"), the enterprise may decide to return the goods or request an allowance for the unsatisfactory services. A *purchase return* is the transfer of title (usually concurrent with transfer of physical custody) of goods from the enterprise back to the vendor. Several documents may represent tasks that make up the purchase return event: requests to return goods, packing lists, and bills of lading.

A *request to return goods* (Exhibit 4-11, for example) is a notification to a vendor of the enterprise's dissatisfaction with goods that seeks permission to return those goods instead of paying for them (or in exchange for a refund). In response, the enterprise receives return authorization information from the vendor via a paper document, an e-mail, or a phone call.

Inventory clerks (or other agents, such as shipping clerks) complete *returns packing lists* (Exhibit 4-12, for example), which detail the contents of each package shipped to an external business partner. If the goods are returned via common carriers, bills of lading usually are also prepared. A *bill of lading* is a document that indicates the transfer of custody of goods from the enterprise to a common carrier, including details about how many packages comprise the shipment, the dimensions and/or weight of those packages, the shipping costs, and the party responsible for shipping costs. Packing lists list the items and quantities of each item returned; bills of lading list the number and dimensions of boxes in which the returned goods are packed.

Sometimes a vendor will negotiate with the enterprise such that the enterprise will keep the unsatisfactory product and the vendor will refund part of the enterprise's purchase price. That refund is called a *purchase allowance*. Because purchase allowances do not involve the return of the product, no packing list or bill of lading need be created.

Tables following Exhibit 4-12 include data related to purchase returns, with new data to be added when purchase return 3 is made indicated in red, bold, italic font.

REQUEST TO RETURN FROM →

Ret. Request No. ___3___
Date of Request ___5/15/2020___

Joe's Favorite Vendor
89056 Ransom Hwy
Metro Village, USA 54321

VENDOR: V7

RETURN CODES:

A Overstock
B DAMAGED
C DEFECTIVE
D WRONG PRODUCT BILLED & SHIPPED
E CORRECT PRODUCT BILLED BUT
   WRONG PRODUCT SHIPPED
F OTHER

All returns will be clean, in saleable condition, and shipped prepaid. A prompt reply will be greatly appreciated. Thank you for your cooperation.

☐ Cash Refund – Please

☒ Outstanding Invoice Reduction

Invoice Number _____

FOR CLARIFICATION CONTACT

Name ___Patrick Wellesley___

Phone ___555-3333___

DEPT.	QUAN. REQ.	PRODUCT NUMBER	DESCRIPTION	RETURN CODE	INVOICE NO.	QUAN. RET.	LIST PRICE	COST OR DISC.	EXTENSION
Sales	200	LIS1	Little Stuff	C	4167	200		$35.50	$7,100.00

Your Source Company
Your Source for Everything You Need
123 Main St., Anytown, USA 12345

Patrick Wellesley, E5

Return requested by

TOTAL	$7,100.00

Exhibit 4-11: Request to Return Goods Document

Your Source Company
Your Source for Everything You Need
123 Main St.
Anytown, USA 12345

RETURNS PACKING LIST 22
Clerk ID 137

If there are any questions about this shipment, contact our sales department (999) 555-3333

Joe's Favorite Vendor	**RETURN AUTHORIZATION NUMBER:** 485
89056 Ransom Hwy	**ORIGINAL PURCHASE NUMBER:**
Metro Village, USA 54321	**DATE:** 5/17/2020
Contact: Trina Weeble	

PART NUMBER	QUANTITY RETURNED	UNIT OF MEASURE	ITEM DESCRIPTION
LIS1	200	each	Little Stuff

Exhibit 4-12: Returns Packing List

PurchaseReturn (Economic Increment Reversal Event)

Purchase ReturnID	Date	Dollar Amount	Packing Slip#	CashRefund or InvoiceReduction	Receiving ReportID^{FK}	Vendor ID^{FK}	Dept SuperID^{FK}	Shipping ClerkID^{FK}
PR3	*05/17/2020*	*$7,100.00*	*22*	*InvoiceReduction*	*RR18*	*V90*	*E5*	*E41*

Stockflow6PurchaseReturnInventoryType

PurchReturnID	Item ID	QuantityReturned	ActualUnitCost
PR3	*LIS1*	*200*	*$35.50*

DepartmentSupervisor (Internal Agent)

DeptSupervisorID	Name	Address	Telephone	DateOfBirth
E5	Patrick Wellesley	53125 Fenton Dr.	555-1112	03/04/1958

ShippingClerk (Internal Agent)

ShippingClerkID	Name	Address	Telephone	DateOfBirth
E41	Amy Milano	8892 Eddy Ave.	555-9557	01/03/1964

Vendor (External Agent)

VendorID	Name	Address	Telephone	PerformanceRating
V7	Joe's Favorite Vendor	89056 Ransom Hwy.	555-7655	Excellent
V14	Reliable Rudy's	34125 Michigan Ave.	555-1199	Very Good

CONCLUDING COMMENTS

This chapter reviewed the workflow activities, documents, REA models, and relational database tables commonly used in the acquisition business process. Whether an enterprise sells hot dogs at a small stand outside a university library or sells custom-made computers via orders placed on its website, whether it sells dental services, insurance, or come combination of products and services, the activities in their acquisition business processes fit the REA pattern. The class names for an enterprise may differ from those used in this textbook; therefore, the concepts learned here cannot be routinely applied with rote memorization. The key to discovering the pattern fit for a specific enterprise requires one to think about the nature of the events and the resources affected by the events. Thinking at the value system level first may help – what resources does the enterprise exchange with its customers and vendors? Thinking at the value chain level next may also help – what resources are provided to the acquisition business process and what does the acquisition business process in turn make available to other business processes?

You may feel a bit overwhelmed if you try to model too much of the process at once. We recommend that you start by modeling the core exchange, i.e., the duality association with the related economic and decrement events. Then it should be relatively straightforward to determine the commitment events and instigation events that lead to each economic event and then to connect resources, internal agents, and external agents to each event as needed. Then consider what additional relationships apply, such as custody, assignment, or others that are unique to the enterprise you are modeling. As long as the foundation of the model is consistent with REA, additional constructs may be added without compromising the advantages provided by the pattern for automated reasoning and inter-enterprise integration.

Use the company's documents, along with interviews of key personnel to determine what attributes to include, and the most appropriate classes and associations to which to assign the attributes. Use company business policies together with common understandings of the process to assign multiplicities to each association.

Once you have modeled a company's acquisition process(es), you would next model its payroll, revenue, and conversion processes, as introduced in chapters 5, 6, and 7, and then integrate the business process models into a single model, following steps introduced in chapter 5. The next step is to follow the guidelines outlined in chapter 3 to convert your integrated model into relational database tables and then to implement those tables in a relational database software application such as Microsoft Access.

KEY TERMS AND CONCEPTS
Bill of lading
Check
Commitment event
Economic decrement event
Economic increment event
Economic reversal event
External agent
Fulfillment association
Instigation event
Internal agent
Mutual commitment
Open purchase order
Performance
Proposition association
Purchase allowance
Purchase event
Purchase order
Purchase requisition
Purchase return
Receiving report
Rental (acquisition)
Request to return goods
Reservation association
Resource
Resource type
Returns packing list
Reversal association
Service acquisition
Service agreement or service order
Stockflow association
Typification association
Vendor invoice

REVIEW QUESTIONS

R4-1. What are three examples of different types of acquisition processes?

R4-2. Describe the acquisition business process – what main activities make up this process?

R4-3. What are the five questions typically asked in introductory journalism, and how are they typically answered in a business process level REA model?

R4-4. What type of data does each record in an event table contain?

R4-5. What resources, internal agents, and external agents are typically associated with each of the following events?

    a. Purchase requisition

    b. Purchase order

    c. Purchase

    d. Cash disbursement

    e. Purchase return

MULTIPLE CHOICE QUESTIONS

MC4-1. Which classes would be paired in a stockflow association in the acquisition cycle?

    A) Purchase requisition and inventory type

    B) Purchase and inventory type

    C) Purchase order and inventory type

    D) Purchase order and purchase

MC4-2. If a resource class represents individually identified items, the expected multiplicity pattern for its association with an economic event class is

    A) Resource 0..1 – 1..* Economic Event

    B) Resource 1..* – 0..1 Economic Event

    C) Resource 1..1 – 1..0 Economic Event

    D) Resource 1..1 – 0..* Economic Event

MC4-3. Which classes would typically connect to each other in a stockflow association in a REA business process model?

    A) Vendor and inventory

    B) Purchase and cash disbursement

    C) Inventory and cash

    D) Purchase and inventory

MC4-4. In an acquisition process, which classes would be paired in a duality association?

    A) Service acquisition and cash disbursement

    B) Cash disbursement and cash

    C) Purchase and purchase return

    D) Purchase and inventory type

MC4-5. Which of these is NOT a mutual commitment event in an acquisition process?
A) Cash disbursement
B) Purchase order
C) Rental agreement
D) Service agreement

MC4-6. In REA business process level models, resources are connected to economic events using _____ associations
A) Participation
B) Difference
C) Duality
D) Stockflow

MC4-7. In an acquisition process, participation associations typically connect which type of internal agents to economic increment events?
A) Salespeople
B) Receiving clerks
C) Credit card companies
D) Suppliers

MC4-8. For supply acquisitions the associated resource is usually _____, and for operating asset acquisitions the associated resource is usually _____.
A) supply type, operating asset
B) service type, operating asset
C) operating asset, supply type
D) supply, operating asset type

MC4-9. Unfulfilled requests by department supervisors for the purchasing department to acquire goods or services are called?
A) Open purchase orders
B) Closed purchase orders
C) Open purchase requisitions
D) Closed purchase requisitions

MC4-10. In an acquisition process, which association connects an instigation event to the resource that the event proposes to increase or decrease?
A) Reservation
B) Participation
C) Stockflow
D) Proposition

CHAPTER 5

Modeling Payroll Business Processes with REA

LEARNING OBJECTIVES

The primary objective of this chapter is to create detailed REA (Resource-Event-Agent) business process models for payroll business processes. We expand the REA models originally seen in chapter 2 for payroll business processes, and illustrate various types of business documents companies use to capture data about tasks and events in their payroll business processes. After studying this chapter, you should be able to

1. Describe the typical tasks, instigation events, commitment events, and economic events found in most enterprises' payroll business processes
2. Identify the documents commonly used to capture data about the various types of tasks and events in payroll business processes
3. Create a REA business process model for a company's payroll business process

PAYROLL BUSINESS PROCESSES

The *payroll business process* encompasses activities needed to acquire and pay for employee labor. The primary objective of the payroll process is to acquire and provide the human effort and expertise the enterprise needs to function efficiently and effectively. Although specific task activities differ in various enterprises' payroll processes, we discuss the pattern identified as common to most payroll processes. Activities in enterprise human resource divisions include hiring, training, evaluating, terminating, scheduling, and paying employees for their labor, knowledge, and skills. Many companies separate these activities into two sub-processes: personnel and payroll. The *personnel function* hires, trains, evaluates, and terminates employees. The *payroll function* schedules, acquires labor, and processes *paychecks* (compensation to employees for their work). While the REA pattern also applies to the personnel function, in this chapter, we focus on the payroll function.

The payroll process is in essence a special case of the acquisition process. However, the acquisition of and payment for goods and outside services often result in different information needs than do the acquisition of and payment for labor, both with respect to the types of resources acquired and the types of agents from whom they are acquired. That is, enterprises must store very different data with respect to employees than they do for vendors, including dependents, withholdings, and so forth). Employee data is also subject to greater regulations and compliance than is vendor data. Therefore, most enterprises keep their payroll processes separate from their acquisition processes.

PAYROLL BUSINESS PROCESSES IN ENTERPRISE VALUE SYSTEMS

At the value system level, the payroll business process is the point of contact between the enterprise and its employees, as shown in Exhibit 5-1.

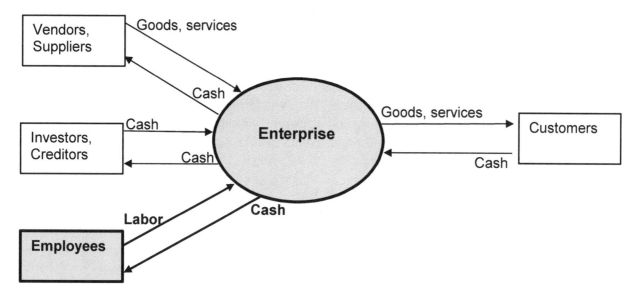

Exhibit 5-1: Payroll Business Process in the Enterprise Value System

At this point of contact, employees are external business partners of the enterprise; in other words, they engage are engaging in arm's length exchanges. In the REA business process level, employees are stereotyped as internal agents; they connect to most events with inside participation associations. In payroll, the general employee class connects to events with outside participation, and the subsets of employees who initiate, authorize, or process payroll events connect to events with inside participation. Those subset employees are also general employees with respect to their own provision of labor.

At arm's length, the enterprise gives cash to the employees in exchange for the employees' labor. Labor is intangible – we cannot directly see or touch labor, therefore when modeling payroll processes, we usually substitute labor type for actual labor. We discuss labor type further in the resources section following Exhibit 5-3. We can see some aspects of the acquisition and consumption of labor by watching employees work; however, we cannot see the knowledge, skills, and mental processes that employees engage while performing work tasks. Because enterprises do not own the employees, the enterprises also typically do not own the employees' knowledge and skills, thus making it difficult to measure and value human resources. We may assume that enterprises capture measurements of those knowledge and skills in employees' salaries and wages, as compensation tends to be higher for more knowledgeable and skilled workers. However, that correlation is imperfect and human resources do not appear on enterprise balance sheets. Today, many enterprises attempt to develop techniques for owning employees' skills and knowledge by creating knowledge bases and artificial intelligence-based decision support systems in which to store the knowledge and procedural decision-making processes of its most valuable knowledge-intensive employees. Although enterprises have made significant progress in the area of knowledge bases and decision support systems, most information systems can still only measure labor acquisition and labor consumption as time-worked.

PAYROLL BUSINESS PROCESSES IN ENTERPRISE VALUE CHAINS
The value chain reveals interfaces between the payroll process and other business processes. Exhibit 5-2 illustrates the typical value chain interfaces.

Partial Value Chain

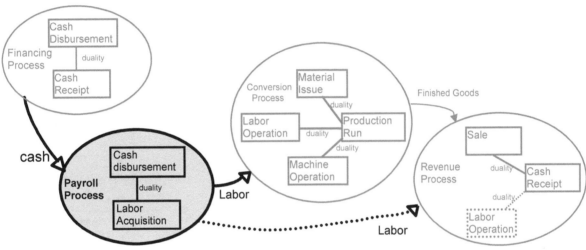

Exhibit 5-2: Payroll Process in the Value Chain

Notice that the solid arrows of Exhibit 5-2 only depict the payroll process making labor available to the conversion process. In many enterprises, conversion is the only process wherein the use of labor is tracked at a specific enough level to justify depicting it in the value chain, as every box and arrow in the value chain must represent measured and recorded phenomena. If we specifically track labor usage in another business process, we similarly show labor as an output of payroll and as an input to the other process. The dashed arrow for labor and the dashed box for labor operation in Exhibit 5-2 indicate that enterprises could choose to track labor usage in the revenue process (or in other processes) as well. Enterprises that track such labor usage would show the labor arrow and the labor operation box as solid (not dashed) lines. Enterprises that choose not to track labor usage in their revenue processes would omit the labor arrow and the labor operation box. We would use a similar depiction for enterprises that specifically track labor usage in the acquisition and financing processes.

PAYROLL BUSINESS PROCESS LEVEL REA MODELS

We begin our business process level discussion of payroll by reviewing some of its more common events. Exhibit 5-3 illustrates the expanded REA business process model for a typical payroll process.

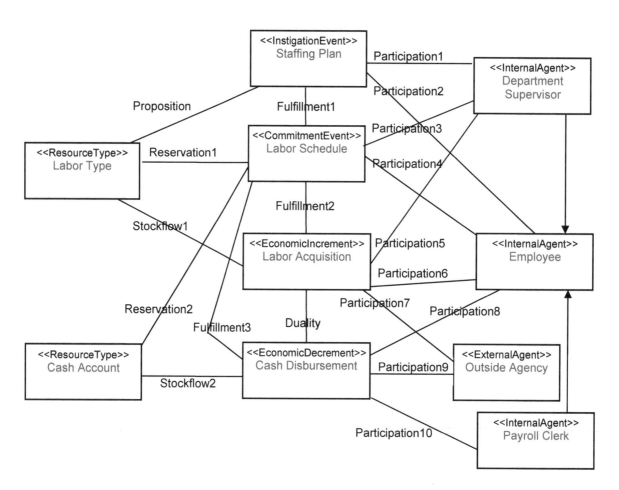

Exhibit 5-3: Expanded REA Business Process Payroll Model

Instigation events in essence make a proposal based on need identification. Mutual commitment events act upon the instigation events and economic events that comprise the exchange of resources fulfill the commitments. These base objects exist in every business process for every enterprise; however, measurement and storage of all details of all objects may not be cost-effective.

The *REA* pattern aids in analyzing business processes and events by highlighting the *what* (the resources involved in the event) and the *who* (the internal and external agents) involved in each event. The *where* and the *when* are stored as attributes of each event. The events, agents, and resources involved in the payroll process vary somewhat from enterprise to enterprise. The general pattern discussed in this chapter can be adapted and applied to meet the exact requirements of any enterprise.

Resources

Human capital is the resource acquired in the payroll process, and is comprised of the work employees perform and the knowledge and skills employees use in performing that work. Because human capital is mostly intangible, it is very difficult to measure. Ownership is also difficult to establish, as discussed earlier in this chapter. If we could resolve the ownership and measurement issues, then we would directly represent the human capital resource as a class in the enterprise's payroll business process model. Instead, we typically substitute a class called labor or labor type that is a resource type. Such a Labor or *Labor type* class represents an inventory of the kinds of labor an enterprise may need to acquire and use in its operations. Some attributes typically captured to represent labor types include an identifier, a description, and a standard (budgeted) hourly wage rate for that type of labor.

Cash is the resource given in exchange for labor. Cash in the payroll process is typically represented by the cash accounts from which paychecks are written. Paychecks are usually written from either a regular checking account or from an imprest checking account. An *imprest checking account* is an account that normally maintains a zero balance. For example, when the amount of cash disbursements needed for a payroll period is determined, a company that uses an imprest checking account transfers the total amount of the paychecks from one of its regular checking accounts to its imprest account. Paychecks to each specific employee are drawn on the imprest checking account. As time passes, if the imprest account balance is positive, that indicates employees are not all cashing their paychecks. If the imprest account balance becomes negative, a mistake likely occurred. Either situation warrants investigation. Attributes typically captured to represent the set of cash accounts include an identifier, type, description, and location of each account. If financial institutions (such as banks or credit unions) maintain most of the cash accounts, then the account numbers assigned by the financial institutions also need to be captured.

Events

We next discuss the events that comprise the expanded payroll process model within the context of the overall documents used by many companies, indicating the REA event types, as well as relational tables, as we did with the acquisition process. Exhibit 5-4 illustrates the typical event sequence for payroll as it corresponds to the generic event sequence. Note that payroll processes typically do not include reversal events.

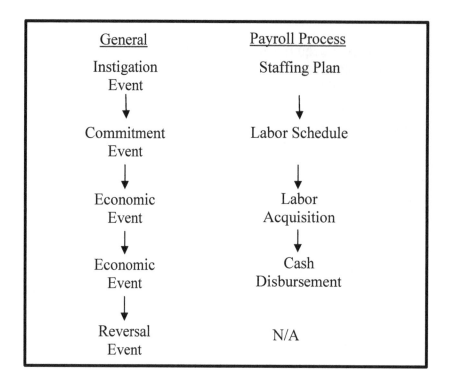

Exhibit 5-4: Stereotypical Series of General and Payroll Process Events

Need Identification – Staffing Plans or Labor Requisitions (Instigation Events)
Supervisors determine the need for labor by monitoring enterprise growth (or lack thereof), production plans, sales forecasts, employee turnover, and other trends and projections. Identification of a need for labor often is labeled as a *staffing plan* or *labor requisition instigation event* as shown in Exhibit 5-3. Labor requests occur on an ongoing basis as part of normal operations and involve identification of the number of hours (or some similar basis) existing employees are needed to provide specific types of labor. The staffing plan event is fulfilled by the scheduling of one or more employees to provide that labor.

Agents involved in instigation events (labor requisitions) in the payroll process usually are department supervisors (agents who authorize the requisition) and employees (agents whose skills and knowledge are the subject of the request). As noted earlier, because labor is intangible it is usually measured via categories and is specified as a resource type. Attributes of staffing plans that typically should be captured include the date and time of the staffing plan. The staffing plan event data should be linked to data regarding the related supervisor, requested employees (if any are specified), and the type of labor requested.

Documentation of need identification for labor may vary widely. Although theoretically we could expect to see a labor requisition form that looks much like a purchase requisition form as shown in the acquisition process chapter, not many enterprises use such forms for routine labor need identification. Indeed, most need for labor is identified by department supervisors who themselves also approve the request based on their own department's budget. A staffing plan is the most commonly used form of documentation on which a department supervisor communicates a department's need for labor for a given time period. Such a plan indicates the types and quantities of labor needed without assigning specific employees to provide the labor. Exhibit 5-5 illustrates a staffing plan.

<table>
<tr><td colspan="11">Your Source Company
Staffing Plan 7
For Period <u>April 1, 2020 – April 7, 2020</u></td></tr>
<tr><td colspan="6">Date Plan Approved <u>2/24/2020</u></td><td colspan="5">Approved by <u>E5</u></td></tr>
<tr><td></td><td colspan="8">Quantity of Labor Needed (in hours)</td><td></td><td></td></tr>
<tr><td>Type of labor needed</td><td>4/1</td><td>4/2</td><td>4/3</td><td>4/4</td><td>4/5</td><td>4/6</td><td>4/7</td><td>Total</td><td>Std Wage Rate</td><td>Ext. Amount</td></tr>
<tr><td>CT2 Cashier duties</td><td>16</td><td>16</td><td>16</td><td>16</td><td>16</td><td>0</td><td>0</td><td>80</td><td>$12.00</td><td>$960.00</td></tr>
<tr><td>US3 Cleaning/janitorial</td><td>8</td><td>8</td><td>8</td><td>8</td><td>8</td><td>12</td><td>0</td><td>52</td><td>$9.00</td><td>$468.00</td></tr>
<tr><td>AP1 Prepare sales tax</td><td>12</td><td>12</td><td>12</td><td>12</td><td>12</td><td>0</td><td>0</td><td>60</td><td>$18.00</td><td>$1,080.00</td></tr>
<tr><td>CT1 Data entry</td><td>12</td><td>12</td><td>12</td><td>12</td><td>12</td><td>12</td><td>12</td><td>84</td><td>$11.00</td><td>$924.00</td></tr>
<tr><td></td><td></td><td></td><td></td><td></td><td></td><td></td><td></td><td></td><td></td><td></td></tr>
<tr><td>Totals</td><td>48</td><td>48</td><td>48</td><td>48</td><td>48</td><td>24</td><td>12</td><td>276</td><td></td><td>$3,432.00</td></tr>
</table>

Exhibit 5-5: Staffing Plan

The relational tables below correspond to Exhibit 5-3's class diagram representation of the staffing plan event, the associations in which it participates (proposition, fulfillment1, participation1, and participation2), and the related classes (labor type, labor schedule, department supervisor, and employee. Alternative tables could be derived depending on the association multiplicities. Data from Exhibit 5-5's staffing plan have been entered into the database tables; however, some of these data (e.g. labor type and employee information) would have existed already in the database tables before the staffing plan data was added to the tables such that only the association information that links them to the event is recorded for those objects. New data recording staffing plan 7 is shown in red, bold, italic font.

Labor Requisition (Instigation Event)

StaffingPlanID	StartDate	EndDate	DatePlanApproved	SuperID[FK]
7	04/01/2020	04/07/2020	02/24/2020	E5

Proposition Association (Labor Requisition – Labor Type)

StaffingPlanID	LaborTypeID	Date	QuantityNeededHours
LR7	CT2	04/01/2020	16
LR7	US3	04/01/2020	8
LR7	AP1	04/01/2020	12
LR7	CT1	04/01/2020	12
LR7	CT2	04/02/2020	16
LR7	US3	04/02/2020	8
LR7	AP1	04/02/2020	12
LR7	CT1	04/02/2020	12
LR7	CT2	04/03/2020	16
LR7	US3	04/03/2020	8
LR7	AP1	04/03/2020	12
LR7	CT1	04/03/2020	12
LR7	CT2	04/04/2020	16
LR7	US3	04/04/2020	8
LR7	AP1	04/04/2020	12
LR7	CT1	04/04/2020	12
LR7	CT2	04/05/2020	16
LR7	US3	04/05/2020	8
LR7	AP1	04/05/2020	12
LR7	CT1	04/05/2020	12
LR7	CT2	04/06/2020	0
LR7	US3	04/06/2020	12
LR7	AP1	04/06/2020	0
LR7	CT1	04/06/2020	12
LR7	CT2	04/07/2020	0
LR7	US3	04/07/2020	0
LR7	AP1	04/07/2020	0
LR7	CT1	04/07/2020	12

Labor Type (Resource Type)

LaborTypeID	Description	StandardWageRate
AP1	Sales tax preparation	$18.00
CT1	Data entry	$11.00
CT2	Cashier duties	$12.00
US3	Cleaning/janitorial	$9.00

Department Supervisor (Internal Agent)

DeptSupervisorID	Name	Address	Telephone	DateOfBirth
E5	Patrick Wellesley	53125 Fenton Dr.	555-1112	03/04/1958

Labor Schedule (Mutual Commitment Event)

A mutual commitment event exists when an enterprise and a business partner have each agreed to exchange specific quantities of resources at a defined future time. In the payroll process a labor schedule serves as a mutual commitment event. A *labor schedule*, also called an employee schedule, is typically prepared by a supervisor with inputs from the employee as to when the employee is, and is not, available to work. This is similar to a purchase agent's preparation of a purchase order with input from a vendor as to the availability of goods or services. The *employee schedule* represents a commitment by the employee to provide the labor as specified and a commitment by the enterprise to pay the employee the contracted wage rate for the labor provided. If the employee does not work his or her scheduled hours, (as when a vendor doesn't fill a purchase order for goods) the enterprise is not obligated to pay for those hours not worked.

Attributes of labor schedule events that typically should be captured include the date the schedule was approved, the total dollar amount to which the schedule commits, and the time period covered by the schedule (often in the form of a beginning date and an ending date). The labor schedule should also be linked to data regarding the related labor types, employees, supervisor, labor acquisition event, and labor requisition event. Data regarding labor schedule events are often captured on a form such as that shown in Exhibit 5-6. This form may either be a paper document, an electronic spreadsheet, or part of a software application interface that is used to update the enterprise database.

Your Source Company
Employee Schedule __7__
For Period <u>April 1, 2020 – April 7, 2020</u>

Date Schedule Approved <u>3/4/2020</u>   Approved by <u>E5</u>

Empl ID	Name	4/1/20	4/2/20	4/3/20	4/4/20	4/5/20	4/6/20	4/7/20	Total Hours	Wage Rate
E15	Donna Davis	7-4	7-4	7-4	7-4	7-4			40	13.50
E16	Nancy Hardaway	9-6	9-6	9-6	9-6	9-6			40	12.75
E17	Joe Thompson	7-4	7-4	7-4	7-4	7-4			40	9.20
E18	Freda Matthews						7-2		6	8.90
E19	John Matthews						7-2		6	8.90
E20	Paula Cosgrove	9-1	9-1	9-1	9-1	9-1	9-1	9-1	28	11.50
E21	Rob Fordham	8-5	8-5	8-5	8-5	8-5			40	11.00
E22	Francis Johnson						8-5	8-5	16	10.75
E23	James Worthwhile	8-8	8-8	8-8	8-8	8-8			60	18.00

Schedule Budgeted Total | $ 3,538.80

Exhibit 5-6: Labor Schedule

The relational tables below correspond to Exhibit 5-3's class diagram representation of the labor schedule event and the associations in which it participates. Other possible tables could be derived, depending on the association multiplicities. Data from the labor schedule in Exhibit 5-6 have been entered into the database tables; however, some of these data (e.g. labor type, supervisor, and employee information) would have existed already in the database tables before the labor schedule data was added to the tables. In such cases, only the association information that links them to the labor schedule is new data. New data entered to record labor schedule 7 are shown in red, bold, italic font.

Labor Requisition (Instigation Event)

StaffingPlanID	StartDate	EndDate	DatePlanApproved	SuperID^FK
LR7	04/01/2020	04/07/2020	02/24/2020	E5

LaborSchedule (Mutual Commitment) Event

Labor ScheduleID	Date Schedule Approved	Begin Date	End Date	Budgeted Total	StaffingPlanID^FK	SuperID^FK
LS7	03/04/2020	04/01/2020	04/07/2020	$3,538.80	LR7	E5

LaborType (Resource Type)

Item ID	Description	Standard Hourly Wage
CT2	Cashier duties	$12.00
US3	Clean sales showroom and stockroom	$9.00
AP1	Prepare quarterly sales tax return	$18.00
CT1	Enter data for sales transactions	$11.00

Reservation Association (LaborSchedule – LaborType)

LaborScheduleID	LaborTypeID	HoursScheduled
LS7	CT2	80
LS7	US3	52
LS7	AP1	60
LS7	CT1	84

Participation Association (LaborSchedule – Employee)

LaborScheduleID	Scheduled EmployeeID	Hours Scheduled	Wage Rate
LS7	E15	40	$13.50
LS7	E16	40	$12.75
LS7	E17	40	$9.20
LS7	E18	6	$8.90
LS7	E19	6	$8.90
LS7	E20	28	$11.50
LS7	E21	40	$11.00
LS7	E22	16	$10.75
LS7	E23	60	$18.00

DepartmentSupervisor (Internal Agent)

SuperID	Authorized Spending Limit
E5	$425,000

Employee (Internal Agent)

EmpID	Name	Address	Telephone	DateOfBirth	Rating	Position	Type	Wage
E5	Patrick Wellesley	53125 Fenton Dr.	555-1112	03/04/1958	Excellent	Supervisor	Salary	$35.50
E15	Donna Davis	149 Rovetta Dr.	555-9932	02/03/1954	Superior	Cashier	Hourly	$13.50
E16	Nancy Hardaway	271 Rovetta Dr.	555-2117	06/11/1956	Excellent	Cashier	Hourly	$12.75
E17	Joe Thompson	535 Olson St.	555-2277	04/24/1947	Excellent	Custodian	Hourly	$9.20
E18	Freda Matthews	3214 Deerlake St.	555-1222	08/06/1940	Good	Custodian	Hourly	$8.90
E19	John Matthews	3214 Deerlake St.	555-1222	10/14/1940	Good	Custodian	Hourly	$8.90
E20	Paula Cosgrove	5006 Jazz Ct.	555-5200	04/18/1958	Excellent	Data Entry	Hourly	$11.50
E21	Rob Fordham	4444 Zephyr Ln.	555-4545	06/04/1975	Excellent	Data Entry	Hourly	$11.00
E22	Francis Johnson	1261 Mason Dr.	555-0129	05/05/1980	Good	Data Entry	Hourly	$10.75
E23	James Worthwhile	5432 Wadsworth Ln	555-7777	04/14/1964	Superior	Accountant	Salary	$18.00
E36	Diane Bowersox	9115 Wolfgang Ct	555-7244	09/15/1963	Superior	Payroll	Hourly	$11.75

Labor Acquisition (Economic Increment Event) - Performance by Employee

As the employees and the enterprise each perform according to the terms of the schedule – called *performance* in contract law – they fulfill the mutual commitment event. Employee performance is the provision of labor to the enterprise – i.e., the enterprise is acquiring labor from the employees. *Labor acquisition* is the primary economic increment event in the payroll business process. Because labor is intangible, the acquisition of labor is also somewhat intangible. While in theory, enterprises acquire labor continuously, most enterprises aggregate labor acquisitions according to defined pay periods. Each instance of the labor acquisition set therefore represents the purchase of labor during a defined work period. The work period may be the same as the enterprise pay period, or it may represent a smaller work period, such as a day's time worked by each employee. Daily (or even more frequent) recording of labor acquisitions allows for a more complete picture of the enterprise on a continual basis because the time lag between the company receiving the benefit of the economic increment event and the recording of that benefit (and the related liability) is minimized.

The primary document prepared by the enterprise in conjunction with the economic increment event is a *timecard*. Employees may complete timecards on a daily, weekly, or other basis. Supervisors typically approve timecards prepared by employees. Timecards list the times employees started working (punched in) and stopped working (punched out) for each day in the covered work period.

Most large enterprises have not used hand-written paper timecards for many years, but instead use electronic time clocks with punch cards that enable automated data processing. Some enterprises have further upgraded systems to allow scanning of employee ID cards or badges upon arrival and departure, with direct transmission of that data to the payroll application. The captured data are similar to the paper timecards; the difference is in the speed with which the system is updated and the level of aggregation of the captured data. Such systems enable the daily or more frequent recording of labor acquisitions recommended earlier.

What about labor acquired from salaried employees, for which no time clock data are collected? For purposes of determining accruals for compensated sick time and vacation time, most enterprises assume such employees work forty hours per week at a wage rate equivalent to their annual salary divided by 2,080 (the number of hours in the year calculated as 52 weeks x 40 hours per week). While they do not require salaried employees to punch a clock, they do typically require them to report sick time or vacation time taken. In many cases, companies require salaried employees to fill out timesheets, either manual or electronic.

Exhibit 5-7 illustrates a timecard representing the type of data collected, regardless of whether the data is captured on paper or electronically, and regardless of whether the data represent actual time worked or assumed time worked.

Timecard # 49						Pay Period		4/1/2020 – 4/7/2020															
Employee ID E23						Employee Name		James Worthwhile															
4/1				4/2				4/3				4/4				4/5				4/6				4/7			
In	Out	In	Out	In	Out	In	Out	In	Out	In	Out	In	Out	In	Out	In	Out	In	Out	In	Out	In	Out	In	Out	In	Out
7	-	-	7	7	-	-	7	7	-	-	7	7	-	-	7	7	-	-	7								

I hereby ascertain that I worked the hours recorded above.

James S. Worthwhile _____   4/5/2020
Employee Signature   Date

Approved by E5 _____ Date: 4/8/2020 _____
Initials   *PW* _____

Exhibit 5-7: Timecard

In addition to the timecard data, to record the labor acquisition event, the enterprise must also use data stored in its system as to any applicable withholdings, also called *payroll deductions*. *Withholdings* represent amounts the enterprise will pay on behalf of the employees to government agencies, benefit providers, or other outside agencies. Some withholdings are statutorily mandated (such as federal income tax), whereas some are voluntary (such as life insurance). While the enterprise does not need withholdings information to determine the cost of the labor acquisition; the enterprise needs withholdings information to determine the amounts that are payable to employees and the amounts that are payable to other outside agencies such as the IRS, state government, or insurance providers. Enterprises record the gross pay dollar amount as wages or salaries expense. *Gross pay* is the amount the employees earned, before subtracting withholdings. Enterprises record the *net pay* (the dollar amount to be paid to the employees, i.e., the gross pay minus the withholdings) as wages or salaries payable. Enterprises record the withholdings according to the types of payables for which the amounts were withheld.

In the United States, amounts withheld for federal income taxes, social security tax, and Medicare tax typically are payable to the Internal Revenue Service. Amounts withheld for state income taxes are payable to the appropriate state government agencies. Amounts withheld for employees' premiums for insurance benefits (health, dental, life, and so forth) are payable to the appropriate insurance providers. Other deductions may be payable to other types of agencies such as charitable organizations.

In theory, enterprises could simply record the gross pay as the labor acquisition cost and then wait to record the various withholdings as part of the duality association once the checks are written to the employees and outside agencies. However, because the amounts are available (either by predefined calculations or reference files) and because the enterprise's economic story is more complete sooner by including them when recording the acquisition event, there is no reason to postpone their recognition. Relational tables with sample data representing labor acquisitions and related phenomena appear below, with new data to record timecard 49 shown in red, bold, italic font. To save space, we depict only James Worthwhile in the employee table – the actual table would include all of the employees previously shown.

LaborSchedule (Mutual Commitment) Event

Labor ScheduleID	Date Schedule Approved	Begin Date	End Date	Total Dollar Amt	LaborReqID^FK	SuperID^FK
LS7	03/04/2020	04/01/2020	04/07/2020	$3,538.80	LR7	E5

Fulfillment Association (LaborAcquisition – LaborSchedule)

LaborScheduleID	LaborAcquisitionID
LS7	*TC49*

LaborAcquisition (Economic Increment) Event

AcqID	BeginDate	EndDate	Hours	GrossPay	FICA	Medical	FIT	SIT	Approval Date	Net Pay	EmpID^FK	SupID^FK
TC49	*04/01/2020*	*04/07/2020*	*60*	*$1,080.00*	*$66.96*	*$15.66*	*$216*	*$43.20*	*04/08/2020*	*$738.18*	*E23*	*E5*

Participation Association (LaborAcquisition – OutsideAgency)

LaborAcquisitionID	AgencyID	Amount
TC49	*IRS*	*$298.62*
TC49	*Mich*	*$43.20*

Stockflow Association (LaborAcquisition – LaborType)

AcquisitionID	LT-ID	Hours worked	Wage
TC49	*AP1*	*60*	*$18.00*

DepartmentSupervisor (Internal Agent)

SuperID	Authorized Spending Limit
E5	$425,000

LaborType (Resource Type)

Item ID	Description	Standard Hourly Wage
CT2	Cashier duties	$12.00
US3	Clean sales showroom and stockroom	$9.00
AP1	Prepare quarterly sales tax return	$18.00
CT1	Enter data for sales transactions	$11.00

OutsideAgencies (External Agent)

AgencyID	AgencyName	MailingAddress
S315	Internal Revenue Service	PO Box 123512
S320	State Government	PO Box 321533
S325	Blue Health	31253 Elm St.
S330	Best Dental	1472 Beech St.

Employee (Internal Agent)

EmplD	Name	Address	Telephone	DateOfBirth	Rating	Position	Type	Wage
E23	James Worthwhile	5432 Wadsworth Ln	555-7777	04/14/1964	Superior	Accountant	Salary	$18.00

Payments to Employees (Economic Decrement Event)

While the employees' contractual performance was the provision of labor, the enterprise's contractual performance is payment to the employees. Such cash disbursements by enterprises to employees are often called paychecks. Cash disbursements in the payroll process may be made via paper check, electronic funds transfer (direct deposit), or less commonly, cash payment. Paycheck or direct deposit stubs typically contain information such as gross pay, net pay, and the various withholdings that make up the difference between gross and net pay (such as income tax, social security tax, Medicare tax, health insurance premiums, and retirement plan contributions). Exhibit 5-8 illustrates a direct deposit stub.

Your Source Company Direct Deposit Notification Employee ID _23_ Name James Worthwhile	Time card 49	Gross Pay $1,080	Federal Income Tax W/H $216.00	FICA W/H $66.96	Medicare W/H $15.66	State Income Tax W/H $43.20	No. __147__ Net Pay $738.18

Your Source Company	No. __147__
   James S. Worthwhile	Date _____ 4/14/2020
	Your net pay has been transmitted electronically (EFT) to your financial institution according to your instructions

Exhibit 5-8: Direct Deposit Notification

Cash disbursements may occur at various times during the payroll business process. Most enterprises pay employees only after acquiring labor from the employees. Some enterprises do offer "advances" to employees; advance payments for which the employee is obliged either to provide the corresponding labor or to repay the cash with interest. Attributes captured for cash disbursements usually include an identifier (such as a disbursement voucher number), date, amount paid, payee identification (for paychecks, that is the employee who supplied labor or the outside agency who benefitted from the employee supplying labor), clerk identification (i.e., the employee who wrote the check), the cash account number from which the cash is disbursed, and the voucher or check number of the payment.

Relational tables with sample data representing payments to employees and related phenomena follow. To save space, the employee table only depicts James Worthwhile; however, the actual employee table would include all employees previously depicted. Data to record cash disbursements 147-149 are shown in red, bold, italic font.

CashDisbursement (Economic Decrement) Event

Cash AccountID	Check Number	Payment Date	Dollar Amount	Payroll ClerkID^{FK}
Ca987654	147	04/14/2020	$738.18	E36
Ca987654	148	04/14/2020	$298.62	E36
Ca987654	149	04/14/2020	$43.20	E36

Participation Association (Cash Disbursement – Employee)

Cash AccountID	Check Number	EmployeeID
Ca987654	147	E23

Participation Association (Cash Disbursement – Outside Agency)

Cash AccountID	Check Number	AgencyID
Ca987654	148	S315
Ca987654	149	S320

Duality Association (LaborAcquisition – CashDisbursement)

LaborAcquisitionID	CheckNumber	Amount Applied
TC49	147	$738.18
TC49	148	$298.62
TC49	149	$43.20

Cash (Resource Type)

CashAccountID	AccountType	Location
Ca123501	Checking	1st Local Bank
Ca987654	Imprest checking	1st Local Bank

LaborAcquisition (Economic Increment) Event

AcqID	BeginDate	EndDate	Hours	GrossPay	FICA	Medical	FIT	SIT	Net Pay	EmpID^{FK}	SupID^{FK}
TC49	04/01/2020	04/07/2020	60	$1,080.00	$66.96	$15.66	$216	$43.20	$738.18	E23	E5

PayrollClerk (Internal Agent)

PayrollClerkID	Fidelity Bond Rating
E36	AA

Employee (Internal Agent)

EmpID	Name	Address	Telephone	DateOfBirth	Rating	Position	Type	Wage
E23	James Worthwhile	5432 Wadsworth Ln	555-7777	04/14/1964	Superior	Accountant	Salary	$18.00

Outside Agencies (External Agent)

AgencyID	AgencyName	MailingAddress
S315	Internal Revenue Service	PO Box 123512
S320	State Government	PO Box 321533
S325	Blue Health	31253 Elm St.
S330	Best Dental	1472 Beech St.

Agents

Employees are stereotyped as internal agents, but as noted earlier, they sometimes play an outside participation role. External agents in payroll for many enterprises include outside payroll processors (only for those that outsource that function) and the many types of vendors to whom withholdings are paid – government agencies, insurance providers, and so forth.

CONCLUDING COMMENTS

This chapter reviewed the workflow activities, documents, models, and relational database tables commonly used in the payroll process. You probably noticed similarities between the acquisition process in the previous chapter and the payroll process in this chapter. In case you need further clarification, Exhibit 5-9 compares and contrasts activities in the acquisition and payroll processes. Note that economic events in the payroll process are not typically reversed.

Activity	Acquisition Process	Payroll Process
Need identification	Purchase Requisition	Labor Requisition or Staffing Plan
Mutual Commitment	Purchase Order	Labor Schedule
Economic Increment	Purchase – Receiving Report representing receipt of goods or services	Labor Acquisition – Timecard representing receipt of labor
Economic Decrement	Cash Disbursement	Cash Disbursement
Economic Increment Reversal	Purchase Return or Allowance	Not applicable
Economic Decrement Reversal	Refund of cash paid	Not applicable

Exhibit 5-9: Comparison of Acquisition and Payroll Activities

KEY TERMS AND CONCEPTS
Direct deposit notification
Employee
Gross pay
Human capital
Imprest checking account
Labor acquisition event
Labor requisition instigation event
Labor schedule
Labor type
Net pay
Paycheck
Payroll deduction
Payroll function
Personnel function
Staffing plan
Timecard
Withholdings

REVIEW QUESTIONS
R5-1. What is the primary objective of the payroll business process?

R5-2. Which functions in enterprise human resource processes are typically considered as personnel functions, and which functions are typically considered as payroll functions?

R5-3. How does the payroll business process connect to the conversion, revenue, acquisition, and financing business processes?

R5-4. What resources, internal agents, and external agents (if any) typically connect to these events in a payroll business process?
   a. Employee schedule (commitment to economic increment event)
   b. Labor acquisition (economic increment event)
   c. Staffing plan or labor requisition (instigation event)
   d. Cash disbursement (economic decrement event)

R5-5. What kinds of information does each of these typically need to perform their roles in enterprise human resource processes?
   a. Management
   b. Payroll
   c. Accounting
   d. Personnel

MULTIPLE CHOICE QUESTIONS

MC5-1.   Which document typically represents the same phenomena as the labor acquisition (economic increment) event?
- A) Payroll register
- B) Operations list
- C) Timecard
- D) Schedule

MC5-2.   The payroll process represents the point of contact between the enterprise and which set of external business partners?
- A) Investors and Creditors
- B) Suppliers
- C) Customers
- D) Employees

MC5-3.   The resource made available by the payroll process to the conversion process in a typical enterprise value chain is:
- A) Inventory
- B) Property, plant, and equipment
- C) Labor
- D) Cash

MC5-4.   Which classes are usually paired in a stockflow association in the payroll process?
- A) Labor acquisition and Employee
- B) Labor type and Schedule
- C) Cash and Cash Disbursement
- D) Employee and Supervisor

MC5-5.   Which of these documents the commitment of the enterprise to receive an employee's labor in a future time period?
- A) Employee schedule
- B) Labor acquisition
- C) Cash budget
- D) Cash disbursement

MC5-6.   The payroll process is in essence a special case of which other business process?
- A) Acquisition
- B) Conversion
- C) Financing
- D) Revenue

MC5-7. What is true about an enterprise's use of an imprest checking account?
   A) Paychecks are usually written from the regular checking account, not the imprest account.
   B) The imprest account normally maintains a zero balance
   C) A negative balance in the imprest account indicates that some employees are not cashing their paychecks
   D) A positive balance in the imprest account usually means a mistake occurred

MC5-8. In which business process are employees most likely to play an outside participation role for some events?
   A) Acquisition
   B) Conversion
   C) Payroll
   D) Revenue

MC5-9. In a payroll process, what type of event does a direct deposit notification typically document?
   A) Commitment
   B) Instigation
   C) Economic increment
   D) Economic decrement

MC5-10. Which payroll process event often doesn't specify related individual employees?
   A) Staffing plan
   B) Employee schedule
   C) Labor acquisition
   D) Cash disbursement

CHAPTER **6**

Modeling Revenue Business Processes with REA

LEARNING OBJECTIVES

The primary objective of this chapter is to discuss the kinds of workflow commonly found in revenue business processes. We expand the REA (Resource-Event-Agent) business process models originally seen in chapter 2 for the revenue process to include instigation and commitment events and the associations between those events and other classes. We also illustrate various types of business documents used by companies to capture data about tasks and events in the revenue process. Once you get through the first part of this chapter, you will have learned how to model acquisition, payroll, and revenue business processes (assuming you studied chapters 4 and 5). In the last part of this chapter, we discuss the procedures for combining the models such that the combined model may be implemented as a single database. After studying this chapter, you should be able to

1. Describe the typical tasks, instigation events, commitment events, economic events, economic reversal events found in most enterprises' revenue business processes
2. Identify the documents commonly used to capture data about the various types of tasks and events in the revenue transaction process
3. Create a REA business process model for a company's revenue process
4. Integrate multiple REA business process models into a single model.

REVENUE BUSINESS PROCESSES

The *revenue business process* encompasses activities needed to provide goods or services to customers in exchange for cash. The acquisition process (discussed in chapter 4) and the revenue process are comprised of the same overall activities viewed from different perspectives. An exchange of goods or services for cash is, to the buyer (cash payer) a purchase, and to the seller (goods or service deliverer) a sale. Therefore, the business process conceptual models for the two processes are similar, and hopefully much of the content in this chapter will feel familiar.

REVENUE BUSINESS PROCESSES IN ENTERPRISE VALUE SYSTEMS

At the value system level, the revenue process is the point of contact between the enterprise and its customers, as shown in Exhibit 6-1.

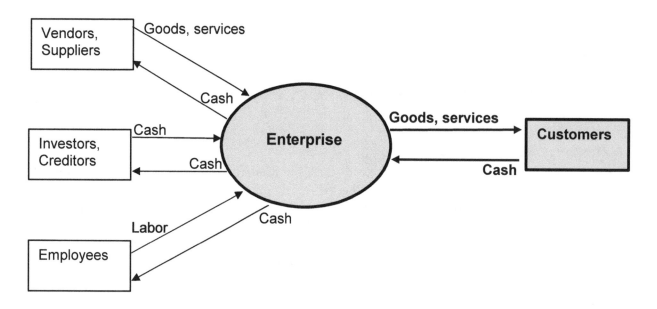

Exhibit 6-1: Revenue Process in the Enterprise Value System

The enterprise delivers goods and services to the customers and receives cash in exchange. Goods may be products the enterprise manufactured (i.e., finished goods inventory), products the enterprise bought from other suppliers (i.e., merchandise inventory), or temporary use of products (e.g. rental of buildings, vehicles, or equipment). Services may be sold individually or services may be combined with products. For example, one might sell accounting services to customers – in which case, the service consists of providing time, skills, knowledge, and effort to the customer. Note that such services are similar to labor as discussed in the payroll process (chapter 5) and share the same measurement difficulty. One might sell automobile repair services, which are in essence sales of time, skills, knowledge, and effort combined with products in the form of parts inventory.

REVENUE BUSINESS PROCESSES IN ENTERPRISE VALUE CHAINS

The value chain reveals interfaces between the revenue process and other business processes. Exhibit 6-2 illustrates the typical value chain interfaces. The labor arrow going from payroll to revenue, and the corresponding labor usage box within revenue are dashed instead of solid to indicate that many enterprises do not track labor usage within their revenue processes, and therefore would not include the labor arrow and labor usage box in their value chains. Only enterprises that provide services as their primary revenue-generating activity are likely to track the usage of labor in their revenue processes. Even those who provide services may track the labor usage as part of their service provision event rather than as a separate event, so often you will not include labor usage as an economic decrement event in the revenue process or labor as a resource. When labor usage is tracked as a separate event, you should show the labor arrow and the labor usage event using solid lines rather than dashed lines.

Partial Value Chain

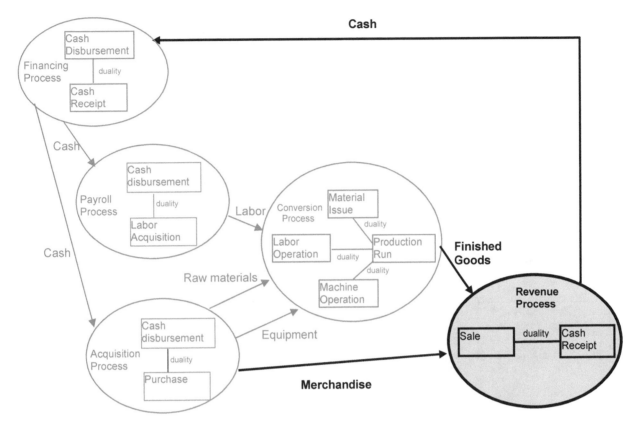

Exhibit 6-2: Revenue Process in the Value Chain

Notice also that the value chain illustrated in Exhibit 6-2 makes both finished goods and merchandise available for sale in the revenue process. The conversion process makes finished goods (products manufactured by the enterprise) available to the revenue process. The acquisition process makes merchandise (products purchased for resale by the enterprise) available to the revenue process. An enterprise value chain should only include whichever resource arrows are appropriate for that enterprise. As noted in chapter 5, if the enterprise specifically tracks labor usage in its revenue process, the value chain would also need to show a labor arrow from payroll to revenue and an event box inside the revenue process that uses up that labor. Many enterprises choose not to specifically track labor usage within their revenue process, thus we omitted the labor arrow and labor operation event from Exhibit 6-2.

REVENUE BUSINESS PROCESS LEVEL REA MODELS

As we expand the revenue process bubble on the enterprise value chain to the business process level, we get a model such as the one illustrated in Exhibit 6-3. This model represents an enterprise that sells products rather than services.

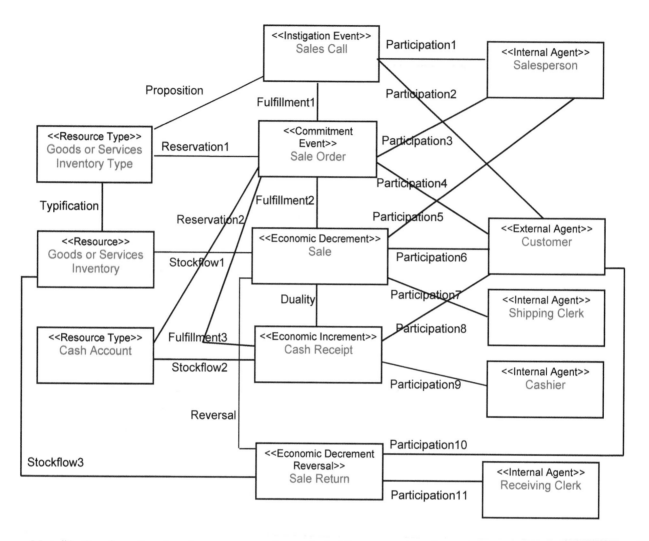

Note#1: Goods or Services Inventory may be excluded for enterprises for which it is not cost effective to use specific identification; if so, stockflow1 and stockflow3 should connect to the Goods or Services Inventory Type class. In other cases, the mutual commitment event may specify an instance of goods or services inventory; if so, reservation1 should connect to the Goods or Services Inventory class.

Exhibit 6-3: Expanded REA Revenue Business Process Model

Resources

Cash is the resource acquired in the revenue process, and is typically represented by the cash accounts into which cash receipts are deposited. Attributes typically captured to represent the set of cash accounts include an identifier, type, description, and location of each account. If financial institutions (such as banks or credit unions) maintain most of the cash accounts, then the account numbers assigned by the financial institutions also need to be captured.

Finished Goods, Merchandise, and *Service Types* are the most common resources that enterprises give up by delivering them to customers. Finished goods and merchandise may simply be called

Inventory and may be tracked as resources or as resource types depending on the degree of traceability that is desirable and practical. Usually only high dollar value, low volume items are tracked as resources. Most inventory is tracked as resource types. The service type resource represents an inventory of the kinds of services an enterprise may sell. Some attributes typically captured to represent inventory and inventory types (including service types) include an identifier, a description, standard (budgeted) unit costs, list unit selling prices, and various dimensions (size, weight, color, and so forth).

Events

We next discuss the events that comprise the expanded revenue process model within the context of the overall workflow and documents used by many companies. We also illustrate the relational database tables that would store revenue process data.

To exchange goods and services for cash with the customers, enterprises must attract customers, then help those customers select goods and services, deliver the goods and services requested, and collect payments for the goods and services. Generating revenue is the key to achieving growth and profitability. Enterprises can produce an abundance of goods and create a variety of services, but the real test of value is whether someone will pay a price that covers the cost of goods and services and provide the enterprise with an acceptable return on invested funds. Exhibit 6-4 illustrates the typical sequencing of revenue process events that correspond to the generic event sequence. Note that the instigation event may alternatively be a customer inquiry or a marketing event instead of a sales call.

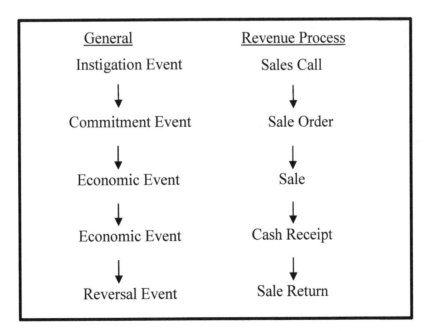

Exhibit 6-4: Typical Sequence of Generic and Revenue Process Events

Need Identification - Marketing Events, Sales Calls, Customer Inquiries (Instigation Events)
Instigation events may be internally instigated (i.e., by the enterprise) or externally instigated (i.e., by an external business partner of the enterprise). The revenue process is instigated by the attraction of a customer's decision to buy the enterprise's goods or services.

Sometimes customers know they want a particular product or service and they search for a source for that product or service. They may call an enterprise to see if the product or service they need is available, without having participated in a marketing event. Such *customer inquiries* are externally generated instigation events.

In an effort to influence customer decision making, an enterprise plans, executes, and evaluates a variety of marketing events (e.g., sales calls, advertising campaigns, and promotions) intended to inform customers about products and services and hopefully influence them to trigger the revenue process. Therefore, marketing efforts are typically considered to be internally generated instigation events. Advertisements on websites are also considered instigation events, and they have the benefit of direct traceability to orders placed by customers. Whereas often we have difficulty tracing marketing-related instigation events to orders, with website advertisements the customers click through to place the orders, providing great data as to what instigated their commitment.

A *sales call* is an event in which an enterprise representative describes features of products or services to potential customers in an attempt to generate sales to those customers (the Sales Call to Inventory Type association is illustrated in Exhibit 6-3). Usually sales calls are pre-arranged and face-to-face and may involve product demonstrations. Data regarding sales calls are often captured on a *sales call report* form such as that in Exhibit 6-5. This form may either be a paper document or a software interface (web page). Either way, similar data are captured and stored.

Note: for simplicity's sake, not all of the data on the Sales Call report in Exhibit 6-5 appears in the tables shown below. All data on that report could be captured, but would result in at least one additional table and added fields that do not easily fit on a page. Some data would have already been in the tables; new data added as a result of the sales call are shown in red, bold, italic font.

Sales Call (Instigation) Event

Sales Call ID	Date	StartTime	EndTime	Location	SalesRepID^{FK}	CustomerID^{FK}
42	05/04/2020	9:12 a.m.	10:00 a.m.	Customer	E23	C2323

Proposition Association (Sales Call – Inventory)

Sales Call ID	Item ID	Customer Reaction to Product
42	BIS1	Negative
42	LIS1	Positive
42	HUS1	Negative
42	TIS1	Positive
42	MIN1	Undecided

Sales Representative (Internal Agent)

Sales Rep ID	Name	Address	Telephone	DateOfBirth
E23	Jimmy Vitale	425 ConAir Drive	555-5678	08/18/1962

Your Source Company
Your Source for Everything You Need
123 Main St.
Anytown, USA 12345

Sales Call Report
No. _42_

Salesperson Name	Jimmy Vitale		Salesperson #	E23
Customer Name	Needmore Stuff		Customer #	C2323

Sales Call Location	Needmore Stuff warehouse

Date	5/4/2020	Start Time	9:12 a.m.	End Time	10:00 a.m.

Customer Representative Called on	Sarah Gibson
What is this person's position?	Procurement supervisor

What products/services were presented at this sales call?

Big stuff (Item BIS1)

Little stuff (Item LIS1)

Huge stuff (Item HUS1)

Tiny stuff (Item TIS1)

Did a sale order result from this sales call?   Yes ☒ Order Number __14, 15__   No ☐

If yes, what products/services were ordered by the customer?

TIS1

LIS1

Follow-up comments (e.g. customer reaction to products, other notes):

Customer likes small things! Had no interest at all in big or huge stuff, don't bother presenting again.
The smaller the better!

Exhibit 6-5: Sales Call Report

Inventory Type (Resource Type)

Item ID	Description	UnitOfMeasure	Standard Cost	List Price
BIS1	Big Stuff	Each	$20.00	$50.00
HUS1	Huge Stuff	Each	$30.00	$70.00
LIS1	Little Stuff	Box of 6	$36.00	$72.00
MIN1	Miniature Stuff	Box of 24	$56.00	$110.00
TIS1	Tiny Stuff	Box of 12	$48.00	$96.00
TTP12	Tiara	Each	$10.00	$25.00

Customer (External Agent)

Customer ID	Name	Address	Telephone	Credit Rating
C2323	Needmore Stuff	86906 Enterprise Court	555-8989	A+

Agreements/Contracts (Commitment Events)

In the revenue process the most common commitments/contracts are sale orders, rental agreements, and service agreements. They are the same activities as we discussed for the acquisition process, but viewed from the seller's perspective. A commitment event doesn't always happen at a discrete point in time; often it involves a series of activities. Typically, a customer places an order with the enterprise for goods or services. A customer order is information in the customer's own format regarding what goods and services the customer is committing to purchase from an enterprise. Sales or customer service representatives and/or order entry clerks may assist the customer and collect the order data. The enterprise determines whether to commit by checking the availability of requested goods or services, verifying all price and date information, and contacting the customer if necessary to adjust pricing or dates promised. The enterprise also determines whether to extend credit to the customer, therefore the credit department will also play a role in the activities associated with the commitment event.

These determinations are important because the enterprise should not commit unless it is confident both parties can fulfill their parts of the sales transaction (i.e., the enterprise must be able to fill the order and the enterprise must be confident that the customer has the ability to pay). An approved customer order becomes a *sale order* – a mutual commitment event in which the enterprise agrees to transfer title of goods to a customer at an agreed upon future time and price and the customer agrees to pay for those goods. Ideally, an enterprise wants to be able to trace each commitment to a sales call or other instigation event (e.g., through a fulfillment association as illustrated in Exhibit 6-3 between the Sales Call and Sale Order). Sometimes it is impossible to determine which marketing effort led to a commitment. Other times, for example in vacation ownership (time share) sales, a commitment typically occurs only as part of a marketing event. In those rare cases, it is very clear whether the instigation activities were successful in generating the commitments and eventual sales. Linking marketing efforts to commitment events provides valuable information with which to evaluate marketing effectiveness, so enterprises should consider the feasibility and cost of materializing this link. The sale order commitment has two reservation associations with the resources that are going to be given and taken in the exchange (see Exhibit 6-3).

Data regarding sale order events are often captured on sale order forms such as that shown in Exhibit 6-5. This form may either be a paper document or part of a software interface (web page) that is used to update the enterprise database. Notice the similarity between the sale order in Exhibit 6-5 and the acquisition process's purchase order in Exhibit 4-6. For many enterprises, the data for sale orders are obtained from customer purchase order forms, commonly referred to as customer orders. The primary difference between a customer order and a sale order is that the customer order is in the customer's format, whereas the sale order is in the seller's format. Sale orders for which the enterprise has not yet delivered the specified products or services are called *open sale orders*.

Data related to sale orders are shown in the tables that follow Exhibit 6-5. Some data would already have been in the tables. New data recorded as a result of the new sale order are shown in red, bold, italic font. Because Sales Call 42 results in two sale orders, data in the tables reflects both Sale Orders 14 and 15; however, Exhibit 6-6 shows just Sale Order 14 as an example of a sale order document.

Your Source Company
Your Source for Everything You Need
123 Main St.
Anytown, USA 12345

Sale Order

ORDER NO: 14

DATE: 5/4/2020

Ordered By:	Ship To:
Sarah Gibson	Needmore Stuff
	86906 Enterprise Dr.
	Anytown, USA 12345

SALESPERSON	P.O. NUMBER	EST. SHIP DATE	TO SHIP VIA	TERMS
E23	Verbal	5/5/2020	FedEx	N/30

QUANTITY	STOCK #	DESCRIPTION	UNIT PRICE	AMOUNT
2	LIS1	Little Stuff, box of 6	$70.00	$ 140.00
10	TIS1	Tiny Stuff, box of 12	$96.00	$ 960.00
		SUBTOTAL		$1,100.00
		SALES TAX		0
		SHIPPING & HANDLING		0
		ORDER TOTAL		$1,100.00

Exhibit 6-6: Sale Order

Sale Order (Mutual Commitment) Event

Sale Order ID	Order Date	Date Needed	Dollar Total	Sales Tax	Shipping Charge	Sales CallID[FK]	Sales RepID[FK]	Customer ID[FK]
14	05/04/2020	05/07/2020	$1,100.00	$0	$0	42	E23	C2323
15	05/05/2020	05/08/2020	$880.00	$0	$0	42	E23	C2323

Reservation Association (Sale Order – Inventory Type)

Sale Order ID	Item ID	Quantity Ordered	Quoted Unit Price
14	LIS1	2	70.00
14	TIS1	10	96.00
15	MIN1	8	880.00

Inventory Type (Resource Type)

Item ID	Description	UnitOfMeasure	Standard Cost	List Price
BIS1	Big Stuff	Each	$20.00	$50.00
HUS1	Huge Stuff	Each	$30.00	$70.00
LIS1	Little Stuff	Box of 6	$36.00	$72.00
MIN1	Miniature Stuff	Box of 24	$56.00	$110.00
TIS1	Tiny Stuff	Box of 12	$48.00	$96.00
TTP12	Tiara	Each	$10.00	$25.00

Sales Representative (Internal Agent)

Sales Rep ID	Name	Address	Telephone	DateOfBirth
E23	Jimmy Vitale	425 ConAir Drive	555-5678	08/18/1962

Customer (External Agent)

Customer ID	Name	Address	Telephone	Credit Rating
C2323	Needmore Stuff	86906 Enterprise Court	555-8989	A+

Similar types of data are captured on similar forms (again, either in software interfaces or on paper documents) for other mutual commitment events such as service agreements and rental contracts. Exhibit 6-7 shows a service agreement; note the similarities in the types of data captured regarding the service agreement and the sale order events. Similar data would also be captured for rental agreements.

Exhibit 6-7: Service Agreement

Performance by Enterprise - Sale, Delivery, Shipment, Rental, or Service Engagement (Economic Decrement Events)

The enterprise's delivery of the products or services specified in the commitment represents the revenue-generating activity of the enterprise and may also be called the enterprise's performance. If the revenue generating activity involves the sale of merchandise, the event may be called sale, delivery, or shipment depending in part on whether the customer is on-site to accept possession of the goods or whether the enterprise must deliver or ship the goods to the customer. The important consideration is that the *sale* occurs when the title to the merchandise transfers from the seller to the buyer. If the title has not transferred, then revenue has not been earned. The sale event will have a stockflow association with the related resource(s) being sold (see Exhibit 6-3). The sale order event is fulfilled by the sale event and by the cash receipt event (shown as fulfillment associations in Exhibit 6-3).

If the enterprise sells services rather than goods, then the resource given up to the customers is a set of employee services, making those services unavailable to provide to someone else. Such an event is usually called *service engagement* or something that more specifically describes the kinds of services performed by the enterprise (such as repair service, audit engagement, or consultation). If the service obligation does not occur, then revenue is not earned. In the case of enterprises that rent merchandise to customers, the revenue generating activity is usually called rental. A *rental* is an event that does not involve the transfer of title of goods, but instead involves a transfer of the right to use goods for an agreed upon length of time. The rental event begins when the right to temporary possession of the goods transfers from the lessor to the lessee and ends when possession of the goods transfers back from the lessee to the lessor.

Notice the similarity between this description and that of the performance by vendor in the acquisition process discussion. The activities are identical if viewed from an independent perspective. They are part of the acquisition process if viewed from the customer's perspective and they are part of the revenue process if viewed from the vendor's perspective.

Whether the revenue-generating activity is a sale, delivery, shipment, rental, or service, these economic decrement events in the revenue process do not always happen at discrete points in time. Rather, they are often made up of a series of workflow activities. The fulfillment of an enterprise's commitment is accomplished by the tasks that make up the economic decrement event. For enterprises that sell or rent merchandise that must be shipped to the customer location, these tasks include picking the inventory from the warehouse, packing the inventory into boxes, and shipping the boxes to the customer via a common carrier. The rental event also includes receiving the returned merchandise, inspecting it, and returning it to the warehouse. Economic decrement events for service enterprises generally require active involvement of trained employees who perform the services. The enterprise must identify the requirements of the services to be rendered and select an individual or group of individuals to perform the services. Services may be provided over an extended period of time by a variety of people.

An enterprise may have multiple revenue generating activities. For example, some enterprises ship finished products to customers and also provide services. Some enterprises provide various combinations of products/services for different customers. For example, a computer manufacturer may serve one customer by shipping a new computer and letting the customer install it and handle the conversion. For another customer, the enterprise may deliver the computer, assist with installation, and convert existing applications for processing on the new computer. Yet another customer may request the enterprise to repair a computer that the enterprise had previously sold to the customer.

Several documents may be prepared in conjunction with the activities that comprise the revenue-generating activities: picking lists, packing lists, bills of lading, and sale invoices. A *picking list* is a document that identifies the goods taken out of the warehouse and made available to be shipped (see Exhibit 6-8). Other names for this document include pick ticket, picking ticket, pick list, and picking slip.

Your Source Company			**PICKING LIST 15**	

Your Source Company
Your Source for Everything You Need
123 Main St.
Anytown, USA 12345

PICKING LIST 15
Clerk ID 137

Order Number: 14   **Order Date:** 5/4/2020   **Warehouse:** WH1

Sold To: Needmore Stuff	**Ship To:** Needmore Stuff
86906 Enterprise Dr.	86906 Enterprise Dr.
Anytown, USA 12345	Anytown, USA 12345

CUST NUMBER	**P.O. NUMBER**	**TERMS**	**REP NUMBER**	
E2323	Verbal	n/30	E23	
SHIP VIA	**DATE-TO-SHIP**			
FedEx	5/5/2020			

ITEM ID	**DESCRIPTION**	**QTY ORDERED**	**QTY PICKED**
LIS1	Little Stuff, box of 6	2	2
TIS1	Tiny Stuff, box of 12	10	10

LINE ITEMS	**TOTAL QUANTITY**
2	12

Exhibit 6-8: Picking List

Often a picking list is initially prepared by the sale order clerk and sent to the warehouse to authorize an inventory clerk to "pick" the goods out of the warehouse. The inventory clerk then completes the picking list. Sometimes the pick ticket is actually a copy of the sale order with the cost column replaced by a "quantity picked" column (picking list carbon copies may be designed to accomplish this without having to fill out separate documents; or a mobile computing device could be used by the clerk). The inventory clerk notes the quantities of each item picked, notes any stockout problems, and signs the form to indicate the transfer of custody of those goods to the shipping area.

A *packing list* (sometimes called a packing slip) is a document that identifies the goods that have been shipped to an external business partner (see Exhibit 6-9). Often the packing list is a copy of the picking list on which a shipping clerk fills in the quantities of each item packed (again, this could be on a mobile computing device), notes any discrepancies from the picking list, and signs to indicate the transfer of custody of the goods to a common carrier.

Your Source Company *Your Source for Everything You Need* 123 Main St. Anytown, USA 12345	**PACKING LIST 15** Clerk ID 137 If there are any questions about this shipment, contact our sales department (999) 555-3333

Needmore Stuff	YOUR PURCHASE ORDER NUMBER
86906 Enterprise Dr.	Verbal
Anytown, USA 12345	
Contact: Sarah Gibson	**# Items Ordered: 2**

WAREHOUSE LOCATION	YOUR SOURCE PART #	FILL QUANTITY	ITEM DESCRIPTION	YOUR LINE	YOU ORDERED	WE SHIPPED
WH1	LIS1	2	Little Stuff	1	2	2
WH1	TIS1	10	Tiny Stuff	2	10	10

Exhibit 6-9: Packing List

The bill of lading also indicates transfer of custody of goods from the enterprise to a common carrier; however, it contains different data from the packing list. Rather than documenting details about each type of item shipped and the quantities of those items, the bill of lading documents details about how many boxes made up the shipment and the dimensions and/or weight of those boxes. See the bill of lading in Exhibit 6-10.

Sale invoices (electronic or paper) communicate to customers that the enterprise has fulfilled its commitment and request the customer to remit payment to fulfill its commitment. If the customer already paid for the merchandise, the invoice indicates that no balance is due. Exhibit 6-11 shows a sale invoice. A sale invoice represents an information event; that is, it does not communicate anything new but rather confirms details that were previously known and agreed upon by the buyer and seller. As noted when discussing the acquisition process, invoices may be reengineered out of a system as long as some mechanism is in place to ensure payment results directly from the non-cash economic event. Elimination of vendor invoices is much less concerning for management to consider than is elimination of sale invoices, but keep in mind they both documents represent the same phenomena – simply from two different perspectives.

Creating separate documents for the picking, packing, and shipment of inventory and for customer billing is not a requirement of any enterprise information system, nor is it required that those activities be separated into four tasks. An interface to an enterprise-wide information system may make approved sale order data available on the company intranet and the shipping function may be integrated with the warehousing function. Thus an inventory clerk may view the approved order details, pick, pack, and ship the goods and transmit an electronic invoice to the customer's information system all in one task, with no need to document transfers of custody (i.e., the picking and packing) because custody did not change until the goods were shipped to the customer.

UNIFORM STRAIGHT BILL OF LADING – Domestic	Document No. 15

Your Source Company   Shipper's No. __14789B__
Your Source for Everything You Need   Carrier's No. __8796801__
123 Main St.   Date __5/5/2020__
Anytown, USA 12345

__Federal Express__
(Name of Carrier)

Route: Vehicle Number:

No. shipping units	Kind of Packaging, Description of Articles, Special Marks and Exceptions	Weight (Subject to Correction)	Rate	Charges (for Carrier use only)
1	Box, stuff	15 lbs.	1.14	

REMIT
C.O.D. TO: N/A
ADDRESS

COD
Amt:$ 0.00

C.O.D. FEE: $ N/A
PREPAID ☐
COLLECT ☐

Note – Where the rate is dependent on value, shippers are required to state specifically in writing the agreed or declared value of the property.
  The agreed or declared value of the property is hereby specifically stated by the shipper to be not exceeding.

$ __1,200.00__   per __box__

Subject to Section 7 of the conditions, if this shipment is to be delivered to the consignee without recourse on the consignor, the consignor shall sign the following statement:
  The carrier shall not make delivery of this shipment without payment of freight and all other lawful charges.

_____
(Signature of Consignor)

Total Charges $ 17.10

FREIGHT CHARGES
Check Appropriate Box:
☐ Freight prepaid
☒ Bill to shipper
☐ Collect

Received subject to the classifications and tariffs in effect on the date of the issue of this Bill of Lading, the property described above in apparent good order, except as noted (contents and condition of contents)
Shipping Clerk ID: 137

Exhibit 6-10: Bill of Lading

Data related to sales are illustrated in the tables following Exhibit 6-11, with new sales data shown in red, bold, italic font. Other data would have existed in the tables before the sales were made. Data in the tables reflect fulfillment of both Sale Orders 14 and 15; however just one example of each related document is illustrated in the exhibits.

Your Source Company
Your Source for Everything You Need
123 Main St.
Anytown, USA

Sale Invoice

INVOICE NO: ____12____
DATE: ___5/5/2020___

Sold To:

Needmore Stuff
86906 Enterprise Dr.
Anytown, USA 12345

Ship To:

Needmore Stuff
86906 Enterprise Dr.
Anytown, USA 12345

SALESPERSON	P.O. NUMBER	S.O. NUMBER	DATE SHIPPED	SHIPPED VIA	TERMS
E23	verbal	14	5/5/2020	FedEx	N/30

QUANTITY	STOCK NO.	DESCRIPTION	UNIT PRICE	AMOUNT
2	LIS1	Little Stuff, box of 6	$70.00	$ 140.00
10	TIS1	Tiny Stuff, box of 12	$96.00	$ 960.00
		SUBTOTAL		$1,100.00
		SALES TAX		0
		SHIPPING & HANDLING		0
		TOTAL DUE		$1,100.00

Make all checks payable to: Your Source Company

THANK YOU FOR YOUR BUSINESS!

Exhibit 6-11: Sale Invoice

Fulfillment2 Association (Sale Order – Sale)

Sale Order ID	Sale ID
14	12
15	13

Sale (Economic Decrement) Event

Sale ID	Date	Dollar Total	PickListID	PackListID	BOL#	SalesRepID[FK]	CustomerID[FK]
12	05/05/2020	$1,100.00	15	15	15	E23	C2323
13	05/06/2020	$880.00	16	16	16	E23	C2323

Stockflow Association (Sale – Inventory)

Sale ID	Item ID	Quantity Sold	Actual Unit Price
12	LIS1	2	70.00
12	TIS1	10	96.00
13	MIN1	8	110.00

Customer (External Agent)

Customer ID	Name	Address	Telephone	Credit Rating
C2323	Needmore Stuff	86906 Enterprise Court	555-8989	A+

Inventory Type (Resource Type)

Item ID	Description	UnitOfMeasure	Standard Cost	List Price
BIS1	Big Stuff	Each	$20.00	$50.00
HUS1	Huge Stuff	Each	$30.00	$70.00
LIS1	Little Stuff	Box of 6	$36.00	$72.00
MIN1	Miniature Stuff	Box of 24	$56.00	$110.00
TIS1	Tiny Stuff	Box of 12	$48.00	$96.00
TTP12	Tiara	Each	$10.00	$25.00

Sales Representative (Internal Agent)

Sales Rep ID	Name	Address	Telephone	DateOfBirth
E23	Jimmy Vitale	425 ConAir Drive	555-5678	08/18/1962

Performance by the Customer – Payments to Enterprise (Economic Increment Events)

Payments made by the customer to the enterprise are often referred to as *cash receipts*. These cash receipts are economic increment events that increase the enterprise's cash balance (requiring a stockflow association as shown in Exhibit 6-3). Cash receipts may take the form of checks, currency, or coins – anything that can be deposited into a cash account held either in a bank or on hand in petty cash. Notice that if a customer pays with a credit card, the enterprise has not yet received cash; the cash receipt does not occur until the credit card company pays the enterprise. In the latter case, the cash receipt must be connected to two external agents – the customer, whose accounts receivable balance will be decreased as a result of the cash receipt, and the credit card company, from whom the cash was literally received.

Cash receipts occur at various times in the revenue process. Some cash receipts may occur as orders are placed (i.e., a prepayment); other cash receipts may occur at the point of sale or upon delivery of goods or services; still other cash receipts may occur days or weeks after sales take place (with either one or several individual customer payments). The receipt of cash is a custodial function. Two documents are typically involved in task activities that comprise the cash receipt event: remittance advices and deposit slips. When payment is received, cashiers, accounts receivable clerks, or other company employees verify the payment information is correctly recorded on a remittance advice. A *remittance advice* is a document (usually the portion of a customer invoice or customer statement that says "return this stub with payment") that advises the enterprise the customer is remitting payment. A *customer statement* is a document that summarizes the economic transactions for a customer and reflects the customer's account balance status. Exhibit 6-11 shows a customer statement with a detachable remittance advice.

A *deposit slip* is promptly prepared summarizing all payments for a prescribed time period (usually a day). The deposit slip and payments are deposited into one of the enterprise's bank accounts. Due to the risk of loss, cash should be deposited at least daily, all employers who have access to cash should be bonded, and two employees should verify cash transactions. In addition to having customers mail or bring payments directly to the business, an enterprise can use the lockbox method or electronic funds transfers to collect customer payments. When the lockbox method is used, customers mail their checks to a post office address, and for a fee, a bank will pick up, total, and directly deposit the funds into the company's account. In such situations the post office serves as an external agent. The bank then sends a copy of the deposit information and the remittance advices to the company. Electronic funds transfers reduce human involvement with cash by having customers electronically transfer funds from their bank accounts directly to the company's bank account. The form of payment is incidental to the occurrence of the event.

Enterprise systems should include the ability to record a cash receipt without linking it to a specific customer. For example, suppose someone sends a check, but neglects to send the remittance advice and the name on the check does not correspond to the name of any existing customer account. The enterprise should be able to deposit the funds and tag the transaction as "unapplied cash" (a cash payment that was received but was not posted to a customer's receivable balance). If this occurs, the system should generate a listing of "unapplied cash" transactions and, as with all errors, they should be investigated and corrected as soon as possible. The enterprise system should also allow enterprises to choose how they want to link customer payments to customer accounts. Two methods include specific invoice (or open invoice) and balance forward. As the name implies, the specific invoice method involves matching payments to specific sale invoices. When enterprises use a balance forward approach, they apply payments to a customer's total account balance, rather than any specific invoice. Exhibit 6-12 is an example of the specific invoice method; Remittance Advice 20 is being applied to Invoices 12 and 13.

Data related to cash receipts is shown in the tables below. Some data would already have been in tables prior to new cash receipts being entered. New data is shown in red, bold, italic font.

Duality Association (Sale – Cash Receipt)

SaleID	CashReceiptID	AmountApplied
12	RA20	$960.00
13	RA20	$880.00

Cash Receipt (Economic Increment) Event

CashReceiptID	Date	Dollar Total	CashAccountID[FK]	CustomerID[FK]	CashierID[FK]
RA20	05/19/2020	$1,840.00	Ca123501	C2323	E111

Cash (Resource Type)

CashAccountID	AccountType	Location	DateAccountEstablished
Ca123501	Checking	1st Local Bank	04/01/2020
Ca789125	Savings	1st Local Bank	04/01/2020
Ca351235	Petty	Onsite - Cashier Desk drawer	04/15/2020
Ca351327	Petty	Onsite - CEO Assistant's File Cabinet	04/22/2020

Cashier (Internal Agent)

CashierID	Name	Address	Telephone	DateOfBirth
E111	Missy Witherspoon	1710 Crestwood Dr.	555-9392	05/11/1970

Customer (External Agent)

Customer ID	Name	Address	Telephone	Credit Rating
C2323	Needmore Stuff	86906 Enterprise Court	555-8989	A+

Your Source Company
Your Source for Everything You Need
123 Main St.
Anytown, USA 12345

PAGE
1

STATEMENT

PAGE
1

**REMITTANCE ADVICE # 20 **

Needmore Stuff
86906 Enterprise Court
Anytown, USA 12345

DATE	CUSTOMER NUMBER
5/19/2020	C2323

DATE	CUSTOMER NUMBER
	C2323

← PLEASE DETATCH HERE AND RETURN THIS STUB WITH YOUR REMITTANCE
TO: Your Source Company
123 Main St.
Anytown, USA 12345

TERMS: N/30

INVOICE NUMBER	DATE	CURRENT	PAST 1-30	PAST 31-60	PAST 61-90	PAST 91-120	INVOICE NUMBER	AMOUNT APPLIED
12	5/5/2020	1,100.00					12	$ 960.00
13	5/6/2020	880.00					13	$ 880.00
TOTAL DUE		**TOTAL CURRENT**	**TOTAL PAST 1-30**	**TOTAL PAST 31-60**	**TOTAL PAST 61-90**	**TOTAL PAST 91-120**	**TOTAL DUE**	**TOTAL REMITTED**
$1,980.00		**$1,980.00**	**$0**	**$0**	**$0**	**$0**	**$1,980.00**	**$ 1,840.00**

REVIEWED BY _____ E16 _____

Exhibit 6-12: Customer Statement with Remittance Advice

Post-Sale Activities: Sale Returns & Allowances (Economic Decrement Reversal Events)
The same "unhappy path" activities we discussed previously for the acquisition process also occur in the revenue process. Just as the purchase/sale activities are identical when viewed from an independent perspective, the purchase return and allowance/sale return and allowance activities are also identical when viewed from an independent perspective. If products do not meet quality standards represented in the sale agreement or the product specifications of the customer; or if the customer's needs changed while the goods were in transit, the customer will not want to keep the goods. Three options are available to handle disagreements like these: The enterprise may allow the customer to keep the product and receive an adjustment or allowance in the price, or the enterprise may allow the customer to return the product and decrease the customer's account receivable or issue a cash refund. Alternatively, the enterprise may take a "no returns – all sales final" approach.

A *sale return* is the transfer of title (usually concurrent with transfer of physical custody) of goods from a customer back to the seller. Several documents may be used in workflow tasks that make up a sale return event, including return authorizations, receiving reports, and credit memos. A *sale return authorization* is a document that gives permission for the customer to return merchandise and is typically prepared in response to a customer's request to return goods through the mail or via a common carrier. In retail stores a modified document is used that combines the customer request, and store authorization; it indicates what inventory items were returned. Receiving reports are completed by inventory or receiving clerks when returned goods are received from customers. The receiving report lists the items and the quantities and condition of each item received. If the customer already paid for the merchandise, the enterprise issues a cash refund (either in currency/coin or via check). If the customer did not already pay for the merchandise, or if the enterprise policy only allows returns for credit toward future customer purchases, then the enterprise will reduce the amount the customer owes the enterprise. A *credit memorandum* (also called credit memo) is an internal document used to communicate to the accounting department that the amount owed by the customer should be reduced by the specified amount. A copy may also be sent to the customer to confirm to them that they were given credit. Exhibits 6-13 through 6-15 illustrate a sale return authorization, receiving report, and credit memorandum. Because the receiving report indicates the actual return of physical custody of the goods back to the selling enterprise, the receiving report is the most appropriate document to represent the sale return.

Return Authorization ___1___

Date ___5/12/2020___

Your Source Company
Your Source for Everything You Need
123 Main St.
Anytown, USA 12345

Customer # ___C2323___

Address: ___36069 Enterprise Dr.___
___Anytown, USA 12345___

For clarification contact:
Name ___Sarah Gibson___
Phone ___555-8989___

All returns must be clean, in saleable condition, and shipped prepaid.
Thank you for your cooperation.

Customer Return Request No. ___3___

Date of Request ___5/9/2020___

RETURN CODES:

A OVERSTOCK
B DAMAGED
C DEFECTIVE
D WRONG PRODUCT BILLED & SHIPPED
E CORRECT PRODUCT BILLED BUT WRONG PRODUCT SHIPPED
F OTHER

[ ] Cash Refund – Please

[x] Credit to Account – Please

ITEM ID	DESCRIPTION	RETURN CODE	INVOICE NUMBER	QUANTITY RETURNED	UNIT PRICE	EXTENSION
LIS1	Little stuff	F – too big	12	2	$70.00	$140.00
AUTHORIZED BY _____					TOTAL	$140.00

Exhibit 6-13: Sale Return Authorization

<table>
<tr><td colspan="3">RECEIVING REPORT</td><td>NO. __25__</td></tr>
</table>

Your Source Company
Your Source for Everything You Need
123 Main St.
Anytown, USA 12345

DATE 5/12/2020	PURCH ORD NO./ SALE RETURN AUT H NO.	SR1	
RECEIVED FROM	Needmore Stuff		PREPAID 10
ADDRESS	86906 Enterprise Dr. Anytown, USA 12345		COLLECT
FREIGHT CARRIER **Federal Expre ss**		FREIGHT BILL NO. **FE78901256**	

	QUANTITY	ITEM NO	DESCRIPTION
1.	2	LIS1	Little Stuff
2.			
3.			
4.			
5.			
6.			
7.			
8.			
9.			

REMARKS: CONDITIONS, ETC.
 Perfect condition

RECEIVED BY E111	DELIVERED TO E23

BE SURE TO
MAKE THIS RECORD
ACCURATE AND COMPLETE

Exhibit 6-14: Receiving Report

CREDIT MEMO

Your Source Company   No. ___1___
Your Source for Everything You Need
123 Main St.
Anytown, USA 12345

                                          5/19/2020

CREDIT TO   Needmore Stuff   DATE _____

                                  CUSTOMER
                                  ACCOUNT NO.   C2323

RETURN AUTH NO.	INVOICE NO.	INVOICE DATE	RECEIVING REPORT NO.	
SR1	12	5/5/2020	25	
ITEM NUMBER	DESCRIPTION	QUANTITY	PRICE EACH	AMOUNT
LIS1	Little Stuff	2	70. 00	140. 00
			TOTAL CREDIT	140. 00

You must present this copy when applying to future orders.

APPLY ON FUTURE ORDER ONLY ☐

REFUND BY CHECK ☐

CREDIT ACCOUNT ☒

Prepared by

Elmore Kirk
Credit Manager Emp# __16__

Exhibit 6-15: Credit Memorandum

Data related to sale returns is illustrated in the following tables. Some data would already have been entered into tables prior to sale returns. New data is shown in red, bold, italic font.

Sale Return (Economic Decrement Reversal) Event

Sale ReturnID	Date	Dollar Amount	Receiving ReportNo.	SupervisorID^{FK}	SaleID^{FK}	CustomerID^{FK}	Receiving ClerkID^{FK}
SR1	05/12/2020	$140.00	RR6	E5	S1	C2323	E247

Stockflow3 Association (Sale Return – Inventory)

Sale Return ID	Item ID	Quantity Returned	Actual Unit Price	Condition of Goods	Reason Returned
SR1	LIS1	2	70.00	Perfect	Too big

Receiving Clerk (Internal Agent)

ClerkID	Name	Address	Telephone	DateOfBirth
E247	Kenneth Barki	4312 Monticello Dr.	556-4891	04/14/1955

Customer (External Agent)

Customer ID	Name	Address	Telephone	Credit Rating
C2323	Needmore Stuff	86906 Enterprise Court	555-8989	A+

VIEW INTEGRATION

We initially create REA business process models separately for each business process because each process presents a manageable set of events and related resources and agents; in other words, this is a problem decomposition strategy to deal with the complexity. Furthermore, in some cases this would allow for design teams to divide up and focus on individual business processes. We call the creation of separate models for different parts of a system *view modeling*. To create a database that can serve as the foundation for an integrated enterprise-wide information system; however, we must integrate the separate views to form a comprehensive model. Although we introduced the conversion of a conceptual model to a logical model, followed by the implementation into a physical database as if those steps would be part of each separate business process analysis, in fact, we should integrate the separate conceptual models for each business process view before we convert the conceptual model to the logical and physical levels. We call this step *view integration*.

When you use the full REA ontology as a foundation for designing an enterprise-wide database, the first step is to consider the enterprise in the context of its external business partners and to create an REA value system model. The second step is to consider the resource flows among the business processes within the enterprise and to create an REA value chain model. Identifying the resource flows at the value chain level helps to identify the points of integration of the business processes and, thereby helps to identify points of integration for the conceptual models of those business processes.

View integration may be used in the normal course of database design for a single enterprise; alternatively, it may be used to consolidate separate databases because of a corporate merger, acquisition, or other form of business consolidation. Whether in the original design phase for a single enterprise or in the consolidation of separate databases, view integration involves three basic steps:

1. Identify the common classes in two views.
2. Merge the common classes, resolving any class conflicts and performing a set union of their attributes.
3. Examine each association and resolve any association conflicts.

Conceptual models are integrated based on their common classes. The resources that flow from one business process to another in a value chain are classes that are common to both business processes; sometimes the processes also share common agent or event classes. One potential class conflict is *class name conflict*; this occurs when the same class included in different conceptual models is not labeled identically. Often different people on the same design team separately model the different views and may use synonymous labels. Even the same individual who models different views at different times, may use synonyms (different words that have the same meaning) for the same class based on how employees in the enterprise use terminology. For example, the class representing disbursements of cash may be labeled payment in the financing process and it may be labeled cash disbursement in the payroll process.

Another type of name conflict occurs when conceptually different classes are given the same label. For example, say two enterprises merged operations and need to merge their databases. One enterprise labeled its sale order class (mutual commitment event) as Sales. The other enterprise labeled its sale class (economic decrement event) as Sales. That is a case of a *homonym* – the same word to represent two different things.

Attribute conflict exists if different attributes have been identified as important for describing the same class in various views. The most extreme attribute conflict exists when different attributes are assigned as primary key identifiers for the same classes. Perhaps one designer assigned a unique identifier called Employee ID as the primary key for the Employee class, and another designer used social security number for the same purpose. Other attribute conflicts include overlapping but non-identical sets of attributes assigned to the same class in different cycles. For example, a person who modeled *Inventory Type* in the acquisition process may have included the attributes *item ID, description, unit of measure*, and *standard unit cost* as attributes. A different person who modeled *Inventory Type* in the revenue process may have included *item ID, description, unit of measure*, and *list selling price* as attributes. All necessary attributes of a class that are needed for any business processes in which that class occurs should be included in an enterprise-wide database.

To resolve class name conflicts and attribute conflicts, choose a common label for each common class, choose the most appropriate primary key, and perform a set union of the attributes needed for the different cycles. Once the classes that are shared by the views to be integrated are identified, relabeled, and assigned the complete set of attributes, the associations must be examined and relabeled if necessary to resolve any association conflicts. An *association name conflict* is a discrepancy in the labels on associations - either the same association with different names or different associations with the same name. Each association should have a unique name to avoid any possible confusion in communications about relationships in the database. Association name conflicts are resolved in the same way as class and attribute name conflicts. An *association structure conflict* is a discrepancy in the multiplicities on an association. One example is when the same association has different multiplicities in different views. Another example is when an association's multiplicities need to be changed once views are integrated.

Exhibits 6-16 through 6-20 illustrate the process of view integration. Exhibits 6-16 and 6-17 show separate view models for the revenue and acquisition process of a company that sells custom-made surfboards. Exhibit 6-18 reorganizes the conceptual models to align shared classes. Exhibit 6-19 illustrates the merging of the models with the set union of attributes for each shared class. This exhibit also illustrates that when a class participates in multiple associations and it is inconvenient to place those associations close to each other, a *copy of the class* is portrayed with a diagonal slash across the corner and with no attributes included in the class. A reader who sees a class illustrated in such a manner should look elsewhere within the diagram to see the details of that class. Exhibit 6-20 illustrates the re-labeling of the associations so that each association has a unique name. The result is an integrated conceptual model containing the core events, resources, and agents for a revenue and acquisition process of a small enterprise.

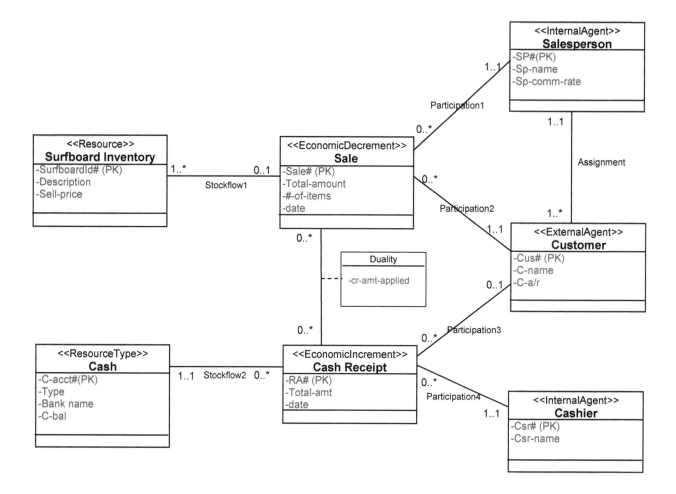

Exhibit 6-16: Revenue Process View Model

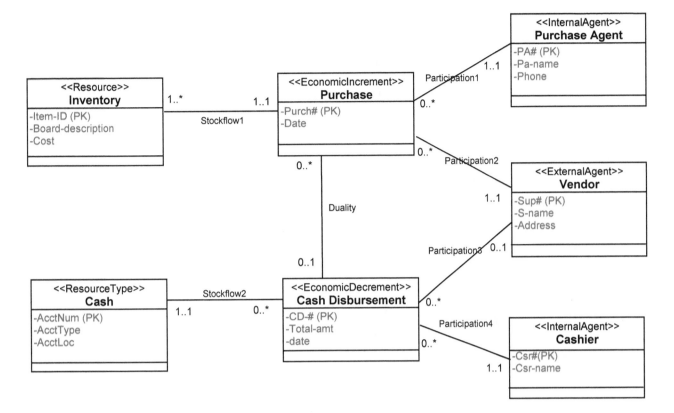

Exhibit 6-17: Acquisition Process View Model

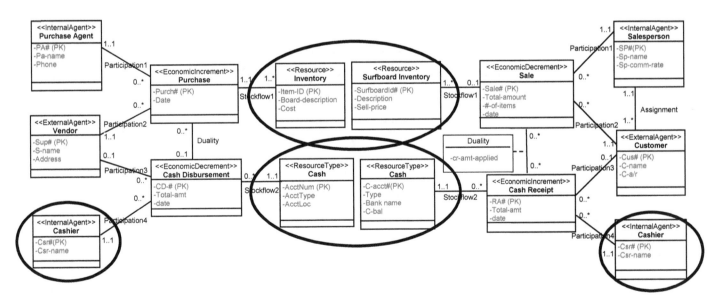

Exhibit 6-18: Identify Common Classes

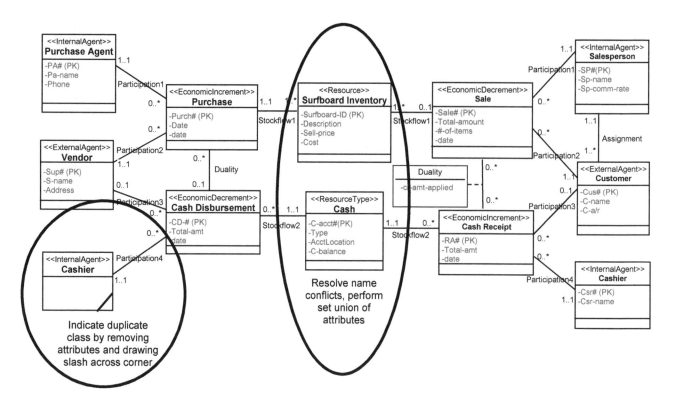

Exhibit 6-19: Merge on Common Classes

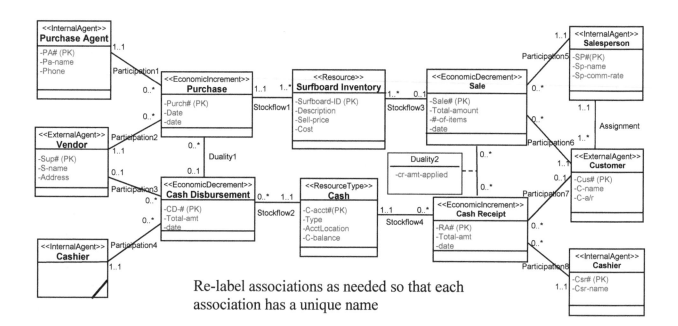

Exhibit 6-20: Resolve Association Name Conflicts

CONCLUDING COMMENTS

This chapter reviewed the workflow activities, documents, REA business process models, and relational database tables commonly used in the revenue process. Whether an enterprise sells hot dogs at a small stand outside a university library or sells custom-made computers via orders placed on its website, whether it sells dental services, insurance, or come combination of products and services, the activities in these processes fit the REA pattern. We also discussed the procedures for integrating business process models from two different processes into a single model, class name, attribute, and association conflicts.

KEY TERMS AND CONCEPTS

Association name conflict
Association structure conflict
Attribute conflict
Class name conflict
Copy of class
Credit memorandum
Customer order
Customer statement
Deposit slip
Homonym
Open sale order
Packing list
Picking list
Remittance advice
Rental (revenue)
Revenue process
Sale invoice
Sale order
Sales call
Sales call report
Sale return
Sale return authorization
Service engagement
View integration
View modeling

REVIEW QUESTIONS

R6-1. What are three different types of revenue processes an enterprise may have?

R6-2. Describe the revenue business process. What main activities make up this process?

R6-3. What non-key attributes might an enterprise store to describe its customer class? List at least six.

R6-4. What association in an enterprise revenue business process allows one to identify open sale orders?

R6-5. What three basic steps are involved in view integration?

MULTIPLE CHOICE QUESTIONS

MC6-1. Each of the following is an instigation event in the revenue cycle, EXCEPT:
   A) Sales call
   B) Advertising campaign
   C) Customer inquiry
   D) Shipment

MC6-2. What type of event is a customer order?
   A) Instigation Event
   B) Mutual Commitment Event
   C) Economic Decrement Event
   D) Economic Increment Event

MC6-3. In the revenue cycle, which of the following association(s) involve an economic decrement event?
          I. Duality   II. Fulfillment   III. Stockflow   IV. Reversal
   A) I and II only
   B) I, II, and III
   C) II and III only
   D) I, II, III, and IV

MC6-4. What kind of event is a sale return?
   A) Economic increment reversal event
   B) Economic decrement reversal event
   C) Instigation event
   D) Economic increment event

MC6-5. What relationship in the sales/collection process represents the association between a commitment event and the resource the event commits to increase or decrease?
   A) Proposition relationship
   B) Participation relationship
   C) Reservation relationship
   D) Fulfillment relationship

MC6-6. Which classes would be paired in a revenue process participation association?
   A) Customer and salesperson
   B) Sale and inventory
   C) Sale and sale return
   D) Service engagement and employee

MC6-7. The creation of separate models for different portions of a system is called:
   A) View integration
   B) Logical level implementation
   C) Decomposition
   D) View modeling

MC6-8. What conflict exists if different attributes have been identified as important for describing the same entity in various views?
A) Attribute conflict
B) Name conflict
C) View conflict
D) Integration conflict

MC6-9. The name conflict that results from the use of different names to describe the same entity or process involves the use of:
A) Homonyms
B) Synonyms
C) Antonyms
D) Amalgams

MC6-10. Which of the following is typically an integration point between the revenue and acquisition business processes for a wholesale distributor?
A) Salesperson
B) Supplier
C) Inventory
D) Sale Order

CHAPTER 7

Modeling Conversion Business Processes with REA

LEARNING OBJECTIVES

The primary objective of this chapter is to create detailed REA models for conversion business processes. We discuss activities that are common to many enterprise conversion processes, and illustrate various types of business documents with which companies capture data about conversion tasks and events. After studying this chapter, you should be able to

1. Describe the typical tasks, commitment events, and economic events found in most enterprises' conversion business processes
2. Explain similarities and differences between different types of conversion processes
3. Identify the documents commonly used to capture data about the various types of tasks and events in conversion business processes
4. Create a REA business process model for a company's conversion business process

CONVERSION BUSINESS PROCESSES

The conversion process includes the business events associated with converting raw inputs such as materials, labor, machinery, and other assets into finished outputs. Often the conversion process involves the manufacture or production of finished goods, so some call it the manufacturing process or the production process. As you analyze and model a business process, you must clearly understand its purpose and objectives. You will better understand this process if you can base your understanding on some personal experience. Have you ever been involved in a conversion process? Perhaps you do not have experience in the manufacturing process of a corporation or other business entity; however, most people have participated in the production of some type of finished product. Have you ever cooked, made crafts, created something on a computer, written a story, or made lemonade? If so, then you have some real life experience with conversion process activities. In this chapter, we use the example of baking cookies to demonstrate many of the concepts.[29] If you have never baked cookies before, we recommend you find a recipe and bake a batch of your favorite cookies before reading the rest of this chapter.

You may think that the conversion processes for most firms will be different because the products they produce are so different. Indeed, the specific workflow tasks vary greatly among enterprises. However, the REA business process level pattern underlies all conversion processes. Before detailing the business process level conversion pattern, let's review how the conversion process fits into typical enterprise value systems and value chains.

---

[29] Thank you to Julie Smith David of the American Accounting Association for the idea of using cookie baking to illustrate conversion process concepts.

CONVERSION BUSINESS PROCESSES IN ENTERPRISE VALUE SYSTEMS

As discussed in chapter 2 and highlighted in Exhibit 7-1, conversion is an internal business process that typically does not provide a point of contact with any external agents. Although an enterprise may need information from external agents or may need to provide information to external agents regarding the conversion process, keep in mind that the value system level depicts *resource* flows, *not* information flows. Typically, any resource flows between the enterprise and the external agents are part of either the acquisition or the revenue processes that interface with the conversion process.

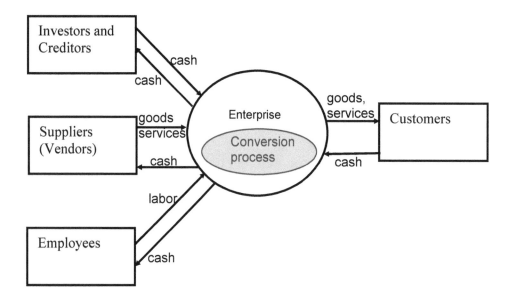

Exhibit 7-1: Conversion Process in an Enterprise Value System

CONVERSION BUSINESS PROCESSES IN ENTERPRISE VALUE CHAINS

Consider also the value chains we discussed in chapter 2. Exhibit 7-2 illustrates the typical value chain for manufacturers. Materials and machinery are made available to the conversion process as a result of the acquisition process. Labor is made available to the conversion process as a result of the payroll process. The conversion process turns those inputs (materials, machinery, and labor) into finished products, which are made available to the revenue process. In order to convert the labor, materials, equipment, and overhead items such as utilities and supplies into finished goods, the conversion process must include economic events that use up those inputs (labor operation uses up labor, raw material issuance uses up materials, and machine operation uses equipment) and an economic event that produces the finished products (i.e., the *production run*).

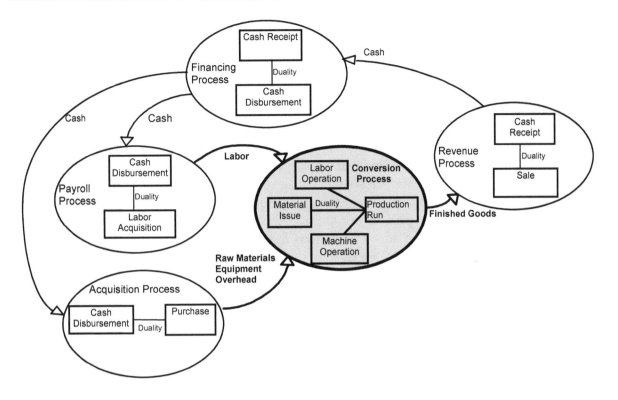

Exhibit 7-2: Sample Value Chain for a Manufacturer

CONVERSION BUSINESS PROCESS LEVEL REA MODELS

Conversion processes are broadly categorized into two types: batch processes and continuous processes. Batch processes involve the production of an established number of units of a product, or they may involve the completion of a job such as a car repair, a consulting engagement, or the printing of 300 copies of a customized wedding invitation. Continuous processes produce a homogeneous product somewhat continuously. Examples include the production of breakfast cereal, petroleum products, flour, and beer.

The main difference between batch processes and continuous processes is that for batch processes, natural starting and ending points exist for assigning costs to the production run, whereas for continuous processes, artificial starting and ending points must be created for cost assignment purposes. Usually these start and end points are arbitrarily chosen boundaries of a time period. The time period may span minutes, hours, days, weeks, or even months, depending on the nature of the enterprise's conversion process. Presumably the time periods should be chosen such that they are long enough to include the production of at least one identifiable resource. For example, the time period used for the economic increment event for an agricultural crop may be designated as the growing season, whereas an hour may be deemed an appropriate time period for a production run of breakfast cereal. Once the production run event is determined as either a batch, job, or time period, cost assignment is relatively straightforward. To assign manufacturing costs to units produced, simply divide the manufacturing costs (accumulated either by job, batch, or time period) by the number of units produced in that job, batch, or time period.

We begin our detailed discussion of the conversion process by reviewing some of its more common events in the context of cookie baking. While it is true that a wide variety of workflow activities may be included in a conversion process, and as a result the task level modeling will vary accordingly, a pattern exists in which the activities can be categorized for data storage and for data exchange purposes for most, if not all, enterprises.

Recall that the REA pattern captures data to answer the *who, what, where, when,* and *why* questions regarding a business process. Answers to the *when* and *where* questions are typically stored as attributes, unless the location is also a resource, e.g., a specific warehouse or machine. Answers to the *who, what,* and *why* questions are provided by the associations captured in the core REA pattern as illustrated for the conversion process in Exhibit 7-3. The participation associations identify the *who* for each event, and the stockflow associations indicate the *what* for each event. The duality association reveals *why* the enterprise engages in the economic events of the process.

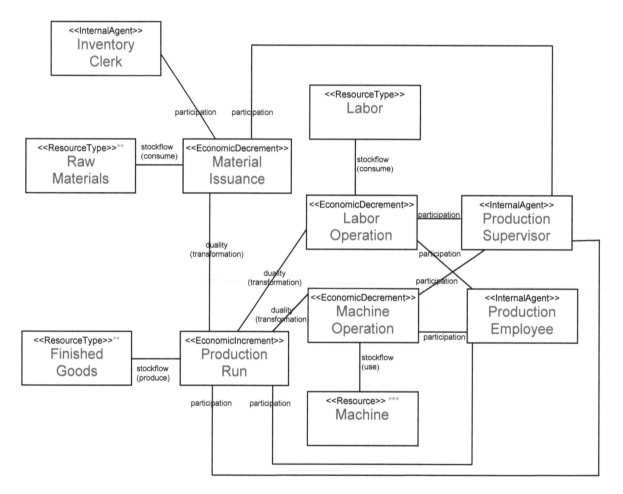

** If each physical instance of raw material or of finished good is uniquely identified, then the stereotype would be Resource rather than Resource Type.
*** If Machines are not uniquely identified, the stereotype would be Resource Type rather than Resource.

Exhibit 7-3: Conversion Business Process Core REA Pattern

Core REA Conversion Process Pattern

The core REA pattern for the conversion process consists of the same components as the core pattern for the acquisition and payroll processes. Recall that the core REA pattern for those processes contains economic increment events paired by duality associations with economic decrement events. Each economic event is associated with the resource or resource type that the event increases or decreases, and each economic event is associated with at least one initiator agent (who may be internal or external) and at least one responsible agent (who is typically internal). In the conversion process instead of only two paired economic exchange events, typically four economic events are tracked in detail. Three of these events are economic decrement events that represent the using up of the machinery, labor, and raw materials. The fourth event is the economic increment event – the production run or batch or job that produces the finished goods. Although the duality association is in essence a 4-way relationship between four events, for ease of implementation, we represent it as three binary relationships, each of which has the inherent causality of duality. The company gives up the labor in the labor operation because it expects to end up with the finished good from the production run. Likewise, the company gives up materials in the material issuance and gives up use of machinery in the machine operation because it expects to end up with the finished good from the production run.

The duality association in the conversion process is slightly different from the duality associations in the acquisition and payroll processes. In the latter processes, duality usually is a *transfer duality association*. That is, the enterprise trades one or more resources for one or more other resources. Usually one of the resources is cash and the other resource is a non-cash resource such as raw materials or finished goods inventory. In the conversion process, the duality association is a *transformation duality association*. That is, the enterprise transforms raw input resources into a finished good resource. It is important to note that there is no requirement that only two economic events be paired in a duality association in the revenue and acquisition processes; in fact, both of those processes also include labor operations that use up the labor resource. Activities in those processes may also use up fixed assets, equipment, utilities, etc. However, the use of labor and fixed assets are typically not tracked at the same level of detail in those processes as they are in the conversion process, because they are usually immaterial compared to the primary economic decrement events and because the necessary measurement tools and techniques are usually cost-prohibitive. In the conversion process, the labor and machine operation costs often exceed the costs of the raw materials and it is cost beneficial and in fact crucial to measure them.

Stockflow associations in the conversion process may be more specifically described as use, consume, or produce. A *use stockflow association* indicates a resource is partially used up by an economic decrement event. For example, equipment is only partially used up by a machine operation – that is, the equipment still exists once the machine operation is complete, and simply has some wear and tear. A *consume stockflow association* indicates a resource is completely used up by an economic decrement. For example, raw materials are completely subsumed into the finished good; they no longer exist separate from that finished good. Produce stockflows indicate a resource is created by an economic increment event. For example, a production run produces finished goods.

Expanded REA Conversion Process Pattern

As with the acquisition and payroll processes, the core REA pattern has been extended to include commitment events and additional associations such as reservation, reciprocal, fulfillment, linkage, and custody. A *linkage association* connects two resource types to depict the fact that one is composed of the other. Exhibit 7-4 illustrates a partial extended conversion process pattern for the business process level of the REA enterprise ontology. Agents are omitted from this illustration to improve readability of the diagram; however, the complete model should attach at least one internal agent to each event (commitments and economic events) in the diagram. Usually two internal agents are connected to each event – one who authorizes the event (such as a supervisor) and one who executes the event (such as a production employee). A *production employee* is a worker who participates in the manufacture of finished goods.

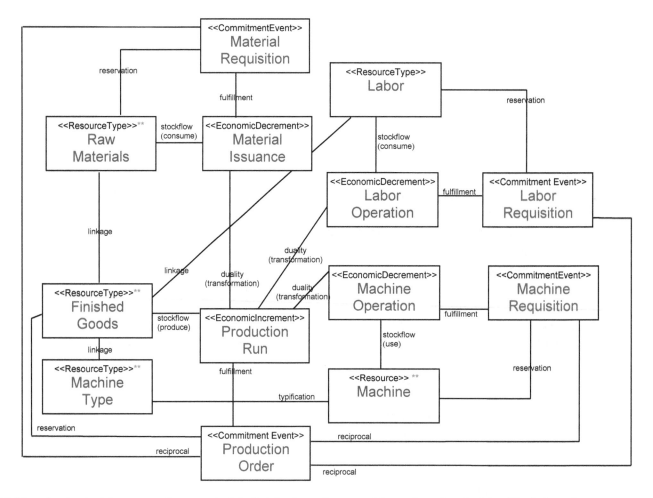

** If each physical instance of raw material, finished good, or machinery is uniquely identified, then the stereotype should be Resource; if not uniquely identified, the stereotype should be Resource Type

Exhibit 7-4: Expanded REA Conversion Business Process Model

As in the acquisition, revenue, and payroll processes, the specific labels on the resources, events, and agents will differ depending on the nature of the enterprise's operations. Exhibit 7-5 illustrates labels that an enterprise whose conversion process involves cookie baking could use.

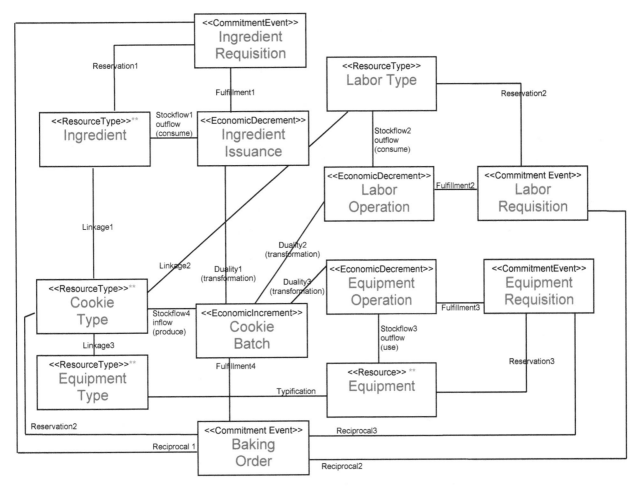

** If each physical instance of raw material, finished good, or machinery is uniquely identified, then the stereotype should be Resource; if not uniquely identified, the stereotype should be Resource Type

Exhibit 7-5: Cookie Baking Example Conversion Business Process Level Model

We next discuss the events in the expanded conversion process model, including typical documents used by many companies. You may notice that instead of beginning this discussion with a need identification (instigation) event, we begin the workflow discussion with reciprocal commitment events. The reason is that the need identification step often takes place outside the conversion process and then triggers activities in the conversion process. A common means by which a need to produce goods is identified is that a customer order for a product is received in the revenue process. If fulfillment of that order will deplete the inventory of that product below an established quantity, that will trigger the conversion process activities. Specifically, it will trigger a production order – a commitment to produce finished goods. That production order then generates commitments to use various inputs in the production process – thus it yields equipment requisitions, labor requisitions, and material requisitions. If any of the requisitioned resources are unavailable/out of stock, those requisitions may then trigger activities in the acquisition and payroll processes, in essence serving as need identifications for those processes.

Production Order (Commitment Event)

In the conversion process the commitments that make up a mutual commitment event are typically not bundled together into a single event as they are in the revenue and acquisition processes. Therefore, in the conversion process, three events are commitments to three economic decrement events and another event is a commitment to an economic increment event. In theory, a commitment event precedes each economic event. The *production order event* represents the enterprise's commitment to engage in a production run (i.e., the production run fulfills the production order and this association is illustrated in Exhibit 7-4). That is, the production order is the commitment to an economic increment event that will increase the finished goods resource. The production order also has three reciprocal associations with the labor requisition, material requisition, and machine requisition events (see Exhibit 7-4). Production order information is typically captured on a *production order document* or application interface. Exhibit 7-6 illustrates a production order document.

Production Order No. _____								
Date _____		Product Number _____		Description _____				
Approved by: _____		Deliver to: _____		Begin Date: _____			Complete by: _____	
WorkCenter	Operation	Quantity Completed	Labor Type Description	Start Date	Time	End Date	Time	

Exhibit 7-6: Production Order

The following relational tables illustrate some of the data attributes that may be captured with respect to the production order (baking order) event and its associations with finished cookies, baking employees, baking supervisors, and with the cookie batch event. The production order table stores the event data that pertains to each production order, such as the order date, the requested completion date, and who authorized it (supervisor). The finished cookies table stores the resource data that describes the finished goods the production order is committing to increase. The reservation table stores the data needed to identify how many of each finished cookie type is going to be produced when the production order is fulfilled. We can see in this example that baking order BO1 committed the company to produce 40 frosted sugar cookies and called for Larry, Moe, and Curly to be the baking employees and for Ricky to be the supervisor for the job. We can also see that baking order BO2 committed the company to produce 48 snickerdoodles and called for Fred and Ethel to be the baking employees and for Lucy to be the supervisor for the job. Some data would already have been entered into tables prior to any new baking order. New data is shown in red, bold, italic font.

BakingOrder (Commitment)

BakingOrderID	BakingOrder Date	Scheduled BeginDate	Requested CompletionDate	SupervisorID^FK	CookieTypeID^FK	Quantity Ordered
BO1	*07/14/2020*	*07/15/2020*	*07/15/2020*	*S2*	*FSCS*	*40*
BO2	*07/14/2020*	*07/15/2020*	*07/15/2020*	*S1*	*SN*	*48*

CookieType (Resource Type)

CookieID	Description	UnitsPerPackage	ListPrice
CC	Chocolate chip plain	12	$2.99
CCP	Chocolate chip with pecans	12	$2.99
FSCS	Frosted sugar cookies with candy sprinkles	10	$3.59
M	Molasses	12	$3.29
OR	Oatmeal raisin	12	$2.99
PB	Peanut butter	12	$2.99
SC	Sugar cookies plain	12	$2.99
SN	Snickerdoodles	12	$3.59

BakingSupervisor (Internal Agent)

SupervisorID	SupervisorName	SupervisorPhone
S1	Lucy	1-1234
S2	Ricky	1-4321
S3	Louie	1-5432

ParticipationBakingEmployeeScheduledForBakingOrder

EmployeeID	BakingOrderID
PE1	*BO2*
PE2	*BO2*
PE3	*BO1*
PE4	*BO1*
PE5	*BO1*

BakingEmployee (Internal Agent)

EmployeeID	EmployeeName	EmployeePhone	SupervisorID[FK]
PE1	Fred	1-6789	S2
PE2	Ethel	1-9876	S2
PE3	Larry	1-7698	S1
PE4	Moe	1-6798	S1
PE5	Curly	1-8796	S1

Material Requisition (Commitment Event)

A material requisition is a commitment event that is reciprocal to the production order. Whereas the production order commits to producing finished goods, in order to produce those goods, the company must use up some materials. The material requisition is thus the commitment to using up the materials necessary to fulfill the production order commitment (the association is a reservation between Material Requisition and Raw Materials in Exhibit 7-4).

Because the word requisition may bring to your mind a purchase requisition (an instigation event in the acquisition process), we must point out that a material requisition is not the same thing as a purchase requisition. A *material requisition* (sometimes called a raw material requisition) is a commitment event whereby the inventory clerk or warehouse supervisor commits to the production supervisor to transfer materials from the materials warehouse to the production floor. A *production supervisor* is an internal agent who authorizes events in the conversion process. A material requisition assumes the raw materials are available within the enterprise, and is reserving them for use. In contrast, warehouse personnel initiate purchase requisitions to indicate the need to acquire the materials or other items from an external source. Thus, if a material requisition is initiated for which insufficient materials are on-hand in the warehouse, this will likely trigger a purchase requisition and thereby instigate events in the acquisition process. However, the raw material requisition event occurs within the conversion process and the purchase requisition event occurs within the acquisition process.

Data captured regarding raw material requisitions typically includes the date/time of requisition and information about the resources and agents involved in the event. Each requisition is assigned a unique identifier. Requisition data is typically captured on a document or data entry screen that is called a material requisition. Exhibit 7-7 illustrates a material requisition form.

Material Requisition No. _____				
Date _____		Production Order Number _____		
Approved by _____		Deliver to _____		
Material ID	Description	Quantity	Unit Cost	Total Cost

Exhibit 7-7: Material Requisition

The following relational tables illustrate some of the data attributes that may be captured with respect to the material (ingredient) requisition event and its associations with ingredients, inventory clerks, baking supervisors, and with the production order event. The ingredient requisition table stores the event data that pertain to each ingredient requisition, such as requisition date, requested completion date, and the authorizing supervisor. The baking supervisor table stores details about the supervisors. The participation table stores information about which inventory clerks participated in which ingredient requisitions; whereas the inventory clerks table stores details about the inventory clerks. The ingredients table stores the resource data that describes the ingredients available for reservation by the ingredient requisition. The reservation association table depicts which ingredients the ingredient requisition commits to decrease.

We can see in this example that supervisor Ricky authorized ingredient requisition 1002 to reserve the ingredients needed for baking order P01 (for 40 frosted sugar cookies), and that inventory clerk Ted participated in the requisition event. We can also see that supervisor Lucy authorized ingredient requisition 1003 to reserve the ingredients needed for baking order BO2 (for 48 snickerdoodles), and that inventory clerk Alice participated in the requisition event. Some data would have already been entered into tables prior to any new material requisition. New data resulting from ingredient requisitions is shown in red, bold, italic font.

IngredientRequisition (Commitment)

RequisitionID	RequisitionDate	SupervisorID[FK]	BakingOrderID[FK]
1002	*07/14/2020*	*S2*	*BO1*
1003	*07/14/2020*	*S1*	*BO2*

BakingOrder (Commitment)

BakingOrderID	BakingOrder Date	Scheduled BeginDate	Requested CompletionDate	SupervisorID^{FK}	CookieTypeID^{FK}	Quantity Ordered
BO1	07/14/2020	07/15/2020	07/15/2020	S2	FSCS	40
BO2	07/14/2020	07/15/2020	07/15/2020	S1	SN	48

BakingSupervisor (Internal Agent)

SupervisorID	SupervisorName	SupervisorPhone
S1	Lucy	1-1234
S2	Ricky	1-4321
S3	Louie	1-5432

ParticipationInventoryClerkIngredientRequisition

InventoryClerkID	IngredientRequisitionID
IC1	1002
IC2	1003

InventoryClerk (Internal Agent)

InventoryClerkID	ClerkName	ClerkPhone
IC1	Ted	1-5678
IC2	Alice	1-8765

ReservationIngredientRequisitionIngredient

IngredientID	IngredientRequisitionID	QuantityReserved	Unit of Measure
CN	1003	0.5	cup
CS	1002	1	cup
EG	1002	4	each
EG	1003	4	each
FL	1002	8	cups
FL	1003	6	cups
ILFS	1002	4	each
ILSN	1003	4	each
PK	1002	4	each
PK	1003	4	each
SH	1002	2.67	cups
SH	1003	1.75	cups
SL	1002	2	teaspoons
SL	1003	1.75	teaspoons
VN	1002	4	teaspoons
VN	1003	2.75	teaspoons
WS	1002	6	cups
WS	1003	4.66	cups

Ingredient (Resource Type)

IngredientID	Description	UnitOfMeasure	StandardCostPerUnitOfMeasure
BS	Brown sugar	50 lb bag	$9.47
BU	Butter	10 lb box	$3.98
CM	Chocolate morsels	10 lb bag	$19.49
CN	Cinnamon	16 oz tin	$3.29
CS	Candy sprinkles	1 lb tin	$3.18
EG	Eggs, large AA grade	2 dozen carton	$1.29
FL	Flour, white sifted	100 lb bag	$20.00
ILFS	Ingredient label - frosted sugar	each	$0.01
ILSN	Ingredient label - snickerdoodle	each	$0.01
PB	Peanut butter	10 lb jar	$8.37
PE	Pecans	2 lb bag	$5.32
PK	Plastic container	each	$0.12
SH	Shortening	10 lb can	$12.10
SL	Salt, iodized	5 lb bag	$1.00
VN	Vanilla, pure	1 liter bottle	$20.00
WS	White sugar	50 lb bag	$10.00

Labor Requisition (Commitment Event)

Just as the material requisition is a commitment event that is reciprocal with the production order, so also is the *labor requisition commitment event*. In order to fulfill the production order, labor must be used. A labor requisition in the conversion process is a commitment to use some labor, and in essence involves the production supervisor scheduling employees to perform labor operations for a production run. The association is a reservation between Labor Requisition and Labor Type in Exhibit 7-4. A document to represent such a commitment event can take many forms and may not even exist on paper. Many companies use the labor schedule made in the payroll process or the production order itself to document this commitment. The data captured for a labor requisition event should include the production order to which the labor requisition applies, the requesting supervisor, the types of employees needed to perform the labor operations, and the quantity of hours of each type of labor needed. The requisition may also specify the location at which the labor will be performed and the supervisor to which scheduled employees should report to begin the labor operations.

The following relational database tables illustrate some of the data attributes that may be captured for the labor requisition event and related resources, events, and agents. We can see that supervisor Louie scheduled labor requisition LR1, specifying the need for two employees for one hour to fill baking order BO2. LR1 specified eight different labor types to be done by the two employees. We can also see that labor requisition LR2 specified the need for three employees for one hour to fill baking order BO1, with those employees performing eleven different labor types.

LaborRequisition (Commitment)

LaborReqID	DateOfRequisition	Number Employees Needed	Hours Needed	SchedulingSupervisor[FK]	Baking Order ID[FK]
LR1	07/14/2020	2	1.00	S3	BO2
LR2	07/14/2020	3	1.00	S3	BO1

BakingSupervisor (Internal Agent)

SupervisorID	SupervisorName	SupervisorPhone
S1	Lucy	1-1234
S2	Ricky	1-4321
S3	Louie	1-5432

BakingOrder (Commitment)

BakingOrderID	BakingOrder Date	Scheduled BeginDate	Requested CompletionDate	SupervisorID^{FK}	CookieTypeID^{FK}	Quantity Ordered
BO1	07/14/2020	07/15/2020	07/15/2020	S2	FSCS	40
BO2	07/14/2020	07/15/2020	07/15/2020	S1	SN	48

ReservationLaborRequisitionLaborType

LaborReqID	LaborTypeID
LR1	L1
LR1	L2
LR1	L3
LR1	L7
LR1	L8
LR1	L9
LR1	L10
LR1	L13
LR2	L1
LR2	L2
LR2	L3
LR2	L6
LR2	L7
LR2	L8
LR2	L9
LR2	L10
LR2	L11
LR2	L12
LR2	L13

Equipment Requisition (Commitment Event)

Similarly, an *equipment requisition* (also called a *machine requisition*) is a commitment event that is reciprocal with the production order, whereby the production supervisor schedules various fixed assets of the company to be used in operations for a production run (the association is a reservation between Machine Requisition and Machine in Exhibit 7-4). A document to represent such a commitment event can take many forms and may not even exist on paper. Many companies simply create an equipment schedule that serves as summarized documentation of all equipment requisitions for a time period. The information captured for a machine/equipment requisition event should include the production order to which the requisition applies, the requesting supervisor, what types of machines/equipment are needed, and for what quantity of hours. The requisition may also specify the supervisor who will be in charge of the machine operations that fulfill the machine/equipment requisition.

The following relational database tables illustrate some of the data attributes that may be captured for the equipment requisition event and related resources, events, and agents. We can see that supervisor Louie scheduled equipment requisition ER1, specifying the need for an oven, cookie sheet, heavy duty mixer, and measuring device set, to be used on 7/15/20 for baking order BO2. We can further see that equipment operations EO15 and EO16 fulfilled ER1 on 7/15/2020 from 6:30-6:45am and from 6:40-7:00am, respectively. Similarly, we can see that equipment requisition ER2 specified the need for an oven, a heavy duty mixer, a measuring device set, a cookie sheet, and frosting utensils. We can further see that equipment operations EO12, EO13, and EO14 fulfilled ER2 on 7/15/2020 from 6:30-6:45am, from 6:51-7:03am, and from 7:08 to 7:12am, respectively. New data resulting from equipment requisitions are shown in red, bold, italic font.

EquipmentRequisition (Commitment)

EquipReqID	EReqDate	DateEquipmentNeeded	BakingOrderID^{FK}	SchedulingSupervisor^{FK}
ER1	*07/13/2020*	*07/15/2020*	*BO2*	*S3*
ER2	*07/13/2020*	*07/15/2020*	*BO1*	*S3*

BakingOrder (Commitment)

BakingOrderID	BakingOrder Date	Scheduled BeginDate	Requested CompletionDate	SupervisorID^{FK}	CookieTypeID^{FK}	Quantity Ordered
BO1	07/14/2020	07/15/2020	07/15/2020	S2	FSCS	40
BO2	07/14/2020	07/15/2020	07/15/2020	S1	SN	48

EquipmentOperation (Economic Decrement Event)

Equipment OperationID	StartTime	EndTime	EmployeeID^{FK}	SupervisorID^{FK}	EquipReqID^{FK}
EO12	07/15/2020 6:30:00 AM	07/15/2020 6:45:00 AM	PE5	S2	ER2
EO13	07/15/2020 6:51:00 AM	07/15/2020 7:03:00 AM	PE5	S2	ER2
EO14	07/15/2020 7:08:00 AM	07/15/2020 7:12:00 AM	PE3	S2	ER2
EO15	07/15/2020 6:30:00 AM	07/15/2020 6:45:00 AM	PE2	S1	ER1
EO16	07/15/2020 6:40:00 AM	07/15/2020 7:00:00 AM	PE2	S1	ER1

ReservationEquipReqEquipment

EquipReqID	EquipmentID
ER1	*EQ2*
ER1	*EQ6*
ER1	*EQ8*
ER1	*EQ9*
ER2	*EQ1*
ER2	*EQ3*
ER2	*EQ4*
ER2	*EQ5*
ER2	*EQ7*

Equipment (Resource)

EquipmentID	EquipmentTypeName	Acquisition Date	Cost	Estimated LifeYears	Estimated SalvageValue
EQ1	Oven	01/03/2020	$400.00	10	$50.00
EQ2	Oven	04/02/2019	$500.00	3	$100.00
EQ3	Heavy duty mixer	03/17/2019	$150.00	3	$0.00
EQ4	Measuring device set	02/16/2019	$80.00	5	$10.00
EQ5	Cookie sheet	02/18/2019	$10.00	3	$0.00
EQ6	Cookie sheet	01/03/2020	$15.00	3	$0.00
EQ7	Frosting utensils	01/03/2020	$10.00	5	$0.00
EQ8	Heavy duty mixer	02/15/2020	$170.00	3	$0.00
EQ9	Measuring device set	02/15/2020	$75.00	5	$10.00

Production Run, Job, or Batch (Economic Increment Event)

The production run, job, or batch is the event that achieves the overall objective of the conversion process – i.e., the production of a finished good resource (the association is a stockflow between Production Run and Finished Goods in Exhibit 7-4). Because this event increases a resource, it is an economic increment event. Some of the data typically captured regarding a production run event include an assigned identifier for the event, the date/time the event started, and the date/time the event ended. Data are also recorded as to what resources and agents are involved, and the production run location (e.g., assembly line #6).

Documentation of the production run often consists of filling in additional details on the production order that committed to the production run. For example, a company that uses a production order such as that pictured in Exhibit 7-6 would fill in the header information – i.e., the top three rows of data upon making the commitment to produce a finished good. As the production run occurs, a supervisor would enter data into the columns to complete the bottom section of the form.

The following relational database tables illustrate some of the data attributes that may be captured for the production run (cookie batch) event and related resources, events, and agents. We can see that supervisor Ricky and baking employees Larry, Mo, and Curly began cookie batch WJ1 on 7/15/2020 at 6:30am and finished the same day at 7:15am. They produced 40 frosted sugar cookies with candy sprinkles, exactly the scheduled quantity. We can also see that supervisor Lucy and baking employees Fred and Ethel began cookie batch WJ2 on 7/15/2020 at 6:30am and finished the same day at 7:37am. They produced 48 snickerdoodles, which was the same as the quantity scheduled. New data entered as a result of cookie batches is shown in red, bold, italic font.

CookieBatch (Economic Increment Event)

BatchID	StartTime	CompletionTime	Scheduled Quantity	Actual Quantity	Supervisor ID[FK]	Baking OrderID[FK]
WJ1	7/15/2020 6:30:00 AM	7/15/2020 7:15:00 AM	40	40	S2	BO1
WJ2	7/15/2020 6:30:00 AM	7/15/2020 7:37:00 AM	48	48	S1	BO2

StockflowCookieBatch-CookieType

BatchID	FinishedCookieTypeID
WJ1	FSCS
WJ2	SN

CookieType (Resource Type)

CookieID	Description	UnitsPerPackage	ListPrice
CC	Chocolate chip plain	12	$2.99
CCP	Chocolate chip with pecans	12	$2.99
FSCS	Frosted sugar cookies with candy sprinkles	10	$3.59
M	Molasses	12	$3.29
OR	Oatmeal raisin	12	$2.99
PB	Peanut butter	12	$2.99
SC	Sugar cookies plain	12	$2.99
SN	Snickerdoodles	12	$3.59

BakingSupervisor (Internal Agent)

SupervisorID	SupervisorName	SupervisorPhone
S1	Lucy	1-1234
S2	Ricky	1-4321

Baking Employee (Internal Agent)

EmployeeID	EmployeeName	EmployeePhone	SupervisorID[FK]
PE1	Fred	1-6789	S2
PE2	Ethel	1-9876	S2
PE3	Larry	1-7698	S1
PE4	Moe	1-6798	S1
PE5	Curly	1-8796	S1

ParticipationCookieBatchBakingEmployee

BatchID	EmployeeID
WJ1	PE3
WJ1	PE4
WJ1	PE5
WJ2	PE1
WJ2	PE2

Material Issuance (Economic Decrement Event)

As the production run occurs, various inputs to the process are used or consumed. Materials typically are consumed during a production run, job, or batch. Those raw materials are usually transformed into finished goods and lose their own identity and nature in the process. Thus the *material issuance* is an economic decrement event, i.e., an event that decreases the materials resource (the association is a stockflow between Material Issuance and Raw Materials in Exhibit 7-4). Data typically captured regarding material issuance events are an assigned identifier for the issuance, the date/time of the issuance, and the location of the issuance. Data are also recorded as to what resources and agents are involved and the underlying production order that the production run fulfills.

The following relational tables illustrate some of the data attributes that may be captured with respect to the ingredient issuance event and its associations with ingredients, inventory clerks, supervisors, and with the cookie batch event. The duality table identifies which ingredient issuances apply to which cookie batches. The ingredient issuance table stores the event data that pertains to each issuance, such as when and where it occurred, who authorized it (supervisor) and who executed it (inventory clerk). In the example shown, the participation associations between baking supervisor and ingredient issuance and between inventory clerk and ingredient issuance are not represented by separate tables, but are traceable via posted foreign keys of supervisor id and employee id in the ingredient issuance table.

The ingredients table stores the resource data that describes the types of ingredients available for use in the production process. As with the finished cookies, the ingredients are not individually identified but instead are identified at the type or category level (i.e., each separate kind of ingredient is assigned a different identification code). The stockflow table stores the data needed to identify which type of ingredient (and how much of each) was actually issued in each ingredient issuance event.

In this example, we can see that Ted and Alice issued several different ingredients to Ricky and to Lucy for the frosted sugar cookie and snickerdoodle cookie batches on July 15, 2020 between 6:20 and 6:30 a.m. Each of the ingredients was issued to the workcenter where the initial work involving the ingredients was to take place. New data for ingredient issuances is shown in red, bold, italic font.

DualityCookieBatch-IngredientIssuance

BatchID	IngredientIssuanceID
WJ1	RMI4238
WJ1	RMI4239
WJ1	RMI4240
WJ2	RMI4241
WJ2	RMI4242
WJ1	RMI4243
WJ2	RMI4244
WJ1	RMI4245
WJ2	RMI4246

StockflowIssuanceofIngredient

IngredientID	IngredientIssuanceID	QuantityIssued	UnitOfMeasure
WS	RMI4238	5	cups
FL	RMI4238	7	cups
EG	RMI4239	4	each
SH	RMI4239	2	cups
VN	RMI4239	3	teaspoons
SL	RMI4238	2	teaspoons
CS	RMI4240	1	cup
WS	RMI4241	6	cups
FL	RMI4241	8	cups
EG	RMI4242	4	each
SH	RMI4242	3	cups
VN	RMI4242	4	teaspoons
SL	RMI4241	2	teaspoons
CN	RMI4241	1	cup
PK	RMI4243	4	each
PK	RMI4244	4	each
ILFS	RMI4245	4	each
ILSN	RMI4246	4	each

IngredientIssuance (Economic Decrement Event)

Ingredient IssuanceID	IssuanceTime	Location	InventoryClerkID[FK]	SupervisorID[FK]	Ingredient RequisitionID[FK]
RMI4238	7/15/2020 6:20:00 AM	WorkcenterA	IC2	S2	1002
RMI4239	7/15/2020 6:22:00 AM	WorkcenterB	IC2	S2	1002
RMI4240	7/15/2020 6:24:00 AM	WorkcenterC	IC2	S2	1002
RMI4241	7/15/2020 6:28:00 AM	WorkcenterD	IC1	S1	1003
RMI4242	7/15/2020 6:26:00 AM	WorkcenterE	IC1	S1	1003
RMI4243	7/15/2020 6:29:00 AM	WorkcenterC	IC2	S2	1002
RMI4244	7/15/2020 6:29:30 AM	WorkcenterE	IC1	S1	1003
RMI4245	7/15/2020 6:29:00 AM	WorkcenterC	IC2	S2	1002
RMI4246	7/15/2020 6:29:30 AM	WorkcenterE	IC1	S1	1003

Ingredient (Resource Type)

IngredientID	Description	UnitOfMeasure	StandardCostPerUnitOfMeasure
WS	White sugar	50 lb bag	$10.00
EG	Eggs, large AA grade	2 dozen carton	$1.29
FL	Flour, white sifted	100 lb bag	$20.00
VN	Vanilla, pure	1 liter bottle	$20.00
SL	Salt, iodized	5 lb bag	$1.00
PB	Peanut butter	10 lb jar	$8.37
CN	Cinnamon	16 oz tin	$3.29
CM	Chocolate morsels	10 lb bag	$19.49
PE	Pecans	2 lb bag	$5.32
SH	Shortening	10 lb can	$12.10
CS	Candy sprinkles	1 lb tin	$3.18
BU	Butter	10 lb box	$3.98
BS	Brown sugar	50 lb bag	$9.47
PK	Plastic container	each	$0.12
ILFS	Ingredient label - frosted sugar	each	$0.01
ILSN	Ingredient label - snickerdoodle	each	$0.01

InventoryClerk (Internal Agent)

InventoryClerkID	ClerkName	ClerkPhone
IC1	Ted	1-5678
IC2	Alice	1-8765

BakingSupervisor (Internal Agent)

SupervisorID	SupervisorName	SupervisorPhone
S1	Lucy	1-1234
S2	Ricky	1-4321
S3	Louie	1-5432

Labor Operation (Economic Decrement Event)

The *labor operation event* is an economic decrement event that represents the performance of a specific activity in the conversion process by a production employee, thereby using up the resource of that person's labor. Many people often are confused as to the difference between labor (also called labor type) and labor operation. Labor Type is a resource-type class that represents a list of the types of labor that can be performed during labor operations. Labor operations are the actual instances that use up (consume) the available labor (the association is a stockflow between Labor Operation and Labor Type in Exhibit 7-4). Data typically captured to describe labor types are the description and standard or budget information such as the standard hourly cost of each type of labor. Data typically captured to describe labor operations are the starting and ending date/time of the labor operation events and the total elapsed time of each labor operation.

Keep in mind that data regarding labor types and labor operations will only be captured and stored if measurement techniques exist and are cost-effective, and this may vary across processes. In the acquisition and revenue processes, labor operations and labor types are typically not measured and recorded. In the conversion process, labor operations are often (but not always) measured and recorded.

When they are measured and recorded, labor operations are usually documented on *job time tickets*, documents that detail start and stop times and descriptions of labor operations on a specific date by a specific employee. Some enterprises call these documents time tracks instead of job time tickets. Either way, the document number typically serves as an identifier for the labor operation event. Exhibit 7-8 illustrates a job time ticket.

Job Time Ticket No._____					
Employee ID _____		Name _____		Date _____	
Start time	Stop time	Total time	Rate	Total Amount	Job Number
Approved by _____ Department Supervisor					

Exhibit 7-8: Job Time Ticket

The following relational tables illustrate some of the data attributes that may be captured with respect to the labor operations event and its associations with labor, baking employees, baking supervisors, and with the cookie batch event. The duality table identifies which labor operations apply to which cookie batches. The labor operations table stores the event data that pertains to each labor operation, such as when it began and ended, who authorized it (supervisor) and who executed it (employee). The labor table stores the resource data that describes the types of labor available for use in the production process. The stockflow table stores the data needed to identify which type of labor (and how much of each) was actually used in each labor operation event.

The participation association between baking supervisor and labor operation is not represented with a separate table, but is traceable via a posted foreign key of supervisor id in the labor operations table. Similarly, the participation association between baking employee and labor operations is represented with the employee id posted as a foreign key in the labor operations table.

In this example, we can see that to make the frosted sugar cookies, Larry took 10 minutes to mix the dry ingredients while Moe took 12 minutes to mix the moist ingredients. Curly took 5 minutes to combine the dry and moist ingredients. Larry took 5 minutes to form the cookies into dough and put them onto a cookie sheet. Curly took 1 minute to put the cookie sheet into the oven and set the timer. Twelve minutes later, Curly took the cookies out of the oven. Four and a half minutes later Larry took 4 minutes to frost the cookies, then Moe took 1 minute to add candy sprinkles and Curly took 2 minutes to package the final cookies.

Meanwhile, to bake the snickerdoodles, Fred took 10 minutes to mix the dry ingredients while Ethel took 10 minutes to mix the moist ingredients. Ethel then took 5 minutes to combine the dry and moist ingredients and then she took 2 minutes to form the dough and put the cookies onto the cookie sheet. Fred took 1 minute to put the cookies into the oven and set the timer. Twelve minutes later Fred took 30 seconds to take the cookies out of the oven. Nearly 35 minutes later, Ethel took 2 minutes to package the finished cookies. Notice that one of the things the tables don't show us is the reason for significant gaps in time – for example, why did they wait 35 minutes to package the cookies? It turns out that Fred thought Ethel had packaged them already, whereas Ethel thought that was Fred's responsibility. Lucy was in a comic mood and had been keeping them so well entertained they didn't realize they weren't finished until Ricky came in to gloat to Lucy that his crew had already finished their cookies even though they had the harder cookies to make (harder in that they involved more labor operations). New data reflecting the labor operations is shown in red, bold, italic font.

LaborOperation (Economic Decrement Event)

LaborOperationID	StartTime	EndTime	EmployeeID^{FK}	SupervisorID^{FK}	LaborReqID^{FK}
LO21	7/15/2020 6:30:00 AM	7/15/2020 6:40:00 AM	PE3	S2	LR2
LO22	7/15/2020 6:30:00 AM	7/15/2020 6:40:00 AM	PE4	S2	LR2
LO23	7/15/2020 6:40:00 AM	7/15/2020 6:45:00 AM	PE5	S2	LR2
LO24	7/15/2020 6:45:00 AM	7/15/2020 6:50:00 AM	PE3	S2	LR2
LO25	7/15/2020 6:50:00 AM	7/15/2020 6:51:00 AM	PE5	S2	LR2
LO26	7/15/2020 7:03:00 AM	7/15/2020 7:03:30 AM	PE5	S2	LR2
LO27	7/15/2020 7:08:00 AM	7/15/2020 7:12:00 AM	PE3	S2	LR2
LO28	7/15/2020 7:12:00 AM	7/15/2020 7:13:00 AM	PE4	S2	LR2
LO29	7/15/2020 7:13:00 AM	7/15/2020 7:15:00 AM	PE5	S2	LR2
LO30	7/15/2020 6:30:00 AM	7/15/2020 6:40:00 AM	PE1	S1	LR1
LO31	7/15/2020 6:30:00 AM	7/15/2020 6:40:00 AM	PE2	S1	LR1
LO32	7/15/2020 6:40:00 AM	7/15/2020 6:45:00 AM	PE2	S1	LR1
LO33	7/15/2020 6:45:00 AM	7/15/2020 6:47:00 AM	PE2	S1	LR1
LO34	7/15/2020 6:47:00 AM	7/15/2020 6:48:00 AM	PE1	S1	LR1
LO35	7/15/2020 7:00:00 AM	7/15/2020 7:00:30 AM	PE1	S1	LR1
LO36	7/15/2020 7:35:00 AM	7/15/2020 7:37:00 AM	PE2	S1	LR1

BakingEmployee (Internal Agent)

EmployeeID	EmployeeName	EmployeePhone	SupervisorID^{FK}
PE1	Fred	1-6789	S2
PE2	Ethel	1-9876	S2
PE3	Larry	1-7698	S1
PE4	Moe	1-6798	S1
PE5	Curly	1-8796	S1

DualityCookieBatch-LaborOperation

BatchID	LaborOperationID
WJ1	LO21
WJ1	LO22
WJ1	LO23
WJ1	LO24
WJ1	LO25
WJ1	LO26
WJ1	LO28
WJ1	LO29
WJ2	LO30
WJ2	LO33
WJ2	LO34
WJ2	LO35
WJ2	LO36

LaborType (Resource Type)

LaborTypeID	Description
L1	Mix dry ingredients
L2	Mix moist ingredients
L3	Combine dry and moist ingredients
L4	Add morsels to mixed dough
L5	Add nuts to mixed dough
L6	Form dough into cookies
L7	Put cookies onto cookie sheet
L8	Put cookie sheet into oven
L9	Set cookie timer
L10	Take cookie sheet out of oven
L11	Frost cookies
L12	Sprinkle cookies
L13	Package cookies

StockflowLaborTypeinLaborOperation

LaborTypeID	LaborOperationID
L1	LO21
L2	LO22
L3	LO23
L6	LO24
L7	LO24
L8	LO25
L9	LO25
L10	LO26
L11	LO27
L12	LO28
L13	LO29
L1	LO30
L2	LO31
L3	LO32
L7	LO33
L8	LO34
L9	LO34
L10	LO35
L13	LO36

Machine or Equipment Operation (Economic Decrement Event)

Along with using up (consuming) materials and labor, conversion processes also often use up machinery and equipment. An economic decrement event, a *machine operation* captures the consumption of a portion of the machine's useful life (the association is a stockflow between Machine Operation and Machine in Exhibit 7-4). The machine or equipment operation event is slightly different in nature from the material issuance and labor operation economic decrement events, in that the machinery typically still exists in its original form (although with some added wear and tear) after the machine operation occurs. In contrast, the material issuance and labor operation events result in the materials and available labor being completely used up – they no longer exist in their original form but have been transformed into finished goods. Nevertheless, part of the machine or equipment item's useful life has been used up, and represents a resource decrease that in some cases is cost-beneficial to measure and record; at a minimum, depreciation expense will be calculated according to chosen accounting conventions. Although machine operations could be tracked using a separate document similar to a job time ticket, usually machine operations are tracked on the production order's bottom section.

In our cookie baking example it makes sense to label this event as equipment operation as that more closely describes the types of machines used in baking cookies: ovens, mixers, utensils, pans, and measuring devices. Notice that we are using the term machine loosely – to represent any fixed asset used in production; some enterprises may prefer to only track consumption of fixed assets that exceed a certain cost value. The following relational tables illustrate some of the data attributes that may be captured with respect to the equipment operation event and its associations with equipment, baking employees, baking supervisors, and with the cookie batch event. The duality table identifies which equipment operations apply to which cookie batches. The equipment operation table stores the event data that pertains to each equipment operation, such as when it began and ended, who authorized it (supervisor) and who executed it (employee). The equipment table stores the resource data that describes the equipment available for use in the production process. Each piece of equipment or machine is specifically identified with a unique id; that is, this is a token-level class rather than a type-level class. Specific identification of fixed assets allows the tracking of cost allocation in accordance with generally accepted accounting principles. The stockflow table stores the data needed to identify which equipment was actually used in each equipment operation event. The equipment does not get completely used up in the equipment operation; rather, it is partially consumed. Thus the stockflow association between equipment and an equipment operation event is called a use stockflow association. The same piece of equipment can thus be used in multiple equipment operations.

The participation associations between baking supervisor and equipment operation and between baking employee and equipment operation are not represented with separate tables, but are traceable via posted foreign keys of supervisor id and employee id in the equipment operations table.

In this example, we can see that the sugar cookie production run (batch) required three equipment operations. The first was a measure and mix operation that partially consumed a heavy duty mixer and measuring device set. The second was a baking operation that partially consumed a cookie sheet and an oven. The third was a finishing operation that partially consumed frosting utensils. The snickerdoodle batch required only two equipment operations. The first was a measure and mix operation that partially consumed a heavy duty mixer and a measuring device set. The second was a baking operation that partially consumed a cookie sheet and an oven. New data entered for equipment operations is shown in red, bold, italic font.

DualityCookieBatchEquipmentOperation

BatchID	EquipOperationID
WJ1	EO12
WJ1	EO13
WJ1	EO14
WJ2	EO15
WJ2	EO16

EquipmentOperation (Economic Decrement Event)

EquipmentOperationID	StartTime	EndTime	EmployeeID[FK]	SupervisorID[FK]	EquipReqID[FK]
EO12	7/15/2020 6:30:00 AM	7/15/2020 6:45:00 AM	PE5	S2	ER2
EO13	7/15/2020 6:51:00 AM	7/15/2020 7:03:00 AM	PE5	S2	ER2
EO14	7/15/2020 7:08:00 AM	7/15/2020 7:12:00 AM	PE3	S2	ER2
EO15	7/15/2020 6:30:00 AM	7/15/2020 6:45:00 AM	PE2	S1	ER1
EO16	7/15/2020 6:40:00 AM	7/15/2020 7:00:00 AM	PE2	S1	ER1

Equipment (Resource)

EquipmentID	EquipmentTypeName[FK]	Acquisition Date	Cost	Estimated LifeYears	Estimated SalvageValue
EQ1	Oven	01/03/2020	$400.00	10	$50.00
EQ2	Oven	04/02/2019	$500.00	3	$100.00
EQ3	Heavy duty mixer	03/17/2019	$150.00	3	$0.00
EQ4	Measuring device set	02/16/2019	$80.00	5	$10.00
EQ5	Cookie sheet	02/18/2019	$10.00	3	$0.00
EQ6	Cookie sheet	01/03/2020	$15.00	3	$0.00
EQ7	Frosting utensils	01/03/2020	$10.00	5	$0.00
EQ8	Heavy duty mixer	02/15/2020	$170.00	3	$0.00
EQ9	Measuring device set	02/15/2020	$75.00	5	$10.00

StockflowEquipmentinEquipmentOperation

EquipmentID	EquipOperationID
EQ1	EO13
EQ2	EO16
EQ3	EO12
EQ4	EO12
EQ5	EO13
EQ6	EO16
EQ7	EO14
EQ8	EO15
EQ9	EO15

Bill of Materials

A *bill of materials* (BOM) is a document that lists the names and quantities of all the materials needed to produce a specified size batch of finished product. It is similar to the ingredient list portion of a recipe. The BOM is represented by the linkage association between Raw Material and Finished Good in Exhibit 7-4. An example bill of materials is illustrated in Exhibit 7-9.

Bill of Materials _____		
Product ID _____ Standard Batch Quantity_____		
Product Description_____		
Material ID	Material Description	Quantity Needed

Exhibit 7-9: Bill of Materials

Operations List

An *operations list* is a document that identifies the labor types and standard processing and setup times for each of those labor types needed to produce a specified size batch of finished product. It is similar to the instruction portion of a recipe, but with more detail. Exhibit 7-10 illustrates an example operations list document.

Operations List _____				
Product ID _____ Standard Batch Quantity _____				
Description _____				
			Standard Time/Unit	
WorkCenter	Labor Type	Description	Setup	Processing

Exhibit 7-10: Operations List

The following relational tables illustrate some of the attributes often stored with respect to the linkage associations between raw materials and finished goods, between labor and finished goods, and between equipment and finished goods. Such information provides standards against which actual commitments and production may be compared for variance analyses and performance evaluations. The bills of materials and operations lists are typically used in the planning stages of the conversion process for made-to-stock finished goods. These documents are used to help in preparing the production order document that represents the commitment to the economic increment event. New data reflecting linkages is shown in red, bold, italic font.

LinkageIngredientsNeededForFinishedCookies

CookieTypeID	IngredientID	QuantityNeeded	UnitOfMeasure	CookieBatchSize
FSCS	CS	0.25	Cup	10
FSCS	EG	1	Each	10
FSCS	FL	1.75	Cups	10
FSCS	ILFS	1	Each	10
FSCS	PK	1	Each	10
FSCS	SH	0.5	Cup	10
FSCS	SL	0.5	Teaspoon	10
FSCS	VN	0.75	Teaspoon	10
FSCS	WS	1	Cup	10
SN	CN	3	Teaspoons	12
SN	EG	1	Each	12
SN	FL	1.5	Cups	12
SN	ILSN	1	Each	12
SN	PK	1	Each	12
SN	SH	0.67	Cup	12
SN	SL	0.5	Teaspoon	12
SN	VN	1	Teaspoon	12
SN	WS	1.5	Cups	12

Ingredient (Resource Type)

IngredientID	Description	UnitOfMeasure	StandardCostPerUnitOfMeasure
BS	Brown sugar	50 lb bag	$9.47
BU	Butter	10 lb box	$3.98
CM	Chocolate morsels	10 lb bag	$19.49
CN	Cinnamon	16 oz tin	$3.29
CS	Candy sprinkles	1 lb tin	$3.18
EG	Eggs, large AA grade	2 dozen carton	$1.29
FL	Flour, white sifted	100 lb bag	$20.00
ILFS	Ingredient label - frosted sugar	each	$0.01
ILSN	Ingredient label - snickerdoodle	each	$0.01
PB	Peanut butter	10 lb jar	$8.37
PE	Pecans	2 lb bag	$5.32
PK	Plastic container	each	$0.12
SH	Shortening	10 lb can	$12.10
SL	Salt, iodized	5 lb bag	$1.00
VN	Vanilla, pure	1 liter bottle	$20.00
WS	White sugar	50 lb bag	$10.00

CookieType (Resource Type)

CookieID	Description	UnitsPerPackage	ListPrice
CC	Chocolate chip plain	12	$2.99
CCP	Chocolate chip with pecans	12	$2.99
FSCS	Frosted sugar cookies with candy sprinkles	10	$3.59
M	Molasses	12	$3.29
OR	Oatmeal raisin	12	$2.99
PB	Peanut butter	12	$2.99
SC	Sugar cookies plain	12	$2.99
SN	Snickerdoodles	12	$3.59

LaborType (Resource Type)

LaborTypeID	Description
L1	Mix dry ingredients
L2	Mix moist ingredients
L3	Combine dry and moist ingredients
L4	Add morsels to mixed dough
L5	Add nuts to mixed dough
L6	Form dough into cookies
L7	Put cookies onto cookie sheet
L8	Put cookie sheet into oven
L9	Set cookie timer
L10	Take cookie sheet out of oven
L11	Frost cookies
L12	Sprinkle cookies
L13	Package cookies

LinkageLaborNeededForFinishedCookieType

CookieTypeID	LaborTypeID
FSCS	L1
FSCS	L2
FSCS	L3
FSCS	L6
FSCS	L7
FSCS	L8
FSCS	L9
FSCS	L10
FSCS	L11
FSCS	L12
FSCS	L13
SN	L1
SN	L2
SN	L3
SN	L7
SN	L8
SN	L9
SN	L10
SN	L13

LinkageEquipTypeCookieType

EquipmentTypeName	CookieType	Quantity Needed	Unit of Measure
Cookie sheet	FSCS	1	Each
Cookie sheet	SN	1	Each
Frosting utensils	FSCS	1	Set
Heavy duty mixer	FSCS	1	Each
Heavy duty mixer	SN	1	Each
Measuring device set	FSCS	1	Set
Measuring device set	SN	1	Set
Oven	FSCS	1	Each
Oven	SN	1	Each

EquipmentType (Resource Type)

EquipmentTypeName	Standard Cost	Average Expected Life
Cookie sheet	$12.00	3
Frosting utensils	$10.00	4
Heavy duty mixer	$160.00	3
Measuring device set	$78.00	5
Oven	$450.00	7

By examining the LinkageIngredientsNeededForFinishedCookies association table in our example, we can see the quantity and unit of measure for each ingredient needed to make a batch of 10 frosted sugar cookies and the quantity and unit of measure for each ingredient needed to make a batch of 12 snickerdoodles. Note that this table is incomplete, as it should also include the ingredients, quantities, and units of measure needed to make batches of the other six cookie types produced by this company. That would have required approximately 60 additional rows of data that would not fit well on a page; therefore, we chose to omit those data and leave the table incomplete. The batch size used for the materials linkage association is an arbitrary choice depending on the needs of the enterprise. Some enterprises will attempt to list the quantity needed to produce a single unit of the finished product. Such an approach would require us to divide each of the quantities in the Linkage table by 10 for the frosted sugar cookies and by 12 for the snickerdoodles. Keeping the measurement at such a fine level of detail may not always be practical or useful. How do you divide an egg by 10 or 12?

By examining the LaborType, CookieType, and LinkageLaborNeededForFinishedCookieType tables in our example, we can see the eleven different types of labor require to make a batch of 10 frosted sugar cookies with candy sprinkles and the eight different types of labor required to make a batch of 12 snickerdoodles. We can also see that the tables in our example do not indicate a specific quantity of labor for each finished cookie type. However, such an attribute could be added as a standard to which actual labor use could be compared. If a quantity (e.g. number of minutes) of each labor type is indicated, a batch size would also need to be included similar to that shown for the linkage1 association table. In this example it was determined that although you could double the quantity of materials needed for a batch size that was twice as big and get a valid measure, you couldn't double the number of minutes for each labor type for a double-sized batch and get a meaningful number, therefore the attributes were not captured. In other words, if it takes 4 minutes to mix the dry ingredients (1 cup of white sugar, 1 3/4 cups of flour, and a ½ teaspoon of salt) to make a batch of 10 cookies, it will likely not take 16 minutes to mix the dry ingredients (4 cups of white flour, 7 cups of flour, and 2 teaspoons of salt) to make a batch of 40 cookies. Note that this table is also incomplete, as it should also include rows for the types of labor needed to make the other six types of cookies in the CookieType table; these were omitted to save space.

Finally, by examining the CookieType, EquipmentType, and LinkageEquipTypeCookieType tables, we can see the five different types of equipment needed to make a batch of frosted sugar cookies with candy sprinkles and the four different types of equipment needed to make a batch of snickerdoodles. The linkage association table includes the quantity and unit of measure for equipment needed for a single batch. To produce multiple batches, you may need to multiply some of these, but not others. Once again, we have included an incomplete table with just enough data to give you the idea of what such a table would encompass. This table would need to specify all types of equipment needed for each of the other six cookie types this company can produce.

To help you make sense of the three kinds of linkage associations, you can think of them as parts of a recipe. Recipes in a cookbook typically contain a list of ingredients along with the quantities needed to make an identified quantity of a food dish. Recipes also include a list of instructions with steps (i.e. labor types) and equipment types needed to prepare the food dish.

CONCLUDING COMMENTS

This chapter reviewed the workflow activities, documents, models, and relational database tables commonly used in the conversion process and demonstrated the expanded REA business process model as it applies to conversion. Whether enterprises produce cereal, video games, furniture, or some other type of resource, the REA pattern for the necessary components of their conversion processes will be similar to each other. Designing an information system that supports the complexities and intricacies of a conversion process requires a careful analysis and a detailed understanding of the objectives of the process. By using the REA ontology to design an integrated enterprise information system, organizations can derive financial statement information and other information needed to support a variety of programs (including activity-based costing, quality management, just-in-time inventories, and material requirements planning).

KEY TERMS AND CONCEPTS
Bill of materials
Consume stockflow association
Conversion process
Equipment requisition
Job time ticket
Labor operation event
Labor requisition commitment event
Linkage association
Machine operation
Machine requisition
Material issuance
Material requisition
Operations list
Production employee
Production order (document)
Production order (event)
Production run
Production supervisor
Reciprocal association
Transfer duality association
Transformation duality association
Use stockflow association

REVIEW QUESTIONS
R7-1. What is the primary objective of the conversion process?

R7-2. How does the conversion process relate to the financing, acquisition, payroll, and revenue processes?

R7-3. What is the difference between a material requisition and a purchase requisition?

R7-4. What resources and agents connect to each of these events in the conversion process?
    a. Material requisition (commitment to economic decrement)
    b. Material issuance (economic decrement)
    c. Labor operation (economic decrement)
    d. Machine operation (economic decrement)
    e. Production order (commitment to economic increment)
    f. Production run (economic increment)

R7-5. What documents in a conversion process capture the information found in the linkage associations?

MULTIPLE CHOICE QUESTIONS

MC7-1. Which kind of association in a conversion process reveals *why* the enterprise uses up materials, labor, and equipment?
A) Duality
B) Stockflow
C) Fulfillment
D) Reservation

MC7-2. In the REA ontology, a relationship in which an enterprise trades one or more resources for one or more different resources is called a(n) _____ duality association.
A) Transformation
B) Trade
C) Exchange
D) Transfer

MC7-3. Which is NOT an economic decrement event in the conversion cycle?
A) Production run
B) Material issuance
C) Labor operation
D) Machine operation

MC7-4. Which statement is FALSE regarding labor operations in a conversion process?
A) Labor Operations are the actual using up of labor
B) Labor Type is a resource-type class that represents the types of labor that can be performed in the labor operations
C) When they are measured and recorded, labor operations are usually documented on move tickets, which serve as identifiers for the labor operations events
D) Labor operation are economic decrement events

MC7-5. What association connects commitment events to each other?
A) Linkage
B) Reciprocal
C) Custody
E) Reservation

MC7-6. What resource does the payroll process typically provide to the conversion process?
A) Cash
B) Labor
C) Machinery
D) Raw materials

MC7-7. Which business process typically includes an event called Material Issuance?
          A) Acquisition
          B) Payroll
          C) Conversion
          D) Revenue

MC7-8. On which class or association should one focus to answer the question of when the most recent material requisition occurred?
          A) Material Requisition event
          B) Material Issuance event
          C) Fulfillment relationship between Material Requisition and Material Issuance
          D) Stockflow relationship between Material Issuance and Raw Materials

MC7-9. A conversion process custody association most likely connects which two classes?
          A) Cash and Cashier
          B) Materials Inventory and Inventory Clerk
          C) Materials Inventory and Production Run
          D) Inventory Clerk and Material Issuance

MC7-10. Where are conversion process activities illustrated in an enterprise value system model?
          A) In the resource flows between the enterprise and its investors and creditors
          B) In the resource flows between the enterprise and its suppliers
          C) In the resource flows between the enterprise and its employees
          D) They aren't – conversion is an internal process within the enterprise

CHAPTER 8

Modeling Workflow

LEARNING OBJECTIVES

The objective of this chapter is to introduce two types of diagrammatic representations for the REA "task level" (also known as "workflow level"): flowcharts and business process model and notation (BPMN). The events and activities (detailed in Chapters 4 through 7) for the various business processes provide context with which we can demonstrate the application of flowcharting or BPMN constructs to enterprise activities. After studying this chapter, you should be able to:

1. Explain the difference between a REA business process level model and a task level (workflow) model

2. Explain why some workflow activities should not be represented as base objects in a REA business process model

3. Describe tools used in practice for modeling workflow

4. Create an enterprise workflow model in BPMN format from a narrative description of the relevant activities

5. Create an enterprise workflow model in flowchart format from a narrative description of the relevant activities

6. Create a narrative to describe the activities represented in an enterprise workflow model in BPMN format

7. Create a narrative to describe the activities represented in an enterprise workflow model in flowchart format

8. Ask relevant questions to clarify how information flows from point of data capture to financial statements when a workflow model or narrative is insufficient

TASK LEVEL MODELING

We define *tasks* as the individual steps involved in accomplishing the essential events in an enterprise. The events themselves are in fact also tasks; however, tasks are not by definition events for two reasons. First, in some instances, there are tasks for which measurements are either not feasible or not cost effective; these tasks will not be represented as events. Second, there are certain tasks that we could re-engineer away without substantively changing the nature of the business; these tasks will not be represented as events. Events are foundational elements in an REA accounting system; tasks that are subject to elimination, or significant change, should not serve as foundational elements.

The purpose of REA task level models is very different from the purpose of REA business process level models. REA business process models form the blueprint of an enterprise-wide database. REA task models document the sequential flow of data through an enterprise (sometimes called *workflow*). Tasks are included in the workflow for an enterprise, even when they are not represented as base objects in the enterprise database. Data captured as a result of tasks may be included in the tables as attributes (which also means that these attributes could be added to classes and associations in the REA business process level model), and data needed to accomplish tasks may be retrieved from the database via queries. Sometimes tasks are important enough to represent as classes and associations which are incremental additions to the REA business process level model.

Pattern discovery at the task level is not as straightforward as at the value system, value chain, and business process levels; as we move from higher to lower levels of abstraction, there is more opportunity for inter-enterprise variation. Although best practices specify how enterprises may accomplish various activities, workflow may include steps or activities that could be substantially altered or even eliminated without substantively changing the nature of the enterprise; this is one objective of business process reengineering.

Tasks may also occur in various sequences for different enterprises (or for different areas within an enterprise) and task level models must portray the sequencing. UML class diagrams are about data and relationships between data. The UML class diagrams for the REA business process level do not necessarily represent a sequencing of events (and there is nothing in the class diagram notation to indicate an overall sequence of any classes; that is not the intent of class diagrams). A sale may come before a cash receipt, or vice versa; the order does not matter for establishing the architecture of the enterprise system's core database as long as one can be traced to the other. Of course, there is some overlap, so that a sales call event can result in a sale order, the sale order can result in a sale, and the sale can result in a cash receipt; the associations between the classes would allow for the data to be related throughout this event sequence. For the task level, sequencing is important, as enterprises need to document details about the procedural aspects of the business activities and corresponding data entry into, and information retrieval from, the enterprise system.

Many different types of documentation may be used to represent tasks, including flowcharts, data flow diagrams, process models, and narrative descriptions. This chapter is limited to flowcharts and business process models. Prior to discussing these two task level models, we discuss the important distinction between the REA business process level and the task level.

COMPARISON OF REA'S BUSINESS PROCESS AND TASK LEVELS

The primary purpose of creating business process level REA models is to design the enterprise database. The primary purpose of creating task level models is to document the specific workflow procedures in such a way that any user can see what physical processes are used. Such documentation is especially useful for identifying enterprise risks and internal control strengths and weaknesses, as discussed further in Chapter 9. An example of REA business process level modeling as compared to task level modeling may help you to understand the difference.

Jayvision, Inc. is an enterprise that creates video games for children. At the REA business process level, Jayvision's UML class diagram for its acquisition/payment process is shown in Exhibit 8-1 (for simplicity, attributes and multiplicities are not illustrated).

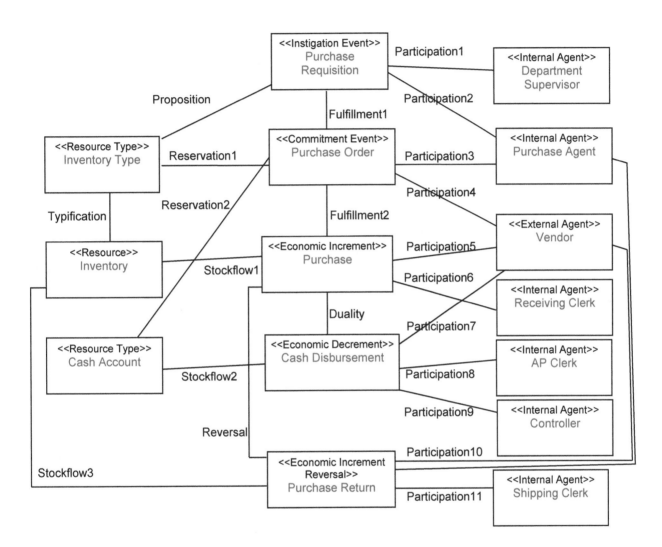

Exhibit 8-1: Jayvision UML Class Diagram (Acquisition Process)

In its acquisition process, Jayvision originally (i.e., prior to business process reengineering) had the following procedures at the REA task level:

- A department supervisor identified (or confirmed) the need to acquire a particular product or service, and submitted a requisition form to the purchasing department through the company mail.
- An agent in the purchasing department opened the mail, approved (or disapproved) the requisitions, and sorted the approved requisitions into piles according to the

type of products and services needed. The disapproved requisitions were returned to the department supervisor with explanations as to why the requisitions were denied.

- An agent in the purchasing department identified appropriate vendors for the requested products and services. Often this entailed searching the catalogs of established vendors to determine pricing and availability; sometimes the purchasing agent contacted the vendor's sales representative to obtain details about the products and services; sometimes the purchasing agent needed to prepare a request for quote or to issue requests for competitive bids from potential suppliers.

- Once the purchasing agent selected appropriate vendors, the purchasing agent prepared purchase orders (based on one or more purchase requisitions) and mailed or faxed them to the vendors. A copy of the purchase order was sent to the accounts payable department, where it was filed in a temporary file in vendor number order awaiting further processing.

- An agent in Jayvision's receiving department received the products. Upon receipt of the products, a clerk manually counted the products and filled out a receiving report (listing the product identification number, quantity received, and a note describing the condition of the items). A copy of the receiving report was sent to the accounts payable department where it was filed in a temporary file in vendor number order awaiting further processing.

- Jayvision's accounts payable department received vendor invoices in the mail. For each vendor invoice received, an accounts payable clerk retrieved the purchase order and receiving report copies for that vendor. The clerk verified that each line item amount on the vendor invoice represented the correct amount for a product or service that had been both ordered and received. The clerk also double-checked the invoice for mathematical accuracy. If everything was deemed okay, the accounts payable clerk wrote a check to the vendor for the amount of the invoice and forwarded the check with its underlying documentation to the controller. The controller signed the check and gave it to an accounting clerk to copy and send to the vendor. The copy was filed along with the supporting documentation in a permanent file in the accounting department.

- Sometimes a purchasing agent authorizes a return of previously purchased inventory. In such cases, a specific shipping clerk will handle the packaging and shipping of the returned goods using the quantities and inventory items listed on the return authorization document.

Jayvision re-engineered its acquisition process workflow, and the new procedures at the REA task level are described as follows:

- A department supervisor identifies or confirms the need to acquire a particular product or service, and enters requisition data into the enterprise database. This entry triggers an electronic notification that is sent to the purchasing department.
- Upon receipt of the electronic notification, the purchasing department examines and approves (or disapproves) the requisitions. Notices regarding disapproved requisitions are electronically sent to the department supervisor with explanations as to why the requisitions were denied.

- The purchasing department identifies appropriate vendors for the requested products and services. Often this entails searching the catalogs of established vendors to determine pricing and availability; sometimes the purchasing agent contacts the vendor's sales representative to obtain details about the products and services; sometimes the purchasing agent needs to prepare a request for quote or to issue requests for competitive bids from potential suppliers.

- Once appropriate vendors are selected, purchase order data are entered into the enterprise database and purchase order forms are electronically generated and are either e-mailed or printed and faxed to the vendors.

- The receiving department for Jayvision receives the products. Upon the products' receipt, a receiving clerk checks the enterprise database to verify that the data for the products received matches the data on the related purchase order. The clerk manually counts the products and enters the appropriate receipt data into the enterprise database.

- Each day the enterprise database's interface displays a list (based on the purchase order and purchase data in the database) of the unpaid purchases (receipts of products and services) that are due within three business days. The accounts payable clerk reviews for accuracy each electronic payment suggested by the enterprise database interface and then electronically notified the controller to authorize the disbursement. The authorized electronic payments are sent to the vendors' bank accounts and recorded in the enterprise database.

- Sometimes a purchasing agent enters the enterprise system and authorizes a return of previously purchased inventory. In such cases, a specific shipping clerk will handle the packaging and shipping of the returned goods based upon inventory data retrieved from the enterprise system.

Even though the steps to accomplish the workflow associated with the events changed significantly from the original workflow to the reengineered workflow, the REA business process level pattern (UML class diagram in Exhibit 8-1) is identical. Both the original and reengineered workflows included need identification (purchase requisition) as an instigation event, ordering of goods or services (purchase order) as a commitment event, receipt of goods (purchase) as an economic increment event, payment of cash (cash disbursement) as an economic decrement event, and returning goods (purchase return) as an economic increment reversal event. Thus, the business process level model and resulting database design contain the same classes and associations under both workflow scenarios. However, representation of the document processing and data flows is quite different for the two scenarios. You will learn how to create workflow models in both BPMN and flowchart formats in this chapter.

DIAGRAMMING WORKFLOW

Whether you create BPMN diagrams, flowcharts, activity diagrams, or some other type of workflow diagrams, you may find the following steps useful.

1. Know why you are diagramming the workflow – if you are trying to find process errors, you may create your diagram at a different level of granularity than if you are trying to document how data flows from source documents to the enterprise's general ledger.

2. Determine the scope of the workflow you are diagramming – how does the business process start and how does it end? In other words, what is the first task that occurs and what is the last task that signals that the business process is complete?

3. Before representing tasks in diagram format, make a list or rough sketch of everything that happens between the starting and ending points you identified in step 2, and indicate the areas of responsibility for each task. Creating a rough sketch will be easier if you don't have to worry about specific notations as you draw, and creating a final diagram will be much easier when starting from a rough sketch.

4. Consider as you sketch whether alternative pathways are possible. Most workflow diagramming tools provide notation to indicate a business process could continue this way or that way depending on the result of what happened thus far.

5. Make note of any tasks or procedures you recognize as providing internal control over the workflow you are diagramming. Even if your reason for diagramming the workflow is not to identify internal controls, those notes will be useful for that purpose and make someone else's job easier.

6. Walk through your diagram with someone who knows the process to verify that you have faithfully and completely represented the workflow, making any necessary changes or additions.

Next we discuss the specifics of creating BPMN diagrams and flowcharts. Most enterprises won't care which tool you use to diagram workflow as long as you are accurate and thorough; however, you should be familiar with both tools, as you are likely to encounter both in practice.

BPMN MODELS

Systems implementation and reengineering efforts make extensive use of business process models (which are workflow level models, not to be confused with the business process level REA models we introduced in chapters 4 through 7). The most widely used notation for such workflow models is *Business Process Model and Notation (BPMN)* 2.0. To avoid confusion between business process level REA (conceptual) models and business process (workflow) models, we will refer to the latter as BPMN models or diagrams.

The BPMN Version 2.0.2 specification was published in December 2013 by the Object Management Group (OMG). The OMG also published the UML Version 2.5.1 specification in

December 2017. We have discussed only one kind of UML diagram in this textbook thus far – UML class diagrams. UML also includes activity diagrams that are similar to BPMN diagrams (and some speculate that the two notations will be harmonized in the future). Both BPMN and UML are incorporated in international standards: ISO/IEC 19510:2013 and ISO/IEC 19505-2:2012, respectively. According to the BPMN specification (OMG 2013, p. 1):

> The primary goal of BPMN is to provide a notation that is readily understandable by all business users, from the business analysts that create the initial drafts of the processes, to the technical developers responsible for implementing the technology that will perform those processes, and finally, to the business people who will manage and monitor those processes. Thus, BPMN creates a standardized bridge for the gap between the business process design and process implementation.

> Another goal, but no less important, is to ensure that XML languages designed for the execution of business processes, such as WSBPEL (Web Services Business Process Execution Language), can be visualized with a business-oriented notation.

Because the technical developers are concerned with implementation details (i.e., making BPMN "computable" with code), the full BPMN notation can be very complex. However, keeping in mind the primary goal of BPMN (providing a notation understandable by all business users), the developers of BPMN ensured that a subset of notation elements could be used by end users (accountants, auditors, managers, etc.). For our study of BPMN, we will proceed by limiting our BPMN element set to the essentials that enable end users to describe business processes; see Exhibit 8-2. It is important to recognize that we will not be describing the entire breadth of notation.

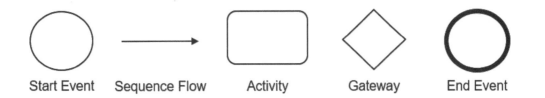

Exhibit 8-2: Minimum Subset of BPMN Elements/Notation

The events, activities, and gateways are categorized as flow objects; these objects define the behavior of a business process. The *sequence flow* represents one way to connect flow objects. The circle element (Exhibit 8-2) shows where a business process starts and ends (BPMN also includes a special intermediate event element that we will not use). The *start event* is the first event in the process, and the circle depicting it is not bold. The *end event* is the last event in the process, and the circle depicting it is bold. Arguably the most important element is the activity. Sequence flows will connect from the start event to various activities and/or gateways, and finally, to the end event. Generally, the sequencing will proceed from left-to-right. The *activity* element can be used to show the performance of specific work within a business process. Activities can be described as either atomic or non-atomic. Atomic activities cannot be further decomposed. Non-atomic activities can be decomposed, and additional notation must be added to the activity element. We will limit our discussion to atomic activities known as tasks (we will not discuss a second type of atomic activity known as a choreography task). Tasks can be manual or automated. Tasks can be performed by people, or they can be performed by automated scripts, web services, or bots.

The *gateway* element shows a divergence control of either branching or forking, and may also indicate a convergence control of merging or joining. Branching (sometimes called exclusive branching) allows for one (but only one) of two or more sequence flows to be followed. Branching may be represented with the empty diamond shape shown in Exhibit 8-2 or by the same symbol with an X inside the diamond. Forking allows for two or more sequence flows to be followed in parallel, though not necessarily concurrently. Forking is represented by adding a plus sign to the inside of the gateway diamond shape.

Merging allows for the control of two or more sequence flows coming together. Merging is exclusive and uses the same element as branching (either with, or without the X inside the gateway element). Joining allows for the control of two or more parallel sequence flows coming together such that all parallel flows must be completed before moving out of the gateway. Joining uses the same element as forking (a plus sign inside the gateway).

An easy-to-follow BPMN example of cookie baking is shown in Exhibit 8-3. As you see, the small set of elements from Exhibit 8-2 allows for the fundamental representation of the process. Once a particular recipe is read and the yield is identified, say as two dozen cookies, the baker can decide whether to proceed with the recipe as written, or to calculate a new yield for four dozen cookies. Then the key tasks are followed until the cookie baking is complete. Note that some tasks like "Measure Ingredients & Combine in Bowl" could be viewed as sub-processes (non-atomic), so if it was important to understand the sub-processes we would have to modify the notation which is currently being limited to atomic tasks.

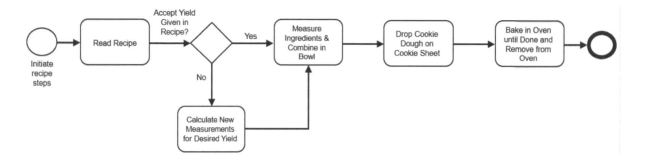

Exhibit 8-3: Simple Cookie Baking BPMN Example

While one may create a basic BPMN diagram using the limited notation in Exhibit 8-2, one may relatively easily extend the notation with the elements shown in Exhibit 8-4. These additional symbols allow for a richer representation, but still keep the overall set of elements to a manageable subset of the BPMN notation.

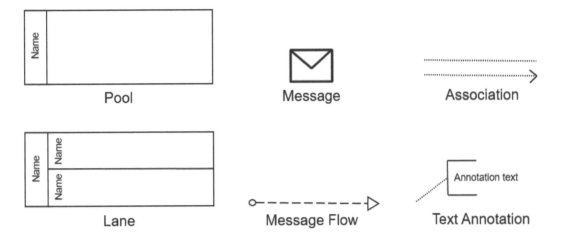

Exhibit 8-4: Some Additional Elements/Notation

Pools and lanes (also called swimlanes) allow the grouping of tasks into areas of responsibility. An *area of responsibility* is a department, section within a department, or an individual employee who is held accountable for the flow of information or physical objects through a system. BPMN designers typically draw pools and lanes horizontally but may instead draw them vertically. Areas of responsibility allow the modeler to indicate who is responsible for the tasks in each swimlane.

Exhibit 8-3 could have been drawn inside of a pool named Bakery. *Pools* are necessary when illustrating two or more participants (business partners) in a collaboration. Collaborations are most commonly business-to-business (B2B), but may be business-to-customer (B2C). Modelers may treat pools as empty "black boxes" in which only the business entity is identified in the pool without its corresponding processes. Modelers use *lanes* to divide pools into subset activities. They may create lanes to represent internal roles or departments, or to represent specific IT systems. Both pools and lanes must cover the entire length of the diagram.

Because collaborations may show a business process of two or more business partners, the diagram can have multiple points of view, or perspectives. This differs from flowcharts which always have an internal point of view.

Earlier we introduced sequence flows as one way to connect flow objects. Now we introduce message flows as a second way. Sequence flows can travel across lanes, but will never travel across pools. Message flows only travel across pools – they never connect objects within a pool. These rules are illustrated in Exhibit 8-5. A third way to connect flow objects is with associations (dotted line), which can be drawn either with arrowheads to show flow direction (which may be bi-directional), or without arrowheads, as shown in Exhibit 8-4. *Associations* link information and artifacts to flow objects. The *text annotation* element attaches to an object with an association.

A *message* element represents the contents of communication between two trading partners. *Message flows* show the flow of messages between two trading partners. One may show message flows without explicitly showing messages (as Exhibit 8-5 illustrates). Sometimes one may want to distinguish an initiating message from a non-initiating message; to denote a non-initiating message, add shading to the element shown in Exhibit 8-4.

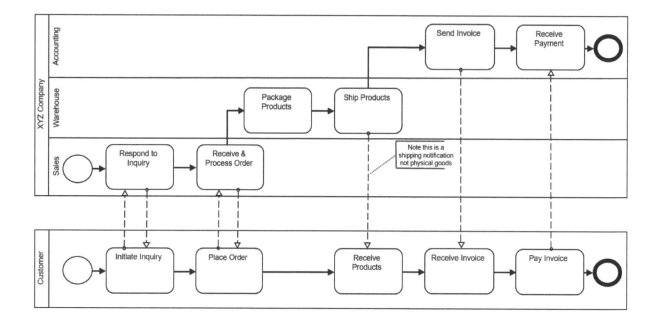

Exhibit 8-5: Example BPMN for Sales Process

BPMN SUMMARY
We introduced BPMN as a technique for representing the task/workflow level of REA. BPMN has a logical orientation, and uses just a few symbols to represent a wide range of activities. The complete BPMN can be quite complex – and useful for designing executable business processes. Rather than attempt to describe the entire BPMN, we limited our discussion to the set of elements that are useful for managers, auditors, and business analysts and left out the elements that are useful for programmers.

FLOWCHARTS
Flowcharts are graphical representations of the inputs, processes, and outputs of an information system; they include physical and logical details about the system components. Despite standardization efforts, various types of flowcharts are used in practice, with various guidelines for how to create flowcharts (e.g., ISO 5807:1985). In this chapter, we discuss the symbols for creating document/procedure flowcharts (focused on paper document creation, flow, use, and storage) and systems flowcharts (focused on information system data creation, flow, use, and storage). Many flowcharts combine features of document/procedure flowcharts with systems flowcharts, and for ease of exposition, we simply use the general term "flowchart."

Managers often create flowcharts to document internal controls in an enterprise. Internal and external auditors may create and/or evaluate flowcharts during the course of their audits. Auditors also use flowcharts as a form of documentation in their work papers (in addition to other documentation such as questionnaires, checklists, and written narratives). Flowcharts show accountability, segregation of duties, and other key internal controls (some people refer to these as internal control flowcharts). As a general rule, the more the complexity of business processes increases, the more auditors will rely on flowcharts.

Broader than solely focusing on internal controls, enterprises need to document details about workflow – who is responsible for particular tasks, what happens, in what order, and what details are captured, maintained, and reported by the information system. Flowcharts can efficiently communicate workflow details and leverage the benefits of diagrammatic representations (e.g., directing attention to sequences, collocation of tasks with the responsible agents). *Flowchart symbols* are specific shapes used to represent task elements, such as data capture and computer processing; numerous symbols represent different elements, as we describe next. *Flow lines* indicate the movement of documents, physical objects, or data to the next point in a system. Some flowcharts distinguish document flows from information flows by using a solid line arrow and dotted line arrow, respectively; for simplicity, we will always use a solid line arrow. Flowcharts focus on the physical aspects of information flows and processes. Similar to the use of pools and lanes in BPMN, many flowcharts include areas of responsibility to show which agents, departments, or functions have responsibility for which tasks. All flowchart symbols should be clearly labeled. Including a legend is often useful to aid flowchart readers, especially if the flowchart contains abbreviations.

Because many information flows are document-related, document processing typically makes up a large portion of flowcharts. The entire information system is made up of a series of input, process, and output activities. The inputs and outputs may be (1) paper documents or (2) electronic data; and, likewise, the processes may be (1) manual or (2) computerized (paper documents are only used with manual processes; electronic data is only used in computer processes). The outputs from the various processes may be used for decision-making purposes or they may serve as inputs to other processes. The pattern *input* → *process* → *output* generally holds in both manual and computerized processes. One may create flowcharts manually, either freehand or with the help of a flowchart template – a stencil that allows users to trace the outline of the various flowchart symbols. Professionals use software packages, such as Lucidchart, Microsoft Visio, or SmartDraw, to create flowcharts. Even word processing, spreadsheet, and presentation software packages often include flowchart symbols among their drawing tools (e.g., the Shapes objects in Microsoft Office).

Manual processes represent tasks that are done primarily by people; such processes involve activities such as filling out forms and reconciling different sources of related information. Although some manual process tasks may use calculators or cash registers as aids, the people using these devices are doing a significant portion of the work. Many such processes are the focus of business process reengineering efforts, and more recently – robotic process automation (RPA). Both the inputs to, and the outputs from, manual processes are paper (as shown in Exhibit 8-6). We use two types of symbols for paper: the traditional *paper document symbol* shown in the top left of Exhibit 8-6, and the *calculator/register tape* shown directly underneath the paper document symbol in Exhibit 8-6. Calculator tape is the paper that comes out of a ten-key adding machine/calculator, whereas register tape is the paper receipt provided at the point of sale (e.g. by a cash register at a grocery store). In this textbook, we depict any other paper document with the traditional paper document symbol. In practice you may come across flowcharts that use parallelograms to represent traditional accounting records like journals and ledgers; for simplicity, we do not use that symbol.

The *file for stored paper* (upside down triangle) symbol in Exhibit 8-6 represents paper storage in a file folder and/or file cabinet. Flowchart designers may indicate how the paper is organized within the file with symbols such as N (numerical), A (alphabetical), C (chronological). Flowchart designers may also use the letter T to indicate a file is temporary. Even though you may think of filing documents as a manual task, the action of filing is not considered significant enough to represent with a manual process symbol. Instead, the filing of documents is represented with a document symbol connected by a flow line to the file symbol.

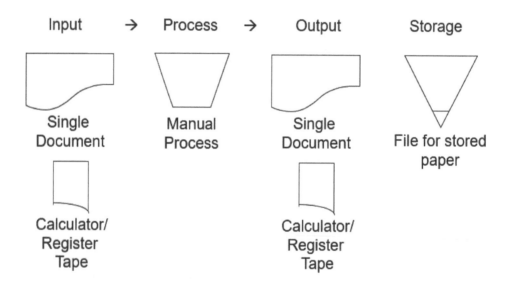

Exhibit 8-6: Flowchart Symbols for Manual Processes

Computer processes represent tasks that are done primarily by computers; such processes involve things like saving accounting transactions that have been entered via keyboard, or the updating of customers' accounts receivable records. Although you may think a person performing a data entry task is manual, that task is not shown with a manual process symbol. Instead, the computer's processor gets the focus because it is accepting the inputted data and doing something with the data. In other words, the computer is doing more work than the person, therefore convention considers the task to be a computerized process rather than a manual process. Exhibit 8-7 shows the symbols that represent inputs to, and outputs from, computer processes.

Visualizing a personal computer (PC) may help you to see how some of the symbols in Exhibit 8-7 are used. A traditional PC has a keyboard (input device symbol), a tower housing the computer processor (computer process symbol), and a monitor (display symbol). Data that is entered via keyboard represents an input. Data that is displayed on a monitor is an output managed by the computer processor. In observing Exhibit 8-7 you may wonder why the document symbol is there when it was previously shown as part of manual processes. Some computer processes involve data entry operations in which the original data was located on a document. These processes are shown by connecting the paper symbol with a flow line to the input device symbol (which, in turn, would connect with a flow line to the computer process symbol). On the other hand, the document symbol is also used to show paper being printed (as an output) from a computer process.

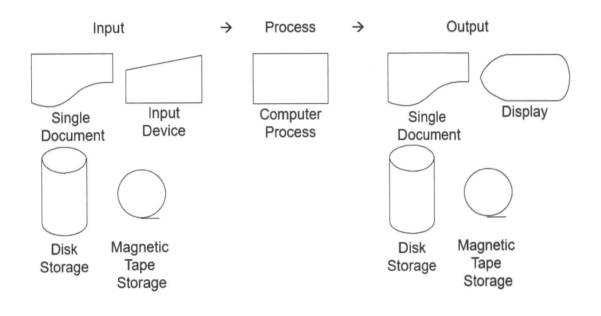

Exhibit 8-7: Flowchart Symbols for Computer Processes

Exhibit 8-7 also shows symbols for disk storage and tape storage, both of which represent electronic data storage (differentiating it from the triangle symbol for paper storage). These symbols can represent either inputs to computer processes, or outputs from computer processes. We will use the disk storage symbol as a default (i.e., unless we specifically refer to tape storage, we mean disk storage). However, we will have some examples that use tape storage.

The most important thing to know about tape storage is that the data are stored sequentially and may only be accessed sequentially. Also the tape only moves one direction (forward) during processing. This affects access and use of the data. While your personal technology is not likely to include tape storage (unless you have an old VCR that uses VHS tapes or an old tape recorder that uses audio cassettes), tape storage is popular in corporate settings. In practice magnetic tapes are most often used to store backup data, but some older systems still use magnetic tapes for operational transaction and master files. Inputs to computer processes from electronic data stores are sometimes called "reads"; outputs from computer processes to electronic data stores are sometimes called "writes." When you open one of your saved files in an application such as Excel, the computer processor reads the data from the electronic data store (disk drive) into random access memory (RAM). When you save the file, the computer processor writes the data to the electronic data store. All reads and writes are mediated by computer processes. We discuss tape and disk storage further later in this chapter.

Exhibit 8-8 shows additional flowchart symbols that go beyond the basic input, process, output logic. We have already discussed the arrow representing data/information flow; this is a required symbol that always connects two other symbols. The remaining symbols should be used as necessary, but they should not be over-used, otherwise the flowchart may become too cluttered.

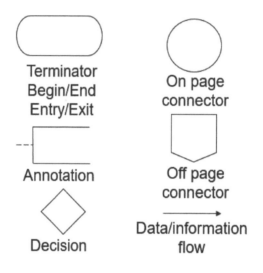

Exhibit 8-8: Additional Flowchart Symbols for Both Manual and Computer Processes

The *terminator* symbol indicates the beginning or ending of a flowchart or points of entry to and exit from the flowchart. The *annotation symbol* allows the preparer to provide clarification as needed, and is often used to describe and document particular internal controls (the dashed line of the annotation symbol can connect to any other symbol as necessary). The *decision symbol* indicates decisions that involve divergent data/information flows; many times the decision has underlying if-then logic such that if "yes" one action happens and if "no" another action happens. The remaining symbols are connectors, both on page and off page. Flowchart designers use *on page connectors* when the data/information flow "jumps" from one part of a page to another part of the same page; e.g. when a document is forwarded from a department on the far left side of the page to a different department on the far right side of the page. Rather than drawing a huge continuous flow line across the entire page, the on page connectors allow for a cleaner look. Matching symbols (usually numbers) must be used on the inside of the on page connectors to remove any ambiguity in determining the continuity of the flow. See Exhibit 8-9 for an example of these connectors. *Off page connectors* basically work the same way, but are used with multi-page flowcharts in which the flow crosses pages. Page references along with unique symbol identifiers (usually letters) must be included inside the off page connector symbols. The off page connector on the sending page will include the page number on which flow will continue, along with the unique symbol identifier. The off page connector on the receiving page will include the page number from which flow is continuing, along with the matching unique symbol identifier.

Exhibit 8-9 shows an example flowchart in which documents move through manual processes. This flowchart represents a subset of tasks that occur during an acquisition business process. Two areas of responsibility are shown: Manufacturing and Purchasing. The vertical orientation of area of responsibilities allows readers to quickly see which tasks are taking place in which departments (auditors can also assess the segregation of duties). The terminator symbol is used to show Manufacturing initiating the requisition which leads to the manual process of creating a purchase requisition document. On page connector 1 allows for a concise depiction of the document flow from Manufacturing to Purchasing. Note how forwarded documents must be shown both in origination and destination areas of responsibility. Purchasing has a manual process to approve or deny the purchase requisitions. The denied purchase requisitions are returned to Manufacturing, and the approved purchase requisitions move on to a manual process of creating a purchase order.

The overlapping/cascading document symbols represent the fact that three copies of the purchase order are created. In such cases of use, these documents should be numbered sequentially, and the document numbers should remain on the document symbols as the documents move to subsequent tasks or destinations. In the example, you see that one copy of the purchase order goes to the vendor, a second copy goes to the Accounts Payable department, and the third copy gets stored in a file within the Purchasing department.

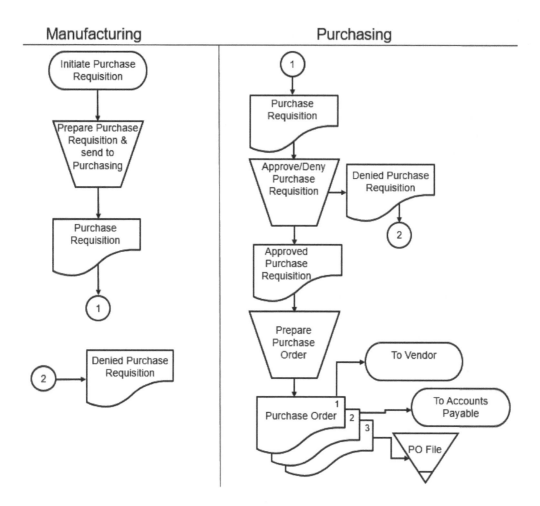

Exhibit 8-9: Example Flowchart with Documents and Manual Processes

In Exhibit 8-10 we slightly modify the Exhibit 8-9 example and show the second copy of the purchase order being sent to the Data Entry department so that the data on the purchase order can be input into the computer system and saved to a purchase order file.

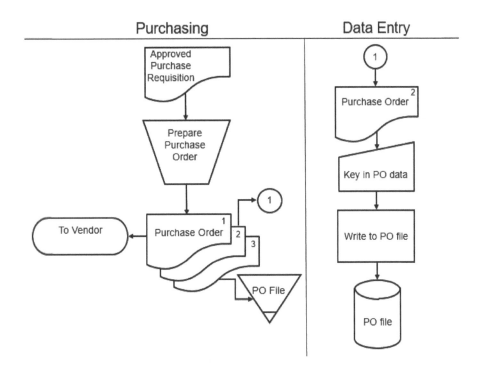

Exhibit 8-10: Example Flowchart with Computer Process

We will revisit disk storage and tape storage symbols (Exhibit 8-7) after discussing some general file concepts and processing methods.

FILE TYPES, MEDIA, AND PROCESSING METHODS

Because system flowcharts reflect the physical media on which data are stored and the automation level of each process, they are difficult to prepare or to interpret without adequate understanding of some features of the common physical media, file types, and tools involved in the information processes. Therefore, this section provides a description of some common file types, media on which files are stored, and some common processing methods.

File Types

Files store data and processing instructions. Each file is named and saved on a storage medium such as a hard disk or magnetic tape. You create files when you save data when using applications such as Microsoft Word or Intuit TurboTax). The two most common types of files you use in your computing are executable files and data files. Executable files are also called program or application files, and they usually have an .exe extension. Executable files read, change, and write data. Data files store the data produced or used by executable files. Data files are seen in many contexts: e.g., transaction data, business reference data, word processing data, spreadsheet data, and graphics data. Often files are referred to by their type or content. When you use Microsoft

Access, every database table (in fact, every Access object), is saved in one Access database file. In practice you may also encounter "file-based" information systems. Most file-based systems include several types of data files: master files, transaction files, history files, reference files, and suspense files.

Master files contain balance data or the status of an entity at a point in time. Examples of master files in enterprise systems are customer, employee, inventory, fixed asset, and supplier master files (to name a few). Enterprise systems often refer to the data stored in master files as master data. Master files do not contain event or activity data; instead they contain balances that are updated with event or activity data. For example, a customer master file may contain an accounts receivable balance field that will be updated with sales and cash receipt activity data.

Transaction files contain activity data that are used to update the balances on master files. Examples of transaction files in enterprise systems are cash disbursement, cash receipt, payroll, purchase, and sales transaction files (to name a few). When a transaction file is used to update a master file, it is often said the transaction file is "run against" the master file. Master files evolved from paper-based ledgers; transaction files evolved from paper-based journals, thus you can think of a general ledger as a master file and a general journal as a transaction file.

History files or archive files, as the names suggest, contain inactive past or historical data. Examples of history files include data files from years past that are no longer subject to updates. History files are distinguished from backup files, which are copies of files created in case the original files are destroyed. At least one backup file should be stored at a location other than where the original files are stored in case of a disaster such as a fire or flood that could potentially damage or destroy both the original and the backup files. If you back up your personal laptop data on an external hard drive or flash drive, you should not carry the backup device in the same carrying case as theft of the carrying case would result in you losing all your stored data. However, if you don't carry the backup device with you, any changes you made since the last time you backed up would be lost anyway. Cloud backup that is set to occur automatically as you make changes to your stored data files is a good option to avoid data loss.

Reference files contain referential data such as tax rate schedules or customer price lists. Suspense files are files of data that are awaiting some action to complete their processing. Examples include records identified as incomplete or erroneous that need correction and reentry for processing (e.g., a payment by a customer who is not listed in the customer master file or a journal entry that doesn't balance).

As discussed in chapter 3, the REA ontology exists independent of any specific technology. In this book we chose to implement REA using relational database technology. We could instead implement REA using file-based technology. For example, we could create master files with Resource and Agent data we could create transaction files with Event data. Because relational database has proven to be a better technology for data management, we chose that over file-based technology. Because relational databases do not use master files and transaction files, using file-based terminology is not applicable (relational data are stored in specific tables within a single database file).

Media

Data are typically stored on media of three types: paper, magnetic tape, and disk. While many companies are striving to go paperless, paper is probably still the most common form of media used in enterprises. Source documents (documents that contain details about transactions) are used as inputs for many information processes, and paper reports are produced as outputs for many information processes. Paper is the media type many people prefer to use. Although increasingly people are asked to read output screens, reports, and even textbooks on computer screens, many still prefer to print the files and read them on paper. Although paper has many advantages, including ease of use and lack of dependence on electricity, paper also has many disadvantages such as bulk (for storage), lack of search and automated processing capability, and susceptibility to destruction (although all media types may be easily destroyed).

Magnetic tape storage stores data from source documents and reports in a format that is computer readable, but its defining feature is sequential ordering (storage and access) of data. As noted earlier, if you have used audiocassette tape recordings of music, or videocassette tape recordings of movies, then you have used magnetic tape media (but this is becoming a "generation gap" example in the age of iTunes and Google Play Music). *Sequential storage* implies that records are stored one after another in some order (chronologically, by account number, alphabetically, etc.). *Sequential access* requires that all data be read in sequential order to find a particular record. For example, suppose you purchase a cassette tape containing songs performed by your favorite recording artist. The songs are stored sequentially (one after another) on the tape. To listen to your favorite song, you must fast forward or rewind (searching the songs one after another) to sequentially access the desired song – there is no faster access option. Enterprises may use magnetic tape cartridges and open reel tapes to store transaction and report data, and those files require sequential storage and access of data. The storage capacity of tape exceeds that of disk; also, tape is more reliable, and has a longer life than disk. While you may not have experience with magnetic tape in your personal life, do not assume that it is an outdated technology. If you use Google's email service Gmail, your emails are backed up on tape (see for example, http://www.cnn.com/2011/TECH/web/03/01/gmail.lost.found/index.html).

Disk technology is increasingly replacing magnetic tape as the preferred media type, both for personal computing (and audio-visual needs), and for certain enterprise processing applications. Examples of *disk storage* include internal and external hard disks, thumb drives, SD cards, CDs, and DVDs. From an information processing standpoint, the primary advantage of disk-based storage over magnetic tape storage is the random storage and direct access capability of disk technology. *Random storage* allows information to be stored in any order on the disk device; in fact, a file need not be stored in its entirety in a single location on a disk – part of it may be stored in one location and part of it in another location, although processing is more efficient if the files are not "fragmented" in that manner. *Direct access* allows each record to be retrieved without reading all the records that precede it in the file. The computer maintains an index to keep track of the location of each record, thus allowing the computer to retrieve any record requested by the user regardless of its physical position in a file. There is no need to sequentially search part or all of the other records stored on the storage device. Suppose instead of purchasing a cassette tape of songs performed by your favorite recording artist you instead purchased a CD containing those songs. With the CD player you can choose your favorite song from the index and listen to it without having to listen to (or fast-forward through) the other songs on the CD.

The most obvious distinction between these media types for system flowcharting is that different symbols are used to represent paper, tape, and disk storage. Another important distinction is whether updates are made to the same physical file or *whether a new file must be created* that merges the original data with the updates. If a master file is stored on magnetic tape, updates cannot be made to the same physical medium, but rather a new magnetic tape must be used. First, the data are read from the old master file (on magnetic tape) into the computer's RAM. Next, the transaction file containing the updates is read into the computer's RAM. Third, the updated records are written onto the new master file (a different magnetic tape). The reason the updates may not be written directly to the old master file is that they may take up a different amount of space on the tape, and could potentially destroy existing data. For example, if you taped four 30-minute television shows on a VCR tape and you want to replace one of those shows with a 60-minute television show, you couldn't do that without destroying one of the other 30-minute television shows. To clarify this even further, suppose the four shows (in order) on your tape were episodes of *Gilligan's Island*, *Seinfeld*, *I Love Lucy*, and *Cheers*. Further supposed you only wanted to keep the episodes of *Gilligan's Island* and *I Love Lucy*, and you wanted to record a one-hour episode of *Matlock*. So you have a 2-hour tape and you want to end up with 2 hours of shows, deleting two 30-minute episodes and replacing them with one 60-minute episode. If you position the tape so that it begins recording where *Seinfeld starts*, you will end up replacing *I Love Lucy* instead of replacing *Cheers*. There is no way to tell the tape to skip over the *I Love Lucy* episode when it comes to it and then start recording again.

Contrast that with the updating of a master file stored on disk. Updates may be written directly to the disk, because it doesn't matter where physically the data is located on the disk. As long as space is available for all the needed data, if you update a customer street address that was 123 Pine St. to 12345 Appleyard Ave. (notice the new address is longer) it will realize the allotted space is not big enough and will add a pointer to a new location on the disk that has adequate space. The logical view (what the user sees when the computer displays this data) does not show the fact that the data is stored in fragments, but physically it is stored in that manner. If the data becomes stored in too many fragments, processing efficiency may decrease; that is why your personal computer may occasionally send a message suggesting that you "defrag" your hard disk drive. The defragment process rearranges the physical locations of data on the drive to make processing more efficient.

In Exhibit 8-11 we illustrate the difference between updating a master file that is stored on tape versus disk. Note that the bidirectional arrow reflects the "reading" of the "old" A/R balances from, and the "writing" of the "new" A/R balances to the same physical disk.

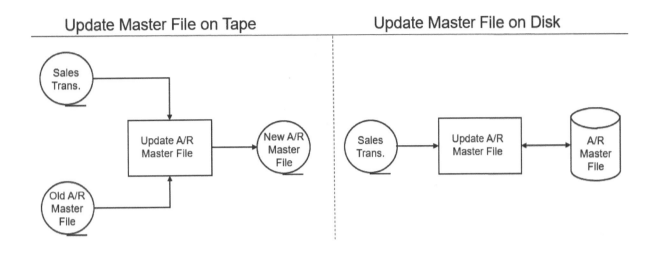

Exhibit 8-11: Examples Updating Master File (Tape versus Disk)

Processing Methods

The timing of processing reveals the point at which activity data are posted to update the master files. The update time does not necessarily synchronize with the actual activity time Therefore the processing method determines the timeliness of the data stored in master files. Processing is often identified by type: batch versus real-time.

Batch processing accumulates transaction data for a period of time to collect a *batch*, or group, of transaction data. Then all of the transactions in the transaction file are posted to the master file (or database) in one processing run. Therefore, processing (i.e., updating of the master file or database) occurs after a group of transaction data is collected. Processing involves merging the data in the transaction file with the current master data to create an *updated* master file (or database). Thus, with batch processing, transaction data may not be entered into the computer system until some time after a business activity occurs, and master files may be updated even later. The only time the master file is accurate and up-to-date is immediately after a batch of transaction data has been processed.

Real-time processing updates master files as business activities occur, which requires that data be entered into the system as the business activities occur. When you use your debit card for a transaction, that activity is typically processed in real-time and your account balance will immediately reflect the decrease.

A different category of processing that focuses on the output side of the system (as opposed to the prior processing methods which focus on the input side) is report-time processing. *Report-time processing* means the data needed to generate the requested report is processed as the report is created. Most event data are stored in a detailed (disaggregated) format and the relevant data are selected, processed, and any master files are updated as the information customer's report is generated.

Due to the sequential access limitations of tape, tape storage media always use batch processing. Disk storage media can handle both batch and real-time processing.

We end this section by illustrating a conceptual difference between file-based accounting systems and relational database enterprise systems. In Exhibit 8-11 we saw different files being used for sales data versus accounts receivable data in a file-based system. In Exhibit 8-12 we demonstrate a relational database system has just one file: the database file. That one file contains multiple table in which data are stored. In a pure REA enterprise database, a credit sale would typically require addition of a new row in a Sales table and addition of one or more new rows of inventory (line-items) in a StockFlow table. Additional rows of data may also be added to Participation and/or Fulfillment tables, depending on whether multiplicities allowed foreign keys to be posted into the Sale table.

Some enterprise systems may store the data in the form of a debit/credit entry in which accounts receivable would be adjusted. Note that other departments besides Sales could be added to the flowchart, but the Enterprise System area of responsibility would remain as shown; the additional departments would simply have arrows drawn from keyboards in their areas to the Enterprise System server computer process. For simplicity in Exhibit 8-12, we only show a keyboard in the Sales area of responsibility, but we could add a rectangle symbol to show the Sales computer's processor and a *display* symbol to show that the Sales end-user would see the enterprise system interface. Furthermore, we illustrate only one server for simplicity (in reality there would be multiple servers).

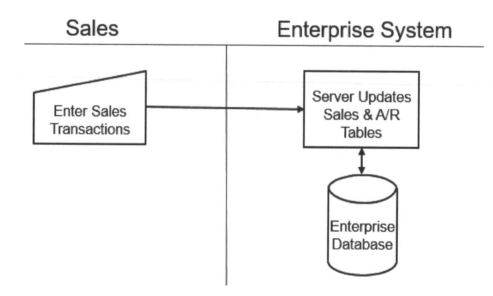

Exhibit 8-12: Example Enterprise Database

FLOWCHART PREPARATION GUIDELINES
While flowchart preparation is as much art as it is science, designers should follow several guidelines to enhance the readability, and thereby enable the validation of their flowcharts.

Flowchart Organization
In general, flowcharts should be organized such that they can be read either from left to right or from top to bottom. A flowchart organized in such a manner need not include arrows on its flow lines. Anytime a flowchart deviates from the presumed flow of top to bottom or left to right, the flow lines must include arrows to ensure the navigation is clear.

Document Resolution
Flowcharts must clearly indicate the origin an eventual termination of all documents. Documents should not appear from nowhere, nor should they be left hanging such that their final destinations are unclear. Thus all documents must come from either a file symbol, from another area of responsibility on the flowchart, or from a terminator symbol. Similarly, all copies of documents must eventually flow to any of a file symbol, a terminator symbol, or a black box that indicates destruction of the document (e.g. the document when no longer needed is shredded).

Minimize Clutter
A flowchart is an important analytical and design tool; however, great amounts of detail reduce a flowchart's readability. To minimize clutter, place areas of responsibility that have the most frequent interchange of data adjacent to each other to avoid the need for long arrows or on/off-page connectors. Also enter text only within flowchart symbols and judiciously use annotations for other narrative. Avoid explaining with narrative what the flowchart already adequately describes.

Ensure Clear Document Progression
Diagram a document before and after a process is performed, when entering or leaving a file, and on entering or leaving a page. Change the name of documents that are altered (e.g., updated, signed, or approved), to indicate their current status. For example, notice in Exhibit 8-2 that once the reimbursement request is approved by the payables clerk, it is re-labeled as approved reimbursement request. Similarly, notice the flow of the check. The computerized process in the data processing department generates the check, which at that point is unsigned. Copies 1 and 2 are sent to the payables supervisor, who performs a manual double-check and signing process. The check is re-labeled as signed check and is sent to the employee, while the copy along with the underlying request and supporting documents is filed in a permanent file.

Follow Input-Process-Output-Storage Convention
Be sure to include all major steps in the business or information process you are modeling. It is often helpful to remember that systems are simply a combination of inputs, processes, outputs, and storage of data. There are three actions that you might view as manual, but that are *not* represented

by the manual process symbol. The first action is "forwarding" an item (like a document of a file) from one area of responsibility to another; in this case, you just show the item with a flowline to the subsequent area of responsibility (usually redrawing the symbol in the subsequent area of responsibility so that all symbols within an area of responsibility are shown). The second action is the act of "filing" a document; in this case, you just show a document with a flow line to a manual storage symbol. The third action is keying; in this case, the important representation is showing the keyboard connected to a computer process.

FLOWCHART SUMMARY

Following the preceding instructions can guide the development of an effective flowchart for analyzing an information process or system. The flowchart is one of the easier types of documentation for people to understand, although it takes effort to create one. Often, auditors use system and document flowcharts to document and assess internal controls.

To test whether you are beginning to understand how to read and prepare flowcharts, go back to Exhibit 8-2, and write a short narrative of the process. Compare your narrative to the narrative provided earlier in this chapter to see how accurately you read the flowchart.

Although many individuals and organizations still use flowcharts, their usefulness is limited to decisions or information needs that require knowledge of the physical information flows and system characteristics. Often the conceptual essence of the system is somewhat obscured by the physical artifacts; other documentation techniques may be useful for information needs that focus on the concepts. Because many accounting and auditing analyses (such as risk assessment and control evaluation) require consideration of the physical tasks, media, and areas of responsibility, system flowcharts are still widely used.

CONCLUDING COMMENTS

This chapter presented overviews of two workflow modeling tools: BPMN and flowcharts, and introduced some of the associated information processing considerations. Practitioners use many different notations for documenting workflow - some organizations and consultants have even developed their own diagramming techniques. Whether you use BPMN, flowcharts, narrative descriptions, or some other tool, is a matter of preference and objective. Diagramming tools such as BPMN and flowcharts combine the efficiency of graphics and the rigor of rules to communicate the nature of the process being modeled. You will benefit from developing the skills to read and create workflow documentation. Workflow documentation tools work very well for summarizing the specific activities and responsible employees for enterprises in such a way that inefficient processes or weak internal controls are often revealed.

Please remember that UML class diagrams as introduced in chapter 3, and workflow models portrayed with BPMN or flowcharts serve different purposes. UML class diagrams determine the architecture of the data storage ;they are similar to a blueprint. Workflow models communicate the areas of responsibilities and the activities to be done in business processes and describe how the information associated with those activities is entered, processed, and reported.

KEY TERMS AND CONCEPTS
Activity (in BPMN)
Annotation symbol
Area of responsibility
Association (in BPMN)
Batch processing
BPMN
Calculator/register tape
Computer process
Data/information flow
Decision symbol
Direct access
Disk storage
Display
End event (in BPMN)
File for stored paper
Flow line
Flowchart
Flowchart symbols
Gateway
Input device
Lane
Magnetic tape storage
Manual process
Master file
Message
Message flow
Off page connector
On page connector
Output
Pool
Random storage
Real-time processing
Report-time processing
Sequence flow
Sequential access
Sequential storage
Single document
Start event (in BPMN)
Task
Terminator
Text annotation
Transaction file
Workflow

REVIEW QUESTIONS

R8-1. What is the difference between REA business process modeling and workflow (task-level) modeling?

R8-2. Why should some workflow activities not be represented as base objects in a REA business process model?

R8-3. Draw the BPMN symbols and describe the use of each.

R8-4. What conventions should you follow to make a flowchart easier to understand?

R8-5. Draw the flowcharting symbols and describe the use of each.

MULTIPLE CHOICE QUESTIONS

MC8-1. The purpose of task level modeling in the REA ontology is
A) To design a database
B) To represent the specific workflow activities that combine to form events in a business process, and to document the flow of data through an enterprise
C) To represent the enterprise in the context of its external business partners
D) To represent the resource interconnections among the enterprise business processes

MC8-2. In BPMN, which symbol represents an activity?

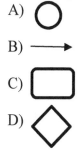

A) ◯

B) ⟶

C) ▢

D) ◇

MC8-3. In BPMN, the grouping of tasks into areas of responsibility is done with
A) Circles
B) Messages
C) Annotation text
D) Pools and lanes

MC8-4. In BPMN, the element that shows either a divergence control of branching or forking or a convergence control of merging or joining is a
A) Gateway
B) Sequence flow
C) Atomic activity
D) End event

MC8-5. One difference between BPMN diagrams and flowcharts is this:
   A) Flowcharts may have multiple points of view, whereas BPMN diagrams always have an internal point of view
   B) BPMN diagrams may have multiple points of view, whereas flowcharts always have an internal point of view
   C) Flowcharts connect objects with messages, whereas BPMN diagrams connect objects with sequence flows
   D) BPMN diagrams connect objects with messages, whereas flowcharts connect pools with text annotations

MC8-6. Which of the following can best be described as a master file?
   A) A file of event data
   B) An income statement
   C) A trial balance
   D) An accounts payable subsidiary ledger

MC8-7. System flowcharts combine these three simple graphical elements to represent various types of physical information flows and processes:
   A) Charts, lines, and documents
   B) Charts, symbols, and annotations
   C) Symbols, lines, and documents
   D) Symbols, flow lines, and areas of responsibility

MC8-8. Which type of processing occurs during the course of a business event and provides immediate response to an information user's request
   A) Online processing
   B) Batch processing
   C) Report-time processing
   D) Real-time processing

MC8-9. In the following flowchart segment, the most likely action to take with the customer remittance advices once they've been keyed into the system, AND the corresponding symbol to replace oval **A** is

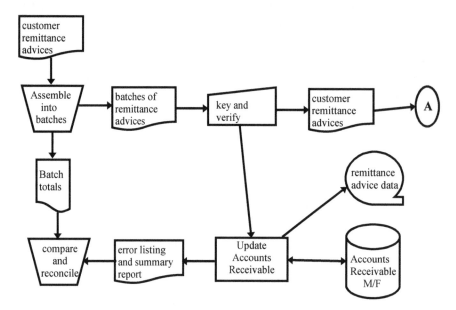

   A) Discard them immediately; manual process symbol
   B) Forward them to the internal audit department for review; dashed line
   C) Forward them to the treasurer to compare with the monthly bank statement; dashed line
   D) File them by customer number; file symbol

MC8-10. In a system flowchart, which symbol should be used to represent a backup of the general ledger master file that can only be accessed sequentially?

   A) ▱

   B) ▭

   C) ⛁

   D) Q

CHAPTER 9

Assessing and Controlling Enterprise Risk

LEARNING OBJECTIVES

Managers, auditors, and system designers must carefully consider enterprise risks and controls. Managers should assess risk, determine the control activities that will best prevent, control, and detect the loss if the threat becomes reality, keeping the cost-benefit tradeoff in mind. Auditors must assess potential and existing clients' risks as part of determining whether or not to take them on or keep them as clients. Auditors must also issue opinions on the adequacy of their clients' internal controls. At the behest of management, system designers should build automated controls into the systems they design. Managers and auditors often use workflow models such as those introduced in chapter 8 to gain understanding of company operations and to identify potential areas of risk and potential places to add controls. Managers and auditors also interview various company representatives and use other sources of information, including social media, to identify potential risks and controls.

In this chapter, we discuss the regulatory mandates and authoritative guidance regarding risk and controls, the efficacy of the REA ontology as a framework for risk assessment, various types of enterprise risk and means by which enterprise system controls may mitigate such risks. After studying this chapter you should be able to:

1. Explain PCAOB's auditing standard 2201 (formerly AS5)
2. Explain the control objectives, components, and principles of internal control prescribed by the COSO (Community of Sponsoring Organizations) framework
3. Classify risks as economy, industry, enterprise, business process, or information risks
4. Identify common sources of enterprise risk, using the REA ontology as a framework
5. Identify specific controls commonly used in enterprises to prevent, detect, and recover from enterprise, business process, and information process risks

PUBLIC COMPANIES AND CORPORATE GOVERNANCE

Public companies have two important characteristics. First, a public company's common shares (stock) are traded on a stock exchange (this will be our focus, but note that there is also an option to trade "over the counter" which is beyond our scope; we will also consider "preferred shareholders" as beyond our scope). Because the U.S. Securities and Exchange Commission (SEC) regulates stock exchanges, public companies have to follow the SEC's requirements. Second, public companies have a corporate structure that separates ownership and control, meaning that the shareholder/owners do not operate the company. Shareholders, as capital providers/owners, are able to share in a company's profits (distributed as dividends), and have a right to vote at shareholder meetings. Shareholders get to vote on the membership of the board of directors.

All public companies have boards of directors that provide corporate governance and oversight. A board of directors essentially make decisions on behalf of the shareholders. People serving as directors are classified as inside (current employee) or outside (independent). It is common for a company's CEO to be an inside director; outside directors are not company employees, and do not serve any company stakeholders other than the shareholders. As a general rule, corporate governance is stronger with more outside/independent directors. Boards of directors often form committees, consisting of subsets of board members. Two types of committees worth highlighting here are the compensation committee and the audit committee, both of which need to only have outside directors. The compensation committee focuses mainly on the top executives and how to design their compensation contracts to align the executives' and shareholders' interests. The audit committee provides *oversight* to corporate financial reporting and internal control over financial reporting. Note the term oversight; it is important to highlight that the company's management is responsible for both corporate financial reporting and internal control over financial reporting. Additionally, the audit committee makes decisions regarding hiring, compensating, retaining (or changing), and overseeing the independent registered public accounting firm (i.e., the external auditor). Finally, the company's internal audit function (i.e., the internal auditor) will report to the audit committee.

REGULATORY MANDATES AND AUTHORITATIVE GUIDANCE

In the beginning of the 21st century, massive accounting frauds changed the financial reporting landscape and the accounting profession. You are probably familiar with the companies at the center of the frauds: Enron, WorldCom, and Tyco International. Enron engaged in accounting practices that fraudulently inflated revenues and hid debt from its balance sheet. WorldCom capitalized billions as investments that should instead have been recognized as expenses. Tyco executives stole money via unapproved loans and unauthorized stock sales (some of the stolen money was spent on a $2 million birthday party for the CEO's wife). The stock market was in peril; investors did not know when the next scandal would arrive or which company would be involved. Something needed to be done to restore investors' confidence in financial reporting. In 2002, the United States Congress passed the Sarbanes-Oxley Act that requires senior management of publicly traded companies to issue reports on their assessments of the effectiveness of internal controls over financial reporting along with their annual reports. Company management is responsible for establishing and maintaining adequate internal controls over financial reporting (ICFR). Sarbanes-Oxley also requires auditors to attest to and report on management's assessments of the internal controls and financial reporting procedures.

Another result of Sarbanes-Oxley was the creation of the PCAOB, that is, the Public Company Accounting Oversight Board, which sets and enforces standards for auditors of publicly traded companies (the PCAOB conducts inspections of registered public accounting firms). The PCAOB's Auditing Standard (AS) #2201[30] (prior to the PCAOB's renumbering, it was AS#5): "An Audit of Internal Control Over Financial Reporting that is Integrated with an Audit of Financial Statements." AS#2201 prescribes a top-down, risk-based approach "to obtain sufficient evidence to support the auditor's opinion on internal control over financial reporting as of year-

---

[30] https://pcaobus.org/Standards/Auditing/Pages/AS2201.aspx

end, and to obtain sufficient evidence to support the auditor's control risk assessments for purposes of the audit of financial statement."

It is important to know how the PCAOB defines ICFR in AS#2201 Appendix A:

Internal control over financial reporting is a process designed by, or under the supervision of, the company's principal executive and principal financial officers, or persons performing similar functions, and effected by the company's board of directors, management, and other personnel, to provide reasonable assurance regarding the reliability of financial reporting and the preparation of financial statements for external purposes in accordance with GAAP and includes those policies and procedures that -

(1) Pertain to the maintenance of records that, in reasonable detail, accurately and fairly reflect the transactions and dispositions of the assets of the company;

(2) Provide reasonable assurance that transactions are recorded as necessary to permit preparation of financial statements in accordance with generally accepted accounting principles, and that receipts and expenditures of the company are being made only in accordance with authorizations of management and directors of the company; and

(3) Provide reasonable assurance regarding prevention or timely detection of unauthorized acquisition, use, or disposition of the company's assets that could have a material effect on the financial statements.

Note: The auditor's procedures as part of either the audit of internal control over financial reporting or the audit of the financial statements are not part of a company's internal control over financial reporting.

Note: Internal control over financial reporting has inherent limitations. Internal control over financial reporting is a process that involves human diligence and compliance and is subject to lapses in judgment and breakdowns resulting from human failures. Internal control over financial reporting also can be circumvented by collusion or improper management override. Because of such limitations, there is a risk that material misstatements will not be prevented or detected on a timely basis by internal control over financial reporting. However, these inherent limitations are known features of the financial reporting process. Therefore, it is possible to design into the process safeguards to reduce, though not eliminate, this risk.

According to AS#2201, Securities and Exchange Commission rules[31] require managers of publicly traded companies to evaluate the effectiveness of its company's internal control over financial reporting using "a suitable, recognized control framework (also known as control criteria) established by a body or group that followed due-process procedures, including the broad distribution of the framework for public comment." AS#2201 specifies that auditors should use the same recognized control framework to evaluate the company's internal control effectiveness that its management used to develop its internal controls.

---

[31] Securities Exchange Act Rules 13a-15(c) and 15d-15(c), 17 C.F.R. §§ 240.13a-15(c) and 240.15d-15(c).

General Data Protection Regulation (GDPR)

The General Data Protection Regulation (GDPR) is an important legislation for enterprises that have operations, activities, customers, suppliers or other business partners in the European Union (EU). Passed in 2016, and in force as of May 25, 2018, GDPR applies not only to companies within the EU, but to all companies processing and holding the personal data of people residing in the EU regardless of the company's location. Many U.S. companies sell products to EU residents via their websites; therefore, this regulation applies to them. The potential global reach of this regulation is a tremendous change with respect to data privacy regulation, and all companies with any connection to EU residents should pay attention. Companies who violate GDPR may be fined up to 4% of total gross revenues or 20 million euros, whichever is greater.

Highlights of GDPR include consent conditions, breach notification rights, right to access, right to be forgotten, data portability, privacy by design, and data protection officers. Consent conditions of GDPR require the request for consent to use clear and plain language, to include the purpose for the processing of related data, and that it must be as easy to withdraw consent as it is to give it. Breach notification rights require companies to notify those affected within 72 hours of first having become aware of a breach. Right to access means that individuals may obtain confirmation to data controllers as to whether or not personal data concerning them is being processed, where, and why, and the data controllers must provide individuals with electronic copies of such data, free of charge. Right to be forgotten, also called data erasure, means individuals may request data controllers to erase their personal data, stop distributing the data, and may have third parties stop processing the data. Data portability allows individuals to obtain data collected about them from one data controller and transmit that data to another controller. Privacy by design requires companies to build data protection into systems as they are designed rather than adding them on after the systems are designed. Data protection officers are employees or external providers hired by companies whose core activities require regular and systematic large-scale monitoring of individuals' data, or whose core activities require sensitive data. Data protection officers must have expert knowledge on data protection law and practices, be provided sufficient resources to be effective, report directly to the highest level of management, and not have conflict of interest.

Committee of Sponsoring Organizations (COSO) Internal Control – Integrated Framework

Most companies (management and board of directors) use the Committee of Sponsoring Organizations (COSO) Internal Control – Integrated Framework as principles-based guidance for developing and evaluating their systems of internal control. COSO is an independent, private sector initiative that consists of five "sponsoring organizations":

1. American Accounting Association (members are mostly accounting professors)
2. American Institute of Certified Public Accountants (members are mostly practicing CPAs)
3. Institute of Internal Auditors (members are mostly practicing internal auditors)
4. Institute of Management Accountants (members are mostly practicing corporate accountants)
5. Financial Executives International (members are mostly high level financial executives such as Chief Financial Officers or controllers.

Representatives from each of these organizations worked together to author the original 1982 COSO Internal Control – Integrated Framework, which was revised in 2013.

The definition of internal control used by the 2013 COSO framework is:

"Internal control is a process, affected by an entity's board of directors, management, and other personnel, designed to provide reasonable assurance regarding the achievement of objectives relating to operations, reporting, and compliance."

The deliberate use of the word process indicates that internal control is not an outcome, rather it is an ongoing commitment by management to take actions and ensure objectives are met. These objectives will be described next, as they are part of the COSO cube.

The COSO cube, as shown in Exhibit 9-1, depicts the relationship between an entity's three categories of objectives, the five internal control components required to achieve the objectives, and the four common levels of corporate organizational structure.

Exhibit 9-1: The COSO cube

The columns on the top face of the cube represent the internal control objectives. Organizations need to think about control objectives with respect to (1) the effectiveness and efficiency of their operations, (2) the reliability, timeliness, and transparency of internal and external, financial and non-financial reporting of their operations, and (3) their compliance with various laws and regulations. The rows on the front face of the cube are the five integrated components of the internal control framework: the control environment (also known as the tone at the top), risk assessment, control activities, information and communication, and monitoring activities. The columns on the right face of the cube, i.e., the third dimension, represent the organizational structure – when thinking about internal controls one needs to consider controls at the entity level, within each division, within operating units inside divisions, and within functions inside (or sometimes across) operating units.

The COSO framework will be used in different ways by different parties. Managers will use a broad perspective when applying the COSO framework, as they are responsible for controlling many different kinds of risk and for complying with many different kinds of regulations. External auditors will use a somewhat narrower perspective when applying the COSO framework, as they primarily need to consider risk that impacts financial reporting.

The 2013 update to the COSO Internal Control Integrated Framework introduced seventeen principles of effective internal control into its discussion of the five components of internal control.

Control Environment
The *control environment* is the tone set by management of an organization, which influences how control conscious its employees are likely to be. Although the control environment is at the top of the cube, it is actually the foundation upon which all other internal control components are built. If management has a laissez faire attitude toward internal control, its employees are likely to be unconcerned as well. If management makes clear both in words and actions, that controls are important, employees will respond accordingly. Five of COSO's seventeen principles have to do with the control environment:

1. Demonstrate commitment to integrity and ethical values
2. Exercise oversight responsibility
3. Establish structure, authority, and responsibility
4. Demonstrate commitment to competence
5. Enforce accountability

The level of importance that management places on each of these principles establishes the control environment. Auditors can explore the extent to which these principles are evident through interviews with and observation of management and company employees to determine the tone set by management. The stronger the control environment, the more effective the remaining components are likely to be.

Risk Assessment
Managers are responsible for assessing its company's risk. Auditors evaluate how effectively managers assessed their risk, which means auditors must also assess the company's risk and then compare their own assessments to those of management. In this *risk assessment* component of control, managers and auditors identify and analyze the relevant risk associated with the organization achieving its objectives, thus revealing what risks need to be controlled and suggesting controls required to manage the risks. Four of COSO's seventeen principles (#6-9) relate to risk assessment:

6. Specify suitable objectives
   a. Operations objectives reflect management's choices, its risk tolerance, include operations and financial performance goals, and determines how management will commit resources.
   b. External financial reporting objectives ensure the company complies with applicable accounting standards, considers materiality, and reflects the entity's activities.
   c. External non-financial reporting objectives ensure the company complies with externally established standards and frameworks, considers the required level of precision for such reporting, and reflects the entity's activities.
   d. Internal reporting objectives reflect management choices, considers the required level of precision, and reflects entity activities.
   e. Compliance objectives reflect external laws and regulations and considers management's risk tolerance.
7. Identify, analyze, and respond to risk
8. Assess fraud risk
9. Identify and analyze significant changes

Principles 6 through 9 portray the importance of risk assessment as an ongoing, iterative process that considers risk at all levels of the entity and takes necessary responsive actions. Principle 8 requires management and auditors to specifically consider the potential for various types of fraud, encouraging them to assess incentives, pressures, opportunities, attitudes, and rationalization. Principle 9 requires an assessment of changes in the company's external environment, its business model, and leadership.

Control Activities

Control activities are the actions established by policies and procedures to help enforce management directives to mitigate risks. In other words, these are activities performed to minimize or eliminate risks. Control activities are often classified as preventive or detective. *Preventive controls* focus on stopping *errors* (unintended mistakes), or *irregularities* (intentional efforts to cause loss to the company) before they occur or are entered into the system. For example, a data entry control that doesn't allow someone to enter a sale into the system without specifying a valid salesperson is a preventive control. Keeping cash locked in registers to protect it from theft is another preventive control. *Detective controls* identify that an error or irregularity has occurred. Bank reconciliations that compare the cash balance reported by the bank to the cash balance reported by the general ledger cash account are detective controls. When considering ICFR, preventive controls aim to prevent errors or fraud that ultimately result in misstatement of financial reports; detective controls identify errors or fraud that have occurred and that could ultimately result in misstatement of financial reports. However, preventative and detective controls (with perhaps different objectives) could be implemented in contexts outside of ICFR as well.

If all else is equal, it is best to prevent errors, irregularities, and disasters. However, cost and impracticality may prohibit prevention of all risk. Consider the risk of theft with respect to merchandise displayed in a retail store. Displaying the merchandise in locked transparent cases such that a customer has to work one-on-one with a salesperson to be able to touch or try on the merchandise is a preventive control. In some retail stores, such as high-end jewelry stores, such a control is cost beneficial. However, can you imagine how difficult grocery shopping would be if all the groceries were locked in transparent cases? Preventing theft in that manner would inconvenience customers so much that they would shop elsewhere.

Enterprises should certainly take steps to prevent risks that have a high impact and a high likelihood of occurrence. Management should prevent risks that have a low impact and a high likelihood of occurrence only if the cumulative cost of the controls is less than the cumulative probable loss based on the risk. Management needs to identify and control risks such that the benefit of controlling the risk exceeds the cost of the controls, while balancing enterprise efficiency and effectiveness.

Prevention is not always possible, especially in the case of disasters such as fire, flood, tornados, hurricanes, and earthquakes. Many enterprises purchase insurance to mitigate risks that have a high impact and a low likelihood of occurrence. Insurance is sometimes called a *corrective control*, i.e. a control that focues on recovering from, repairing the damage from, or minimizing the cost of threats. Insurance doesn't prevent a disaster from occurring; however, it minimizes the financial impact of the damage. For example, having automobile insurance doesn't prevent you from being involved in a car accident; however, having insurance helps to soften the financial blow of repairing or replacing your car and paying for medical expenses necessitated by the accident.

Three of COSO's seventeen principles (#10-12) involve control activities.

10. Select and develop control activities
11. Select and develop general controls over technology
12. Deploy through policies and procedures

Principle 10 specifies that companies should integrate their control activity selection with their risk assessment, consider entity-specific factors, determine the relevant business processes, evaluate a mix of control activity types, consider the level at which control activities are applied, and address segregation of duties. *Segregation of duties* prohibits one employee from performing two or more of the following functions: authorization of transactions involving assets, custody of assets, record keeping, and reconciliation. Separating those functions reduces the opportunity for an employee to steal enterprise assets and to conceal the theft in the normal course of his or her work. *Collusion* (two or more employees in different positions working together to perpetrate fraud) is still a risk even with segregation of duties.

Principle 11 reminds companies to determine the dependency between the use of technology in business processes and technology general controls. *General controls* include controls over data center operations, access security, software acquisition, development and maintenance, and operating systems. Companies are to establish relevant technology infrastructure controls, security management processes, and controls over its technology acquisition, development, and maintenance processes.

Principle 12 specifies that companies are to deploy control activities through policies and procedures. Companies are to establish the policies and procedures with clear responsibility and accountability for their execution, assurance that competent personnel will perform the activities in a timely manner, take corrective action when needed, and will periodically re-assess them.

Information and Communication

Three of COSO's seventeen principles (#13-15) apply to its *information and communication* component:

13. Obtain or generate and use relevant, quality information to support the functioning of other components of internal control
14. Internally communicate information, including objectives and responsibilities for internal control, necessary to support the functioning of other components of internal control
15. Communicate with external parties regarding matters affecting the functioning of other components of internal control

Principle 13 encourages companies to identify information requirements, capture data from internal and external sources, process relevant data into information, maintain quality throughout the processing of the data, and to consider the costs and benefits of the information. Principle 14 emphasizes the importance of communicating with the board of directors, providing separate communication lines, and selecting relevant methods of communication. Principle 15 encourages companies to enable inbound communications, communicate with external parties and the board of directors, to provide separate communication lines, and select relevant methods of communication.

Monitoring

Monitoring activities are selected, developed, and performed to ascertain whether or not each control component continues to exist and function as intended, and whether any change is needed. *Monitoring* is a key input in the organization's assessment of internal control effectiveness, as unmonitored control activities are likely to cease or become ineffective.

Two of COSO's seventeen principles (#16-17) apply to monitoring:

16. Conduct ongoing and/or separate evaluations
17. Evaluate and communicate deficiencies

For principle 16, ongoing evaluations require continuous monitoring, which is important for some types of processes (similar to a fuel gauge in your vehicle that constantly monitors how much fuel remains). Even for processes that benefit from continuous monitoring, companies may consider also implanting separate evaluations. In deciding how often to monitor and evaluate a process, companies should employ knowledgeable personnel, establish a baseline understanding of the process, consider the likely rate of change related to the process, integrate the monitoring with the business process, adjust the scope and frequency as needed, monitor any outsourced service providers that are part of the process, and use technology as needed to accomplish the monitoring. Ideally, the company will make the monitoring as unobtrusive and automated as possible.

Principle 17 is important, because if the company doesn't assess the results of its monitoring efforts, or fails to communicate any deficiencies revealed by the monitoring, its efforts were in vain. Once corrective actions are taken with respect to any noted deficiencies, the company should also monitor those corrective actions to determine their effectiveness or lack thereof.

Requirements for Effective System of Internal Control (COSO)
According to COSO (2013):

"An effective system of internal control reduces, to an acceptable level, the risk of not achieving an objective relating to one, two, or all three categories of objectives – that is, operations, reporting, and compliance. It requires that (i) each of the five components of internal control and relevant principles is present and functioning, and that (ii) the five components are operating together in an integrated manner." (p. 3) (Source: https://www.coso.org/Documents/COSO-FAQs-May-2013-branded.pdf)

The words *present* and *functioning* map into AS#2201 such that auditor testing of *design effectiveness* is related to the 5 components (and related 17 principles) being *present* (i.e., designed and implemented), and auditor testing of *operating effectiveness* is related to the 5 components (and related 17 principles) *functioning* (i.e., operating as designed/intended).

Although the COSO framework (2013) addresses internal control deficiencies (and major deficiencies), it acknowledges the judgement necessary to conclude effectiveness of internal controls and states that regulators and standard-setters "may establish criteria for defining the severity of, evaluating, and reporting internal control deficiencies" (p. 4) (Source: https://www.coso.org/Documents/COSO-FAQs-May-2013-branded.pdf). Relatedly, AS#2201 (Appendix A) contains the following definitions:

"A control objective provides a specific target against which provides a specific target against which to evaluate the effectiveness of controls. A control objective for internal control over financial reporting generally relates to a relevant assertion and states a criterion for evaluating whether the company's control procedures in a specific area provide reasonable assurance that a misstatement or omission in that relevant assertion is prevented or detected by controls on a timely basis.

A deficiency in internal control over financial reporting exists when the design or operation of a control does not allow management or employees, in the normal course of performing their assigned functions, to prevent or detect misstatements on a timely basis.

- A deficiency in design exists when (a) a control necessary to meet the control objective is missing or (b) an existing control is not properly designed so that, even if the control operates as designed, the control objective would not be met.

- A deficiency in operation exists when a properly designed control does not operate as designed, or when the person performing the control does not possess the necessary authority or competence to perform the control effectively.

A significant deficiency is a deficiency, or a combination of deficiencies, in internal control over financial reporting that is less severe than a material weakness, yet important enough to merit attention by those responsible for oversight of the company's financial reporting.

A material weakness is a deficiency, or a combination of deficiencies, in internal control over financial reporting, such that there is a reasonable possibility that a material misstatement of the company's annual or interim financial statements will not be prevented or detected on a timely basis.

> Note: There is a reasonable possibility of an event, as used in this standard, when the likelihood of the event is either "reasonably possible" or "probable," as those terms are used in Financial Accounting Standards Board Statement No. 5, Accounting for Contingencies ("FAS 5")."

A material weakness requires the external auditor to issue an adverse opinion on ICFR. Significant deficiencies are important enough to that they must be presented to the audit committee, but do not result in an adverse opinion. A number of factors go into deficiency-related judgements. First, did a misstatement actually occur or not. Second, what is the magnitude of the misstatement or potential misstatement. Finally, is there a reasonable possibility that internal controls failed to prevent/detect a misstatement or potential misstatement.

An important part of the external auditor's control work is evaluating and testing IT general controls (ITGCs) and application controls. We will cover these later in the chapter. Next we will discuss another framework created by COSO as it relates to risk management, which REA may facilitate.

COSO ERM, RISK IDENTIFICATION, AND THE REA ONTOLOGY

In addition to the COSO Internal Control – Integrated Framework, COSO developed a second, complementary framework, the COSO Enterprise Risk Management (ERM) – Integrated Framework (first version was in 2004, followed by a revision in 2017). While some confusion exists as to the difference between COSO's Internal Control Framework and its ERM framework, the two were designed to work together. The former focuses on controls, which of course requires one to think about risk. The latter focuses on risk, which requires one to think about controlling the risk. The COSO ERM framework is broader than the COSO internal control framework, especially at the strategic level. For example, management may contemplate a strategic decision to launch a new product line; this action would be within the scope of ERM, but would not have a direct association with the internal control framework (although if management ended up pursuing the strategy, there would be internal control implications). Management has four options for addressing risk. A common option is risk mitigation, taking actions to reduce risk (e.g., implementing internal controls or implementing a hedging strategy). A second option is sharing/transferring the risk through means such as insurance or outsourcing. Sometimes management either accepts the risk or avoids the risk.

In an attempt to clear up some misconceptions about ERM, COSO states:

"Enterprise risk management is not a function or department. It is the culture, capabilities, and practices that organizations integrate with strategy-setting and apply when they carry out that strategy, with a purpose of managing risk in creating, preserving, and realizing value." (see https://www.coso.org/Documents/2017-COSO-ERM-Integrating-with-Strategy-and-Performance-Executive-Summary.pdf)

Just as the COSO internal control "cube" has 5 components, COSO ERM has 5 components: (1) governance and culture, (2) strategy and objective-setting, (3) performance, (4) review and revision, and (5) information, communication, and reporting. These ERM components are supported by 20 principles, summarized in Exhibit 9-2, taken from page 7 of the framework's executive summary[32].

Exhibit 9-2: COSO ERM Principles
https://www.coso.org/Documents/2017-COSO-ERM-Integrating-with-Strategy-and-Performance-Executive-Summary.pdf, p.7

The COSO ERM framework, with its twenty principles, emphasizes the strong connection between risks, strategy, and performance, and clarifies that risk isn't something to be avoided altogether, but something to be managed. Opportunities come with risk, so to take advantage of opportunities, one must accept some risk. The key is to not blindly accept risk, but to see and respond to the risk.

The first five principles are categorized as governance and culture. They relate to the company's mission, vision, and values, and also to the control environment element of the COSO internal control framework. The governance aspect emphasizes the importance of and the responsibility for risk oversight and management. The culture aspect communicates the entity's understanding of risk and its commitment to ethical values and nurturing of desired behavior by its management and employees. Best practices for these principles include a board of directors trained in ERM, with ERM deemed the board's responsibility, a board charter that defines its risk appetite and tolerance, and board minutes documenting consideration of risk impact on its decisions.

Principles six through nine are categorized as strategy and objective-setting principles. They establish the importance of defining the enterprise's risk appetite in alignment with its strategy,

[32] https://www.coso.org/Documents/2017-COSO-ERM-Integrating-with-Strategy-and-Performance-Executive-Summary.pdf, p.7.

and implementing the strategy with specific business objectives. Best practices for these principles include maintenance of a business context report that documents consideration of internal and external factors, analysis of competitors and peers risk responses, documentation of risk appetite and consideration of multiple strategies for addressing risk, and documentation of business objectives that shows alignment with budgets, forecasts, and strategic plans.

Principles 10 through 14 are categorized as performance principles. Applying these principles, enterprises identify and assess risks that threaten the achievement of its strategy and business objectives. Enterprises then prioritize risk by severity according to their risk appetites and they select risk responses, ensuring that the overall level (a portfolio view) of risk meets their defined appetites. Best practices for these principles include a risk/severity inventory, i.e., a list of identified risks, indicating severity, that includes measures of impact, likelihood, and frequency, ranked by priority, and a risk response plan that indicates the response for each risk on the inventory.

Principles 15 through 17 are categorized as risk and revision principles. Similar to the monitoring activities component of COSO's internal control framework, these principles reflect an enterprise's consideration of how well its risk management is functioning over time and bearing in mind any significant changes in its context, and determination of any needed improvements. Best practices for these principles include change management documentation indicating consideration of risks associated with the change, and documented risk and performance reviews.

Principles 18 through 20 are categorized as information, communication, and reporting principles. Similar to the information & communication component of COSO's internal control framework, these principles require ongoing information gathering and sharing, using internal and external sources and various technologies, at all levels of the enterprise. Best practices for these principles include the use of software designed for ERM, sample reports from the ERM software, evidence that employees are trained to use the ERM software, copies of risk communications, and reports of actions taken to address risk.

The common subject of all 20 principles is risk. Thinking about risk may be somewhat abstract without some guidance to make it more concrete. The REA ontology provides a framework to help identify risks and thereby consider controls to mitigate those risks. Enterprise risks occur at several levels: economic, industry, value system, value chain, business process, and information process. Exhibit 9-3 illustrates these levels and lists some types of risk at each level.

Because our discussion of REA in this textbook focuses primarily on business process representation, it is most useful for risk identification at the business and information process levels. However, we also discuss value system and value chain level risks in the context of the economy and industry in which the enterprise operates, and those risks that pertain to the enterprise as a whole. Keep in mind that the risks identified in Exhibit 9-3 are not a comprehensive list. In fact, a comprehensive list is impossible because the environment, technology, and people change constantly, and new risks continually arise.

Also, please realize that the categorization of risks is not an exact science. Overlaps may sometimes make it difficult to distinguish an economic risk from an industry risk, an industry risk from a value system risk, and so forth. The most important objective is for you to recognize the risks as potential threats of loss, whether they are economic, industry, value system, value chain, business process, or information process risks. You must apply critical thinking for risk identification; however, this framework will provide guidance for your thinking.

Economic risks	Example risks associated with factors that affect an entire global or local economy • Economic downturns – global or local • Wars • Epidemics • Terrorist attacks • Environmental disasters (widespread floods, hurricanes, etc.)
Industry risks	**Risks associated with factors that affect the enterprise's industry** e.g. Industry-wide cost increases Industry-wide decrease in demand for products Economic risk that is especially bad for a specific industry Unexpected competition from another industry
Enterprise risks	Internal factors e.g. Lack of ethics Low employee morale Employee incompetence Strategic related risk External factors e.g. Increased competition from other enterprises Reduction of perceived brand quality and/or firm reputation Crises involving business partners (value system relationships) Catastrophe that causes an interruption of operations Merger or acquisition involving another enterprise
Business process risks	**Risks associated with actual business process objects** Resources (R's) Events (E's) Agents (A's) Resource-Event relationships Event-Event relationships Event-Agent relationships Resource-Agent relationships
Information process risks	**Risks associated with** Recording information about R's, E's and A's Maintaining information about R's, E's and A's Reporting information about R's, E's and A's

Exhibit 9-3: Risk Identification Levels

Economic and Industry Risks

Enterprises do not operate in a vacuum; they operate within industries that are part of local and global economies. Failure to consider local and global economic risks and industry risks and to adequately address those risks may prove disastrous for enterprises. *Economic risks* are threats to an entire economy; examples include those resulting from war, epidemics, financial market changes, terrorist attacks, and natural disasters such as floods, hurricanes, and drought. Many of these factors can lead to a global or local economic downturn. Sometimes economic risks devastate selected industries and thereby become industry risks. *Industry risks* are those that affect an entire industry. For example, the terrorist attacks of September 11, 2001 not only contributed to global economic downturn; they were especially damaging to selected industries such as travel and tourism.

Another type of industry risk is a widespread cost increase that particularly affects a specific industry. For example, if the cost of raw materials that are used intensively in an industry increases significantly, the entire industry is negatively affected. A sudden increase in a product's price may lead to a sudden decrease in demand for that product. Decreased product demand is an industry risk that is sometimes independent of price increases. Such decreases may result from simple trend shifts (e.g. the popularity of fad products is ever-changing) or from the development of superior replacement products developed in another industry (e.g. many years ago the invention of the telephone replaced much of the demand for telegraph and personal messenger services; cell phones replaced the need for most – but not all – pagers and two-way radios).

Enterprise Risks

Enterprise risks reflect potential threats of loss to the enterprise as a result of internal actions/circumstances and external actions/circumstances. Internal risk factors include such threats as low employee morale, lack of ethics in the enterprise, and employee incompetence, and strategic risks. These internal risk factors are largely determined by management's philosophy and operating style, therefore interviews with management may identify the extent to which these risk factors represent a concern. If management's philosophy and operating style encourage a high-risk environment, greater risk also exists at the business process and information process levels. Questions that may help to identify a high-risk environment include:

- Is the enterprise committed to hiring competent people who possess the knowledge and skills needed to perform their assigned jobs?
- Does management have a conservative or reasonable approach in accepting business risks and in reporting the financial results of operations?
- If there is a board of directors, are there outside representatives on the board?
- Does an audit committee oversee the audit of its financial statements? Who serves on the audit committee?
- Does the company have a well-defined organizational structure with the appropriate division of duties and responsibilities? Are the identified reporting relationships established so that important activities are planned, executed, controlled, and monitored on a timely basis?
- Do employees understand the company's policies and practices, what they are individually responsible for, and to whom they report?

- Has management developed a culture that emphasizes integrity and ethical behavior?
- Does the enterprise have a "whistleblower" policy that encourages employees to inform management or the board of directors of fraudulent activities observed in the firm's operations?

Enterprises that can answer these questions in the affirmative likely have favorable control environments. Enterprises that have not taken these and similar steps to encourage integrity and competence face a high degree of internal enterprise risk. Strategic risks must also be considered as internal factors. Enteprise risk increases when the enterprise's strategy does not align with its mission and vision, when enterprises fail to consider IT as part of its strategy, and so forth. When any strategy is pursued, executives must anticipate risks along with the potential rewards.

Enterprise risk also results from external factors such as increased competition from other enterprises within the industry, loss of perceived brand quality or firm reputation, catastrophes that cause business interruptions, crises involving one or more of the enterprise's external business partners, and risks resulting from mergers or acquisitions. Increased competition may lower the enterprise's market share. Events that cause a perceived loss of brand quality or firm reputation (e.g. if quality control fails to prevent a defective batch of products from being sold and the market generalizes the problem to all of the firms' products) may result in long-term negative consequences for the enterprise. All enterprises face some risk of *business interruption*, a temporary halt in normal operations, due to catastrophes such as fire, flood, tornado, power outages, or technology failures. While such catastrophes were noted as economic risks, that section referred to large-scale events such as the Great Chicago Fire or Hurricane Katrina that affected many enterprises in a large enough area to be considered at least a local economy. Such events can also be limited such that they affect only one enterprise – or a small enough number of enterprises so as not to rise to the level of economic risk. All enterprises also face risks that one or more of its external business partners may experience a business interruption catastrophe that will in turn cause a threat to the enterprise. For example, a warehouse fire that destroys a key supplier's entire inventory and interrupts the supplier's business for several months may cause the enterprise to be unable to fulfill customer orders until an alternative source is found. Another external enterprise risk enterprises sometimes face is involvement in a business combination such as a merger or acquisition. While a voluntary business combination may appear to be an attractive option during negotiations, sometimes plans fail to consider all circumstances and unexpected negative consequences result. The risk of such a consequence is an enterprise risk.

Business Process Risks

Because the REA pattern represents an enterprise's business processes, it provides a useful framework to help system designers, managers, and auditors identify *business process risks*. In this section we provide some examples of risks specific to resource, events, agents, and various relationships in the REA pattern for business processes. The examples in this section do not provide a comprehensive list of business process risks; indeed a comprehensive list cannot exist because as controls for known risks are developed, additional means for misappropriating enterprise assets and misstating results of operations for enterprises are also being created that existing controls may not sufficiently mitigate. Thus, although the REA pattern provides a useful framework, we discourage students from adopting a checklist mentality when considering risks (and controls).

Business process risks are defined for this textbook as risks associated with actual business process objects, including resources, events, agents, and relationships among resources, events, and agents. Some of the resources most commonly found in enterprises are inventory, supplies, operating assets, and cash. Risks associated with resources include threats associated with theft or loss, obsolescence, waste, and damage (either intentional or unintentional). Risks associated with events include failure to execute an event that should occur, execution of an event that should not occur, or executing an event at the wrong time (too soon or too late). Risks associated with agents include assigning an inappropriate agent to an event.

Most risks do not involve resources or events in isolation, but rather involve some combination of resources, events, and/or agents (and relationships among them). Risks associated with resource-to-event relationships include execution of an event involving an incorrect resource, an incorrect quantity of a resource, or an incorrect cost or price for a resource. Risks associated with resource-to-resource relationships include an incorrectly specified correspondence of one resource to another resource. An example is a bill of materials for a finished good inventory type that specifies an incorrect raw material or an incorrect quantity of a raw material. The primary risk associated with event-to-event relationships is incorrect sequencing of corresponding events. For example, if a company has a policy requiring all sales to be accompanied by cash receipts (down payments) equal to at least 50% of the selling prices, a risk is that a sale will be accepted without receiving the required cash receipt. Similarly, a risk exists that a cash disbursement may be made without confirmation that the goods were actually received for which the cash is disbursed.

Event-to-agent relationships in the REA enterprise ontology represent participation relationships linking internal and external agents to events. Risks include execution of events involving unauthorized external agents (e.g. sales made to non-existent customers) or unauthorized internal agents, (e.g. cash disbursements made by inventory clerks). Resource-to-agent relationships reflect custody arrangements (i.e. internal agents responsible for physical custody of a resource type); risks include unauthorized agents having custody of resources. Examination of single relationships is useful for risk identification; however, full risk analysis also requires simultaneous examination of multiple relationships. For example, queries may be formulated to evaluate whether linked purchase orders, purchases, and cash disbursements are all related to the same vendor. If not, there may be a data entry error or an irregularity that warrants investigation.

Information Process Risks
Information process risks are threats of loss associated with recording, maintaining, and reporting information about resources, events, agents, and relationships among them. On the surface, these risks may seem very similar to business process risks. The difference is that business process risks have to do with the actual execution of the events and the actual physical resources and agents. Information process risks have to do with the information that gets recorded, maintained, and reported about those objects. For example, if a sale is made to a non-existent customer, it is a business process error. If a sale is actually made to an approved customer, but a data entry error is made such that it appears the sale is made to a non-existent customer, it is an information

processing error. Information process risks include recording, maintaining, or reporting information that is incomplete, inaccurate, or invalid. Incomplete information reflects failure to record, maintain, or report information about resources, events, agents, or relationships. Inaccurate information reflects the recording, maintaining, and reporting of data that is incorrect as to the reality it represents. Invalid information reflects the recording, maintaining, and reporting of information about non-existent resources, events, agents, or relationships. All of these types of information processing risks need to be controlled.

IDENTIFICATION OF MITIGATING CONTROLS

Once risks have been identified at the various levels of detail outlined in Exhibit 9-3 for an enterprise, its management must make choices about those risks. As mentioned above, management can choose to mitigate, share/transfer, accept, or avoid risks. Because our intended reader is primarily interested in the risk of material misstatement in financial statements, we limit our focus primarily to risk mitigation with an internal control mindset.

Controls for Economic and Industry Risks

You may be wondering what an enterprise could possibly do to shield itself from economic and industry risks. These risks can be very difficult, if not impossible, to control. One control that is likely to be cost effective is the gathering and monitoring of enough information to be able to predict trends and product replacements. Enterprises that focus inwardly and tend to ignore the environment in which they operate are likely to be caught unaware by economic and industry risks. Enterprises that focus outwardly and pay attention to industry and economic trends and market demands are likely to be prepared for most shifts in prices and quantities at the economy and industry levels. Economic and industry risks can be managed to some extent with financial instruments and strategies such as hedges.

Controls for Enterprise Risks

Like economic and industry risks, external enterprise risks are often difficult to predict and identify and are therefore difficult to control. Constant analysis and awareness of the external environment may help enterprises anticipate and prepare for increased competition. Strong commitment to quality and extra quality control procedures may help to prevent loss of perceived brand quality or firm reputation; effective responsiveness to the market in case of a quality problem may help to correct any loss of perceived brand quality or firm reputation (possibly at the expense of a short-term financial loss). For example, it may cost a manufacturer a significant dollar amount to recall a production run of a defective product and replace the products at no cost to the customers; however, the cost of not recalling and replacing the products would likely result in a much costlier loss of perceived brand quality and firm reputation.

Enterprises may purchase insurance to mitigate some external risks such as business interruptions caused by natural disasters or computer disruptions such as hard disk crashes or attacks by hackers, viruses, or worms. Companies may also create contingency plans such that in case of business interruptions operations may be transferred to a backup location. A *contingency plan* is a set of procedures to enact if a disaster occurs. Business interruptions of external business partners are more difficult to insure. A supplier whose warehouse burned down may have insurance to replace lost inventory, but usually that insurance does not compensate the supplier's customer who lost money because the inventory was not available when it needed to be issued to the production floor. To help mitigate such risks, enterprises should consider identifying multiple sources for each type of raw material or merchandise inventory they use in their conversion and revenue processes.

Management's philosophy and operating style dictate many of the controls for enterprise risks. Some high level policies that contribute to a well-controlled enterprise include sound human resource policies and practices. Human capital is often considered to be the most important resource for many enterprises. However, employees who are mismatched with their job responsibilities or who are not managed properly may become more of a liability than a resource. Human resource policies and practices relate to hiring, orienting, training, evaluating, counseling, promoting, compensating, and terminating employees.

Sound personnel practices are essential in controlling both operating activities and information processes. This is becoming increasingly important as enterprises empower employees in an attempt to streamline operations and cut costs. The quality of an enterprise's employees directly influences the quality of the goods and services provided to the customers. Generally speaking, competent, trustworthy employees are more likely to help the enterprise create value. Controls that help ensure success in hiring and retaining quality employees include completion of background checks, full explanation of enterprise policies and procedures, clear definition of promotion and personal growth opportunities as well as termination policies, and clear definition of work schedules. Many enterprises have suffered significant losses at the hands of individuals who had histories of incompetence, fraud, or other dishonest acts. Simple background checks could have prevented these losses. The other controls mentioned are summarized in a phrase: effective communication with employees. Employees must understand what is expected of them and they must be equipped with the training and tools they need to meet those expectations. They also need to be very aware of the consequences of not meeting expectations.

Controls for Business Process Risks

Resource Controls
Some of the resources most commonly found in enterprises are inventory, supplies, operating assets, and cash. Risks associated with resources include threats associated with theft or loss, obsolescence, waste, and damage (either intentional or unintentional).

Segregation of Duties
As described earlier in this chapter, segregation of duties is an important control to lessen the opportunity for theft of all types of resources.

Resource Theft and Loss: Cash
Theft of resources is a rampant problem for many enterprises, costing billions of dollars worldwide every year. Because cash is the most liquid of all resources and is universally desirable, it is particularly susceptible to theft and enterprises need strict controls over those who have access to

cash. Perhaps this is why many advocate moving to a cashless economy. NPR says that Sweden recently reached a point in which only 13% of people reported using cash for their most recent purchase.[33]. Sweden reached that point very quickly compared to the United States, in which 70% of people still use cash regularly. NPR notes that the speed at which Sweden is becoming cashless is likely because Sweden is considered a pioneer in digital technology and most of its citizens are tech-savvy. Still, others appear to be following suit. Britain saw nearly 500 cash point (ATM) machines close every four weeks during 2018 due to increased use of digital payments and less need for physical cash.[34] Why cashless? Much of the move is driven by banks, for whom cash is expensive. Governments also benefit from greater traceability of digital payments, which make hiding cash assets (and revenue) more difficult, if not impossible. Problems with going cashless certainly exist, which is why even Sweden is not 100% cashless. Some people are unable to have bank accounts or credit cards because of immigration status or poor life choices. Requiring a payment system that prohibits such people from being able to buy anything would be horrific. Risk of identity theft would likely increase use of biometric payment authorizations, and biometrics have a one percent failure rate.[35] Businesses benefit from lessened costs of handling cash and lessened likelihood of theft of cash.

Cash is most often stolen by employees, but could potentially be stolen by customers. *Physical access controls*, which are features, barriers, or procedures designed to prohibit unauthorized people from touching a resource, are especially important when the resource is cash. Currency should obviously be kept locked in a container to which only authorized employees have access. In the revenue process most enterprises keep cash in cash registers that may only be opened under certain circumstances. Control over the enterprise checkbook is especially important in the acquisition, payroll, and financing processes, as access to the checkbook provides access to the cash in the checking account. *Bonding* of employees who handle cash is a form of insurance whereby if an employee with an adequate rating from the bonding (insurance) company is proven to have stolen cash from the enterprise, the bonding company recompenses the enterprise. Bonding is considered a corrective control. Just as the purchase of automobile insurance does not prevent a driver from being involved in a car accident, bonding does not prevent a seemingly trustworthy employee from deciding to steal cash from the company. The purpose of buying automobile insurance is so that if an accident occurs, the owner may be recompensed for the loss incurred. Similarly the purpose of bonding employees is so that if a theft occurs, the enterprise may be recompensed for the loss incurred.

Enterprises may take advantage of electronic funds transfers for cash transactions as a means of reducing theft. In electronic funds transfers-in, customers send cash receipts directly to the bank; the bank deposits the cash directly into the enterprise cash account. In electronic funds transfers-out, the enterprise authorizes the bank to directly transfer funds from the enterprise cash account to a designated vendor. Such transfers also ensure accuracy of record keeping because the transaction data are usually made available to be automatically input into the enterprise information system.

[33] https://www.npr.org/2019/02/11/691334123/swedens-cashless-experiment-is-it-too-much-too-fast
[34] https://www.telegraph.co.uk/personal-banking/savings/nearly-500-atms-close-month-britains-rush-cashless-society-accelerates/
[35] https://www.moneycrashers.com/biometrics-cashless-society/

Lapping is a method of stealing cash that enterprises need to control. To accomplish lapping an employee steals cash from a customer payment and delays posting a payment to the customer's account. The employee uses funds from a subsequent customer payment to post to the first customer's account. This process continues with the employee continually stealing from subsequent customer payments to post as prior customer payments. Employees who engage in lapping often attempt to conceal the fraud by writing off as uncollectible customer accounts that have actually been paid. Eventually, lapping becomes so difficult to hide that the perpetrator leaves the company or the lapping is detected.

One of the most important detective controls with respect to cash and other assets are periodic *reconciliations of physical to recorded quantities*. Such reconciliations compare a physical count of the on-hand dollar values of the assets to the dollar values the information system reports as being on-hand. An example with which you are probably familiar is the monthly reconciliation of a bank statement. Bank statement reconciliation compares details of the inflows and outflows depicted on the bank statement with the details of the inflows and outflows for the same account as recorded in the enterprise information system. Discrepancies in the bank statement versus the records in the enterprise system may reveal fraudulent cash-related activities as well as bank or enterprise errors. An employee with no other cash responsibilities should perform the monthly reconciliation.

Periodic counts of actual cash and reconciliation to account balances in the information system records (similar to bank statement reconciliation) help to detect theft or loss due to errors in petty and on-hand cash accounts such as those stored in cash registers.

Resource Theft and Loss: Inventory, Supplies, and Operating Assets
Restriction of access to non-cash resources is the most common preventive control to reduce theft of those resources. In enterprises for which inventory, supplies, and operating assets are delivered to the enterprise via common carriers or suppliers, the receiving dock should be secured, and the goods immediately transferred from the receiving dock to a locked storeroom or warehouse to which only authorized employees are allowed access. The goods may then be transferred to less secure environments as needed. In enterprises for which merchandise is sold via shipments (e.g., mail order catalog companies or internet stores), inventory is typically kept locked in the storeroom or warehouse with access limited to authorized employees. In other enterprises customers need to be able to physically examine inventory, so the inventory must be transferred to a less secure sales floor. For high value items, access is still often limited. For example, in retail stores, high priced items that are small enough to be easily stolen are typically kept in locked display cases and can only be examined by customers under the direct supervision of a sales representative.

When supplies and operating assets are made available to the business processes in which they are to be used up, their access should still be restricted when practical. For example, employee offices containing furniture, computer equipment, and other operating assets should be locked when not in use. Buildings in which offices are located should be locked during non-working hours. Precautions such as tagging each operating asset with a permanent id tag help to deter theft and to facilitate periodic counts of operating assets and reconciliation of the counts with the recorded assets on hand. As with cash, all enterprise resources should periodically be counted and the balances compared to the recorded balances in the enterprise information system. Discrepancies should be brought to management's attention.

Supplies are the resources employees are most likely to steal from enterprises. Most supplies are small, relatively inexpensive, and easily mixed in with employees' personal supplies. Many employees don't consider personal use of enterprise supplies as theft; and some firms may view personal use of supplies by employees as acceptable. Enterprises that want to monitor supply use typically keep supplies locked in a cabinet, closet, or room that can only be opened under the watchful eye of an employee who is assigned custody of those assets. The enterprise may require documentation of what supplies were removed and by whom to help detect excessive or unnecessary use of supplies. Such procedures have become more important in recent years, as employees have developed personal needs for more expensive supplies such as printer toner, computer storage media, etc.

When people are made aware of detective controls, those detective controls may also serve as deterrents. That does not make their primary purpose preventative; however, prevention will be a secondary purpose. Such detective controls don't prevent all people from stealing; however, they may deter some people due to their fear of getting caught. One such primarily detective control that may also have secondary preventive benefit is the use of surveillance equipment such as security cameras to identify theft or damage as or after it occurs and to identify those responsible for theft or damage. Companies frequently use surveillance equipment in the less secure environments such as the sales floor, and employee offices, but also use them in the more secure storerooms and warehouses.

Tracking the chain of custody of resources is a preventive and detective control for loss. Several technologies exist to assist with tracking the chain of custody of inventory. One is the application of barcodes to inventory and/or inventory containers and the subsequent scanning of the barcode labels as the inventory and/or inventory containers move throughout the enterprise's acquisition and sales processes. An example of the use of barcodes to track the location and chain of custody of assets with which you may be familiar is that offered by enterprises such as Federal Express and UPS. When you ship a package with one of these enterprises, a barcode is applied to the package. At each location, and when custody of the package changes hands, the barcode is scanned to update the database with the current status of the package in the chain of custody. To enhance customer service, these companies provide customers with tracking numbers that correspond to the barcodes applied to their packages. Customers may enter the tracking numbers on the company websites or via telephone to determine the location and status of the packages.

Radio frequency identification (RFID) tags are another type of technology available to track the chain of custody of resources. *RFID tags* communicate electronically with a reader via radio waves, thus eliminating the need to scan the tags with barcode readers. The readers are connected to a networked information system. Items or containers of items are automatically tracked as they move from location to location. Some envision these tags playing a role in future grocery shopping, allowing shoppers to simply associate their shopping cart with a debit or credit card (or even a virtual wallet phone app such as ApplePay); put desired items into bags in their carts and then leave the store with the merchandise. The readers would transmit details to the networked information system and the customer's authorized payment vendor would transfer the digital payment to the store.

Resource Obsolescence and Waste

The risk of obsolescence is the likelihood of a resource becoming outdated or superseded by new products. This risk is particularly great for inventory, but is also a concern for some operating assets and supplies. Some types of resources are more susceptible to decreased value due to obsolescence than are other types of resources. To control the risk of obsolescence, enterprises need to avoid purchasing or producing more inventories, supplies, and operating assets than they expect to sell or use up in a reasonable timeframe. An enterprise system can help to mitigate the risk of obsolescence by shortening the entire cycle from estimating the demand for a product to acquiring the raw materials, manufacturing the product, selling the product, and collecting the cash.

Resource Damage: Inventory and Supplies

Another risk associated with resources is the risk of damage while in storage or while in transit. Damage could result from various causes, including a lack of climate control, inadequate packaging, careless handling, haphazard placement of inventory on storage shelves, etc. Well-communicated inventory storage and handling procedures and employee training of those procedures are preventive controls for such damage. Insurance is a corrective control; it will not necessarily prevent the damage from occurring but the firm will be compensated for the loss.

Event and Association Controls

Business and information process risks associated with events and the associations in which they participate generally include

- Failure to execute an event that should occur
- Failure to record an event that did occur
- Execution of an event that should not occur
- Recording of an event that did not occur
- Execution of an event at an incorrect time or location, or involving the incorrect resources and/or agents
- Incorrect recording of event details (such as time, location, affected resources, and agents involved)

We next examine specific risks that fit into these general categories for each type of event in various business and information processes.

Instigation Event Risks and Controls

Some risks reduce the likelihood of the enterprise fulfilling its strategic and operational objectives with respect to its instigation events. Instigation events are those events that initiate the chain of events within each business process. For the revenue process, instigation events include marketing efforts, sales calls, and customer inquiries. Some examples of risk associated with such instigation events include:

- Failure to make potential customers aware of product features that would entice them to buy the product.

- Mistakes made in the advertising or promotions regarding the products or services available for sale.

- A sales call presentation to a customer, including products the customer has no reason to be interested in, or for which they have previously declared no interest.

- Inability of customer making an inquiry to find the information they need about desired products or services.

- Inability to track which customer orders result from each separate marketing effort (tracking is desired in order to know which marketing efforts to continue, which to discontinue, which to further develop, etc.).

- Salespeople spending too much time with non-target customers, i.e., people who never buy anything or who don't buy enough to justify the time commitment of marketing personnel.

- Salespeople spending time doing unproductive things that do not influence potential customers.

In the acquisition process the most common instigation event is a purchase requisition. When a department supervisor identifies a need for a good or service and communicates that need to the Purchasing department, that communication is a purchase requisition. Some examples of risk associated with purchase requisition instigation events include:

- Failure to identify needs for resources in a timely manner.

- Requisitioning resources that are not actually needed by the enterprise or that do not have the features the enterprise needs.

- Inability to locate a reliable source from which to obtain needed items.

- Failure to approve a requisition for items for which need was appropriately identified.

- Requisitioning items for which they do not have available funding in their budgets.

This list is only a beginning; many risks exist that may inhibit an enterprise achieving its strategic and operational objectives for instigation events. The list of possible controls to mitigate risks associated with instigation events is even longer, thus we do not attempt to provide an exhaustive list. However, one major control is an effective enterprise information system. The more complete the design of the enterprise-wide database, the more information-related risks are mitigated. For example, if the database is designed in conformance with the REA pattern (and if data are entered correctly and completely) the enterprise will be able to track which instigation events lead to customer orders. Sales and marketing personnel should be able to run queries to effectively identify desirable customers and to help schedule their activities to minimize wasted time. The information system can also accurately report salespeople's activities. Merely recording and reporting the activities performed and the amount of time spent on each activity encourages effective use of time. Similarly, if production schedule data from the conversion process is integrated with the acquisition process, the need for the raw materials involved in upcoming production runs can be communicated automatically. Such an information system can also integrate information linking departmental budgets to requisitions to determine whether funding is available or whether the proposed purchase will cause budget overruns.

Mutual Commitment Event Risks and Controls

Mutual commitment events in the REA ontology are those events that obligate the enterprise to participate in a future exchange with an external business partner that will result in one or more economic events that increase a resource and will also result in one or more economic events that decrease a resource. In the revenue and acquisition processes, sale orders and purchase orders are the most common mutual commitment events. Risks associated with these events include:

- Failure to accept an order that both the enterprise and the potential customer would have been willing and able to fulfill.

- Acceptance of an order from an undesirable or unauthorized customer (e.g., a bad credit risk, thus increasing bad debt losses).

- Acceptance of an order for a product or service that is not currently sold by the company and can't be made available.

- Acceptance of an order by an unauthorized internal agent.

- Commitment to provide products or services with an unrealistic delivery date.

- Commitment to provide products or services at an unprofitable price.

- Failure to place a purchase order for items the enterprise needs and can pay for, and which a reliable vendor could fill.

- Placement of a purchase order from an undesirable or unauthorized vendor.

- Placement of a purchase order for items the company no longer needs, or for too many items as compared to the quantity needed by the enterprise.

- Placement of a purchase order by an unauthorized employee.

- A purchasing agent placing an order for a dollar amount that is higher than his or her authorized limit.

- Failure to provide adequate lead-time to vendors when placing orders, leading to impossible situations or leading to exorbitant shipping and handling costs.

- Failure to obtain the lowest possible cost for the highest possible quality items.

Some of these risks can be controlled declaratively within an enterprise system. For example, the interface can be programmed to prevent placement of a purchase order with an unauthorized vendor, and to prevent acceptance of a sale order from a customer who is not in the system as an approved customer. The interface can also be programmed to allow only items on the "approved list of goods and services" to be purchased or sold, to allow them to be purchased and sold only by selected internal agents (identified by passwords and access codes), to automatically insert the quoted costs and selling prices from the master cost sheet and price list (and possibly to allow adjustments within a specified range), and to automatically calculate line item extensions and total order amounts. Such automation not only improves the efficiency of the business processes, it also improves control over business and information process risks.

Economic Decrement Event Risks and Controls

Because economic decrement events involve an outflow of economic resources such as inventory or cash, this type of event is particularly susceptible to risks associated with theft of those resources (see *Resource Risks* earlier in this chapter). Risks associated with sales, shipments, or service engagements in the revenue process include:

- Failure to ship goods in response to a sale order commitment.
- Shipment of goods that were not ordered by a customer.
- Shipment of goods by an unauthorized internal agent.
- Shipment of goods to the wrong customer or to an unauthorized location.
- Shipping the wrong product or the incorrect amount of product.
- Shipping poorly packaged products.
- Selecting a poor carrier or route.
- Losing sales due to untimely shipments.

An effective enterprise system can help control several of these risks. The system itself can verify who ships products and to whom they are shipped. Passwords can prevent an unauthorized internal agent from gaining access to the system to ship products. Computer generated address labels can prevent shipping products to the wrong customers and product bar codes can help prevent shipping the wrong products.

Risks associated with cash disbursements include:

- Failure to pay for goods that were received, or making late payments, thus earning a bad credit rating.
- Recording a cash disbursement that did not in fact occur.
- Making duplicate cash disbursements for the same purchase.
- Recording incorrect details about cash disbursements
- Failure to take advantage of early payment discounts.

A common control for mitigating some of these risks associated with cash disbursements is having one person check another person's work – known as an *independent check on performance*. For example, one employee may write checks based on the supporting documentation, and another employee may verify the accuracy of the checks and the entries to record them. Alternatively as the underlying acquisitions are made, the system may generate and record the checks and an employee may verify their accuracy and sign them.

Economic Increment Event Risks and Controls

Because economic increment events involve resource inflows, these events are also particularly susceptible to risks associated with theft (see *Resource Risks* earlier in this chapter). In the revenue and financing processes, the most common economic increment event is the receipt of cash. Risks associated with cash receipts include:

- Failure to receive cash as a result of a sale, or failure to record cash that was received.

- Recording a cash receipt that did not in fact occur.
- Accepting duplicate cash receipts for the same sale.
- Recording incorrect details about cash receipts
- Failure to deposit cash into the bank in a timely manner, or depositing cash into the wrong cash account.

When cash is received in the mail, two employees should open the mail together. One employee should take the money and prepare the deposit and the other person should send a receipt to the customer and record the receipt in the company's information system. The system should compare the deposit total with the total of the receipts to verify their equality. A control to reduce the risk of data entry errors is the use of computer-readable remittance advices. If a customer pays the exact amount of an invoice and returns the remittance advice with the payment, the computer can read the information on the remittance advice and know the amount of the payment and the customer information needed to correctly process the payment.

In the acquisition process, the most common economic increment is the receipt of inventory, supplies, services, or operating assets. Risks associated with such acquisition events include:
- Failure to receive goods or services in response to a purchase order commitment.
- Receipt of goods or services that the enterprise did not order.
- Receipt of the wrong goods or services or an incorrect quantity of goods or services.
- Damaging goods during unpacking on the receiving dock.
- Failure to receive goods or services in a timely manner.
- Failure to record acquisitions quickly enough to take advantage of early payment discounts.

Access restriction controls for resource-related theft risks as described earlier in this chapter should also be enforced for acquisition events. An effective enterprise system can help control several of the other risks identified. The system can be used during the acquisition event to verify the goods received were in fact ordered. An automated system records the receipt of goods as the goods are received, ensuring that early payment discounts may be taken. The system may also be queried on a regular basis to identify and follow up with vendors regarding unfilled purchase orders (i.e., orders for which goods have not yet been received).

Economic Decrement Reversal Risks and Controls
Economic decrement reversal events in the revenue process should be subject to close scrutiny because they are the alternative to the expected economic increment event and because they involve custody of inventory. Sale returns are sometimes used as a means to cover up theft of cash (e.g., without proper controls, a clerk may steal a customer payment for an invoice and then process a sale return for the invoice amount). Other risks associated with sale returns include:
- Failure to accept a sale return for which a customer has a legitimate reason.
- Acceptance of returned goods that were not originally sold by the enterprise.
- Approval of a sale return by an unauthorized employee.

- Recording a sale return that did not in fact occur.

These risks may be controlled with the aid of an enterprise system. No person without a proper password or access code should be able to authorize a sale return event. Access restriction controls and chain of custody tracking should be enforced for the receipt of the returned merchandise into the warehouse.

Economic Increment Reversal Risks and Controls
Similarly, economic increment reversal events in the acquisition process are the alternative to the expected economic decrement event and they involve custody of inventory. Purchase returns are sometimes used as a means to cover up theft of inventory, supplies, or operating assets (e.g., without proper controls, a clerk may steal goods and then process a fictitious purchase return for the purchase amount). Other risks associated with purchase returns may include:

- Failure to return goods that did not satisfy the enterprise's needs.
- Return of goods that the enterprise does in fact need.
- Approval of a purchase return by an unauthorized employee.
- Recording a purchase return that did not in fact occur.

These risks may be controlled with the aid of an enterprise system. No person without a proper password or access code should be able to authorize a purchase return event. Restriction of access controls should be employed in the activities of packaging and shipping the goods back to the appropriate vendor. The enterprise system may be used to verify who ships goods and to whom they are shipped to help resolve any dispute with a vendor as to whether goods were actually returned. Passwords can prevent unauthorized employees from gaining access to the system to ship products. Computer generated address labels can prevent shipping products to the wrong vendors and product bar codes can help prevent returns of the wrong products.

Controls for Information Process Risks
Many of the controls for business process risks involved information system controls that overlap with controls for information process risks. Indeed, it is often difficult to distinguish between controls over actual business process objects and the recording, maintenance, and reporting of information about those objects. This section focuses on information processing risks and controls that are reasonably separable from the business process objects themselves.

Although all information processing errors and irregularities are undesirable, those that occur during the recording and maintenance processes are particularly harmful. Why? The old adage, "Garbage in, Garbage out!" If inaccurate, invalid, or incomplete data are either recorded or maintained, the result is erroneous reporting. Since important decisions regarding the enterprise's strategy and direction are based on reports produced by the system, the errors may prove disastrous.

Controls for information process risks check the accuracy, completeness, and authorization of information to be recorded, maintained, and reported. Such controls typically are categorized as either IT general controls (ITGCs) or application controls. ITGCs relate to the general IT environment in which technology and applications are bought, developed, used, and protected. *Application controls* are features included in software programs that help to ensure that transactional data are authorized, complete, and accurate. Exhibit 9-4 illustrates the relationship between the general controls and the application controls in a typical environment. The IT general controls mitigate risk associated with access to the enterprise software programs and to the data, with development of the enterprise software programs, with changes to the enterprise software programs, and with computer operations. Enterprise systems often use a three-tier architecture as shown in Exhibit 9-4. In such environments, the first tier consists of end user computers which are clients on the network. The second tier consists of web/application servers and the third tier consists of a database server.

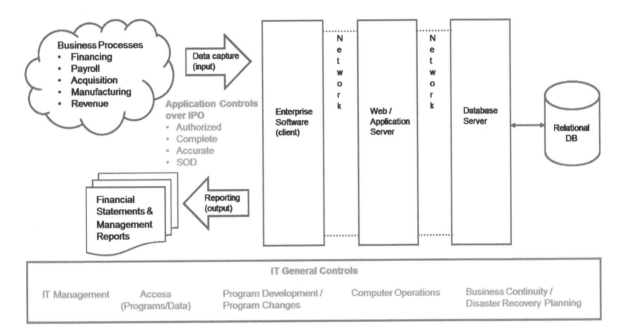

Exhibit 9-4: Generic IT Environment

End users interact directly with the client tier, where they log into the enterprise system applications. The applications have controls to ensure data entered is authorized, complete, and accurate. End user accounts are assigned to roles that control what data the users can view, add, edit, and delete. Such roles can, and should, be established according to segregation of duties principles. For example, the role "HR" is set up such that users with that role have the authority to add new employees, but not to disburse paychecks to employees; whereas the role "Payroll" is set up such that users with that role have the authority to disburse paychecks to employees, but not to add new employees. Proper segregation of duties would ensure that a single user account not have the power of both of these roles, to prevent a user from both adding a new (fictitious) employee and issuing paychecks to the new (fictitious) employee. The principle of least privilege, i.e., only provide privileges as minimally necessary to perform job functions, should be applied to roles and to user accounts assigned to roles.

As Exhibit 9-4 illustrates, the ITGCs span all three tiers of the client-server architecture, as well as the data capture, storage, and reporting. While application controls are effective within specific software packages, Exhibit 9-4 shows potential access vulnerabilities that could allow one to circumvent the application controls. For example, one could potentially access data directly through the network operating system or the database that underlies an application without effective ITGCs preventing such access. Implementing and testing such controls requires specific technical training and expertise that most accountants don't have, and are beyond the scope of this book. Instead, we focus on the ITGCs that accountants typically implement and test.

Information Technology General Controls (ITGCs)

We chose to focus on five categories of ITGCs: (1) IT Management, (2) Access to Programs and Data, (3) Program Development and Changes, (4) Computer Operations, and (5) Business Continuity/Disaster Recovery Planning. ITGCs apply to all system components, processes, and data present in an enterprise. ITGCs aim to maintain integrity of computer operations, including program and data files.

IT Management

Possibly the most important control for information process risks is to ensure that whomever is in charge of IT and IT controls is a high level executive who reports to the president of the enterprise - in other words, an executive who sits in the C-suite, such as a Chief Information Officer (CIO) or Chief Risk Management Officer (CRMO). Having such an individual responsible and accountable for the enterprise's IT and related controls greatly increases the likelihood that information process risks will be well-managed. The executive in charge of IT should work with a steering committee, composed of several other key officers of the enterprise, to develop a plan that identifies the strategic use of information technology within the enterprise and prioritizes the development of individual components. This plan should align IT with the enterprise's business objectives and should be well-communicated with all business process owners and other relevant employees throughout the enterprise.

IT management should create and maintain documentation for all significant IT activities, processes and controls, and establish appropriate metrics to monitor and evaluate those activities, processes and controls. IT management should also create and maintain an inventory of all key systems and data and identify owners of those systems and data. The enterprise should maintain documentation of the system/data owners' responsibilities, with owners' acknowledgement of, and agreement to, those responsibilities. IT management should also ensure segregation of duties within the IT area such that no single individual could undermine a critical process. IT management should provide to all staff continuing education programs that include ethical conduct, integrity standards, system security, and confidentiality training.

Access to Programs and Data

Enterprises must protect their programs and data both from unauthorized physical access and from unauthorized logical access.

In the business process risk section we discussed the need to restrict access to enterprise resources. The enterprise system is made up of resources to which access should be restricted. Critical system hardware such as file servers should be locked in restricted areas. Other components of networked information systems usually need to be accessible to authorized users to complete business and information processes. Unauthorized access to systems represents a tremendous risk to enterprises, so prevention of unauthorized system access is important. Controlling access is critical when systems have online, real-time transaction processing capabilities. Any computer that is connected to the Internet is vulnerable to attempted break-ins by unauthorized users. Unauthorized users are sometimes referred to as hackers. Hackers may seek personal gain from intruding into an enterprise's information system, or they may seek only to cause destruction to the enterprise such as has been accomplished by denial of service attacks. In a denial of service attack, an intruder typically logs into the system and launches an application that inundates the server with logins such that it gets overloaded and has insufficient resources to serve legitimate users' needs. The most likely way to ensure the secrecy of data that is stored on a computer is to keep the computer as a standalone (i.e., never connect it to the Internet) and keep that computer locked in a secure place. The movie *Mission Impossible* illustrates this, wherein a computer that contains a list is a standalone computer, locked in a well-controlled room within CIA headquarters. A team devises a plan to circumvent the many physical access controls (including a retinal scanner to prevent unauthorized entry, floor sensors and temperature change sensors to detect unauthorized entry, and many more). Most enterprises can't operate effectively with standalone computers; therefore they must implement logical access controls at all possible layers of entry.

Firewalls block unauthorized access while allowing outward communication from enterprise computers. Intrusion detection systems consist of devices or software applications that monitor the network for suspicious activity and policy violations and issue alerts administration when such problems are identified. Enterprises should periodically conduct vulnerability assessments, i.e., identify, classify, quantify, and prioritize the vulnerabilities in its computer systems, network infrastructure, and software applications to understand and control the risk associated with these weak points. Such vulnerability assessments may include ethical hacking and social engineering.

Ethical hacking (also called penetration testing) involves computer security experts employing the same procedures as malicious hackers use to expose weaknesses in the enterprise system. These experts are expected to communicate all identified weakness to management so that management can strengthen the system to fend off malicious hackers. Social engineering within a vulnerability assessment involves computer security experts attempting to deceive and manipulate employees into revealing confidential information such as passwords or bank account numbers. Such attempts may include phone pretexting, email phishing, USB drive baiting, and physical access. In phone pretexting, a social engineer pretends to be someone authorized to obtain confidential information to trick the employee into providing that information. They may spoof their caller id such that the call appears to be coming from a legitimate source. Phishing emails likewise may appear to come from a legitimate sender, asking the employee to click on a link that ends up filling the employee's computer with malware that steals confidential information or passwords. Employees should never plug an unknown USB drive into their computers. USB drive baiting, therefore, attempts to get employees to do just that. Perhaps the social engineer drops a USB drive on an employee's desk or into a desk drawer while the employee is away from their desk. Perhaps the social engineer sends a USB drive to the employee in the mail. If the employee takes the bait and plugs in the USB drive, it fills their computer with malware that steals confidential information or passwords. Physical access social engineers may drop by the employee's desk pretending to be from IT and needing to access the employee's computer for a legitimate sounding reason such as upgrading the enterprise software on the employee's computer. They will simply ask for the employee's password. If the employee isn't present when they arrive, they may look around the employee's workstation to see if they employee has written their password and left it in an accessible place. They will check to see if the employee left their computer while still logged in, thus allowing unauthorized access to the enterprise system. As in ethical hacking, the security expert social engineer uses the same techniques a malicious social engineer would use, to determine points of weakness in the enterprise so that management can strengthen those points by re-training employees to resist such attempts.

Logical access controls restrict unauthorized access to the programs and data in systems. Networked information systems have several layers of potential access points, each of which must be secured. Besides controlling access to the enterprise's application software packages, it is also necessary to control access to the underlying database, and to the overall network operating system. If adequate controls are not built into the system at each layer, unauthorized users may gain access to the application software through a back door in the network operating system or in the underlying database. System access controls involve the use of passwords and an access control matrix.

A *password* is a unique identifier that only the user should know and is required to enter each time he/she logs onto the system. Passwords are a weak form of protection. Unless passwords are formally assigned, routinely changed, and protected from use by other people, they will quickly get into the wrong hands and provide unauthorized access to the system. An *access control matrix* identifies the functions each user is allowed to perform and what data and programs the user can access once he or she gains access to the system. For example, only a limited number of individuals are allowed access to payroll data. Some users are only allowed to read data, while other users are given the right to read and update the data. Access controls require users to authenticate themselves (i.e. give evidence that they are who they say they are) by providing something they know, something they possess, or something they physically are. Examples of access controls that represent things users know are passwords and personal identification numbers (PINs). Examples of access controls that represent things users possess are identification cards or tokens. Examples of access controls that require physical characteristics as input include voice recognition, fingerprint identification, retinal scanners, and digital signature recognition technology.

Enterprises can also use terminal identification codes to prevent access by unauthorized terminals over communication lines. A host computer can require a terminal to electronically transmit its identification code that identifies it as an authorized terminal and defines (and limits) the type of transaction a terminal user can perform. The host computer compares the identification code it receives from the terminal with a list of approved terminal identification codes to verify that it is an approved terminal.

Encryption is used to protect highly sensitive and confidential data. *Encryption* is a process of encoding data entered into the system, storing or transmitting the data in coded form, and then decoding the data upon its use or arrival at its destination. This prevents unauthorized access to the data while it is stored or as it is transmitted. Unauthorized users can easily intercept information broadcast over networks by applications that do not use encryption.

Given that the last few paragraphs has discussed the difference between authorized and unauthorized users, all of the controls we discussed could be circumvented if the enterprise hasn't adequately developed procedures for the creation, change, and deletion of authorized user accounts. New employees should be given access privileges commensurate with their responsibilities in a timely manner; as their responsibilities change, their access privileges should change accordingly. Access privileges of terminated employees (whether termination was voluntary or involuntary) should be revoked in a timely manner.

Program Development and Program Changes

Systems software consists of the computer programs that make the computer hardware run. They include the operating system, networking and communication software, and various utilities programs to back up and maintain files. Application software consists of the programs that process the business events of the enterprise such as the acquisition of goods and services and the production of finished products. Because of the high cost to develop custom software, there is a growing trend to purchase both systems and application software and modify them as necessary to meet the needs of the enterprise. Care must be taken in specifying the requirements of the software, analyzing available software to see which package best meets the requirements, modifying the software as necessary, and testing individual applications and the entire system to make sure it processes the data accurately.

User departments are generally responsible for developing the list of software requirements. People from the user departments, the systems analysts, and the programmers work together to identify potential software packages in the market and compare their features with those desired by the enterprise. When modifications are required, the systems analysts design the changes and the computer programmers write the code to make the changes. Test data are generally used to verify that the programs and the entire system work correctly. Test data reflect a set of business events to test every logic path within the programs. The correct results from running the test data are developed independently from the system being tested and are compared with the results obtained when processed by the new system. If the new system correctly processes the test data we assume it has been modified correctly. The data control group is responsible for reviewing the testing and the test results to verifying that they are adequate and that the systems is ready for use.

This same process must be followed every time a modification is required in a program. The request comes from the user department. Systems analysts design the change, programmers write the code and use test data to verify that the program functions properly, and the data control group verifies the program is ready for use. Once the modification is complete, it is turned over to the operating people and controlled by the systems librarian. Controls over developing and maintaining a system are very important. The way a system is developed is as important as how it is operated in preventing errors and irregularities. For example, this separation of duties within the software development area may prevent a programmer from inserting code in enterprise software that transfers miniscule monetary amounts from individual transactions to their own bank accounts that accumulate to large sums. Hollywood movies such as Superman III and Office Space include scenes whereby programmers scam companies in this manner. What's the true magnitude of the financial shrinkage due to fraudulent software? No one knows.

Computer Operations

ITGCs for computer operations have the objective of ensuring that all systems and programs are available and processing accurately. Some of the ITGCs we discussed as physical and logical access controls, such as firewalls and intrusion detection systems, also help to achieve this objective. The enterprise may need to prohibit use of unauthorized software by employees on enterprise computers. Additional ITGCs include file security controls, configuration testing, batch job processing and monitoring controls, incident management controls, tests of spreadsheets and other user-developed systems, and system backups.

File security controls attempt to verify that the correct file is being updated and to prevent inadvertent destruction or inappropriate use of files. Some of these controls include the following:

> *External file labels* (as simple as stick-on labels) identify a storage media's contents and help prevent someone from inadvertently writing over the contents of the disk or tape.

> *Internal file labels* record the name of a file, the date it was created, and other identifying data on the file medium to be read and verified by the computer. Internal labels include *header labels* and *trailer labels*. Header labels are a file description recorded at the beginning of a file. Trailer labels mark the end of a file and contain control or summary data about the contents of the file.

> *Lockout procedures* are used by database management systems to prevent two applications or users from updating the same record or data item at the same time.

> *The read-only file designation* is used to mark data available for reading only. The data cannot be altered by instructions from users, nor can new data be stored on the device.

Configuration testing is periodic testing and assessment performed to confirm that the software and network infrastructure is appropriately configured and is operating as intended. This includes a review of any configuration changes, additions, or deletions to determine whether or not they were properly approved based on demonstrated need.

Batch job processing and monitoring controls are implemented to help ensure that authorized programs are run as scheduled and that deviations from the plan are identified and investigated. Management should document job schedules, and the procedures in place to monitor job completeness. Chronological information from job processing should be recorded and stored in logs to enable the review, examination, and reconstruction of system and data processing.

Incident management controls provide reasonable assurance that the enterprise adequately responds to, records, resolves, or investigates any problems and incidents in computer operations. One such control is an incident management system that records, analyzes, and resolves data integrity and access control incidents and reports them to management. Such a system should include an audit trail that allows management to trace the incident to its underlying cause. Another such control is a documented process for investigating incidents with examples of how to resolve problems that may arise.

Tests of spreadsheets and other user-developed systems are crucial in any enterprise that relies on data maintained in or generated by such systems. Spreadsheets are the most common type of user-developed system in practice, so we focus our discussion on them. Because spreadsheets are susceptible to a high error rate, as users may mis-type formulae or inadvertently overwrite data, they should be documented and regularly reviewed for processing integrity. Enterprises should periodically use test data to evaluate whether the spreadsheets sort and calculate that data accurately. If at all possible, enterprises should move away from user-developed systems and instead use systems that are less susceptible to inadvertent modification. In addition to their error susceptibility, if such systems are maintained by multiple employees in multiple locations, version control will likely become a problem, as will their vulnerability to unauthorized access and tampering.

Until we have a fail-safe technology, we must guard against possible failures in the computer hardware and its power source, as well as protect system hardware from the environment. Such failures can result in the interruption of business operations and the loss of data. As a preventive measure, enterprises should properly maintain computer equipment and facilities, and operate equipment in an appropriate physical environment (environmental controls). For larger systems, specially prepared rooms are sometimes necessary to house computer equipment. Some enterprises have backup system components (e.g., extra disk storage devices, extra printers, and extra communication channels) so that if a component fails, processing can quickly be transferred to another component without interrupting the flow of processing for an extended period of time.

Not only can computer components fail, but the power source for the components can also fail or provide an irregular power supply. The loss of power shuts down the entire operation and any data in temporary storage will be lost. Protection from the loss of power is usually provided through the use of special battery units called uninterruptable power supplies (UPS). These devices provide battery support and sound an alarm when power is interrupted. This allows needed time to stop computer processes and back up data and instructions (programs). An irregular power supply can damage or destroy the computer hardware. Sudden and dramatic increases in power are called power surges or spikes. Protecting against surges or spikes involves the use of a surge protector or line conditioning. Conditioning power lines is sometimes provided by utility companies, but can also be provided by a simple and relatively low cost, device called a surge protector.

Regardless of the controls taken to secure the computer and prevent problems, files are occasionally lost and programs are occasionally destroyed. Therefore, it is necessary to maintain backup or duplicate copies of current data files, programs, and documentation. At least one set of backup copies of all these items should be stored at a location that is physically removed from the computer facilities, in case whatever destroyed the original data also destroys the backup. For example, if a thief steals a laptop and the backup external hard drive that is with the laptop, data recovery may be impossible. Cloud storage (computers stored at other locations to which data are transmitted electronically) offers enterprises an easy solution for offsite backup. Enterprise that do not want to store data in the cloud should regularly transport backups to an offsite location to avoid losing both original and backup data simultaneously. Enterprises should develop policies for how long to retain backup copies. The length of time will depend on the managerial and regulatory requirements of the enterprise. System backups should be automated, if at all possible, as humans tend to forget or procrastinate, as other tasks seem to be much more important. Until they lose hours, days, weeks, or months of work as a result of failing to back up their data.

Business Continuity/Disaster Recovery Planning

The backup process we discussed in the previous section is to protect against routine hardware failures and human errors. However, it also helps enterprises to keep their businesses running and to recover when disasters ensue. Such disasters include natural disasters such as earthquakes, fire, floods, tornadoes, and hurricanes as well as unnatural disasters such as terrorist attacks or other events that cause major hardware and software failures. A global enterprise that suffers such a failure in one location must be able to continue its operations in other locations. If the failure occurs at its primary system location, lack of business continuity/disaster recovery planning could render the entire enterprise unable to operate.

Enterprises should document disaster recovery plans for critical systems and should test those plans annually. Such plans should detail specific procedures to be followed in various scenarios – i.e., what if location X becomes unavailable but all other locations are operational, what if locations X and Y are both unavailable but all other locations are operational; what if half of the locations are unavailable, and so forth. Disaster recovery plans should include arrangements for alternate work sites. For example, an enterprise may have multiple data centers at different locations such that they may take on each other's workload if one center goes down. Alternatively, enterprises may create reciprocal agreements other enterprises such that if one has a disaster, the other will take on their workload. In both of these examples, the enterprises involved must ensure that they have sufficient technical infrastructure to handle double the workload in emergency situations.

Some elements of business continuity and disaster recovery plans exist to help minimize the extent of disasters. For example, enterprises should install smoke alarms and fire extinguishers and keep flashlights on hand at all business locations. Being alerted and having the means to put out small fires may avert disaster altogether. Having flashlights on hand allows selected employees to guide others out of buildings with power outages. Similarly, ensuring that electronic equipment is stored on raised surfaces, with water sensors below them may enable employees to move the equipment to safer locations when flooding begins. Although in some flooding situations, safe recovery of the equipment will be impossible, enterprises should still take measures to protect themselves in case of less disastrous situations.

Just as insurance provides corrective control for the resources discussed in the business process risk portion of this chapter, so also insurance provides corrective control for IT resources as part of business continuity and disaster recovery plans. Insurance for natural and human-made disasters will help to ensure that enterprises experiencing such disasters will have the resources they need to replace the damaged system components

Application Controls

Application controls are controls that apply to the processing within individual software programs. These controls help ensure that transactions are valid, properly authorized, and completely and accurately processed. Our discussion of application controls will be divided into data input controls, processing controls, and file controls.

Data Input Controls

Some of the most important controls are those dealing with the accuracy and completeness of data as the data are entered into the computer. Accuracy of input data is checked by event processing rules, data entry verification, and several edit checks.

Event processing rules should be built into the system to verify that prescribed business rules are followed when executing an event. Some examples of potential business rules include:

> A customer may exist in our database before participating in a related sale event, but it is not permissible to record a sale event without identifying the related customer.

> Products can be shipped (Sale event) only after a valid customer order has been taken (Sale Order event).

> Each customer order can have one or more types of inventory associated with it; each inventory type can be involved in many customer orders; and information about inventory types may be entered into the system before any orders are taken.

As we discussed in previous chapters, business rules such as these can be designed into the relational database table definitions by specifying the multiplicities that correspond to the business rules. Alternatively such rules or business logic can be programmed into the user interface software. In some cases these event processing rules and programmed business logic can help enterprises detect errors or irregularities; in other cases it will help prevent errors.

If data are entered after the events actually occurred, the control is detective rather than preventive. The data entry clerk will not be able to enter the data into the system and will need to bring it to a manager's attention, thereby identifying the error or irregularity. For example, consider a mail order company that does not normally have prepaid sales and very rarely generates cash sales. Because the company also receives cash from non-sale sources (such as bank loans), the information system must allow cash receipts to be entered without having previously processed a corresponding sale. A risk exists that a cash receipt that actually resulted from a sale was not matched to any corresponding sale in the system. To detect such a case, a query may be developed to identify any unmatched cash receipts in the system so that someone can verify whether they match loans or whether they should have been matched to a sale. That investigation could reveal that the sale was inadvertently not recorded in the system (the enterprise's error). Alternatively a query could identify "overmatched" cash receipts in the system – those for which the cash receipt amount exceeded the related sale amount(s); such a query could reveal that a customer paid for the same sale twice (the customer's error, but the enterprise should return the overpayment).

Event processing rules can also help prevent errors or fraud, if the data input functions are embedded in the business process procedures. That is, if the data are entered on a real-time basis as the events occur, enforcement of business rules by the database or user interface software will prevent the noncompliant events from being recorded which will then result in non-execution of the events. In other words, the system can note activities that represent exceptions to the prescribed rules and send exception messages to a responsible person for review. Based on the authorized person's response, the system can allow or prevent execution of the activity. For example, is a shipment normally necessary to record an order? No; instead, an order event should precede the shipping event. Is an order necessary to execute a shipment? For many enterprises the answer is yes! The authorization for a shipment is the existence of a valid order. Without a valid order, the shipping event should not be executed. An IT application could deny the execution and recording of a shipment that is not supported by a valid order. If shipping personnel can only generate shipping labels through the system, the likelihood of shipping merchandise without an order is reduced significantly. Notice that if an enterprise does not embed the data entry function into the business process procedures, but instead inputs data after the events have occurred; then the system's ability to prevent errors and irregularities is substantially reduced; it can only detect rather than prevent.

Data Entry Verification. As event data are entered into systems they must be checked to verify the accuracy of the record being updated and the accuracy of the data itself. Two controls often applied in this area are closed loop verification and key verification.

> *Closed-loop verification* uses one input data item to locate the record to be updated and displays other data from the record so the data entry person can verify it as the correct record to be processed. For example, if a sale order clerk enters a customer number for a customer buying merchandise on account, the computer uses the number to locate the customer record, then display additional customer data (such as name and address) on the computer screen. This way the user can verify that the correct customer record is being updated.

> *Key verification* (also called rekeying) requires one data entry employee to key input data twice, or requires two different data entry employees to enter the same data. The computer compares the data entered on the second keying operation with the original data and highlights any differences. The clerk verifies and corrects any differences.

Edit checks are incorporated into computer instructions to verify and validate the completeness, reasonableness, and/or accuracy of the data. Edit checks can help reduce both operating risk and information processing risk. Their use is not limited to one type of risk or circumstance. The following is an overview of some of the edit check logic used in information systems. Edit checks may be applied to individual fields, records, or batches of records.

Several edit checks can be used to check the accuracy, reasonableness, and completeness of individual data input fields.

> *Check digit.* A formula can be applied to an account number, part number, or similar standard number to calculate a check digit. The check digit is appended to and maintained

as part of the number (usually as the last digit). For example, suppose we want a five-digit account number (including the check digit) and the first four digits of the account number (based on style, division, color, and product type) are 1534. A check digit formula is used to add the fifth digit. There are several check digit formulas, and one rather simple, but less than adequate, formula adds the account number digits and extracts the second digit of the sum. The resulting account number using this formula is 15343 (the 3 is the second digit of $1 + 5 + 3 + 4 = 13$).

Completeness check. A *completeness check* verifies that all critical field data are entered. It checks for missing data or blanks.

Default value. *Default values* set the field contents to a pre-specified (default) value. In some cases the default values may be overridden, while in other cases they may not.

Field or mode check. A *field or mode check* verifies that the entered data type is the appropriate mode for a field. For example, if a field is declared as a text or an alphanumeric field, the data input should be alphanumeric (letters and numbers). Other field modes include numeric, date, logical, counters, memo, and embedded objects (such as video, audio, or graphics).

Range check. A *range check* compares entered data to a predetermined acceptable upper and/or lower limit. Data values are not accepted without special authorization if the data fall outside the specified limits.

Validity check. A *validity check* compares entered data against pre-specified data stored within the computer to determine its validity. For example, to determine the validity of a user identification number, the computer would compare the entered primary key of the user to a stored list of valid user numbers.

The next level of edit checks examines an entire record, generally a record in the file being updated by business event data. Some of the more common record edit checks are:

Master reference check. A *master reference check* verifies that an event/transaction record has a corresponding master record to be updated. An error occurs when there is no corresponding master record for the transaction record. For example, there is an error if you input a sale for a customer not currently included in your customer data files.

Reasonableness check. *Reasonableness checks* verify whether the amount of an event/transaction record appears reasonable when compared to other elements associated with each item being processed. For example, if an employee is coded as a clerk, it is probably unreasonable that her pay per week is $5,000. Note that a reasonableness check is not the same as a limit check. It might be reasonable for the president to have a weekly check of $5,000. The reasonableness of the pay is based on the relationship between position (clerk versus president) and the amount of the pay, not a fixed dollar amount.

Referential integrity. *Referential integrity* is a safeguard to ensure that every posted foreign key attribute relates to a primary key attribute. For example, suppose you have two tables: a Salesperson table and a Sales event table. Since the two tables have a relationship (a salesperson participates in each sale), you must include the primary key attribute of the Salesperson table (e.g., salesperson number) in the Sale event table; salesperson number is a foreign key attribute in the Sales event table. You want to enforce referential integrity to ensure a valid relationship between the two tables. Referential integrity prevents recording a sale in the Sale event table without a valid salesperson number from the Salesperson table. It also prevents deleting a sales person from the Salesperson table as long as that salesperson has sales in the Sale event table.

Valid sign check. The *valid sign check* is used to highlight illogical balances in a master file record. For example, a negative balance for the quantity on hand for a particular item in inventory is a likely error.

The third level of edit checks is for an entire batch of events or transactions. Sometimes business events can be grouped into batches for a period of time, such as one day, and processed together. Controls are needed to make sure none of the events are lost, no unauthorized events are added, and that all events are in the proper sequence and correctly processed.

Sequence check. A *sequence check* verifies the records in a batch are sorted in the correct sequence. For sequential processing (often used in batch processing), the transaction records must be sorted in the same order as the master file's primary key. A sequence check can be used to highlight missing batch items (e.g. a missing check).

Transaction type check. A *transaction type check* verifies that all transactions included within the batch are of the same category or type. For example, we would not want to confuse the addition of a new customer with the addition of a new employee.

Batch control totals. When transactions are processed in batches, each batch should be dated and assigned a unique batch number. A *batch control total* is an internal control used to verify that all transactions within a batch are present and have been processed. They verify that no transactions were added or deleted during processing. There are several types of batch control totals. Let's use a record that includes a customer number field and an invoice amount field to illustrate three types of control totals: hash, financial/numeric, and record count control totals.

Hash control total. A *hash control total* is the sum of an attribute in a file that has no real meaning or use. For example, the sum of the customer number field of all the records in a batch is a meaningless number for purposes other than as a control total. But, if it is calculated when the batch is first assembled, the computer can recalculate it after the records have been entered for processing. If the computer-generated sum is the same as the original amount, we have some assurance that all records were accurately processed. If they are not the same, one or more transactions may have been either added or deleted from the batch.

Financial/numeric control total. A *financial control total* is the sum of a financial field, such as the invoice amount, of all records in a batch. Usually, this is a meaningful numeric or financial field. For example, the total of the invoice amounts is meaningful because it represents the increase in account receivable and it is useful to evaluate the effectiveness of those taking orders for the day.

Record count control total. A *record count control total* is a total of the number of records in a batch. So if a batch contains 46 records, the record count is 46.

All the control totals can be used to verify batch input, processing, and output. For example, suppose a clerk enters 46 customer invoices totaling $14,678.93 in charge sales into a computer file. Also assume that the sum of the customer account numbers on the invoices is 738476846. Once these records are entered into a batch transaction file, the file should include 46 records (the record count), the customer number field should total 738476846 (a hash total), and the sum of the invoice amount field should total $14,678.93 (a financial total). When the records are processed to update the customer receivable master file, the update run should show that 46 records were affected, and the accounts receivable total should increase by $14,678.93.

Batch control totals may be generated by one computerized process compared with another computerized process that uses the same batch as input; in those cases, a hash total is as easy as a record count or financial/numeric control total. Often, however, the initial batch control total is generated manually with a ten-key adding machine as the batch is created. The batch control total (usually a financial total, but sometimes a record count) is written on the batch header along with the batch number and date. Once a manual batch control total is computed and the batch is processed in a computerized process, the computer process should generate a control total of the same type (financial, numeric, record count, or hash) and the manual total should be compared to the computerized total. If they match, the enterprise has a reasonable confidence that all items in that batch were in fact processed in the computer system processes.

Notice that batch totals do not identify errors in individual records. Batch totals only highlight errors in the group as a whole. Batch totals do not ensure that individual records are updated correct. For example, if the total of an accounts receivable subsidiary ledger equals the total in a general ledger accounts receivable control account, this does not signify that the posting to the individual customer accounts are correct. It only indicates that the same total amount was posted; some individual items could have been posted to the wrong customer's account.

CONCLUDING COMMENTS

This chapter introduced you to the importance of understanding enterprise risks and provided some examples of controls that are available to reduce enterprise risks. Some of the control examples cited are useful for preventing errors and irregularities, while others are helpful in detecting and correcting errors and irregularities. Just as change has become a constant feature of enterprises and information technology, the need for creativity and innovation in identifying risks and developing control procedures to reduce risks is also becoming constant across enterprises. The tools provided in this chapter are only a beginning; as new risks arise, new controls must also be developed. The key is to adequately assess risks, determine which of the risks need to be controlled, and design cost-effective controls to mitigate those risks. When measuring the cost of controls, any decreases in operational efficiency and effectiveness must be considered. Although this chapter may seem long to you, please know that it is by no means a comprehensive discussion of enterprise risks and controls. Entire books are available that cover these topics in greater depth. Our goal was simply to provide a broad overview to start you thinking about enterprise risk and control, especially the usefulness of REA as a framework for systematically identifying and assessing risk.

KEY TERMS AND CONCEPTS
Access control matrix
Application controls
Batch control total
Bonding
Business interruption
Business process risks
Check digit
Closed loop verification
Collusion
Completeness check
Contingency plan
Control activity
Control environment
Corrective controls
Default value
Detective controls
Economic risks
Edit check
Encryption
Enterprise risks
Error (risk and control context)
Field (mode) check
Financial/numeric control total
General controls
Hash control total
Independent check on performance
Industry risks
Information and communication
Information process risks
Internal control
Irregularity (risk and control context)
Key verification (rekeying)
Lapping
Logical access controls
Master reference check
Monitoring

KEY TERMS AND CONCEPTS (continued)
Passwords
Physical access controls
Preventive controls
Range check
Reasonableness check
Reconciliation of physical to recorded quantities
Record count control total
Referential integrity
RFID (radio frequency identification) tags
Risk
Risk assessment
Segregation of duties
Sequence check
Transaction type check
Valid sign check
Validity check

REVIEW QUESTIONS
R9-1. Who is ultimately responsible for internal controls within an enterprise?
R9-2. What is the PCAOB and why was it created?
R9-3. When and how does GDPR apply to American enterprises?
R9-4. What are the five components of internal control that make up the COSO Internal Control Integrated Framework?
R9-5. How can the REA ontology help enterprise managers assess risk?

MULTIPLE CHOICE QUESTIONS
MC9-1. Who does PCAOB's AS#2201 require to evaluate the effectiveness of publicly traded companies' internal control over financial reporting?
　　A) Managers
　　B) Auditors
　　C) Creditors
　　D) Both managers and auditors

MC9-2. The right to be forgotten portion of the General Data Protection Regulation (GDPR) means what?
   A) The request for consent must use clear and plain language, to include the purpose for the processing of related data, and it must be as easy to withdraw consent as it is to give it
   B) Individuals may obtain confirmation to data controllers as to whether or not personal data concerning them is being processed, where, and why, and the data controllers must provide individuals with electronic copies of such data, free of charge
   C) Individuals may request data controllers to erase their personal data, stop distributing the data, and may have third parties stop processing the data
   D) Individuals may obtain data collected about them from one data controller and transmit that data to another controller

MC9-3. The Control Environment component of the COSO Internal Control Integrated Framework is also called
   A) Privacy by design
   B) Tone at the top
   C) Data erasure
   D) Operational compliance

MC9-4. What is the common subject of all twenty principles of the COSO ERM framework?
   A) Risk
   B) Communication
   C) Technology
   D) Accuracy

MC9-5. What is collusion?
   A) Collusion is an internal control designed to prevent fraud.
   B) Collusion is the act of two or more employees acting together to conspire in a fraud.
   C) Collusion is the act of two internal controls contradicting each other and negating the intended benefit.
   D) Collusion is a clash or disagreement between two middle-tier managers.

MC9-6. Which of these is an example of an enterprise risk?
   A) A global epidemic
   B) Unexpected competition from another industry
   C) An industry-wide cost increase
   D) A merger with or acquisition of another enterprise

MC9-7. Which of these is an example of an economy risk?
   A) Loss of brand quality
   B) The increasing cost of computer memory chips
   C) Sales made to non-existent customers
   D) A change in the financial market

MC9-8. Which risks are associated primarily with recording, maintaining, and reporting information about resources, events, agents, and relationships among them?
A) Business process risks
B) Information process risks
C) Industry risks
D) Enterprise risks

MC9-9. What kind of control is bonding (i.e., buying insurance to protect against theft by cash-handling employees)?
A) Primarily preventive
B) Primarily detective
C) Primarily corrective
D) Primarily substitutive

MC9-10. What identifies the functions each user is allowed to perform and specifies which data and programs the user can access after gaining access to the system?
A) Passwords
B) Logical access controls
C) Access control matrix
D) Application controls

CHAPTER 10

REA Policy and Scheduling Layers

LEARNING OBJECTIVES

The objective of this chapter is to introduce the policy and scheduling infrastructure layers of the REA ontology and to discuss REA implementation compromises commonly used in database design. After studying this chapter, you should be able to

1. Explain the difference between the accountability, policy, and scheduling infrastructures in REA modeling
2. Explain the difference between typification, grouping, and generalization
3. Explain meronymic associations
4. Create REA business process models that include typification, grouping, generalization, and meronymic associations
5. Explain common reasons for compromising implementations
6. Identify and create common conceptual level, logical level, and physical level implementation compromises

ACCOUNTABILITY, POLICY, AND SCHEDULING INFRASTRUCTURES IN REA

REA business process conceptual models have three layers: the accountability (also called operational) infrastructure, the policy (also called planning) infrastructure, and the scheduling infrastructure. The *accountability infrastructure* (aka *operational infrastructure*) represents the economic activities and related phenomena that actually have happened in an economic exchange. This layer is composed of the daily activities of the enterprise carrying out its mission. We introduced to you the accountability layer in chapter 2, and we built upon that in chapters 4 through 7. The *policy infrastructure* represents the economic activities and related phenomena that should, could, or must happen in a company. The policy infrastructure reflects the results of planning and control efforts by the enterprise management, and is composed of the rules, procedures, policies, and goals set by enterprise management. The scheduling infrastructure represents commitments that have been made and specifies the types of resources, events, and agents to be affected by the fulfillment of those commitments.

Most of the REA constructs introduced thus far in this book are part of the accountability infrastructure. Economic resources, economic events, and economic agents and the associations among them represent the economic activities that have already happened. Colors are often used to divide the layers represented in a REA business process model. In a full color REA business process model, accountability/operational constructs appear in green. Scheduling layer constructs, including instigation and commitment events, and the proposition, reservation, fulfillment, and participation associations in which those events participate, appear in purple or red. Yellow depicts the policy layer constructs in a full color REA model. The policy infrastructure extends the accountability and scheduling layer concepts with mechanisms such as generalization, typification, and grouping.

GENERALIZATION

Generalization is the abstraction from a class of objects to a superclass (that captures the commonalities between subclass instances, resulting in a less detailed higher level construct) via the creation of an "is-a" relationship between the subclass and superclass. Such relationships are called generalization hierarchies. Subclasses contain more specific instances of superclasses. For example, the classes oboe, bassoon, and English horn all participate in an "is-a" relationship with the double-reed instrument class. Note that no name is attached to the arrows – anytime you see an arrow on a REA class diagram, you should assume it represents a generalization hierarchy. If you want to label the arrows with "is-a" you may do so, but it is unnecessary. Note that generalization is a bottom up approach – where we start with subclasses and find shared attributes which lead us to generalize to a superclass. Specialization is the same concept, except we work from the superclass to the subclasses based on finding attributes that only apply to instances of the subclasses and not to the superclass. For ease of reading, because specialization and generalization are different names for the same hierarchies, simply viewed from opposite perspectives, we will refer to them as generalization hierarchies.

Generalization hierarchies may have multiple layers, as illustrated in Exhibit 10-1.

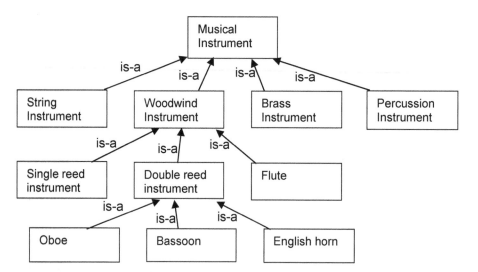

Exhibit 10-1: A multi-layered generalization hierarchy

For example, an oboe is a double-reed instrument, a double-reed instrument is a woodwind instrument, a woodwind instrument is a musical instrument. We use generalization hierarchies in conceptual modeling primarily to avoid storing null values when some of the characteristics that we want to include in a model are common to all instances of the superclass, but other characteristics are unique to specific subclasses. Subclasses inherit the characteristics of the superclass as well as possessing their own attributes. Subclasses may also be created because of specific associations in which the subclasses participate.

Consider the Employee class for an enterprise. Employees hold many kinds of positions in a typical enterprise, and the enterprise may need to store different attributes for employees in different positions. For example, the enterprise may want to store the CPA license number for its accountants, the driver's license numbers for its truck drivers, and the fidelity bond rating for its cashiers. The values of those attributes would be null for all employees who do not hold those respective positions, therefore, the enterprise should not store those attributes for all employees. Other attributes should be stored for all employees, such as employee id, last name, first name, address, telephone number, date of birth, and so forth.

Generalization allows us to store the attributes that are common to all employees as attributes of the Employee superclass and to store the others as attributes of the appropriate subclass. Exhibit 10-2 illustrates these concepts in conceptual model form and provides representative example data in the corresponding relational tables. Notice that the conceptual model uses arrows to point from the subclasses to the superclass. Multiplicities are not displayed for generalization associations – by definition each member of the subclass is also a member of the superclass, and each member of the superclass cannot repeat in a particular subclass. Instead of multiplicities, we show generalization constraints. The first generalization constraint communicates whether a relationship between the superclass and its subclasses is complete or incomplete. Complete means that every instance of the superclass must appear in one of the subclasses, and is denoted as "c". Incomplete means that some superclass members may not appear in any of the subclasses, and is denoted as "i". The second generalization constraint communicates whether a relationship between the superclass and its subclasses is disjoint or overlapping. Disjoint means that an instance may only be a member of one subclass, and is denoted as "d"; whereas, overlapping means that an instance may be a member of multiple subclasses, and is denoted as "o".

While generalization hierarchies may be implemented with relational databases, they are better-suited to object-oriented database technologies, for reasons beyond the scope of this book. In the relational tables, you should not use a foreign key to implement the generalization association because the superclass and subclasses already share the same primary key. You should establish a relationship between those primary keys in an Access relationship layout. Whenever we use generalization, we will show the same primary key throughout all subclasses and superclasses in the conceptual model.

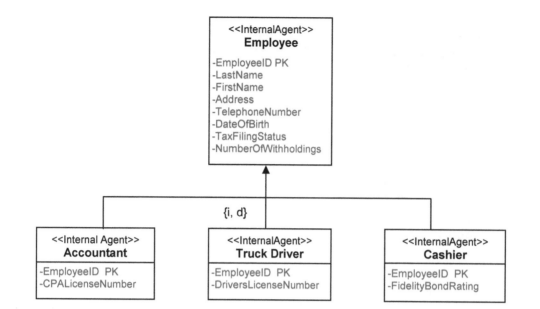

Employee

EmployeeID	Last Name	First Name	Address	Telephone Number	Date of Birth	Tax Status	Number of Withholdings
E1	Frank	Ryan	123 Neat St.	616-342-1235	08/27/1990	S	1
E2	Daniels	Jackie	83156 Elm St.	616-531-1381	04/05/1980	MFJ	3
E3	Burger	Chase	921 Oak St.	517-326-5213	10/03/1966	MWS	2
E4	Newman	Marcus	444 Ash St.	616-883-9980	06/10/1964	MFJ	6
E5	Q	Susie	765 Beech St.	616-892-2638	11/05/1989	HH	2
E6	Tuttle	Franklin	329 Maple St.	517-319-5130	07/07/1989	S	1
E7	Grace	Sal	901 Oak St.	517-513-3123	01/03/1970	HH	4
E8	Place	Sharon	2991 Birch St.	616-883-1269	05/05/1964	MFJ	5
E9	Maxx	Angel	3552 Rider Dr.	616-831-9056	03/14/1990	S	1

Accountant

EmployeeID	CPA License Number
E7	M12351
E8	M90123

Truck Driver

EmployeeID	Driver's License Number
E2	D500315120531289
E9	M800312315012986

Cashier

EmployeeID	Fidelity Bond Rating
E3	AA
E5	A

Exhibit 10-2: Generalization Conceptual Model and Corresponding Relational Tables

Notice that the instances of the subclasses are also instances of the superclass. For example, the E7 who is an accountant is the same E7 who is an employee and the E3 who is a cashier is the same E3 who is an employee. To get all details of any specific employee, you would join the Employee table to the relevant subclass table. For example, joining Employee to Truck Driver would allow us to get all details for Jackie Daniels and for Angel Maxx. You may notice that some of the employees in the Employee superclass table are not included in any of the subclass tables. That simply indicates that no separate attributes are stored for employees in their positions in this enterprise, and those types of positions do not participate in any special associations with other classes. So those employees are members of the superclass, but they are not members of any subclasses (which is why the constraint shown in Exhibit 10-2 is incomplete). The disjoint constraint means that, in this enterprise, employees cannot be both cashiers and truck drivers, or both cashiers and accountants, or both accountants and truck drivers.

TYPIFICATION

As defined in chapter 4, *typification* is an association between a category and individual instances of that category. Typification allows us to store characteristics that describe categories, or types, of objects. For example, an enterprise may want to track certain characteristics of the categories of employees it has such as the pay range and benefit plan for which each employee position type is eligible. We saw typification in earlier chapters for inventory.

Recall that inventory may be specifically identified with unique tags or serial numbers for each separate physical unit, as is often the case with vehicles or electronics. Earlier in this book we called this token-level representation. Alternatively, model numbers, catalog product numbers, part numbers, ISBNs, or SKUs may be used to identify inventory (as "inventory type"), in which case each identifier represents many different physical units. That is often the case with groceries, books, office supplies (other than electronics), clothing, and many other products. Earlier in this book, we called this type-level representation. Type-level representation is appropriate when each instance of the type has identical values for the characteristics of interest. The association between uniquely identified inventory (a resource) and catalog inventory (inventory type, a resource-type) is typification.

Even enterprises that track inventory at the token level may also find it useful to track inventory at the type level. For example, a computer manufacturer advertises information about the types of computers it has available to sell by assigning model numbers to identify the specific features a finished computer will have. Customers order by model number to indicate the bundle of features they want – not by serial number to indicate the exact physical computer. As long as the company sends the customer a computer that has all the ordered features, the customer won't care whether the computer has serial number xyz1235123-1235y or whether it has serial number xyz3e212351231sah-235. Once the enterprise actually sells the computer, then the enterprise will track the specifically identified computer. Exhibit 10-3 shows a conceptual model for a typification association between Employee and Employee Type and the corresponding relational database tables.

Employee

EmployeeID	Last Name	First Name	Address	Telephone Number	Date of Birth	Tax Status	Number of Withholdings	EmployeePositionType^{FK}
E01	Frank	Ryan	123 Neat St.	616-342-1235	08/27/1990	S	1	Line Worker
E02	Daniels	Jackie	83156 Elm St.	616-531-1381	04/05/1980	MFJ	3	Truck Driver
E03	Burger	Chase	921 Oak St.	517-326-5213	10/03/1966	MWS	2	Cashier
E04	Newman	Marcus	444 Ash St.	616-883-9980	06/10/1964	MFJ	6	Executive
E05	Q	Susie	765 Beech St.	616-892-2638	11/05/1989	HH	2	Cashier
E06	Tuttle	Franklin	329 Maple St.	517-319-5130	07/07/1989	S	1	Line Worker
E07	Grace	Sal	901 Oak St.	517-513-3123	01/03/1970	HH	4	Accountant
E08	Place	Sharon	2991 Birch St.	616-883-1269	05/05/1964	MFJ	5	Accountant
E09	Maxx	Angel	3552 Rider Dr.	616-831-9056	03/14/1990	S	1	Truck Driver
E10	Curie	George	6312 Peach Ct.	616-315-1235	02/12/1956	MWS	2	Executive

Employee Type

EmployeePositionType	Benefit Plan	Minimum of Pay Range	Maximum of Pay Range
Accountant	Full	$40,000.00	$152,000.00
Truck Driver	Full	$25,000.00	$56,000.00
Cashier	Health only	$22,000.00	$36,000.00
Line Worker	Health only	$22,000.00	$42,000.00
Admin Assistant	Health only	$25,000.00	$56,000.00
Executive	Full	$60,000.00	$999,000.00

Exhibit 10-3: Typification Conceptual Model and Corresponding Relational Tables

Notice that the typification association in this example is implemented with the primary key of Employee Type (Employee Position Type) posted as a foreign key in the Employee table. If, instead, the multiplicities had indicated that one employee could hold multiple position types, then the association would have been implemented with a separate table.

Also notice that the instances of the Employee Type table are the position types, not the individual employees. That is the key to understanding the difference between generalization and typification. With generalization, the instances of the subclasses are also instances of the super class. With typification, the instances of the object class and the typified object class are different things – the instances of the object class are the objects and the instances of the typified object class are categories to which the objects belong. Notice what this mechanism accomplishes. Without typification, the attributes assigned to Employee Type could instead be assigned to Employee. The first disadvantage of that approach is that the values of those attributes would be identical for every instance of employee that had the same position type. For example, the benefit plan value would be "Full" and the maximum of pay range value would be "$152,000" for every employee who is an accountant. That violates the one fact, one place rule introduced in chapter 3, as their values depend not on the EmployeeID, but on the PositionType attribute.

The second disadvantage of that approach is the increased number of data fields required, with no additional information value. Our small example in Exhibit 10-3 would only add six cells - the new table would have twelve columns and ten rows, for a total of 120 cells, compared to the 114 total cells in our illustrated tables (90 in Employee and 24 in Employee Type). This increase is only 5%. However, many enterprises' Employee tables would have many more rows, and their Employee Type tables would have many more rows and columns. This approach for an enterprise whose Employee table contains 40 columns and 1,200 rows and whose Employee Type table contains 12 columns and 30 rows, would yield 14,040 additional cells of data (52*1200 = 62,400 cells in the combined table, compared to 40*1200 + 12*30 = 48,360 cells in the separate tables), an increase of 29% stored cells of data, with no increased information value.

Often generalization hierarchies have a superclass that is associated with a type class in which aggregate data is collected about the subclasses. Therefore, Exhibits 10-2 and 10-3 could be combined (think "view integration") on the employee (super)class, as illustrated in Exhibit 10-4.

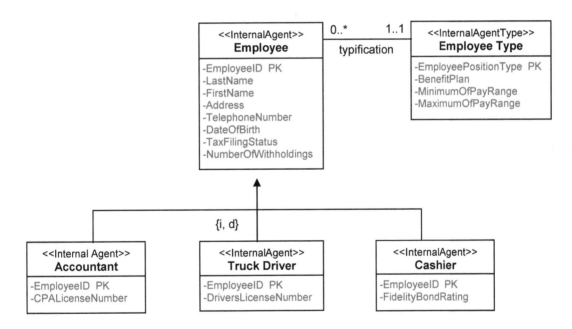

Exhibit 10-4: Generalization and Typification Combined

Typification Chains
Not only can we typify objects once, but we can then further typify the object types. Recall the example of the specific computers categorized into model numbers, resulting in a typification association between finished computers and computer types. We could then further classify the computer types into categories such as premium gaming computers, premium business computers, moderate gaming computers, moderate business computers, and economy computers, as illustrated

in Exhibit 10-5. This example enterprise allows deviation in processor speed, drive capacity, and RAM within a model. For example, the base model for a M25 has a 2.7Ghz processor, a 256Gb hard drive, and 4Gb RAM. However, customers may upgrade the processor to 3.5Ghz and they may upgrade the hard drive to 512Gb, and they may upgrade the RAM to 8Gb. Therefore the finished computer table must store the actual configurations of each physical computer as manufactured; whereas the computer type table stores the standard configurations.

<<Resource>> **FinishedComputer**	0..* 1..1 typification	<<ResourceType>> **Computer Type**	0..* 1..1 typification	<<ResourceType>> **Computer Category**
-SerialNumber PK -DateManufactured -ActualProcessorSpeed -ActualDriveCapacity -ActualRAM		-ModelNumber PK -ModelName -StdProcessorSpeed -StdDriveCapacity -StdRAM		-CategoryName PK -AvgMfgCost -YTDSalesDollars -YTDSalesQuantity

Finished Computer

SerialNumber	Date Manufactured	Actual ProcessorSpeed	ActualDrive Capacity	ActualRAM	ModelNumber[FK]
Y3150321AG89	04/29/2020	4.9Ghz	1T	16Gb	M57
Z93Z12354L28	04/30/2020	3.5Ghz	256Gb	8Gb	M25
K02356MN589	05/01/2020	3.5Ghz	256Gb	4Gb	M31
K023PR3829H	05/02/2020	4.9Ghz	512Gb	16Gb	M57
R6521KW4392	05/02/2020	3.5Ghz	512Gb	8Gb	M25

Computer Type

ModelNumber	ModelName	StdProcessorSpeed	StdDriveCapacity	StdRAM	Category[FK]
M17	Ghane	2.3Ghz	128Gb	4Gb	Economy
M25	Plenit	2.7Ghz	256Gb	4Gb	BasicBusiness
M31	Modesto	3.5Ghz	256Gb	8Gb	BasicBusiness
M44	Nikad	4.3Ghz	1T	16Gb	PremiumBusiness
M49	Anilai	4.3Ghz	512Gb	16Gb	PremiumGaming
M57	Gliz	4.9Ghz	512Gb	16Gb	PremiumGaming

Computer Category

CategoryName	AvgMfgCost	YTDSalesDollars	YTDSalesQuantity
Economy	$125	$995,413	5002
BasicBusiness	$187	$1,396,577	4499
PremiumBusiness	$289	$1,533,072	2915
PremiumGaming	$318	$2,278,629	4777

Exhibit 10-5: Typification Chain Conceptual Model and Logical Model (Tables)

GROUPING

Grouping is a mechanism in which objects are grouped into collections based on shared characteristics. Typification and grouping are similar; in fact, typification is considered a strong form of grouping. Typification groups objects based on the object instances sharing an archetypal essence; whereas grouping groups objects based on shared classification or membership. For example, specific instances of airplanes may be categorized as plane types (e.g. Boeing 747, Boeing 767) and also as members of fleets (e.g. Delta's fleet, United's fleet)[36]. The categorization as plane types is typification, as it groups them according to what they are. The categorization as members of fleets is grouping, as it groups them according to shared membership.

Grouping has the same purpose as typification; that is, to store characteristics of object categories in such a way as to minimize the number of cells needed to communicate the information and to comply with the one fact, one place rule introduced in chapter 3.

TIME EXPANSION OF ACCOUNTING WITH REA

Exhibits 10-6, 10-7, and 10-8 further illustrate the time expansion of REA modeling (the past/near present, the foreseeable present, and the future). Although we introduced commitment events in earlier chapters, the commitments had more in common with the operational level than they did with the policy level (in Exhibit 10-6, this is the commitment to the event association; the event is shown with a dashed line because it is formally part of the operational level at the bottom of Exhibit 10-6). We tracked the resources that we expected to give or take, we tracked the economic events that fulfilled the commitment events, and we tracked the agents who participated in the agreements. However, we did not track other details of what the commitment events specified.

To more fully describe the enterprise activities and to help bridge the policy and accountability infrastructures, Geerts & McCarthy advocate tracking the resource types, event types, and agent types that are specified by a commitment event (as shown in Exhibit 10-7). The specification between a commitment and a resource type, as previously discussed, is a reservation. The commitment reserves a resource or resource type so that it is available when the economic event occurs to which the commitment agreed. However, a commitment may also specify the type of event and the type of agent to be involved in the event to which the agreement applies. None of our previously introduced associations are equivalent to the specifications between commitment and event type and between commitment and agent type. Although we related commitment events to the economic events that fulfilled them, that fulfillment association is different from the specification of the type of event to which a commitment agreed. Similarly, although we tracked the agents responsible for or who participated in commitment events, such participation differs from specification of the types of agents a commitment agrees will participate in the eventual fulfilling events. Such specifications are essentially part of the policy infrastructure and one may compare them to the operational events after they occur to monitor compliance with the specifications to which the commitments agreed. Management should address findings of non-compliance to avoid negative impressions of the external agents involved in those commitments.

---

[36] Geerts, G. and McCarthy, W.E., 2006. Policy-level specifications in REA enterprise information systems. *Journal of Information Systems*, 20(2), 37-63.

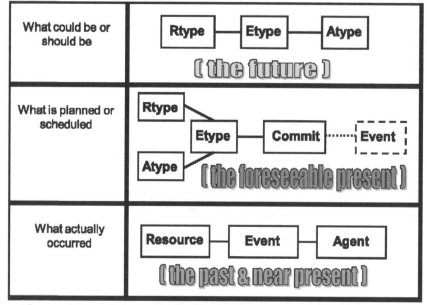

the elevator pitch for time expansion

Exhibit 10-6: Three layers of time expansion with REA
Source: William McCarthy, Michigan State University

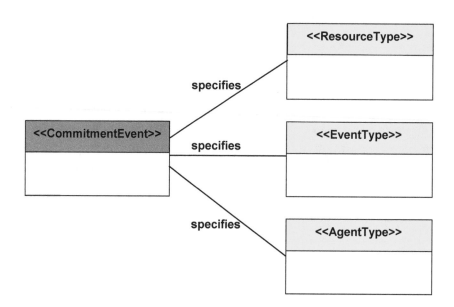

Exhibit 10-7: Abstract specification of commitments

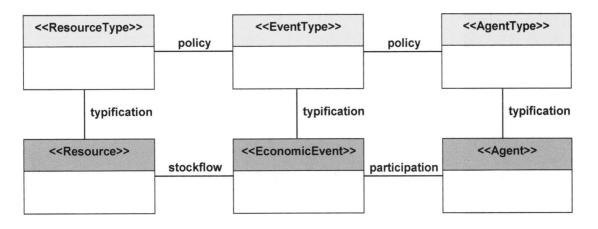

Exhibit 10-8: Policy formation between typified REA constructs

Grouping, typification, and generalization are used in the policy infrastructure component of REA conceptual models – that is, the part of the model that identifies what could, should, or must occur. Any object class may be typified if doing so is useful for planning, controlling, or evaluating the company's activities. That is, you may have Event Types and Agent Types as well as the Resource Types we previously introduced.

As illustrated in Exhibit 10-8, policy specification often involves associations between types. For example, a company may classify its salespeople according to experience such that it has master salespeople, senior salespeople, associate salespeople, and staff salespeople. The company may also classify its customers such that the company has relationship customers, choice customers, and transaction customers. Extending the REA conceptual model to include types allows a company to specify a policy as to which types of salespeople may be assigned to which types of customers. For example, company policy may specify that only master salespeople and senior salespeople may be assigned to relationship customers and that staff salespeople may only be assigned to transaction customers. The time focus of policy specifications is on the future. However, we can analyze operational data *post hoc* to determine its compliance with policies. Adherence to company policy can be validated by comparing the policy layer to the operational layer using a database query to see, for example, whether any specific salespeople typed as staff are assigned to specific customers typed as relationship or choice.

Adding the policy infrastructure dimension to REA is an important advancement to facilitate the COSO (Committee of Sponsoring Organizations) internal control framework objectives. Recall from chapter 9 that COSO objectives include designing control activities (policies and procedures that enterprises use to ensure that necessary actions are taken to minimize risks associated with achieving enterprise objectives) and monitoring the quality of internal control performance over time. Declaring such policies in the database structure allows querying to identify instances of non-compliance that management can address.

ATTRIBUTES OF TYPE AND GROUP CLASSES

To help you understand the instances of type and group classes (i.e., classes that result from typification and grouping), let's consider three kinds of attributes that we want to track for such classes:

1. Essential characteristics of a class
2. Standards, budgets, or guidelines
3. Aggregations

An essential characteristic is one that describes a common value for all instances of a type or group. For example, an essential characteristic of animal type instances in an animal type class is the sound the type of animal makes (e.g., "meow" for a cat, "neigh" for a horse). Benefit plan, minimum and maximum pay range values are essential attributes for employee type tracked in Exhibit 10-3. For the company in that example, all accountants have the full benefit plan.

Standards, budgets, or guidelines are expected values based on history, planning, and/or policy. For example, companies often store the standard unit cost and manufacturer's suggested retail price for inventory types. The standard processor, hard drive, and memory configurations in the Computer Type table in Exhibit 10-5 are stored standards. Aggregations are counts, sums, averages, and so forth, that summarize the instance values within a given type or group. The YTD (year-to-date) sales dollars and sales quantities in the Computer Category table in Exhibit 10-5 are stored aggregations. Companies may also often store computed totals for policy associations. Such associations often are many-to-many relationships, and the association class construct is used to represent such attributes.

MERONYMIC ASSOCIATIONS

A *meronymic association* is a whole-part association. In REA, many economic events (especially in the revenue process) consist of many separate parts and we need to capture data for the whole as well as for the parts. Any event for which tickets are sold in advance has a meronymic association between the overall event and the individual tickets sold. Concerts, theater productions, sporting events, train rides, and airplane rides are some examples of economic events that commonly have advance ticket sales. In such cases, the information the enterprise needs to track differs for the whole versus the parts. In the case of a concert, the individual ticket sales (part) connect to the customers to whom the enterprise sold the tickets and to the cash receipts for those tickets. The actual concert occurrence connects to the resources used up and the agents involved in the occurrence. The REA pattern in essence changes to that shown in Exhibit 10-9, with the meronymic association for a concert shown in Exhibit 10-10. Note that Exhibit 10-9 uses general terms instead of specific stereotypes, because the pattern can apply in various scenarios, some which have economic decrements as part-whole events and some which have economic increments as part-whole events. Whether resources or resource types are involved, and the specific types of agents that are involved are also situation specific. Exhibit 10-10's concert example illustrates that one common type of meronymic association with the related duality.

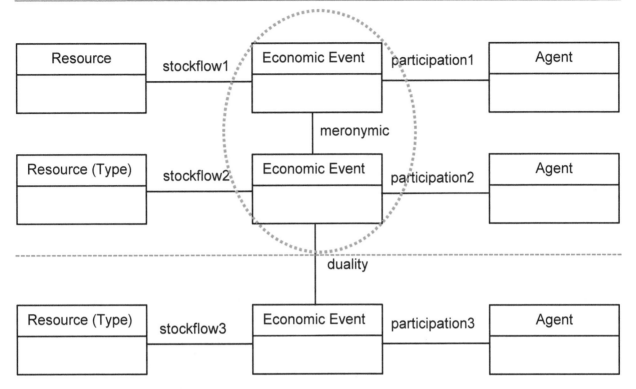

Exhibit 10-9: Core REA Pattern with Meronymic Association
Source: William E. McCarthy, Michigan State University

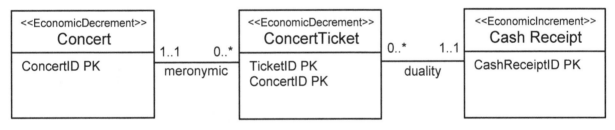

Exhibit 10-10: Meronymic Association for a Concert Event with Tickets Sold

IMPLEMENTATION COMPROMISE

Models that are, in theory, ideal, are not always practical or possible to implement in working information systems; sometimes implementation compromises are necessary. *Implementation compromises* are deviations from a theoretically pure conceptual model due to practical considerations, insufficient measurement techniques, and other constraints. In this section, we discuss some common implementation compromises in the design of enterprise-wide databases. Some of the implementation compromises we discuss apply to the conceptual level, some apply to the logical level, and some apply to the physical implementation level. Although the word compromise inherently carries a negative connotation, many of the compromises discussed in this chapter are made for good reasons and result in improved databases; so do not think of implementation compromises as something to avoid.

Conceptual Level Modeling Compromises

A *conceptual level compromise* is the use of less than theoretically ideal representation in a conceptual model because of an inability or lack of need to completely and accurately represent an object. Such compromises occur anytime we determine we cannot adequately represent or measure an object in reality. Common compromises made at the conceptual level include

- Exclusion of a class or association because of inadequate measurement mechanisms or because no decision need exists for that data.
- Consolidation of conceptually congruent classes.
- Materialization of tasks as event classes.

It is only practical to include measurable and definable phenomena in a conceptual model from which a database will be designed. Often we can identify the existence of phenomena that we cannot measure; it is an implementation compromise to exclude those objects from the conceptual model. For example, we may be aware that an enterprise's revenue process uses many different resources in the process of generating revenue. Fixed assets such as the storefront display room, the warehouse, the shelving within those facilities, equipment such as cash registers, supplies such as cash register tape, pens, and staplers, and the labor of sales personnel and support staff are consumed to varying degrees within the revenue process. However, trying to measure the extent to which the process consumes each of those resources is a challenge. Until cost-effective means for directly measuring and tracing the resources consumed to the resources acquired as a result, the conceptual model for the revenue process must be compromised to exclude those immeasurable items. The cost of those resources may still be tracked via the acquisition process conceptual model; however, those costs must be represented only as period expenses rather than directly matched to the revenues they helped to produce.

In other cases, measurement mechanisms may exist, but no decision need exists and therefore an enterprise may decide to exclude a class or association. For example, if an enterprise has only one purchasing agent, and intends to always have only one purchasing agent, then there is no need to track which internal agent is responsible for purchases. Or if an enterprise sells merchandise only to cash customers and has no need to track information about individual customers, the enterprise could choose not to model a customer class.

Sometimes an enterprise chooses not to implement all of the associations prescribed by the REA pattern. For example, an enterprise may make a declarative/procedural trade-off, whereby it decides to exclude the declarative duality association between purchase and cash disbursement because the enterprise determines no need to apply payments directly to individual purchases and by procedurally tracing purchases and cash disbursements each to the related vendor, the enterprise may be able to determine accounts payable by vendor (though not by purchase). This type of accounting method is sometimes called "balance forward" whereas the matching of payments to specific purchases is sometimes called "open item" accounting.

In some enterprises, certain pairs or groups of events always occur simultaneously. Such events are called *conceptually congruent events*. The practical compromise is to collapse, or consolidate, the classes for conceptually congruent events. For example, consider Only Gas, a gas station/convenience store that sells only gasoline and has never needed non-sales sources of cash.

Only Gas sells gasoline for cash – no credit cards, checks, or sales on account are permitted. Only Gas's procedures are as follows:

- Customers are required to bring their car keys and driver's licenses to the cashier's window, which is conveniently located adjacent to the gas pumps.
- Cashiers unlock the appropriate pumps, enabling the customers to pump gas.
- Customers pump gas into vehicles or containers, then return to the cashier's window; pay for the gas, retrieve their car keys and driver's licenses, and drive away.

These activities encompass multiple events within the revenue process, including the sale order, sale, and cash receipt. There is no identifiable need to separate these events for Only Gas, because they are conceptually congruent. That is, each occurrence of a sale order is automatically accompanied by an occurrence of sale and an occurrence of cash receipt. Another way of looking at this is that the multiplicity pattern is

Sale Order 1..1 – 1..1 Sale 1..1 – 1..1 Point Of Sale Cash Receipt.

A sale order would not be entered into Only Gas's system without also entering exactly one sale and exactly one cash receipt. This allows the classes to be collapsed (consolidated) into a single class in the conceptual model. Therefore instead of the normal conceptual model reflecting

The compromised conceptual model could be portrayed as follows:

The consolidation of conceptually congruent events simplifies the conceptual model as compared to the full REA ontology pattern.

Another type of implementation compromise – *materialization of tasks as classes*, i.e., the representation of an activity that could be re-engineered away as a base object class – increases the complexity of the conceptual model. Recall from earlier chapters that workflow tasks that comprise an event may involve preparation of multiple documents. For example, the sale event as described in the workflow chapter may sometimes involve picking, packing, and shipping of inventory and may involve preparation of as many as four documents: picking list, packing list, bill of lading, and sale invoice. Similarly, the purchase requisition event may or may not involve requesting quotes or bids from potential vendors to help determine the vendor with whom to place a purchase order. Some companies may determine they have a need to keep the attributes from each of these tasks separate from each other rather than combining them into the event they comprise. Therefore, a company may choose to model the requests for quotes and the receipt of quotes from vendors as events between the purchase requisition and purchase order as follows:

| Purchase Requisition | Request for Quote | Vendor Quote | Purchase Order | Purchase |

Such a model deviates from the standard REA representation. Why does REA not include request for quote and vendor quote as events in its pattern? Because an enterprise could choose not to request and obtain vendor quotes in its acquisition process and the process would still be an acquisition process. The tasks in the workflow of the process would differ, but the tasks would still comprise acquisition. REA attempts to portray as events the parts of a process's workflow that are unlikely to change if an enterprise decides to change its workflow, but not its overall business plan. Does that mean an enterprise should never include vendor quote as a class in an acquisition process REA model? No, but the enterprise should be aware that if it ever decides to stop obtaining vendor quotes as part of its acquisition process, its database modifications will be more extensive than if the vendor quote data had been included as attributes within the traditional REA model's classes.

Because the enterprise also would need to track each resource and agent involved with each of these activities, the complexity added to the conceptual model may be burdensome. As noted, if workflow changes in the future, the database design will need to change. Enterprises should exercise caution in determining whether or not to materialize tasks as classes. To make the determination, enterprises should consider what is needed to plan, control, execute, and evaluate its activities and employees. If the attributes can be stored and retrieved effectively for the needed decisions using the standard REA template, then the standard template should be used. If the attributes cannot be stored and retrieved effectively in the standard template for an enterprise, then separate classes should be created in which to store the task attributes.

Logical Level Modeling Compromises

Compromises are also made at the logical level. *Logical level compromises* are the deviations from pure theory made when converting a conceptual model into database objects such as relational tables. Some database designers compromise the logical level by posting a foreign key for some multiplicity patterns that would result in some null values as long as the *load* (the percentage of non-null values for a posted foreign key) is high. A theoretically pure relational database would never allow a null value in a table, and the steps outlined in this book for converting a conceptual model into relational tables results in only non-null values. However, some database designers would allow associations with multiplicity patterns of 0..1-0..1; 0..1-0..*; 0..1-1..*; 0..*-0..1; and 1..*-0..1 to be implemented with foreign keys as long as the foreign key values for most instances would be non-null.

Such an implementation requires less storage space and decreases the complexity of queries that involve multiple tables. Because queries often focus on associations, associations that are implemented with separate tables often require the use of three tables (instead of two). By compromising the logical level for associations for which a posted foreign key results in a relatively low number of null values, an enterprise usually can reduce query complexity.

A similar type of compromise is sometimes made when a class is related to two or more other classes and the associations are mutually exclusive; that is, an instance of Class A will be related to either an instance of Class B or to an instance of Class C. For example, Cash Disbursement is an event in multiple business processes. In the payroll process, cash disbursements are made to employees. In the acquisition process, cash disbursements are made to vendors. In the financing process, cash disbursements are made to creditors or investors. However, each cash disbursement is made to an instance of only one of those related classes.

Panel A of Exhibit 10-11 illustrates the integrated conceptual model with the cash disbursement class participating in three separate associations with various agents. Theoretically these three associations would require three separate tables to represent them in the database.

An implementation compromise could be made to post a single foreign key; for example, Payee, to implement all three associations. Such posting of a single foreign key to implement multiple associations is called ***combined class key posting***. Panel B of Exhibit 10-11 illustrates this compromise. The value for the Payee would be an employee foreign key for a record that disburses cash to an employee, the value would be a supplier foreign key for a record representing cash disbursed to a supplier, and the value would be a creditor or investor foreign key for a record representing cash disbursed to a creditor or investor.

Panel A: Conceptual Model

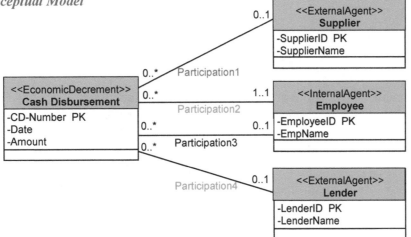

Note: Participation2 represents the association with the employee who processes payments (e.g., cashier, A/P clerk, or payroll clerk). Participation3 represents the association with the employee to whom the cash disbursement is made (e.g., a worker being paid in the payroll process).

Panel B: Logical Relational Model

Cash Disbursement (Economic Decrement Event)

CashDisbursement#	Date	Amount	EmplID^FK	Payee^FK

Employee (Internal Agent)

EmplID	Name

Supplier (External Agent)

Supplier ID	Name

Lender (External Agent)

Lender ID	Name

Participation1 is implemented via Supplier Payee ID posted from Supplier into Cash Disbursement.
Participation2 is implemented via EmplID posted from Employee into Cash Disbursement.
Participation3 is implemented via Employee Payee ID posted from Employee into Cash Disbursement.
Participation4 is implemented via Lender Payee ID posted from Lender into Cash Disbursement.

Exhibit 10-11: Combined Class Key Posting

A disadvantage that results from combined class key posting is the inability to enforce referential integrity. In the example shown, the value for Payee could be posted from any of three different tables and referential integrity only verifies the value against one reference table. Therefore referential integrity for Participation1, Participation3, and Participation4 cannot be enforced. An alternative implementation compromise that could be used is to combine agents of different types about which similar attributes need to be stored into a single class. For example, employees, suppliers, and lenders could be combined into one class without the use of a generalization hierarchy as long as no specific attributes need to be stored about each subtype. The conceptual model for the previous example could be compromised as shown in Exhibit 10-12.

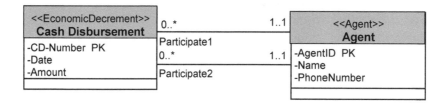

Exhibit 10-12: Combination of Classes Without Generalization

In this case, Participate1 portrays the association of the cash disbursement to the internal agent who processes it and Participate2 represents the association of the cash disbursement to the agent to whom it is sent. Becausee internal and external agents have been combined into one class, the stereotype is changed to Agent. Referential integrity may now be enforced. Because this company tracks the same attributes for lenders, employees, and suppliers, it is relatively easy to consolidate all the data values into a single agent table, rather than to keep three separate agent tables.

Physical Implementation Compromises
Compromises may also be made at the physical implementation level. A *physical level compromise* is a deviation from the theoretical ideal when implementing the logical database model in vendor-specific database software. Physical implementation compromises include storage of *derivable attributes* (attributes whose value can be calculated from the values of other stored attributes) and event activity roll-ups. As described in a previous chapter, we recommend the storage of static derivable attributes because the cost of the extra storage space taken up by those attributes is likely outweighed by the benefit of less complexity, and therefore less processing power needed for queries that use those attributes.

For example, if the enterprise sells mass-produced merchandise inventory, attributes such as quantity sold and actual unit selling price may be used to derive the total dollar amount of a sale. Total dollar amount of a sale is a static derivable attribute; that is, once the total dollar amount for Sale 1 is computed, it does not change as additional sales are added to the enterprise system. If the total sale dollar amount is stored as an attribute in the Sale event table, it simplifies all additional queries the enterprise needs that include total sales dollar amounts as components (e.g., accounts receivable, deferred revenue, or total sales by salesperson)

Another physical implementation compromise is that of *event activity roll-up* – the aggregation of a group of event records into a single summary record once historical detail is no longer needed. This compromise recognizes that enterprise databases exist in a finite storage space and also recognizes that the larger the size of the database, the less efficient querying becomes. A benefit of enterprise information systems founded on enterprise-wide databases is the ability to produce financial statements without actually closing the books. This is sometimes called a virtual close. The disadvantage of never closing the books is the uncontrolled growth of the database – the database may quickly grow too large for optimized, proficient querying. One means of controlling that growth is to wait until such a time as event activity detail is not needed and then roll that data up into a single event occurrence and continue entering additional data into the table. In Exhibit 10-13 we illustrate event activity roll-up. Clearly in practice an enterprise would never roll up a mere seven rows; this is to help you understand the concept.

Sale – Original table

SaleID	Date	Amount	Customer[FK]	Salesperson[FK]
S1	1/1	$400.00	C23	SP4
S2	1/1	$450.00	C17	SP2
S3	1/5	$875.00	C46	SP3
S4	1/5	$125.00	C72	SP4
S5	1/6	$350.00	C14	SP3
S6	1/7	$500.00	C17	SP2
S7	1/8	$700.00	C46	SP3

Sale table with event activity for S1-S7 rolled up

SaleID	Date	Amount	Customer[FK]	Salesperson[FK]
SR1	1/1	$3,400	C0	SP0
S8	1/9	$520.00	C23	SP4
S9	1/9	$317.00	C72	SP4

SR1 represents the set of sales 1 through 7.
C0 is set up as a placeholder customer (a customer number that indicates we can't track the customer).
SP0 is set up as a placeholder salesperson (indicates we can't track the salesperson).
Note: because the date field likely has a date data type, it can't store a date range. Based on its needs, the enterprise may decide to use the first date of the range, the last date of the range, or a midpoint.

Exhibit 10-13: Event Activity Roll-up

CONCLUDING COMMENTS

In this chapter, we discussed some advanced concepts used in the accountability, policy, and scheduling infrastructure components of the REA ontology to support enterprise planning and control activities. Generalization, typification, grouping, and meronymic associations allow for rich policy specifications to be embedded in the enterprise database and validated by querying to compare actual transactions to enterprise policies. We also discussed the value of making implementation compromises to circumvent practical constraints such as hardware limitations and available measurement tools. We must apply such compromises with full understanding of the benefits the compromises may provide but also with consideration of what opportunities they prevent. In other words, we must apply typical cost/benefit analysis.

KEY TERMS AND CONCEPTS
Accountability infrastructure
Combined class key posting
Conceptual level compromise
Conceptually congruent events
Derivable attribute
Event activity roll-up
Generalization
Grouping
Implementation compromise
Load
Logical level compromise
Materialization of tasks as classes
Meronymic association
Operational infrastructure
Physical level compromise
Policy infrastructure
Typification

REVIEW QUESTIONS
R10-1 Explain the difference between typification and generalization.

R10-2. Explain the difference between the operational, policy, and scheduling layers of the REA ontology.

R10-3. What is a specification association?

R10-4. What is a meronymic association?

R10-5. What kinds of implementation compromises may one want to make when designing a REA-based database with Microsoft Access?

MULTIPLE CHOICE QUESTIONS
MC10-1. What abstraction mechanism creates an "is-a" relationship between a super-class and one or more sub-classes?
   A) Generalization
   B) Typification
   C) Conversion
   D) Fulfillment

MC10-2. In the REA ontology, a relationship between two types (e.g. resource type and event type or event type and agent type) likely represents
   A) Typification
   B) Specification
   C) Policy
   D) Internal Control

MC10-3. In the REA ontology, a relationship between a commitment event and a resource type or an agent type likely represents
A) Typification
B) Specification
C) Policy
D) Internal Control

MC10-4. In the REA ontology, representation of what could be, should be, or must be is part of the
A) Operational layer
B) Accountability layer
C) Policy layer
D) Scheduling layer

MC10-5. Exclusion of a class or association because of inadequate measurement mechanisms is what kind of implementation compromise?
A) Conceptual level.
B) Logical level
C) Physical level
D) Meta-physical level

MC10-6. In some enterprises, certain pairs or groups of events always occur simultaneously. These events are called:
A) Logically congruent events
B) Physically congruent events
C) Conceptually congruent events
D) Economically congruent events

MC10-7. Which of the following is a disadvantage that results from combined class key posting?
A) Inability to run queries
B) Inability to enforce referential integrity
C) Uncontrolled growth of the database
D) The need for outer join queries

MC10-8. Which of the following is a physical level compromise?
A) Event activity (or event history) roll-up
B) Combined entity key posting
C) Consolidation of conceptually congruent event classes
D) Materialization of tasks as event classes

MC10-9. Posting a foreign key to implement an association when doing so results in a high load is an example of a:
A) Physical level implementation compromise
B) Logical level implementation compromise
C) Conceptual level implementation compromise
D) None of the above.

MC10-10. Which compromise recognizes that enterprise databases exist in a finite storage space and also recognizes that the larger the size of the database, the less efficient querying becomes?
A) Event activity (or event history) roll-up
B) Storage of derivable attributes
C) Combined entity key posting
D) Consolidation of conceptually congruent event entities

CHAPTER 11

Introduction to Querying

LEARNING OBJECTIVES

Sound database design is a necessary, but not sufficient, requirement for data analysis in a relational database environment. Querying logic and skills are also necessary for valid information retrieval. An incorrectly designed database is bound to produce inefficient and potentially meaningless information; however, even a correctly designed database may produce meaningless information with inaccurate querying. The most common query language is SQL: Structured Query Language. Even most databases that have proprietary visual interfaces use SQL behind the scenes. In addition to the SQL syntax, one must understand wildcard characters, comparison operators, logical operators, pattern matching, aggregations/functions, and different ways to join tables. These fundamental skills transfer to other data analysis settings (such as the use of generalized audit software). In addition to the underlying SQL, we introduce the Microsoft Access querying interface – essentially a tool for generating SQL syntax.

After studying this chapter, you should be able to
1. Identify and understand the primary clauses of a simple SQL query statement
2. Identify and explain the purpose of:
    a. wildcard characters
    b. comparison operators
    c. logical operators
    d. aggregations/functions
3. Explain how to apply pattern matching in SQL queries
4. Explain the mechanics of inner joins, left joins, right joins, and full outer joins, and describe situations in which each join type would be most appropriate
5. Create SQL queries using SQL syntax to retrieve requested information from a relational database
6. Create SQL queries using the Access query tool to retrieve requested information from a relational database

QUERYING RELATIONAL DATABASES

People in various parts of an enterprise need information in many different formats to support different types of decisions. Much of the information is derived from the same underlying data, but that data must be aggregated in different ways. For example, the marketing manager for the southeast region may need to know last month's sales dollar value specifically calculated for the southeast region. That same marketing manager may also need to know what last month's sales quantity was for a particular product or product line in the southeast region. The accountant preparing an income statement needs to know last month's total sales for the entire enterprise (not just the southeast region). The sales supervisor needs to have sales details separately for each salesperson. These different reporting needs are based on the same underlying data – that is, the disaggregated sales data, including sale dates, locations, actual selling prices of products, and quantities of products sold. The accounts receivable manager also needs sales data, separately for each customer, and also needs to know details of cash receipts received in exchange for those sales Different queries are needed to retrieve, aggregate, and display the data in appropriate formats for these three information needs.

In the past, business people typically had to ask information technology personnel to write computer programs and run queries to generate reports for them. But today, many business systems offer users the capability of *ad hoc querying* – direct querying by end users, whereby no pre-formulated queries or interfaces were developed in anticipation of needing the information. A *query* is a request for information submitted to a database engine. Querying is asking questions about the data in the database, and the answers to the questions are a result of combining and manipulating the data in different ways. We can isolate certain rows from tables, we can isolate certain columns from tables, we can join tables together, we can create calculations based on various data items, and so forth.

To query a database, users must know whatever querying language the enterprise database requires. Most relational databases require SQL, even if they also include a graphical interface such as Microsoft Access' Design View (a derivative of Query by Example, QBE, the first graphical query language). While users do less SQL coding with a graphical interface, they still must understand the database design, SQL syntax, the various kinds of operators, aggregations, functions, and join types to use, and apply querying logic. It is sometimes easy to misuse graphical queries because they hide the actual SQL syntax being created; actually, the syntax is available but it may be disregarded. Therefore, understanding of SQL syntax is important – even for those preferring to use the graphical query interface. Having covered database design in previous chapters, we next turn to queries.

Throughout this chapter, we use the conceptual model in Exhibit 11-1 and the corresponding tables that follow that exhibit to illustrate the operators, aggregations, join types, and querying logic. In this particular database, queries will allow us to understand the data about departments, employees, training courses, and related relationships.

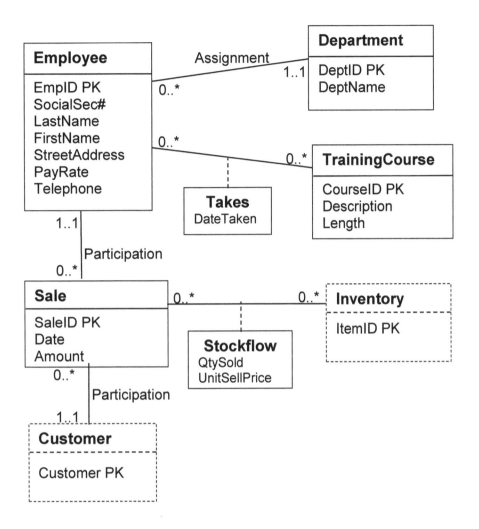

Exhibit 11-1: Conceptual Model for Database to Query

Note: Inventory and Customer are included on the conceptual model as dashed classes to indicate where they would fit, but are not included in the database tables, as none of the queries we demonstrate required their use. We include the item ID as the primary key of Inventory, as that becomes part of the concatenated primary key of the Stockflow table. We include Customer as the primary key of Customer, because that becomes a foreign key in the Sale table.

Employee

EmpID	SocialSec#	LastName	FirstName	StreetAddress	PayRate	Telephone	DeptID^FK
E1	123345678	Adams	Anita	144 Apple St.	$10.00	555-1234	D4
E2	234456789	Boston	Benjamin	255 Banana Rd.	$12.00	555-2345	D2
E3	345567890	Crabb	Charlie	366 Cherry Ave.	$14.00	555-3456	D2
E4	456678901	Davis	Deborah	477 Dip Dr.	$32.00	555-4567	D1
E5	567789101	Engler	Edward	588 Eggplant St.	$11.00	555-5678	D4
E6	678891012	Folkert	Fawn	699 Fruity Ave.	$23.00	555-6789	D3
E7	987563210	Green	Greta	177 Oak St.	$18.00	555-9876	D5
E8	831521336	Hasta	Hilda	189 Oak St.	$18.00	555-8315	D5

Department

DeptID	DeptName
D1	Executive Management
D2	Accounting
D3	Information Systems
D4	Operations
D5	Sales

TrainingCourse

CourseID	Description	Length
AC1	Accounting Fundamentals	2 days
AC2	Chart of Accounts	5 days
IS1	Basic Information Systems	5 days
IS2	Database Design	5 days
MD100	ERP Systems	10 days

EmployeeTakesCourse

EmpID	CourseID	DateTaken
E3	AC1	May 1-2
E3	AC2	June 24-28
E4	AC1	Oct 14-15
E6	IS1	June 24-28
E6	IS2	July 8-12

Sale

SaleID	Date	Amount	Customer^{FK}	SalespersonID^{FK}
S108	04/26/2020	$432.00	C76	E7
S109	04/26/2020	$118.00	C83	E8
S110	04/27/2020	$625.00	C19	E8
S111	04/28/2020	$375.00	C38	E7
S112	04/28/2020	$864.00	C76	E7

StockflowSaleInventory

ItemID	SaleID	QtySold	UnitSellPrice
I1	S108	10	$25.00
I1	S109	4	$25.00
I1	S111	15	$25.00
I2	S108	10	$15.00
I2	S112	41	$14.00
I3	S108	4	$8.00
I3	S109	2	$9.00
I3	S112	29	$10.00
I5	S110	25	$25.00

First, note the database design in the tables following Exhibit 11-1.

- Employee has EmpID as its primary key.
- Department has DeptID as its primary key.
- The Assignment association between Employee and Department is represented with Department's primary key posted as a foreign key in the Employee table.
- TrainingCourse has CourseID as its primary key.
- The Takes association class between Employee and TrainingCourse is represented with a separate table called EmployeeTakesCourse. Note that the primary keys of the Employee and TrainingCourse tables are posted into the EmployeeTakesCourse table as a concatenated primary key, and the table has an attribute of its own called DateTaken.
- Sale has SaleID as its primary key.
- The participation association between Sale and Employee is represented with Employee's primary key posted as a foreign key in the Sale table, labeled SalespersonID.

- The Stockflow association class between Sale and Inventory is represented with a separate table called StockflowSaleInventory. Note that the primary keys of the Sale and Inventory tables are posted into the StockflowSaleInventory table as a concatenated primary key, and the table has attributes of its own called QtySold and UnitSellPrice.

Once you understand how the tables in Exhibit 11-1 fit together, you are ready to learn some basic SQL and querying logic. When we say "how the tables fit together" we formally mean, how the tables are joined together. Tables can be joined together when they share a common attribute – either as a result of a primary key/foreign key relationship or as a result of a primary key/concatenated primary key relationship. Employee and Department may be joined on the shared DeptID field; Sale and Employee may be joined on the shared EmpID field; Employee and EmployeeTakesCourse may be joined on the shared EmpID field; TrainingCourse and EmployeeTakesCourse may be joined on the shared CourseID field; Sale and StockflowSaleInventory may be joined on the shared SaleID field. Later in this chapter, we will discuss several different types of joins.

STRUCTURED QUERY LANGUAGE

Structured Query Language (SQL) is the most commonly used querying language for relational databases. While SQL may be used to create, update, insert, and delete data, in this chapter, we focus only on its use to retrieve data from tables; this type of query is sometimes called a "select query."

SQL uses a standard format for every retrieval query to simplify the task of query development. In SQL, every retrieval query follows a structured, pre-defined Select-From-Where syntax as follows:

> SELECT <u>attribute name(s)</u>
> FROM <u>table name(s)</u>
> WHERE <u>condition criteria are met</u>;

Some relational databases require a semi-colon while others do not. The semi-colon is a standard way to separate SQL statements; the semi-colon allows more than one SQL statement to be executed in the same call to a database server, because it indicates to the database software that the end of the query statement has been reached. Access does not require a semi-colon; however, if you create a query in the Access Design View, a semi-colon will automatically be generated in the SQL syntax. Most current relational database software packages automatically put the semi-colon at the end of the statement to help avoid the syntax error that may occur when it is missing. The SELECT and FROM clauses are required in SQL (select) queries, whereas the WHERE clause is optional. Some queries do not require the WHERE clause, and some queries require additional clauses; however, in general this Select-From-Where format is a great starting point for building queries. The capitalization of the clauses is only for emphasis here; SQL is not case-sensitive.

The first clause of each SQL statement (that is, the ***SELECT clause***) is required, and specifies which attributes the query's answer should include. Recall that attributes are the names of a table's columns, and are also called fields.

The second clause of each SQL statement (that is, the *FROM clause*) is also required, and specifies the tables that contain the data to include in the answer. The FROM clause may specify a single table or multiple tables.

The third clause of each SQL statement (that is, the WHERE clause) is optional. The *WHERE clause* specifies criteria rows of data must meet to be included in the answer. If no such criteria exist, the WHERE clause is not specified. Multiple criteria can be specified in the WHERE clause.

Next, we use SQL to demonstrate some simple queries using the tables following Exhibit 11-1.

Say we want to generate a list of all employees' names and phone numbers to use for an emergency phone tree. A query to produce this list will keep all of the employees in the answer – that is, we do not want to specify any criteria by which to select only a subset of the employees. Thus, the WHERE clause is unnecessary and omitted from the SQL statement. The only attributes needed in the answer to this query are the employees' last name, first name, and telephone number. We simply need to ask the database to tell us the values of those three attributes for every employee in the Employee table.

The SQL statement is:

```
SELECT LastName, FirstName, Telephone
FROM Employee;
```

The result of running this query is

LastName	FirstName	Telephone
Adams	Anita	555-1234
Boston	Benjamin	555-2345
Crabb	Charlie	555-3456
Davis	Deborah	555-4567
Engler	Edward	555-5678
Folkert	Fawn	555-6789
Green	Greta	555-9876
Hasta	Hilda	555-8315

SQL allows users to specify how query results are sorted through the use of the *ORDER BY clause* (this optional clause is the final clause in the SQL statement when it is used). The clause is followed by the column name you wish to sort, and then the sorting order ascending/descending (the default option is to put data in ascending order; to specify descending order, add desc after the column name as shown below). Here is an example, sorting the prior query result in descending order by LastName:

```
SELECT LastName, FirstName, Telephone
FROM Employee
ORDER BY LastName desc;
```

Here is the revised query result:

LastName	FirstName	Telephone
Hasta	Hilda	555-8315
Green	Greta	555-9876
Folkert	Fawn	555-6789
Engler	Edward	555-5678
Davis	Deborah	555-4567
Crabb	Charlie	555-3456
Boston	Benjamin	555-2345
Adams	Anita	555-1234

Next, say we want to generate a list of employees (including all employee attributes) whose pay rate is less than $15 per hour. This query specifies criteria (payrate < $15) by which to select only a subset of the employees.

The SQL statement is:
    SELECT *
    FROM Employee
    WHERE PayRate <15.00;

Note that the * (asterisk) is a *wildcard character* that tells the database to include all attributes in the query result. The result of running this query is

EmpID	SocialSec#	LastName	FirstName	Street Address	PayRate	Telephone	DeptID
E1	123345678	Adams	Anita	144 Apple St.	$10.00	555-1234	D4
E2	234456789	Boston	Benjamin	255 Banana Rd.	$12.00	555-2345	D2
E3	345567890	Crabb	Charlie	366 Cherry Ave.	$14.00	555-3456	D2
E5	567789101	Engler	Edward	588 Eggplant St.	$11.00	555-5678	D4

Notice that the first query above kept all the rows, but a subset of the columns of the Employee table, and the second query kept all the columns but a subset of the rows of the Employee table. The next query keeps only a subset of the columns and only a subset of the rows.

Say we want to retrieve the last and first names, and telephone numbers, of the employees whose pay rate is less than $15 per hour. This data would allow us to call those employees to tell them we are giving them a raise of $1.50 per hour. The following SQL statement combines what the two previous statements accomplished into a single statement.

    SELECT LastName, FirstName, Payrate, Telephone
    FROM Employee
    WHERE PayRate <15.00;

The result of running this query is

LastName	FirstName	PayRate	Telephone
Adams	Anita	$10.00	555-1234
Boston	Benjamin	$12.00	555-2345
Crabb	Charlie	$14.00	555-3456
Engler	Edward	$11.00	555-5678

It is important to understand some additional characteristics of queries. In Access, there are three views of a query: Design View, SQL View, and Datasheet View. Design View is a visual interface that creates SQL syntax. *SQL View* shows SQL syntax; you can enter syntax directly into the SQL View, or you can just view the syntax created by the actions performed in the Design View. The Datasheet View is the output (result) of running a query. When you save a query in Access, you are saving the SQL syntax, not the result of the query that you see in the Datasheet View (you can "save" the query result, for example, by copying it to a Word document). The query result that you see in the Datasheet View looks like a table, but it does not change the underlying tables (at least not when using a select query). If the data in the tables change, rerunning a saved query on the tables will take into account the changes to the tables. Finally, note that you can query an existing query (as opposed to querying a table).

COMPARISON OPERATORS

The less than symbol (<) in the previous two queries is a comparison operator. Table 11.1 presents commonly used comparison operators with the purpose of applying them in queries. Symbols used to express these operators are included when applicable. Some operators are only expressed as words, not as symbols. In such cases, the operators' words are given in all caps.

Queries may apply comparison operators to numeric, text, and date fields. Their application to numeric data is self-evident, e.g., smaller numbers are less than larger numbers. When applied to text, values that begin with letters that appear earlier in the English alphabet are considered to be less than values that begin with letters that appear later in the English alphabet. Perhaps when you were a child, you played message decoding games in which you were given a set of numbers and you had to convert each number into the corresponding letter of the alphabet in order to read the message. In such codes, A = 1, B = 2, C = 3, and so on, through X = 24, Y = 25, and Z = 26. Similarly, in querying, words that begin with letters that come later in the alphabet are considered greater than words that begin with letters that come earlier in the alphabet. For example, green is greater than brown. Queries differentiate words that begin with the same letter by considering the second letters. For example, brown is greater than blue because r is greater than l. Words that begin with the same two letters are differentiated by their third letters, and so on.

Table 11.1 Comparison Operators

Operator (symbol, if any)	Purpose
Equal to (=)	Include records for which a field's value equals a specific value
Less than (<)	Include records for which a field's value is less than a specific value
Less than or equal to (<=)	Includes records for which a field's value is either less than or equal to a specific value
Greater than (>)	Include records for which a field's value is greater than a specific value
Greater than or equal to (>=)	Includes records for which a field's value is either greater than or equal to a specific value
Not Equal to (<>) or (!=)	Includes records for which a field's value does not equal a specific value
BETWEEN X and Y, where X and Y are endpoints of a range of values	Includes records for which a field's value falls within the given range, including the end points of the range. An alternative way of saying >= X and <= Y.
IS NULL	Includes records for which a specified field's value is empty, also called null.
EXISTS or IS NOT NULL	Includes records for which a specified field's value is something other than empty or null.
LIKE	Includes records that match the pattern specified after the LIKE operator. Often includes wildcard characters as part of the pattern.

When applied to dates, comparison operators consider dates that are earlier in time as less than dates that are later in time. For example, January 1, 2020 is less than January 2, 2020. Most database software stores Julian dates rather than the text format of dates. Julian developed a date valuation system by assigning a value of 1 to January 1, 4713 BCE (before common era). Next, Julian assigned a value of 2 to January 2, 4713, and then incremented each subsequent day's value by 1. Today's Julian date value (depending on when you are reading this) is likely somewhere in the 2.5-3 million range.

BETWEEN is a comparison operator that identifies records for which a field's value is within a specific range of values. The endpoints of the range are included. Use of a BETWEEN operator is equivalent to using a combination of "less than or equal to" with "greater than or equal to." For example, a query to include all sales for the month of June 2020 in its answer could be constructed using WHERE SaleDate >=6/1/2020 AND SaleDate <=6/30/2020, or it could be constructed using WHERE SaleDate BETWEEN 6/1/2020 and 6/30/2020.

IS NULL is a comparison operator that identifies records for which a specific field's value does not exist (i.e., the field is empty; no data has been entered). Null is not the same as zero, which is a value. For a field's value to be empty, it must have no value entered into it at all. *EXISTS* and *IS NOT NULL* are comparison operators that identify records for which a specific field's value contains non-null values. In other words, these operators retrieve the opposite records from those retrieved by the IS NULL operator. Although any theoretically pure relational database will not have any null values, most enterprise databases in practice are not theoretically pure. Even theoretically pure databases may contain data entry errors that resulted in null values. In such cases, the IS NULL operator would be useful in identifying those errors.

LIKE is a comparison operator that identified records for which a field's value fits a specific pattern. The pattern can be an exact pattern match. For example, the SQL statement

    Select *
    From TrainingCourse
    WHERE CourseID LIKE 'AC1';

would return the result

CourseID	Description	Length
AC1	Accounting Fundamentals	2 days

However, the true power of the LIKE operator is realized when the LIKE operator is combined with one or two wildcard symbols (like * or ?). Access actually supports two SQL standards: ANSI-89 and ANSI-92. For our purposes, we will focus on ANSI-89 which contains the following wildcard characters: *, ?, [ ], !, -, and #. Also note that SQL generally requires that text search terms be included in single quotation marks (e.g., 'AC1' above), but Microsoft Access alternatively accepts double quotation marks too.

The asterisk symbol (*) may be used to represent zero, one, or multiple characters. Values matching the pattern 'A*' would include all values that start with A (AC1 and AC2 in the example). Values matching the pattern 'AC*' would include AC, AC1, AC23, and ACCOUNTING.

The question mark (?) symbol may represent only a single character. Values matching the pattern 'AC?' would include AC1 and AC2, but would not include AC, AC23, or ACCOUNTING.

The * and ? wildcards may be used together to more completely specify the pattern to which potential field values should be compared. For example, WHERE CourseID LIKE '?C*' would isolate any rows for which the CourseID field contained the letter C in the second position, with any one character before the C, and any number of characters after the C. WHERE CourseID LIKE 'AC??' would isolate any rows for which the CourseID field started with AC and contained two additional characters.

The [ ] will match any single character inside the square brackets. LIKE 't[ae]n' will identify "tan," and "ten," but not "ton." The ! will match any character not in square brackets; LIKE 't[!ae]n' will identify "ton," but not "ten" or "tan."

The - (hyphen) inside square brackets will match any one character out of an ascending range of characters. LIKE 't[a-o]n' will identify tan, ten, ton, and any data that begins with "t" followed by any character from "a" to "o" and ending in an "n."

The # is used to match a single numeric digit. LIKE '5#5' matches to 505, 515, 525, etc. Comparison operators are used to isolate rows in the tables of interest – retrieving a subset of the records for which the comparison criteria are met – therefore they are included in the WHERE clauses of SQL statements.

LOGICAL OPERATORS

Queries often include *logical operators*, which are Boolean search terms used to define which records are included in the query result. Example logical operators include AND, OR, and NOT. The *AND operator* is similar to a set intersection in mathematics set theory. In other words, an answer to a query connecting two criteria with an AND operator will contain only the instances that meet both criteria. The *OR operator* is similar to a set union in mathematics set theory. In other words, an answer to a query connecting two criteria with an OR operator will contain all instances that meet at least one of the criteria. The *NOT operator* identifies instances that do not meet one or more conditions. The SQL statement

> SELECT *
> FROM Employee
> WHERE PayRate < 13 AND DeptID = 'D2';

applied to the tables following Exhibit 11-1 returns a result of

EmpID	SocialSec#	LastName	FirstName	Street Address	PayRate	Telephone	DeptID
E2	234456789	Boston	Benjamin	255 Banana Rd.	$12.00	555-2345	D2

In contrast, the SQL statement

> SELECT *
> FROM Employee
> WHERE PayRate < 13 OR DeptID = 'D2';

applied to the same tables returns a result of

EmpID	SocialSec#	LastName	FirstName	Street Address	PayRate	Telephone	DeptID
E1	123345678	Adams	Anita	144 Apple St.	$10.00	555-1234	D4
E2	234456789	Boston	Benjamin	255 Banana Rd.	$12.00	555-2345	D2
E3	345567890	Crabb	Charlie	366 Cherry Ave.	$14.00	555-3456	D2
E5	567789101	Engler	Edward	588 Eggplant St.	$11.00	555-5678	D4

Notice that the result of applying the OR operator is a larger set of records than is the result of applying the AND operator. That is because the AND operator has more stringent criteria to meet. The NOT operator can be combined with LIKE, as in "NOT LIKE." For example, NOT LIKE 'S*' returns all values that do not begin with "S."

AGGREGATION FUNCTIONS (VERTICAL CALCULATIONS) IN SQL QUERIES

Queries may include two types of calculations. *Aggregation functions* are mathematical operations performed within a particular column of data values, such as a computation of the average of a set of values; they are also called *vertical calculations*. Several different aggregation functions are standard in SQL. The *average (AVG) aggregation function* computes the average of a column of data values, to apply it, simply add AVG( ) to the field name (the field name is inside the parentheses) in the SELECT clause of the SQL statement. For example, if we wanted to compute the average pay rate for all of our employees, we could specify:

> SELECT AVG(PayRate) AS AveragePayRate
> FROM Employee;

Producing the result:

AveragePayRate
$17.25

Note that in the prior SQL statement, "AS" allows you to assign a name to a column and is known as an alias; once you apply a function to the column name "PayRate" the result of the function appears under the column name "AveragePayRate." You will see us continue to use AS in some of the examples below.

Other aggregation functions (that are applied the same way) include *SUM* (to add a column), *MAX* (to find the largest value in a column), *MIN* (to find the smallest value in a column), and *COUNT* (to tell how many data values are in a column).

When we use aggregation functions in queries, sometimes we want subtotals within columns rather than the grand total for the entire column. For example, we may want to calculate the total sales for each date in a time period, or we may want to know the total purchase amount for each vendor. *GROUP BY* is an additional clause that may be included after the WHERE clause in a SQL statement as a sub-totaling mechanism. Whatever field(s) the query is asked to group by will be grouped together and any aggregation function that is used will be applied to the subgroups rather than to the entire table. Examine the Sale table following Exhibit 11-1.

If you wanted to calculate total sales separately for each date, you will need to GROUP BY date, and SUM amount. The query is formulated as follows:

> SELECT Date, SUM(Amount) AS SumofAmount
> FROM Sale
> GROUP BY Date;

The answer that results from applying this query to the Sale table is:

Date	SumofAmount
04/26/2020	$550.00
04/27/2020	$625.00
04/28/2020	$1,239.00

If instead, you want to calculate total sales separately for each customer, you will need to GROUP BY customer. The query is formulated as follows:

> SELECT Customer, SUM(Amount) AS SumofAmount
> FROM Sale
> GROUP BY Customer;

The answer that results from applying this query to the Sale table is:

Customer	SumofAmount
C19	$625.00
C38	$375.00
C76	$1,296.00
C83	$118.00

In the preceding example, we instead might have been interested in aggregating sales amounts by customers, but only displaying the customers that have over $500 in sales. The solution is similar to using the WHERE clause to identify rows meeting criteria, but the WHERE clause cannot be used with aggregate functions. The *HAVING clause* is what we need:

> SELECT Customer, Sum(Amount) AS SumofAmount
> FROM Sale
> GROUP BY Customer
> HAVING Sum(Amount)>500;

The answer is a subset of the prior query result:

Customer	SumofAmount
C19	$625.00
C76	$1,296.00

Although a query cannot use the where clause related to a field in an aggregate function, the where clause can still be used with other fields not part of an aggregate function. For example, in the prior query, we could have used the WHERE clause on a date field to have the group by clause, aggregate function, and having clause be applied only on rows that fall on a certain date (or between a certain date range):

> SELECT Customer, Sum(Amount) AS SumofAmount
> FROM Sale
> WHERE Date=#04/28/2020#
> GROUP BY Customer
> HAVING Sum(Amount)>500;

This SQL produces the following query result:

Customer	SumofAmount
C76	$864.00

Note that Customer C76 only has one sale (for $864.00) on 4/28/2020 so there isn't any data to aggregate beyond the one data value. But if there had been multiple sales involving C76 on 4/28/2020 the aggregation would have been executed.

When GROUP BY is used alone, without any aggregation functions applied to any columns, it eliminates repeating data values. The following SQL statement

> SELECT Customer
> FROM Sale
> GROUP BY Customer;

produces this result (note that in the underlying table being queried, C76 appears twice, but in the query result it appears once):

Customer
C19
C38
C76
C83

EXPRESSIONS (HORIZONTAL CALCULATIONS) IN SQL QUERIES

A *horizontal calculation* or expression manipulates data values from two or more different fields in the same record. Examine the Stockflow table following Exhibit 11-1. To calculate the sale line extension for all rows of data, a new field must be created and defined as the product of QtySold and UnitSellPrice (below this will be named as "SaleLineExtension").

The query is formulated as follows (assuming you only want to see the SaleLineExtension data):

> SELECT QtySold*UnitSellPrice As SaleLineExtension
> FROM Stockflow;

Here is the result:

SaleLineExtension
$250.00
$100.00
$375.00
$150.00
$574.00
$32.00
$18.00
$290.00
$625.00

To accomplish your desired result, sometimes you may need a series of queries that build on each other. You will sometimes end up with a wrong answer, or get an error message indicating the query is too complex, if you mix horizontal calculations with aggregations (which are vertical calculations) in the same query, as the database engine may not perform the calculations in the order you intend. The answer will be different if the database engine aggregates before performing the horizontal calculation than it will be if the database engine calculates horizontally before aggregating. To be certain the calculations are done in the desired order, consider creating one query that performs the horizontal calculations, and then creating a second query (using the first query as the starting object) that aggregates vertically. Or vice versa, depending on the query objective.

JOINING TABLES

A JOIN query combines two (or more) tables (or queries) on the basis of common attributes. Recall from earlier chapters that associations between classes are represented in relational database tables by posting attributes from some tables into other tables (e.g., by posting a primary key into another table as a foreign key, or by posting primary keys from two related class tables into a new table as a concatenated primary key). Join queries often use these links between tables when information from two (or more) related tables is needed to answer a question or create a report. Four join types are possible, although many database systems can only process three of these types.

The most common join type is an inner join. An *inner join* combines tables (queries), including in the query result only the records that have the same values in the fields that are joined. An *outer join* combines tables (queries) including records even when the joined fields don't have the same values in three different ways: as left, right, or full outer joins.

A *left join* (also called a left outer join) includes all records from whichever table is on the left (which is determined by the order that the tables enter the FROM clause of the SQL statement), and matches those records from the table that is on the right, for which values in the joined fields are equal. The combined table records from the left table for which the joined field values don't match will contain null values for the fields from the right table. The records from the right table for which the joined field values don't match values from the left table are excluded from the combined table.

A *right join* (also called a right outer join) includes all records from whichever table is on the right, and matches those records from the table that is on the left, for which values in the joined fields are equal. The combined table's records from the right table for which the joined field values don't match will contain null values for the fields from the left table. The records from the left table for which the joined field values don't match values from the right table are excluded from the combined table.

A *full outer join* (not possible in some database systems) includes all records from both the left and right tables, displaying null values in columns for which the joined fields didn't contain matching values.

It is critical to note that if a data value in one of the joined fields repeats (regardless of join type), there will (relatedly) be repeating rows of data in the query result. Furthermore, any data that depends on the repeating values will also repeat. Not recognizing this can lead to erroneous data analysis, especially if the data is going to be aggregated. We will follow up on these points below when we examine the joins.

Some find it helpful to illustrate the join types using diagrams such as those in Exhibit 11-2.

Exhibit 11-2: Join Types Illustrated

Consider the TrainingCourse (left table) and EmployeeTakesCourse (right table) following Exhibit 11-1. Joining the two tables with an inner join on the CourseID field will yield a result that includes only the courses AC1, AC2, IS1, and IS2. Course MD100 is excluded from the result because there is not a matching value in the CourseID fields in both tables. Joining the two tables with a left join will include MD100 in the result, with null values appearing in the EmplID and DateTaken fields. Joining the two tables with a right join will yield the same result as the inner join, as there are no CourseIDs in the right table that aren't also in the left. However, joining the two tables with a full outer join will yield the same result as the left join for the same reason.

The SQL syntax for the joins, and the results of applying them to the tables following Exhibit 11-1, are as follows:

Inner join query

```
SELECT *
FROM TrainingCourse
INNER JOIN EmployeeTakesCourse ON TrainingCourse.CourseID =
EmployeeTakesCourse.CourseID
ORDER BY TrainingCourse.CourseID;
```

Result of inner join query

CourseID	Description	Length	EmplID	CourseID	DateTaken
AC1	Accounting Fundamentals	2 days	E4	AC1	Oct 14-15
AC1	Accounting Fundamentals	2 days	E3	AC1	May 1-2
AC2	Chart of Accounts	5 days	E3	AC2	June 24-28
IS1	Basic Information Systems	5 days	E6	IS1	June 24-28
IS2	Database Design	5 days	E6	IS2	July 8-12

As mentioned above, you have to understand that data can repeat as a result of a join. In the inner join above, "AC1", "Accounting Fundamentals", and "2 days" repeats in the query result. This happens because two different employees have taken the same course; this fact is observed by looking at the EmployeeTakesCourse table (you will see that employees E3 and E4 have both taken that accounting course). In this particular join, the "AC1" in the Training Courses table is being joined with the two instances of "AC1" in the EmployeeTakesCourse table. This is exactly how a join is supposed to work. However, the data analyst needs to understand that it would be inappropriate to add up the length in the query result and say that AC 1 lasts for 4 days (when it only lasts for 2 days as indicated in the Training Courses table). Any time you create a join, you have to be careful of how you aggregate and interpret the query result.

Left join query

```
SELECT *
FROM TrainingCourse
    LEFT JOIN EmployeeTakesCourse ON TrainingCourse.CourseID =
    EmployeeTakesCourse.CourseID
    ORDER BY TrainingCourse.CourseID;
```

Result of left join query

CourseID	Description	Length	EmplID	CourseID	DateTaken
AC1	Accounting Fundamentals	2 days	E4	AC1	Oct 14-15
AC1	Accounting Fundamentals	2 days	E3	AC1	May 1-2
AC2	Chart of Accounts	5 days	E3	AC2	June 24-28
IS1	Basic Information Systems	5 days	E6	IS1	June 24-28
IS2	Database Design	5 days	E6	IS2	July 8-12
MD100	ERP Systems	10 days			

Right join query:

```
SELECT *
FROM TrainingCourse
    RIGHT JOIN EmployeeTakesCourse ON TrainingCourse.CourseID =
    EmployeeTakesCourse.CourseID
    ORDER BY TrainingCourse.CourseID;
```

Result of right join query

CourseID	Description	Length	EmplID	CourseID	DateTaken
AC1	Accounting Fundamentals	2 days	E4	AC1	Oct 14-15
AC1	Accounting Fundamentals	2 days	E3	AC1	May 1-2
AC2	Chart of Accounts	5 days	E3	AC2	June 24-28
IS1	Basic Information Systems	5 days	E6	IS1	June 24-28
IS2	Database Design	5 days	E6	IS2	July 8-12

Note that while some databases include explicit full outer join syntax, Access does not (so the following example will not run in Access).

Full outer join query

```
SELECT *
FROM TrainingCourse
    FULL OUTER JOIN EmployeeTakesCourse ON TrainingCourse.CourseID =
    EmployeeTakesCourse.CourseID
    ORDER BY TrainingCourse.CourseID;
```

Result of full outer join query

CourseID	Description	Length	EmplID	CourseID	DateTaken
AC1	Accounting Fundamentals	2 days	E4	AC1	Oct 14-15
AC1	Accounting Fundamentals	2 days	E3	AC1	May 1-2
AC2	Chart of Accounts	5 days	E3	AC2	June 24-28
IS1	Basic Information Systems	5 days	E6	IS1	June 24-28
IS2	Database Design	5 days	E6	IS2	July 8-12
MD100	ERP Systems	10 days			

Because it is impossible for an employee to take a course that is not in the course listing (i.e., the TrainingCourse table), the full join does not have a different result than the left join.

In Access, you can obtain a full outer join via the use of a UNION query. Union queries are beyond the scope of our discussion, but here is the SQL in Access to allow for the creation of the full outer join described above:

```
SELECT *
FROM TrainingCourse
    LEFT JOIN EmployeeTakesCourse ON TrainingCourse.CourseID
        =EmployeeTakesCourse.CourseID
UNION
SELECT *
FROM TrainingCourse
    RIGHT JOIN EmployeeTakesCourse ON TrainingCourse.CourseID
    =EmployeeTakesCourse.CourseID
WHERE TrainingCourse.CourseID IS NULL
ORDER BY TrainingCourse.CourseID;
```

We end this section with a word of caution. If you do not join tables (queries) on a common attribute, you will get a Cartesian product (also called a cross product or a cross join. Such a result will match every row from one table (query) with every row from the other table (query). Rarely would you want such a result. You can watch out for Cartesian products by keeping track of the number of records in the objects that you are querying. For example, if you have one table with 100 rows and another table with 120 rows, if you get a query result with 12,000 rows, you will know it is the result of a product (100 x 120).

PARAMETER QUERIES

Users often need to re-use queries, changing only the date criteria. For example, a marketing manager who wants to know the total sales for a specific inventory item for a week or for a month could use the same query with different date constraints. A *date constraint* is a restriction placed on a date field in a query to limit the query results to include only records for which the date values meet the restriction (accomplished with the WHERE clause). To increase the re-usability of queries, database software offers the option of creating parameter queries.

A *parameter query* specifies variables in lieu of data values as part of the query's selection criteria, allowing the user to specify different data values to be used each time the query is run. Consider a query that specifies a date range as the criteria: BETWEEN #1/1/19# and #1/31/19#. If the user wants to re-use this query in the future for a different date range (e.g., BETWEEN #2/1/19# and #2/28/19#), he or she must change the design of the query to change the date constraint. A parameter query for this situation would not specify the exact dates; instead, it would include parameter names for each date, for example BETWEEN [BeginDate] and [EndDate]. Each time the query is run, the database engine will conclude that it doesn't know what the values for BeginDate and EndDate are, so the software will prompt the user to specify the values of these parameters. This enables the user to change the dates each time the query is run without changing the design of the query.

Parameter queries are a powerful concept because financial reports (and other management reports) get created on a recurring basis. A balance sheet report could prompt users to enter a specific balance sheet date, and that same date could be passed to all of the individual queries (e.g., cash, accounts receivable, inventory) being used to generate the balance sheet (and the date would only need to be entered one time).

DESIGN VIEW (QUERY BY EXAMPLE) IN MICROSOFT ACCESS

Although most relational database software can run queries that are created in SQL syntax, most packages also offer a visual interface intended to make querying have more of a "point and click" feel. Such an interface was originally called Query By Example (QBE) because it has the user provide an example of what they want the answer to their query to look like. Microsoft Access refers to this as the Design View. The user doesn't need to learn the precise SQL syntax in order to generate many useful queries (although knowledge of syntax is important). However, it is very important to understand exactly what the different elements of the Design View interface accomplish when developing a query. If you do not ask the correct question, you will not get the correct answer! Using Design View can seem easier than it really is, and it is easy to make mistakes and obtain unintended query results. Think about this: the less you understand the language of a person (or computer software) to whom you are asking a question, the more likely you are to make a mistake in asking that question. *You* may understand what you are trying to ask, but if you cannot adequately communicate the question to the database software, you will not get the answer you need. The dangerous thing is that you may not even realize the answer is incorrect! Of course that warning is also true for users explicitly querying with SQL syntax, but our own anecdotal experience leads us to believe Design View is more likely than SQL View (syntax) to cause a false sense of security for untrained users. Most users trained in SQL syntax are instructed to test their query construction before relying on the result; whereas many Design View users do not receive such instruction.

Because we are using Microsoft Access as our physical implementation software, we will next examine some elements of querying with the Design View interface in Access. Note that you can enter Access queries directly in SQL syntax using the SQL
View, so you may choose to bypass the Design View interface.

To create a new query in Microsoft Access, you first need to open a database (assuming it isn't open). It is important for you to have a solid understanding of both the design and content of the tables from which you are trying to retrieve information before you create any queries. The overall approach to using Design View in Access is as follows

(1) Select the table(s) and/or query(ies) that contain the fields that eventually need to appear in the query result, and establish any joins that are needed (make sure to use the appropriate join type). This will generate the FROM clause syntax.

(2) Drag the fields that need to be manipulated, or that need to appear in the query result, into the query grid (the lower half of the Design View into which fields are dragged and in which aggregations or horizontal calculations may be created to establish the desired logic for a query). This will generate the SELECT clause.

(3) Complete whatever additional (optional) steps are needed to develop the answer

    a. Set criteria to filter out irrelevant records (generate WHERE clause)

    b. Use aggregation functions within the fields for which such calculations are appropriate OR create calculated fields using standard mathematical operators

    c. Apply any other needed functions such as Group By, Order BY, or Having (generate GROUP BY, ORDER BY, or HAVING clauses)

Keep in mind that you may need to accomplish your query objective (end result) with a series of queries that build on each other. You will generally end up with a wrong answer if you mix horizontal calculations (which are row computations that combine data from multiple columns of one or more tables), and vertical calculations (which aggregate data values within a column according to specified functions). Access doesn't know which to do first, the vertical calculations or the horizontal calculations and if the query runs at all, it may create an answer that includes every possible combination of everything. It is best to create one query that applies the aggregation functions, and then create a new query (using the first query as the starting object) that accomplishes the horizontal calculations, or vice versa, depending on the query demands.

To allow a comparison and contrast, we next use some of the same queries introduced earlier with SQL for discussing Access Design View. The database we use therefore consists of the same tables we used earlier in the chapter. We display them here in Microsoft Access as Exhibit 11-3 so you can see that we are using the same data. You are also provided with the Access database file in case you want to follow along on a computer as you read.

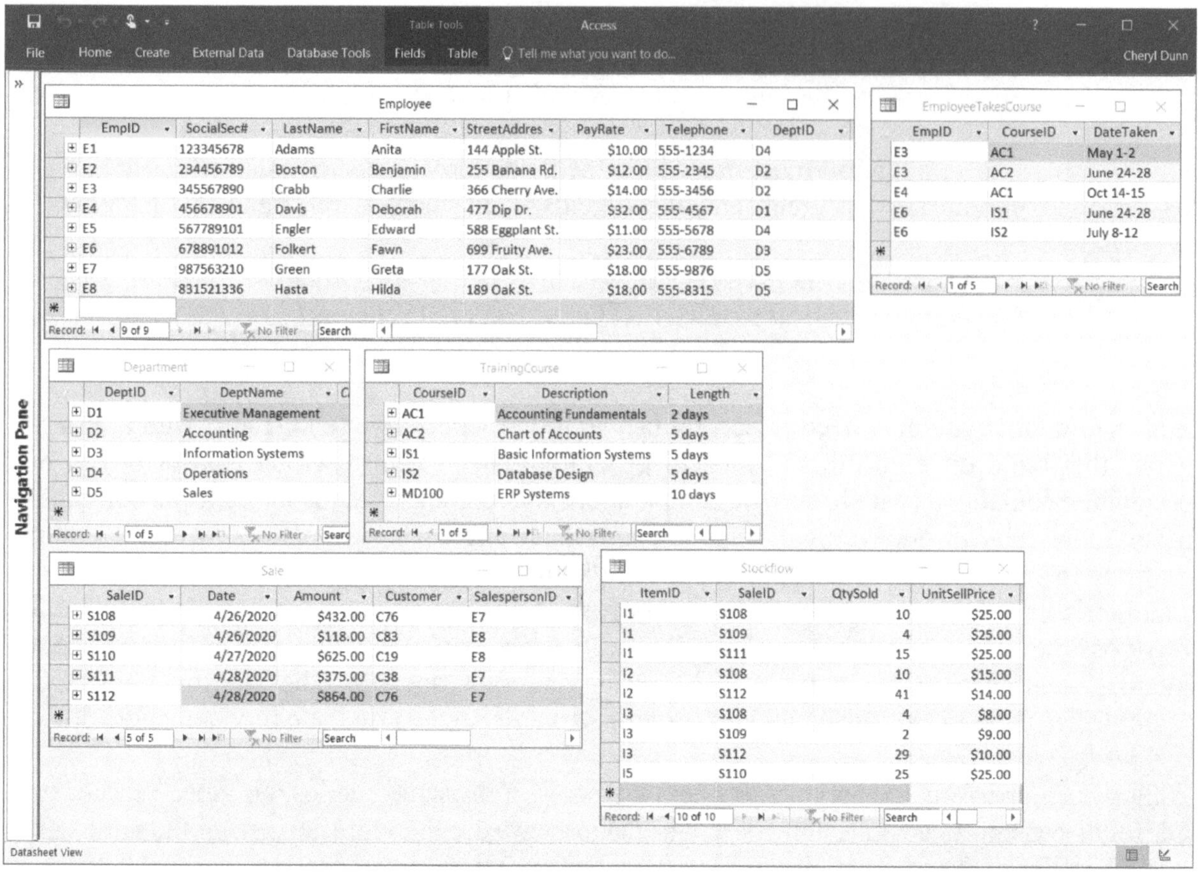

Employee

EmpID	SocialSec#	LastName	FirstName	StreetAddres	PayRate	Telephone	DeptID
E1	123345678	Adams	Anita	144 Apple St.	$10.00	555-1234	D4
E2	234456789	Boston	Benjamin	255 Banana Rd.	$12.00	555-2345	D2
E3	345567890	Crabb	Charlie	366 Cherry Ave.	$14.00	555-3456	D2
E4	456678901	Davis	Deborah	477 Dip Dr.	$32.00	555-4567	D1
E5	567789101	Engler	Edward	588 Eggplant St.	$11.00	555-5678	D4
E6	678891012	Folkert	Fawn	699 Fruity Ave.	$23.00	555-6789	D3
E7	987563210	Green	Greta	177 Oak St.	$18.00	555-9876	D5
E8	831521336	Hasta	Hilda	189 Oak St.	$18.00	555-8315	D5

EmployeeTakesCourse

EmpID	CourseID	DateTaken
E3	AC1	May 1-2
E3	AC2	June 24-28
E4	AC1	Oct 14-15
E6	IS1	June 24-28
E6	IS2	July 8-12

Department

DeptID	DeptName
D1	Executive Management
D2	Accounting
D3	Information Systems
D4	Operations
D5	Sales

TrainingCourse

CourseID	Description	Length
AC1	Accounting Fundamentals	2 days
AC2	Chart of Accounts	5 days
IS1	Basic Information Systems	5 days
IS2	Database Design	5 days
MD100	ERP Systems	10 days

Sale

SaleID	Date	Amount	Customer	SalespersonID
S108	4/26/2020	$432.00	C76	E7
S109	4/26/2020	$118.00	C83	E8
S110	4/27/2020	$625.00	C19	E8
S111	4/28/2020	$375.00	C38	E7
S112	4/28/2020	$864.00	C76	E7

Stockflow

ItemID	SaleID	QtySold	UnitSellPrice
I1	S108	10	$25.00
I1	S109	4	$25.00
I1	S111	15	$25.00
I2	S108	10	$15.00
I2	S112	41	$14.00
I3	S108	4	$8.00
I3	S109	2	$9.00
I3	S112	29	$10.00
I5	S110	25	$25.00

Exhibit 11-3: Example Tables in Microsoft Access

We know of no convenient way to display all of these tables on the screen simultaneously. We opened each one in data sheet view and resized the table windows so they would fit on the screen. We next display the relationship layout as Exhibit 11-4 so you can familiarize yourself with the relationships between tables that are formed by the use of posted keys.

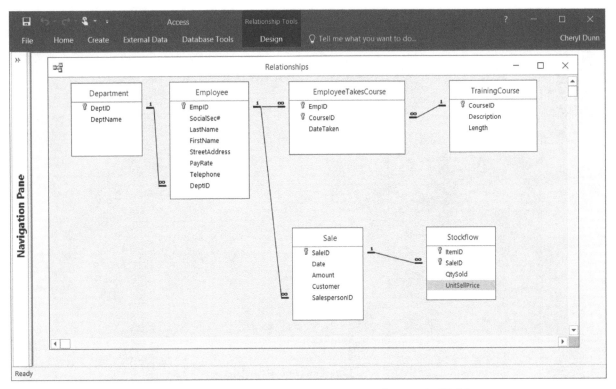

Exhibit 11-4: Relationship Layout for Example Tables

Please note that this is not intended to be a complete database. Only the tables necessary to illustrate the query examples are included. In addition to looking at the relational layout and the data in each table, you should also familiarize yourself with each table's design. Partial views of the table designs are displayed as Exhibit 11-5; however, as noted after the exhibit, you can't see everything in a single picture of the table design view because the field properties in the bottom section vary for each field in the table.

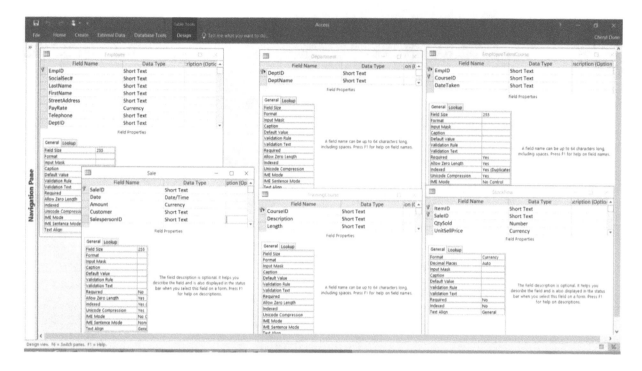

Exhibit 11-5: Database Table Design View

You must be familiar with the structure of the database tables you are querying to effectively design queries. Keep in mind that you should look at the design view of the tables within Microsoft Access itself (rather than relying on the chapter exhibits), because the field properties panel may be different for each field. To view each field's property, you need to click on each field within the design view of each table and then examining the field properties panel. From the upper panel you can see the data type, which in many cases is all you need to know about each field when using it in a query. Knowing the data type is important because you can only use most mathematical functions on number and currency fields; you can also perform limited mathematical functions on date fields, for example to compute the difference between two dates or between a stored date and the current date. The latter is useful for calculating information such as the number of days an invoice is past due; the former is useful for calculating information such as the average delivery time for a particular vendor.

Starting a Query and Adding the Appropriate Table(s) and/or Query(ies)
In the Database window, click the Query button and choose "New." Microsoft Access will then display the "New Query" dialog box (See Exhibit 11-6). Choose Design View (the **Design View** is the mode that depicts the logic of the query in QBE format -- do NOT use query wizards without having a complete understanding of the assumptions the wizards make).

Panel (a)

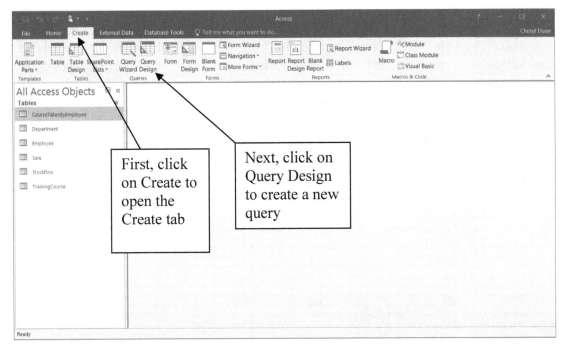

The result of clicking on Query Design will be the following windows – notice Show Table is a separate window that is on top of the query window. The query window is the screen in which the query is created – in that window the user may toggle between Design View, SQL View, and Datasheet View.

Panel (b)

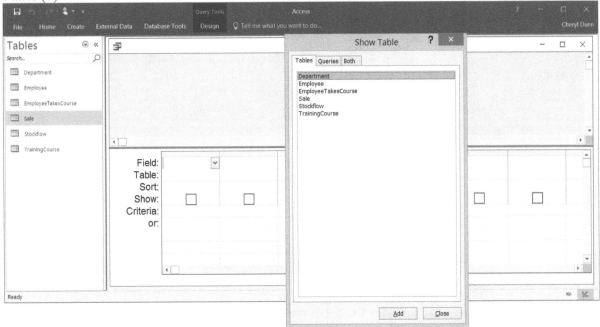

Exhibit 11-6: Starting a New Query

The show table window displays a list of tables and queries in your database (the default is to show the tables; if you want to base a query on an existing query, you can click on either the Queries tab or the Both tab). To include table(s) in the query, either double-click on each table name or click each table name and click the Add button. To select multiple tables and add them simultaneously, press the Ctrl key while you click on the table names and when all the chosen table names are highlighted, click on Add. When all appropriate tables and/or queries are added to the query window, click on Close. For our first query (generate a list of employees' names and phone numbers to be used for an emergency phone tree) we only need the Employee table, so simply double-click on Employee, then click on Close as shown in Exhibit 11-7.

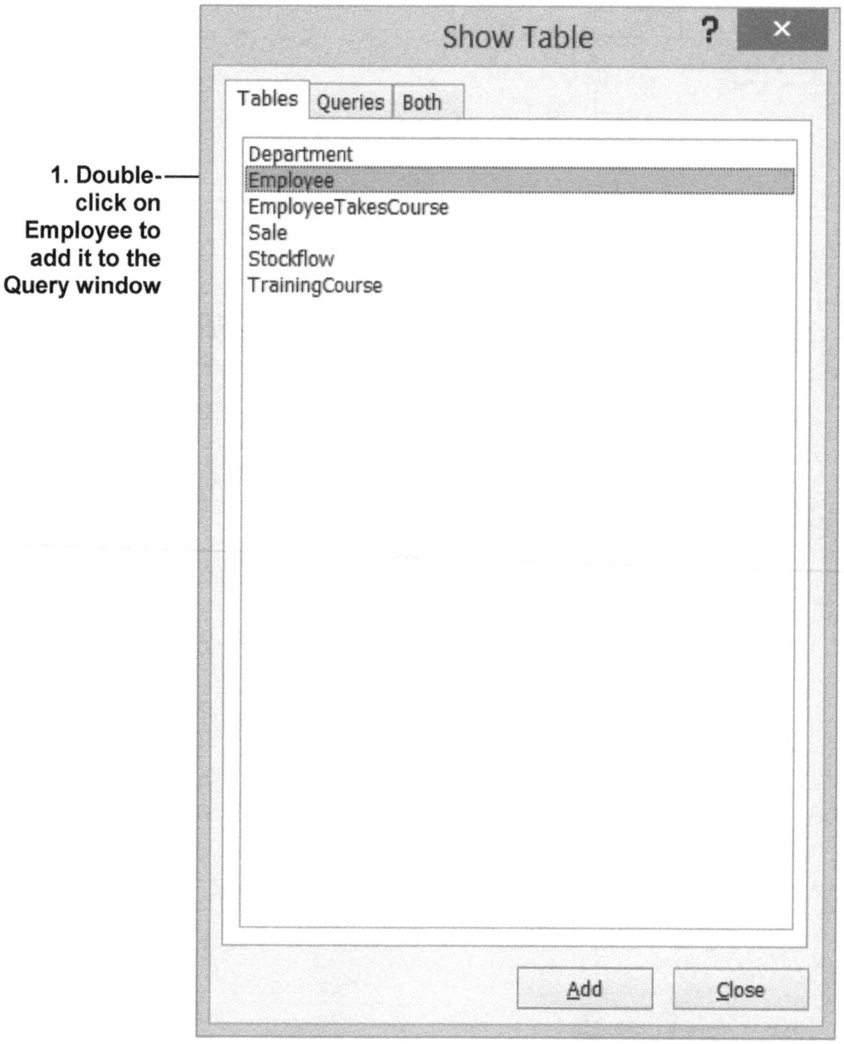

Exhibit 11-7: Show Table window

Resize the Query window and the Employee table window that appear so you can see all the fields in the Employee table and still see the lower panel of the query window as shown in Exhibit 11-8. To resize windows, simply click and drag on the edges or corners.

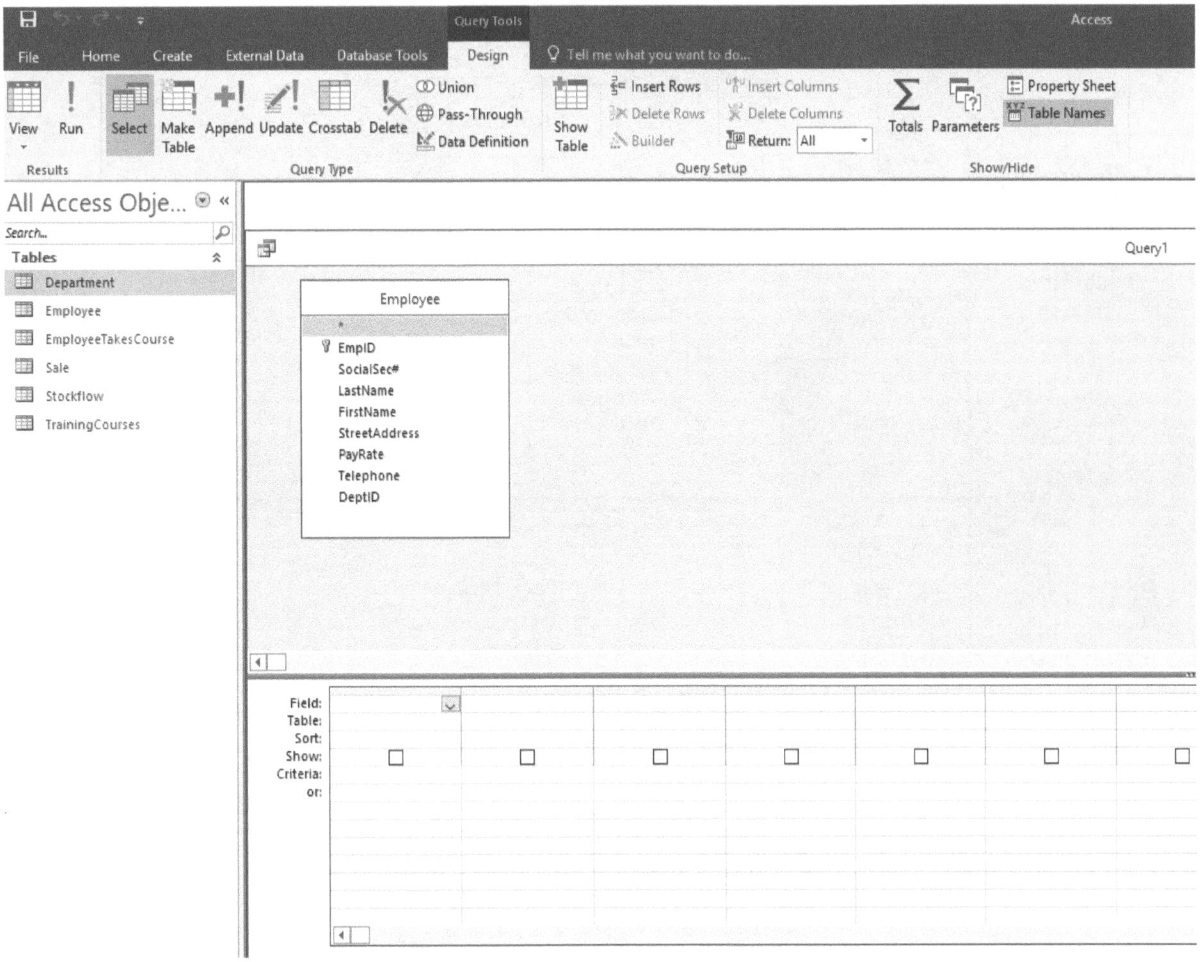

Exhibit 11-8: Query Window

The next step is to add field names from the table to the query grid. This can be accomplished either by clicking the field name(s) and dragging them down to the grid or by double-clicking each field name to add it to the grid. For our query we need only the names and phone numbers for the emergency phone tree. Therefore, we add Last Name, First Name, and Telephone to the query grid as illustrated in Exhibit 11-9. This action will automatically generate the syntax in the underlying SQL SELECT clause (as long as the "Show:" checkbox is checked; removing the check mark removes the field from the SELECT clause).

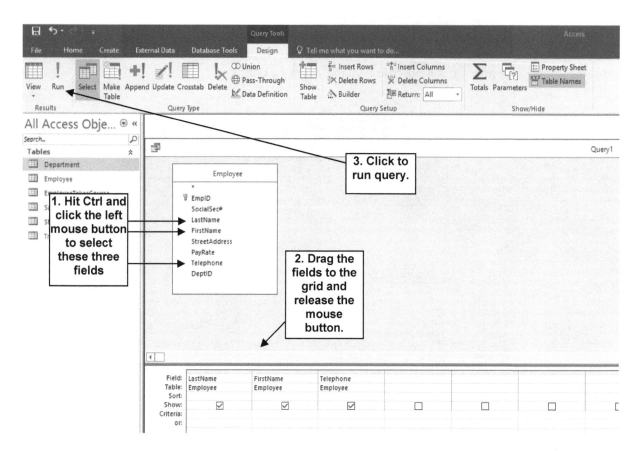

Exhibit 11-9: Employee Phone Tree Query Design

Because our query keeps all rows of data, thus not requiring a WHERE clause, our query is complete. To see the results of the query, either click on the icon that looks like an exclamation mark (!), or switch to Datasheet View (the view that is row/column format and looks like a table) by clicking datasheet toolbar button or by selecting View, Datasheet View.

A query's answer in Microsoft Access is not actually a table, but is instead a dynaset. A *dynaset* looks and behaves like a table, but is not actually stored as a table -- it is generated as a view each time the query is run. New data added to the database that affects the query result is reflected in the dynaset the next time the query is run. The answer to our first query is shown in Exhibit 11-10.

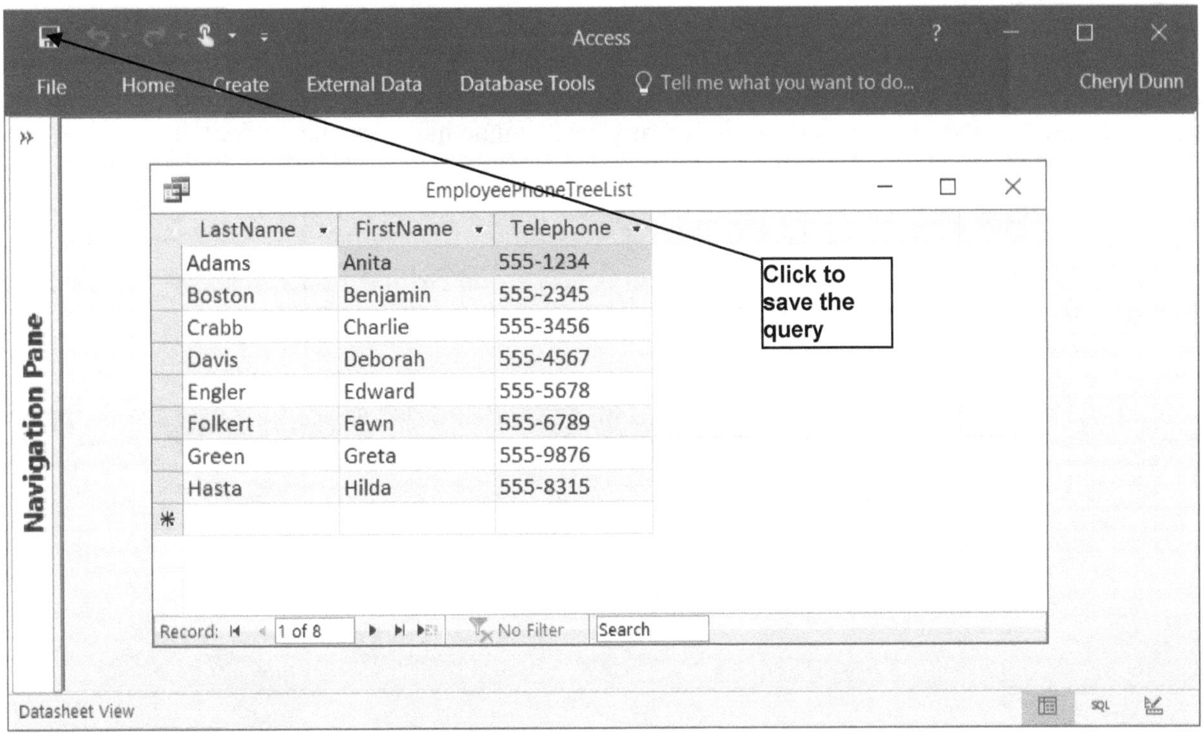

Exhibit 11-10: Employee Phone Tree Query Result

Once we are certain our query is executing properly, we need to save the query so we can run it again as needed. To save the query, either click on the Save icon as indicated on Exhibit 11-10, or click on File, Save on the menu. That will bring up a "Save As" window into which you can type a meaningful name for your query and click on OK. See Exhibit 11-11. Your saved queries will appear under the listing of tables. When you run a query, the query name will appear above the dynaset (just like a table name appears above the actual table columns and rows). Prior to you naming the query, Access will assign it a default name of Query1 as shown in Exhibit 11-10.

Exhibit 11-11: "Save As" window

To begin our second query (a list of all attributes of employees whose pay rate is less than $15), create a new query and add the Employee table to the query window following the same steps illustrated in Exhibits 11-6 through 11-8. The next step is to add all the fields from the Employee table to the query grid. Then specify the criteria by which the horizontal subset (i.e., a selected group of rows from one or more tables) is to be defined. In this example, the field for which the criterion needs to be specified is PayRate, and the criterion is <15. The query grid includes a line labeled "Criteria" on which to enter the logical operator expression. Criteria should be entered on the same line in the appropriate fields for any query that includes the logical operator AND. Criteria should be entered in the Criteria line for one of the appropriate fields and on the "Or" line for the other appropriate field for a query that includes the logical operator OR.

Exhibit 11-12(a) illustrates the appropriate query design, and Exhibit 11-12(b) shows the resulting dynaset, along with a query name (EmployeesWithPayRateLessThan15).

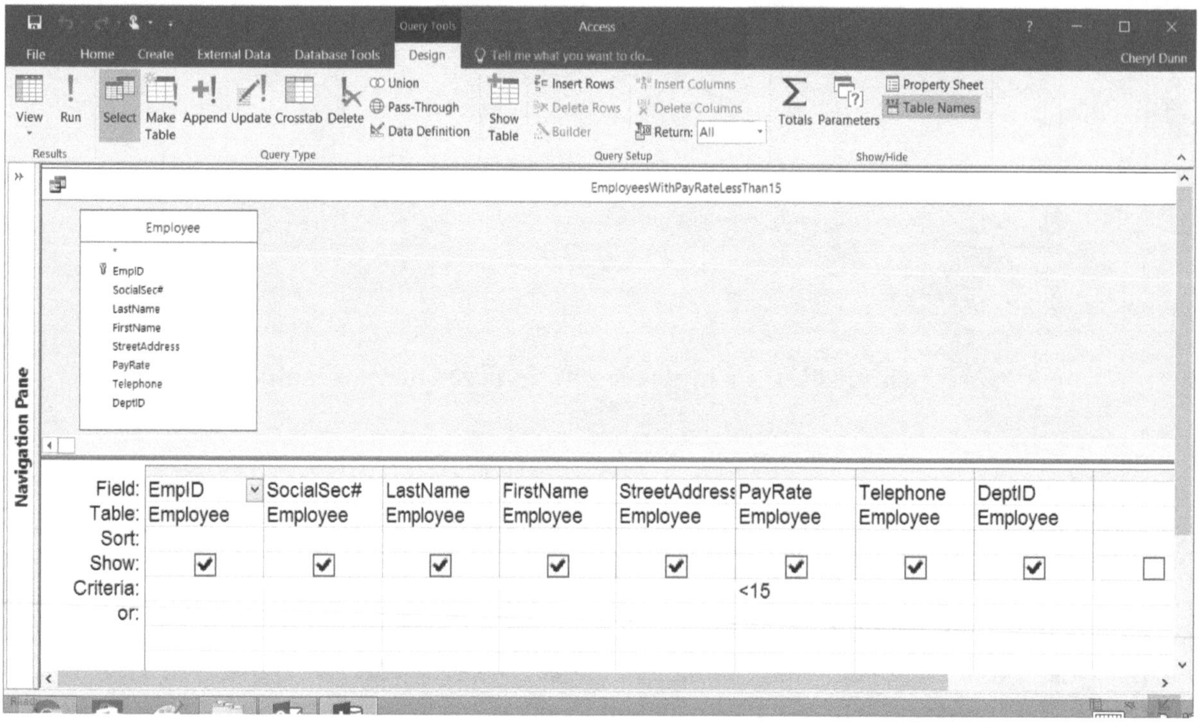

Exhibit 11-12(a): Employees with PayRate <15 Query Design

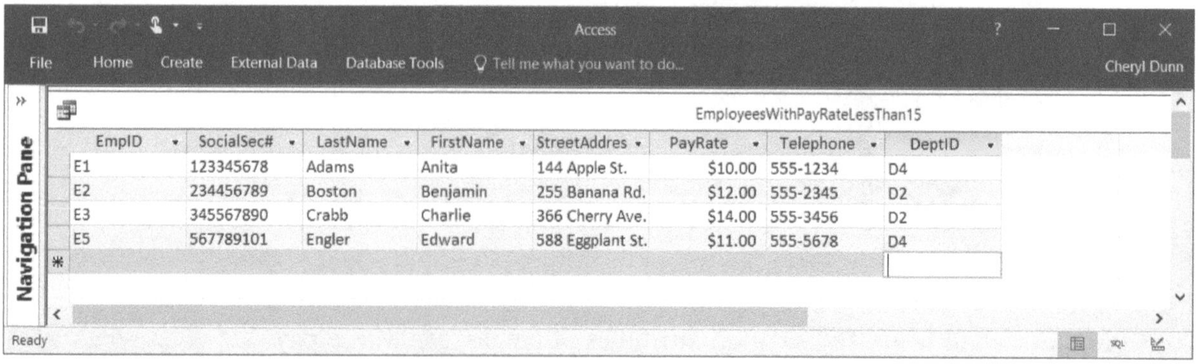

Exhibit 11-12(b): Employees with PayRate < 15 Query Result

Exhibit 11-12(c) shows an alternative query approach to that depicted in Exhibit 11-12(a). If you look closely at the top of the Employee table, you will see an asterisk (*). This is the wild card to select all columns in the table. It can be brought into the query grid instead of specifying all of the columns on a one-by-one basis. Criteria, however, cannot be used on the wild card; the solution is to add the columns that have criteria and then remove the "show" checkmark (so that the data does not display twice, once as part of the wild card and once as part of the criteria filter). In this example, the PayRate field is added and the "<15" is used as the criteria.

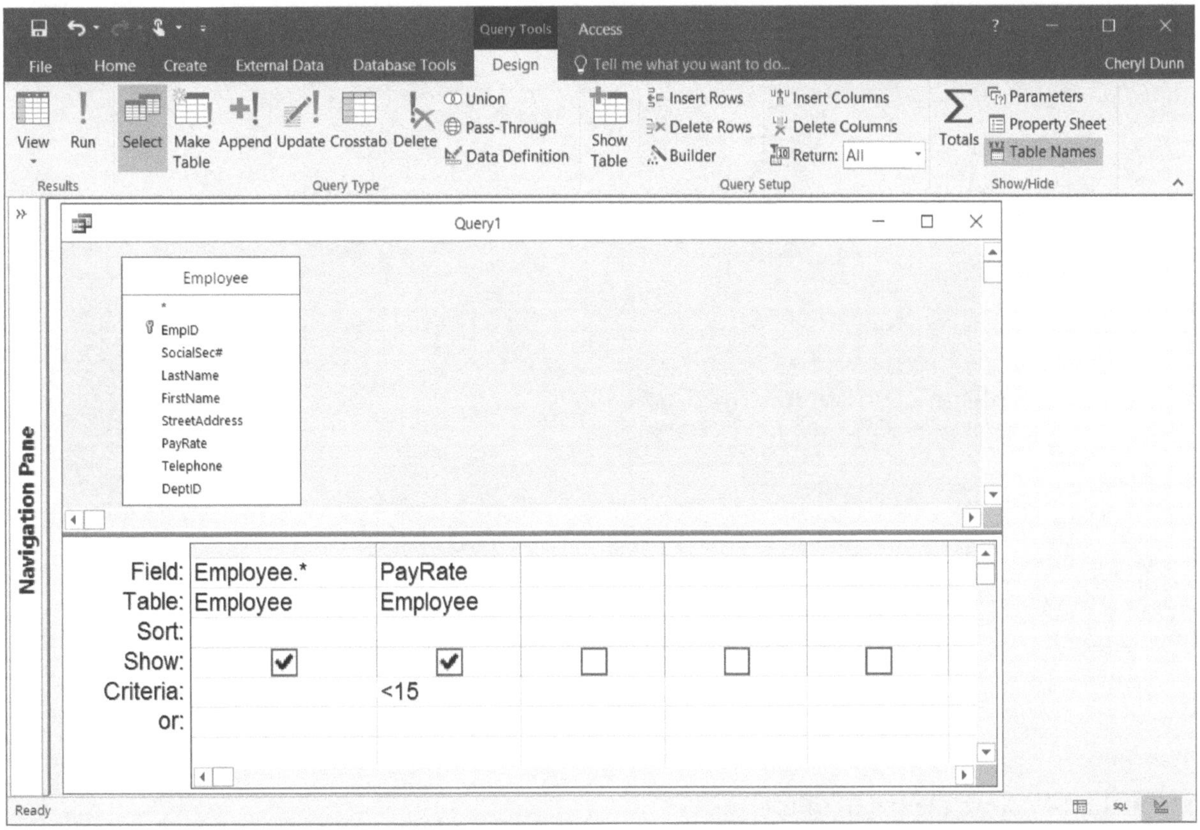

Exhibit 11-12(c): Employees with PayRate < 15 Query Result (alternative query approach)

Another query we generated earlier in this chapter using SQL created a list of employees and the names of the departments to which they are assigned. This query joined two tables, and included only the employee name column and department name column in the result. To formulate this query in Design View, follow the steps introduced earlier in Exhibits 11-6 through 11-8 adding both the Employee and the Department tables to the query window. Then add the LastName and FirstName fields from the Employee table and add the DeptName field from the Department table to the query window. Exhibit 11-13 shows the result of these steps. Notice that a join line automatically appeared between Employee and Department, linking the Department ID field in the Department table with the DeptID field in the Employee table. This line represents the join that was established in the relationship layout as Access's means for knowing that DeptID in the

Employee table is a posted foreign key from the Department table. The Access Design View uses the inner join as the default join type.

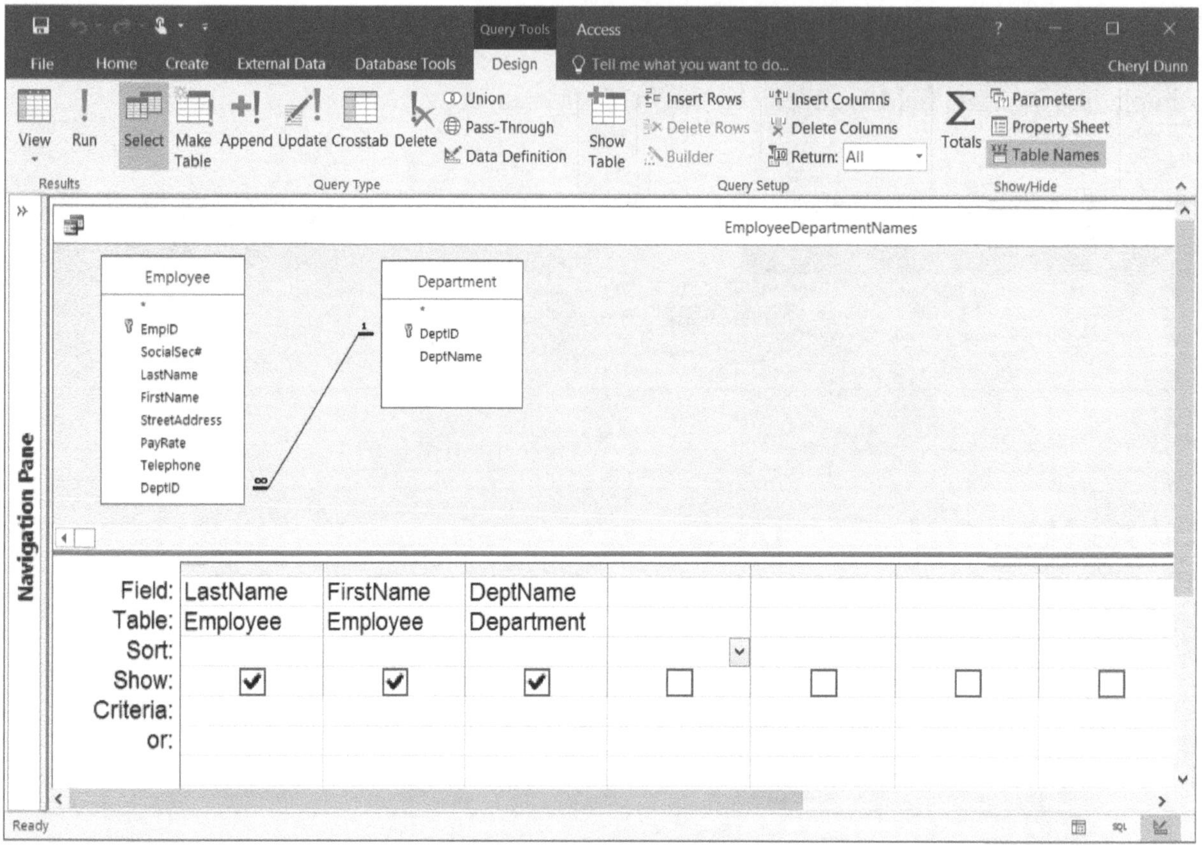

Exhibit 11-13: Employee and Department Names JOIN Query Design

Exhibit 11-14 shows the result of this query.

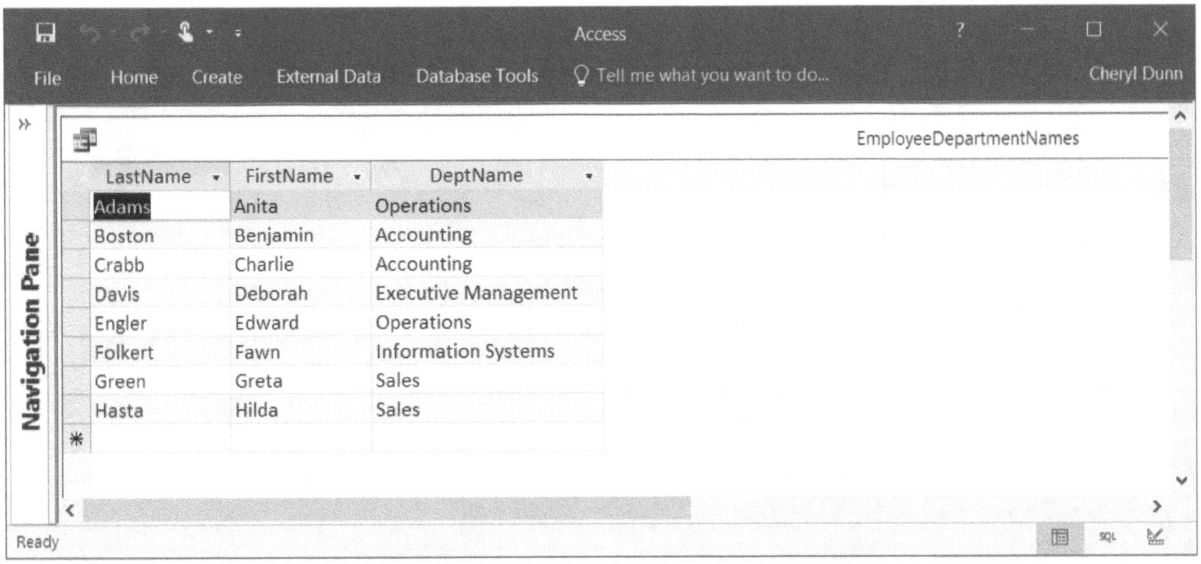

LastName	FirstName	DeptName
Adams	Anita	Operations
Boston	Benjamin	Accounting
Crabb	Charlie	Accounting
Davis	Deborah	Executive Management
Engler	Edward	Operations
Folkert	Fawn	Information Systems
Green	Greta	Sales
Hasta	Hilda	Sales

Exhibit 11-14: Employee and Department JOIN Query Result

Another query we examined previously in this chapter listed all employees and the training courses they have taken. To formulate this query in Design View, add the tables Employee, EmployeeTakesCourse, and TrainingCourse to the query window. The joins established in the relationship layout appear in the query window (between the EmplID fields in the Employee and EmployeeTakesCourse tables and between the CourseID fields in the EmployeeTakesCourse and TrainingCourse tables). Next, add the appropriate field names to the query grid (LastName, FirstName, CourseID, Description). At this point, your query design should resemble Exhibit 11-15(a).

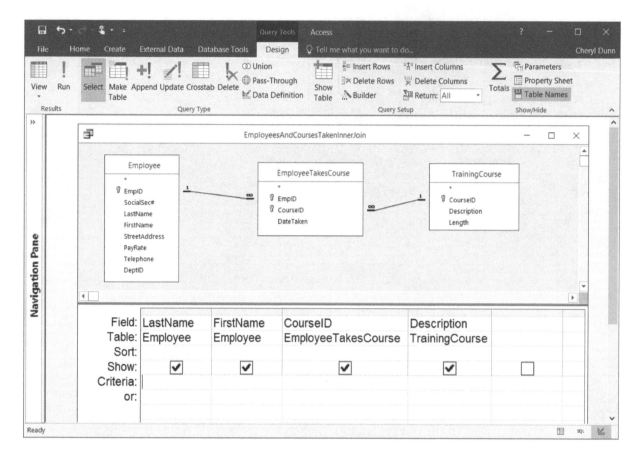

Exhibit 11-15(a): Initial Query Design Employees and Courses Taken

Running this query results in the dynaset shown in Exhibit 11-15(b). What does this answer tell you about the type of join Access uses by default? It must be an inner join, because only those employees who have actually taken courses show up in our answer.

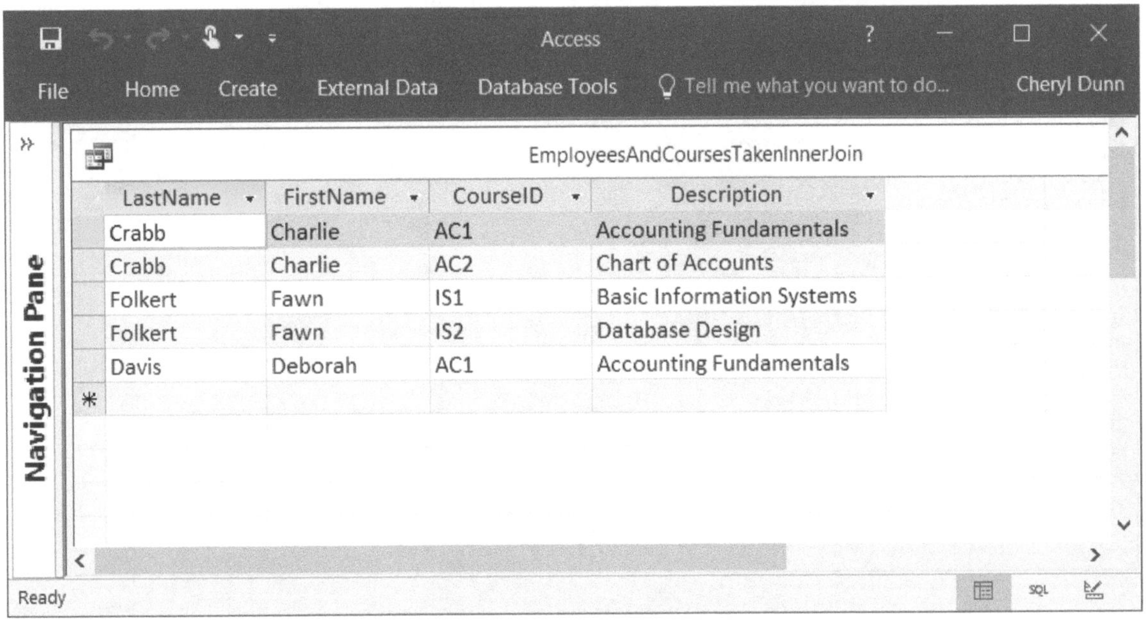

Exhibit 11-15 (b): Result of Initial Query Design Employees and Courses Taken

To include ALL employees in the list, showing null values in course-related data for those who have not taken any training courses, the join types must be changed to an outer join (with the Employee table being the focus of the outer join). To change the join types, go back to the query design and double-click on the join line between Employee and EmployeeTakesCourse. A window will appear similar to the one shown in Exhibit 11-16. The window shows which table is "left" and which is "right" (reading this will help you think about which type of join you should choose). The *join properties window* displays three possible join types and you can change the join type by clicking on the appropriate join description. Option 1 is always an inner join (the default join type); option 2 is always a left (outer) join and option 3 is always a right (outer) joins however, whether a table is left or right depends on the order that the tables were added to the query. When you first enter Join Properties, the window display confirms the join was established as an inner join, as it says (option 1) "Only include rows where the joined fields from both tables are equal." This needs to be changed to "Include ALL records from 'Employee' and only those records from 'EmployeeTakesCourse' where the joined fields are equal." Notice that with Access's Design View, options 1, 2, and 3 don't explicitly use the words "inner join," "left join" or "right join" – you simply choose the option that describes what you are trying to accomplish.

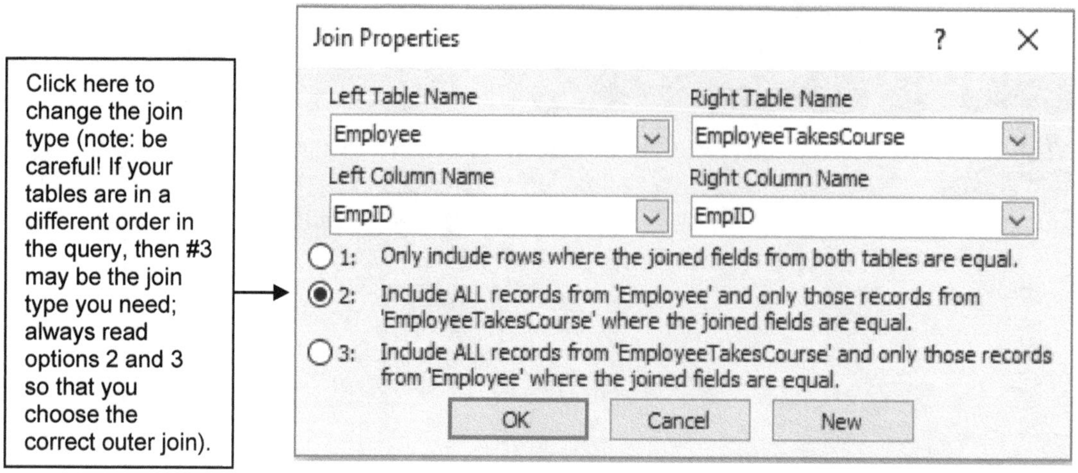

Click here to change the join type (note: be careful! If your tables are in a different order in the query, then #3 may be the join type you need; always read options 2 and 3 so that you choose the correct outer join).

Join Properties   ?   ✕

Left Table Name   Right Table Name

Employee   ⌄   EmployeeTakesCourse   ⌄

Left Column Name   Right Column Name

EmpID   ⌄   EmpID   ⌄

○ 1:   Only include rows where the joined fields from both tables are equal.

◉ 2:   Include ALL records from 'Employee' and only those records from 'EmployeeTakesCourse' where the joined fields are equal.

○ 3:   Include ALL records from 'EmployeeTakesCourse' and only those records from 'Employee' where the joined fields are equal.

OK   Cancel   New

Exhibit 11-16: Join Properties Window

Once you have chosen the appropriate option, click on OK. You will see a result that is shown in Exhibit 11-17(a). Notice that when you specify a left or right join, the join lines change to arrows, as illustrated in Exhibit 11-17(a) and (b) (if you do not see an arrow on a join line, then you know it is an inner join). The arrows point from the table for which all records will be included and toward the table for which the records whose joined fields are equal will be included.

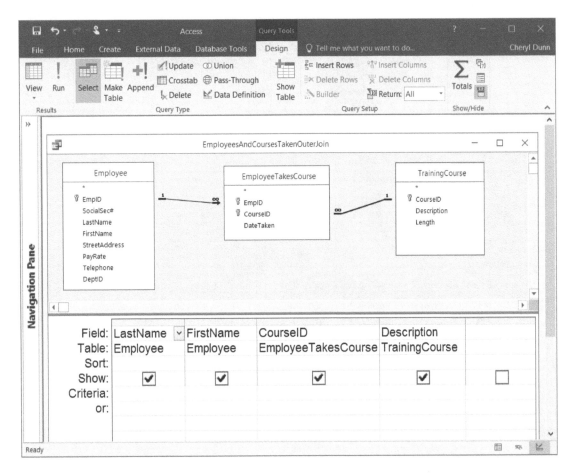

Exhibit 11-17(a): One Outer Join Established

If you try to run the query as illustrated in Exhibit 11-17(a), you will get an error message indicating the use of an ambiguous outer join. When this happens, there is ambiguity regarding whether to run the outer join or inner join first. This distinction could change the query result and the ambiguity must be resolved. This is usually done by breaking the query up into sub-queries. Alternatively, there is no need to break the query up if (1) all of the outer joins/arrows point in the same direction, or (2) the outer join table is primary and the other tables are secondary, so that the outer join arrows always point from the primary table to the secondary tables. The solution we will employ here is to have all of the outer joins point in the same direction, as described next.

Change the join type for the join between EmployeeTakesCourse and TrainingCourse to include all records from 'EmployeeTakesCourse' and only those records from 'TrainingCourse' where the joined fields are equal (again, make sure you read options 2 and 3 in Join Properties).

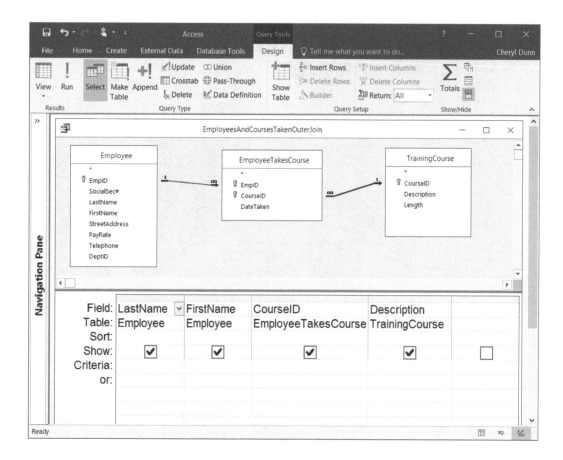

Exhibit 11-17(b): Revised Outer Join Lines

When you run the query again, your answer should resemble Exhibit 11-18.

LastName	FirstName	CourseID	Description
Adams	Anita		
Boston	Benjamin		
Crabb	Charlie	AC1	Accounting Fundamentals
Crabb	Charlie	AC2	Chart of Accounts
Davis	Deborah	AC1	Accounting Fundamentals
Engler	Edward		
Folkert	Fawn	IS1	Basic Information Systems
Folkert	Fawn	IS2	Database Design
Green	Greta		
Hasta	Hilda		

Exhibit 11-18: Result of Revised Query Design Employees and Courses Taken

Another query we examined earlier calculated the average pay rate for our employees. This query requires an aggregation function called AVG. In Design View aggregation functions may be added to the query grid by clicking on an icon that looks like a summation symbol and is labeled as Totals. When that icon is clicked, a "Total" line is added to the query grid. When this line is added, it defaults to a "Group By" aggregation. If you click on Group By, a drop down menu will appear from which you can select "Avg." Exhibit 11-19(a) illustrates the appropriate query design, and Exhibit 11-19(b) illustrates the query result.

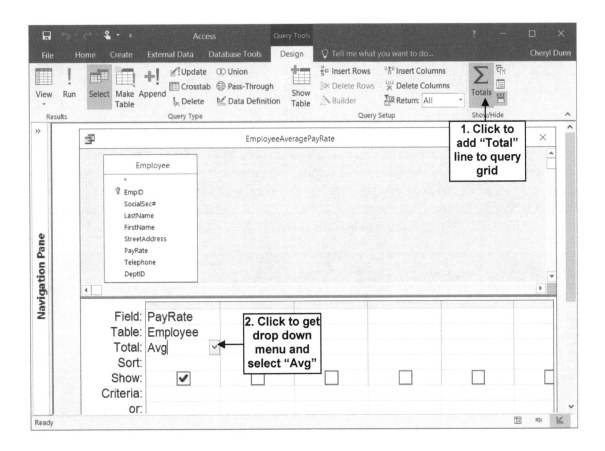

Exhibit 11-19(a): Average PayRate Query Design

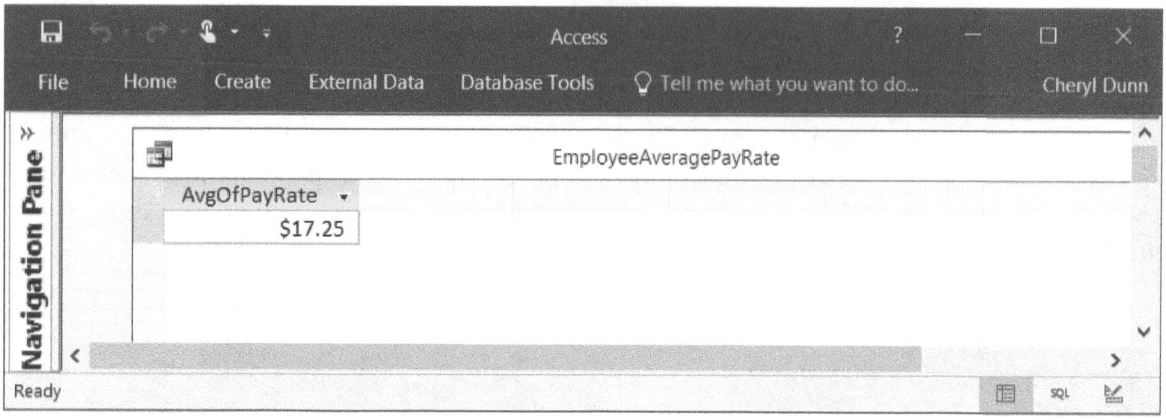

Exhibit 11-19(b): Average Pay Rate Query Result

Another query we examined earlier in this chapter calculated total sales separately for each date. In Design View, this query is accomplished by adding the Sale table to the query window, dragging the date and amount fields to the query grid, adding the Total line to the query grid, and setting the Total line to Group By for the Date field, and to Sum for the Amount field. This query design is illustrated in Exhibit 11-20(a) and the result is displayed in Exhibit 11-20(b).

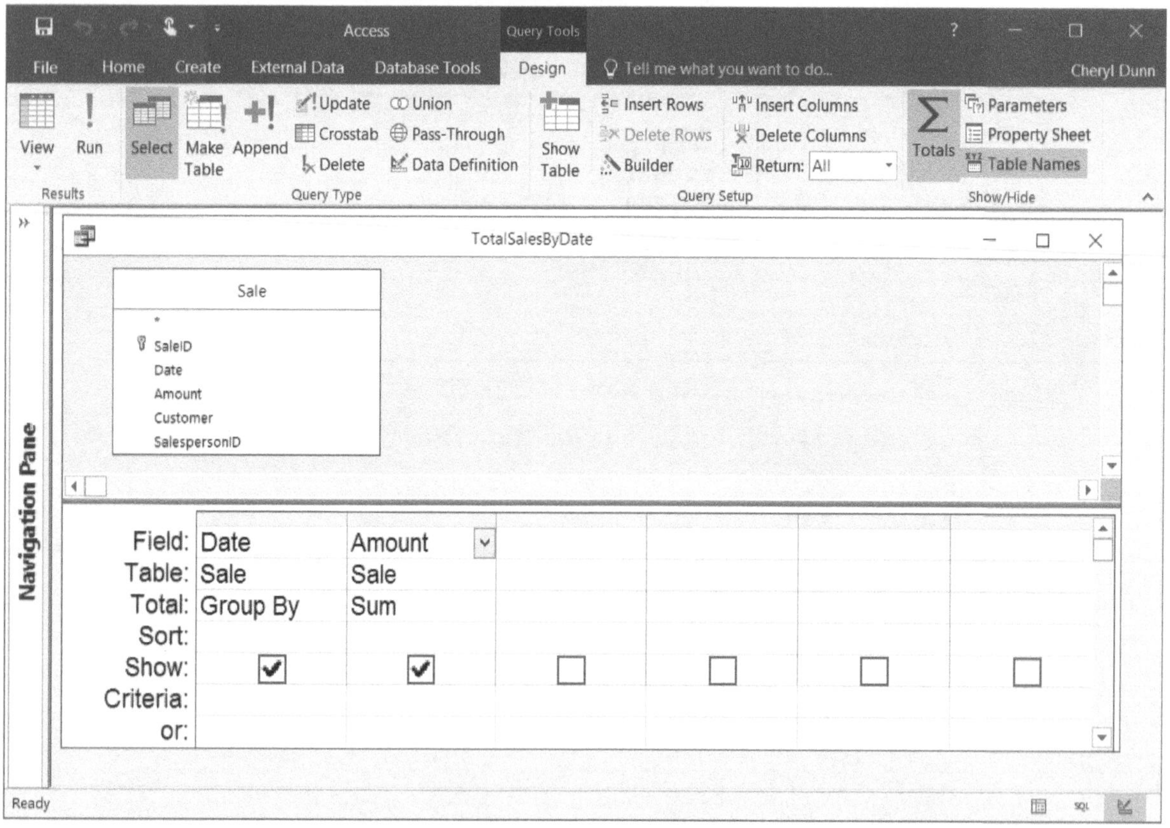

Exhibit 11-20(a): Total Sales By Date Query Design

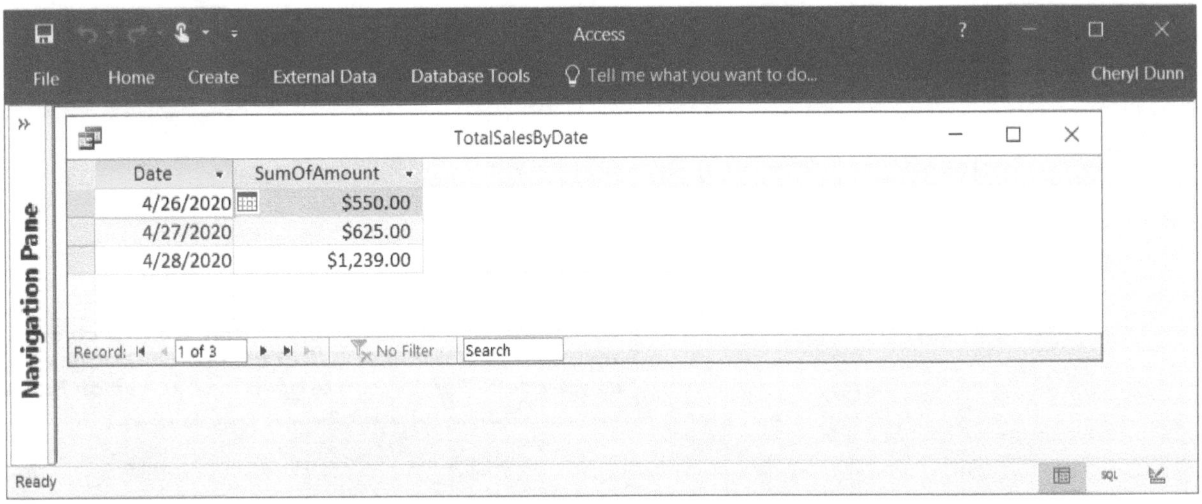

Exhibit 11-20(b): Total Sales by Date Query Result

If instead, you wanted to calculate total sales separately for each customer, you would need to drag the Customer and Amount fields to the query grid, GROUP BY Customer and SUM Amount (not depicted with an Exhibit). It is important when you are using aggregation functions that you only drag the fields to the query grid that actually participate in an aggregation. If, for example, you drag the Date, Customer, and Amount fields, Access will first group by Date, and then group by Customer (or vice versa depending on which field is listed first). This will not give you the sum you want!

The final query we examined earlier required a calculation of quantity sold multiplied by the unit sales price to compute a sale line extension. To accomplish this query in Design View, add the Stockflow table to the query window. Drag all the fields to the query grid. Save the query as SaleLineExtension. Saving the query with fields in the query grid makes those fields readily available as expression categories for manipulation in a tool called the Expression Builder. The *Expression Builder* is an application within Microsoft Access that assists in creating horizontal calculations within queries.

Place your cursor in the next available blank field in the query grid, and click on the icon that looks like a magic wand to open the Expression Builder, as illustrated in Exhibit 11-21. Once the Expression Builder is open, double-click on the QtySold field to place it in the expression window. Then click on the asterisk symbol for multiplication. Double-click on the UnitSellPrice field to place it into the expression window. The expression tells Access this field should store the multiplication of QtySold and UnitSellPrice. Access will use a default expression name (which is also a field name) of Expr1 (this is really an alias, and you can always rename it; we will leave the default name and you will see it in Exhibit 11-22). Click on OK to close the Expression Builder. Next, run the query.

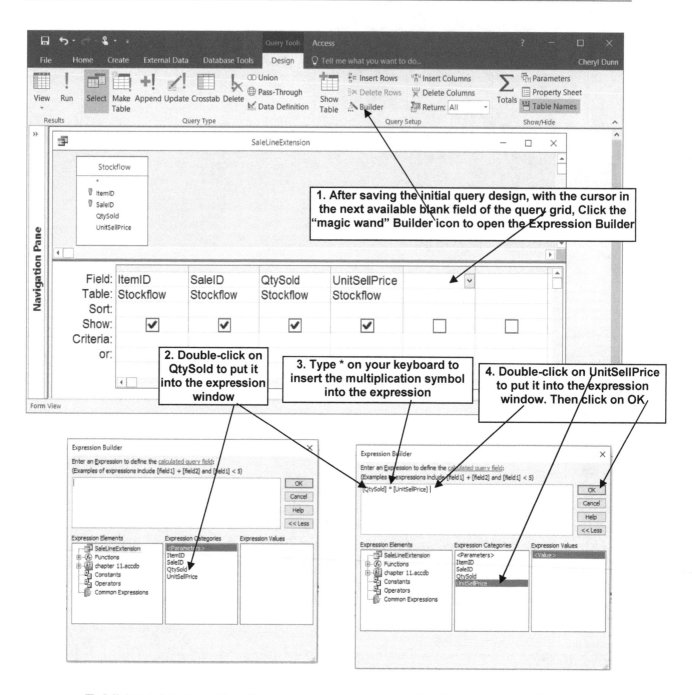

Exhibit 11-21: Sale Line Extension Query – Using the Expression Builder

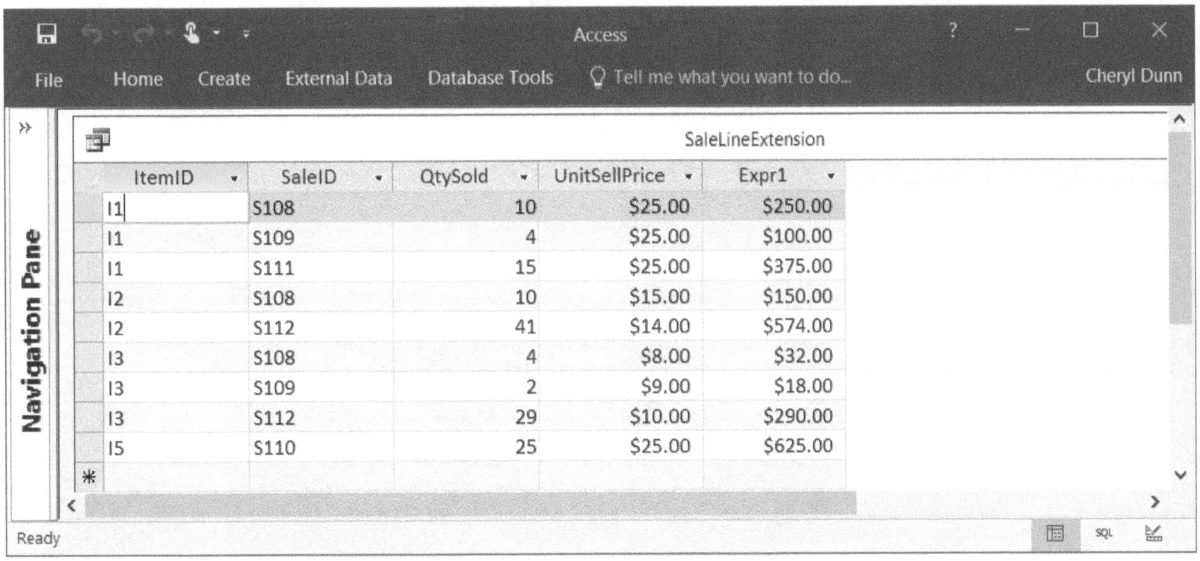

ItemID	SaleID	QtySold	UnitSellPrice	Expr1
I1	S108	10	$25.00	$250.00
I1	S109	4	$25.00	$100.00
I1	S111	15	$25.00	$375.00
I2	S108	10	$15.00	$150.00
I2	S112	41	$14.00	$574.00
I3	S108	4	$8.00	$32.00
I3	S109	2	$9.00	$18.00
I3	S112	29	$10.00	$290.00
I5	S110	25	$25.00	$625.00

Exhibit 11-22: Sale Line Item Extension Query Result

Exhibit 11-22 shows the result of running the SaleLineExtension query. In the dynaset, you see the expression (field) is labeled with the default "Expr1". To change this to a more meaningful name, switch back to the query's design view and in the expression's field, highlight the Expr1 and type the more meaningful name, as shown in Exhibit 11-23.

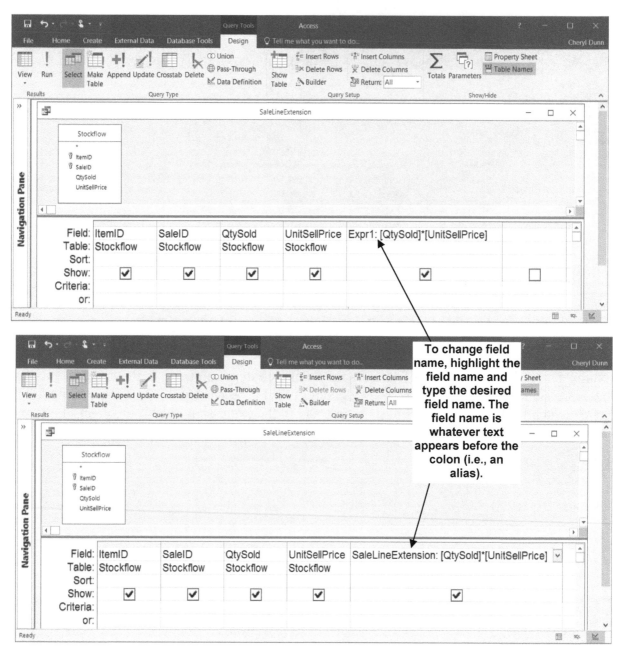

Exhibit 11-23: Renaming a Field

We noted earlier that Access allows query entry via a SQL View as an alternative to the Design View. Let's enter the (final) SQL statement directly into Access instead of using the Design View interface. Create a new query, and when the Show Table window appears, hit close without adding any tables or queries to your query window. In the upper left corner, the SQL with the small down arrow next to it indicates the path to switch to SQL view. Click on the arrow next to SQL to display the SQL view, as shown in Exhibit 11-24.

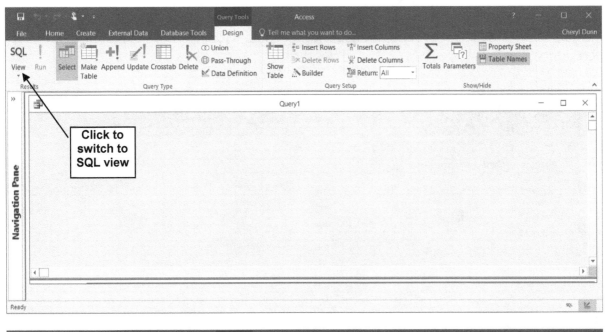

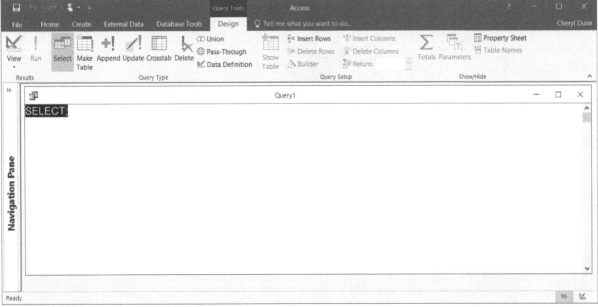

Exhibit 11-24: Creating a Query in Microsoft Access SQL View

The SQL View appears with the word SELECT followed by a semicolon. Access knows that every SQL statement begins with the word SELECT, and ends with a semicolon. All that is needed is the detail that goes in between. Type the SQL statement in as shown in Exhibit 11-25, then run the query to see the same dynaset that resulted earlier using Design View. Compare Exhibit 11-25 with Exhibit 11-22; the only difference is the other ItemID, SaleID, QtySold, and UnitSellPrice attributes do not appear in Exhibit 11-25. That is because the SQL statement (Exhibit 11-25) did not specifically ask for those to be included. A slight revision to the SQL statement will cause those fields to appear in the dynaset, as follows (not shown in an Exhibit):

SELECT ItemID, SaleID, QtySold, UnitSellPrice, QtySold*UnitSellPrice AS SaleLineExtension
FROM Stockflow;

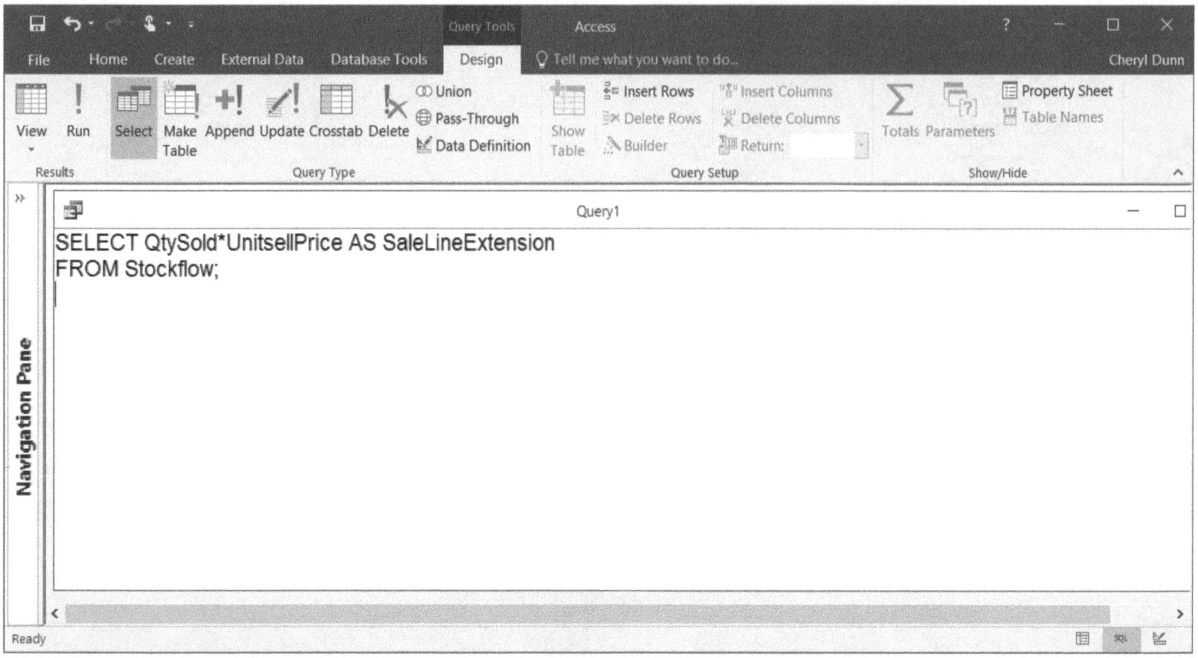

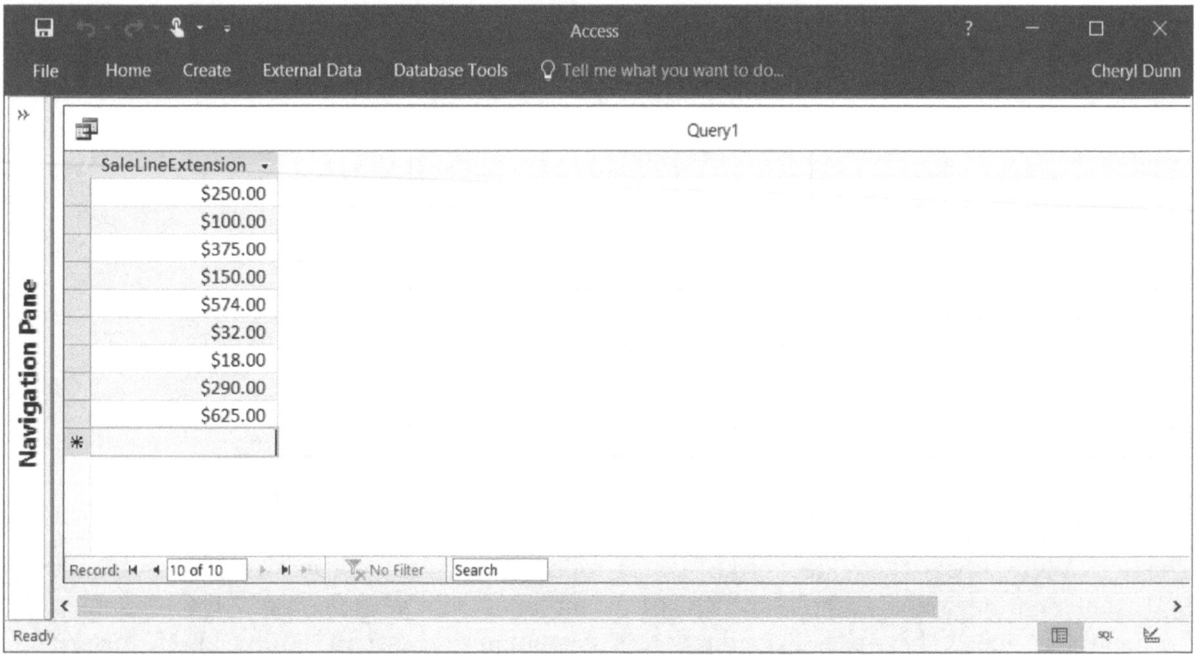

Exhibit 11-25: SQL Statement and Resulting Dynaset

CONCLUDING COMMENTS

So far, in this book, you have learned how to create a conceptual representation of an enterprise's reality and convert it, first into a logical set of relational tables and then into a physical implementation of relational tables using Microsoft Access 2016 software. You also learned how to retrieve information from the tables using a structured approach (SQL). It is in the querying capabilities that the real power of the relational database is manifested; however, a solid understanding of table design is foundational for a good understanding of querying. In turn, a solid understanding of querying is foundational for retrieval of valid data, which is crucial for sound decision-making. Perhaps it is now becoming clear to you (if it wasn't already clear) why all enterprise system users (that is, anyone who might someday form an *ad hoc* query of a relational database) must understand the basics of relational database design. Hopefully seeing the translation of the conceptual models into an actual working database has helped clarify some of the concepts that we covered in earlier chapters by making them more concrete. You may find it worthwhile to go back and re-read those chapters now that you have a better understanding of the end result.

Once you unlock the mystery of query construction, whether with SQL or a proprietary software interface, you can tap into the wealth of information that is at your fingertips in a well-designed relational database. Enterprises today typically store vast amounts of data in relational databases that one can retrieve in a variety of formats for different decision-making purposes. To ensure the information retrieved is valid, users should be well versed in relational database design, semantic query logic, and the syntax of the particular query language used. This chapter provides you with only a cursory introduction to SQL querying. To become proficient at querying, you MUST practice and learn through trial and error.

If you do an Internet search using a search engine such as www.google.com and keywords "SQL tutorial" you will find several sites that provide help with understanding SQL syntax. Note, however, that you will not find solutions for the semantic nature of queries you need to formulate. Rather, you must first figure out where the desired information is in your database and determine how to get that information. Try using a pencil and a calculator (or exporting data to a spreadsheet) to figure solutions out manually with some test data before attempting to create a computerized query. That ensures that you understand the logic of the query before enveloping the logic into the syntax of SQL, and it also gives you some "check figures" to use in determining whether the computerized query is functioning as planned. Comprehensive testing of queries that are intended to be re-used is crucial to ensure they will work for different dates (if date constraints are included), and after new data is entered into the database.

KEY TERMS AND CONCEPTS
Ad hoc querying
Aggregation function
AND operator
Average (AVG) aggregation function
BETWEEN operator
COUNT aggregation function
Date constraint
EXISTS operator
Expression Builder
FROM clause
Full outer join
GROUP BY clause
HAVING clause
Horizontal calculation
Inner join
IS NOT NULL operator
IS NULL operator
Join properties window (in Microsoft Access)
Left join
LIKE operator
Logical operators
MAX aggregation function
MIN aggregation function
NOT operator
OR operator
ORDER BY clause
Outer join
Parameter query
Query
Right join
SELECT clause
Structured Query Language (SQL)
SUM aggregation function
Vertical calculation
WHERE clause
Wildcard character

REVIEW QUESTIONS
R11-1. What is the standard format of a SQL query statement?

R11-2. What is the advantage of a query that includes a date constraint as a parameter query?

R11-3. What is the difference between an aggregation (vertical calculation) and an expression (horizontal calculation)?

R11-4. Give an example of a query for which you would use an outer join instead of an inner join.

R11-5. What does a Group By clause in a query accomplish?

MULTIPLE CHOICE QUESTIONS

MC11-1. Which of the following is necessary for effective information retrieval?

    A) The database is well designed

    B) The query designer has a thorough knowledge of the database table structures and the nature of the data in the tables.

    C) The query designer adequately understands the desired output.

    D) The query designer knows the querying language used to retrieve information from the enterprise's database.

    E) All of the above are necessary for effective information retrieval.

MC11-2. If a table contained 50 rows and you want to use only 20 of the rows that meet a specific criterion, you would create a query to get

    A) A vertical subset

    B) A horizontal subset

    C) A diagonal subset

    D) A JOIN

MC11-3. What is currently the most commonly used querying language?

    A) Relational Algebra

    B) Structured Query Language (SQL)

    C) Query By Example

    D) Fortran

MC11-4. In SQL, queries follow what structured, predefined syntax?

    A) SELECT *attribute name(s)*, FROM *table name(s)*, WHERE *condition criteria is met*;

    B) SELECT *attribute name(s)*, JOIN *table name(s)*, WHERE *condition criteria is met*;

    C) SELECT *attribute name(s)*, QUERY *table name(s)*, WHEN *condition criteria is met*;

    D) SELECT *attribute name(s)*, FROM *table name(s)*, WHEN *condition criteria is met*;

MC11-5. Which of the following is true regarding the use of an outer join in SQL?

    A) The outer join must be specified in the SELECT clause of an SQL statement.

    B) The outer join need not be specified as an outer join, because most database software automatically recognizes whether a join should be inner or outer.

    C) The outer join must be specified as a Left Join or a Right Join.

    D) An outer join is also commonly called an Equi-Join.

MC11-6. What does the asterisk (*) in SQL mean?

    A) The asterisk (*) is a standard symbol used to end most or all queries

    B) The asterisk (*) is a wildcard symbol that requests inclusion of all attributes

    C) The asterisk (*) is a wildcard attribute that means to disregard any attributes that follow its use

    D) The asterisk (*) is an interruption symbol used to abort a query if it takes longer to process than a prescribed time length.

MC11-7. Which SQL statement will multiply Table A's Field P by Table A's Field Q?
- A) Select Field P From Table A Where Field Q = Field P * 2;
- B) Select Sum (Field P, Field Q) From Table A;
- C) Select (Field P * Field Q) From Table A;
- D) Select Table A Field P and Table A Field Q, Multiply P*Q;

MC11-8. If Table A is on the left and Table B is on the right, a right outer join will include in its answer
- A) Only the rows for which the values of the two tables' common attribute match exactly.
- B) All the rows from Table A, with the corresponding detail of Table B for those rows for which the values of the two tables' common attribute match exactly.
- C) All the rows from Table B, with the corresponding detail of Table A for those rows for which the value of the two tables' common attribute match exactly.
- D) All rows from both Table A and Table B.

MC11-9. A query's answer in Microsoft Access is referred to as a
- A) Project
- B) Dynaset
- C) Dataset
- D) Interface

MC11-10. In Access query design view, how should one calculate the average pay rate for all employees, using an Employee table that has EmplID as its primary key, and SocialSecurityNo, LastName, FirstName, StreetAddress, PayRate, Telephone, and DeptID as additional attributes?
- A) Drag PayRate to the query grid and type Avg on the Criteria line under PayRate.
- B) Click the summation sign to add the Total line to the query grid. Drag EmplID and PayRate to the query grid, click Group By on the Total line under EmplID and click Avg on the Total line under PayRate.
- C) Click the summation sign to add the Total line to the query grid. Drag PayRate to the query gird. Click Avg on the Total line under PayRate.
- D) Drag EmplID and Payrate to the query grid. Type Group By on the Criteria line under EmplID and click Avg on the Criteria line under Payrate.

CHAPTER 12

Acquisition and Revenue Accounting Analytics – Single Process

LEARNING OBJECTIVES

This chapter illustrates use of the REA ontology to determine and meet information needs within the acquisition and revenue business processes. Some of these information needs require relatively uncomplicated queries that involve single classes or associations within each process. Other information needs are more complicated and require sets of queries that require use of multiple associations, either within the acquisition process or within the revenue process. In chapter 13, we illustrate even more complicated queries that integrate tables from both acquisition and revenue processes. After studying the current chapter, you should be able to

1. Identify common information needs within the acquisition process
2. Identify common information needs within the revenue process
3. Create queries to meet common information needs within the acquisition process
4. Create queries to meet common information needs within the revenue process

INFORMATION NEEDS IN THE ACQUISITION AND REVENUE PROCESSES

Information customers, i.e., people who need information in order to make decisions, often need information found within the acquisition and revenue process.

Within any business process, information needs fit into the following categories:
- Internal users need information about internal phenomena.
- Internal users need information about external phenomena.
- External users need information about internal phenomena.

For example, salespeople (internal users) need information about the products they sell (internal phenomena). Salespeople also need information about customers to whom they make sales (external phenomena). Vendors (external users) need information about products the company wants to purchase (internal phenomena). Purchase agents (internal users) need information about new products its vendors offer (external phenomena).

We next analyze each class and association in the business process level REA pattern to provide guidance as to the types of queries that satisfy common information needs. The queries presented are not a comprehensive set (there exist too many to list them all). However, the set provided should guide you to create similar queries to satisfy similar needs. To demonstrate these example queries we use the database tables in Exhibit 12-1.

Cash (Resource Type)

CashAccountID	AccountType	Location	DateAccountEstablished
Ca123501	Checking	1st Local Bank	04/01/2020
Ca789125	Savings	1st Local Bank	04/01/2020
Ca351235	Petty	Onsite - Cashier Desk drawer	04/15/2020
Ca351327	Petty	Onsite - CEO Assistant's File Cabinet	04/22/2020

InventoryType (Resource Type)

ItemID	Description	UnitOfMeasure	StandardCost	ListPrice
BIS1	Big Stuff	Each	$20.00	$50.00
HUS1	Huge Stuff	Each	$30.00	$70.00
LIS1	Little Stuff	Box of 6	$36.00	$72.00
MIN1	Miniature Stuff	Box of 24	$56.00	$110.00
TIS1	Tiny Stuff	Box of 12	$48.00	$96.00
TTP12	Tiara	Each	$10.00	$25.00

SalesCall (Instigation Event)

SalesCallID	Date	StartTime	EndTime	Location	SalesRepID[FK]	CustomerID[FK]
SC1	05/04/2020	9:12 AM	10:00 AM	Customer	E23	C2323
SC2	05/04/2020	9:27 AM	10:35 AM	Ours	E26	C4731
SC3	05/05/2020	10:30 AM	11:15 AM	Customer	E23	C6125
SC4	05/20/2020	8:30 AM	9:15 AM	Customer	E26	C4731

PurchaseRequisition (Instigation Event)

PurchaseReqID	Date	MaxBudgetforPurchase	DateNeeded	SupervisorID[FK]	PurchaseAgentID[FK]
R1	4/22/2020	$30,000.00	05/02/2020	E5	E12
R2	5/5/2020	$1,400.00	05/23/2020	E5	E12
R3	5/6/2020	$5,500.00	05/20/2020	E5	E12
R4	5/15/2020	$200.00	05/25/2020	E5	E12
R5	5/18/2020	$7,500.00	05/26/2020	E5	E12

SaleOrder (Mutual Commitment Event)

SaleOrderID	OrderDate	DateNeeded	DollarTotal	SalesTax	Shipping Charge	Sales CallID[FK]	Sales RepID[FK]	CustomerID[FK]
SO1	05/04/2020	05/07/2020	$1,100.00	$0.00	$0.00	SC1	E23	C2323
SO2	05/04/2020	05/12/2020	$3,050.00	$0.00	$0.00	SC2	E26	C4731
SO3	05/06/2020	05/09/2020	$4,305.00	$0.00	$0.00	SC1	E23	C2323
SO4	05/08/2020	05/17/2020	$8,280.00	$0.00	$0.00	SC2	E26	C4731
SO5	05/24/2020	06/03/2020	$4200.00	$0.00	$0.00	SC4	E26	C4731
SO6	06/01/2020	06/10/2020	$3,890.00	$0.00	$0.00	SC3	E23	C6125

PurchaseOrder (Mutual Commitment Event)

PurchaseOrderID	OrderDate	DateNeeded	DollarTotal	PurchaseReqID[FK]	PurchaseAgentID[FK]	VendorID[FK]
PO1	04/24/2020	05/02/2020	$28,450.00	R1	E12	V7
PO2	05/05/2020	05/08/2020	$1,100.00	R2	E12	V14
PO3	05/05/2020	05/12/2020	$200.00	R2	E12	V90
PO4	05/06/2020	05/10/2020	$3,240.00	R3	E12	V14
PO5	05/06/2020	05/24/2020	$2,000.00	R3	E12	V7
PO6	05/16/2020	05/24/2020	$220.00	R4	E12	V14

Exhibit 12-1: Database Tables for Example Queries

Sale (Economic Decrement Event)

SaleID	Date	DollarTotal	PickListID	PackListID	BOL#	SalesRepID[FK]	CustomerID[FK]
S1	05/05/2020	$1,100.00	15	15	15	E23	C2323
S2	05/07/2020	$3,050.00	16	16	16	E26	C4731
S3	05/08/2020	$2,100.00	17	17	17	E23	C2323
S4	05/10/2020	$2,205.00	18	18	18	E23	C2323

CashReceipt (Economic Increment Event)

CashReceiptID	Date	DollarTotal	CashAccountID[FK]	CashierID[FK]
RA1	04/01/2020	$50,000.00	Ca123501	E111
RA2	05/19/2020	$3,060.00	Ca123501	E111
RA3	05/24/2020	$3,050.00	Ca123501	E111
RA4	05/24/2020	$4,200.00	Ca123501	E111
RA5	06/01/2020	$3,890.00	Ca123501	E111

Purchase (Economic Increment Event)

Receiving ReportID	Date	Dollar Amount	Receiving ClerkID[FK]	VendorID[FK]	Vendor InvoiceNbr	Invoice Amount
RR1	04/30/2020	$28,450.00	E247	V7	VI4167	$28,450.00
RR2	05/08/2020	$1,100.00	E247	V14	821536	$1,100.00
RR3	05/10/2020	$3,240.00	E247	V14	821983	$3,240.00
RR4	05/12/2020	$2,000.00	E251	V7	VI5213	$2,000.00
RR5	05/12/2020	$480.00	E247	V90	312353	$480.00

CashDisbursement (Economic Decrement Event)

DisbVoucherID	VoucherDate	DollarAmount	CheckNumber	CashAcctID[FK]	APClerkID[FK]	PayeeID[FK]
CD1	05/15/2020	$746.57	41234	Ca123501	E36	E23
CD2	05/25/2020	$30,450.00	41235	Ca123501	E36	V7
CD3	05/29/2020	$398.12	41236	Ca123501	E36	E41
CD4	05/30/2020	$2,000.00	41237	Ca123501	E36	V7

SaleReturn (Economic Decrement Reversal Event)

SaleReturnID	Date	Dollar Amount	Receiving Report#	SupervisorID	SaleID[FK]	CustomerID[FK]	ReceivingClerkID[FK]
SR1	05/12/2020	$140.00	RR6	E5	S1	C2323	E247

PurchaseReturn (Economic Increment Reversal Event)

Purchase ReturnID	Date	Dollar Amount	Packing SlipNbr	Debit MemoNbr	Receiving ReportID[FK]	VendorID[FK]	SupervisorID[FK]	Shipping ClerkID[FK]
PR1	05/17/2020	$480.00	22	3	RR5	V90	E5	E41

Customer (External Agent)

CustomerID	Name	Address	Telephone	CreditRating
C2323	Needmore Stuff	86906 Enterprise Court	555-8989	A+
C2831	Targeted One	41352 Price Ln.	555-1771	B+
C4731	Gottahave Moore	1207 Emperor Dr.	555-5688	B
C6125	Don't Wantmuch	3421 Carradine St.	555-9098	A+

Exhibit 12-1 (cont.): Database Tables for Example Queries

Vendor (External Agent)

VendorID	Name	Address	Telephone	PerformanceRating
V7	Joe's Favorite Vendor	89056 Ransom Hwy.	555-7655	Excellent
V14	Reliable Rudy's	34125 Michigan Ave.	555-1199	Very Good
V90	Trina's Trinkets	1612 Myway Rd.	555-2424	Very Good

PurchaseAgent (Internal Agent)

PurchaseAgentID	FirstName	LastName	Address	Telephone	DateOfBirth
E12	Joy	Berwick	437 Oak Dr.	555-9617	04/20/1982

Cashier (Internal Agent)

CashierID	FirstName	LastName	Address	Telephone	DateOfBirth
E111	Missy	Witherspoon	1710 Crestwood Dr.	555-9392	05/11/1970
E222	Eponine	Eldridge	1003 Zenker Dr.	555-9099	07/29/1982

ReceivingClerk (Internal Agent)

ReceivingClerkID	FirstName	LastName	Address	Telephone	DateOfBirth
E247	Kenneth	Barki	4312 Monticello Dr.	556-4891	04/14/1955
E251	Rita	Barki	4312 Monticello Dr.	556-4891	05/22/1958

SalesRepresentative (Internal Agent)

SalesRepID	FirstName	LastName	Address	Telephone	DateOfBirth
E23	Jimmy	Vitale	425 ConAir Drive	555-5678	08/18/1962
E26	Cyndie	North	122 Front St.	555-6353	04/04/1961
E30	Wayland	Stindt	3506 Carthan St.	555-0621	12/29/1973

ShippingClerk (Internal Agent)

ShippingClerkID	FirstName	LastName	Address	Telephone	DateOfBirth
E41	Amy	Milano	8892 Eddy Ave.	555-9557	01/03/1964

Supervisor (Internal Agent)

SupervisorID	FirstName	LastName	Address	Telephone	DateOfBirth
E5	Patrick	Wellesley	53125 Fenton Dr.	555-1112	03/04/1958

AccountsPayableClerk (Internal Agent)

APClerkID	FirstName	LastName	Address	Telephone	DateOfBirth
E36	Diane	Bowersox	9115 Wolfgang Ct.	555-7244	09/15/1963

ParticipationPurchaseRequisitionVendor (Participation Association)

PurchaseReqID	Recommended VendorID
R1	V7
R2	V14
R3	V7
R5	V7

Exhibit 12-1 (cont.): Database Tables for Example Queries

PropositionSalesCallInventoryType (Proposition Association)

SalesCallID	ItemID	CustomerReactiontoProduct
SC1	BIS1	Negative
SC1	HUS1	Negative
SC1	LIS1	Positive
SC1	MIN1	Undecided
SC1	TIS1	Positive
SC2	BIS1	Positive
SC2	HUS1	Positive
SC2	LIS1	Undecided
SC2	MIN1	Negative
SC2	TIS1	Negative
SC3	BIS1	Negative
SC3	HUS1	Negative
SC3	LIS1	Negative
SC3	MIN1	Negative
SC3	TIS1	Negative

PropositionPurchaseRequisitionInventoryType (Proposition Association)

PurchaseReqID	ItemID	QuantityNeeded	EstimatedUnitCost
R1	BIS1	100	$20.00
R1	HUS1	150	$30.00
R1	LIS1	200	$36.00
R1	TIS1	300	$48.00
R2	MIN1	20	$56.00
R2	TTP12	20	$10.00
R3	BIS1	100	$20.00
R3	MIN1	60	$56.00
R4	TTP12	20	$10.00
R5	LIS1	200	$36.00

ReservationSaleOrderInventoryType (Reservation Association)

SalesOrderID	ItemID	QuantityOrdered	QuotedUnitPrice
SO1	LIS1	2	$70.00
SO1	TIS1	10	$96.00
SO2	BIS1	40	$60.00
SO2	HUS1	13	$50.00
SO3	MIN1	41	$105.00
SO4	LIS1	120	$69.00
SO5	LIS1	60	$70.00
SO6	TIS1	22	$95.00
SO6	HUS1	36	$50.00

Exhibit 12-1 (cont.): Database Tables for Example Queries

ParticipationCashReceiptCustomer (Participation Association)

CashReceiptID	CustomerID
RA2	C2323
RA3	C6125
RA4	C4731
RA5	C6125

ReservationPurchaseOrderInventoryType (Reservation Association)

PurchaseOrderID	ItemID	QuantityOrdered	OrderedUnitCost
PO1	BIS1	100	$20.00
PO1	HUS1	150	$29.00
PO1	LIS1	200	$35.50
PO1	TIS1	300	$50.00
PO2	MIN1	20	$55.00
PO3	TTP12	20	$10.00
PO4	MIN1	60	$54.00
PO5	BIS1	100	$20.00
PO6	TTP12	20	$11.00

FulfillmentSaleOrderSale (Fulfillment Association)

SaleOrderID	SaleID
SO1	S1
SO2	S2
SO3	S3
SO3	S4

FulfillmentPurchasePurchaseOrder (Fulfillment Association)

PurchaseOrderID	ReceivingReportID
PO1	RR1
PO2	RR2
PO3	RR5
PO4	RR3
PO5	RR4

StockflowSaleInventoryType (Stockflow Association)

SaleID	ItemID	QuantitySold	ActualUnitSellingPrice
S1	LIS1	2	$70.00
S1	TIS1	10	$96.00
S2	BIS1	40	$60.00
S2	HUS1	13	$50.00
S3	MIN1	20	$105.00
S4	MIN1	21	$105.00

StockflowSaleReturnInventoryType (Stockflow Association)

SaleReturnID	ItemID	QuantityReturned	ActualUnitSellPrice	ConditionOfGoods	ReasonReturned
SR1	LIS1	2	$70.00	perfect	too big

Exhibit 12-1 (cont.): Database Tables for Example Queries

StockflowPurchaseInventoryType (Stockflow Association)

ReceivingReportID	ItemID	QuantityPurchased	ActualUnitCost
RR1	BIS1	100	$20.00
RR1	HUS1	150	$29.00
RR1	LIS1	200	$35.50
RR1	TIS1	300	$50.00
RR2	MIN1	20	$55.00
RR3	MIN1	60	$54.00
RR4	BIS1	100	$20.00
RR5	TTP12	48	$10.00

StockflowPurchaseReturnInventoryType (Stockflow Association)

PurchReturnID	ItemID	QuantityReturned	UnitCostAllowed
PR1	TTP12	48	$10.00

DualitySaleCashReceipt (Duality Association)

SaleID	CashReceiptID
S1	RA2
S2	RA3
S3	RA2

DualityPurchaseCashDisbursement (Duality Association)

Receiving ReportID	Disb VoucherID
RR1	CD2
RR4	CD2

DualityPurchaseReturnCashReceipt (Duality Association)*

PurchReturnID	CashReceiptID

DualitySaleReturnCashDisbursement (Duality Association)*

SaleReturnID	CashDisbursementID

*Note: These two tables contain no data because this company has not yet received cash for any purchase returns nor has it disbursed cash for any sale returns. For the purchase return that has occurred, the vendor reduced the balance due from this company, and this company reduced the balance due from its customer for the sale return.

Exhibit 12-1 (cont.): Database Tables for Example Queries

Resource Queries in the Acquisition and Revenue Processes

A *resource query* asks a question that can be answered with data in a single resource or resource type table. Internal and external users may need information regarding an enterprise resource or resource type. The resources and resource types most commonly present in the Acquisition and Revenue processes are inventory or services (specifically identified inventory, inventory types, or service types), operating assets (not shown in the database above), and cash. Users may need either detailed or summarized information about each resource instance or about only those resource instances meeting specific criteria. That information may include all characteristics of the resource instances, or it may include only a subset of the characteristics.

Information regarding inventory, service types, operating assets, and cash that may be needed by internal users (such as salespeople) and by external users (such as customers) includes:

- A list of each inventory item, item type, or service type offered for sale by an enterprise
- A list of all inventory items, item types, or service types that possess certain characteristics (e.g., all books, real estate listings with lake frontage, toys with selling prices within a certain range, video games in Game Boy Advance format, and preventive dental care services)
- Quantity on hand of an inventory item type as of a specified date
- Total cost value of inventory on hand as of a specified date
- A list of all cash accounts owned by an enterprise as of a specified date
- Balance in a specific cash account as of a specified date
- Total balance in all cash accounts as of a specified date
- A list of general and administrative supply and service types the enterprise purchases and for which the enterprise maintains descriptive data
- A list of fixed assets owned by an enterprise
- Book value of a depreciable fixed asset owned by an enterprise on a specified date
- Average age of an enterprise's machinery on a specified date

Notice that some of the information needs listed above fall completely within either the acquisition process or the revenue process; others require data from both processes and cannot be provided by single-table queries unless the database allows the storage of volatile derivable attributes (triggers). For example, calculation of quantity on hand of inventory requires the use of quantities purchased of inventory along with the quantities sold of inventory. Purchased quantities are part of the acquisition process and quantities sold are part of the revenue process. Therefore, unless quantity on hand is stored as a triggered update field attribute in the inventory table, the query will be complex and will involve tables from multiple business processes. Similarly, calculation of the total cash balance requires the use of cash receipts from multiple business processes (primarily financing and revenue) and the use of cash disbursements from multiple business processes (primarily from acquisition, payroll, and financing). Therefore, unless the balance of each cash account is stored as a triggered update field in the cash resource type table, the query will involve multiple tables from multiple business processes. We will review such multiple business process queries in chapter 13.

A list of each inventory item or item type offered for sale by an enterprise is a query that can be answered using a single-table query of the inventory or inventory type table. The SQL query based on the tables in Exhibit 12-1 is

```
SELECT *
FROM InventoryType;
```

The asterisk (*) is a wild card that indicates all fields in the InventoryType table are to be included in the answer. No WHERE clause is included, because all instances of inventory type are to be included. Exhibit 12-2 illustrates the Access design view that accomplishes this same query.

ItemID	Description	UnitOfMeasure	StandardCost	ListPrice
BIS1	Big Stuff	Each	$20.00	$50.00
HUS1	Huge Stuff	Each	$30.00	$70.00
LIS1	Little Stuff	Box of 6	$36.00	$72.00
MIN1	Miniature Stuff	Box of 24	$56.00	$110.00
TIS1	Tiny Stuff	Box of 12	$48.00	$96.00
TTP12	Tiara	Each	$10.00	$25.00

ListingOfInventoryTypes

Exhibit 12-2: List Each Inventory Item Type

Notice that because this query doesn't limit the rows or columns to be included, the answer is simply a listing of the InventoryType table. In most database software, one can view the same information simply by opening the InventoryType table, thus a query would be unnecessary.

This single-table query could easily be revised to list only the inventory item types that possess specific characteristics, such as those with list selling prices less than $70.00 or those with "each" as a unit of measure. The query also could include only selected attributes. For example, when providing inventory information to customers, the enterprise likely doesn't want to include the standard costs. To meet such an information need, a query could be constructed similar to the following query that lists only the description, unit of measure, and list price of those items that have list prices less than $70.00. The SQL query based on the tables in Exhibit 12-1 is

> SELECT Description, UnitOfMeasure, ListPrice
> FROM InventoryType
> WHERE ListPrice < 70;

The query result is

Description	UnitOfMeasure	List Price
Big Stuff	Each	$50.00
Tiara	Each	$25.00

Exhibit 12-3 illustrates the Access design view and result for this query.

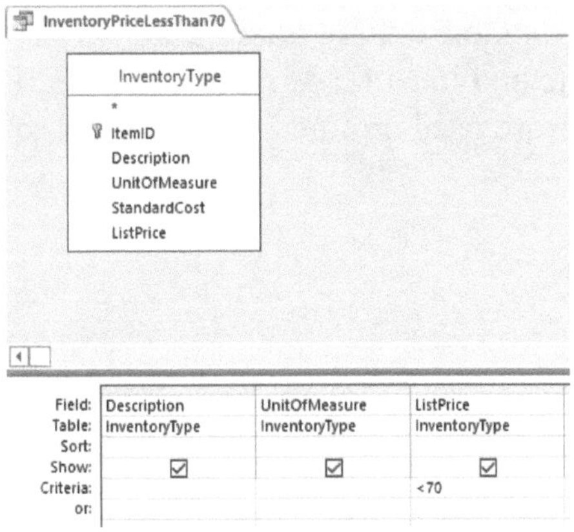

Description	UnitOfMeasure	ListPrice
Big Stuff	Each	$50.00
Tiara	Each	$25.00

InventoryPriceLessThan70

Exhibit 12-3: List Selected Characteristics of Items with List Price < $70.00

Event Queries in the Acquisition and Revenue Processes

Internal and external users may need information regarding events. An *event query* asks a question that can be answered by using a single table that contains data detailing a set of events. The most common events in the acquisition process are purchase requisitions, purchase orders, purchases, cash disbursements, and purchase returns. The most common events in the revenue process are sales calls, sale orders, sales, cash receipts, and sale returns. Users may need either detailed or summarized information about each event or about only those event instances meeting specific criteria.

Examples of information needs in the acquisition and revenue processes are
- Total number of purchase requisitions, purchase orders, purchases, payments, or purchase returns made during a specified time period
- Total dollar amount for a specific purchase requisition, purchase order, general and administrative service and supplies acquisition, operating asset acquisition, inventory acquisition, payment, or purchase return
- Total or average dollar amount of all acquisition events of a specified type for one or more specified time periods.
- Seller's tracking number for an expected purchase event.
- Date a specified purchase requisition, purchase order, purchase, payment, or purchase return event occurred
- Location of a sales call
- Total number of sales calls, sale orders, or sales that occurred at a specified location or during a specified time period
- Total dollar amount for a specific sale order, sale, cash receipt, or sale return event
- Total or average dollar amount of all sale orders, sales, cash receipts, or sale returns for one or more specified time periods
- Total or average dollar amount of sale orders, sales, cash receipts, or sale returns in a specific location for one or more specified time periods
- Sales tax applicable to a specified sale event
- Shipper's tracking number for a shipment sale event
- Date a sale event occurred
- Length of a sales call (end time minus start time)

Using the tables from Exhibit 12-1, we next create some example queries for similar information needs. For one query, a user wants to know the date and location of sales call SC3. The sales call ID is defined as a text data type so quotation marks are used around SC3. The SQL query is

```
SELECT SalesCallID, Date, Location
FROM SalesCall
WHERE SalesCallID="SC3";
```

The result of this query is

Sales Call ID	Date	Location
SC3	5/05/2020	Customer

Exhibit 12-4 illustrates the Access design view and result for this query.

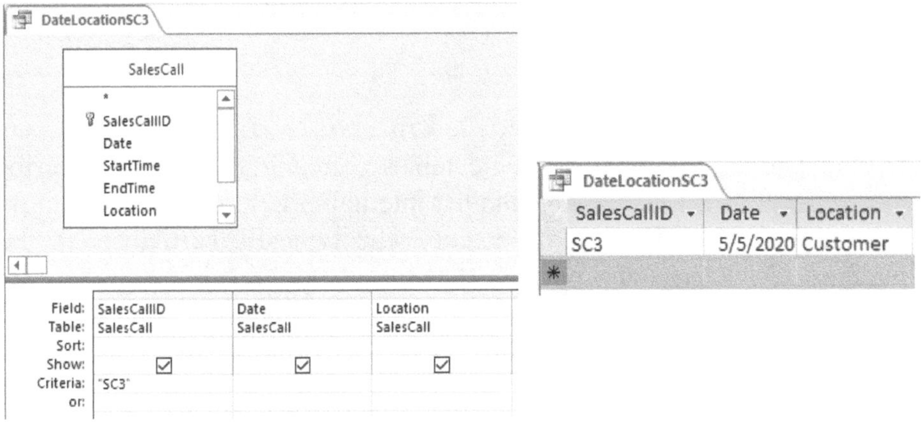

Exhibit 12-4: Query and Result for Date and Location of Sales Call SC3

An event query with an aggregation based on the tables in Exhibit 12-1 is the total sales dollar amount for a specified time period. Say the accountants need that figure for the income statement they are preparing for the week May 1-7, 2020. The SQL query is

> SELECT Sum(DollarTotal) AS SumOfDollarTotal
> FROM Sale
> WHERE Date BETWEEN #5/1/2020# AND #5/7/2020#;

The result is

SumOfDollarTotal
$4,150.00

Exhibit 12-5 illustrates the same query and result in Access design view.

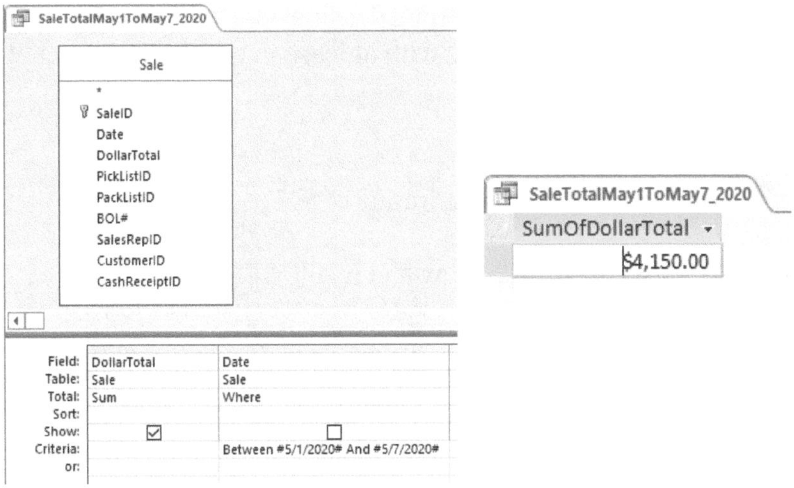

Exhibit 12-5: Query and Result for Total Sales May 1-7, 2020

As a reminder, accountants would need to revise the dates within this query's design for every new income statement they prepare. Using parameters for the dates (i.e., Between [begin date] and [end date]) would be a more flexible query.

Agent Queries in the Acquisition and Revenue Processes

Agent queries are queries that involve single tables containing data that describe internal or external agents; typically such queries' results list internal or external agents who possess one or more specific characteristics. The internal agents who typically participate in the acquisition process are purchase agents, accounts payable clerks, inventory/receiving clerks, and supervisors. The internal agents most often present in the revenue process are salespersons, credit managers, inventory/shipping clerks, cashiers, and various service-providing employees (such as consultants, medical care providers, and waitresses). The external agents most likely to participate in the acquisition process are suppliers or vendors. The external agents usually associated with the revenue process are customers, clients, patrons, or patients. These lists are not intended to be comprehensive but simply to provide a representative set of agents found in those processes. Users may need either detailed or summarized information about each agent or about only those agent instances that meet specific criteria.

Examples of information needs with respect to various types of agents in the revenue and acquisition processes include (but are not limited to):

- A list of all salespeople, cashiers, inventory clerks, credit managers, purchase agents, accounts payable clerks, inventory clerks, or supervisors for an enterprise
- A list of all employees that possess certain characteristics (e.g., all waiters and waitresses who are at least 21 years old, all staff auditors who have passed the CPA exam, or all salespeople whose pay is commission-based)
- A list of all employee names and telephone numbers for an emergency phone tree
- A list of all customers who live in a specific zip code
- A list of all suppliers who are ISO compliant

An example agent query that can be constructed using the tables in Exhibit 12-1 is one that identifies and lists all attributes of customers with at least an "A" credit rating. The SQL code is

```
SELECT *
FROM Customer
WHERE CreditRating ="A" or CreditRating="A+";
```

Exhibit 12-6 illustrates the Access design view and result.

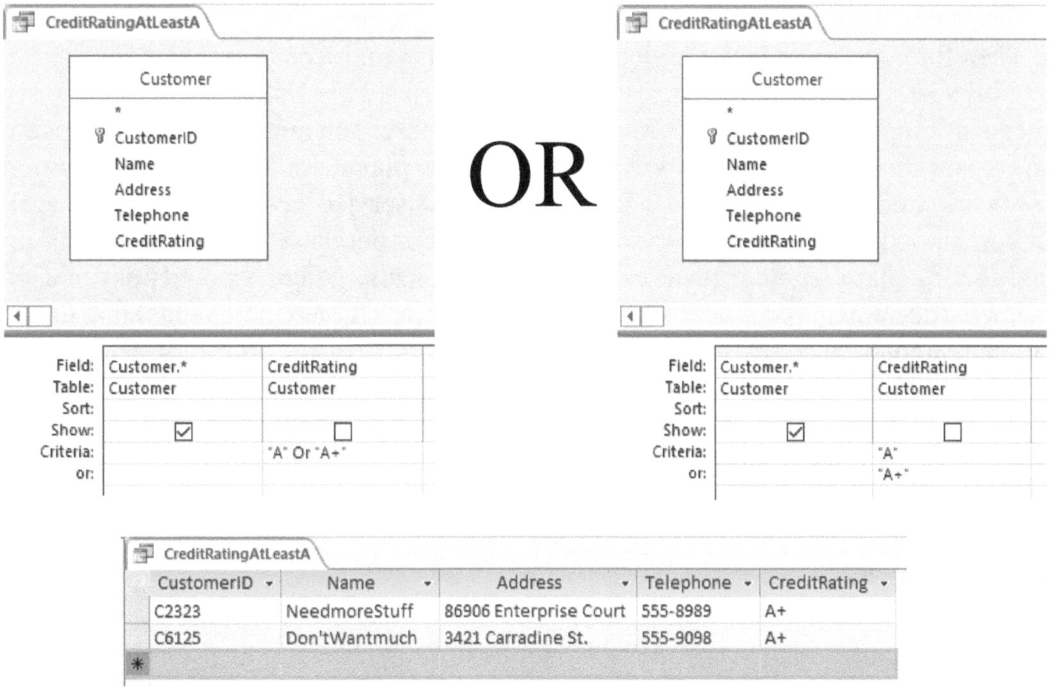

Exhibit 12-6: Query and Result for Customers with Credit Rating A or A+

ASSOCIATION QUERIES

Although resource, event, and agent queries satisfy some information needs, many information needs can only be satisfied by combining information about resources, events, and/or agents. For example, one may not just want to know what event happened, or when or where it happened. One may also want to know what resources were affected by (or involved in) the event, who was affected by (or involved in) the event, why did the event occur (e.g., what other events led to the event) or what was the result of the event (what subsequent events occurred)? Therefore, let's examine each association in the REA business process pattern to study what types of queries help to satisfy information needs arising from these relationships.

Duality Association and/or Reversal Association Queries

Duality associations represent exchanges comprised of two or more events, and reversal associations represent the negation of part or all of an exchange. *Duality association queries* ask questions about economic exchanges, and *reversal association queries* ask questions about the negations of exchanges. Some types of information needs with respect to duality associations in general are

- Identification as to whether a specified exchange is completed
- Identification of completed exchanges for a specified time period
- Identification of incomplete exchanges for a specified time period
- Calculation of the amount of claims, such as prepaid expenses, payables, unearned revenues, or receivables, either in total or for a specific exchange event
- Calculation of the total or average length of the timing differences between the events involved in one or more exchanges

Queries involving economic events often include adjustments for any reversals of the economic events. Therefore, our focus is not only on duality but also on reversal associations.

In the acquisition process the most common economic increment and economic decrement events that participate in duality and reversal associations are purchases or service acquisitions, cash disbursements, and purchase returns. If a purchase or service acquisition (increment) occurs without corresponding cash disbursements (decrements) or purchase returns (increment reversals) that total the purchase amount, there exists a claim typically called accounts payable. If a cash disbursement (decrement) occurs without corresponding purchases (increments) that total the cash disbursement amount, there exists a claim typically called prepaid expense. If data entry controls were not established to prevent a purchase return (increment reversal) from being entered without corresponding purchases (increments) that equal or exceed the purchase return amount, querying can reveal this as an error because something that never happened cannot be reversed.

Some information needs for which queries can be created using the duality association in the acquisition process are
- Calculation of the outstanding payable balance for a purchase or service acquisition
- Calculation of total accounts payable at a point in time
- Calculation of prepaid expenses at a point in time
- Aging of accounts payable
- Calculation of the average number of days it takes to pay vendor invoices

Similarly, in the revenue process the most common economic decrement and economic increment events that participate in duality and/or reversal associations are sales, rentals, or service engagements, cash receipts, and sale returns. Although the association between a sale and a sale return is reversal rather than duality, the reversal of a sale indicates the sale will not be requited by a cash receipt. If a sale (decrement) occurs without corresponding cash receipts (increments) or sale returns (decrement reversals) that total the sale amount, then there exists a claim that is typically called accounts receivable. The sale invoices that represent the sales for which cash receipts have not yet occurred in full are called open sale invoices. If a cash receipt (increment) occurs without corresponding sales (decrements) that total the cash receipt amount, then there exists a claim that is typically called deferred revenue. If data entry controls were not established to prevent a sale return (decrement reversal) from being entered without corresponding sales (decrements) that equal or exceed the sale return amount, querying can reveal this as an error because something that never happened cannot be reversed.

Some information needs for which queries can be created using the duality association in the revenue process are:
- Calculation of the outstanding receivable balance for a sale, rental, or service engagement invoice
- Creation of an open sale invoice file (a list of open sale invoices)
- Calculation of total accounts receivable at a point in time
- Calculation of prepaid revenue at a point in time
- Aging of accounts receivable
- Calculation of the average number of days it takes to collect receivables

Accounts Receivable

Using the tables in Exhibit 12-1 we can construct a query to calculate the total dollar amount of accounts receivable on a particular date (we call it the balance sheet date because accounts receivable is a line item on an enterprise's balance sheet). Consider the information needed for such a query. Accounts receivable is calculated as the total dollar amount of all sales minus any cash receipts applicable to those sales and minus any sale returns. The calculation should only include those events that occurred during the time period up to and including the balance sheet date. For example, if a sale for $1,000 occurred on June 29, then $200 of the merchandise was returned on July 6 and the customer paid the remaining $800 on July 15, then as of June 30 accounts receivable for the sale was $1,000; as of July 7, accounts receivable for the sale was $800; and as of July 31 accounts receivable for the sale was $0. If the dates are not properly constrained or if the information is not linked together correctly in constructing the query, the result may be incorrect. Notice that there is no beginning date constraint; even if the sale took place last year, if it was not returned nor was cash received to settle the receivable, then it is still a receivable. When bad debts exist, an enterprise may need to add an event class to the conceptual model for bad debt write-offs that would also be subtracted from sales in calculating accounts receivable (we ignore write-offs in the chapter database).

Procedures for computing accounts receivable in aggregate are generally as follows:

1) Calculate total sales dollar value through the balance sheet date by using the sale table (assuming that the dollar amount of the sale is stored in the sale table).

2) Calculate total cash receipts that applied to sales, for which the cash receipts occurred before or on the balance sheet date, using the duality association to isolate only those cash receipts that applied to sales (because the cash receipt table may include other cash receipts from financing or purchase returns).

3) a. If the duality association is represented with a separate table, join the cash receipt table to the duality table, establish the constraint on the cash receipt date, and sum the cash receipt amounts.

   b. If duality is represented with the cash receipt identifier posted as a foreign key in the sale table, then join the cash receipt table to the sale table and establish the constraint on the cash receipt date. Then, in another query, sum the cash receipt amounts (Note: Do not combine these steps into one query, because any cash receipt that paid for multiple sales will be counted multiple times in the sum and your query result will be incorrect.) Note that if you need to calculate accounts receivable, then a posted cash receipt identifier in the sale table as a foreign key is likely an implementation compromise (see chapter 10), as if all sales immediately have cash receipts to enter there would be no accounts receivable.

4) Calculate total sale returns that occurred through the balance sheet date, using the sale return table.

5) Subtract the amounts calculated in steps 2 and 3 from the amount calculated in step 1.

These procedures cannot be accomplished in a single query because steps 1 through 3 each involve vertical aggregations based on different tables and step 4 involves a horizontal calculation using those results. Multiple strategies exist to formulate the queries needed to generate this accounts receivable figure; the queries shown below present one possibility. We will use parameter queries which will allow accounts receivable to be calculated for any date.

A/R Query Step 1: Sum sales through the balance sheet date using the Sale table

        SELECT Sum(Sale.DollarTotal) AS SumOfDollarTotal
        FROM Sale
        WHERE (((Sale.Date)<=[bsdate]));

Exhibit 12-7 illustrates this query in Access design view.

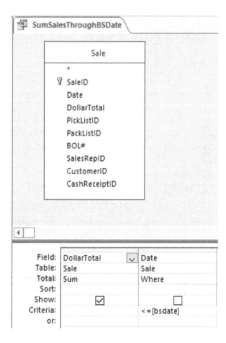

Exhibit 12-7: A/R Query Step 1

A/R Query Step 2a: Identify and sum cash receipts that occurred through the balance sheet date and that applied to sales that were made prior to the balance sheet date.

        SELECT Sum(DualitySaleCashReceipt.AmountApplied) AS SumOfAmountApplied
        FROM Sale INNER JOIN (CashReceipt INNER JOIN DualitySaleCashReceipt ON
            CashReceipt.CashReceiptID = DualitySaleCashReceipt.CashReceiptID) ON
            Sale.SaleID = DualitySaleCashReceipt.SaleID
        WHERE (((CashReceipt.Date)<=[bsdate]) AND ((Sale.Date)<=[bsdate]));

Exhibit 12-8 illustrates this query in Access design view.

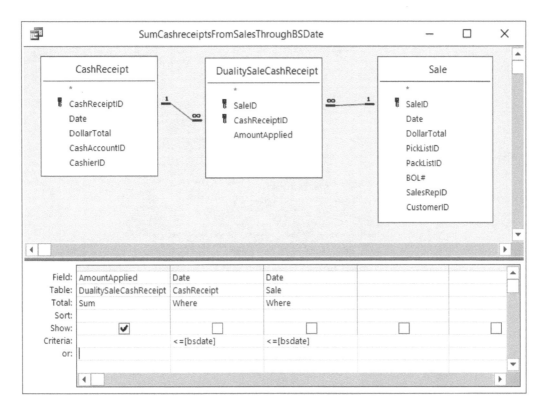

Exhibit 12-8: A/R Query Step 2

A/R Query Step 3: Sum Sale Returns through the balance sheet date using the SaleReturn table

> SELECT Sum(SaleReturn.DollarAmount) AS SumOfDollarAmount
> FROM SaleReturn
> WHERE (((SaleReturn.Date)<=[bsdate]));

Exhibit 12-9 illustrates this query in Access design view.

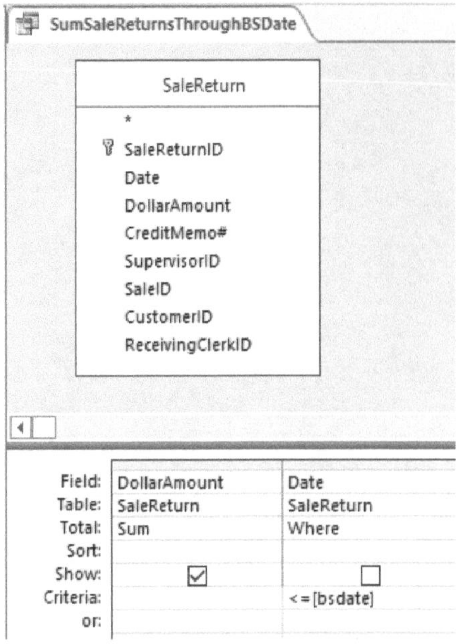

Exhibit 12-9: A/R Query Step 3

A/R Query Step 4: Calculate Query 1 Result – Query 2 Result – Query 3 Result

> SELECT SumSalesThroughBSDate.SumOfDollarTotal,
>   SumCashReceiptsForSalesThroughBSDate.SumOfDollarTotal,
>   SumSaleReturnsThroughBSDate.SumOfDollarAmount,
>   Nz([SumSalesThroughBSDate.SumOfDollarTotal])-
>   Nz([SumCashReceiptsForSalesThroughBSDate.SumOfDollarTotal])-
>   Nz([SumOfDollarAmount]) AS AR
> FROM SumSalesThroughBSDate, SumCashReceiptsForSalesThroughBSDate,
>   SumSaleReturnsThroughBSDate;

Exhibit 12-10 illustrates this query in Access design view.

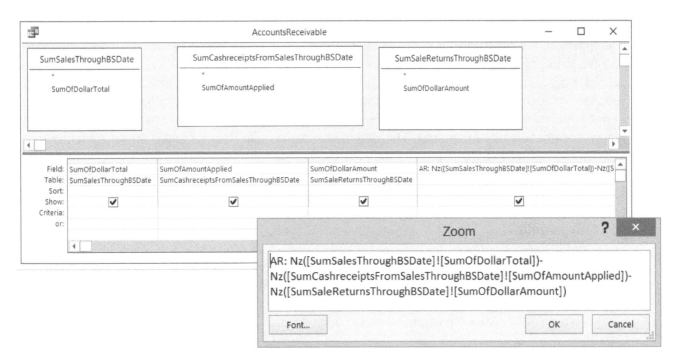

Exhibit 12-10: A/R Query Step 4

You may wonder why A/R Query Step 4 includes Nz three times. This is a function called *Null to zero* that instructs the database engine to treat as zero any null value of whatever variable or expression is in the parentheses following the Nz. This enables the software to avoid returning a null value as the answer, as in mathematics, the result of an equation that includes the empty set as a factor is the empty set. In most business scenarios, if the value of a factor doesn't exist, it means for our decision-making purposes the value is zero. For example, if we haven't yet had any sale returns, the dollar value of the sale returns is zero.

Correct placement of the Nz is important. Note that Nz(a-b-c) will yield a different result from Nz(a)-Nz(b)-Nz(c) if either (a), (b), or (c) is null. Mathematical order of operations dictates that what is inside the parentheses is calculated first, before whatever function precedes the parentheses is applied. If (a) is 100 and (b) is 40 and (c) is null, Nz(a-b-c) would first calculate the value of (100-40-null) as null and then treat the null result as if it is zero (the answer would appear as blank, because Access doesn't change the null to zero, it merely treats it as if it is zero. Nz(a)-Nz(b)-Nz(c) would become Nz(100) - Nz(40) - Nz(null), or 100-40-0, yielding a result of 60.

Unearned Revenue
Whereas Accounts Receivable represents sales that have occurred without the corresponding cash receipt; Unearned Revenue represents cash receipts that have occurred without the corresponding sales. Unearned Revenue is a liability to the company that received the cash but hasn't yet fulfilled its obligation of providing goods or services. You may wonder how one would know from looking at the database that the cash receipts are for sales if the sales haven't yet happened, as no duality entry would yet exist. The answer is that such cash receipts would be related by fulfillment to sale orders. As noted in an earlier chapter, many companies' sale orders are mutual commitments that

are fulfilled by both any related shipment/sale events and also by any related cash receipt events. The timing of the sale orders, sales, and cash receipts may be such that the order precedes the sale and the sale precedes the cash receipt (resulting in accounts receivable), or such that the order precedes the simultaneous sale and cash receipt (resulting in no accounts receivable nor unearned revenue) or such that the order and cash receipt are simultaneous and precede the sale (resulting in unearned revenue), or such that all three events occur simultaneously (resulting in no accounts receivable nor unearned revenue). The only combination that doesn't make sense is for the sale and/or cash receipt to happen prior to the order.

Using the tables in Exhibit 12-1, we can construct a set of queries to calculate the total unearned revenue on a balance sheet date. Procedures for computing unearned revenue in aggregate are generally as follows:

1) Calculate total cash receipts that applied to sale orders, for which the cash receipts occurred before or on the balance sheet date, using the fulfillment association to isolate only those cash receipts that applied to sale orders (because the cash receipt table may include other types of cash receipts, such as from financing or purchase returns).

2)
    a. If the fulfillment association is represented with a separate table, join the cash receipt table to the fulfillment table, establish the constraint on the cash receipt date, and sum the cash receipt amounts.

    b. If fulfillment is represented with the cash receipt identifier posted as a foreign key in the sale order table, then join the cash receipt table to the sale order table and establish the constraint on the cash receipt date. Then, in another query, sum the cash receipt amounts (Note: Do not combine these steps into one query, because any cash receipt that paid for multiple sale orders will be counted multiple times in the sum and your query result will be incorrect.)

3) Calculate the total dollar value for all sales that resulted from sale orders through the balance sheet date by using the sale table (assuming that the dollar amount of the sale is stored in the sale table) and the fulfillment sale order-sale table. Note that it is important to only include sales that resulted from orders, as any non-ordered sales would not relate to the cash receipts included in step 1.

4) Calculate the total dollar value of any sale returns that resulted from ordered sales through the balance sheet date by using the sale return table (assuming that the dollar amount of the sale return is stored in the sale return table), the reversal sale-sale return, sale, and fulfillment sale order-sale table.

5) Calculate step 2 minus step 3, then subtract that result from step 1. In other words, subtract the unreturned sales through the balance sheet from the cash received for sale orders.

We next use parameter queries that allow one to calculate unearned revenue for any date.

Unearned Revenue Query Step 1: Sum cash receipts applied to sale orders through the balance sheet date using the Sale Order, Cash Receipt and FulfillmentSaleOrderCashReceipt tables.

```
SELECT Sum(FulfillmentSaleOrderCashReceipt.AmountApplied) AS
        SumOfAmountApplied
FROM SaleOrder INNER JOIN (CashReceipt INNER JOIN
        FulfillmentSaleOrderCashReceipt ON CashReceipt.CashReceiptID =
        FulfillmentSaleOrderCashReceipt.CashReceiptID) ON SaleOrder.SaleOrderID =
        FulfillmentSaleOrderCashReceipt.SaleOrder
WHERE (((CashReceipt.Date)<=[bsdate]) AND ((SaleOrder.OrderDate)<=[bsdate]));
```

Exhibit 12-11 illustrates this query in Access design view.

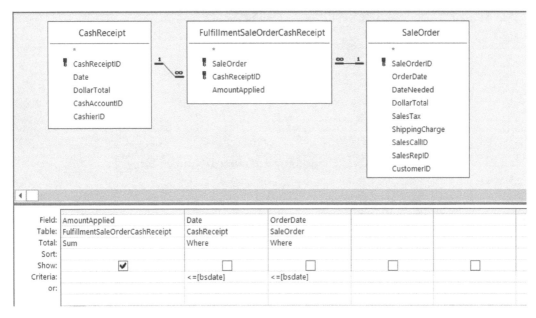

Exhibit 12-11: Unearned Revenue Query Step 1

Unearned Revenue Query Step 2: Sum sale amounts through the balance sheet date

```
SELECT Sum(Sale.DollarTotal) AS SumOfDollarTotal
FROM Sale INNER JOIN FulfillmentSaleOrderSale ON Sale.SaleID =
        FulfillmentSaleOrderSale.SaleID
WHERE (((Sale.Date)<=[bsdate]));
```

Exhibit 12-12 illlustrates this query in Access design view.

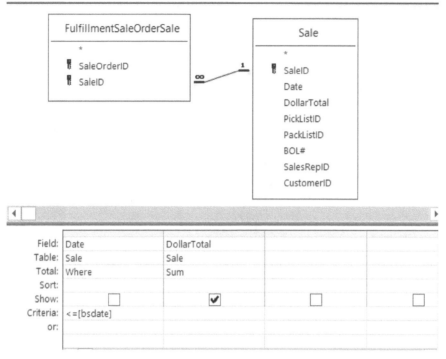

Exhibit 12-12: Unearned Revenue Query Step 2

Unearned Revenue Step 3: Calculate returns of sales that resulted from orders through the balance sheet date.

SELECT Sum(SaleReturn.DollarAmount) AS SumOfDollarAmount
FROM (Sale INNER JOIN FulfillmentSaleOrderSale ON Sale.SaleID =
        FulfillmentSaleOrderSale.SaleID) INNER JOIN SaleReturn ON Sale.SaleID =
        SaleReturn.SaleID
WHERE (((SaleReturn.Date)<=[bsdate]));

Exhibit 12-13 illustrates this query in Access design view.

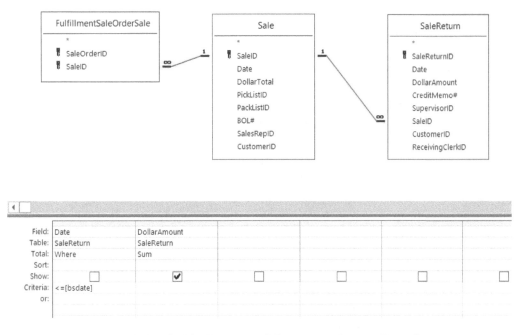

Exhibit 12-13: Unearned Revenue Query Step 3

Unearned Revenue Step 4: Subtract unreturned ordered sales from cash receipts for orders

SELECT SumOfAmountApplied, SumOfDollarTotal, SumOfDollarAmount,
    [SumOfAmountApplied]-(Nz([SumOfDollarTotal])-Nz([SumOfDollarAmount]))
    AS UnearnedRevenue
FROM SumCashReceiptsFromSaleOrdersThroughBSDate,
    SumSaleReturnsFromOrderedSalesThroughEndDate,
    SumSalesFromOrdersThroughEndDate;

Exhibit 12-14 illustrates this query in Access design view.

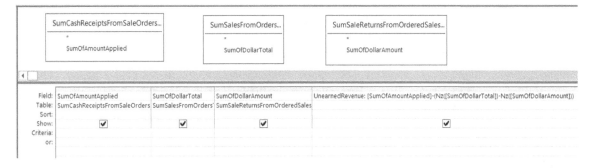

Exhibit 12-14: Unearned Revenue Query Step 4

Accounts Payable

Using the tables in Exhibit 12-1, we can construct a set of queries to calculate the total dollar amount of accounts payable on a balance sheet date. Accounts payable is calculated as the total dollar amount of all acquisitions minus any cash disbursements applicable to those purchases and minus any purchase returns. The calculation should include only those events that occurred during the time period up to and including the balance sheet date. For example, if a purchase for $3,000 occurred on June 29, and then $600 of the merchandise was returned on July 6 and the company paid the remaining $2,400 on July 15, then as of June 30 accounts payable for the purchase was $3,000; as of July 7, accounts payable for the purchase was $2,400; and as of July 31 accounts payable for the purchase was $0. If the dates are not properly constrained in the query or if the query does not link the fields together properly, the result will be inaccurate. Notice that there is no beginning date constraint; even if the purchase took place last year, if it was not returned nor paid for, then it is still payable.

Procedures for computing accounts payable in aggregate are generally as follows:
Determine what kinds of acquisitions are represented in your database (do NOT include labor acquisitions, because unpaid labor acquisitions are called wages payable rather than accounts payable) and for each kind of acquisition follow these steps:

1. Determine which table contains the acquisition date and dollar amount (usually these are found in the acquisition event table). Sum the acquisitions that happened through the balance sheet date (with no beginning date constraint).

2. Determine which tables contain the cash disbursements that applied to those acquisitions and calculate the applicable cash disbursements total. To determine this, examine the duality association.

   a. When the duality association is represented with a separate table, join the duality table to the cash disbursement table, establish the ending date constraint on the cash disbursement date field (with no beginning date constraint), and sum the cash disbursement amount applied to the acquisition.

   b. When the duality association is represented with the cash disbursement identifier posted as a foreign key into the acquisition table, join the cash disbursement table to the acquisition table, establish the ending date constraint on the cash disbursement date field (with no beginning date constraint), and sum the cash disbursement amounts.

3. Calculate total purchase returns that occurred through the balance sheet date, using the purchase returns table.

4. Subtract the results of steps 3 and 4 from the result of step 2 to get accounts payable as of the balance sheet date.

These procedures should not be combined in a single query because steps 1 through 4 each involve vertical aggregations based on different tables and step 5 involves a horizontal calculation using those results. We next outline a set of queries to calculate accounts payable for inventory acquisitions for the tables in Exhibit 12-1. Additional queries would be needed to calculate accounts payable for operating asset purchases and general and administrative supply and service acquisitions (notice that the partial set of tables in Exhibit 12-1 does not include sufficient detail of those acquisitions to be able to calculate the payables for those). This set of queries uses parameters for the dates of interest increase re-usability, and the final query uses the Nz function for the same reasons discussed with respect to the accounts receivable queries.

A/P Query Step 1 Sum acquisition amounts that happened through the balance sheet date

```
SELECT Sum(Purchase.DollarAmount) AS SumOfDollarAmount
FROM Purchase
WHERE (((Purchase.Date)<=[bsdate]));
```

Exhibit 12-15 illustrates this query in Access design view.

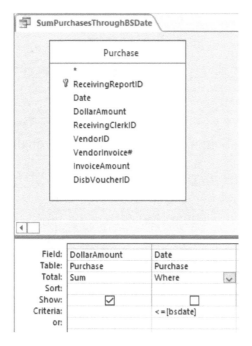

Exhibit 12-15: Accounts Payable Query Step 1

Accounts Payable Query Step 2: Sum payments made through the balance sheet date that applied to purchases made through the balance sheet date.

```
SELECT Sum(DualityPurchaseCashDisbursement.[Amount Applied]) AS
        [SumOfAmount Applied]
FROM CashDisbursement INNER JOIN DualityPurchaseCashDisbursement ON
        CashDisbursement.DisbVoucherID =
        DualityPurchaseCashDisbursement.DisbVoucherID
WHERE (((CashDisbursement.VoucherDate)<=[bsdate]));
```

Exhibit 12-16 illustrates this query in Access design view.

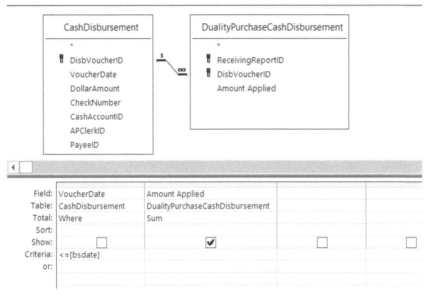

Exhibit 12-16: Accounts Payable Query Step 2

Accounts Payable Query Step 3: Sum total purchase returns through balance sheet date

SELECT Sum(PurchaseReturn.DollarAmount) AS SumOfDollarAmount
FROM PurchaseReturn
WHERE (((PurchaseReturn.Date)<=[bsdate]));

Exhibit 12-17 illustrates this query in Access design view.

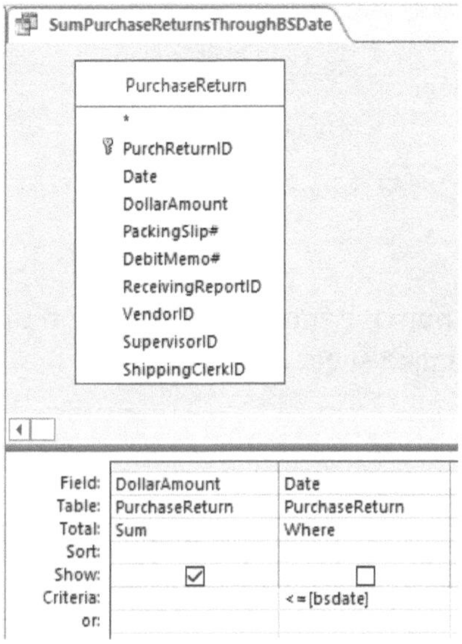

Exhibit 12-17: A/P Query Step 3

Accounts Payable Query Step 4: Calculate Query 1 result – Query 2 result – Query 3 result

> SELECT SumPurchasesThroughBSDate.SumOfDollarAmount,
>   SumPurchaseReturnsThroughBSDate.SumOfDollarAmount,
>   SumCashDisbursementsForPurchasesThroughBSDate.[SumOfAmount Applied],
>   Nz([SumPurchasesThroughBSDate]![SumOfDollarAmount])-
>   Nz([SumPurchaseReturnsThroughBSDate]![SumOfDollarAmount])-
>   Nz([SumOfAmount Applied]) AS AP
> FROM SumPurchasesThroughBSDate,
>   SumCashDisbursementsForPurchasesThroughBSDate,
>   SumPurchaseReturnsThroughBSDate;

Exhibit 12-18 illustrates this query in Access design view.

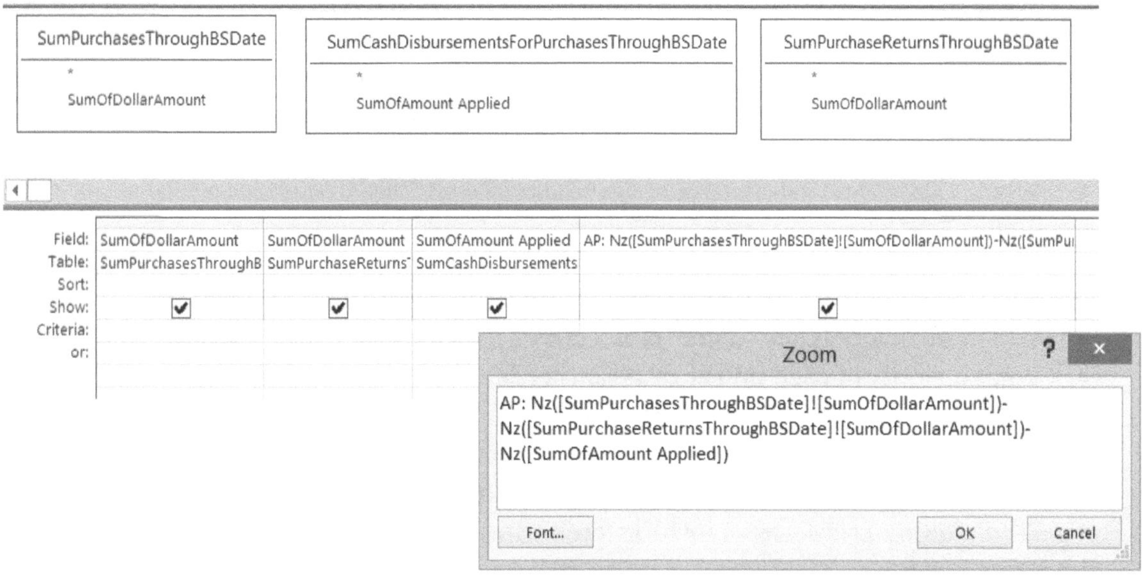

Exhibit 12-18: Accounts Payable Query Step 4

Stockflow Association Queries

Stockflow associations represent relationships between economic increment or decrement events and the resources that are increased or decreased by those events. A *stockflow association query* is one that attempts to satisfy information needs about the effect of economic events on resources or about the resources involved in events. Some common information needs are:

- What resources or resource types were increased or decreased by an economic event?
- What quantity of a resource or resource type was increased or decreased by an economic event?
- What dollar value of a resource or resource type was increased or decreased by an economic event?

- When did an event increase or decrease a specific resource or resource type?
- Where did an event increase or decrease a specific resource or resource type?

Such information needs can require detailed descriptions of specific transactions or they may require aggregations such as sums or averages. The preceding types of information may be used as part of a trend analysis to project future events and their expected effects on resources or resource types, and/or they may be compared to similar information for competitors to gauge the level of competitive advantage (or disadvantage) the enterprise may have.

Within the acquisition process, some common information needs of these types are
- Which inventory types were increased by a specific purchase event?
- What quantity of each inventory type was increased by a specific purchase event?
- Which inventory types were decreased by a purchase return event?
- What quantity of each inventory type was decreased by a specific purchase return event?
- What unit cost was charged for an inventory type on a specific purchase event?
- What unit cost was granted as credit for an inventory type on a specific purchase return event?
- What was the total dollar value of purchases for a specified time period? (Note: If the total purchase dollar amount is stored in the purchase event table, then it is not necessary to use the stockflow association to meet this information need.)
- What is the average dollar value of purchases of a specified inventory type for a specified time period?

Within the revenue process, some common information needs of these types are
- Which inventory types were decreased by a specific sale event?
- What quantity of each inventory type was decreased by a specific sale event?
- Which inventory types were increased by a sale return event?
- What quantity of each inventory type was increased by a specific sale return event?
- What selling price was charged for an inventory type on a specific sale event?
- What selling price was granted as credit for an inventory type on a specific sale return event?
- What was the total dollar value of sales for a specified time period? (Note: If the total sale amount is stored in the sale event table, then it is not necessary to use the stockflow association to meet this information need.)
- What is the average dollar value of sales of a specified inventory type for a specified time period?

Assume a marketing manager has requested two reports of sales dollars by inventory item to see which inventory item has generated the most and least sales during two time periods. The first report covers the week of May 1-7, 2020 and the second report covers the week of May 8-14, 2020. In each report, the manager wants the ItemID, the item description, and the total sales dollar amount for each item. How would you construct a query from the tables in Exhibit 12-1 to meet the manager's need?

Begin by examining the tables to see which tables you need. Because this query combines information about sales and inventory, you need to look at the stockflow association and related classes and determine which of the database tables represent those constructs. Then examine those tables to see which contain the relevant information. In this case the Sale, InventoryType, and StockflowSaleInventoryType tables contain the desired information. Be careful; you will see a "DollarTotal" field in the Sale table, but this aggregates the value of all inventory on a sale and is irrelevant to the stated query objective.

We construct two queries (Exhibits 12-19 and 12-20), with dates as parameters so that the same queries may be run for each week, as follows:

Inventory Item Sales Query Step 1: Join tables, constrain dates, and extend line item sale amounts

```
SELECT InventoryType.ItemID, InventoryType.Description, Sale.Date,
       StockflowSaleInventoryType.QuantitySold,
       StockflowSaleInventoryType.ActualUnitSellingPrice,
       [QuantitySold]*[ActualUnitSellingPrice] AS ExtSaleAmt
FROM Sale INNER JOIN (InventoryType INNER JOIN StockflowSaleInventoryType
       ON InventoryType.ItemID = StockflowSaleInventoryType.ItemID) ON
       Sale.SaleID = StockflowSaleInventoryType.SaleID
WHERE (((Sale.Date) Between [begindate] And [enddate]));
```

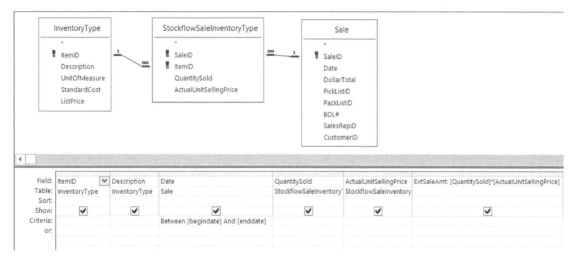

Exhibit 12-19: Inventory Item Sales Query Step 1 in Access Design View

Inventory Item Sales Query Step 2: Sum extended sale amounts for each item

```
SELECT StockflowExtendedSaleAmt.ItemID, StockflowExtendedSaleAmt.Description,
       Sum(StockflowExtendedSaleAmt.ExtSaleAmt) AS SumOfExtSaleAmt
FROM StockflowExtendedSaleAmt
GROUP BY StockflowExtendedSaleAmt.ItemID,
       StockflowExtendedSaleAmt.Description;
```

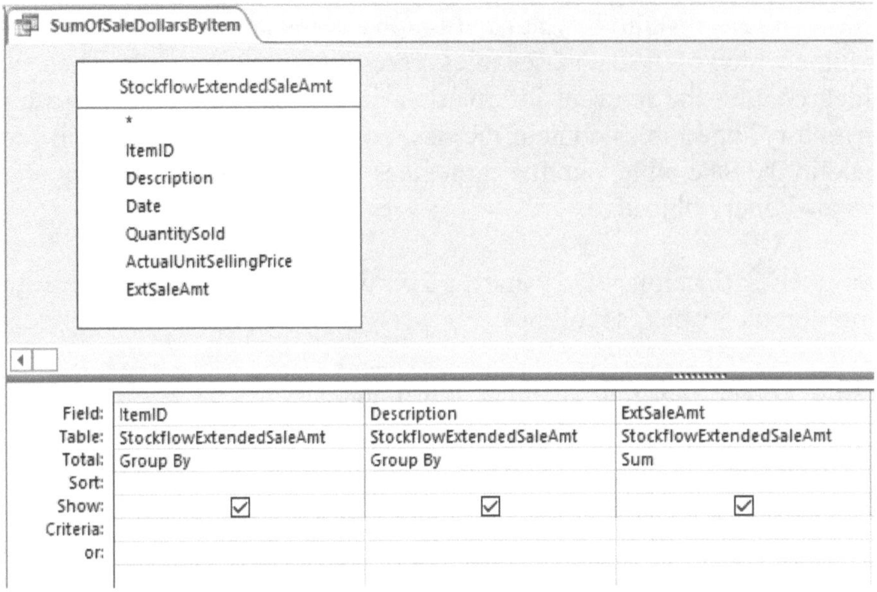

Result for May 1-7, 2020

SumOfSaleDollarsByItem

ItemID	Description	SumOfExtSa
BIS1	Big Stuff	$2,400.00
HUS1	Huge Stuff	$650.00
LIS1	Little Stuff	$140.00
TIS1	Tiny Stuff	$960.00

Result for May 8-14, 2020

SumOfSaleDollarsByItem

ItemID	Description	SumOfExtSa
MIN1	Miniature Stuff	$4,305.00

Exhibit 12-20: Inventory Item Sales Query Step 2 in Access Design View With Results

Examine the results for each of the two weeks. Carefully compare them to each other and to the InventoryType table in Exhibit 12-1. Do these reports meet the marketing manager's need?

No.

Why not? Although the reports allow for easy identification of the items with the highest dollar sales (Big Stuff for May 1-7 and Miniature Stuff for May 8-14), they do not even display the items with lowest dollar sales, which are in fact those items that haven't sold at all. That is because the join type between InventoryType and StockflowSaleInventoryType in the query set is an inner join, which results in a solution that only includes instances with matching values in both tables. To keep instances that exist in the InventoryType table without matching values in the StockflowSaleInventoryType table, the join type between those two tables must be changed to an outer join.

Because the Inventory Item Sales Query Step 1 contains three tables, in some database software packages, we cannot simply change the join between InventoryType and StockflowSaleInventoryType to an outer join, as some database software considers outer joins with three tables to be ambiguous. To include the non-sold items, then, the following query steps should be used, thus better satisfying the marketing manager's information need.

Revised Inventory Item Sales Query Step 1 (Exhibit 12-21): Constrain dates and calculate extended sale amounts for inventory items sold

```
SELECT Sale.Date, StockflowSaleInventoryType.ItemID,
       StockflowSaleInventoryType.QuantitySold,
       StockflowSaleInventoryType.ActualUnitSellingPrice,
       [QuantitySold]*[ActualUnitSellingPrice] AS ExtSaleAmt
FROM Sale INNER JOIN StockflowSaleInventoryType ON Sale.SaleID =
       StockflowSaleInventoryType.SaleID
WHERE (((Sale.Date) Between [begdate] And [enddate]));
```

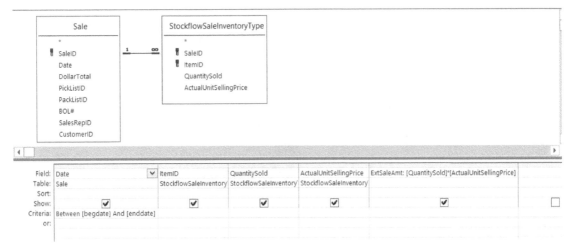

Exhibit 12-21: Revised Inventory Item Sales Query Step 1

Revised Inventory Item Sales Query Step 2 (Exhibit 12-22):

```
SELECT InventoryType.ItemID, InventoryType.Description,
       Sum(InventorySaleAmountsRevised.ExtSaleAmt) AS SumOfExtSaleAmt
FROM InventoryType LEFT JOIN InventorySaleAmountsRevised ON
       InventoryType.ItemID = InventorySaleAmountsRevised.ItemID
GROUP BY InventoryType.ItemID, InventoryType.Description;
```

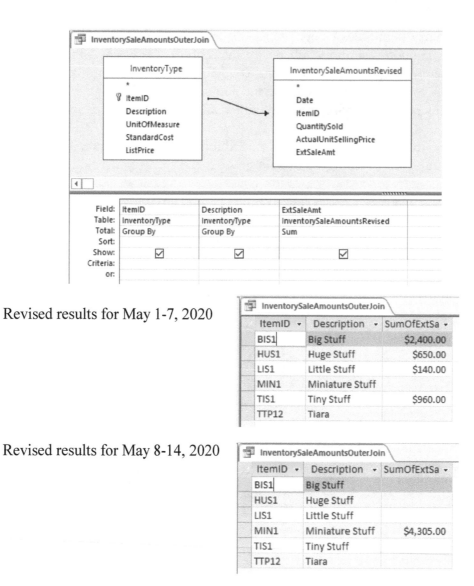

Revised results for May 1-7, 2020

Revised results for May 8-14, 2020

Exhibit 12-22: Revised Inventory Item Sales Query Step 2

Note that using the outer join causes all items to appear in the results whether they have sold during the time period of interest or not, thus allowing the marketing manager to easily identify not only the highest sale totals, but also the non-selling items.

Weighted Average Unit Cost for a time period (NOT for financial statements)
Enterprises commonly need to calculate the weighted average unit cost of inventory items purchased during a specific time period. Such a query involves the stockflow association between purchase and inventory in the acquisition process. The weighted average unit cost of an item is calculated as the total purchase dollar amount for that item during the time period divided by the total quantity purchased of that item during the time period. The general procedures for determining weighted average unit cost (i.e., the weighted average unit cost query steps) for each inventory item during a time period are as follows.

1. Determine which table contains the purchase date attribute (usually this is in the table that represents the purchase economic event).

2. Determine which table contains the purchase quantities and actual unit cost information (usually these attributes are in the table that represents the stockflow association between purchase and inventory).

3. Join the tables together, set the date constraints (beginning and ending dates for desired time period) and multiply the quantities purchased by the actual unit costs to get the total purchase line-item amounts. Note: If the total purchase line-item amount is already stored as a derivable attribute in the stockflow table, then you don't need to calculate it.

4. Group the result from step 3 by inventory item and sum the purchase quantity and the total purchase line-item dollar amount.

5. Start with the result from step 4 and, still grouping by inventory item, divide the sum of the total purchase line item by the sum of the total purchased quantity.

Note on Weighted Average Unit Costing for Financial Statements
The procedures described are only for use in the time period in which the items are purchased. When using weighted average unit cost for valuing Cost of Goods Sold on the Income Statement or Inventory on the Balance Sheet, Step 3 will need to be modified to use only an ending date constraint. The modification is needed because the time period for which the Income Statement is calculated may not be the same as the time period in which the inventory items are purchased. For example, items that are purchased in March may be sold in April. If the query is intended to value cost of goods sold for the month of April, the seemingly logical beginning date constraint to use is April 1. However, if April 1 is set as a beginning date constraint, those items will not be assigned a cost value because they weren't purchased during April. Because the weighted average unit cost flow assumption indicates no physical matching of items sold to items purchased, no beginning date constraint can be used. To avoid having unreasonably old inventory costs assigned to Cost of Goods Sold and Inventory, a company may instead want to use a moving weighted average which would require programming and is beyond the scope of this book.

We next display the queries that provide the requested information for the weighted average unit cost for inventory types purchased in a specified time period. The queries specify dates as parameters to allow re-use for alternative time periods.

WAUC Query Step 1 (Exhibit 12-23): Join Purchase and StockflowPurchaseInventoryType tables, constrain purchase date, calculate purchase line item extensions

SELECT StockflowPurchaseInventoryType.ItemID,
       StockflowPurchaseInventoryType.QuantityPurchased,
       StockflowPurchaseInventoryType.ActualUnitCost,
       [QuantityPurchased]*[ActualUnitCost] AS LineItemExtension, Purchase.Date
FROM Purchase INNER JOIN StockflowPurchaseInventoryType ON
       Purchase.ReceivingReportID =
       StockflowPurchaseInventoryType.ReceivingReportID
WHERE (((Purchase.Date) Between [begindate] And [enddate]));

Exhibit 12-23: WAUC Query Step 1 – NOT FOR FINANCIAL STATEMENTS

WAUC Query Step 2 (Exhibit 12-24): Sum purchase quantities and line item extensions for each item type

SELECT LineItemPurchaseExtensionsDuringPeriod.ItemID,
       Sum(LineItemPurchaseExtensionsDuringPeriod.QuantityPurchased) AS
       SumOfQuantityPurchased,
       Sum(LineItemPurchaseExtensionsDuringPeriod.LineItemExtension) AS
       SumOfLineItemExtension
FROM LineItemPurchaseExtensionsDuringPeriod
GROUP BY LineItemPurchaseExtensionsDuringPeriod.ItemID;

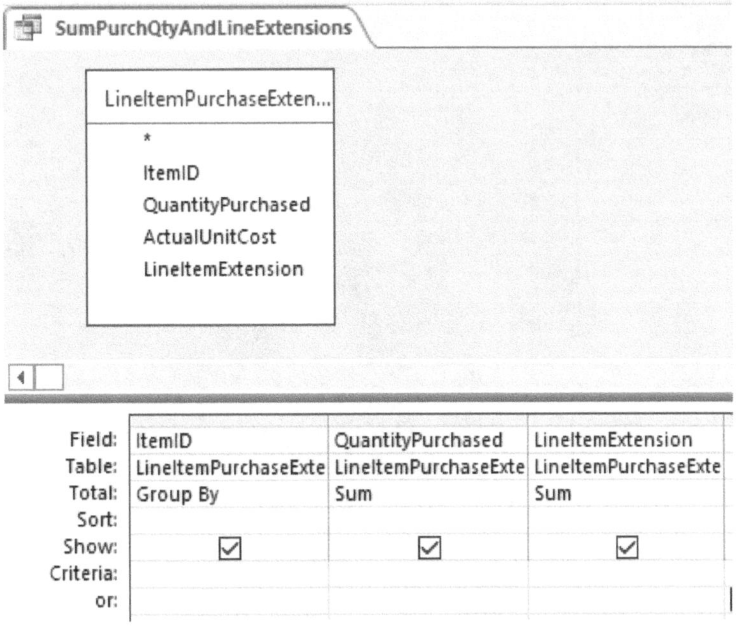

Exhibit 12-24: WAUC Query Step 2 – NOT FOR FINANCIAL STATEMENTS

WAUC Query Step 3 (Exhibit 12-25): Divide line extension sums by total purchase quantities for each item type

```
SELECT SumPurchQtyAndLineExtensions.ItemID,
       SumPurchQtyAndLineExtensions.SumOfLineItemExtension,
       SumPurchQtyAndLineExtensions.SumOfQuantityPurchased,
       [SumOfLineItemExtension]/[SumOfQuantityPurchased] AS WAUC
FROM SumPurchQtyAndLineExtensions;
```

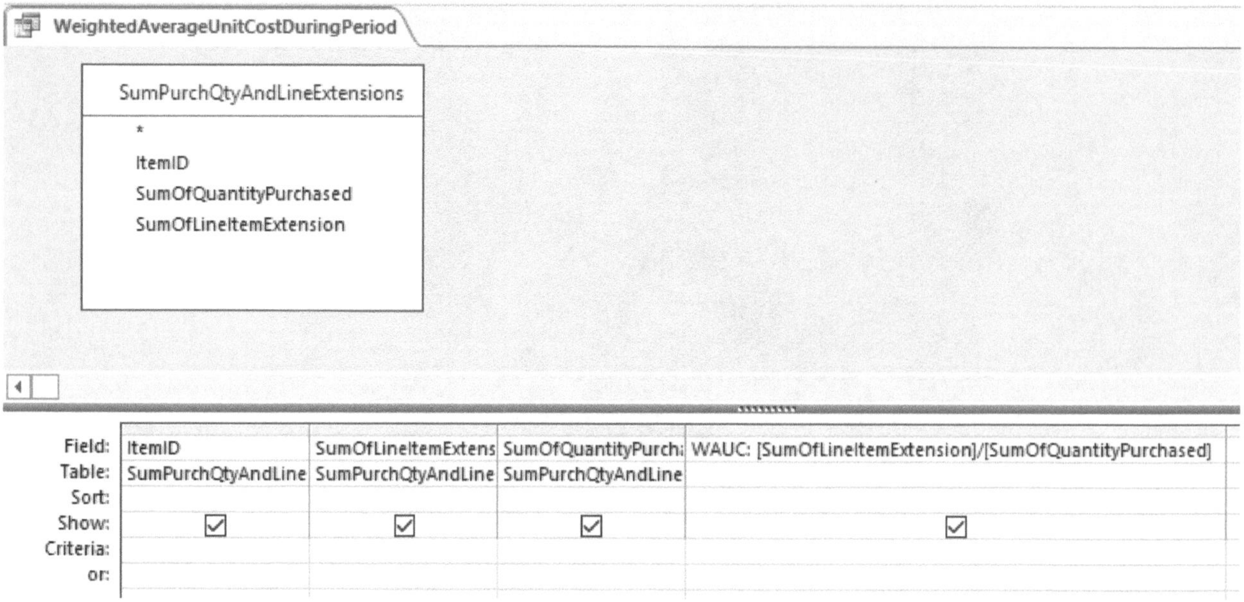

Result for May 1-31, 2020

WeightedAverageUnitCostDuringPeriod

ItemID	SumOfLineItemExtension	SumOfQuantityPurchased	WAUC
BIS1	$2,000.00	100	20
MIN1	$4,340.00	80	54.25
TTP12	$480.00	48	10

Exhibit 12-25: WAUC Query Step 3 – NOT FOR FINANCIAL STATEMENTS

Note that the WAUC data is not formatted with a dollar sign. When the database divides the currency data type by the number data type to create the WAUC expression, it returns a number data type for WAUC (this is called conversion or coercion). If you would like WAUC to be formatted as currency, simply go back to the Design View, put your cursor in the WAUC expression, right-click to bring up the Property Sheet, and then choose Currency formatting from the dropdown menu. You can do this any time you encounter a data type conversion; there are also data type conversion functions available in Access (e.g., if you would like to change a text data type to a number).

Fulfillment Association Queries

Fulfillment associations are similar to duality associations in that both associations represent relationships between events. Whereas duality associations focus on economic exchanges, fulfillment associations focus on events that led up to the economic exchanges. A ***fulfillment association query*** is one that answers one or more questions about the relationship between an instigation event and the commitment event to which it led, or about the relationship between a commitment event and the resulting economic event. Therefore, some of the information needs to be satisfied with fulfillment associations include:

- Identification of unfulfilled commitments or instigation events
- Identification of fulfilled commitments or instigation events

- Identification of commitment events that were not preceded by instigation events, or identification of economic events that were not preceded by commitment events
- Calculation of length of time between instigation and commitment events or between commitment and economic events
- Identification of causes of commitments and/or of economic events
- Identification of results of instigations and/or of commitment events

In the acquisition process the most common instigation events are purchase requisitions; the most common commitment events that fulfill the purchase requisitions are purchase orders; and the most common economic increment events that fulfill the purchase orders are purchases (i.e., receipt of goods or services). If a purchase requisition occurs without a corresponding purchase order, the purchase requisition is unfulfilled. If a purchase order occurs without a corresponding purchase, the purchase order is unfulfilled. Some information needs for which queries can be created using the fulfillment associations in the acquisition process are:
- List of unfilled purchase orders
- Identification of filled purchase requisitions (i.e., those purchase requisitions that resulted in purchase orders)
- Calculation of average number of days the enterprise takes to fill purchase requisitions for a given time period
- Identify the purchase order that corresponds to a purchase

In the revenue process the most common instigation events are sales calls; the most common commitment events that fulfill the sales calls are sale orders, rental contracts, or service engagement contracts; and the most common economic decrement events that fulfill the sale orders are sales, rentals, or service engagements. If a sales call occurs without a corresponding sale order, the sales call is unfulfilled. If a sale order occurs without a corresponding sale, the sale order is unfulfilled. A list of unfilled sale orders is often called an open sale order file. Some example information needs for which queries can be created using the fulfillment associations in the revenue process are
- List of open sale orders
- Identification of successful sales calls (i.e., those sales calls that resulted in orders)
- Calculation of number of average days the enterprise takes to fill sale orders

Using the tables in Exhibit 12-1, we can construct a query to calculate the number of days the enterprise took to fill each sale order, and a further query to calculate the average number of days the enterprise takes to fill sale orders for that time period. Note that the date fields must be designed as Date/Time fields rather than text fields in order to subtract the fields to calculate the number of days to fill each order. We next show each of the queries needed to satisfy these information needs.

Sale Order Fulfillment Query 1 (Exhibit 12-26): Number of Days to Fill Each Order

SELECT SaleOrder.OrderDate, Sale.Date, [Date]-[OrderDate] AS DaysToFill
FROM SaleOrder INNER JOIN (Sale INNER JOIN FulfillmentSaleOrderSale ON
        Sale.SaleID = FulfillmentSaleOrderSale.SaleID) ON SaleOrder.SaleOrderID =
        FulfillmentSaleOrderSale.SaleOrderID
WHERE (((SaleOrder.OrderDate) Between [begindate] And [enddate]));

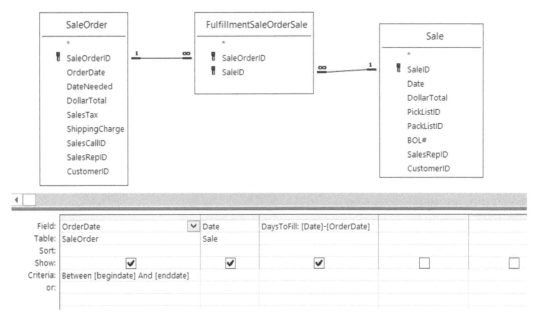

Exhibit 12-26: Sale Order Fulfillment Query 1

Sale Order Fulfillment Query 2 (Exhibit 12-27): Average Number of Days to Fill Orders (builds
on Query 1)

SELECT Avg(DateDiffSaleOrderSale.DaysToFill) AS AvgOfDaysToFill
FROM DateDiffSaleOrderSale;

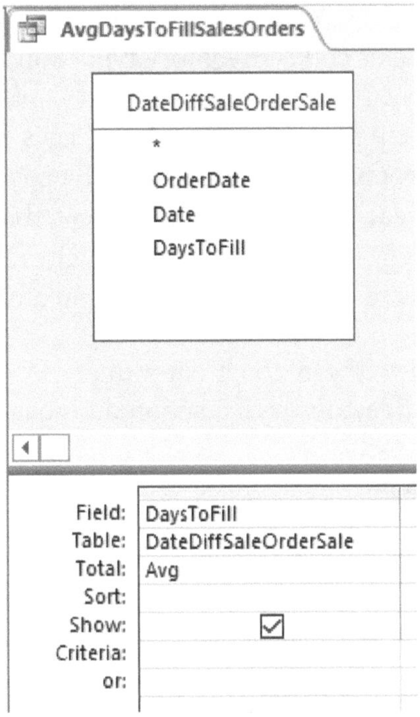

Exhibit 12-27: Sale Order Fulfillment Query 2

Proposition Association Queries
Proposition associations represent relationships between instigation events and the resources the events propose to increase or decrease. A *proposition association query* is one created to satisfy information needs about the proposed effect of instigation events on resources or about the resources involved in instigation events. Some common information needs are

- What resources or resource types does the instigation event propose to increase or decrease?
- What quantity of a resource or resource type is the proposed increase or decrease for an instigation event?
- When did an instigation event propose to increase or decrease a specific resource or resource type?

Within the acquisition process, the most common instigation events are purchase requisitions, and the most common resource involved in a purchase requisition is inventory type. Some common information needs within the acquisition process are

- Which inventory types were identified as needed in a purchase requisition event?
- What unit cost was estimated for an inventory type in a purchase requisition event?
- How many times has a specified inventory type been requisitioned during a time period?
- How many types of inventory were requisitioned in a purchase requisition event?

Within the revenue process, the most common instigation events are sales calls, and the most common resource involved in a sales call is inventory type. Some common information within the revenue process are

- Which inventory types were presented as part of a sales call event?
- What selling price was proposed for an inventory type in a specific sales call event?
- What was the reaction to each inventory type presented in a specific sales call event?
- Have any inventory types never been presented in any sales call event?
- How many different types of inventory were presented in a specific sales call event?

Using the tables in Exhibit 12-1, we can construct a query to identify which (if any) inventory items have <u>never</u> received a positive customer reaction during a sales call, as follows:

Query Step 1 (Exhibit 12-28): Identify items in sales calls with "not positive" reactions

```
SELECT PropositionSalesCallInventoryType.ItemID,
     PropositionSalesCallInventoryType.CustomerReactiontoProduct
FROM PropositionSalesCallInventoryType
WHERE
     (((PropositionSalesCallInventoryType.CustomerReactiontoProduct)<>"Positive"));
```

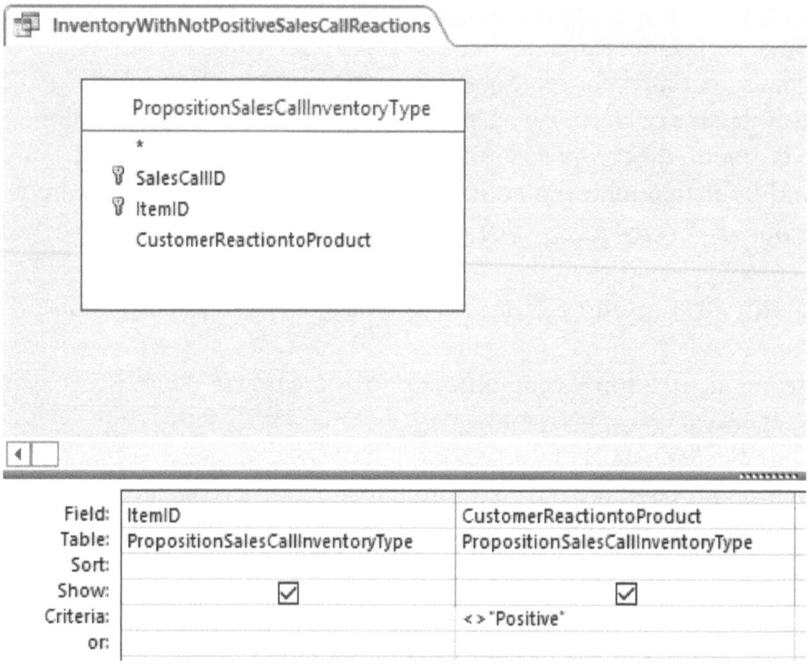

Exhibit 12-28: Items With Positive Customer Reaction Query

Query Step 2 (Exhibit 12-29): Outer join InventoryType to prior query, identifying those items that were not included in the sales call (and therefore, have no customer reaction including a positive reaction; these will appear as null values).

SELECT InventoryType.ItemID, InventoryType.Description,
 InventoryWithNotPositiveSalesCallReactions.CustomerReactiontoProduct
FROM InventoryType LEFT JOIN InventoryWithNotPositiveSalesCallReactions ON
 InventoryType.ItemID = InventoryWithNotPositiveSalesCallReactions.ItemID;

Exhibit 12-29: Items Without Positive Customer Reactions Query

Reservation Association Queries

Reservation associations represent relationships between commitment events and the resources the events are committing to increase or decrease. A *reservation association query* is one that attempts to satisfy information needs about the eventual effect of commitment events on resources or about the resources involved in commitment events.

Some common information needs are
- What resources or resource types is a commitment event agreeing to increase or decrease?
- What quantity of a resource or resource type is a commitment event agreeing to increase or decrease?
- What dollar value of a resource or resource type is a commitment event agreeing to increase or decrease?
- When did an event commit to increase or decrease a specific resource or resource type?
- Where did an event commit to increase or decrease a specific resource or resource type?

Within the acquisition process, the most common commitment events are purchase orders and the most common resource associated with commitment events is inventory type. Some common information needs of these types within the acquisition process are

- Which inventory types does a specific commitment event agree to increase?
- What quantity of each inventory type does a specific commitment event agree to increase?
- What unit cost was quoted for each inventory type in a specific commitment event?
- What was the total dollar value of purchase orders for a specified time period? (Note: If total dollar amount is stored in the purchase order event table, then it is not necessary to use the reservation association to meet this information need.)
- What is the average dollar value of purchase orders of a specified inventory type for a specified time period?

Within the revenue process, the most common commitment events are sale orders and the most common resource associated with commitment events is inventory type. Some common information needs of these types within the revenue process are

- Which inventory types does a specific commitment event agree to decrease?
- What quantity of each inventory type does a specific commitment event agree to decrease?
- What selling price was quoted for each inventory type in a specific commitment event?
- What was the total dollar value of sale orders for a specified time period? (Note: If the total dollar amount is stored in the sale order event table, then it is not necessary to use the reservation association to meet this information need.)
- What is the average dollar value of sale orders of a specified inventory type for a specified time period?

Because these queries are very similar to the examples already illustrated for the proposition and stockflow association queries, no additional examples are displayed in detail.

Participation Association Queries

Participation associations represent relationships between various events and the agents who participate in the events. A *participation association query* is one that attempts to satisfy information needs for identification of which agents participated in events or the events in which agents have participated. Any common information needs on this list could be required for either internal or external agents.

- Which agents participated in a specified event?
- In how many events of a specified type has a specified agent participated?
- What is the total dollar value of events of a specific type in which a specified agent has participated for a specified time period?
- When did a specified event in which a specified agent participated occur?
- Where did a specified event in which a specified agent participated occur?

Within the acquisition process, some common information needs of these types are:
- From which supplier was a purchase made?
- By which purchase agent was a purchase order placed?
- How many purchase orders did a purchase agent make during a time period?
- What is the total or average dollar amount of purchases made by each purchasing agent during a specified time period?
- When was a purchase received, and by which receiving clerk (include clerk's Id, name, and telephone number)?
- To which supplier have the most purchase returns been made?

Within the revenue process, some common information needs of these types are
- To which customer was a sale made?
- By which salesperson was a sale order accepted?
- How many sales calls did a specified salesperson make during a specified time period?
- What is the total (or average) dollar amount of sales made by each salesperson during a specified time period?
- When was a shipment sent to a customer?
- Where did a sales call to a customer take place?

Using the database tables in Exhibit 12-1, we can construct a query to calculate the number of sales calls made by each salesperson for a time period (as well as display salespeople who did not make sales calls during the time period). The tables needed are SalesCall and SalesRepresentative, as the relevant participation association is implemented with SalesRepID posted as a foreign key in the SalesCall table.

Sales Calls by Salesperson Query Step 1 (Exhibit 12-30): Constrain dates on sales calls

```
SELECT SalesCall.SalesCallID, SalesCall.Date, SalesCall.SalesRepID
FROM SalesCall
WHERE (((SalesCall.Date) Between [begindate] And [enddate]));
```

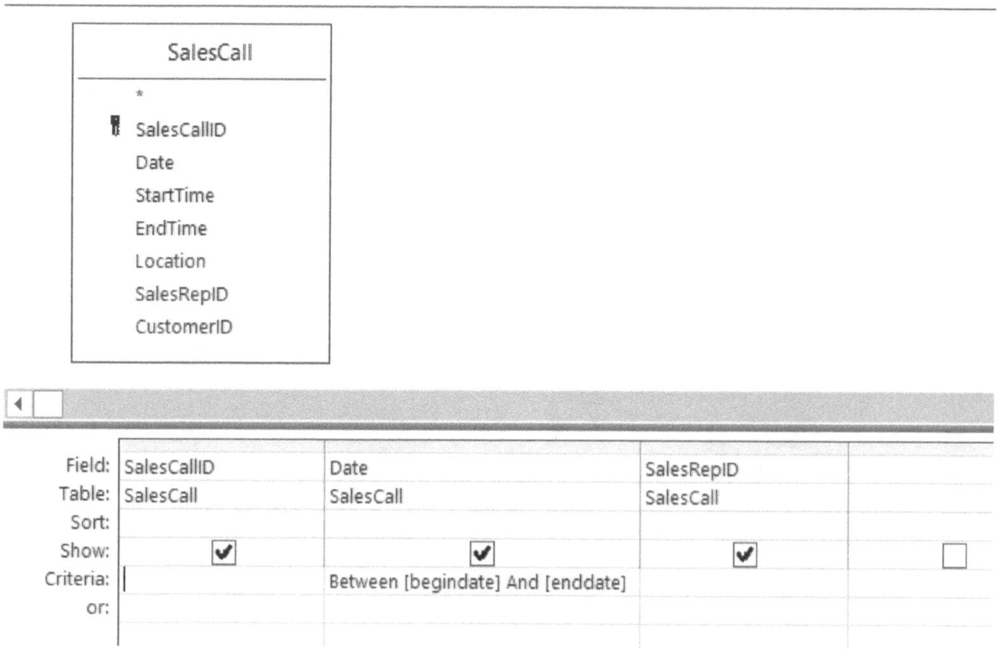

Exhibit 12-30: Sales Calls by Salesperson Query Step 1

Sales Calls by Salesperson Query Step 2 (Exhibit 12-31): Outer join sales representatives to sales calls and count the sales calls made by each representative

    SELECT SalesRepresentative.SalesRepID, SalesRepresentative.Name,
        Count(SalesCallsforTimePeriod.SalesCallID) AS CountOfSalesCallID
    SELECT SalesRepresentative.SalesRepID, SalesRepresentative.FirstName,
        SalesRepresentative.LastName, Count(SalesCallsForTimePeriod.SalesCallID) AS
        CountOfSalesCallID
    FROM SalesRepresentative LEFT JOIN SalesCallsForTimePeriod ON
        SalesRepresentative.SalesRepID = SalesCallsForTimePeriod.SalesRepID
    GROUP BY SalesRepresentative.SalesRepID, SalesRepresentative.FirstName,
        SalesRepresentative.LastName;

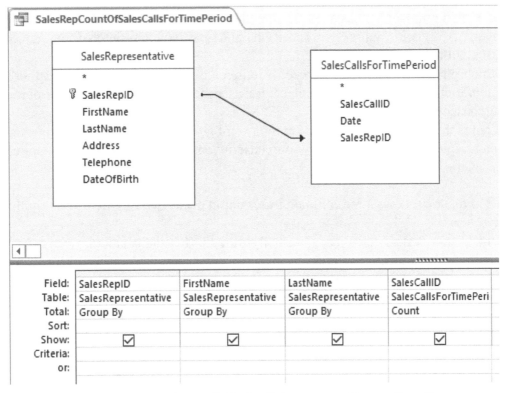

Exhibit 12-31: Sales Calls by Salesperson Query Step 2

You may be wondering why this query was constructed in two steps rather than combining both steps into one. If both steps are combined, any sales representative who has not made any sales calls during the time period identified by the date constraints will not appear in the query result at all (because of the date constraint filter being applied to rows of dates).

ADDITIONAL QUERIES REQUIRING MULTIPLE ASSOCIATIONS
Sometimes information that crosses multiple associations must be retrieved to satisfy an information need. For example, a query that requires information about both a resource and an agent that were involved in an economic event needs to use both a stockflow association and a participation association. These types of queries are the most complicated to construct, and yet are typically the most powerful tools for meeting information needs.

Within the acquisition process, some common information needs that require use of multiple associations are:
- Which purchase orders have been partially filled? (requires stockflow, reservation, and fulfillment-purchaseorder-purchase associations)
- What is the total dollar value of accounts payable to a given supplier at a point in time? (requires duality, participation-supplier-purchase, and participation-supplier-cash disbursement associations)

- On which requisitions has a specific vendor been the recommended supplier for a given inventory type? (requires proposition and participation-purchaserequisition-supplier associations)
- Which purchase agent ordered a specific inventory type from a given supplier? (requires reservation, participation-supplier-purchaseorder, and participation-purchaseagent-purchaseorder associations)
- What is the total dollar amount of purchases of an inventory type made from suppliers in a given region? (requires stockflow-purchase-inventory and participation-supplier-purchase associations)

Within the revenue process, some common information needs that require use of multiple associations are:

- Which sale orders have been partially filled? (Requires stockflow, reservation, and fulfillment-sale-order-sale associations.)
- What is the total dollar value of accounts receivable for a specific customer at a point in time? (Requires duality, participation-customer-sale, and participation-customer-cash receipt associations.)
- What inventory types have been presented to a specific customer in sales calls during a specified time period? (Requires proposition and participation-customer-sales-call associations.)
- Which salesperson presented a specific inventory type to a specific customer? (Requires proposition, participation-customer-sales call, and participation-salesperson-sales-call associations.)
- What is the total dollar amount of sales of an inventory type that have been made to customers in a specific region? (Requires stockflow and participation-customer-sale associations.)
- In what region have sales calls involving a specific inventory type been the most successful? (Requires proposition, fulfillment-sales-call-sale-order, and reservation associations.)

In the earlier discussion of fulfillment association queries, we designed a query set to calculate the average number of days an enterprise had taken to fill sale orders. That query set has one weakness; it does not distinguish a completely filled sale order from a partially filled sale order. As long as the enterprise has sent something from a customer's order to the customer, it counts the order as having been filled for purposes of calculating the days it took to fill the order. When the remainder of the order is filled, that sale date is also factored into the calculation of days to fill the order; in the average calculation it is as if the two parts of the order that are shipped separately are two different orders with the same order date. Over a reasonably long time frame, this distinction is not usually crucial so the query set as shown may be useful. If, however, the enterprise does not want to count an order as filled until it is *completely* filled, or if the firm wants to determine which sale orders have been only partially filled, additional association information is needed.

Using the database tables in this chapter, a query can determine which sale orders have been only partially filled. This query requires information from the sale order event, reservation association, fulfillment association, sale event, and stockflow association. The data needed regarding the sale order event are the order ID (to link to the reservation and fulfillment associations) and the date on which the order was placed. The data needed regarding the sale event are the sale ID (to link to the fulfillment and stockflow associations) and the date on which the sale occurred. In a previous query we saw that it is useful to complete date constraints as a preliminary step in queries that join multiple items together, as it helps to prevent filtering out records that should be included in an answer. The first two steps of the query set next demonstrated thus isolate the sale orders through a user-specified date along with the line items in the reservation table, and isolate the sales through a user-specified date, along with the line items in the stockflow table.

The third step joins the date-constrained reservation result to the fulfillment association table to add the related sale ID to each reservation record; similarly, the fourth step joins the date-constrained stockflow result to the fulfillment association table to add the related sale order ID to each stockflow record. The fifth step joins the results from steps 5 and 6 together based on sale ID, sale order ID, and inventory item ID. The quantity sold field is summed so that if multiple sales applied to the same sale order the total sold can be compared to the quantity ordered. The final (sixth) step subtracts that total sold from the quantity ordered to calculate the unfilled quantity of each item on sale orders that have been at least partially filled.

This series of query steps does not include sale orders that have not been filled at all; additional steps would be needed to include those in the answer. As you can see, queries of multiple associations can become quite complex. It is important to organize your thinking and not combine too many steps.

Partially Filled Orders Query Step 1 (Exhibit 12-32): Constrain sale order date through ending date

```
SELECT SaleOrder.SaleOrderID, SaleOrder.OrderDate,
       ReservationSaleOrderInventoryType.ItemID,
       ReservationSaleOrderInventoryType.QuantityOrdered,
       ReservationSaleOrderInventoryType.QuotedUnitPrice
FROM SaleOrder INNER JOIN ReservationSaleOrderInventoryType ON
       SaleOrder.SaleOrderID = ReservationSaleOrderInventoryType.SaleOrderID
WHERE (((SaleOrder.OrderDate)<=[enddate]));
```

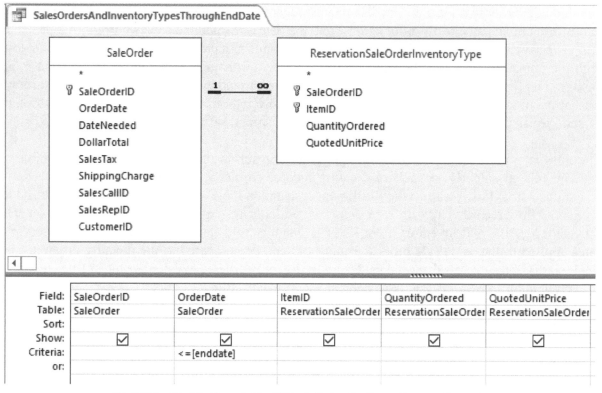

Exhibit 12-32: Partially Filled Sale Orders Query Step 1

Partially Filled Orders Query Step 2 (Exhibit 12-33): Constrain sale date through ending date

    SELECT Sale.SaleID, Sale.Date, StockflowSaleInventoryType.ItemID,
        StockflowSaleInventoryType.QuantitySold,
        StockflowSaleInventoryType.ActualUnitSellingPrice
    FROM Sale INNER JOIN StockflowSaleInventoryType ON Sale.SaleID =
        StockflowSaleInventoryType.SaleID
    WHERE (((Sale.Date)<=[enddate]));

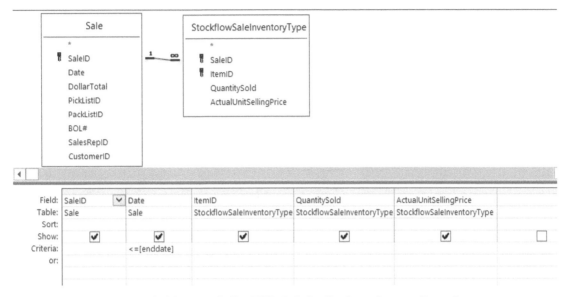

Exhibit 12-33: Partially Filled Sale Orders Query Step 2

Partially Filled Orders Query Step 3 (Exhibit 12-34): Join step 1 result with fulfillment association to link sale orders to sale ids

```
SELECT SalesOrdersAndInventoryTypesThroughEndDate.SaleOrderID,
    SalesOrdersAndInventoryTypesThroughEndDate.ItemID,
    SalesOrdersAndInventoryTypesThroughEndDate.QuantityOrdered,
    FulfillmentSaleOrderSale.SaleID
FROM SalesOrdersAndInventoryTypesThroughEndDate
LEFT JOIN FulfillmentSaleOrderSale ON
    SalesOrdersAndInventoryTypesThroughEndDate.SaleOrderID =
    FulfillmentSaleOrderSale.SaleOrderID;
```

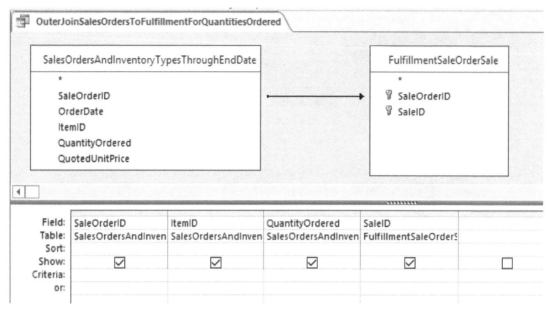

Exhibit 12-34: Partially Filled Sale Orders Query Step 3

Partially Filled Orders Query Step 4 (Exhibit 12-35): Join step 2 result with fulfillment association to link sales to sale order ids

> SELECT FulfillmentSaleOrderSale.SaleOrderID, FulfillmentSaleOrderSale.SaleID,
>   SalesAndInventoryTypesThroughEndDate.ItemID,
>   SalesAndInventoryTypesThroughEndDate.QuantitySold
> FROM SalesAndInventoryTypesThroughEndDate INNER JOIN
>   FulfillmentSaleOrderSale ON SalesAndInventoryTypesThroughEndDate.SaleID
>   = FulfillmentSaleOrderSale.SaleID;

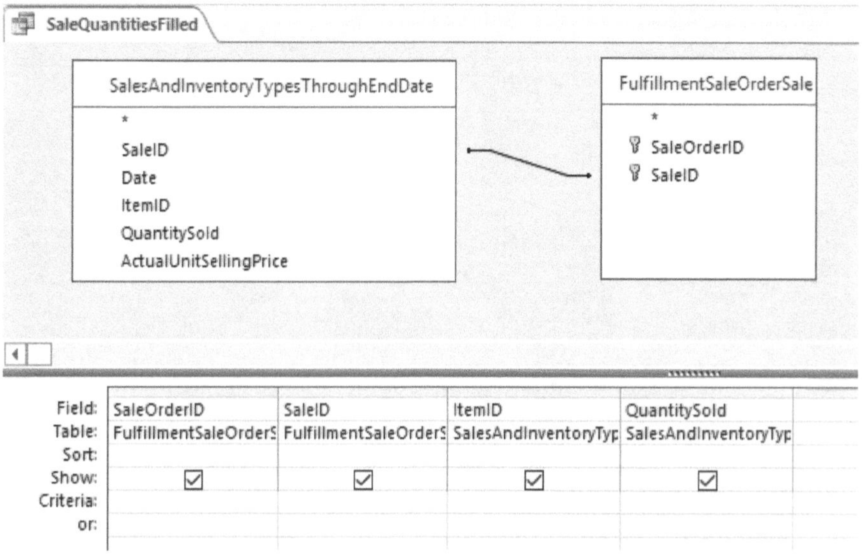

Exhibit 12-35: Partially Filled Sale Orders Query Step 4

Partially Filled Orders Query Step 5 (Exhibit 12-36): Join step 3 and step 4 results, linking by sale id, order id, and item id. Group by sale order id, item id, quantity ordered, and sum the quantities sold

```
SELECT OuterJoinSalesOrdersToFulfillmentForQuantitiesOrdered.SaleOrderID,
     OuterJoinSalesOrdersToFulfillmentForQuantitiesOrdered.ItemID,
     OuterJoinSalesOrdersToFulfillmentForQuantitiesOrdered.QuantityOrdered,
     Sum(SaleQuantitiesFilled.QuantitySold) AS SumOfQuantitySold
FROM OuterJoinSalesOrdersToFulfillmentForQuantitiesOrdered INNER JOIN
     SaleQuantitiesFilled ON
     (OuterJoinSalesOrdersToFulfillmentForQuantitiesOrdered.SaleID =
     SaleQuantitiesFilled.SaleID) AND
     (OuterJoinSalesOrdersToFulfillmentForQuantitiesOrdered.ItemID =
     SaleQuantitiesFilled.ItemID) AND
     (OuterJoinSalesOrdersToFulfillmentForQuantitiesOrdered.SaleOrderID =
     SaleQuantitiesFilled.SaleOrderID)
GROUP BY OuterJoinSalesOrdersToFulfillmentForQuantitiesOrdered.SaleOrderID,
     OuterJoinSalesOrdersToFulfillmentForQuantitiesOrdered.ItemID,
     OuterJoinSalesOrdersToFulfillmentForQuantitiesOrdered.QuantityOrdered;
```

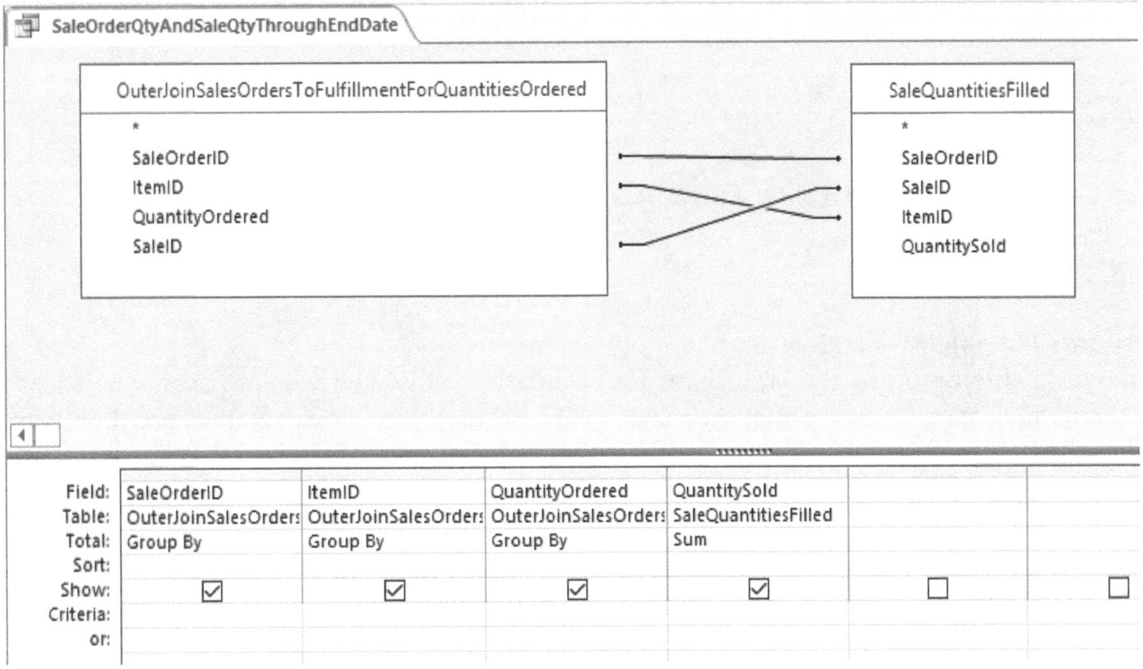

Exhibit 12-36: Partially Filled Sale Orders Query Step 5

Partially Filled Orders Query Step 6 (Exhibit 12-37): Using Step 5 result, subtract sum of quantity sold from quantity ordered to get unfilled quantities of partially filled orders; then exclude differences equal to zero (zeros indicate that the quantity filled is equal to quantity ordered). Test your query using 5/8/2020.

```
SELECT SaleOrderQtyAndSaleQtyThroughEndDate.SaleOrderID,
       SaleOrderQtyAndSaleQtyThroughEndDate.ItemID,
       SaleOrderQtyAndSaleQtyThroughEndDate.QuantityOrdered,
       SaleOrderQtyAndSaleQtyThroughEndDate.SumOfQuantitySold,
       [QuantityOrdered]-[SumOfQuantitySold] AS UnfilledQuantity
FROM SaleOrderQtyAndSaleQtyThroughEndDate
WHERE ((([QuantityOrdered]-[SumOfQuantitySold])<>0));
```

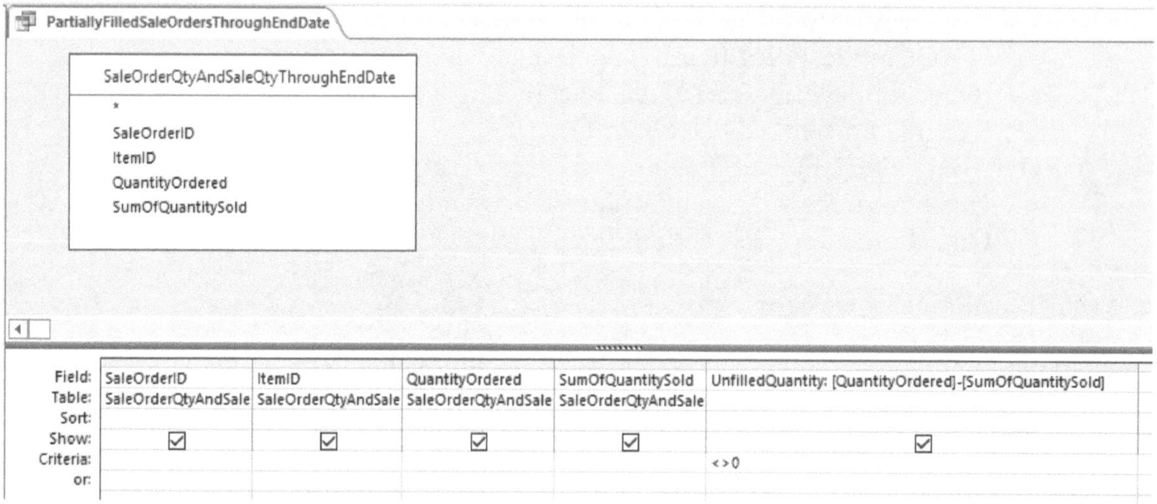

Exhibit 12-37: Partially Filled Sale Orders Query Step 6

Accounts Payable By Vendor

In the acquisition process, the procedures for calculating individual vendor payable balances are similar to those for calculating total accounts payable in aggregate; however, they are slightly more complicated by the addition of the participation associations. The general procedures are as follows:

Determine what kinds of acquisitions are represented in your database (except for labor acquisitions) and for each kind of acquisition follow these steps:

1. Determine which tables contain the acquisition date, dollar amount, and related vendor (usually these are found in the acquisition event table). Group by vendor, and sum the acquisition amount through the balance sheet date (with no beginning date constraint).

2. Determine which tables contain the cash disbursements that applied to those acquisitions. To determine this, examine the duality-purchase-cashdisbursement association.

a. If the duality association is represented with a separate table, join the duality table to the cash disbursement table, establish the ending date constraint on the cash disbursement date field (with no beginning date constraint), group by vendor, and sum the cash disbursement amount applied to the acquisition.

b. If the duality association is represented with the cash disbursement identifier posted as a foreign key into the acquisition table (not likely, unless an implementation compromise was made, as if all purchases have related cash disbursements they would not have accounts payable), join the cash disbursement table to the acquisition table, establish the ending date constraint on the cash disbursement date field (with no beginning date constraint), group by vendor and sum the cash disbursement amounts.

3. Determine which tables contain purchase returns that applied to those acquisitions. To determine this, examine the reversal-purchase-purchasereturn association

a. If the purchase-purchase return association is represented with a separate table, join the purchase return table to the acquisition table, establish the ending date constraint on the purchase return table date field (with no beginning date constraint), group by vendor and sum the purchase return amount applied to the acquisition.

b. If the purchase-purchase return association is represented with purchase ID posted as a foreign key in the purchase return table, establish the ending date constraint on the purchase return table date field (with no beginning date constraint), group by vendor and sum the purchase return amount applied to the acquisition.

4. Subtract the results of steps 2 and 3 from the result of step 1 to get accounts payable for each vendor as of the balance sheet date.

Vendor A/P Query Step 1 (Exhibit 12-38): Constrain purchase date and sum purchase amount per vendor

```
SELECT Purchase.VendorID, Sum(Purchase.DollarAmount) AS SumOfDollarAmount
FROM Purchase
WHERE (((Purchase.Date)<=[enddate]))
GROUP BY Purchase.VendorID;
```

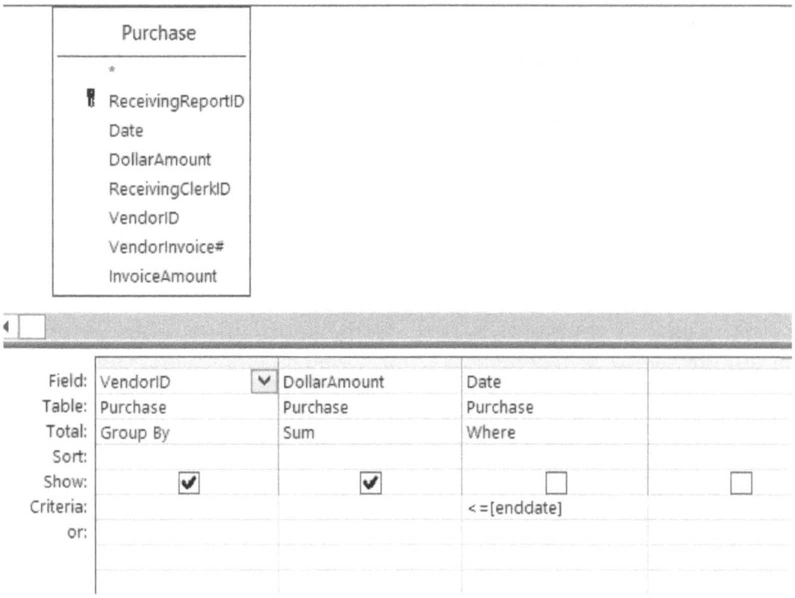

Exhibit 12-38: Accounts Payable Per Vendor Query Step 1

Vendor A/P Query Step 2 (Exhibit 12-39): Join CashDisbursement, Purchase, and DualityPurchaseCashDisbursement tables, group by vendor, constrain payment date, sum amount applied

SELECT CashDisbursement.PayeeID, Sum(DualityPurchaseCashDisbursement.[Amount
    Applied]) AS [SumOfAmount Applied]
FROM Purchase INNER JOIN (CashDisbursement INNER JOIN
    DualityPurchaseCashDisbursement ON CashDisbursement.DisbVoucherID =
    DualityPurchaseCashDisbursement.DisbVoucherID) ON
    Purchase.ReceivingReportID =
    DualityPurchaseCashDisbursement.ReceivingReportID
WHERE ((((CashDisbursement.VoucherDate)<=[enddate]))
GROUP BY CashDisbursement.PayeeID;

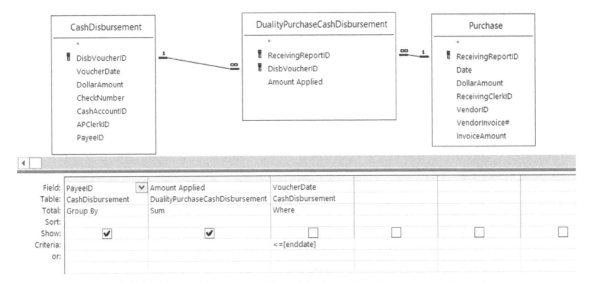

Exhibit 12-39: Accounts Payable Per Vendor Query Step 2

Vendor A/P Query Step 3 (Exhibit 12-40): Join Purchase and PurchaseReturn tables, constrain return date

```
SELECT PurchaseReturn.VendorID, Sum(PurchaseReturn.DollarAmount) AS
        SumOfDollarAmount
FROM PurchaseReturn
WHERE (((PurchaseReturn.Date)<=[enddate]))
GROUP BY PurchaseReturn.VendorID;
```

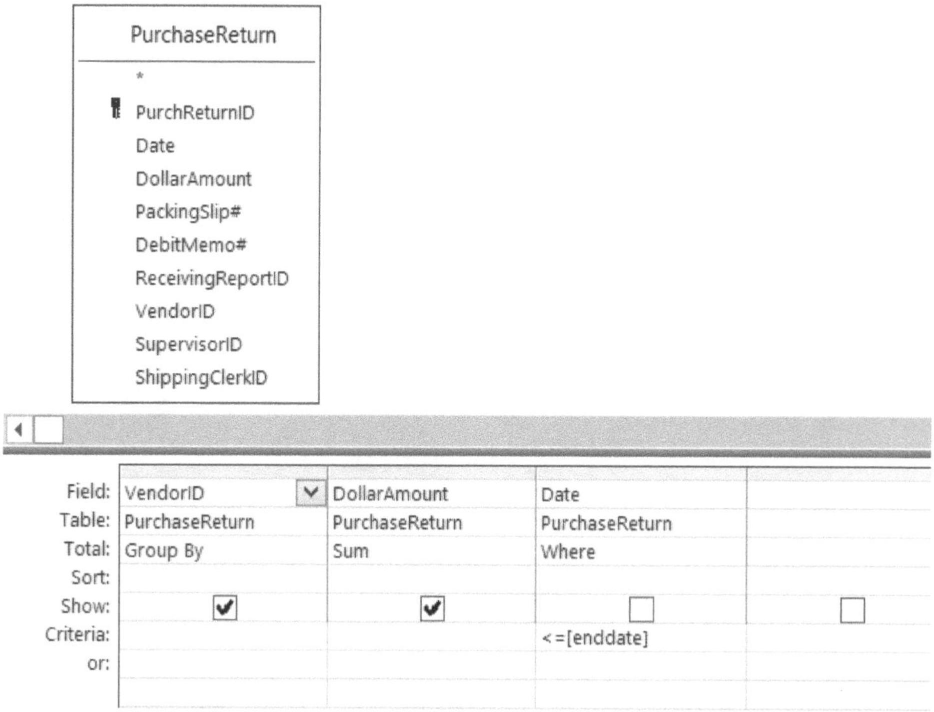

PurchaseReturn

- PurchReturnID
- Date
- DollarAmount
- PackingSlip#
- DebitMemo#
- ReceivingReportID
- VendorID
- SupervisorID
- ShippingClerkID

Field:	VendorID	DollarAmount	Date	
Table:	PurchaseReturn	PurchaseReturn	PurchaseReturn	
Total:	Group By	Sum	Where	
Sort:				
Show:	✔	✔	☐	☐
Criteria:			<=[enddate]	
or:				

Exhibit 12-40: Accounts Payable Per Vendor Query Step 3

Vendor A/P Query Step 4 (Exhibit 12-41): Join query steps 1 and 3 to calculate unreturned (net) purchases per vendor

```
SELECT PurchasesByVendorThroughEndDate.VendorID,
      Nz([PurchasesByVendorThroughEndDate]![SumOfDollarAmount])-
      Nz([PurchaseReturnsByVendorThroughEndDate]![SumOfDollarAmount]) AS
      UnreturnedPurchases
FROM PurchasesByVendorThroughEndDate LEFT JOIN
      PurchaseReturnsByVendorThroughEndDate ON
      PurchasesByVendorThroughEndDate.VendorID =
      PurchaseReturnsByVendorThroughEndDate.VendorID;
```

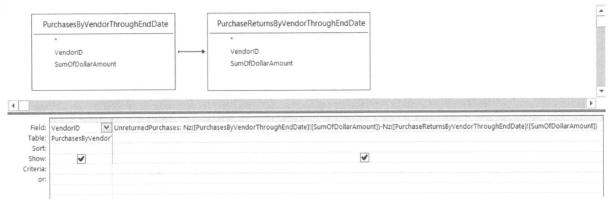

Exhibit 12-41: Accounts Payable Per Vendor Query Step 4

Vendor A/P Query Step 5 (Exhibit 12-42): Join query steps 4 and 2 to calculate unpaid, unreturned purchases (i.e., accounts payable) per vendor

SELECT UnreturnedPurchasesByVendorThroughEndDate.VendorID,
   Nz([UnreturnedPurchasesByVendorThroughEndDate]![UnreturnedPurchases])-
   Nz([IDAndSumCDAppliedToPurchasesByVendor]![SumOfAmount Applied])
   AS AcctsPayable
FROM UnreturnedPurchasesByVendorThroughEndDate LEFT JOIN
   IDAndSumCDAppliedToPurchasesByVendor ON
   UnreturnedPurchasesByVendorThroughEndDate.VendorID =
   IDAndSumCDAppliedToPurchasesByVendor.PayeeID;

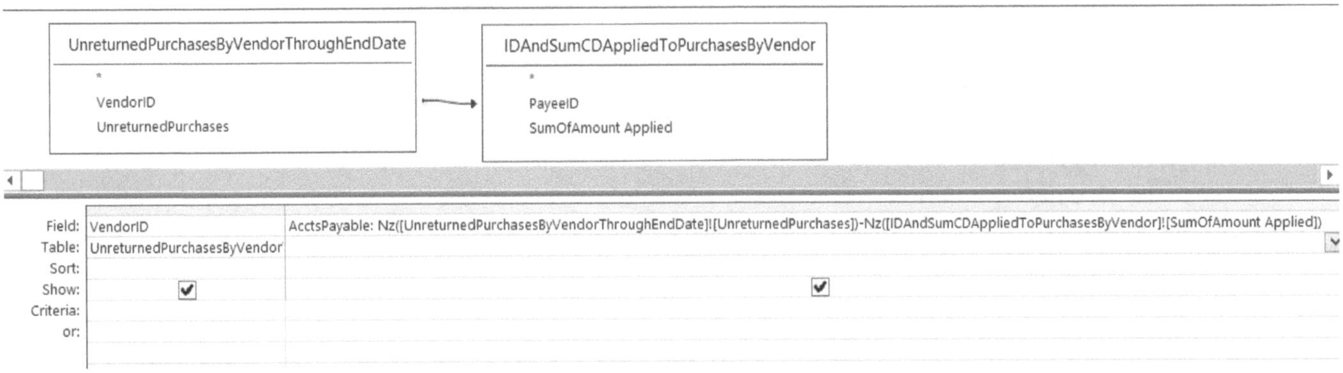

Exhibit 12-42: Accounts Payable Per Vendor Query Step 5

Note that query steps 4 and 5 should not be combined into a single query step because outer joins are needed to include purchases from vendors to whom neither payments nor returns have been made. Inclusion of two outer joins in the same query is too ambiguous for some database engines to process.

CONCLUDING COMMENTS

This chapter applied the information retrieval concepts discussed in chapter 11 to the revenue and acquisition business processes to illustrate how to create queries to satisfy representative information needs. Some queries were relatively simple, requiring information from within one class or association. Other queries were complex, requiring information from multiple classes and associations. The queries presented represent only a tiny fraction of the many different information needs that enterprises have on a daily basis. One goal of this chapter is to enable students who will one day face the task of meeting enterprise information needs to think creatively and generate queries to meet those information needs. The database tables presented in this chapter are not comprehensive. Database tables in real-world enterprise system applications have dozens (sometimes even hundreds) of attributes. Examination of the attributes available in an enterprise system database is a critical step in developing queries that report values of those attributes in the format a specific user needs. Practicing the queries illustrated in this chapter is a good starting point, but you will need to exercise your creativity and critical thinking to apply similar thinking to build queries for the same information needs using alternative databases and to build queries for different information needs.

KEY TERMS AND CONCEPTS

Accounts payable query steps
Accounts receivable query steps
Acquisition process queries
Agent queries
Duality association queries
Event queries
Fulfillment association query
Null-to-zero (Nz) function in Microsoft Access
Partially filled order query steps
Participation association queries
Proposition association queries
Reservation association queries
Resource queries
Revenue process queries
Reversal association queries
Single process queries
Stockflow association queries
Unearned revenue query steps
Weighted average unit cost query steps

REVIEW QUESTIONS

R12-1. For a neighborhood pizza restaurant, list three kinds of information one should be able to obtain with a resource or resource type query in the acquisition or revenue process.

R12-2. For a dentist with just one location, list three kinds of information one should be able to obtain with a fulfillment association query in either the acquisition or revenue process.

R12-3. What is the Nz function in Microsoft Access, and why would one want to use it?

R12-4. In Microsoft Access query design view, what are the two ways to accomplish a logical OR operation? I.e., to find a field's values that are either A or B.

R12-5. On what revenue process association should one focus when designing queries to calculate both accounts receivable and unearned revenue?

MULTIPLE CHOICE QUESTIONS

MC12-1. Which of the following information needs in the acquisition/payment process requires multiple relationships?
   A) To which supplier have the most purchase returns been made?
   B) Which inventory types were identified as needed in a purchase requisition event?
   C) On which requisitions was a specific inventory type requested from a specific recommended supplier?
   D) When was a specific purchase received, and by which receiving clerk?

MC12-2. Which of the following information needs can be met using only one relationship in the revenue cycle?
   A) Which sale orders have been partially filled?
   B) Which salesperson presented a specific inventory type to a specific customer?
   C) Which inventory types were delivered in a specific sale event?
   D) What is the total dollar value of accounts receivable for a specific customer at a point in time?

MC12-3. Which of the following is an example of an information need that could be satisfied by an event query in the revenue cycle?
   A) What is the name and address of the salesperson with the highest dollar sales for a specific time period?
   B) A list of open sale orders
   C) What is the total dollar amount of a specific sale?
   D) A list of inventory items that have a list selling price higher than $100

MC12-4. Which of the following information needs in the acquisition/payment process requires multiple relationships?
   A) To which supplier have the most purchase returns been made?
   B) Which inventory types were identified as needed in a purchase requisition event?
   C) On which requisitions was a specific inventory type requested from a specific recommended supplier?
   D) When was a specific purchase received, and by which receiving clerk?

MC12-5. A list of all science fiction titles owned by a bookstore is an information need that could be answered by what type of query?
   A) Event query
   B) Agent query
   C) Resource query
   D) Fulfillment query
   E) Duality query

MC12-6. Which operation would you use to total purchases for each individual purchase agent?
   A) GROUP BY
   B) WHERE
   C) EQUALS
   D) BETWEEN

MC12-7. Examine the relational tables depicted below. A user needs a query that includes InventoryStockID, and Description from the inventory table and the corresponding SaleIDs and Quantities Sold from the Stockflow1 table. Inventory items that have not yet been sold should be included in the query result, with blanks showing for the corresponding Sale IDs and Quantities Sold. What kind of join is required to generate the desired result? Assume the Inventory table is the left table and the Stockflow table is the right table.

Inventory

InventoryStockID	Description	List Price	Standard Cost
ABC123	Huge	$475	$208
BCD234	Large	$360	$190
CDE345	Medium	$245	$165

Stockflow1

SaleID	InventoryStockID	QuantitySold	ActualUnitPrice
100001	ABC123	5	$450
100001	BCD234	10	$340
100002	ABC123	1	$460
100003	BCD234	50	$330

   A) A left inner join is required
   B) A right inner join is required
   C) A right outer join is required
   D) A left outer join is required

MC12-8. Which information need focuses on a Stockflow association in the revenue process?
   A) Calculation of the quantity of each inventory type that was increased by a specific sale return event
   B) Creation of an open sale order file
   C) Identification of the customer to whom a specific sale was made
   D) Identification of which types of inventory were presented in a specific sales call

MC12-9. Examine the tables from Stanwood Company's database. Calculate the total dollar amount of sales made by Jayne Joseph for the time period covered by this database.

Sale-Inventory-Line-Item

Sale ID	Stock Number	Sale Quantity	Sale Unit Price	Extended Sale Line
06050800	1234	2,000	$1.90	$3,800
06050800	3456	1,000	$12.00	$12,000
06050800	5678	700	$13.00	$9,100
06060900	1234	1,000	$2.10	$2,100
06081000	1234	2,000	$1.90	$3,800
06100800	7890	1,000	$20.00	$20,000
06130800	1234	2,000	$1.90	$3,800
06190800	3456	4,000	$11.00	$44,000
06190800	5678	1,500	$12.00	$18,000
06211000	1234	2,000	$1.90	$3,800
06260800	5678	800	$13.00	$10,400

Sale

Sale ID	Invoice Number	Customer Number[FK]	Salesperson Number[FK]	Cash Receipt ID[FK]
06050800	1	C100	E304	06210800
06060900	2	C101	E304	06210900
06081000	3	C102	E301	06230800
06100800	4	C100	E304	06210800
06130800	5	C100	E304	06210800
06190800	6	C105	E304	
06211000	7	C104	E301	
06260800	8	C101	E301	

Inventory

Stock Number	Description	Weighted Avg Unit Cost
1234	A	$1.00
3456	B	$6.00
5678	C	$7.00
7890	D	$10.00

Employee

Employee Number	First Name	Last Name	City Address	Street Address	Pay Rate	Birth Date	Employee Category
E300	Bob	Cronk	Lake City	Colorado Dr	$40.00	1968	President
E301	Tess	Smith	Lake City	Colorado Dr	$36.00	1969	Sales
E302	Linda	Kay	Hillview	Clinton St	$28.00	1969	Cashier
E303	Lorie	Elitzr	Hillview	Pleasant St	$30.00	1966	AP-Pr Clerk
E304	Cheryl	Lindon	Lake City	France Dr	$36.00	1964	Sales
E305	James	Woodrof	Lake City	92nd St	$32.00	1962	Buyer

A) $ 18,000
B) $130,800
C) $ 3,800
D) $ 32,200

MC12-10. Given the following tables and query (provided in both Access design view and SQL formats), what is the most likely output to result?

Sale

SaleID	SaleDate	SaleAmount
42	06/10/2020	$5,000.00
43	06/10/2020	$3,000.00
44	06/11/2020	$1,000.00
45	06/12/2020	$750.00

SaleCR

SaleID	CRID	AmountApplied
42	17	$500.00
42	19	$4,000.00
43	18	$3,000.00
45	18	$750.00

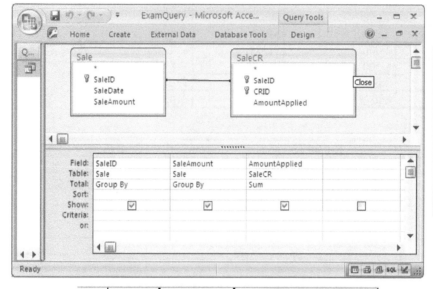

SELECT Sale.SaleID,
Sale.SaleAmount,
Sum(SaleCR.AmountApplied) as
SumOfAmountApplied
FROM Sale INNER JOIN SaleCR
ON Sale.SaleID = SaleCR.SaleID
GROUP BY Sale.SaleID,
Sale.SaleAmount;

A)

SaleID	SaleAmount	SumOfAmountApplied
42	$5,000.00	$4,500.00
43	$3,000.00	$3,000.00
44	$1,000.00	
45	$750.00	$750.00

B)

SaleID	SaleAmount	SumOfAmountApplied
42	$5,000.00	$4,500.00
43	$3,000.00	$3,000.00
45	$750.00	$750.00

C)

SaleID	SaleAmount	AmountApplied	ARAmt
42	$5,000.00	$500.00	$4,500.00
42	$5,000.00	$4,000.00	$1,000.00
43	$3,000.00	$3,000.00	$0.00
45	$750.00	$750.00	$0.00

D)

SaleID	SaleAmount	SumOfAmountApplied	ARAmt
42	$5,000.00	$4,500.00	500
43	$3,000.00	$3,000.00	0
44	$1,000.00		1000
45	$750.00	$750.00	0

CHAPTER 13

Acquisition and Revenue Accounting Analytics – Multiple Process

LEARNING OBJECTIVES
This chapter illustrates the increased complexity of satisfying information needs that combine data from both the acquisition and revenue business processes. Queries that satisfy such information needs will always involve multiple steps with queries that build on other queries. Many such queries focus on resources that are common to multiple business processes (recall the REA value chain models from previous chapters that illustrate how resources connect business processes). After studying this chapter, you should be able to

1. Identify information needs that require information across multiple associations and across multiple business processes
2. Create queries to satisfy information needs that require information from multiple business processes

INFORMATION NEEDS WITH DATA FROM MULTIPLE BUSINESS PROCESSES
Multiple process queries require data from two or more business processes. The thought process for how to combine the processes is similar to what we discussed for view integration in chapter 6. Classes that are common across the different processes (usually resource or agent classes) are natural points of integration. For acquisition and revenue processes, the common classes are often cash and inventory. In this chapter we will base our queries on the tables in chapter 12, Exhibit 12-1. You should already be familiar with those tables from working with them in chapter 12.

Cash Balance
The calculations of cash balances (either for one or more specific accounts, or for the total balance of all cash accounts) are typically affected by all business processes except the conversion process. In a database these accounts are usually represented in a cash class table; however, the account balance is a volatile derivable attribute that is not stored unless the software is capable of triggers. Therefore, a set of queries is needed to calculate the total cash receipts through the date for which the balance is needed; then to calculate the total cash disbursements through the date for which the balance is needed; and finally to subtract the total cash disbursements from the total cash receipts. If the cash receipt amounts and the cash disbursement amounts are stored as attributes in the cash receipt and cash disbursement tables, respectively, the querying is quite simple. If the company only stores amounts in duality association tables, then all the appropriate duality tables need to be joined to the cash receipt and disbursement event tables to apply the date constraints and get the totals. Most companies recognize the value of storing the amount field in the cash receipt and disbursement event tables, so we consider that case and ignore the more complicated possibility.

The process for querying to provide the cash balance on a given date is typically as follows.

1. Determine which table contains the cash receipt date (usually this is in the table that represents the cash receipt event) and make sure the same table also contains the cash receipt amount field.

2. Determine which table contains the cash disbursement date (usually this is in the table that represents the cash disbursement event) and make sure the same table also contains the cash disbursement amount field.

3. Create a query that establishes the ending date constraint (with no beginning date constraint) and **sum** the dollar amount field in the table identified in step 1.

4. Create a query that establishes the ending date constraint (with no beginning date constraint) and sum the dollar amount field in the table identified in step 2.

5. Create a query that subtracts the total in step 4 from the total in step 3.

Cash Query Step 1 (Exhibit 13-1): Sum cash receipt amounts through a balance sheet date

    SELECT Sum(CashReceipt.DollarTotal) AS SumOfDollarTotal
    FROM CashReceipt
    WHERE (((CashReceipt.Date)<=[enddate]));

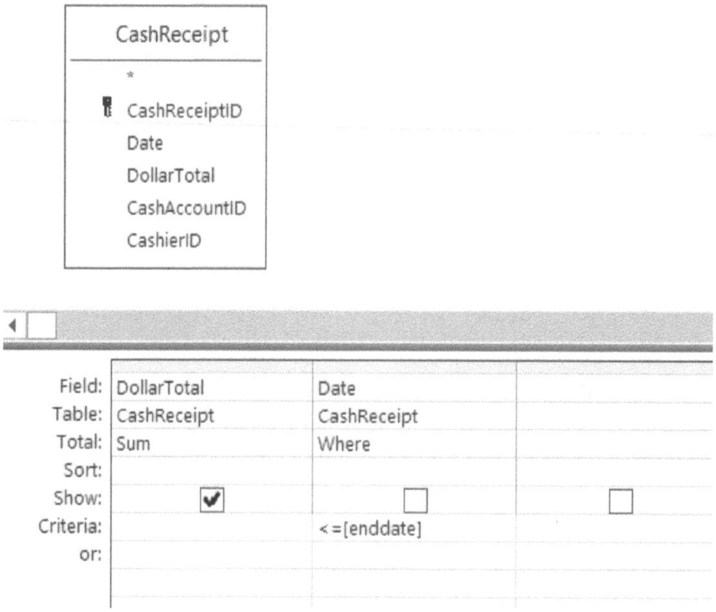

Exhibit 13-1: Cash Balance Query Step 1

Cash Query Step 2 (Exhibit 13-2): Sum cash disbursement amounts through balance date

```
SELECT Sum(CashDisbursement.DollarAmount) AS SumOfDollarAmount
FROM CashDisbursement
WHERE (((CashDisbursement.VoucherDate)<=[enddate]));
```

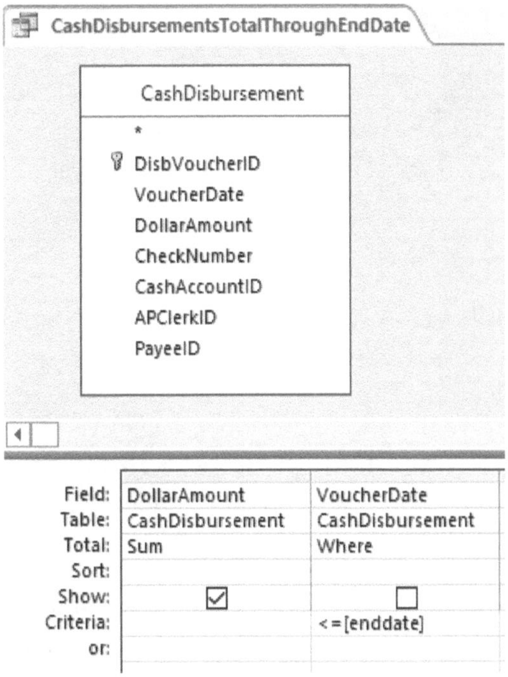

Exhibit 13-2: Cash Balance Query Step 2

Cash Query Step 3 (Exhibit 13-3): Subtract step 2 result from step 1 result

```
SELECT CashReceiptsTotalThroughEndDate.SumOfDollarTotal,
    CashDisbursementsTotalThroughEndDate.SumOfDollarAmount,
    Nz([CashReceiptsTotalThroughEndDate]![SumOfDollarTotal])-
    Nz([CashDisbursementsTotalThroughEndDate]![SumOfDollarAmount]) AS
    Balance
FROM CashReceiptsTotalThroughEndDate, CashDisbursementsTotalThroughEndDate;
```

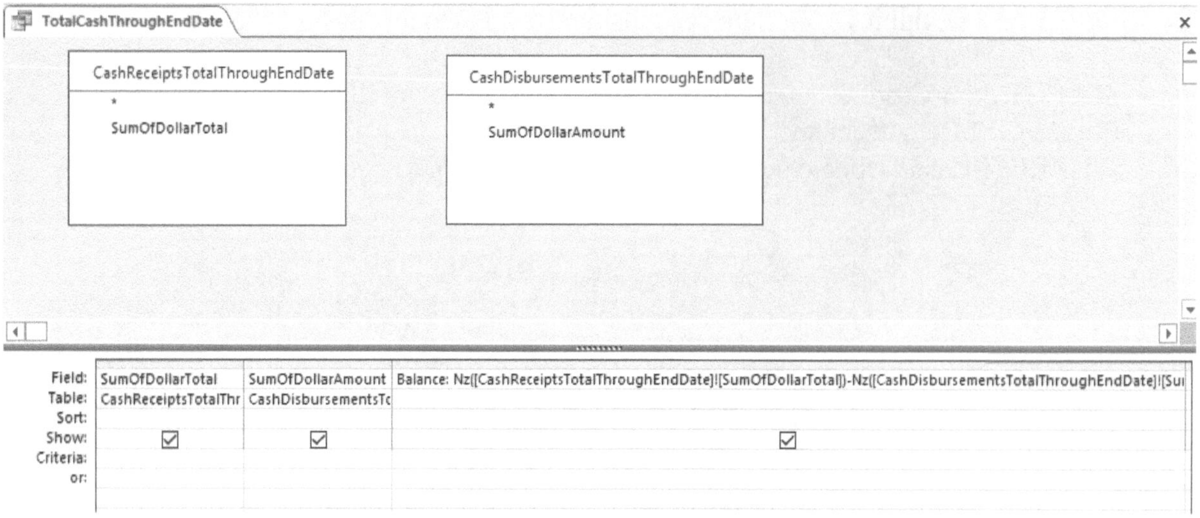

Exhibit 13-3: Cash Balance Query Step 3

INVENTORY INFORMATION ACROSS BUSINESS PROCESSES

Several needs for inventory-related information require integration of data from multiple business processes. Examples include calculations of the quantity on hand for inventory on a given date, calculations of the dollar cost value of inventory on hand on a specific date, and calculations of the dollar cost value of inventory that was sold during a given time period. We first demonstrate an example query set to calculate the quantity on hand of each inventory item based on the enterprise database tables in chapter 12, Exhibit 12-1. Following that, we demonstrate queries that calculate the cost values of inventory on hand and the cost of inventory sold.

Inventory Quantities On Hand

Quantity on hand consists of quantities purchased minus quantities returned minus quantities sold through a given ending date (with no beginning date constraint). Notice the similarity to the calculation of cash balance, which was the amount of cash receipts minus the amount of cash disbursements through a specific date. The pattern for both calculations is that balance equals inflows minus outflows. An important difference between the queries we illustrated for the total cash balance and the queries we next illustrate for the quantity on hand of each inventory item is the fact that for inventory we calculate a separate balance for each item type whereas for cash query we calculated just one overall balance. Companies with multiple cash accounts will certainly want separate balances calculated for each of their accounts; to meet that need, you would employ similar procedures as those we next describe for inventory.

The procedures for calculating inventory item quantities on hand typically are as follows.

1. Determine which table contains the purchase date attribute (usually this is in the table that represents the purchase economic event).

2. Determine which table contains the purchase quantity attribute and the item ID (usually this is in the table that represents the stockflow association between the purchase economic event and the inventory resource).

3. Determine which table contains the purchase return date attribute (usually this is in the table that represents the purchase return economic event).

4. Determine which table contains the quantity returned attribute and the item ID (usually this is in the table that represents the stockflow association between the purchase return economic event and the inventory resource).

5. Determine which table contains the sale date attribute (usually this is in the table that represents the sale economic event).

6. Determine which table contains the quantity sold attribute and the item id (usually this is in the table that represents the stockflow association between the sale economic event and the inventory resource).

7. Determine which table contains the sale return date attribute (usually this is in the table that represents the sale return economic event).

8. Determine which table contains the quantity returned attribute and the item ID (usually this is in the table that represents the stockflow association between the sale return economic event and the inventory resource).

9. Join the tables identified in steps 1 and 2, group by inventory item, set the ending date constraint (with no beginning date constraint) and sum the quantity purchased to get the total quantity purchased per inventory item. Make sure to include the inventory item identifier attribute in the query result to provide a means for linking to the results of other steps.

10. Join the tables identified in steps 3 and 4, group by inventory item, set the ending date constraint (with no beginning date constraint) and sum the quantity returned to get the total quantity returned per inventory item. Make sure to include the inventory item identifier attribute in the query result to provide a means for linking to the results of other steps.

11. Join the tables identified in steps 5 and 6, group by inventory item, set the ending date constraint (with no beginning date constraint) and sum the quantity sold to get the total quantity sold per inventory item. Make sure to include the inventory item identifier attribute in the query result to provide a means for linking to the results of other steps.

12. Join the tables identified in steps 7 and 8, group by inventory item, set the ending date constraint (with no beginning date constraint) and sum the quantity returned to get the total quantity of sale returns per inventory item. Be sure to include the inventory item identifier attribute in the query result to provide a means for linking to the results of other steps.

13. Join the results from steps 9 and 10. Change the join type to include all records from the total quantity purchased query and the matches from the total quantity returned query. The null to zero (Nz) function is necessary in the calculation to subtract the total quantity returned from the total quantity purchased. For example, this calculation expression would look something like this (depending on the query's variable names):

   Nz(SumPurchaseQty) – Nz(SumQtyReturned).

   This formula results in the unreturned purchase quantities for each item.

14. Join the results from steps 11 and 12. Change the join type to include all records from the total quantity sold query and the matches from the total sale return quantity. The null to zero (Nz) function is necessary in the calculation to subtract the total quantity returned from the total quantity sold. For example, this calculation expression would look something like this (depending on the query's variable names):

   Nz(SumQtySold)-Nz(SumSaleReturnQty).

15. Join the results from step 13 with the results from step 14. Change the join type to include all records from the total unreturned quantities purchased query and the matches from the total unreturned quantities sold query. The null to zero (Nz) function is needed in the calculation to subtract the total unreturned quantity sold from the total unreturned purchase quantity. For example, this calculation expression would look something like this (depending on the query's variable names):

   Nz(SumUnreturnedPurchaseQty) – Nz(SumUnreturnedSaleQty)

   This query result yields the total quantity on hand separately for each inventory item.

Inventory QOH Query 1 (Exhibit 13-4): Accomplish steps 1, 2, and 9 – Constrain purchase date, sum quantities by type

```
SELECT StockflowPurchaseInventoryType.ItemID,
       Sum(StockflowPurchaseInventoryType.QuantityPurchased) AS
       SumOfQuantityPurchased
FROM Purchase INNER JOIN StockflowPurchaseInventoryType ON
       Purchase.ReceivingReportID =
       StockflowPurchaseInventoryType.ReceivingReportID
WHERE (((Purchase.Date)<=[enddate]))
GROUP BY StockflowPurchaseInventoryType.ItemID;
```

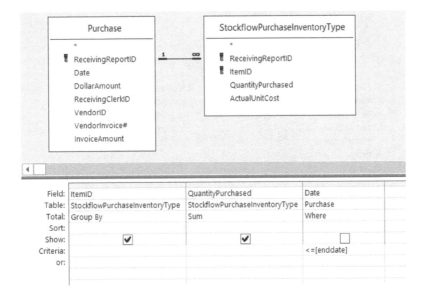

Exhibit 13-4: Inventory Quantity On Hand Query 1

Inventory QOH Query 2 (Exhibit 13-5): Accomplish steps 3, 4, and 10 – Constrain return date, sum quantities by type

> SELECT StockflowPurchaseReturnInventoryType.ItemID,
>   Sum(StockflowPurchaseReturnInventoryType.QuantityReturned) AS
>   SumOfQuantityReturned
> FROM PurchaseReturn INNER JOIN StockflowPurchaseReturnInventoryType ON
>   PurchaseReturn.PurchReturnID =
>   StockflowPurchaseReturnInventoryType.PurchReturnID
> WHERE (((PurchaseReturn.Date)<=[enddate]))
> GROUP BY StockflowPurchaseReturnInventoryType.ItemID;

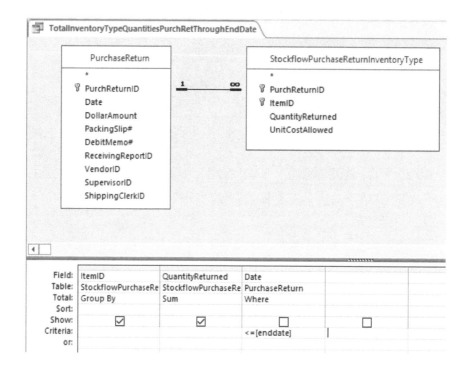

Exhibit 13-5: Inventory Quantity on Hand Query 2

Inventory QOH Query 3 (Exhibit 13-6): Accomplish steps 5, 6, and 11 – Constrain sale date; Sum quantities sold by type

```
SELECT StockflowSaleInventoryType.ItemID,
       Sum(StockflowSaleInventoryType.QuantitySold) AS SumOfQuantitySold
FROM Sale INNER JOIN StockflowSaleInventoryType ON Sale.SaleID =
       StockflowSaleInventoryType.SaleID
WHERE (((Sale.Date)<=[enddate]))
GROUP BY StockflowSaleInventoryType.ItemID;
```

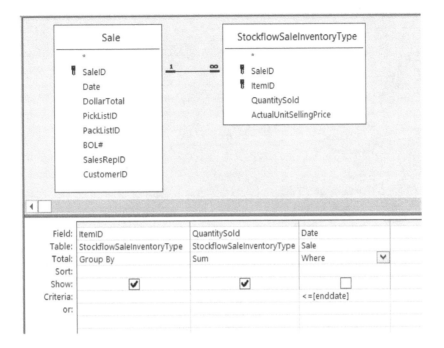

Exhibit 13-6: Inventory Quantity on Hand Query 3

Inventory QOH Query 4 (Exhibit 13-7): Accomplish steps 7, 8, and 12 - Constrain sale return date, sum quantities by type

```
SELECT StockflowSaleReturnInventoryType.ItemID,
        Sum(StockflowSaleReturnInventoryType.QuantityReturned) AS
        SumOfQuantityReturned
FROM SaleReturn INNER JOIN StockflowSaleReturnInventoryType ON
        SaleReturn.SaleReturnID = StockflowSaleReturnInventoryType.SaleReturnID
WHERE (((SaleReturn.Date)<=[enddate]))
GROUP BY StockflowSaleReturnInventoryType.ItemID;
```

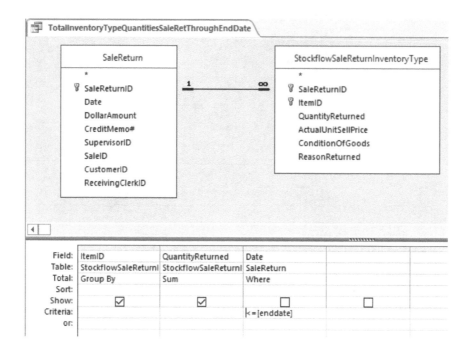

Exhibit 13-7: Inventory Quantity on Hand Query 4

Inventory QOH Query 5 (Exhibit 13-8): Accomplish step 13 – Calculate unreturned purchase quantities by item

```
SELECT TotalInventoryTypeQuantitiesPurchasedThroughEndDate.ItemID,
    TotalInventoryTypeQuantitiesPurchasedThroughEndDate.SumOfQuantityPurchased,
    TotalInventoryTypeQuantitiesPurchRetThroughEndDate.SumOfQuantityReturned,
    Nz([TotalInventoryTypeQuantitiesPurchasedThroughEndDate]![SumOfQuantityPurchased])
    -Nz([TotalInventoryTypeQuantitiesPurchRetThroughEndDate]![SumOfQuantityReturned])
    AS NetPurchaseQuantity
FROM TotalInventoryTypeQuantitiesPurchasedThroughEndDate
LEFT JOIN TotalInventoryTypeQuantitiesPurchRetThroughEndDate ON
    TotalInventoryTypeQuantitiesPurchasedThroughEndDate.ItemID =
    TotalInventoryTypeQuantitiesPurchRetThroughEndDate.ItemID;
```

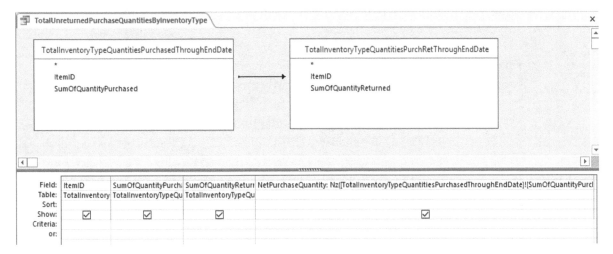

Exhibit 13-8: Inventory Quantity on Hand Query 5

Inventory QOH Query 6 (Exhibit 13-9): Accomplish step 14 – Calculate unreturned sale quantities by item

> SELECT TotalInventoryTypeQuantitiesSoldThroughEndDate.ItemID,
>   TotalInventoryTypeQuantitiesSoldThroughEndDate.SumOfQuantitySold,
>   TotalInventoryTypeQuantitiesSaleRetThroughEndDate.SumOfQuantityReturned,
>   Nz([TotalInventoryTypeQuantitiesSoldThroughEndDate]![SumOfQuantitySold])-
>   Nz([TotalInventoryTypeQuantitiesSaleRetThroughEndDate]![SumOfQuantityReturned])
>   AS UnreturnedQtySold
> FROM TotalInventoryTypeQuantitiesSoldThroughEndDate
> LEFT JOIN TotalInventoryTypeQuantitiesSaleRetThroughEndDate ON
>   TotalInventoryTypeQuantitiesSoldThroughEndDate.ItemID =
>   TotalInventoryTypeQuantitiesSaleRetThroughEndDate.ItemID;

Exhibit 13-9: Inventory Quantity on Hand Query 6

Inventory QOH Query 7 (Exhibit 13-10): Accomplish step 15 - Calculate quantity on hand by item

```
SELECT TotalUnreturnedPurchaseQuantitiesByInventoryType.ItemID,
    TotalUnreturnedPurchaseQuantitiesByInventoryType.NetPurchaseQuantity,
    TotalUnreturnedSaleQuantitesByInventoryType.UnreturnedQtySold,
    Nz([TotalUnreturnedPurchaseQuantitiesByInventoryType]![NetPurchaseQuantity])
    -Nz([TotalUnreturnedSaleQuantitesByInventoryType]![UnreturnedQtySold]) AS
    QOH
FROM TotalUnreturnedPurchaseQuantitiesByInventoryType
LEFT JOIN TotalUnreturnedSaleQuantitesByInventoryType ON
    TotalUnreturnedPurchaseQuantitiesByInventoryType.ItemID =
    TotalUnreturnedSaleQuantitesByInventoryType.ItemID;
```

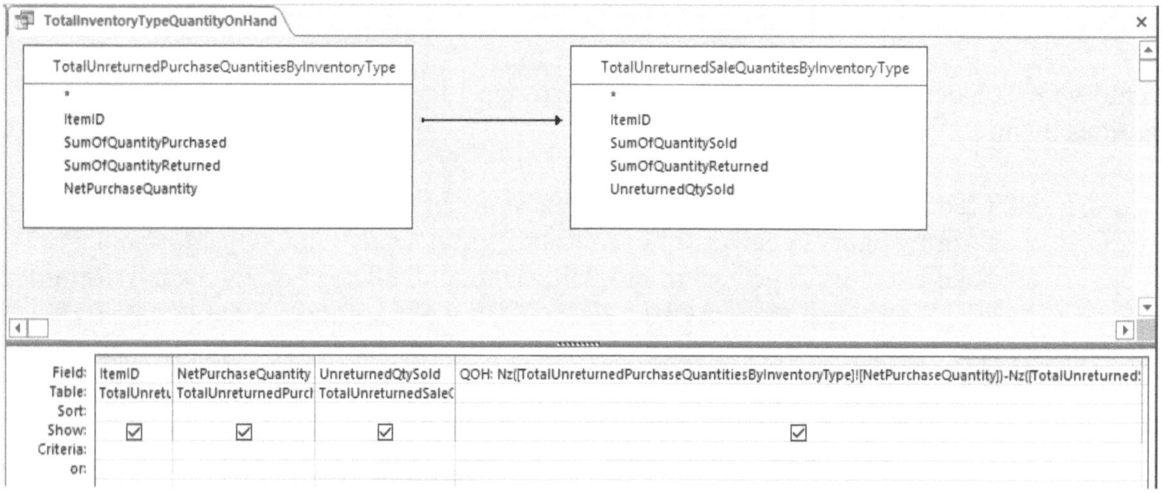

Exhibit 13-10: Inventory Quantity on Hand Query 7

Inventory Cost (Dollar Value for Balance Sheet)

Once the quantities on hand of inventory types are calculated for a given date, an enterprise also may want to assign cost values to those inventory types. Various cost assumptions may be used to assign costs to inventory types, including weighted average unit cost, first-in-first-out (FIFO), and last-in-first-out (LIFO). The assignment of costs based on FIFO or LIFO entails the writing of program code that is too complex for this book. The assignment of weighted average unit costs to inventory types on hand is less complex and can be accomplished without extensive program code, as previously demonstrated in this chapter when we calculated the weighted average unit cost of inventory purchased during a time period. As the next set of queries demonstrates, we can modify the time period weighted average calculation to eliminate the beginning date constraint (as costs incurred in previous time periods may be applicable to items sold in the current period) and multiply the result by the QOH query result to calculate the total cost value of each inventory type on hand. We can then sum the item types to get the overall cost value of inventory for the balance sheet.

Modified WAUC Query Step 1 (Exhibit 13-11): Join Purchase and StockflowPurchaseInventoryType tables, constrain purchase date, calculate purchase line item extensions

```
SELECT Purchase.Date, Purchase.ReceivingReportID,
        StockflowPurchaseInventoryType.ItemID,
        StockflowPurchaseInventoryType.QuantityPurchased,
        StockflowPurchaseInventoryType.ActualUnitCost,
        [QuantityPurchased]*[ActualUnitCost] AS ExtPurchLine
FROM Purchase INNER JOIN StockflowPurchaseInventoryType ON
        Purchase.ReceivingReportID =
        StockflowPurchaseInventoryType.ReceivingReportID
WHERE (((Purchase.Date)<=[enddate]));
```

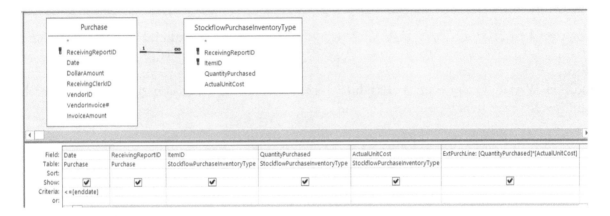

Exhibit 13-11: Modified Weighted Average Unit Cost (for Financial Statements) Step 1

Modified WAUC Query Step 2 (Exhibit 13-12): Sum purchase quantities and line item extensions for each item type

```
SELECT PurchaseInventoryExtLineItemsThroughEndDate.ItemID,
        Sum(PurchaseInventoryExtLineItemsThroughEndDate.QuantityPurchased) AS
        SumOfQuantityPurchased,
        Sum(PurchaseInventoryExtLineItemsThroughEndDate.ExtPurchLine) AS
        SumOfExtPurchLine
FROM PurchaseInventoryExtLineItemsThroughEndDate
GROUP BY PurchaseInventoryExtLineItemsThroughEndDate.ItemID;
```

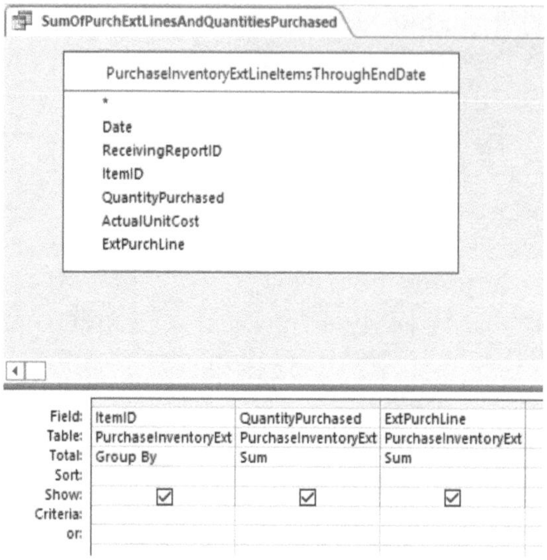

Exhibit 13-12: Modified Weighted Average Unit Cost (for Financial Statements) Step 2

Modified WAUC Query Step 3 (Exhibit 13-13): Divide line extension sums by total purchase quantities for each item type

```
SELECT SumOfPurchExtLinesAndQuantitiesPurchased.ItemID,
       SumOfPurchExtLinesAndQuantitiesPurchased.SumOfQuantityPurchased,
       SumOfPurchExtLinesAndQuantitiesPurchased.SumOfExtPurchLine,
       [SumOfPurchExtLinesAndQuantitiesPurchased]![SumOfExtPurchLine]/[SumOf
       PurchExtLinesAndQuantitiesPurchased]![SumOfQuantityPurchased] AS WAUC
FROM SumOfPurchExtLinesAndQuantitiesPurchased;
```

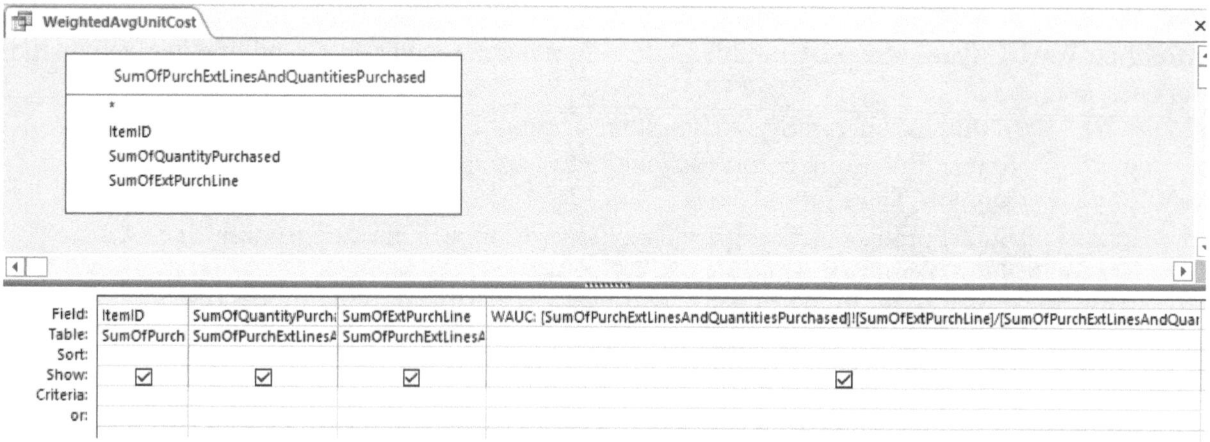

Exhibit 13-13: Modified Weighted Average Unit Cost (for Financial Statements) Step 3

Inventory Balance Sheet Query Step 1 (Exhibit 13-14): Multiply Modified WAUC Step 3 by Inventory QOH Step 7

SELECT TotalInventoryTypeQuantityOnHand.ItemID,
      TotalInventoryTypeQuantityOnHand.QOH, WeightedAvgUnitCost.WAUC,
      [QOH]*[WAUC] AS TotalItemCost
FROM TotalInventoryTypeQuantityOnHand
INNER JOIN WeightedAvgUnitCost ON TotalInventoryTypeQuantityOnHand.ItemID =
      WeightedAvgUnitCost.ItemID;

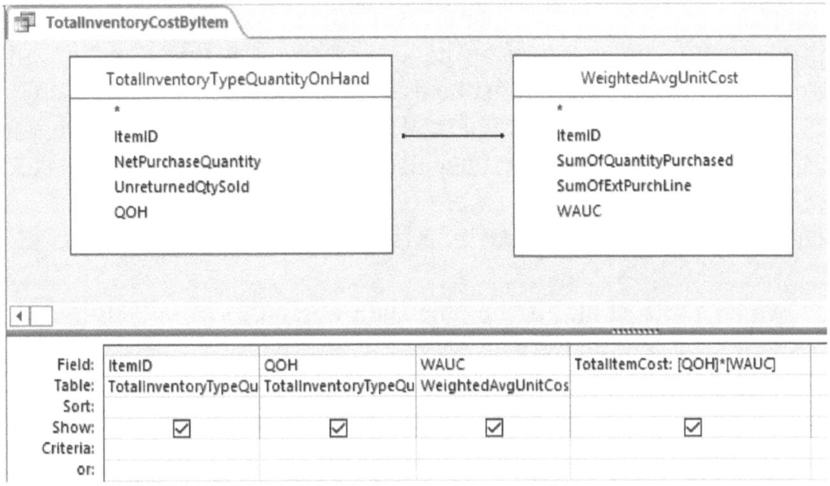

Exhibit 13-14: Inventory on Balance Sheet Query Step 1

Inventory Balance Sheet Query Step 2 (Exhibit 13-15): Sum total item costs from step 1

SELECT Sum(TotalInventoryCostByItem.TotalItemCost) AS SumOfTotalItemCost
FROM TotalInventoryCostByItem;

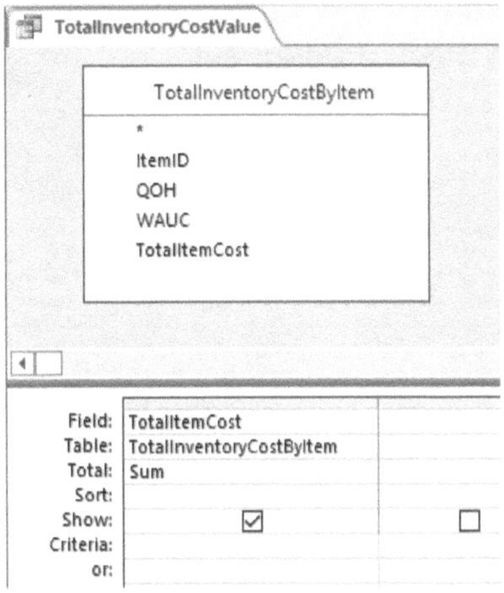

Exhibit 13-15: Inventory on Balance Sheet Query Step 2

A difficult issue associated with the inventory cost queries demonstrated here is that the aggregation of all purchases up to the ending date results in the inclusion of relatively old costs. For some decision needs that may be fine; but other decision needs may require consideration of only the more recent costs. Alternative means for computing moving average unit costs may be employed to allocate the costs differently; for this book we only illustrate the simplest approach.

Cost of Goods Sold

Cost of goods sold is a line item on enterprise income statements that is similar to the calculation of the dollar value of inventory on hand. Whereas the calculation of inventory on hand applies an assumed cost value to the quantities of inventory types on hand; the calculation of cost of goods sold applies an assumed cost value to the quantities of inventory types sold during a specified time period. The total cost value of inventory on hand appears as a line item on enterprise balance sheets. The same cost value assumption must be used in calculating inventory on the balance sheet and cost of goods sold on the income statement. Therefore, if weighted average unit cost is used as the costing assumption for inventory, it must also be used for cost of goods sold.

The overall procedures to calculate cost of goods sold for a given time period are as follows:

1. Determine which table contains the sale date attribute; usually this is in the table that represents the sale economic event.

2. Determine which table contains the sale quantities; usually this is in the table that represents the stockflow association between sale and inventory.

3. Join the tables together; set date constraints for the beginning and ending of the income statement period; group by inventory ID, and sum the quantity sold.

4. Join the result of step 3 with the result of the modified WAUC query step 3 from the balance sheet inventory queries. Join them on Item ID and multiply the quantity sold of each item type by the weighted average unit cost of each item type to get the total weighted average cost of goods sold for each inventory type.

5. Create a final query that sums the weighted average cost per inventory item type sold to get the total COGS for the income statement.

COGS Query 1 (Exhibit 13-16): Accomplish steps 1, 2, 3: Constrain sale date; sum quantity sold by item

SELECT StockflowSaleInventoryType.ItemID,
      Sum(StockflowSaleInventoryType.QuantitySold) AS SumOfQuantitySold
FROM Sale INNER JOIN StockflowSaleInventoryType ON Sale.SaleID =
      StockflowSaleInventoryType.SaleID
WHERE (((Sale.Date) Between [begindate] And [enddate]))
GROUP BY StockflowSaleInventoryType.ItemID;

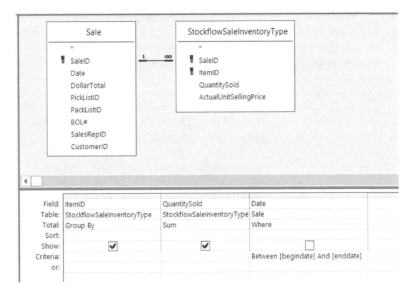

Exhibit 13-16: Cost of Goods Sold Query 1

COGS Query 2 (Exhibit 13-17): Accomplish step 4 – Calculate COGS by item as quantity sold x weighted average unit cost

SELECT InventoryTypeQuantitiesSoldDuringPeriod.ItemID,
      InventoryTypeQuantitiesSoldDuringPeriod.SumOfQuantitySold,
      WeightedAvgUnitCost.WAUC, [SumOfQuantitySold]*[WAUC] AS COGS
FROM InventoryTypeQuantitiesSoldDuringPeriod
INNER JOIN WeightedAvgUnitCost ON
      InventoryTypeQuantitiesSoldDuringPeriod.ItemID =
      WeightedAvgUnitCost.ItemID;

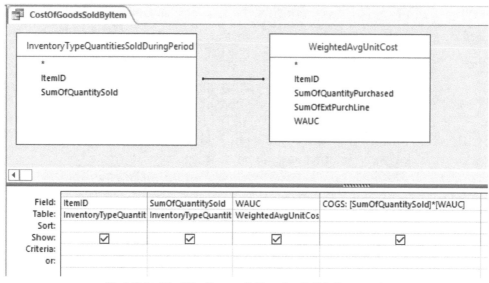

Exhibit 13-17: Cost of Goods Sold Query 2

COGS Query 3 (Exhibit 13-18): Accomplish step 5 - Sum Query 2 result to get total COGS for period

SELECT Sum(CostOfGoodsSoldByItem.COGS) AS SumOfCOGS
FROM CostOfGoodsSoldByItem;

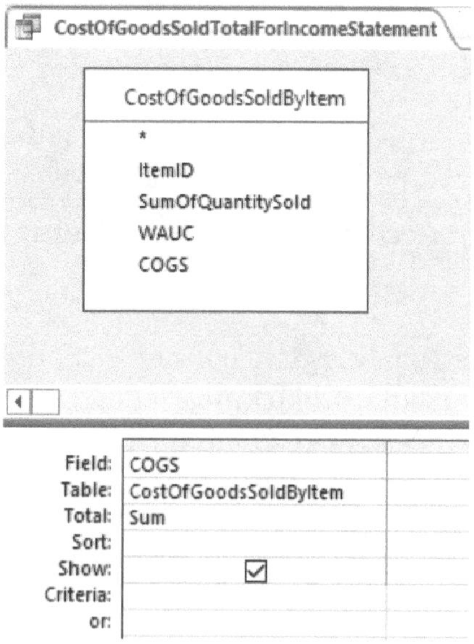

Exhibit 13-18: Cost of Goods Sold Query 3

CONCLUDING COMMENTS

This chapter illustrated complex queries that combine information from multiple classes and associations across both the acquisition and revenue business processes. We focused our attention on cash and inventory, as those are the most common resources shared by acquisition and revenue processes. Many other information needs span multiple business processes. While such queries may seem intimidating, just take them one step at a time. Determine the tables needed, then determine the order in which to combine data, perform aggregations, and create expressions. That order will vary depending on the information need. You will need to think logically and systematically; that will become more natural with practice. The database tables presented in Exhibit 12-1 are purposely smaller than real-world database tables to help you get comfortable with the querying concepts in a more manageable setting. The addition of many more attributes and many more rows of data will not change the overall logic of querying, so once you are accustomed to working with smaller relational databases, you can transfer much of what you know to working with larger relational databases.

KEY TERMS AND CONCEPTS

Cash balance query steps
Cost of goods sold query steps
Inventory cost query steps
Inventory quantity on hand query steps
Multiple process queries
Weighted average unit cost for financial statements query steps

REVIEW QUESTIONS

R13-1. What steps are needed in a set of queries that calculate the total balance of cash on a given date?

R13-2. What steps are needed in a set of queries that calculate the total quantity on hand of each inventory type on a given date?

R13-3. What steps are needed in a set of queries that calculate weighted average unit costs for each inventory type to be used in financial statement numbers such as cost of goods sold and inventory cost?

R13-4. What steps are needed in a set of queries that calculate cost of goods sold on an income statement, assuming you already have a list of inventory types with their weighted average unit costs?

R13-5. What steps are needed in a set of queries that calculate the dollar value to be reported for inventory on a balance sheet, assuming you already have a list of inventory types with their weighted average unit costs?

MULTIPLE CHOICE QUESTIONS

MC13-1. What resources are most likely to be included in information needs that encompass both the revenue and acquisition processes?
A) Raw materials inventory and finished goods inventory
B) Operating assets and salespeople
C) Merchandise (or finished goods) inventory and cash
D) Cash and cashiers

MC13-2. Which financial statement line item requires details from multiple business processes?
A) Sales on the income statement
B) Cost of goods sold on the income statement
C) Accounts receivable on the balance sheet
D) Accounts payable on the balance sheet

MC13-3. What constraint(s) should one use on cash receipt and cash disbursement dates in queries that calculate a company's cash balance?
A) <=[balance_date]
B) BETWEEN [begin_date] and [balance_date]
C) >[balance_date]
D) >[begin_date] and <[balance date]

MC13-4. What constraint(s) should one use on inventory purchase dates in the weighted average cost queries to calculate cost of goods sold?
A) <=[balance_date]
B) BETWEEN [begin_date] and [balance_date]
C) >[balance_date]
D) >[begin_date] and <[balance date]

MC13-5. What constraint(s) should one use on sale dates in queries to calculate cost of goods sold?
A) <=[balance_date]
B) BETWEEN [begin_date] and [balance_date]
C) >[balance_date]
D) >[begin_date] and <[balance date]

MC13-6. Which attribute would NOT need to be included in a set of queries to calculate cost of goods sold using weighted average unit costing? Assume weighted average unit cost is not stored as an attribute in the inventory table.
A) Beginning date of the income statement period for which COGS is needed
B) Actual unit costs of each inventory item on each purchase
C) Quantities sold of each inventory item on each sale
D) Actual unit selling prices of each inventory item on each sale

MC13-7. What kind of join is typically needed in a set of queries that calculates quantities on hand of each inventory type?
A) Inner
B) Outer – keeping all items purchased and related items sold
C) Outer – keeping all items sold and related items purchased
D) Equi

MC13-8. Using the following tables extracted from Carlisle Company's database, calculate the ending cash balance for the checking account Carlisle has located at First Union.

Cash

Cash Account Number	Cash Account Type	Location
1	Petty	Office
2	On hand	Office
89591020	Checking	First Union
78782040	Checking	Capital City
93821001	Cert-Deposit	Nations

Cash Disbursement

Voucher No.	CheckNo.	CashAccount No.	Amount	APClerk Number ^{FK}	PayeeID^{FK}
1	1	89591020	$1,900	33	40207
2	1	78782040	$3,000	33	40208
3	2	89591020	$32,000	33	40205
4	2	78782040	$400,000	33	40200
5	3	89591020	$940,000	33	40201
6	3	78782040	$10,000	33	40206
7	4	78782040	$120,000	33	40202
8	5	78782040	$30,000	33	40203
9	6	78782040	$132,000	33	40202
10	4	89591020	$72,600	33	40209
11	5	89591020	$252,000	33	40200
12	7	78782040	$13,000	33	40204
13	6	89591020	$356,000	33	40200
14	7	78782040	$200,000	33	40201
15	8	78782040	$30,000	33	40203
16	8	89591020	$60,000	33	S40
17	9	89591020	$20,000	33	S41
18	10	89591020	$40,000	33	S42
19	11	89591020	$72,600	33	40209

Cash Receipt

Cash Rect Number	Amount	Cashier Number^{FK}	SenderID^{FK}
099998	$1,500,000	32	S40
988888	$500,000	32	S41
100000	$1,000,000	32	S42
100001	$868,000	32	10000
100005	$60,000	32	10001
100009	$150,000	32	10002

Cash Receipt Inflow of Cash

Cash Rect Number	Cash Acct Nbr	Amount Deposited
099998	89591020	$1,500,000
099999	93821001	$500,000
100000	78782040	$1,000,000
100001	89591020	$868,000
100005	78782040	$60,000
100009	78782040	$15,000

A) $2,368,000
B) $1,847,100
C) $1,292,900
D) $ 520,900

MC13-9. Given the following tables, calculate the quantity on hand of inventory product code 3456 as of March 31, 2020.

Purchase Event

PurchaseID	PurchaseDate
532395	02/14/2020
532893	03/5/2020
541235	04/1/2020

SaleEvent

SaleNumber	Invoice Number	Sale Dollar Amount	Sale Date	CustomerID[FK]	SalespersonID[FK]
06050800	1	$24,900.00	02/22/2020	C100	E304
06060900	2	$2,100.00	02/25/2020	C101	E304
06081000	3	$3,800.00	03/7/2020	C102	E301
06100800	4	$20,000.00	03/15/2020	C100	E304
06130800	5	$3,800.00	03/30/2020	C100	E304
06190800	6	$62,000.00	03/30/2020	C105	E306
06211000	7	$3,800.00	04/1/2020	C104	E301
06260800	8	$10,400.00	04/5/2020	C101	E304
06261400	9	$16,750.00	04/30/2020	C107	E306
06261530	10	$29,000.00	05/3/2020	C102	E301

StockflowPurchaseInventoryType

ProductCode	PurchaseID	PurchaseQuantity	ActualUnitCost
1234	532395	100000	$0.90
1234	532893	50000	$1.20
3456	532395	40000	$6.50
3456	541235	40000	$5.50
5678	532395	70000	$7.00
7890	532893	140000	$10.00

StockflowSaleInventoryType

SaleNumber	ProductCode	Quantity Sold	Unit Selling Price
06050800	1234	2000	$1.90
06050800	3456	1000	$12.00
06050800	5678	700	$13.00
06060900	1234	1000	$2.10
06081000	1234	2000	$1.90
06100800	7890	1000	$20.00
06130800	1234	2000	$1.90
06190800	3456	4000	$11.00
06190800	5678	1500	$12.00
06211000	1234	2000	$1.90
06260800	5678	800	$13.00
06261400	3456	500	$12.50
06261400	7890	500	$21.00
06261530	1234	4000	$1.90
06261530	5678	1000	$13.00
06261530	7890	400	$21.00

A) 35,000
B) 415,600
C) 74,500
D) None of the above

MC13-10. Using the following tables extracted from Carlisle Company's database, calculate cost of goods sold for the time period covered in these tables, assuming Carlisle uses weighted average unit costing and that all information in the database is up to date.

Inventory

Stock Number	Description	Wtd Avg Unit Cost	List Sell Price
854310	Med basic	$21.00	$30.00
962020	Large basic	$42.00	$50.00
789530	Med deluxe	$92.50	$120.00
697350	Large deluxe	$105.00	$150.00
599940	Small basic	$10.00	$15.00

Sale-Inventory-Line-Item

Sale Invoice Number	Stock Number	Sale Quantity
17161911	854310	4,000
17161911	962020	2,000
17161911	789530	1,400
17171011	854310	2,000
17192111	854310	4,000
17192111	599940	2,000
17211911	697350	2,000
17241911	599940	4,000
17241911	854310	4,000
17291911	854310	2,000
17201911	962020	8,000
17201911	789530	3,000
17201911	599940	6,000
17322111	854310	4,000
17471911	789530	1,600
17371911	599940	14,000

Sale

Sale Invoice Number	Sale Date	Customer Number[FK]	Salesperson Number[FK]
17161911	11/01	10000	34
17171011	11/03	10001	34
17192111	11/05	10002	31
17211911	11/08	10000	34
17241911	11/11	10000	34
17291911	11/15	10003	31
17201911	11/07	10005	34
17322111	11/18	10004	31
17371911	11/24	10002	31

A) $1,865,000
B) $ 640,000
C) $2,510,000
D) $4,672,000

CHAPTER **14**

Conversion and Payroll Process Accounting Analytics

LEARNING OBJECTIVES

This chapter illustrates use of the REA ontology to determine and meet information needs within the conversion and payroll business processes. Some of these information needs require relatively uncomplicated queries that involve single classes or associations within each process. Other information needs are more complicated and require sets of queries that require use of multiple associations. After studying this chapter, you should be able to

1. Identify common information needs within the conversion process
2. Identify common information needs within the payroll process
3. Create queries to meet common information needs within the conversion process
4. Create queries to meet common information needs within the payroll process

INFORMATION NEEDS IN THE CONVERSION PROCESS

We use the relational database tables in Exhibit 14-1 in the examples for developing queries in the conversion process. These tables are for a fictitious company that manufactures and sells cookies. While admittedly limited in the number of attributes captured, these tables provide sufficient detail to provide a foundation for identifying and satisfying information needs in the conversion process. After listing the tables, we analyze each of the classes and associations in the conversion process pattern to provide some ideas about the types of queries that may satisfy information needs in the conversion process. The queries presented are not a comprehensive set of queries (there are simply too many potential queries to list them all); however, the set provided should provide you guidance for creating similar types of queries.

CookieBatch

BatchID	StartTime	CompletionTime	Scheduled Batches	Actual Batches	SupervisorID[FK]
WJ1	7/15/2020 6:30:00 AM	7/15/2020 7:15:00 AM	4	4	S2
WJ2	7/15/2020 6:30:00 AM	7/15/2020 7:37:00 AM	4	4	S1

StockflowCookieBatchCookieType

BatchID	CookieTypeID
WJ1	FSCS
WJ2	SN

Exhibit 14-1: Relational Database Tables for an Example Cookie Manufacturer

CookieType

CookieTypeID	Description	UnitsPerPackage	ListPrice
CC	Chocolate chip plain	12	$2.99
CCP	Chocolate chip with pecans	12	$2.99
FSCS	Frosted sugar cookies with candy sprinkles	10	$3.59
M	Molasses	12	$3.29
OR	Oatmeal raisin	12	$2.99
PB	Peanut butter	12	$2.99
SC	Sugar cookies plain	12	$2.99
SN	Snickerdoodles	12	$3.59

BakingSupervisor

SupervisorID	SupervisorName	SupervisorPhone
S1	Lucy	1-1234
S2	Ricky	1-4321

BakingEmployee

EmployeeID	EmployeeName	EmployeePhone	SupervisorID[FK]
PE1	Fred	1-6789	S2
PE2	Ethel	1-9876	S2
PE3	Larry	1-7698	S1
PE4	Moe	1-6798	S1
PE5	Curly	1-8796	S1

ParticipationCookieBatchBakingEmployee

BatchID	EmployeeID
WJ1	PE3
WJ1	PE4
WJ1	PE5
WJ2	PE1
WJ2	PE2

DualityCookieBatchIngredientIssuance

BatchID	IngredientIssuanceID
WJ1	RMI4238
WJ1	RMI4239
WJ1	RMI4240
WJ1	RMI4243
WJ1	RMI4245
WJ2	RMI4241
WJ2	RMI4242
WJ2	RMI4244
WJ2	RMI4246

Exhibit 14-1 (cont.): Relational Database Tables for an Example Cookie Manufacturer

IngredientIssuance

IngredientIssuanceID	IssuanceTime	Location	InventoryClerkID[FK]	SupervisorID[FK]
RMI4238	7/15/2020 6:20:00 AM	WorkcenterA	IC1	S2
RMI4239	7/15/2020 6:22:00 AM	WorkcenterB	IC2	S2
RMI4240	7/15/2020 6:24:00 AM	WorkcenterC	IC2	S2
RMI4241	7/15/2020 6:28:00 AM	WorkcenterD	IC1	S1
RMI4242	7/15/2020 6:26:00 AM	WorkcenterE	IC2	S1
RMI4243	7/15/2020 6:29:00 AM	WorkcenterC	IC1	S2
RMI4244	7/15/2020 6:29:30 AM	WorkcenterE	IC1	S1
RMI4245	7/15/2020 6:29:00 AM	WorkcenterC	IC2	S2
RMI4246	7/15/2020 6:29:30 AM	WorkcenterE	IC2	S1

StockflowIssuanceOfIngredients

IngredientID	IssuanceID	QuantityIssued	UnitOfMeasure
CN	RMI4241	1	Cup
CS	RMI4240	1	Cup
EG	RMI4239	4	Each
EG	RMI4242	4	Each
FL	RMI4238	7	Cups
FL	RMI4241	8	Cups
ILFS	RMI4245	4	Each
ILSN	RMI4246	4	Each
PK	RMI4243	4	Each
PK	RMI4244	4	Each
SH	RMI4239	1.75	Cups
SH	RMI4242	2.67	Cups
SL	RMI4238	1.75	Teaspoons
SL	RMI4241	2	Teaspoons
VN	RMI4239	3	Teaspoons
VN	RMI4242	4	Teaspoons
WS	RMI4238	4.67	Cups
WS	RMI4241	6	Cups

InventoryClerk

InventoryClerkID	ClerkName	ClerkPhone
IC1	Ted	1-5678
IC2	Alice	1-8765

Exhibit 14-1 (cont.): Relational Database Tables for an Example Cookie Manufacturer

Ingredient

IngredientID	Description	UnitOfMeasure	StandardCostPerUnitOfMeasure
BS	Brown sugar	50 lb bag	$9.47
BU	Butter	10 lb box	$3.98
CM	Chocolate morsels	10 lb bag	$19.49
CN	Cinnamon	16 oz tin	$3.29
CS	Candy sprinkles	1 lb tin	$3.18
EG	Eggs, large AA grade	2 dozen carton	$1.29
FL	Flour, white sifted	100 lb bag	$20.00
ILFS	Ingredient label - frosted sugar	Each	$0.01
ILSN	Ingredient label - snickerdoodle	Each	$0.01
PB	Peanut butter	10 lb jar	$8.37
PE	Pecans	2 lb bag	$5.32
PK	Plastic container	Each	$0.12
SH	Shortening	10 lb can	$12.10
SL	Salt, iodized	5 lb bag	$1.00
VN	Vanilla, pure	1 liter bottle	$20.00
WS	White sugar	50 lb bag	$10.00

LaborOperation

LaborOperationID	StartTime	EndTime	EmployeeID[FK]	SupervisorID[FK]	LaborReqID[FK]
LO21	7/15/2020 6:30:00 AM	7/15/2020 6:40:00 AM	PE3	S2	LR2
LO22	7/15/2020 6:30:00 AM	7/15/2020 6:40:00 AM	PE4	S2	LR2
LO23	7/15/2020 6:40:00 AM	7/15/2020 6:45:00 AM	PE5	S2	LR2
LO24	7/15/2020 6:45:00 AM	7/15/2020 6:50:00 AM	PE3	S2	LR2
LO25	7/15/2020 6:50:00 AM	7/15/2020 6:51:00 AM	PE5	S2	LR2
LO26	7/15/2020 7:03:00 AM	7/15/2020 7:03:30 AM	PE5	S2	LR2
LO27	7/15/2020 7:08:00 AM	7/15/2020 7:12:00 AM	PE3	S2	LR2
LO28	7/15/2020 7:12:00 AM	7/15/2020 7:13:00 AM	PE4	S2	LR2
LO29	7/15/2020 7:13:00 AM	7/15/2020 7:15:00 AM	PE5	S2	LR2
LO30	7/15/2020 6:30:00 AM	7/15/2020 6:40:00 AM	PE1	S1	LR1
LO31	7/15/2020 6:30:00 AM	7/15/2020 6:40:00 AM	PE2	S1	LR1
LO32	7/15/2020 6:40:00 AM	7/15/2020 6:45:00 AM	PE2	S1	LR1
LO33	7/15/2020 6:45:00 AM	7/15/2020 6:47:00 AM	PE2	S1	LR1
LO34	7/15/2020 6:47:00 AM	7/15/2020 6:48:00 AM	PE1	S1	LR1
LO35	7/15/2020 7:00:00 AM	7/15/2020 7:00:30 AM	PE1	S1	LR1
LO36	7/15/2020 7:35:00 AM	7/15/2020 7:37:00 AM	PE2	S1	LR1

Exhibit 14-1 (cont.): Relational Database Tables for an Example Cookie Manufacturer

DualityCookieBatchLaborOperation

BatchID	LaborOperationID
WJ1	LO21
WJ1	LO22
WJ1	LO23
WJ1	LO24
WJ1	LO25
WJ1	LO26
WJ1	LO28
WJ1	LO29
WJ2	LO30
WJ2	LO33
WJ2	LO34
WJ2	LO35
WJ2	LO36

LaborType

LaborTypeID	Description
L1	Mix dry ingredients
L2	Mix moist ingredients
L3	Combine dry and moist ingredients
L4	Add morsels to mixed dough
L5	Add nuts to mixed dough
L6	Form dough into cookies
L7	Put cookies onto cookie sheet
L8	Put cookie sheet into oven
L9	Set cookie timer
L10	Take cookie sheet out of oven
L11	Frost cookies
L12	Sprinkle cookies
L13	Package cookies

Exhibit 14-1 (cont.): Relational Database Tables for an Example Cookie Manufacturer

StockflowLaborTypeInLaborOperation

LaborTypeID	LaborOperationID
L1	LO21
L1	LO30
L10	LO26
L10	LO35
L11	LO27
L12	LO28
L13	LO29
L13	LO36
L2	LO22
L2	LO31
L3	LO23
L3	LO32
L6	LO24
L7	LO24
L7	LO33
L8	LO25
L8	LO34
L9	LO25
L9	LO34

DualityCookieBatchEquipmentOperation

BatchID	EquipOperationID
WJ1	MO12
WJ1	MO13
WJ1	MO14
WJ2	MO15
WJ2	MO16

EquipmentOperation

Equipment OperationID	StartTime	EndTime	EmployeeID[FK]	SupervisorID[FK]	EquipReqID[FK]
MO12	7/15/2020 6:30:00 AM	7/15/2020 6:45:00 AM	PE5	S2	ER2
MO13	7/15/2020 6:51:00 AM	7/15/2020 7:03:00 AM	PE5	S2	ER2
MO14	7/15/2020 7:08:00 AM	7/15/2020 7:12:00 AM	PE3	S2	ER2
MO15	7/15/2020 6:30:00 AM	7/15/2020 6:45:00 AM	PE2	S1	ER1
MO16	7/15/2020 6:40:00 AM	7/15/2020 7:00:00 AM	PE2	S1	ER1

Exhibit 14-1 (cont.): Relational Database Tables for an Example Cookie Manufacturer

Equipment

FixedAssetID	EquipTypeName[FK]	Acquisition Date	Cost	Estimated LifeYears	Estimated SalvageValue
FA1	Oven	02/16/2016	$400.00	10	$50.00
FA2	Oven	04/02/2016	$500.00	8	$100.00
FA3	Heavy duty mixer	02/27/2016	$150.00	3	$0.00
FA4	Measuring device set	02/16/2016	$80.00	5	$10.00
FA5	Cookie sheet	02/18/2016	$10.00	3	$0.00
FA6	Cookie sheet	01/03/2020	$15.00	3	$0.00
FA7	Frosting utensils	01/03/2020	$10.00	5	$0.00
FA8	Heavy duty mixer	02/15/2020	$170.00	3	$0.00
FA9	Measuring device set	02/15/2020	$75.00	5	$10.00

StockflowEquipmentInEquipmentOperation

FixedAssetID	EquipmentOperationID
FA1	MO13
FA2	MO16
FA3	MO12
FA4	MO12
FA5	MO13
FA6	MO16
FA7	MO14
FA8	MO15
FA9	MO15

BakingOrder

BakingOrderID	BakingOrderDateTime	RequestedCompletion	SupervisorID[FK]
BO1	07/14/2020 4:30:00 PM	07/15/2020 8:00:00 AM	S2
BO2	07/14/2020 4:31:30 PM	07/15/2020 8:00:00 AM	S1
BO3	07/15/2020 4:45:00 PM	07/16/2020 8:00:00 AM	S1
BO4	07/15/2020 4:46:00 PM	07/16/2020 8:00:00 AM	S1
BO5	07/15/2020 4:50:00 PM	07/16/2020 8:00:00 AM	S2

ReservationBakingOrderCookieType

BakingOrderID	CookieTypeID	NumberOfBatchesOrdered
BO1	FSCS	4
BO2	SN	4
BO3	CC	3
BO3	CCP	2
BO4	PB	3
BO5	M	4

Exhibit 14-1 (cont.): Relational Database Tables for an Example Cookie Manufacturer

ParticipationBakingEmployeeScheduledForBakingOrder

EmployeeID	BakingOrderID
PE1	BO2
PE2	BO2
PE3	BO1
PE4	BO1
PE5	BO1

CookieBatchFulfillsBakingOrder

BatchID	BakingOrderID
WJ1	BO1
WJ2	BO2

IngredientRequisition

IngredientRequisitionID	RequisitionDate	SupervisorID^{FK}	BakingOrderID^{FK}
1001	07/14/2020 4:35:00 PM	S2	BO1
1002	07/14/2020 4:35:30 PM	S1	BO2

ReservationIngredientRequisition

IngredientRequisitionID	IngredientID	QuantityReserved	Unit of Measure
1001	CS	1	cup
1001	EG	4	each
1001	FL	8	cups
1001	ILFS	4	each
1001	PK	4	each
1001	SH	2.67	cups
1001	SL	2	teaspoons
1001	VN	4	teaspoons
1001	WS	6	cups
1002	CN	0.5	cup
1002	EG	4	each
1002	FL	6	cups
1002	ILSN	4	each
1002	PK	4	each
1002	SH	1.75	cups
1002	SL	1.75	teaspoons
1002	VN	2.75	teaspoons
1002	WS	4.66	cups

Exhibit 14-1 (cont.): Relational Database Tables for an Example Cookie Manufacturer

ParticipationInventoryClerkIngredientRequisition

InventoryClerkID	IngredientRequisitionID
IC1	1001
IC1	1002
IC2	1001
IC2	1002

IngredientIssuanceFulfillsIngredientRequisition

IngredientIssuanceID	IngredientRequisitionID
RMI4238	1002
RMI4239	1001
RMI4240	1001
RMI4241	1001
RMI4242	1001
RMI4243	1001
RMI4244	1002
RMI4245	1001
RMI4246	1002

LaborRequisition

LaborReqID	DateOf Requisition	Number Employees Needed	Hours Needed	Scheduling Supervisor[FK]	Baking Order ID[FK]
LR1	07/14/2020	2	1.00	S1	BO2
LR2	07/14/2020	3	1.00	S2	BO1
LR3	07/15/2020	4	2.00	S1	BO3

Exhibit 14-1 (cont.): Relational Database Tables for an Example Cookie Manufacturer

ReservationLaborRequisitionLaborType

LaborReqID	LaborTypeID
LR1	L1
LR1	L2
LR1	L3
LR1	L10
LR1	L13
LR1	L7
LR1	L8
LR1	L9
LR2	L1
LR2	L10
LR2	L11
LR2	L12
LR2	L13
LR2	L2
LR2	L3
LR2	L6
LR2	L7
LR2	L8
LR2	L9

EquipmentRequisition

EquipReqID	EReq	DateEquipmentNeeded	BakingOrderID[FK]	SchedulingSupervisor[FK]
ER1	07/13/2020	07/15/2020	BO2	S1
ER2	07/13/2020	07/15/2020	BO1	S2
ER3	07/15/2020	07/16/2020	BO3	S1
ER4	07/15/2020	07/16/2020	BO4	S1

ReservationEquipReqEquipment

EquipReqID	FixedAssetID
ER1	FA2
ER1	FA6
ER1	FA8
ER1	FA9
ER2	FA1
ER2	FA3
ER2	FA4
ER2	FA5
ER2	FA7

Exhibit 14-1 (cont.): Relational Database Tables for an Example Cookie Manufacturer

LinkageIngredientsNeededInCookieType

CookieTypeID	IngredientID	QuantityNeeded	UnitOfMeasure	CookieBatchSize
FSCS	CS	0.25	cup	10
FSCS	EG	1	each	10
FSCS	FL	1.75	cups	10
FSCS	ILFS	1	each	10
FSCS	PK	1	each	10
FSCS	SH	0.5	cup	10
FSCS	SL	0.5	teaspoon	10
FSCS	VN	0.75	teaspoon	10
FSCS	WS	1	cup	10
SN	CN	3	teaspoons	12
SN	EG	1	each	12
SN	FL	1.5	cups	12
SN	ILSN	1	each	12
SN	PK	1	each	12
SN	SH	0.67	cup	12
SN	SL	0.5	teaspoon	12
SN	VN	1	teaspoon	12
SN	WS	1.5	cups	12

LinkageLaborTypeNeededForCookieType

CookieTypeID	LaborTypeID	SequenceOfLaborTypeInCookieType
FSCS	L1	1
FSCS	L10	8
FSCS	L11	9
FSCS	L12	10
FSCS	L13	11
FSCS	L2	2
FSCS	L3	3
FSCS	L6	4
FSCS	L7	5
FSCS	L8	6
FSCS	L9	7
SN	L1	1
SN	L10	7
SN	L13	8
SN	L2	2
SN	L3	3
SN	L7	4
SN	L8	5
SN	L9	6

Exhibit 14-1 (cont.): Relational Database Tables for an Example Cookie Manufacturer

LinkageEquipmentTypeCookieType

EquipmentTypeName	CookieTypeID	QuantityNeeded	UnitofMeasure
Cookie sheet	FSCS	1	each
Cookie sheet	SN	1	each
Frosting utensils	FSCS	1	set
Heavy duty mixer	FSCS	1	each
Heavy duty mixer	SN	1	each
Measuring device set	FSCS	1	set
Measuring device set	SN	1	set
Oven	FSCS	1	each
Oven	SN	1	each

EquipmentType

EquipTypeName	StandardCost	AverageExpectedLifeYears
Cookie sheet	$12.00	3
Frosting utensils	$10.00	4
Heavy duty mixer	$160.00	3
Measuring device set	$78.00	5
Oven	$450.00	7

Exhibit 14-1 (cont.): Relational Database Tables for an Example Cookie Manufacturer

Resource Queries in the Conversion Process

The resources and resource types that most commonly exist in the conversion process are raw materials inventory, labor type, machinery, and finished goods inventory. For each resource, users may need any of the following:

- Detailed status information at one or more points in time for each resource instance
- Detailed status information at one or more points in time for only those resource instances meeting specified criteria
- Summarized status information at one or more points in time for all resource instances
- Summarized status information at one or more points in time for only those resource instances meeting specified criteria

With regard to each of the above, users may need to know all characteristics of the instances in the answer set, or they may need only a subset of the characteristics.

Raw materials and finished goods inventory may be tracked at the type level and/or may be specifically identified. Therefore, queries may be needed at either of those levels of detail. Labor is typically tracked only at the type level. Machinery and other operating assets are usually specifically identified, but may also be tracked at the category (type) level. For example, most enterprises assign an identification tag to each operating asset that has a cost value exceeding a certain materiality threshold; however, they also keep track of the category to which the asset belongs (e.g., furniture, computer equipment, office equipment). Since (1) the raw materials and machinery resources in the conversion process are the same as those acquired in the acquisition process, and (2) the finished goods resources produced in the conversion process is the same as the inventory resources in the revenue process, any query that focuses solely on a resource table will be very similar to the resource queries displayed in Chapter 8.

Event Queries in the Conversion Process

Users may need information regarding events. The most common events in the conversion process are material requisitions, material issuances, labor operations, machine operations, production orders, and production runs. For each of these types of events, users may need any of the following:

- Detailed information about each event instance (i.e., what happened, when did it begin and end, at which workstation did it occur, etc.)
- Detailed information about each event instance that meets specified criteria (e.g., events of a specified type that occurred during a specified time period or that occurred at a specified workstation)
- Summarized information for all instances of an event type for a specified time period (e.g., total of the event instances during a specified time period)
- Summarized information for only those instances of an event type for a specified time period that meet specified criteria (e.g., average dollar value of the event instances for a specified location during a specified time period)

Examples of information needs in the conversion process regarding events are (among many other possibilities):

- Length of a specific production run (end time minus start time)
- Average length of the production runs within a specified time period
- Total number of production runs that occurred at a specified plant or workstation or during a specified time period
- Date and/or time an issuance of materials occurred

From the event tables in the cookie manufacturing example (IngredientRequisition, BakingOrder, CookieBatch, IngredientIssuance, LaborOperation, and EquipmentOperation) some specific queries (among many possibilities) that may be developed are:

- How long did it take to produce a specific batch of cookies?
  - Using the CookieBatch table, calculate the difference between the StartTime and the CompletionTime for a specific batch.
- Count the number of ingredient issuances that were made to Workcenter E
  - Using the IngredientIssuance table, use the Count function to count the issuances for which the Location field is Workcenter E.
- When did the most recent ingredient requisition take place?
  - Using the IngredientRequisition table, use the Max function to identify the largest (most recent) date in the RequisitionDate field.
- Which baking orders are requested for completion on a particular day?
  - Using the BakingOrder table, specify the desired day as criteria by which to select the corresponding orders.

- How many equipment operations took longer than 14 minutes to complete?
  - o Using the EquipmentOperation table, create an expression to calculate the difference in StartTime and EndTime and then use the expression as criteria by which to select the corresponding equipment operations.

A caution before you try to make each of these example queries. The queries that involve calculations with date/time fields may not provide meaningful results because of the complexities of formatting the results in some database software; these complexities may involve additional coding that is beyond the scope of this book. Therefore, don't panic if you can't make a query run correctly that involves a date/time calculation (of course you can always attempt to find help by doing an internet search).

Agent Queries in the Conversion Process

Because the conversion process does not typically involve external agents, the agent queries center on various types of employees. The employees commonly involved in conversion processes are production supervisors, production workers, and inventory clerks. Production supervisors are the internal agents who authorize conversion process events. Production workers are the internal agents who do the conversion work. Inventory clerks are internal agents who issue materials and equipment into production. Queries may be generated to obtain any of the following:

- Detailed status information at one or more points in time for each employee
- Detailed status information at one or more points in time for each employee who meets specified criteria
- Summarized status information at one or more points in time for all employees
- Summarized status information at one or more points in time for all employees who meet specified criteria

Because the agent tables in the cookie manufacturing example (BakingSupervisor, BakingEmployee, and InventoryClerk) only include employee ids, names, and telephone numbers, not many queries can be constructed other than a list of employees and their telephone numbers. A complete database would typically include many other attributes of employees that could provide useful information for decision-makers.

ASSOCIATION QUERIES IN THE CONVERSION PROCESS
Combining information from various resource, event, and agent tables in accordance with the associations in which they participate can provide much richer data than single table queries. We next discuss queries based on the various types of associations in the conversion process.

Duality Association Queries
As explained in a previous chapter, duality associations in conversion processes represent transformations rather than exchanges. Raw inputs are not exchanged for finished goods; rather they are converted into finished goods. The duality association connects raw material issuances, machine operations, and labor operations – economic decrement events that use up the inputs – to the production runs – economic increment events that produce the finished goods.

Information needs with respect to duality associations in conversion processes include (among other possibilities):
- Identification of labor operations related to one or more specified production runs
- Identification of machine (equipment) operations related to one or more specified production runs
- Identification of raw material issuances related to one or more specified production runs
- Calculation of the time taken for a labor (or machine/equipment) operation as a percentage of a complete production run
- Count the number of raw material issuances (or labor operations or machine operations) related to a specified production run

For the cookie manufacturing example, duality queries could investigate
- Which labor operations (or equipment operations or ingredient issuances) related to batch WJ1 and which related to batch WJ2?
- How many ingredient issuances were associated with each cookie batch?
- How many equipment operations were necessary to make cookie batch WJ1?
  - Join the EquipmentOperation table to the DualityCookieBatchEquipmentOperation table; set the criteria for the BatchID = WJ1 and count the EquipmentOperationID field.
- How much of the total production time for batch WJ1 consisted of equipment operations and how much of the time consisted of labor operations?

As noted earlier, queries that calculate differences in date/time fields are very difficult to successfully create in Microsoft Access so you may want to skip the last one above.

Stockflow Association Queries
Stockflow associations in the conversion process represent the use or consumption of input resources by economic decrement events and the production of finished good resources by economic increment events. Therefore, stockflow associations are commonly used in queries to identify the effect of economic events on resources, or to identify the resources used up – or produced by – the economic events. Some common information needs that can be addressed by stockflow associations are:

- What resources or resource types were increased or decreased by an economic event?
- What quantity of a resource or resource type was increased or decreased by an economic event?
- What dollar value of a resource or resource type was increased or decreased by an economic event?
- When did an event increase or decrease a specific resource or resource type?
- Where did an event increase or decrease a specific resource or resource type?

These information needs may be addressed at a detailed level or they may be aggregated for groups of events and/or resources/resource types. The information may be used in isolation or used as part of a trend analysis to project future events and their expected effects on resources or resource types. Within the conversion process, some common stockflow information needs (among many other possibilities) are:

- Which raw material types were decreased by a material issuance?
- What quantity of each raw material inventory type was decreased by a material issuance?
- What types of labor were used in a labor operation?
- What equipment was used (and/or for how long) in a machine (equipment) operation?
- What finished goods were produced by a production run?
- What quantity of each finished good was produced by a production run?
- What is the standard unit cost of the raw materials used by a material issuance?

In the cookie manufacturing example, questions such as the following could be answered via stockflow association queries:

- How long did it take to sprinkle the cookies in labor operation 28?
    - Because this involves a date/time calculation, you should not attempt this in Microsoft Access.
- How many frosted sugar cookies with candy sprinkles were produced on July 15, 2020 and in which batch(es)?
    - Join the CookieType table to the StockflowCookieBatchCookieType table using Cookie Type ID to determine which batches were for frosted sugar cookies with candy sprinkles. Join StockflowCookieBatchCookieType table to CookieBatch table using the BatchID, constrain the CompletionTime = 7/15/2020 and sum the ActualQuantity.
- What kind of cookies were produced in batch WJ1?
    - Join the CookieType table to the StockflowCookieBatchCookieType table using CookieTypeID. Use criteria setting the BatchID field =WJ1 and display the BatchID, CookieTypeID, and the Description.

Fulfillment Queries in the Conversion Process

Fulfillment associations in the conversion process represent associations between the production order and production run (the production run fulfills the production order) and between the materials (or labor or equipment) requisition and the material issuance (or labor or machine/equipment operation). Fulfillment association queries in the conversion process in general include:

- Identification of unfilled commitment events (e.g., production orders for which production runs have not yet occurred, material requisitions for which material issuances have not yet occurred, etc.)
- Identification of filled commitment events (e.g., production orders for which production runs have occurred, material requisitions for which material issuances have occurred)
- Identification of economic events for which commitments were not made (e.g., production runs that were not ordered or material issuances that were not requisitioned)
- Calculation of length of time between commitment events and economic events (e.g., length of time between production order and production run or between material requisition and material issuance)
- Identification of causes for economic events (e.g., which production order led to a production run or which material requisition led to a material issuance)
- Identification of results of commitment events (e.g., which production run fulfilled a production order or which material issuance fulfilled a material requisition)

In the cookie manufacturing example, questions such as the following could be answered via fulfillment association queries:
- Has baking order BO4 been fulfilled?
  - Join the BakingOrder table to the CookieBatchFulfillsBakingOrder table with an outer join keeping all baking orders; include the BakingOrderID from the BakingOrder table and the BatchID from the CookieBatchFulfillsBakingOrder table; set criteria to select the BakingOrderID = BO4.
- Have any ingredient issuances occurred that were not related to ingredient requisitions?
  - Join the IngredientIssuance and IngredientIssuanceFulfillsIngredientRequisition tables with an outer join keeping all ingredient issuances; include the IngredientIssuanceID from the IngredientIssuance table and the IngredientRequisitionID from the IngredientIssuanceFulfillsRequisition table; set criteria to select null ingredient requisitions.
- What is the average length of time between baking orders and cookie batches for this company?
  - Join the BakingOrder, CookieBatchFulfillsBakingOrder, and CookieBatch tables and subtract the BakingOrderDateTime from the related batch CompletionTime. Then calculate the average of the result. Because this involves a date/time calculation, whether you get a meaningful result may depend on the software you use.
- What baking order triggered cookie batch WJ2?
  - Join the CookieBatch and CookieBatchFulfillsBakingOrder tables; include the BakingOrderID; set the criteria to select BatchID = WJ2.

Reservation Queries in the Conversion Process

Reservation associations in the conversion process represent associations between commitment events such as production orders and material requisitions and the resources those events are committing to increase or decrease. Therefore, reservation associations are commonly used in queries to satisfy information needs about the eventual effect of commitment events on resources

or about the resources involved in commitment events. Some common information needs in the conversion process are:
- What finished good or finished good type is a production order agreeing to produce?
- What quantity of a finished good or finished good type is a production order agreeing to produce?
- What is the dollar value of the finished good or finished good type a production order is agreeing to produce?
- When did a production order commit to produce a specific finished good or finished good type?
- What material or material type is a material requisition agreeing to use up?
- What quantity of each material type is a material requisition agreeing to use up?
- What is the standard or actual unit cost for each material a material requisition is agreeing to use up?
- When did a material requisition commit to using up a material or material type?

In the cookie manufacturing example, questions such as the following could be answered via reservation association queries:
- What kind of cookies is baking order BO5 agreeing to produce and when are they scheduled to be produced?
  - Join the ReservationBakingOrderCookieType table to the CookieType and to the BakingOrder tables to see that BO5 is agreeing to produce molasses cookies by July 16, 2020 at 8:00 a.m.
- How many peanut butter cookies are scheduled to be produced on July 16, 2020 and which production order represents the agreement to produce them?
  - Join ReservationBakingOrderCookieType, CookieType, and BakingOrder tables, include the QuantityReserved, set the criteria for CookieTypeID to equal PB (peanut butter) and the RequestedCompletion date to = July 16, 2020.
- What are the descriptions of the ingredients that were scheduled to be used up by ingredient requisition 1002?
  - Join Ingredient table to ReservationIngredientRequisition. Set criteria for the IngredientRequisitionID to be 1002.

Participation Queries in the Conversion Process
Participation associations in the conversion process typically represent the associations between production orders, material requisitions, material issuances, machine (equipment) operations, labor operations, and production runs and the employees who authorize those events (typically supervisors) and the employees who accomplish the events (typically production workers or inventory clerks). Therefore, participation associations are commonly used in queries to satisfy information needs about the identification of employees who participated in events or about the events in which specified employees participated. Some common information needs are:
- Which production supervisor authorized a machine (equipment) operation?
- By how many production orders has a production employee been scheduled to work?
- How long did a production employee take to perform a labor operation?
- How many production orders have been authorized by a specific production supervisor?

- Which inventory clerk accomplished a material issuance?

In the cookie manufacturing example, questions such as the following could be answered via participation association queries:
- What is the name of the supervisor who authorized equipment operation MO13?
  - o Join the EquipmentOperation table to the BakingSupervisor table; set criteria for the EquipmentOperationID to be MO13 and display the SupervisorName.
- What are the names of the employees who were scheduled on baking order BO2?
  - o Join the ParticipationBakingEmployeeScheduledForBakingOrder and BakingEmployee tables; set criteria for the BakingOrderID to be BO2 and display the EmployeeName.
- What are the names and phone numbers of the inventory clerks who processed ingredient issuances #RMI4240-RMI4245?
  - o Join the IngredientIssuance and InventoryClerk tables; set criteria for the IngredientIssuanceID to be BETWEEN RMI4240 and RMI4245 and display ClerkName and ClerkPhone.
- How many production runs has Lucy supervised?
  - o Join the CookieBatch and BakingSupervisor tables; set criteria for the SupervisorName field to be Lucy; use the Count aggregation function on the BatchID field.

Linkage Queries in the Conversion Process

Linkage associations in the conversion process typically represent the associations between finished goods and raw materials and also between finished goods and labor type. As described earlier, the information content within the linkage between finished goods and raw materials is often captured by enterprises on bill of materials documents, and the information content within the linkage between finished goods and labor types is often captured on operations list documents. Therefore, *linkage association queries* ask the same kinds of questions that could be answered from one of those documents. Some examples are:
- What raw materials are needed to produce a finished good or finished good type?
- What quantity of each raw material is needed to produce a finished good or finished good type?
- Which finished goods contain a specified raw material or a specified labor type?
- What labor types are needed to produce a finished good or finished good type?

In the cookie manufacturing example, questions such as the following could be answered via linkage association queries:
- How much white sugar is needed to make a batch of snickerdoodles?
  - o Join the CookieType, Ingredient, and LinkageIngredientsNeededInCookieType tables; enter criteria =Snickerdoodles in the finished cookie type description field; enter criteria =white sugar in the ingredient Description field; display the QuantityNeeded and UnitOfMeasure fields.
- Which finished cookie types contain brown sugar?

        o Join the CookieType, Ingredient, and LinkageIngredientsNeededInCookieType tables; enter criteria =Brown sugar in the ingredient Description field; display the cookie type Description field.

- Which finished cookie types require the labor type frost cookies?
  - o Join the CookieType, LaborType, and LinkageLaborTypeNeededForCookieType tables; enter criteria =Frost cookies in labor type Description field; display the finished cookie type Description field.

INFORMATION NEEDS IN THE PAYROLL PROCESS

We use the relational database tables in Exhibit 14-2 in the examples for developing queries in the payroll process. While admittedly limited in the number of attributes captured, these tables provide sufficient detail to provide a foundation for identifying and satisfying information needs in the payroll process. After listing the tables, we analyze each of the classes and associations in the payroll process pattern to provide some ideas about the types of queries that may satisfy information needs in the payroll process. The queries presented are not a comprehensive set of queries (there are simply too many potential queries to list them all); however, the set provided should provide you guidance for creating similar types of queries.

LaborRequisition

LaborReqID	Date	MaximumBudget ForRequest	TotalEstimated BudgetRequest	LaborRequestPeriod	SupervisorID[FK]
LR1	02/24/2020	$3,000.00	$1,995.00	4/1/2020-4/7/2020	E5
LR2	03/02/2020	$3,000.00	$1,280.00	4/8/2020-4/14/2020	E5

PropositionLaborRequisitionLaborType

LaborReqID	LaborTypeID	HoursNeeded
LR1	AP1	40
LR1	CT1	40
LR1	CT2	40
LR1	US3	35
LR2	AP1	40
LR2	CT1	40
LR2	CT2	40
LR2	US3	40

Exhibit 14-2: Relational Database Tables for an Example Payroll Process

ParticipationLaborRequisitionEmployee

LaborReqID	RequestedEmployeeID
LR1	E16
LR1	E17
LR1	E21
LR1	E23
LR2	E15
LR2	E18
LR2	E21
LR2	E23

DepartmentSupervisor

SupervisorID	AuthorizedSpendingLimit
E5	$425,000.00

Employee

Employee ID	FirstName	LastName	Address	Telephone	DateOfBirth	Rating	Employee PositionType^{FK}	Wage
E5	Patrick	Wellesley	53125 Fenton Dr.	555-1112	03/04/1958	Excellent	Supervisor	$35.50
E15	Donna	Davis	149 Rovetta Dr.	555-9932	02/03/1954	Superior	Cashier	$13.50
E16	Nancy	Hardaway	271 Rovetta Dr.	555-2117	06/11/1956	Excellent	Cashier	$12.75
E17	Joe	Thompson	535 Olson St.	555-2277	04/24/1947	Excellent	Custodian	$9.20
E18	Freda	Matthews	3214 Deerlake St.	555-1222	08/06/1940	Good	Custodian	$8.90
E19	John	Matthews	3214 Deerlake St.	555-1222	10/14/1940	Good	Custodian	$8.90
E20	Paula	Cosgrove	5006 Jazz Ct.	555-5200	04/18/1958	Excellent	Data Entry	$11.50
E21	Rob	Fordham	4444 Zephyr Ln.	555-4545	06/04/1975	Excellent	Data Entry	$11.00
E22	Francis	Johnson	1261 Mason Dr.	555-0129	05/05/1980	Good	Data Entry	$10.75
E23	James	Worthwhile	5432 Wadsworth Ln	555-7777	04/14/1964	Superior	Accountant	$20.00
E36	Diane	Bowersox	9115 Wolfgang Ct	555-7244	09/15/1963	Superior	Payroll	$11.75

EmployeePositionType

EmployeePositionType	PayType	LowEndOfHourlyPayScale	HighEndOfHourlyPayScale
Accountant	Salary	$19.00	$25.00
Cashier	Hourly	$11.00	$15.00
Custodian	Hourly	$8.50	$11.00
Data Entry	Hourly	$9.00	$12.00
Payroll	Hourly	$10.00	$14.00
Supervisor	Salary	$33.00	$38.00

LaborType

LaborTypeID	Description	StandardHourlyWage
AP1	Prepare taxes	$19.00
CT1	Enter data for sales transactions	$9.00
CT2	Cashier duties	$10.00
US3	Clean sales showroom and stockroom	$8.00

Exhibit 14-2 (cont.): Relational Database Tables for an Example Payroll Process

LaborTypeEmployeePositionType

LaborTypeID	EmployeePositionType
AP1	Accountant
CT1	Data Entry
CT2	Cashier
US3	Custodian

LaborSchedule

LaborScheduleID	DateApproved	BeginDate	EndDate	TotalDollarAmount	LaborReqID^{FK}	SupervisorID^{FK}
LS1	02/25/2020	04/01/2020	04/07/2020	$2,072.00	LR1	E5
LS2	03/03/2020	04/08/2020	04/14/2020	$2,136.00	LR2	E5

ReservationLaborScheduleLaborType

LaborScheduleID	LaborTypeID	HoursScheduled
LS1	AP1	40
LS1	CT1	40
LS1	CT2	40
LS1	US3	35
LS2	AP1	40
LS2	CT1	40
LS2	CT2	40
LS2	US3	40

ParticipationLaborScheduleEmployee

LaborScheduleID	ScheduledEmployeeID	HoursScheduled
LS1	E16	40
LS1	E17	35
LS1	E21	40
LS1	E23	40
LS2	E15	40
LS2	E18	40
LS2	E21	40
LS2	E23	40

LaborAcquisition

LaborAcquisitionID	BeginDate	EndDate	TotalHours	GrossPay	EmpID^{FK}	SupervisorID^{FK}
TC50	04/01/2020	04/07/2020	45	$900.00	E23	E5
TC51	04/01/2020	04/07/2020	40	$440.00	E21	E5
TC52	04/01/2020	04/07/2020	40	$510.00	E16	E5
TC53	04/01/2020	04/07/2020	35	$322.00	E17	E5
TC54	04/08/2020	04/14/2020	45	$900.00	E23	E5
TC55	04/08/2020	04/14/2020	40	$440.00	E21	E5
TC56	04/08/2020	04/14/2020	40	$540.00	E15	E5
TC57	04/08/2020	04/14/2020	32	$284.80	E18	E5

Exhibit 14-2 (cont.): Relational Database Tables for an Example Payroll Process

ParticipationLaborAcquisitionOutsideAgency

LaborAcquisitionID	AgencyID	AmountDueToAgency
TC50	S315	$252.00
TC50	S320	$38.25
TC50	S325	$18.00
TC50	S330	$9.00
TC51	S315	$123.20
TC51	S320	$18.70
TC51	S325	$8.80
TC51	S330	$4.40
TC52	S315	$142.80
TC52	S320	$21.68
TC52	S325	$10.20
TC52	S330	$5.10
TC53	S315	$90.16
TC53	S320	$13.69
TC53	S325	$6.44
TC53	S330	$3.22
TC54	S315	$252.00
TC54	S320	$38.25
TC54	S325	$18.00
TC54	S330	$9.00
TC55	S315	$123.20
TC55	S320	$18.70
TC55	S325	$8.80
TC55	S330	$4.40
TC56	S315	$151.20
TC56	S320	$22.95
TC56	S325	$10.80
TC56	S330	$5.40
TC57	S315	$79.75
TC57	S320	$12.10
TC57	S325	$5.70
TC57	S330	$2.85

StockflowLaborAcquisitionLaborType

LaborAcquisitionID	LaborTypeID	HoursWorkedPerLaborType
TC50	AP1	45
TC51	CT1	40
TC52	CT2	40
TC53	US3	35
TC54	AP1	45
TC55	CT1	40
TC56	CT2	40
TC57	US3	32

Exhibit 14-2 (cont.): Relational Database Tables for an Example Payroll Process

FulfillmentLaborAcquisitionLaborSchedule

LaborScheduleID	LaborAcquisitionID
LS1	TC50
LS1	TC51
LS1	TC52
LS1	TC53
LS2	TC54
LS2	TC55
LS2	TC56
LS2	TC57

OutsideAgency

AgencyID	AgencyName	MailingAddress
S315	Internal Revenue Service	PO Box 123512
S320	State Government	PO Box 321533
S325	Blue Health	31253 Elm St.
S330	Best Dental	1472 Beech St.

CashDisbursement

Disb VoucherID	Voucher Date	Dollar Amount	Check Number	Cash AccountID^{FK}	Payroll ClerkID^{FK}	PayeeID^{FK}	PayeeType^{FK}
100	04/14/2020	$2,172.00	40404	Ca123501	E36	Ca987654	Imprest
101	04/14/2020	$582.75	49	Ca987654	E36	E23	Payroll
102	04/14/2020	$284.90	50	Ca987654	E36	E21	Payroll
103	04/14/2020	330.22	51	Ca987654	E36	E16	Payroll
104	04/14/2020	$208.49	52	Ca987654	E36	E17	Payroll
105	04/14/2020	$608.16	53	Ca987654	E36	S315	IRS
106	04/14/2020	$92.32	54	Ca987654	E36	S320	State
107	04/14/2020	$43.44	55	Ca987654	E36	S325	Health
108	04/14/2020	$21.72	56	Ca987654	E36	S330	Dental
109	04/21/2020	$2,164.80	40405	Ca987654	E36	Ca987654	Imprest
110	04/21/2020	$582.75	57	Ca987654	E36	E23	Payroll
111	04/21/2020	$284.90	58	Ca987654	E36	E21	Payroll
112	04/21/2020	$349.65	59	Ca987654	E36	E15	Payroll
113	04/21/2020	$184.40	60	Ca987654	E36	E18	Payroll
114	04/21/2020	$606.15	61	Ca987654	E36	S315	IRS
115	04/21/2020	$92.00	62	Ca987654	E36	S320	State
116	04/21/2020	$43.30	63	Ca987654	E36	S325	Health
117	04/21/2020	$21.65	64	Ca987654	E36	S330	Dental

Cash

CashAccountID	AccountType	Location
Ca123501	Checking	1st Local Bank
Ca987654	Imprest checking	1st Local Bank

Exhibit 14-2 (cont.): Relational Database Tables for an Example Payroll Process

DualityLaborAcquisitionCashDisbursement

LaborAcquisitionID	VoucherNumber
TC50	100
TC50	101
TC50	105
TC50	106
TC50	107
TC50	108
TC51	100
TC51	102
TC51	105
TC51	106
TC51	107
TC51	108
TC52	100
TC52	103
TC52	105
TC52	106
TC52	107
TC52	108
TC53	100
TC53	104
TC53	105
TC53	106
TC53	107
TC53	108
TC54	109
TC54	110
TC54	114
TC54	115
TC54	116
TC54	117
TC55	109
TC55	111
TC55	114
TC55	115
TC55	116
TC55	117
TC56	109
TC56	112
TC56	114
TC56	115
TC56	116
TC56	117
TC57	109
TC57	113
TC57	114
TC57	115
TC57	116
TC57	117

Exhibit 14-2 (cont.): Relational Database Tables for an Example Payroll Process

PayrollClerk

PayrollClerkID	FidelityBondRating
E36	AA

Exhibit 14-2 (cont.): Relational Database Tables for an Example Payroll Process

Resource Queries in the Payroll Process

Labor type and cash are the resources that most commonly exist in the payroll process. For each resource, users may need any of the following:

- Detailed status information at one or more points in time for each resource instance
- Detailed status information at one or more points in time for only those resource instances meeting specified criteria
- Summarized status information at one or more points in time for all resource instances
- Summarized status information at one or more points in time for only those resource instances meeting specified criteria

With regard to each list item, users may need to know all characteristics of the instances in the answer set, or they may need only a subset of the characteristics.

Labor is typically tracked only at the type level. Cash is tracked by the accounts in which the cash is stored. Some example queries and procedures for creating the queries based on the tables in this chapter are as follows:

- What are the descriptions for all labor types for the enterprise?
  - Use the LaborType table; display all fields.
- Which labor types have standard hourly wage rates less than $10?
  - Use the LaborType table; enter criteria <10 in the StandardHourlyWage field; display labor type Description.
- Does the enterprise own any imprest cash accounts?
  - Use the Cash table; enter criteria LIKE *imprest* in the AccountType field; display the CashAccountID. (The LIKE command coupled with the wild card * symbols will identify any account type that includes the word imprest in the type name).
- What is the average standard hourly wage rate for all labor types?
  - Use the LaborType table; apply the AVG aggregation function to the StandardHourlyWage field.

Event Queries in the Payroll Process

Users may need information regarding events. The most common events in the payroll process are labor requisitions, labor schedules, labor acquisitions, and cash disbursements. For each of these types of events, users may need any of the following:
- Detailed information about each event instance
- Detailed information about each event instance that meets specified criteria

- Summarized information for all instances of an event type for a specified time period
- Summarized information for only those instances of an event type for a specified time period that meet specified criteria

Some example queries to satisfy information needs regarding events in the payroll process are (among many other possibilities) as follows:
- What is the maximum budget amount for labor requisition LR7?
    - Use the LaborRequisition table; set criteria for the LaborReqID to be LR7; apply the MAX aggregation function to the MaximumBudgetForRequest field.
- When was labor schedule LS7 approved?
    - Use the LaborSchedule table; set criteria for the LaborScheduleID to be LS7; display the DateApproved field.
- How many days of labor are included on labor acquisition TC49?
    - Use the LaborAcquisition table; set criteria for the LaborAcquisitionID to be TC49; subtract the BeginDate from the EndDate. Because this involves a date/time calculation, whether you get meaningful results depends on the software you use.
- How many cash disbursements were made on 4/14/2020?
    - Use the CashDisbursement table; set criteria for the VoucherDate to be 4/14/2020; apply the COUNT aggregation function to the DisbVoucherID field.
- What is the dollar value of wages expense for April, 2020?
    - Use the LaborAcquisition table; set criteria for the BeginDate field to be >=4/1/2020 and for the EndDate field to be <= 4/30/2020; apply the SUM aggregation function to the GrossPay field.
    - Note: this query reveals the need for companies to track labor acquisitions at a finer level of detail than in this example. If the desired wages expense period only includes part of the timecard period, it will be impossible to isolate what portion of the gross pay applied to the desired wages expense period.
- What total dollar amount of withholdings should have been added to the payable account for state government as a result of labor acquisitions during April 2020?
    - Use the LaborAcquisition table joined to the ParticipationLaborAcquisitionOutsideAgency table; set criteria for the BeginDate to be >=4/1/2020 and for the EndDate to be <=4/30/2020; apply the SUM aggregation operator to the AmountDueToAgency field where the AgencyID field = S320.

Agent Queries in the Payroll Process
The agents commonly involved in payroll processes are the employees from whom labor is acquired, the department supervisors who authorize labor acquisitions, and the payroll clerks who generate the paychecks (cash disbursements). Queries may be needed to obtain any of the following:
- Detailed status information at one or more points in time for each employee
- Detailed status information at one or more points in time for each employee who meets specified criteria
- Summarized status information at one or more points in time for all employees

- Summarized status information at one or more points in time for all employees who meet specified criteria

Some example queries based on the tables in this chapter are as follows:
- What are the names and positions of the employees who have been rated as excellent?
  - Use the Employee table; set criteria for the rating field to be Excellent; display the FirstName, LastName, and Position fields
- What is the average wage of the data entry employees?
  - Use the Employee table, set criteria for the Position field to be "Data Entry" and use the AVG aggregation function to average the Wage
- What are the names and birth dates of employees who were born in 1960 or earlier?
  - Use the Employee table; set criteria for the DateOfBirth field to be <=12/31/1960; display the FirstName, LastName and DateOfBirth fields

ASSOCIATION QUERIES IN THE PAYROLL PROCESS

Combining information from various resource, event, and agent tables according to the associations in which they participate can provide much richer data than single class queries. We next discuss queries based on the various types of associations in the payroll process.

Duality Association Queries in the Payroll Process

The duality association in the payroll process connects labor acquisitions to cash disbursements, as it represents exchanges of cash for labor. Information needs with respect to duality associations in the payroll process include (among other possibilities):
- Calculation of the outstanding wages payable balance at a point in time
- Identification of the labor acquisition for which a cash disbursement was made
- Identification of cash advances made to employees
- Identification and calculation of amounts withheld from gross pay amounts for employee and employer payroll-related taxes

Based on the tables in this chapter, duality queries could investigate
- Had labor acquisition TC50 been paid for as of 4/10/2020?
  - Join the LaborAcquisition, DualityLaborAcquisitionCashDisbursement, and CashDisbursement tables; set criteria for LaborAcquisitionID to be TC50 and for the VoucherDate to be <=4/10/2020.
- What is the balance of wages payable as of April 30, 2020?
  - Query 1: Wages payable are increased by net pay amounts that represent the cost of labor acquired net of taxes and other withholdings amounts (those amounts are classified into other liability accounts). To find the net pay amounts for labor acquisitions that occurred through April 30, 2020, use the LaborAcquisition table joined to the ParticipationLaborAcquisitionOutsideAgency table; set criteria for the EndDate to be <=4/30/2020, and group by LaborAcquisitionID and GrossPay, and sum the AmountDueToAgency.
  - Query 2: Calculate net pay per LaborAcquisitionID by netting the amounts determined in Query 1.

o <u>Query 3:</u> Wages payable is decreased by paychecks, those are the cash disbursements that applied to the labor acquisitions' net pay amounts (not the cash disbursements that applied to the withheld portions of the labor acquisitions). To find the paycheck amounts that occurred through April 30, 2020, join the CashDisbursement and DualityLaborAcquisitionCashDisbursement tables using the DisbVoucherID. Set criteria for the VoucherDate to be <=4/30/2020, group by the VoucherNumber and DollarAmount where the PayeeType = Payroll.

o <u>Query 4:</u> Sum the DollarAmount from query 3.

o <u>Query 5:</u> Subtract the sum of amounts calculated in query 4 from the sum of net pay amounts calculated in query 2 to get wages payable.

Stockflow Association Queries in the Payroll Process

Stockflow relationships in the payroll process represent the connections between resources labor type and cash and the economic events that increase labor and decrease cash. Some common stockflow information needs in the payroll process (among other possibilities) are:

- Which cash account was decreased by a cash disbursement?
- What is the total dollar amount of cash disbursements made from a specified cash account during a time period?
- What quantity of each labor type was acquired by a labor acquisition event?
- How many different labor types were acquired by a labor acquisition event?
- Which labor acquisitions have involved a specified labor type?

Based on the tables in this chapter, stockflow queries could investigate:

- What total dollar amount of cash disbursements were made from imprest checking accounts during the month of April, 2020?
    - o Join the CashDisbursement and Cash tables; set criteria for the AccountType to be LIKE *imprest* and for the VoucherDate to be BETWEEN 4/1/2020 and 4/30/2020, and sum the cash disbursement DollarAmount.
- How many different types of labor were acquired on labor acquisition TC49?
    - o Join the LaborAcquisition and StockflowLaborAcquisitionLaborType tables, set criteria for the stockflow LaborAcquisitionID to be TC49 and apply the COUNT aggregation operator to the stockflow LaborTypeID field.

Fulfillment Queries in the Payroll Process

The fulfillment associations typically materialized in the payroll process represent relationships between the labor requisitions and labor schedules (the schedules fulfill the requisitions) and between the labor schedules and labor acquisitions (the acquisitions fulfill the schedules). Fulfillment association queries in the payroll process in general include:

- Identification of unfilled commitment events (e.g., schedules for which work has not yet been performed, requisitions for which schedules have not yet been developed)
- Identification of filled commitment events (e.g., schedules for which labor was acquired, labor requisitions for which schedules were developed)
- Identification of economic events for which commitments were not made (e.g., labor acquisitions that were not scheduled)

- Identification of results of commitment events (e.g., which labor acquisitions resulted from a labor schedule, and were there any discrepancies between the scheduled and actual acquisitions)

Based on the example tables in this chapter, questions such as the following could be answered via fulfillment association queries in the payroll process:
- Has staffing plan 1 been fulfilled?
    - Join LaborRequisition and LaborSchedule tables with an outer join that keeps all labor requisitions from the LaborRequisition table; include LaborReqID from LaborRequisition table and LaborScheduleID from LaborSchedule table; set criteria for the LaborReqID to be LR1.
- Have any labor acquisitions occurred that were not scheduled?
    - Join LaborAcquisition and FulfillmentLaborAcquisitionLaborSchedule tables with an outer join that keeps all acquisitions; set criteria for the LaborScheduleID to be IS NULL.
- What staffing plan triggered labor schedule LS1?
    - Join LaborSchedule and LaborRequisition tables; set criteria for the LaborScheduleID to be LS1.

Reservation Queries in the Payroll Process
The reservation association that is typically materialized in the payroll process represent the relationships between labor schedules and the types of labor the schedules commit to acquire. Some enterprises also materialize the reservation associations between the labor schedules and the cash resource the schedules commit to decrease. Therefore, reservation associations in the payroll process are commonly used in queries to satisfy information needs about the eventual effect of labor schedules on cash or about the labor types involved in labor schedules. Some information needs (among many others) in the payroll process are:
- What labor type or types is a labor schedule agreeing to acquire?
- How many hours of a specified labor type is a labor schedule committing to acquire?
- What is the dollar value of cash reserved by a labor schedule?
- On what dates is a labor schedule committing to acquire a specified labor type?

Based on the tables in this chapter, one can answer questions such as the following via reservation relationship queries in the payroll process:
- What are the descriptions of the labor types that labor schedule LS1 commits to acquire?
    - Join the ReservationLaborScheduleLaborType and LaborType tables; set criteria for the LaborScheduleID to be LS1 and display the labor type Description field.
- How many hours of cashier duties does labor schedule LS1 commit to acquire?
    - Join ReservationLaborScheduleLaborType and LaborType tables; set criteria for the labor type Description to be LIKE *cashier* and for the LaborScheduleID to be LS1, and display the HoursScheduled.

Participation Queries in the Payroll Process
Participation associations in the payroll process typically represent the associations between labor requisitions, labor schedules, labor acquisitions, and cash disbursements and the employees who authorize those events (typically supervisors for labor acquisition and payroll clerks for cash disbursements) and the employees who accomplish those events (typically a generalized employee entity set). The labor acquisition and cash disbursement events are also typically associated with outside agencies that benefit from employees' labor, because a portion of the employees' compensation becomes compensation to the agencies. Therefore, participation associations are commonly used in queries to satisfy information needs regarding the identification of employees who participated in events or regarding the events in which specified employees participated. Some common payroll process information needs are:

- Which department supervisor authorized a labor requisition?
- By how many labor schedules has an employee been scheduled to work?
- How many hours did an employee work on a labor acquisition?
- How many labor schedules has a specific department supervisor authorized?
- Which payroll clerk issued a specific cash disbursement?

Based on the tables in this chapter, one can answer questions such as the following via participation association payroll process queries:

- What is the name of the supervisor who authorized labor requisition LR1?
  - Join the LaborRequisition, DepartmentSupervisor, and Employee tables; set criteria for LaborReqID to be LR1 and display the supervisor FirstName and LastName fields.
- What are the names of the employees who were scheduled on labor schedule LS1?
  - Join the ParticipationLaborScheduleEmployee and Employee tables; set criteria for the LaborScheduleID to be LS1, and display the employee FirstName and LastName fields.
- Who worked on labor acquisition TC50 and how many hours did the employee work?
  - Join the LaborAcquisition and Employee tables, set criteria for LaborAcquisitionID to be TC50, display the employee FirstName, LastName, and TotalHours.

CONCLUDING COMMENTS
This chapter explored the kinds of questions one can answer by running queries on databases that portray the conversion and payroll business processes structured consistently with REA. We systematically examined each type of class and each type of association in the two business processes, giving examples of information needs and queries that could address those needs. The information needs identified do not comprise a comprehensive list, but simply a starting point.

KEY TERMS AND CONCEPTS
Conversion process queries
Linkage association queries
Payroll process queries

REVIEW QUESTIONS

R14-1. Give an example of a resource query in the conversion process.

R14-2. Give an example of a duality query in the conversion process.

R14-3. Give an example of a fulfillment query in the conversion process.

R14-4. Give an example of an event query in the payroll process.

R14-5. Give an example of a reservation query in the payroll process.

MULTIPLE CHOICE QUESTIONS

MC14-1. To make a query that finds the date of the most recent material requisition, on which class or association should one focus?

    A) Material requisition event class

    B) Material issuance event class

    C) Fulfillment association between material requisition and material issuance

    D) Reservation association between material requisition and raw materials

MC14-2. Using the tables in Exhibit 14-1, identify the quantity of shortening that a recipe would require to make a batch of 12 snickerdoodles.

    A) 0.5 cup

    B) 0.67 cup

    C) 0.5 teaspoon

    D) 1 cup

MC14-3. Using the tables in Exhibit 14-1, what total quantity of flour was issued into production on 7/15/2020 (for all cookie types produced that day)?

    A) 7 cups

    B) 8 cups

    C) 10.67 cups

    D) 15 cups

MC14-4. Using the tables in Exhibit 14-1, how much total time did Ethel spend mixing moist ingredients on 7/15/2020?

    A) 30 seconds

    B) 4 minutes

    C) 5 minutes

    D) 10 minutes

MC14-5. Using the tables in Exhibit 14-1, how many types of ingredients are needed to make frosted sugar cookies with candy sprinkles?

    A) 16

    B) 9

    C) 18

    D) 11

MC14-6. Using the tables in Exhibit 14-2, how many different types of labor were requisitioned on LR2?
   A) 2
   B) 4
   C) 6
   D) 8

MC14-7. Using the tables in Exhibit 14-2, which labor types have standard hourly wage rates < $10?
   A) CT1 and CT2
   B) CT1 and US3
   C) AP1
   D) CT1, CT2, and US3

MC14-8. Using the tables in Exhibit 14-2, for how many hours is Joe Thompson scheduled from April 8 to April 14, 2020?
   A) 35
   B) 75
   C) 80
   D) 0

MC14-9. Using the tables in Exhibit 14-2, what is the balance of wages payable at the end of the day on April 7, 2020?
   A) $2,172.00
   B) $1,406.36
   C) $ 765.64
   D) $ 0

MC14-10. Using the tables in Exhibit 14-2, did the company come in under or over budget for labor schedule LS2?
   A) Under budget by $28.80
   B) Over budget by $28.80
   C) Over budget by $7.20
   D) Under budget by $7.20

CHAPTER **15**

REA and Emerging Technologies in Accounting

LEARNING OBJECTIVES

Several technologies have emerged in recent years that have the potential to disrupt the current practices of accounting and auditing. REA may facilitate and be facilitated by these emerging, transformative technologies. After studying this chapter, you should be able to:

1. Describe transformative technologies in accounting, including blockchain (distributed ledger technology), cognitive computing, Internet of Things, robotic process automation, and accounting analytics
2. Explain the extent to which REA facilitates (or is facilitated by) adoption of various transformative technologies in accounting
3. Speculate about the extent to which the transformative technologies introduced in this chapter will disrupt the practices of accounting and auditing
4. Explain how accountants can adapt to changes caused by transformative technologies such as those introduced in this chapter

BLOCKCHAIN

Blockchain is a distributed ledger system whereby records conveying offer and acceptance are verified and stored. The immutability and transparency of blockchain provide a layer of trust to the internet. *Immutability* does not literally mean the blockchain cannot be changed – rather, it means that any such change will be immediately revealed and rejected by the blockchain. Transparency means that all participants on a blockchain can see the blocks on the chain, although some blockchains may allow different levels of permission to allow some data to be private. Although blockchain was originally designed to support the cryptocurrency called *Bitcoin*, the applications of blockchain technology to accounting are completely separate from Bitcoin or any other cryptocurrency. *Cryptocurrency* is an encrypted digital currency (not physical like paper currency) that does not need a financial intermediary such as a central bank. We can adopt blockchain technology while using traditional currencies such as U.S. dollars, euros, or yen (with or without using cryptocurrency). There is apparently a lot of naïve mixing of these concepts where we have seen people equating cryptocurrency and blockchain, and it is inappropriate to overgeneralize comparisons between the two.

Multiple kinds of blockchains currently exist. *Public blockchains* are available to anyone and everyone who wants to become a node on the chain and who has the appropriate hardware to join. A *private blockchain* may be within a single enterprise, whereby the blockchain is only available to users within the enterprise who have the appropriate encryption key. A private blockchain may alternatively be a *consortium blockchain*, whereby multiple enterprises have combined efforts to create and jointly lead a blockchain to support a shared endeavor. Consortium blockchains are only available to those participants who have the appropriate encryption key. *Semi-private blockchains* are led by a single enterprise but have participants across enterprises, for example, across a supply chain.

A somewhat simplified explanation of how blockchain essentially works follows.

1. One party initiates a transaction to transfer currency (or some type of tokenized asset) to another party.
2. The transaction is grouped with other transactions to form a block.
3. The block is broadcast to all the nodes on the blockchain network.
4. The nodes agree that the block of transactions is valid, assigning a hash number that builds on the hash number of the most recent previously approved block.
5. The new block is added to the chain, updating all participants' copies of the chain on the network.
6. The currency (or other tokenized asset) is then transferred to the receiving party.

Note that companies may use this not just for payments, but for simple tracking of asset movement across a supply chain.

Immutability in a blockchain means that any changes after a block is added to the chain invalidate that block and all subsequent blocks and thus become evident to all. Any changes to a block on the chain will change the hash number assigned to that block on only the copy of the chain belonging to the node that changed the block. That will likewise change the hash numbers on all subsequent blocks on that copy of the chain. The discrepancy will be revealed as soon as the chain attempts to add another block, as the one node will not generate the same new hash number to assign to the new block. Consensus rules, such that the one node that is out of alignment with all the other nodes will have to replace its copy of the chain with the consensus copy before it can add any more blocks to the chain. If, after a block is added to the chain, an error is discovered in that block, a new block must be added to correct the error, because the original block cannot be changed.

While blockchain is still immature as a technology, and is mostly used for cryptocurrency transactions, some enterprises use blockchain to track physical assets and to store and process smart contracts. Supply chain use cases abound, and the participating enterprises cite major benefits resulting from all parties knowing precisely where in the supply chain the goods reside at any point in time. *Smart contracts* track the flow of economic exchanges from the point of commitment through the happy path economic events and, if applicable, through the unhappy path reversal events. Smart contracts embed the contract terms into computer code such that the exchange moves along the appropriate path as the contracting parties meet (or fail to meet) each contract condition. Currently the smart contract technologies are advancing more quickly than contract law; therefore entering into smart contracts carries some risk.

Of the emerging technologies discussed in this chapter, blockchain has the highest potential to disrupt many business processes and many enterprises. Financial institutions could become significantly disintermediated. Such institutions recognize this threat and are investing heavily in blockchain research, trying to find a way to shift the way in which they provide intermediation in the financial markets, rather than having their role significantly diminished or possibly even eliminated.

Blockchain may significantly disrupt the role of auditors, as the blockchain itself could serve as a public audit trail of all transactions. While designed to be a supporting infrastructure for Bitcoin, blockchain has in fact become a new source of trust. Public accounting firms (long considered sources of trust) are also investing heavily in blockchain research, and the Big Four firms all advertise blockchain auditing services. The extent to which such services are necessary remains to be seen. Until blockchain technology matures and is more fully understood, no one really knows. Tax accounting is also likely to be affected if blockchain is adopted for accounting. Tax reporting could become a thing of the past, if the blockchain is set up such that governmental tax agencies have access to all financial records – both for enterprises and individuals. Don't expect any of this to happen anytime soon; indeed, any change of this magnitude would face political stumbling blocks that could prevent it from ever occurring. In fact, tax authorities currently haven't been able to agree on whether cryptocurrencies are currencies, investments, or some other type of assets for tax purposes.

Blockchain clearly has the potential to provide a certified record of skills obtained by individuals, and it also has the potential to provide a certified record of ownership of assets. The need for property title insurance may disappear, as all property transfers could be public record on a blockchain. Medical records may be stored on a blockchain and accessed (with permission only) by patients, medical care providers, pharmacies, insurance providers, and so forth. Imagine not having to fill out the same medical history information on paper forms for every new doctor you visit, but rather giving the new doctor permission to access your medical history on a blockchain. That blockchain can be set up such that the patient has control over what information each doctor or other provider is permitted to see.

Blockchain is especially useful in scenarios that traditionally have required intermediaries and much back-and-forth sending of paperwork, as the blockchain eliminates the need for the intermediary and provides a shared ledger available to all participants, thus eliminating the need to send paperwork back and forth.

Intermediaries are companies such as banks or title agencies that serve as trust verifiers in financial transactions. The original Bitcoin/blockchain paper resulted from dissatisfaction with the banks in the economic recession that occurred in approximately 2006-2009. With Bitcoin, parties may transfer payment amongst each other without the need for a bank or other intermediary. Because all parties on the blockchain have duplicate copies of the same ledger, the need for a trusted intermediary disappears.

Recall the document flow discussed in the acquisition and revenue business process chapters, and imagine those documents strung together in a supply chain. Picture the following scenario:

The manufacturer stores data about its finished goods in its enterprise database. To get its finished products to its overseas customers, the products must travel by boat, then by train, then by truck. At each stage along the way, documentation must be prepared, with copies sent back and forth between various transportation providers and the manufacturer. Each participant in that chain has its own system in which they enter the relevant data, with the manufacturer updating its own enterprise database based on the documentation received at each step. With a blockchain, as the goods move along in the various modes of transit, the transportation providers would update the blockchain to which all the participants have access, such that all of them can tell where the goods are in real time.

Whether blockchain's potential can be fully realized with multiple types of blockchains as is current practice remains to be seen. Our guess is that to fully realize its potential, there can only be one blockchain, with all participants allowed appropriate levels of access. To have multiple blockchains would be similar to having multiple internets. How would you know which one to search? Time will tell whether our guess has any merit. We are not suggesting that no benefit results from the use of multiple blockchains; simply that more benefit would result from just one.

To fully embrace blockchain technology, accounting must undergo a fundamental shift, from systems that are enterprise centric, to systems that take an independent view. Currently, each party to an economic exchange records the exchange events in its own separate accounting or enterprise system to reflect its perspective of the events. For example, one party to an exchange of goods for cash (say Miller Company) records the exchange as a purchase and a cash payment, and the other party (say Keyton Enterprises) records the exchange as a sale and a cash receipt. The two parties' systems are separate and enterprise-centric, i.e., kept from the perspective of the enterprise. For a blockchain to replace separate accounting and enterprise systems, the recording perspective for each exchange must reflect an independent view. Instead of the events recorded as different phenomena in different systems by Miller and Keyton, the events must be recorded as a transfer of goods with the initiating party being Keyton and the receiving party being Miller, and a transfer of currency with the initiating party being Miller and the receiving party being Keyton. While not easy, the transition from an enterprise-centric to an independent view is possible in an REA-based system; whereas it seems to be impossible in a general ledger based system.

COGNITIVE COMPUTING

If you saw IBM's Watson defeat renowned champions Ken Jennings and Brad Rutter on the U.S. television show *Jeopardy* in 2011, then you have witnessed a demonstration of cognitive computing (you can find videos on YouTube). *Cognitive computing* consists of computerized models that simulate human thought processes, by combining artificial intelligence and signal processing, encompassing machine learning, reasoning, natural language processing, and other technologies to understand, reason, learn, and interact in a specific domain. Experts believe that accounting is a domain ripe for automation with cognitive computing.

Cognitive computing may assist auditors with decisions that in the past have required experience-based judgment skills. Because cognitive computing technologies can digest judgments from thousands of audits across many years, while redacting sensitive client details, such tools may in fact prove superior to any specific human auditor's judgment, which is limited to a relatively smaller number of audits across a relatively smaller time frame. Because of the tremendous processing ability of cognitive technologies, auditors will no longer need to extract and test samples of client data, extrapolating test results to the overall population. Instead, such systems can test clients' entire data sets. KPMG has partnered with IBM Watson to develop cognitive technology audit tools, and H&R Block has also partnered with IBM Watson to develop cognitive technology tax tools. Other large accounting and tax firms are engaging in similar endeavors. Currently the cost of cognitive computing technologies makes them available only to the largest of firms, which puts smaller firms at a tremendous disadvantage, at least until software developers create commercialized software applications to make such technology more accessible to a wider range of users.

Most experts seem to agree that rather than replacing accountants, cognitive technologies will change the nature of accountants' work, allowing them to make better informed decisions and eliminating many mundane, tedious tasks. Because cognitive technologies facilitate continuous audit and allow clients glimpses of their tax position throughout the year, the infamous "busy season" may go away.

REA and cognitive computing have much in common. REA is a form of semantic modeling based on knowledge representation. Semantic modeling and knowledge representation are important components of cognitive computing. Capturing the meaning of economic exchanges should more easily and effectively allow that data to be used by a cognitive computing system than do the general ledger account codes. General ledger coding creates a rather brittle structure – once you decide to code something a certain way, it destroys its ability to be used in a different way.

The generalization associations discussed in chapter 10 come from the field of artificial intelligence. Another cognitive computing concept is augmented intensional reasoning. Intensional reasoning is the use of data structures for automated information retrieval. ***Augmented intensional reasoning*** adds domain knowledge to aid in making such information retrieval meaningful for that domain. While we demonstrated the implementation of REA using relational database technology, REA can also be implemented using cognitive technologies – and such implementations are far more powerful than relational implementations. Consider the conversion of the conceptual models into the logical (relational) models and physical (relational) models (as introduced in chapter 3) and think about what got lost in the process. The facts that a class was stereotyped as a resource type or an economic decrement event, or that an association was labeled as a stockflow or duality are lost in the translation. If we had implemented these constructs using object-oriented programming or another cognitive technology, such tools can reason with the understanding that stockflow and duality relationships are different. As a result, because stockflows and dualities make up the value chain, such tools can reason holistically about the entire value chain.

INTERNET OF THINGS

The ***Internet of Things (IoT)*** is a system of interconnected appliances, machines, vehicles, and other devices that communicate with each other and exchange data using the Internet, without any human intervention or interaction. Computer chips and Wi-Fi capabilities installed in such devices generate huge quantities of data communicating their status and outputs. If you drive a newer model car, most likely your car is constantly sending data to a device at its manufacturer, allowing the manufacturer or a designated representative to contact you when your car needs maintenance. In businesses, production machinery may communicate with production supervisors, notifying them in advance that a component will soon wear out and cause the assembly line to shut down if it is not replaced, thus saving on costly down-time. A freezer may have built-in sensors that alert the enterprise when the temperature inside the freezer becomes warmer than it should, such that the enterprise may (if possible) repair the malfunction, or else move the contents to an alternative freezer before anything spoils

Combining Blockchain with IoT can be a very effective means of tracking and maintaining smart contracts. Consider the supply chain example described in the Blockchain section earlier in this chapter. Say that the goods shipped along that route are perishable and must remain refrigerated at a certain temperature. The manufacturer could install various types of sensors into the refrigerated container in which the goods are shipped. One type of sensor could track the container's location, updating a database as the container moves. Another type of sensor could monitor the temperature inside the container, sending alerts whenever the temperature changes. If the temperature exceeds a safe value, the smart contract conditions could be flagged as out of compliance, triggering penalties or nullifying the contract altogether.

To the extent that IoT encompasses enterprise-controlled resources, it would have implications for the REA model. The IoT device itself would be a resource, however, the stream of data measurements associated with the device over time would be related to one or more events (business events typically, as opposed to an economic event). The implications of IoT stretch beyond enterprise-controlled resources. For example, an appliance or car that an enterprise sells to a customer could collect IoT data that are sent back to the (selling) enterprise – even though the customer owns the resource. This data transfer may support, for example, for error diagnosis, customer service, or warranty claim evaluation. Therefore, REA is extensible beyond enterprise-centric activities to account for these new sources and streams of data that IoT facilitates, and broadens our view of data available for analytics.

IoT sensors measure phenomena such as acoustics, vibration, humidity, moisture, flow, proximity, electricity, magnetics, radio frequencies, and chemicals. Data communicating these measurements are available to enterprises that use IoT technology. Some of these data may result in better accounting measurements – for example, the sensors in manufacturing equipment may enable precise measurement of raw materials that without the sensors would be considered indirect materials. Converting indirect materials to direct materials facilitates cost traceability and cost management. Combining IoT data with ERP, point of sale, and customer relationship management data may help accountants to better predict product defects to improve estimated warranty liabilities.

Enterprises may use IoT data to better manage customer experiences, resulting in increased revenues and improving net income. For example, Disney created wearable MagicBands to improve guests' experiences at its hotels and theme parks, but more importantly to increase efficiencies and revenues.[37] With MagicBands, guests may leave their wallets locked safely in their rooms, as they use their bands for theme park admission, to pay for purchases anywhere on Disney property, and even to unlock their hotel room doors. They also allow guests to pre-select up to three FastPasses (passes that allow guests to wait in a shorter line for a ride, a show, or a

---

[37] https://www.forbes.com/sites/deborahsweeney/2013/01/09/4-benefits-that-magicbands-bring-to-the-wonderful-world-of-disney-parks/#18e63d3a7446

character meet and greet) weeks in advance for each day of their planned park visits. Disney is able to track guests' locations as long as they are wearing their bands on Disney property. As a result, Disney can monitor and communicate wait times for attractions to guests via a smart phone app and via in-park information boards. Disney can monitor buying and dining habits of individuals and tailor offers to them. Guests can choose not to wear the bands and instead opt for a magnetic card park ticket and a magnetic card room key to avoid revealing so much personal data to Disney. However, based on the authors' observations during recent visits, most guests appear to wear and enjoy wearing their MagicBands.

ROBOTIC PROCESS AUTOMATION

If you have ever created or seen an Excel macro, or automated scripts in auditing software, such as IDEAScript in CaseWare's IDEA, then you have seen simple instances of *Robotic Process Automation* (RPA). RPA is the intelligent automation of repetitive tasks that follow prescribed rules or algorithms. Such algorithms may use structured or unstructured inputs. Accounting tasks such as reconciliations of physical counts to accounting records will likely be done by RPA-enabled technologies rather than by humans in the not-so-distant future. Some enterprises are already using drones to count and assess the condition of inventory items, to collect data, to provide security and surveillance, to make repairs, and even to deliver packages. Some enterprises are already using robots to manufacture products and even to assist in surgeries.

RPA does not require a drone or a robot – the key part of the definition is the process automation (also note that some use the term robot, or simply "bot," to refer to a software application that automates a process). Physical tasks need to be automated with physical objects such as drones or robots; whereas mental and document-based tasks may be automated with software applications – such applications are able to read and extract data from documents and write data to documents. While alarmists put forth images of robots replacing accountants, the likely near-term reality is that accountants will be able to substitute tasks that are easy to automate with ones that are more meaningful, judgment-oriented, and mentally engaging. For example, instead of spending time and effort preparing a routine tax filing that a bot can complete,[38] a tax accountant can instead be strategizing and planning for the next year.

An important distinction between RPA and cognitive computing is that RPA doesn't learn as it is processing. One teaches the robot/software exactly what to do, and if anything changes in the structure of what the bot is working with, the bot will either not be able to complete its processing or it will complete it with incorrect results. For example, say a bot's processing involves opening three different spreadsheets, extracting specific data fields from each of the spreadsheets, manipulating the data and writing resulting figures into twelve different fields on a tax form. That automated process will work consistently and accurately every time as long as the inputs remain consistent and reliable. However, if anything changes – e.g., if the spreadsheet software is updated such that its menu commands are slightly different, or if the tax form's layout is modified – the bot will continue following its original instructions and may not recognize that anything changed. If the original instructions still make some process happen, even if it isn't the original process, then the bot will keep operating, but it won't produce the intended results. If the original instructions simply don't work anymore because of the changed software or form layout, then the

---

[38] https://www.youtube.com/watch?v=3Nc-NqfmHSA&feature=youtu.be

bot will simply stop and produce an error message. Either way, the bot is "broken." Cognitive computing, on the other hand, results in the software learning from the examples it has processed so that even if future examples aren't exactly the same, the software can continue processing.

REA has the potential to facilitate RPA because the use of the REA ontology allows for a consistent representation of data and relationships among data. Imagine a scenario where several firms have enterprise systems based on the REA ontology. An external auditor would be able to have a consistent approach to data extraction and analysis that they could automate with RPA software. Additionally, this would create a market for software vendors to create REA-based RPA software. Currently, the potential of REA is limited by the fact that so many enterprises have already invested in ERP with established vendors as opposed to doing "clean slate" design/implementations based on the REA ontology. Although software vendor Workday designed its ERP software in a way that is consistent with many aspects of the REA ontology, most other ERP products bear only surface resemblance to REA, as evidenced by the centrality of their general ledger modules.

The current market leaders in RPA software[39] are Automation Anywhere[40], UiPath[41], Blue Prism[42], Pegasystems[43], and Thoughtonomy[44]. One key advantage of vendor products such as these, is that the programming requirements are typically minimal; in-house RPA development, by definition involves significant programming. While these software products offer tremendous potential, management should treat these tools like any other IT tools. Enterprises must analyze the costs and benefits from both a strategic and a governance viewpoint before deciding whether to invest. Investments in IT are costly and management needs to understand the technology, and resist the temptation to quickly initiate RPA projects just because they are popular. Therefore, management needs to do proof-of-concept and prototype testing before launching a large-scale RPA implementation.

ACCOUNTING ANALYTICS

You may wonder why we include analytics as an emerging technology in this chapter, when the book has analytics in its title and we have already included three chapters on querying, which is one form of analytics. *Accounting analytics* is the process of transforming accounting-related data into knowledge to add value to decisions. Accounting analytics is an emerging technology because its use in practice has changed dramatically over the past few years, and new tools and applications continue to be developed each year. All the major accounting firms are investing in accounting analytics, and they are encouraging colleges and universities to expand their curricula to offer more analytics to help students develop an analytic mindset.

Interestingly, the word analytics has different meanings to different people. Accountants have done some types of analytics for many years. They calculate various financial ratios to analyze liquidity,

---

[39] Sharma, S. "Oven Decision Matrix: Selecting a Robotic Process Automation (RPA) Platform, 2018-19" published by Ovum Consulting, December 11, 2018.
[40] https://www.automationanywhere.com/
[41] https://www.uipath.com/
[42] https://www.blueprism.com/
[43] https://www.pega.com/
[44] https://thoughtonomy.com/

profitability, and solvency. They create pro forma financial statements and use sensitivity analysis to examine the effects of various possible scenarios. They create common size financial statements and analyze trends in financial statements across time. If accountants have been conducting such analytics for many years, then, what makes this an emerging or transformative technology? The quantity and types of data available for accountants to analyze has increased exponentially, and that volume and variety enables and requires new types of analyses. Powerful software is now available with which accountants can easily create many different kinds of visualizations. Further, the amount of analytics work that accountants do is increasing relative to their non-analytics work. For accountants to take advantage of the many types of data and tools with which to analyze these data, they must understand how data are stored and develop the skills to extract and manipulate data. The previous chapters of this book are intended to help you develop that skill set. In addition to the data skills included in this book, accountants also need statistical modeling and optimization skills beyond the scope of this book.

One of the first steps in accounting analytics should be to ask the right questions – determine who needs what information and for what purpose, and then use one's understanding of the enterprise and its value system, value chain, and business processes to know what questions to ask. Once one determines what questions to ask, the next step is extract, transform, and load (ETL) the data that's needed to answer those questions. ETL requires understanding how the data is currently stored, as well as how to convert the data from its current form into one that is useful for analysis. ETL involves collecting the data and cleaning the data – for example, removing duplicate records, ensuring data types are correct, identifying data inconsistencies, and so forth. If the data is stored in a manner that is consistent with the REA pattern, with adequate data entry controls in place, the ETL process should be relatively easy for analytics that require only within-enterprise accounting data.

Most enterprises do not store data in such a manner, and the ETL process can be cumbersome and time consuming. And whenever an enterprise (whether or not it has an REA-based system) wants to analyze data combined from multiple data sources, including data from outside the enterprise, the ETL process may comprise as much as 80 percent of the analytic work. That is dismaying, given that 76 percent of data scientists view collecting data sets and cleaning and organizing data as the least enjoyable part of their work.[45]

Even when the enterprise data is not stored in a manner consistent with REA, having learned the REA ontology should enable one to see how one should be able to connect data during the ETL process. Understanding value system, value chain, and business process connections should assist in cleaning data, especially in identifying data inconsistencies.

Four categories of analytics are useful in business and accounting: descriptive analytics, diagnostic analytics, predictive analytics, and prescriptive analytics. *Descriptive analytics* describe or summarize what has already happened, focusing on the past. Most of the types of analytics we described earlier as those accountants have done for many years, such as ratio, trend, and common size analysis are descriptive in nature. *Diagnostic analytics* explain why something happened, combining what has happened with other types of data. *Predictive analytics* speculate what will

---

[45] https://www.forbes.com/sites/gilpress/2016/03/23/data-preparation-most-time-consuming-least-enjoyable-data-science-task-survey-says/#43541aaf6f63

happen in the future. *Prescriptive analytics* similarly focus on the future, prescribing what should be done.

How can REA facilitate each of these types of analytics? Because the operational layer of REA focuses on the past, describing what has already happened, that layer directs us to the data useful for descriptive analytics. Querying financial statement numbers from the operational data to verify that they agree, and calculating metrics such as cost per customer, inventory availability, or on-time delivery percentages are examples of descriptive analytics. The data for such analytics are in the core pattern classes and associations, i.e., the resources, economic events, agents, duality, stockflow, participation, and reversal associations.

Diagnostic analytics use both the operational and policy layers of REA. Fulfillment, duality, and reversal associations provide useful data for diagnosis, especially when combined across multiple business processes. For example, to explain why an enterprise delivered products late to a customer, one might trace the products from the late sale back to the conversion process to see what raw materials made up those products. One might further trace those materials back to the acquisition process, to see that the enterprise ordered the materials early enough that they should have been available for on-time delivery; however, the vendor delivered the materials later than scheduled. Some diagnostic analytics require comparison of operational and policy layer data. For example, variance analysis and analysis of policy violations both compare actual occurrence data to policy data.

Because the scheduling layer of REA focuses on what enterprises have planned and scheduled, that layer directs us to data useful for predictive analytics. One may obtain data from instigation and commitment event classes, and from proposition, reservation, and specification associations, to make reasonably certain predictions of future economic events, especially combining this data with statistical relationships found in historical data (e.g. in the past, 10% of sale order commitment events went unfilled). One may also compare or combine such data with data from external sources such as social media chatter or customer satisfaction feedback, and run statistical models to adjust one's predictions.

Because the policy layer of REA focuses on what could be or should be, that layer directs us to data useful for prescriptive analytics. Typification and policy associations house some of the prescriptions enterprises make. Combining these data with sophisticated techniques such as self-optimizing algorithms will help enterprises determine the most favorable courses of action to take. The above discussion presumes that enterprise data are stored consistent with REA. However, as noted earlier, rarely in practice do enterprises store data consistent with REA. Most enterprises must extract, transform, and load data from multiple internal systems before conducting analytics. A solid understanding of the REA ontology will help you determine how to combine data from such systems. First, determine where the enterprise stores data for each of the REA constructs for each of the business processes in chapters 4 through 7. Then consider the view integration techniques and the advanced REA constructs in chapter 10. Next, determine how to integrate outside data together with internal systems data. For example, Internet of Things data is likely to connect to internal resource or resource type data, as mentioned above.[46]

---

[46] See Murthy, U.S. & Geerts, G.L. 2017. An REA ontology-based model for mapping big data to accounting information system elements. *Journal of Information Systems*, 31(3), pp. 45-61. Also see Geerts, G.L. & O'Leary,

CONCLUSION

We live in an age of accelerations, in which the rate of technology innovation seems to be ever-increasing. Today's emerging technologies will either become standard or they will disappear. New technologies will emerge. Our hope is that you will do as much as you can to be agile and adaptable throughout your career. Stay abreast of emerging technologies and consider ways in which they affect – and may potentially even disrupt – the field of accounting. Adopt a continuous learning mindset, always considering how new developments may be incorporated to make your work more efficient and more effective. In an ideal world, enterprises would all have systems designed in conformance with the REA ontology, as such systems would yield better analytics, better decisions, and better enterprise management. The more closely a system mirrors the reality it represents, the better the system is. REA was discovered by observation of common elements of hundreds of business transactions, and REA-based systems thus closely mirror the reality they represent. Of course, the world is not ideal, and most enterprises today have multiple legacy systems that were designed with no knowledge of REA. Sure, we hope this book encourages enterprises to replace legacy systems with REA-based systems. However, we will be happy if this book helps people to use REA to better understand enterprise value systems, value chains, and business processes no matter how their enterprise software is structured, and to use this understanding to enhance their analytics and decisions.

KEY TERMS AND CONCEPTS

Accounting analytics
Augmented intensional reasoning
Bitcoin
Blockchain
Cognitive computing
Consortium blockchain
Cryptocurrency
Descriptive analytics
Diagnostic analytics
Immutability of blockchain
Internet of Things (IoT)
Predictive analytics
Prescriptive analytics
Private blockchain
Public blockchain
Robotic process automation (RPA)
Semi-private blockchain
Smart contract

D.E. 2014. A supply chain of things: The EAGLET ontology for highly visible supply chains. *Decision Support Systems*, 63(2014), pp. 3-22.

REVIEW QUESTIONS

R15-1. What is blockchain and how might blockchain disrupt the role of auditors?

R15-2. What kind of shift would accounting need to make in order to fully embrace blockchain?

R15-3. How might data generated by the Internet of Things affect financial reporting?

R15-4. What is Robotic Process Automation, and how concerned should accountants be about the robots taking accountants jobs?

R15-5. How does knowledge of the REA ontology facilitate one's ability to do descriptive, predictive, prescriptive, and diagnostic analytics?

MULTIPLE CHOICE QUESTIONS

MC15-1. Blockchain technology
- A) Requires the use of cryptocurrency, such as Bitcoin
- B) Must be facilitated by financial institutions such as banks
- C) May be public, private, semi-private, or consortium
- D) Has been largely ignored by most financial institutions and accounting firms

MC15-2. Consortium blockchains are available to whom?
- A) Only employees within a single enterprise
- B) Participants across a supply chain
- C) Participants who have the appropriate encryption key
- D) Anyone and everyone who has the appropriate hardware to join and wants to become a node on the chain

MC15-3. Immutability of a blockchain means that
- A) Any changes after a block is added to the chain invalidate that block and all subsequent blocks, and thus become evident to all.
- B) Changes cannot be made to a block by any node on the chain
- C) An error discovered in a block may be corrected by the same node that originally added the block, but not by any other node on the chain
- D) Any node on the chain may authorize a change to an existing block

MC15-4. Computerized models that simulate human thought processes, by combining artificial intelligence, signal processing, machine learning, reasoning, and natural language processing, are also known as
- A) Cognitive computing
- B) Blockchain computing
- C) Internet of Things
- D) Robotic process automation

MC15-5. In the world of accounting analytics and big data, ETL stands for
- A) Entities, typification, and localization
- B) Events, trades, and levels
- C) Extract, track, and locate
- D) Extract, transform, and load

MC15-6. A key difference between cognitive computing and Robotic Process Automation (RPA) is that
A) Cognitive computing software is able to learn and adapt, whereas RPA software can only repeat exactly the same steps it was originally taught
B) RPA software is able to learn and adapt, whereas cognitive computing software can only repeat exactly the same steps it was originally taught
C) Cognitive computing and RPA are both able to learn and adapt, but RPA must be installed in some kind of drone or robot hardware, whereas cognitive computing need not have any drone or robot hardware
D) RPA is considered artificial intelligence, whereas cognitive computing is considered natural intelligence

MC15-7. Delta Airlines began tagging passengers' luggage with tags that contain RFID chips to allow tracking of the tags' (and thus presumably the bags') locations. The tags send messages about their locations to Delta's server, which then sends alerts to passengers when location changes of interest occur, e.g., when their bags are loaded onto their next plane or when their bags are arriving at baggage claim's carousel number two. This technology is an example of
A) Blockchain
B) Cognitive computing
C) Internet of Things
D) RPA

MC15-8. Descriptive analytics
A) Summarize what has already happened
B) Explain why something happened
C) Speculate as to what will happen in the future
D) Prescribe what should be done in the future

MC15-9. Data for diagnostic analytics in REA are found primarily in
A) The core pattern associations within a business process, such as stockflow and participation
B) Fulfillment, duality, and reversal associations, especially when combined across multiple business processes
C) Instigation and commitment classes, and in proposition, reservation, and specification associations
D) Typification and policy associations, especially when combined with self-optimizing algorithms to determine the most favorable course of action to take

MC15-10. What can accountants do to stay agile and adaptable throughout their careers?
A) Adopt a continuous learning mindset, always considering how new developments may be incorporated to make their work more efficient and effective
B) Stay abreast of emerging technologies and ponder the potentially disruptive effects
C) Use REA to better understand enterprise value systems, value chains, and business processes and use that understanding to enhance their analytics and decisions
D) All of the above

GLOSSARY OF KEY TERMS

A

Access control matrix – identifies the functions each user is allowed to perform and what data and programs the user can access once he or she gains access to the system, p.268

Accountability (in early accounting) - keeping track of the assets and measuring the give and the take of economic transactions, p.3

Accountability infrastructure – (aka operational infrastructure) represents the economic activities and related phenomena that actually have happened in an economic exchange. This layer is composed of the daily activities of the enterprise carrying out its mission. p.283

Accountants as visionaries – should be actively engaged in researching new technologies and new business models to determine the potential impacts on their companies and/or on the field of accounting in general, pp.8-9

Accounting analytics – the process of transforming accounting-related data into knowledge to add value to decisions, p. 482

Accounting transactions – those events that directly affected a company's assets, liabilities, or owners' equity accounts, p.6

Acquisition process – involves giving the resource cash in exchange for various resources like raw materials and equipment (give event: cash disbursement; take event: acquisition), p.25

Activity (in BPMN) – an element that can be used to show the performance of specific work within a business process, and can be either atomic or non-atomic, p.215

Ad hoc querying – direct retrieval of information by end-users from a database whereby the retrieval was not planned (i.e. no pre-formulated queries or interfaces were developed in anticipation of needing the information), p.306

Agent – an individual, department, division, or organization that participates in the planning, control, execution, or evaluation of events, p.20

Agent queries – queries that involve single tables containing data that describe internal or external agents; typically such queries' results list internal or external agents who possess one or more specific characteristics, p.366

Aggregation function – mathematical operations performed within a particular column of data values, such as a computation of the average of a set of values; they are also called vertical calculations, p.316

AND operator – similar to a set intersection in mathematics set theory; an answer to a query connecting two criteria with an AND operator will contain only the instances that meet both criteria, p.315

Annotation symbol – a flowcharting symbol that allows the preparer to provide clarification as needed, and is often used to describe and document particular internal controls (the dashed line of the annotation symbol can connect to any other symbol as necessary), p.222

Application control – features included in software programs that help to ensure that transactional data are authorized, complete, and accurate, p.265

Area of responsibility – a department, section within a department, or an individual employee who is held accountable for the flow of information or physical objects through a system, p.217

Assignment – an association between an internal agent and an external agent that is separate from any event in which they might both participate, p.41

Association (in BPMN) – link information and artifacts to flow objects, p.217

Association (in UML) – a relationship between classes, p.54

Association class – a relationship between classes wherein the association has characteristics of its own and for which there can be only one link between the related classes, p.55

Association name conflict – a discrepancy in the labels on associations - either the same association with different names or different associations with the same name, p.167

Association structure conflict – a discrepancy in the multiplicities on an association, p.167

Attribute – a characteristic possessed by a class or an association, p.55

Attribute conflict – different attributes have been identified as important for describing the same class in various views p.167

Augmented intensional reasoning – use of data structures for automated information retrieval, with domain knowledge added to aid in making such information retrieval meaningful for that domain, p.479

Average (AVG) aggregation function – computes the average of a column of data values, to apply it, simply add AVG( ) to the field name (the field name is inside the parentheses) in the SELECT clause of the SQL statement, p.316

B

Barter transaction – exchange of a non-cash resource for a different non-cash resource, p.29

Batch control total – an internal control used to verify that all transactions within a batch are present and have been processed, p.276

Batch processing – accumulates data for a period of time to collect a group of transaction data, after which all transactions are posted to the master file in one processing run, p.229

BETWEEN operator – a comparison operator that identifies records for which a field's value is within a specific range of values, p.313

Bill of lading – a document that indicates the transfer of custody of goods from the enterprise to a common carrier, including details about how many packages comprise the shipment, the dimensions and/or weight of those packages, the shipping costs, and the party responsible for shipping costs, p. 119

Bill of materials – a document that lists the names and quantities of all the materials needed to produce a specified size batch of finished product, similar to the ingredient list portion of a recipe, p.201

Bitcoin – a croptocurrency, a form of electronic cash, p.475

Blockchain – a distributed ledger system whereby records conveying offer and acceptance are verified and stored, p.475

Bonding – the process of purchasing insurance on the employees who handle cash for an enterprise; the insurer performs background checks on the employees, determines the likelihood the employees will steal from the enterprise, and agrees to compensate the enterprise in the case of employee theft; is primarily a corrective control, p.256

BPMN (Business Process Model and Notation) – the most widely used notation for workflow diagrams, p.214

Business entrepreneur script – The stereotypical sequence of enterprise events that says (from the enterprise's point of view) the enterprise gets some cash, engages in value-added exchanges, pays back the cash, and lives off the profit, p.22

Business interruption – a temporary halt in normal operations, p.252

Business process – a term widely used in business to indicate anything ranging from the act of producing a report to the entire set of activities in a transaction cycle; in this text business process is the term used to describe an entire transaction cycle, p.21

Business process risks – risks specific to resource, events, agents, and various relationships in the REA pattern for business processes, p.252

C

Calculator/register tape – a flowcharting symbol used to represent the paper that comes out of a ten-key adding machine (calculator tape), or the paper receipt provided at the point of sale (register tape – e.g., that provided by a cash register at a grocery store), p.219

Candidate key – an attribute value that could be used as a primary key for a class table (not necessarily for the class in whose table it exists), p.61

Cash disbursement – an event that decreases cash; also called a payment, p.8, 117

Cash receipt – an event that has the effect of increasing cash, p.8, 159

Check – a document used to authorize the transfer of cash from one person or enterprise to another, p.117

Check digit – a number that is appended to and maintained as a part of an account number, part number, or other identifier as determined by a predefined formula, p.274-275

Claim – a timing difference between an economic increment event and the related economic decrement event; accounts receivable, deferred revenue, and accounts payable are examples of claims, p.39

Class – a set of entities, i.e., real world objects that have separate physical or conceptual existence, that share the same types of characteristics p.54

Class name conflict – occurs when the same class included in different conceptual models is not labeled identically, p.166

Closed loop verification – an internal control that uses one input data item to locate the record to be updated and displays other data from the record so the data entry person can verify it as the correct record to be processed; e.g., display of a customer's name upon the user entering the customer number, p.274

Cognitive computing – computerized models that simulate human thought processes, by combining artificial intelligence and signal processing, encompassing machine learning, reasoning, natural language processing, and other technologies to understand, reason, learn, and interact in a specific domain, p.478

Collusion – two or more employees acting together to perpetrate a fraud, p.244

Combined class key posting – a logical level implementation compromise whereby a single foreign key is placed into a table to represent two or more different relationships, p.300

Commitment event – an event in which the enterprise enters into agreements expected to result in a future economic event, p.97

Completeness check – an edit check internal control that verifies that all critical field data are entered, p.275

Composite attribute – a characteristic that may be decomposed into other attributes, p.56

Computer processes – tasks that are done primarily by computers, p. 220

Concatenated primary key – a unique and universal identifier for a class or association class that is made up of multiple attributes, p.55

Conceptual database model – a representation of objects and their relationships; is hardware and software independent, p.52

Conceptual level compromise – the use of less than theoretically ideal representation in a conceptual model because of an inability or lack of need to completely and accurately represent an object, p.296

Conceptually congruent events – pairs or groups of events always occur simultaneously, p.296

Consortium blockchain – a blockchain for which multiple enterprises have combined efforts to create and jointly lead a blockchain to support a

share endeavor; are available to those participants who have the appropriate encryption key, p.475-476

Consume stockflow association – indicate a resource is completely used up by an economic decrement, p.179

Contingency plan – a set of procedures to enact if a disaster occurs, p.254

Control activity – one of COSO's five interrelated components of an internal control system; a policy or procedure used to ensure necessary actions are taken to minimize risks associated with achieving enterprise objectives; may be preventive, detective, or corrective in nature, p.243

Control environment – one of COSO's five interrelated components of an internal control system; "the tone at the top;" the foundation that provides discipline and structure upon which all other components of internal control are built, p.242

Conversion process – takes resources like raw materials, equipment, and labor, and gives them in exchange for the production of a finished good resource (give events: material issue, machine operation, and labor operation; take event: production run), p.25

Copy of class – a duplicate representation of a class placed in a separate position on a conceptual model; portrayed with a diagonal slash across the corner and with no attributes included in the class; helps to avoid the creation of duplicate database tables, p.167

Corrective control – a control activity that focuses on recovering from, repairing the damage from, or minimizing the cost of threats, p.244

COUNT aggregation function – determines how many data values are in a column, p.316

Credit memorandum or credit slip – an internal document used to communicate to the accounting department that the amount owed by the customer should be reduced by the specified amount, p.163

Cryptocurrency - an encrypted digital currency (not physical like paper currency) that does not need a financial intermediary such as a central bank, p.475

Custody – associates an agent and a resource such that the agent has physical control over the resource or the agent controls access to the resource. Such a relationship is separate from any event involving the resource, p.41

Customer order – information in the customer's own format regarding what goods and services the customer is committing to purchase from an enterprise, p.152

Customer statement – a document that summarizes the economic transactions for a customer and reflects the customer's account balance status, p.92

D

Data science skills – being able to (1) ask the right questions, (2) manipulate data to answer those questions, and (3) create data visualizations to effectively communicate those answers, p.10

Data type (field property) (in Microsoft Access) – an important field property that determines what kind of data values may be entered into a database table's column, p.72

Data/information flow (in BPMN) - a required symbol that always connects two other symbols, p.222

Database window (in Microsoft Access) – a container for all objects stored in the database, including tables, queries, forms, and reports, p.72

Datasheet view (in Microsoft Access) – a mode that presents a relational table or a query result in row/column format, p.72

Date constraint – a restriction placed on a date field in a query to limit the query results to include only records for which the date values meet the restriction, p.323

Decision symbol – in flowcharts, this diamond-shaped symbol indicates decisions that involve divergent data/information flows; many times the decision has underlying if-then logic such that if "yes" one action happens and if "no" another action happens, p.222

Default value – a software option that sets a data field's contents to a pre-specified (default) value; in some cases the default values may be overridden, while in other cases they may not, p.275

Deposit slip – a document summarizing all payments for a prescribed time period (usually a day), p.92

Derivable attribute – a characteristic of a class or an association class that can be calculated based on the values of other stored characteristics, p.149, p.401

Descriptive analytics - describe or summarize what has already happened, focusing on the past, p.483

Design view (in Microsoft Access table creation) –a mode that displays details about the fields of a table and allows the user to specify various design parameters such as which field(s) comprise the primary key, whether a field is set to required data entry, and the data type for a field, p.72

Design view (in Microsoft Access query creation) – a mode that depicts the logic of a query as an example of how the user wants the answer to their query to be structured, p.324

Detective control – a control activity that focuses on identifying that errors or irregularities have occurred, p.243

Diagnostic analytics - explain why something happened, combining what has happened with other types of data, p.483

Direct access – allows each record to be retrieved without reading all the records that precede it in the file, p.227

Direct deposit notification – a document that contains information about an employee's work-related compensation, such as gross pay, net pay, and the various withholdings that make up the difference between gross and net pay (such as income tax, social security tax, Medicare tax, health insurance premiums, and retirement plan contributions), p.138

Disk storage – electronic data storage on a digital medium that allows random storage and direct access, examples include internal and external hard disks, thumb drives, SD cards, CDs, and DVDs p. 227

Display – flowchart symbol that indicates when data is visually available to a user via a computer screen, p.230

Double-entry bookkeeping – an accounting technique formally described by Pacioli in 1494 that has the components of the accounting equation (Assets = Liabilities + Equity) as foundational elements of the systems' organizing structure, p.3

Duality – the causal relationship between a give (economic decrement) event and a take (economic increment) event, p.34

Duality association queries – queries that ask questions about economic exchanges, involving the tables that comprise a relationship between an economic decrement and an economic increment event such as that between sale and cash receipt or between cash disbursement and purchase; typically such queries are used to identify incomplete exchanges or to calculate dollar values of claims such as accounts receivable and accounts payable, p.367-368

Dynaset (in Microsoft Access) – a query's result; looks and behaves like a table but is not actually stored as a table; it is generated as a view each time the query is run, p.332

E

Economic agent – a person, department, division, or organization who participates in, authorizes, records, or plays other roles in the various events in enterprise business processes, p.9

Economic decrement event – an activity that decreases one or more resources, p.9

Economic event – an activity that changes the quantity or value of economic resources, p.9

Economic increment event – an activity that increases one or more resources, p.9

Economic resources – tangible or intangible things that have value to an enterprise, including assets, skills, knowledge, and digital assets. p.9

Economic reversal event – an activity that negates a previous event that had increased (decreased) a resource; therefore the reversal event decreases (increases) the resource, p.97

Economic risks – threats of loss associated with factors that affect the entire economy, p.251

Edit check – a control incorporated into computer program instructions to verify and validate the completeness, reasonableness, and/or accuracy of data, p.274

Employee schedule – a commitment by the employee to provide the labor as specified and a commitment by the enterprise to pay the employee the contracted wage rate for the labor provided, p.133

Encryption – a process of encoding data entered into a system, storing or transmitting the data in coded form, and then decoding the data upon its use or arrival at its destination to prevent unauthorized access to the data while it is stored or as it is transmitted, p.268

End event (in BPMN) – the last event in the process, depicted with a bold circle, p.215

Enforce referential integrity (in Microsoft Access) – a choice selected in the relationship layout to determine whether data entry will be disallowed if it does not match between the two key fields as the user enters data into the database, p.80

Enterprise ontology – a vocabulary useful for understanding business processes that can guide system implementation using many different technologies, p.9

Enterprise risks– potential threats of loss to the enterprise as a result of internal actions/circumstances and external actions/circumstances, p.251

Entity – a real world object that has either a physical or conceptual existence, p.54

Entity integrity – a principle in the relational database model that requires the values of a relational table's primary key to be (1) unique and (2) non-null (i.e., every row of data must have a primary key value that is different for each row), p.61

Equipment requisition - a commitment event that is reciprocal with the production order, whereby the production supervisor schedules various fixed assets of the company to be used in operations for a production run, p.188

ERP system – a group of software applications integrated to form an enterprise-wide information system solution, p.8

Error (risk and control context) – an unintended mistake on the part of an employee or external business partner, p.243

Event – an activity an enterprise plans, controls, executes, and evaluates, p.20

Event activity rollup – the aggregation of a group of event records into a single summary record once historical detail is no longer needed, p.300

Event queries –asks a question that can be answered by using a single table that contains data detailing a set of events, p.364

EXISTS operator - a comparison operator that identifies records for which a specific field's value contains non-null values, p.313

Expression builder (in Microsoft Access) – an application within Microsoft Access that assists the user in creating horizontal calculations within queries, p.345

Extension – the rows in a relational database table; they represent the specific instances that are members of the entity or relationship set, p.59

External agent – a person or organization with which an enterprise trades resources; also called external business partner, p.21

F

Fact (in database design) – the pairing of a candidate key data value with another attribute data value; facts are found in a table's extension (rows), p.51

Field – a column in a relational database table, p.59

Field (mode) check – an instruction in a computer program that verifies the entered data type is the appropriate mode (e.g. text, numeric, date) for the field into which the data is entered, p.275

Field property (in Microsoft Access) – defines the characteristics of data that is allowed to be entered into a column of a database table, p.72

File for stored paper – a flowchart symbol that is an upside down triangle and represents paper storage in a file folder and/or file cabinet, p.220

Financial/numeric control total – the sum of a financial field, such as an invoice amount, of all records in a batch, p.277

Financing process – business process that is a special case of the acquisition process, in which cash is exchanged for cash at a later point in time, p.33

Flow line – a symbol on a flowchart used to indicate the movement of a document, a physical object, or data to the next point in a system, p.219

Flowcharts – graphical representations of the inputs, processes, and outputs of an information system, including physical and logical details about system components, p.218

Flowchart symbols – specific notations used to communicate constructs on a system flowchart; numerous different symbols are used to represent different constructs, p.219

Foreign key – a column of data that relates to the primary key column of a related table, p.59-60

FROM clause (in SQL) – specifies the table name(s) from which data is to be retrieved, p.309

Fulfillment association – an association between instigation and commitment events whereby the commitment event fulfills the instigation event OR an association between commitment events and economic events whereby the economic event fulfills the commitment event, p.97

Fulfillment association query – a query that answers one or more questions about the relationship between an instigation event and the commitment event to which it led, or about the relationship between a commitment event and the resulting economic event, p.390

Full outer join – combines tables or query results, including all records from both the left and right tables, displaying null values in columns for which the joined fields didn't contain matching values, accomplishes a set union of the two tables, p.319

G

Gateway – an element in BPMN that shows a divergence control of either branching or forking, and may also indicate a convergence control of merging or joining, p.216

General controls – controls over data center operations, access security, software acquisition, development and maintenance, and operating systems, p.244

Generalization – the abstraction from a class of objects to a superclass (that captures the commonalities between subclass instances, resulting in a less detailed higher level construct) via the creation of an "is-a" relationship between the subclass and superclass, p.284

Gross pay – the amount the employees earned, before subtracting withholdings, p.136

GROUP BY – an additional clause that may be included as a subtotaling mechanism after the WHERE clause in SQL, or as a vertical aggregation function in Access query design view, p.316

Grouping - a mechanism in which objects are grouped into collections based on shared characteristics, p.291

H

Hash control total – the sum of an attribute in a file that has no real meaning or use; for example, the sum of the customer number field of all the records in a batch, p.276

HAVING clause – an aggregation mechanism to restrict the records included in an aggregation function, p.317

Homonym – one word used to designate multiple different things, p.167

Horizontal calculation – manipulates data values from two or more different fields in the same record; also called an expression, p.319

Human capital – the resource acquired in the human resource process, made up of the work employees perform and the knowledge and skills employees use in performing that work, p.129

I

Immutability of blockchain – any changes made to previously accepted blocks of data will be immediately revealed and rejected by the blockchain, p.475

Implementation compromise – deviations from a theoretically pure conceptual model due to practical considerations, insufficient measurement techniques, and other constraints, p.295

Imprest checking account – an account that normally maintains a zero balance, into which a company deposits money to cover paychecks and from which paychecks are drawn, p.129

Independent checks on performance – verification of accuracy of an employee's performance by a different employee (or by an automated procedure), p.262

Industry risks – threats of loss associated with factors that affect an enterprise's industry, p.251

Information and communication – one of COSO's five interrelated components of an internal control system; prescribes features of the information system to ensure information quality and also prescribes open channels of communication to ensure employees understand what is expected of them in achieving internal control objectives, p.245

Information process risks– threats of loss associated with recording, maintaining, and reporting information about resources, events, agents, and relationships among them, p.253

Inner join – a join that combines the tables together based on a common attribute, keeping only those rows for which the data values of the common attribute match exactly; also called an equi-join; accomplishes a set intersection of the tables, p.319

Input device – a flowchart symbol that depicts manual data entry to a computer process, p.221

Input → process → output (in flowcharts) – the pattern to be followed when creating flowcharts, p.219

Instigation event – events that identify the need for future *commitment* and *economic events*, thus triggering other activities and events in the business process, p.97

Intension – The columns in a relational database table; they represent the attributes of the entity or relationship set; also called the schema of the table, p.59

Internal agent – an individual, department, or division within an enterprise who participate in events or who control resources while acting on behalf of the enterprise, p.39

Internal control – per COSO, "a process, affected by an entity's board of directors, management, and other personnel, designed to provide reasonable assurance regarding the achievement of objectives relating to operations, reporting, and compliance." , p.241

Internet of Things (IoT) - a system of interconnected appliances, machines, vehicles, and other devices that communicate with each other and exchange data using the Internet, without any human intervention or interaction, p.479

Irregularity – an intentional effort to cause harm to an enterprise; a fraud, p.243

IS NOT NULL operator – a comparison operator that identifies records for which a specific field's value contains non-null values, p.313

IS NULL operator - a comparison operator that identifies records for which a specific field's value does not exist (i.e., the field is empty; no data has been entered), p.313

J

Job time ticket – a document that indicates starting and stopping times and descriptions for labor operations performed on a specific date by a specific employee; also called a time track document, p.195

Join properties window (in Microsoft Access) – a screen that appears when a user double-clicks on a join line to reveal whether the join is an inner join, a left join, or a right join; a user can change the join type in this window; used in the relationship layout and in query designs, p.339

Joint venture – a form of business that is temporarily created for the duration of a combined effort between two or more parties, p.3

K

Key verification (rekeying) – the keying of input data twice, with the computer comparing the two entries and highlighting any discrepancies for correction, p.274

L

Labor acquisition event – the primary economic increment event in the payroll business process ; each instance covers some time period; often represented by a timecard document, p.135

Labor operation – an economic decrement event that represents the performance of a specific activity in the conversion process by a production employee, thereby using up the resource of that person's labor, p.194

Labor requisition commitment event (in conversion process) – commitment to use some labor; is reciprocal with the production order commitment, p.187

Labor requisition instigation event (in payroll process) – identification of the need for labor; most commonly documented by a staffing plan, p.130

Labor schedule – a mutual commitment event in the human resource business process wherein the employee agrees to provide labor as specified in the schedule and the enterprise commits to pay the employee the contracted wage rate for the labor provided, also called employee schedule, p.133

Labor type – a resource type class that represents an inventory of the kinds of labor an enterprise may need to acquire and use in its operations, p.129

Lane – a mechanism in BPMN that is used to divide pools into subset activities, also called swimlane p.218

Lapping – a method of stealing cash whereby an employee steals cash from a customer payment and delays posting a payment to the customer's account, and then uses funds from a subsequent customer payment to post to the first customer's account; the process continues with the employee continually stealing from subsequent customer payments to post as prior customer payments, p.257

Left Join – a combination of tables based on a common attribute that includes unmatched records from the first table in the join and does not include unmatched records from the second table in the join; is a partial outer join, is also called left outer join, p.320

LIKE operator - a comparison operator that identified records for which a field's value fits a specific pattern, wherein the pattern may be exact or may contain wildcard symbols to precisely specify the desired target data, p.315

Linkage association – a relationship between two resource types to represent the fact that one of the resources is composed of the other, p.180

Linkage association queries – ask the kinds of questions that could be answered from referring to a bill of materials or operations list, p.459

Load– the percentage of data values for an attribute that are non-null; if most cells in a column have actual values, the load is high; if most cells in a column have null values, the load is low, p.298

Logical access control – restrict unauthorized access to the programs and data in systems, p.268

Logical database model – in database design, a model into which the conceptual model is converted once the type of database software to be used has been chosen (e.g. relational or object-oriented); is hardware independent and is somewhat software independent (if relational is chosen as the database type, then any relational software may be chosen but object-oriented software may not), p.52

Logical level compromise – a deviation from pure theory made when converting a conceptual model into database objects, p.298

Logical operator – Boolean search terms used in queries to define which records are included in the query result; Examples include AND, OR, and NOT, p.315

M

Machine operation – an economic decrement event that captures the consumption of a portion of a machine's useful life, p.198

Machine requisition - a commitment event that is reciprocal with the production order, whereby the production supervisor schedules various fixed assets of the company to be used in operations for a production run, also called equipment requisition, p.188

Magnetic tape storage – stores data from source documents and reports in a format that is computer readable; examples include audiocassette tapes and vcr tapes, p.227

Mandatory participation – represents a requirement that an instance of a class must be associated with at least one instance of an associated class in order to be included in the database; a minimum multiplicity equal to one, p.57

Manual process – a set of tasks done primarily by people; such processes involve activities such as filling out forms and reconciling different sources of related information; represented by a trapezoid symbol on a flowchart, p.219

Master file – contain balance data or the status of an entity at a point in time, p.226

Master reference check – verifies that an event/transaction record has a corresponding master record to be updated, p.275

Material issuance – an economic decrement event involving the using up of raw materials in the production process; the raw materials are usually transformed into finished goods and lose their own identity and nature in the process; also called raw material issuance, p.191

Material requisition – a commitment event whereby the inventory clerk or warehouse supervisor commits to the production supervisor to transfer materials from the materials warehouse to the production floor, also called raw material requisition, p.184

Materialization of tasks as classes – a conceptual model level implementation compromise in which an activity that could be re-engineered is established as a class (base object), p.297

MAX aggregation function – used in querying, finds the largest value in a column, p.316

Maximum multiplicity – represents the maximum number of times an instance of a class may participate in an association with instances of a related class; the most common possible values are 1 and * (many), p.57

Meronymic association - a whole-part association, used in REA especially to capture events that need to be captured as a whole (such as a concert) and for which parts (such as tickets) aso need to be captured, p.294

Message (in BPMN) – an element that represents the contents of communication between two trading partners, p.217

Message flow (in BPMN) – show the flow of messages between two trading partners, p.217

MIN aggregation function – used in querying, finds the smallest value in a column, p.316

Minimum multiplicity – represents the minimum number of times an instance of a class must participate in an association with instances of a related class; the most common possible values are 0 and 1, p.57

Monitoring – one of COSO's five interrelated components of an internal control system; the process of assessing the quality of internal control performance over time and taking corrective actions as needed, p.245

Multiple process queries – queries that require data from two or more business processes, p.417

Multiplicities – business rules describing how instances of a class participate in an association with instances of another class, p.57

Mutual commitment event – a bundle of commitments that happen simultaneously, that obligate an enterprise to participate in at least two future economic events, one that increments a resource and another that decrements a resource, p.97

N

Net pay – the dollar amount to be paid to employees, calculated as gross pay minus amounts withheld for taxes, insurances, an so forth, p.136

NOT operator – in querying, identifies instances that do not meet one or more conditions, p.315

Null value – a blank cell in a database table; a cell into which no data has been entered, p.55

Null to zero function (in Microsoft Access) – a Microsoft Access procedure used in querying that treats null values as if they are zeros; each factor in an expression that could potentially have a null value should be enclosed in parentheses and preceded by Nz; for example Cash: Nz(CashReceipts)-Nz(CashDisbursements), p.373

O

Object pattern – a commonly observed constellation of things and relationships between those things, p.18

Off page connector – an element of flowcharts that directs readers when the data/information flow jumps from one page to another page, p.222

On page connector – an element of flowcharts that directs readers when the data/information flow jumps from one part of a page to another part of the same page, p.222

One fact, one place rule – a principle in database design that prohibits a pairing of a candidate key value with another attribute value from appearing multiple places in a database table and also prohibits multiple pairings of candidate key values with other attribute values in the same place; helps to ensure well-behaved relational tables, p.61

Open purchase order – A purchase order for which the products or services have not yet been received, p.112

Open sale order – A sale order for which the enterprise has not yet delivered the products or services, p.152

Operational infrastructure – (also called accountability infrastructure) represents the economic activities and related phenomena that actually have happened in an economic exchange. This layer is composed of the daily activities of the enterprise carrying out its mission, p.283

Operations list – a document that identifies the labor types needed to create a finished good; captures the same information as the linkage relationship between labor types and finished goods, p.201

Optional participation – represents a minimum multiplicity of zero; instances of a class may be included in the database without being related to an instance of the associated class, p.57

OR operator – similar to a set union in mathematics set theory; an answer to a query connecting two criteria with an OR operator will contain all instances that meet at least one of the criteria, p.315

ORDER BY clause – SQL allows users to specify how query results are sorted through the use of this optional clause (the final clause in a SQL statement when used); is followed by the column one wants to sort and the sort order – ascending or descending, p.310

Outer join – a combination of tables or queries that includes records even when the joined fields don't have the same values in three different ways: as left, right, or full outer joins, p.319

P

Packing list – sometimes called a packing slip, a document that identifies the goods that have been shipped to an external business partner, p.157

Paper document symbol – in flowcharts, a symbol that represents data stored on paper, other than a calculator or register tape p.219

Parameter query – a query in which variables are used in lieu of data values as part of the query's selection criteria; allows the user to specify the data value to be used each time the query is run, thereby allowing re-use of the same query many times for different decisions, p.323

Participation – a relationship between an event and an internal or external agent, p.40

Participation association query – a query that attempts to satisfy information needs for identification of which agents participated in events or the events in which agents have participated, p.396

Password –a unique identifier that only an authorized user of a system or application should know and that the user is required to enter each time he/she logs onto the system; a weak form of protection; a logical access control, p.268

Pattern – an arrangement of repeated or recognizably consistent objects or actions, p.17

Paycheck – compensation to employees for work performed, p.125

Payroll deduction – amounts withheld from paychecks to be paid on behalf of the employee (sometimes by statute, sometimes voluntarily) to government agencies, benefit providers, or other outside agencies; also called withholdings p.136

Payroll function – the function within the payroll process that schedules and acquires labor, and processes paychecks (compensation to employees for their work), p.125

Payroll process – a special type of acquisition where the resource cash is exchanged for the resource labor (give event: cash disbursement; take event labor acquisition), p.25

Performance (in contract law) – the fulfillment of an obligation in a manner that releases the performer from all liabilities; an activity or action that fulfills an obligation, p.113

Personnel function – function within the payroll process that hires, trains, evaluates, and terminates employees, p.125

Physical access control – features, barriers, or procedures designed to prohibit unauthorized people from touching a resource, p.256

Physical database model – implementations using the chosen vendor-specific database software, p.53

Physical level compromise – a deviation from the theoretical ideal when implementing the logical database model in vendor-specific database software, p.300

Picking list – a document that identifies the goods that have been taken out of the warehouse and made available to be shipped, p.156

Policy infrastructure – in the REA ontology, the economic activities and related phenomena that should, could, or must happen in a company; reflects results of planning and control efforts by enterprise management, and is composed of the rules, procedures, policies, and goals set by enterprise management, p.283

Pool – in BPMN, a means for grouping of tasks into areas of responsibility that is necessary for illustrating two or more participants (business partners) in a collaboration, p.217

Predictive analytics – speculate what will happen in the future, p.483

Prescriptive analytics – prescribe what should be done in the future, p.484

Preventive controls – control activities that focuses on stopping errors or irregularities either from occurring or from being entered into the enterprise information system, p.243

Primary key attribute – a characteristic that must uniquely and universally identify each instance of a class or association, p.55

Private blockchain – a blockchain that operates within a single enterprise, whereby the blockchain is only available to users within the enterprise who have the appropriate encryption key, p.475

Production employee – a worker who participates in the manufacture of finished goods; an internal agent involved in labor operations and production runs in the conversion process, p.180

Production order (document) – a document that captures information about a production order event, p.183

Production order (event) – an event that represents the enterprise's commitment to engage in a future economic increment event (a production run) that will increase the finished goods resource, p.182

Production run – an economic increment event that produces finished products, p.176

Production supervisor – an internal agent who authorizes events in the conversion cycle, p.184

Proposition association – an association that connects an instigation event to a resource or resource type; often specifies quantity and proposed cost or selling price for the item(s) identified as needed, p.98

Proposition association queries – created to satisfy information needs about the proposed effect of instigation events on resources or about the resources involved in instigation events, p.393

Public blockchain – a blockchain that is available to anyone and everyone who wants to become a node on the chain and who has the appropriate hardware to join, p.475

Purchase allowance – A refund of part of a dissatisfied enterprise's purchase price, whereby the enterprise keeps the unsatisfactory product, p.119

Purchase event – an economic increment event in which services or the title to goods transfers from a supplier to the enterprise; also called an acquisition, p.113

Purchase order – a mutual commitment event in which a supplier agrees to transfer title of goods to the enterprise at an agreed upon future time and price and the enterprise agrees to pay for those goods; a document reflecting the terms of the mutual commitment event, p.111

Purchase requisition – an instigation event in which the need for goods or services is identified; an internal document that communicates this need to the enterprise purchasing function, p.110

Purchase return – an economic increment reversal event in which title of goods is transferred (usually concurrently with transfer of physical custody of goods) from the enterprise back to the vendor, p.119

Q

Query – a request for information submitted to a database engine, p.306

R

Random storage – information may be stored in any order on the disk device, p.227

Range check – an instruction in a computer program that compares entered data to a predetermined acceptable upper and/or lower limit and rejects data that falls outside the specified limits unless special authorization is obtained, p.275

REA accounting – an accounting method that supports all of the traditional accounting needs, but it goes beyond that – it can plan and set policies for future accounting transactions and additionally support the decision-making needs of all people in the organization because it considers non-accounting events and activities in addition to accounting events and activities, p.9

REA business process model – a representation of an enterprise's resources, events, agents, and appropriate associations between them within one or more business processes in an enterprise value chain, p.21

REA task level model – a task is a workflow step or activity that may be changed or eliminated without fundamentally changing the nature of the enterprise and therefore should not serve as a foundational element in an enterprise information system; task level models in the REA ontology are graphical representations of workflow processes for which there is no identified pattern, p.21

REA value chain model – a representation that depicts an enterprise's internal resources that flow between interconnected business processes, and the economic events that affect the resource flows, p.21

REA value system model – a representation that depicts the resource exchanges between the enterprise and various business partners, p.21

Real-time processing – updates master files as a business activities occur, p.229

Reasonableness check – an instruction in a computer program to verify whether the amount of an event/transaction record appears reasonable when compared to other elements associated with each item being processed, p.275

Receiving report – a document that lists the items and the quantities and condition of each item received in an acquisition event; the receiving report identifier is often used as the identifier for the acquisition event, p.114

Reciprocal association – a relationship between a commitment to an economic increment and a commitment to an economic decrement; the commitment level equivalent of the duality relationship; in the conversion cycle, represents a schedule of what is to be produced and what will need to be used and consumed in the production process, p.99, p.182

Reconciliation of physical to recorded quantities – a comparison of a quantity of a resource on hand per a count to the quantity listed as on hand in the information system, p.257

Record – a row in a relational database table, p.59

Record count control total – the total number of records in a batch, p.277

Redundancy – in database design, duplicate storage of the same information, p.61

Referential integrity – a principle in relational databases that requires a value for a foreign key attribute to either be null (blank) or to match exactly a data value in the table in which the attribute is a primary key, p.60, 276

Relation – a two dimensional storage structure with rows and columns, more commonly referred to as a table, p.59

Relational model – a logical level database design model based developed by E.F. Codd based on set theory and predicate logic; primary constructs are relations (tables) that represent classes and associations between classes, p.59

Relationship layout (in Microsoft Access) – a window in which relationships between tables are visually depicted, p.77

Remittance advice – a document (usually the portion of a customer invoice or statement that says "return this stub with payment") that advises the enterprise the customer is remitting payment; often used as the identifier for a cash receipt event, p.160

Rental (acquisition) – an economic increment event that begins when the right to temporary possession of an asset transfers from the supplier to an enterprise and ends when possession transfers back from an enterprise to the supplier, p.113

Rental (revenue) – an economic decrement event that does not involve the transfer of title of goods, but instead involves a transfer of the right to use goods for an agreed upon length of time; begins when the right to temporary possession of the goods transfers from the lessor to the lessee and ends when possession of the goods transfers back from the lessee to the lessor, p.155

Repeating group – multiple values stored in the same cell of a table, p.59

Report-time processing – data used to generate a requested report is processed as the report is created, p.229

Request to return goods – notification to a supplier of the enterprise's dissatisfaction with goods that seeks permission to return those goods instead of paying for them (or in exchange for a refund), p.119

Required data entry field property (in Microsoft Access) – a choice specified in table design view; a user will not be allowed to enter a record into the table without including a value for any field(s) for which this property is set to "yes"; a user may leave any field except the primary key field(s) blank for which this property is not set to "yes" (Microsoft Access automatically enforces entity integrity so there is no need to set the required data entry field property to "yes" for primary key fields), p.75

Reservation association – a relationship between a commitment event and a resource or resource type, p.99

Reservation association queries – queries that attempt to satisfy information needs about the eventual effect of commitment events on resources or about the resources involved in commitment events, p.395

Resource – a thing that has economic value (with or without physical substance) that enterprise activities provide, use, consume, and manage, p.20

Resource query – a query that asks a question that can be answered with data in a single resource or resource type table, p.361

Resource type – a resource that is tracked only by the category into which it is classified, such that the enterprise uses one identifier such as a part number or stock keeping unit (SKU) to represent each each resource type, and the individual instances of the resource type are interchangeable and indistinguishable; also may be referred to as a bulk resource, p.38

Responsibility – an association between two types of internal agents that is separate from any event in which they might both participate, p.41

Returns packing list – a packing list specifically for purchase returns, detail the contents of each package shipped to an external business partner, p.119

Revenue process – business process in which finished good resources are exchanged for the cash resource in which goods or services resources are exchanged to customers or clients for cash or some other form of compensation, p.25

Reversal association – a relationship between an economic reversal event and the economic event being reversed or annulled, p.100

Reversal association queries – queries that ask questions about the negation of exchanges, p.367

RFID (Radio frequency identification) tags – tags that communicate electronically with a reader via radio waves that enable tracking of resources, and eliminating the need to scan the tags with barcode readers, p.258

Right join – includes all records from whichever table is on the right, and matches those records from the table that is on the left, for which values in the joined fields are equal, is also called right outer join, p.319

Risk assessment – one of COSO's five interrelated components of an internal control system; the identification and analysis of relevant risks associated with the enterprise achieving its objectives; forms the basis for determining what risks need to be controlled and the controls required to manage them, p.242

Robotic process automation (RPA) – the intelligent automation of repetitive tasks that follow prescribed rules or algorithms that may use structured or unstructured inputs, p.481

S

Sale – an economic decrement event in which title to goods is transferred from the enterprise to a customer; may also be called a shipment or a delivery; if sale involves services instead of goods, the event is usually called service engagement or something similar, p.155

Sale invoice – a document used to communicate to a customer the fact that the enterprise has fulfilled a commitment to transfer title of goods to the customer; sometimes also serves as a request or reminder for the customer to fulfill its commitment and remit payment to the enterprise, p.157

Sale order – a mutual commitment event in which the enterprise agrees to transfer title of goods to a customer at an agreed upon future time and price and the customer agrees to pay for those goods; a document reflecting the terms of the mutual commitment event, p.152

Sale return – the transfer of title (usually concurrent with transfer of physical custody) of goods from a customer back to the seller, p.163

Sale return authorization – a document that gives permission for the customer to return merchandise and is typically prepared in response to a customer's request to return goods through the mail or via a common carrier, p.163

Sales call – an event in which an enterprise representative describes features of products or services to potential customers in an attempt to generate sales to those customers, p.150

Sales call report – a document or software interface that communicate the details of sales a sales call, p.150

Schema – the column headings, or intension, of a relational database table, p.59

Script pattern – a sequence of events that typically occur in combination, p.19

SELECT clause – the first clause of each SQL statement, that specifies which attributes the query's answer should include; a required clause, p.309

Semi-private blockchain – a blockchain that is led by a single enterprise but has participants across enterprises, for example, across a supply chain, p. 476

Segregation of duties – the structuring of employees' job functions such that one employee is prohibited from performing two or more of the following functions: authorization of transactions involving assets, custody of assets, record keeping, and reconciliation; reduces the opportunity for one employee to steal enterprise assets and to conceal the theft in the normal course of his or her work, p.119

Sequence check – a control used to verify the records in a batch are sorted in the correct sequence and/or to highlight missing batch items, p.276

Sequence flow – a way to connect flow objects in a BPMN diagram, they connect from the start event to various activities and/or gateways, and finally, to the end event, p.215

Sequential access – requires all data to be read in sequential order; to find a particular record requires all previous records to be read first, p.227

Sequential storage – records are stored one after another in some order (chronologically, or in numeric order, p.227

Service acquisition – economic increment event in which the acquired resources are services, p.113

Service agreement or service order – a mutual commitment that involves a vendor performing a service rather than providing goods, p.111

Service engagement – an economic decrement event in which an enterprise sells services, rather than goods, to a customer, p.155

Show Table window (in Microsoft Access) – a screen from which the user may choose which table(s) to include in the relationship layout or in a query, p.78, 330

Simple attribute – a characteristic of a class or association that cannot be further decomposed into component characteristics, p.56

Smart card or token – a logical access control that authenticates a user through a hardware device combined with a log-in password process; the smart card generates a random code that changes at predetermined intervals and must be matched against the host system; the user must also enter a password to gain access to the system, p.130

Smart contract – a contract that tracks the flow of an economic exchange from the point of commitment through the happy path economic events, and , if applicable, through the unhappy path reversal events. A contract that embeds the contract terms into computer code such that the exchange moves along the appropriate path as the contracting parties meet (or fail to meet) each contract condition, p.476

SQL view (in Microsoft Access) – a mode for viewing the underlying SQL statement for a query; even if a query was created in design view, Microsoft Access generates a corresponding SQL statement that the user may view to evaluate the query's logic, p.312

Staffing plan – a document on which a supervisor communicates a department's need for labor for a given time period, that indicates the types and quantities of labor needed but does not assign specific employees to provide the labor, p.130

Start event (in BPMN) – the first event in a business process, depicted with a non-bold circle, p.215

Static derivable attribute – an attribute that can be calculated from other fields in the database, but for which the derived value will not change if new data records (also called rows) are entered into the database, p.56

Stockflow – an association between an economic event and a resource or an association between an economic reversal event and a resource; often specifies quantity and actual cost or selling price for the item(s) involved in the event, p.34

Stockflow association query – a query that attempts to satisfy information needs about the effect of economic events on resources or about the resources involved in events, p.381

Structured Query Language (SQL) – the most commonly used querying language for relational databases; uses a standard format for every retrieval query statement (Select-From-Where) to simplify the task of query development, p.309

SUM aggregation function – in SQL, adds the values in a column, p.316

T

Task – an individual step involved in accomplishing an essential event in an enterprise, p.209

Terminator – a symbol that indicates the beginning or ending of a flowchart or a point of entry to or exit from the flowchart, p.222

Text annotation – in BPMN, an element that attaches to an object with an association, p.217

Timecard – the primary document prepared by the enterprise in conjunction with the economic increment event is a time card; may be completed on a daily, weekly, or other basis; are typically completed by employees and approved by supervisors, list the times employees started working (punched in) and stopped working (punched out) for each day in the covered time period, p.135

Token level representation – a representation that uses symbols that each have a one-for-one correspondence to the physical object it represents, p.15

Transaction file – a file that contains activity data that is used to update the balances on master files, p.226

Transaction type check – a batch level internal control that verifies that all transactions within the batch are of the same category or type, p.276

Transfer duality association – a relationship between economic increment and economic decrement events in which the decremented resources are traded for the incremented resources, p.179

Transformation duality association – an association between economic increment and economic decrement events whereby the decremented resources are converted into the incremented resources, p.179

Tuple – a row in a relational database table, also called record or table extension, p.59

Type level representation – a category into which individual objects may be classified; type level representation uses one type to represent as many individual instances as fit the category, p.15

Typification – an association between a category and individual instances of that category, p.99, 287

U

Unified Modeling Language (UML) – a widely accepted notation for system analysis and design that includes several types of diagrams for different levels of analysis; its *class diagrams* are appropriate for conceptual modeling of data, as well as modeling specific REA concepts, p.52

Use stockflow association – an association that indicates a resource is partially used up by an economic decrement event, p.179

V

Valid sign check – an internal control used to assess whether a field's sign (positive or negative) makes sense; is used to highlight illogical values, particularly balances in master file records, p.276

Validity check – an internal control in which a comparison is made between entered data and pre-specified stored data to determine whether the entered data is valid, p.275

Vendor invoice – a document sent by a vendor to the enterprise to communicate the fact that the vendor has fulfilled its commitment to transfer title of the goods to the enterprise, p.114

Vertical calculation – mathematical operations performed within a particular column of data values, such as a computation of the average of a set of values, p.316

View integration – the process of integrating the separate conceptual models for each business process view before we convert the conceptual model to the logical and physical levels, p.166

View modeling – the creation of separate models for different parts of a system, p.166

Volatile derivable attribute – an attribute that can be calculated from other attribute values, and for which the derived value will change if additional transaction data is entered into the database, p.56

W

WHERE clause – in SQL, specifies criteria rows of data must meet to be included in the answer, p.310

Wildcard character – a symbol that tells the database to include all attributes in the query result, p.311

Withholdings – also called payroll deductions, amounts the enterprise will pay on behalf of the employees to government agencies, benefit providers, or other outside agencies, p.136

Workflow – the sequential flow of data through an enterprise, p.210

INDEX

A

Access control matrix, 268
Accountability, 3, 10, 22, 40, 219, 242, 245, 283
Accountability infrastructure, 283, 291
Accountants as visionaries, 7-8
Accounting analytics, 482
Accounting transactions, 6
Accounts payable query steps, 378-381
Accounts payable by vendor query steps, 406-411
Accounts receivable query steps, 369-373
Acquisition event, *see* Purchase event
Acquisition process, 25, 33, 37-39, 42-47, 98, 107-121, 167-170, 211-213, 260-261, 263-264
Acquisition process queries, 355-368, 378-382, 387-391, 393, 396-397, 399-400, 406-411; *also see* Multiple process queries
Ad hoc querying, 306
Activity (BPMN), 215-216
Agent, 9, 21-23, 26, 30, 39-44, 46-47, 58, 95-96, 98-99, 101, 103, 105-106, 126, 128, 166-170, 176, 252-254, 283, 286-289, 291-295, 299-300
Agent queries, 366-367, 396-400, 454, 467-468
Aggregation function, 316-318, 325, 343-345, 459, 466-468
Alternative conceptual modeling notations, 92-94
Analytics, 10, 481-485; *also see* Query
AND operator, 315; *distinguish from* OR operator
Annotation symbol, 222
Application controls, 247, 265-266, 273-277
Area of responsibility, 217, 230-232
Assignment, 40-41, 95-96,
Assignment association, *see* Assignment
Association (BPMN), 217

B

Association (generally, in UML, and in queries), 21, 26, 34, 39-47, 54-60, 64-69, 77-87, 95-109, 128-140, 148-170, 178-205, 210-213, 259, 283-301, 308, 319, 355-361, 367-369, 374, 378, 381-382, 390-401, 455-460, 469-471, 479, 484
Association class, 54-56, 65-67, 83-86, 101, 294, 308
Association class attribute, *see* Association class
Association name conflict, 167-170
Association structure conflict, 167
Attribute, 37-38, 45-46, 55-69, 72-87, 97, 100-103, 108-109, 128-130, 133, 139, 148-149, 166-170, 178, 182, 185, 187, 189-205, 210, 276, 284-289, 294-301, 309-311, 319-323, 362
Attribute assignment, 100-103
Attribute conflict, 167-170
Augmented intensional reasoning, 479
AVG aggregation function, 316, 343, 392-393, 466, 468

B

Barter transaction, 29
Batch control total, 276-277
Batch (conversion/manufacturing), *see* Production run
Batch processing, 229-230
BETWEEN operator, 313, 323, 365-366, 383, 385, 388, 392, 397-398, 433, 459, 469
Bill of lading, 119, 157-158, 297
Bill of materials, 200-201, 253, 459
Bitcoin, 475-477
Blockchain, 475-478, 480
Bonding, 256
BPMN, 209, 214-218
Business entrepreneur script, 22
Business event, 9, 97-98, 480; *also see* Instigation event *and* Commitment event; *distinguish from* Economic event
Business interruption, 252
Business process, 13, 21-26, 33-47, 54, 95-121, 125-140, 145-170, 175-205, 209-213, 214-218, 218-225, 244-245, 249-277, 283-284, 476-478, 483-484

Business process analytics, *see* Business process queries
Business process queries, 355-411, 417-434, 441-471
Business Process Model and Notation (BPMN) 2.0, *see* BPMN
Business process risks, 249-277

C

Calculator/register tape, 219-220; *distinguish from* Magnetic tape storage
Candidate key, 61-64, 69
Candidate key attribute, *see* Candidate key
Cardinality, 92-94; *also see* Multiplicity
Cash balance query steps, 417-420
Cash disbursement event, 8, 25, 37, 39-40, 43-47, 98, 106, 108-109, 117, 127-130, 138-140, 147, 166, 169-170, 177, 211, 213, 253, 262, 296, 298-300, 362, 364, 368, 378, 399, 406-407, 417-420, 466-469, 471
Cash receipt event, 8, 25, 37-39, 68-69, 97, 106, 108, 127, 147-149, 155, 160-161, 168-170, 177, 210, 226, 253, 256, 262-263, 273, 294, 297, 306, 362, 364, 368-371, 373-375, 377, 400, 415, 417-418, 420, 437, 478
Check, 117; *also see* Cash disbursement event
Check digit, 274-275
Chen entity-relationship model, 92-94
Claim, 39; *also see* Duality
Class, 40, 46, 51-69, 74-87, 92-94, 96-106, 128, 148, 166-170, 178, 180-181, 210-213, 284-301, 307-308, 319-323, 355, 479
Class diagram, 40, 43, 45, 47, 51-69, 83, 92-94, 96, 101, 109, 128, 148, 168-170, 178, 180-181, 211, 284, 286, 288-290, 292-293, 295, 299-300, 307; *also see* Class
Class name conflict, 166-170
Closed loop verification, 274
Cognitive computing, 478-479, 481-482
Collusion, 239, 244

505